COMPUTING FUNDAMENTALS WITH JAVA

Rick Mercer

University of Arizona

Franklin, Beedle & Associates, Inc.
8536 SW St. Helens Drive, Suite D
Wilsonville, Oregon 97070
(503) 682-7668
www.fbeedle.com

President and Publisher	Jim Leisy (jimleisy@fbeedle.com)
Developmental Editor	Sue Page
Production	Stephanie Welch
Proofreaders	Tom Sumner
	Senta Gorrie
	Jeni Lee
Cover Design	Ian Shadburne
Marketing	Christine Collier
Order Processing	Krista Brown

Library of Congress Cataloging-in-Publication Data is available from the publisher upon request.

This textbook is dedicated to my mom and dad:
Eleanor Mercer
Ken Mercer

Table of Contents

CHAPTER 6   SELECTION   252

CHAPTER 7   REPETITION   309

CHAPTER 8   ARRAYS   380

CHAPTER 9   A FEW EXCEPTIONS,   439
A LITTLE INPUT/OUTPUT, AND
SOME PERSISTENT OBJECTS

CHAPTER 10   DESIGNING AN   483
INHERITANCE HIERARCHY

CHAPTER 11   MORE ARRAYS   543

CHAPTER 12   SIMPLE RECURSION   591

Preface

This textbook was written for the introductory computer science course at the university level. It is appropriate for students with little or no programming background. Students with programming experience in other languages can use this textbook to learn Java. Preliminary versions of this textbook have been used with groups with no programming experience and in accelerated courses that assumed previous programming experience in some other language.

This book has been class-tested 11 times in a variety of settings. More than 1,400 students have used it. It was developed in courses where students had a wide variety of programming experience, from none to several years experience with other programming languages. This textbook recognizes the relevance and validity of object-oriented programming and design, but not at the expense of traditional computing fundamentals.

After completing the first eight chapters, students should be comfortable with traditional programming concepts such as problem-solving, control structures (selection and repetition), methods (functions), parameters, and arrays. Students will also have learned the main concepts of object-oriented programming, such as partitioning systems into objects, message passing, building classes, polymorphism through inheritance, and polymorphism through Java interfaces. They will be able to write programs that use Java classes and classes written by them for particular applications.

By the end of Chapter 8, students will also have had the opportunity to observe the development of a relatively complex object-oriented system. The system is progressively built in sections of Chapters 3 through 8. This extended case study provides the opportunity for understanding object-oriented programming in Java. This bank teller system directly uses 11 standard Java classes, plus 10 classes written specifically for this application.

Chapters 9 through 12 provide additional material sometimes presented in a first course in programming. These additional topics include exceptions and Java input/output streams. The objects built in the case study can be made persistent (the objects live until the program is run again). Design issues are woven through the text in algorithmic patterns and object-oriented design guidelines. Chapter 10, "Designing an Inheritance Hierarchy," presents an object-oriented software development strategy with role-playing and Class/Responsibility/Collaborator cards. The other major focus of that chapter is the design of a small inheritance hierarchy; design and maintenance considerations are interwoven with the Java constructs needed to obtain polymorphism through inheritance. Chapter 11, "More Arrays," presents two-dimensional arrays and array-processing algorithms typically presented in a first course (binary search and sorting). Chapter 12, "Simple Recursion," introduces the concept of recursion and how it works in programming.

This textbook is the result of 14 years of reasoning about how best to utilize the first course in the computer science curriculum and how best to integrate object-oriented programming and design.

Features

- **Traditional topics:** This textbook recognizes the relevance and validity of object-oriented programming. But it does not sacrifice traditional topics such as problem-solving, design, control structures, and arrays.
- **Objects-early approach:** The first three chapters present the basics of programming and using Java objects. Chapter 4 shows how classes are built in the context of a larger system. Polymorphism through inheritance and Java interfaces are presented in Chapters 4 and 5. Selection and repetition are studied in the context of methods in classes that are part of a larger system. This approach results in the same understanding of traditional topics—such as methods, parameters, selection, loops, and arrays—as would be expected in books that are not object-oriented. Along the way, students are also exposed to the advantages of object-oriented programming, such as the partitioning of systems into objects, the encapsulation of behavior and state, and the polymorphism that comes from inheritance and Java interfaces. This objects-early approach lets students become comfortable implementing small systems of two or three classes while understanding one system (through the bank teller case study) with over 20 different types of objects. Students will see the big picture.
- **Carefully chosen subset of Java:** Because students might have little or no programming experience, this textbook concentrates on a small subset of Java's feature-rich platform. With only one interface and six Java classes, event-driven programming with graphical user interfaces is possible. Java classes that manage calendar dates, collections of objects, and the writing of objects from and to a

file provide glimpses into the power of having a large, readily available, standard library of classes.

■ **Case study (an object-oriented system in Chapters 3–9):** The bank teller system specified at the beginning of Chapter 3 begins with finding the objects and learning how to use one of them. This system becomes a case study as it is developed over seven chapters. By the end of Chapter 8, this object-oriented program ends up using 11 existing Java classes. Ten other classes are developed during the case study. Chapter 9 shows how to make the objects persistent (live to the next program run). This case study reviews the main concepts in each of the chapters. It also provides an example of a relatively large system that is developed in an object-oriented fashion.

■ **Algorithmic patterns:** Algorithmic patterns help beginning programmers design algorithms around a set of common generalities. The first algorithmic pattern, Input/Process/Output, is introduced in Chapter 1. It is reused in subsequent chapters. The Input/Process/Output pattern is especially useful for readers with no programming experience and to laboratory assistants that may be helping them. In Chapter 5, IPO takes the form of user input into a `JTextField` and output into other `JTextFields` and `JLabels`. Other algorithmic patterns include the Guarded Action pattern in Chapter 6 and the Indeterminate Loop pattern in Chapter 7.

■ **Event-driven programming the Java way:** Chapter 5 presents the Java event model. The small subset of graphical components (`JButton`, `JLabel`, `JTextField`, and `JFrame`), along with the `ActionListener` interface and the `GridLayout` manager, allow students to build some small, modern programs (instructors could add other listener interfaces to this small subset). This textbook shows how Java does event-driven programming. Through class testing, the author has found that students have no more trouble with Java's event model than they do with other traditional topics. Because the textbook uses a small subset of graphical components and only one listener interface, after two or three tries students understand the Java event model such that they can use it repeatedly as a pattern for building event-driven programs with a graphical user interface. This textbook does not attempt to hide the Java event model with additional nonstandard classes. Java consistently uses the same design to handle many events, such as mouse clicks and menu selections. Once one listener interface is mastered, other listener interfaces are more easily understood.

■ **Extensively tested in the classroom and laboratory:** Students supplied many useful comments and suggestions concerning manuscript clarity, organization, programming projects, and examples. This textbook was class-tested 11 terms, from Spring 1998 to Fall 2001. It has been used by students at Penn State Berks and (mostly) by students at the University of Arizona. This provided plenty of opportunity for feedback and analysis. In the four years that it took to write this textbook, it went through four moderate modifications. Each modification made it more pedagogically sound and more object-oriented.

Pedagogy

This textbook has many pedagogical features that have made this introduction to programming, design, and object technology accessible to students.

- **Self-Check Questions:** These short questions allow students to evaluate whether they understand the details and terms just presented in the reading. The answers to all self-check questions are located at the end of each chapter.
- **Exercises:** These transitional problems examine the major concepts presented in the chapter. Answers to selected exercises are provided at the end of the book. Answers to all exercises are in the instructor's manual.
- **Programming Tips:** Each set of programming projects is preceded by a set of programming tips intended to help students complete the programs, to warn students of potential pitfalls, and to promote good programming habits.
- **Programming Projects:** Many relatively small-scale problems have been extensively lab-tested to ensure that projects can be assigned and completed with little or no instructor intervention. Chapter 1 has analysis and design projects that can be completed without a computer. Every other chapter has programming projects that represent a wide range of difficulty. Students typically complete from one to four programming projects per week in an acceptable amount of time. These programming projects were not made up at the last minute. Virtually all of the programming projects were assigned and successfully completed by students over the past 12 years.

Chapter Outlines

Chapter 1, "Program Development," is intended for students who have never written a computer program. However, students with some experience might appreciate the introduction to algorithmic patterns presented here. The Input/Process/Output pattern applies to simple text-based programs. Input/Process/Output also applies to event-driven programs with graphical user interfaces (presented in Chapter 5). This chapter does not try to present the history of computers, binary number representation, the Web, networking, operating systems, and so on. While many introductory CS1 books present such topics, this textbook begins by concentrating on the process of writing computer programs, while suggesting that there are things that can be done before going to the computer.

Chapter 2, "A Little Java," introduces the low-level programming constructs, such as primitive types, tokens, assignment, input, and output. Also introduced is the notion of constructing objects with the easy-to-use, author-supplied

TextReader class, which has the readInt, readDouble, readWord, and readLine methods.

Chapter 3, "Using Objects," shows how to use the objects of existing classes. It begins with the specification of a system that will be used as a case study. Students are invited to "find the objects" in this system. The first object used is from this system. Along with a few author-supplied classes (BankAccount, Grid, and GraphicGrid), several interesting Java classes besides String are introduced: ArrayList, GregorianCalendar, DecimalFormat, JFrame, JButton, JLabel, and JTextField. Two exercises invite students to show a Java JColorChooser and JFileChooser object in a JFrame. Students with no experience complete these projects in about eight lines of code.

Throughout this textbook, students are encouraged to view object-oriented programs as collections of objects that send messages to each other. By introducing a few Java classes that are interesting and easy to use, the textbook shows students how much they can accomplish with Java.

Chapter 4, "Classes and Interfaces," shows how to implement Java classes. Methods and parameters are introduced in the context of building a class. These programming constructs are more intuitive. The first example class is in the context of something bigger. Once it is completed, another system is specified (Jukebox) and two classes from this system are built. This example ends with two objects in a "use" relationship—a Song object is passed as an argument to a JukeboxAccount object. At the end of this chapter most students should see that object-oriented programs are about more than an object interacting with other objects—one program is more than just one class.

As in all chapters, programming projects offer the opportunity to implement and test one class, to build something with graphical components, or to build more than one class. In most cases, students are also using one or more existing Java classes.

Chapter 4 introduces the Java interface, which specifies the methods that a class must have. Interfaces are introduced here to allow for event-driven programming in the subsequent chapter and to introduce another way to obtain polymorphism. This reinforces the importance of methods, parameters, and returned values. Perhaps most importantly, the design decisions captured in Java interfaces have proven to be very useful to students writing their first classes.

Chapter 5, "Events, Listeners, and a Little Polymorphism," introduces event-driven programming with a graphical user interface. The small subset of graphical components used will have already been introduced. The Java interface will have already been introduced. This chapter allows an event-driven program with a graphical user interface to be completed here and in the next three chapters.

Chapter 5 introduces inner classes so the listeners can more easily access the objects they need. (*Note:* These are not anonymous inner classes.) Chapter 5 also introduces the polymorphism that comes from inheritance through examples

students have already used. Polymorphism is introduced with Java's
`ActionListener` interface.

Chapter 6, "Selection," introduces selection patterns and the Java constructs
that provide solutions to problems where choices have to be made. This is a
traditional chapter on selection. It shows how to implement the `Comparable`
interface in a few classes to show that any two objects can be compared.

Chapter 7, "Repetition," introduces repetition patterns and the Java constructs
that provide solutions to problems requiring repetition. This is a traditional
chapter on repetitive control structures, with some added concepts such as
iterators and sorting.

Chapter 8, "Arrays," introduces the array object with one subscript. This is a
traditional chapter on arrays. Also introduced is a collection class that reinforces
the use of an array instance variable. This collection has an `iterator` method that
returns an `Iterator` object to demonstrate polymorphism through interfaces.

**Chapter 9, "A Few Exceptions, a Little Input/Output, and Some Persistent
Objects,"** provides a brief introduction to exception handling in Java. The second
section presents some of the Java stream classes for disk and network input and
output. The final section completes the bank teller case study by making the
objects persistent.

Chapter 10, "Designing an Inheritance Hierarchy," summarizes the previous
nine chapters. It pulls together many of the traditional and object-oriented concepts necessary to develop a new system specified at the beginning of the chapter.
Two new topics are presented:

- a methodology for developing object-oriented software
- how to design an inheritance hierarchy

An imaginary team of programmers play the roles of objects. Scripted scenarios
reenact the role-playing performed by this team. The programmers are working
together as they develop Class/Responsibility/Component (CRC) cards. Responsibility-driven design is used to better assign responsibilities to the objects in the
system. Along the way, several objects are found that have some common characteristics and a few differences. Therefore, a class hierarchy is designed using relevant
object-oriented design guidelines.

A collection class that is part of this system shows how different types of objects
understand the same messages but respond in different ways. Polymorphism
through inheritance is demonstrated through an inheritance hierarchy.

Chapter 11, "More Arrays," shows the binary search and selection sort algorithms to reinforce the use of Java arrays and introduce two commonly used array-
processing algorithms. These algorithms are implemented in static methods. Two-
dimensional arrays are introduced. This chapter could be presented any time after
Chapter 8.

Chapter 12, "Simple Recursion," introduces the concept of recursion, recursive solutions that also have iterative solutions, and backtracking. This chapter could be presented any time after Chapter 7.

Concept Summary by Chapter

Chapter	Concepts
1 and 2	A simple program development strategy
	Sequential execution of program statements
	The Input/Process/Output pattern
	Primitive types
	Input and output
	Constructing objects
3	Finding objects in a system
	Sending messages
	Interfaces
	Graphical component layout
	Case Study: Laying out the bank teller window
4	Implementing classes
	Methods
	Argument/parameter association
	Return types
	Finding the objects in another system
	Relationships between objects
	Class constants
	Case Study: A Transaction class
5	Event-driven programming
	Listener objects
	Java's event model (listeners)
	Registering listeners to graphical components
	Polymorphism through inheritance
	Polymorphism through interfaces
	Case Study: Inheritance and listener classes
6	Selection patterns
	Selection control structures (if and if...else)
	Comparing objects (the Comparable interface)
	Case Study: Validating user input

7	Repetition patterns
	Repetitive execution of program statements
	Iterating over a collection
	Sorting
	Case Study: A collection of objects
8	Arrays
	Sequential search
	Building a collection class
	Case Study: Looking up customers in a collection
9	Exception handling
	Text input and output using standard Java classes
	Persistence
	Case Study: Saving the account and transaction collections
10	Finding the objects
	Role-playing and developing CRC cards
	Responsibility-driven design
	Designing an inheritance hierarchy
	Object-oriented design guidelines
	Polymorphism through inheritance
11	More array processing (binary search and selection sort)
	Static methods
	Processing data stored in rows and columns
	Processing elements in two-dimensional arrays
	Nested looping
12	Recursive solutions to some simple problems
	Backtracking

Accompanying Disk

The disk that accompanies this book contains all of the Java source code from the textbook. The disk is divided into a folder for each chapter. Some of these folders hold files that help the student complete the programming assignments. The root directory (folder) on the disk has the files needed by some of the programming projects. These include `TextReader.java`, `Grid.java`, `GraphicGrid.java`, and `BankAccount.java`.

Instructor's Manual

The instructor's manual is available as a CD to teachers who adopt this textbook. The CD includes the following items:

- Solutions to all programming projects.
- Answers to the all exercises (answers to selected exercises are at the end of this textbook).
- Teaching suggestions for each chapter.
- Multiple versions of tests, which were actually used at the University of Arizona.
- Lecture notes for each chapter as Microsoft PowerPoint slides.

To obtain a copy of the CD, contact the publisher, Franklin, Beedle and Associates, at its Web site, **www.fbeedle.com**.

Acknowledgments

Critical feedback from students, teaching assistants, and other interested people is essential. At the University of Arizona (where I have taught since the fall of 1998), I have had the pleasure of working with many bright and highly motivated undergraduate section leaders. The program at the University of Arizona has undergraduates leading recitation sections as they help teach large classes. I acknowledge and thank the students and the section leaders who have provided feedback for the following courses at the University of Arizona:

- C Sc 127A (CS1): Fall 1998, Spring 1999, and Spring 2001
- C Sc 227 (CS1 & CS2): Summer 1998, Summer 1999, Spring 2000, Summer 2000, Spring 2001, Summer 2001, and Fall 2001

Section leaders and students from these courses offered feedback, ideas, corrections, exercises, and programming projects for this textbook. Contributors (listed in reverse alphabetical order) include Wei Xi, Andy Wilt (the GraphicGrid class), Sreshta Wickramasinghe, Marty Stepp, Travis Singleton, Jessica Miller, Ursula McDuffee, Andy Lenards, Richard Kowal, Jignesh Joshi, Kelly Heffner, Valerie Fectau, and Mike Brooks.

As an author at Franklin, Beedle & Associates, I am happy to be part of a team that has enthusiastically expended a great deal of energy in the development of our textbooks. I thank the folks at FBA for their support and expertise in making this all possible: Jim Leisy, Sue Page, Tom Sumner, Stephanie Welch, Ian Shadburne, Christine Collier, and Krista Brown.

I have been fortunate to encounter many excellent educators from academia and industry who care and think about a lot of the same issues I do. The debates and new ideas generated in discussions, both live and through email, have allowed for the plethora of informed decisions necessary for producing a good textbook. I wish to acknowledge the following people (listed in reverse alphabetical order) for their dedication, insight, and willingness to make things better: Suzanne Westbrook, Dave West, Gene Wallingford, Stuart Reges, Rich Pattis, Jim Leisy, Adele Goldberg, Mike Feldman, Ed Epp, Jutta Eckstein, Robert Duvall, Dwight

Duego, Alistair Cockburn, Mike Clancy, Alyce Brady, Robert Biddle, Joe Bergin, Owen Astrachan, and Erzebet Angster.

Too numerous to specifically mention are the many authors and presenters I would like to acknowledge for their opinions, creativity, and technical accuracy, which have influenced me during my 17-year career as a computer science educator.

Reviewers spend countless hours poring over material with critical eyes and useful comments. Because of the quality of their work, criticisms and recommendations were always considered seriously.

Richard Baldwin	*Austin Community College*
Wayne T. Caruolo	*Red Rocks Community College*
Henry A. Etlinger	*Rochester Institute of Technology*
Dennis Heckman	*Portland Community College*
Sridhar Narayan	*University of North Carolina, Wilmington*
Lawrence Carl Petersen	*Texas A&M University*
Carolyn J. C. Schauble	*Colorado State University*
Louis Steinberg	*Rutgers University*

And, finally, thanks to my family for understanding: Diane, Chelsea, Austen, and Kieran.

—Rick Mercer, Tucson, Arizona
mercer@cs.Arizona.edu

Chapter 1

Program Development

Coming Up

First, there is a need for a computer-based solution to a problem. The need may be expressed in a few sentences as a **problem specification**. The progression from understanding a problem specification to achieving a working computer-based solution is known as "program development." After studying this chapter, you will be able to

- follow a case study using a simple program development strategy
- understand the characteristics of a good algorithm
- understand how algorithmic patterns help in program design
- provide a deliverable from the analysis phase of program development
- provide a deliverable from the design phase of program development

Analysis and design projects reinforce your ability to develop programs.

1

1.1   Program Development

There are many approaches to program development. This chapter begins by examining a strategy with these three steps: analysis, design, and implementation.

Phase of Program Development	Activity
Analysis	Understand the problem.
Design	Develop a solution.
Implementation	Make the solution run on a computer.

Our study of computing fundamentals begins with an example of this particular approach to program development.

Each of these three phases will be exemplified with a simple case study—one particular problem. Emphasis is placed on the **deliverables**—the tangible results—of each phase. Here is a preview of the deliverables for each of the three stages:

Phase	Deliverable
Analysis	A document that lists the data that store relevant information
Design	An algorithm that outlines a solution
Implementation	An executable program ready to be used by the customer (or ready to be graded)

Self-Check

1-1   What deliverable can you expect at the end of a successfully completed college career?

1.2   Analysis

Synonyms for analysis: inquiry, examination, study

Program development may begin with a study, or **analysis**, of a problem. Obviously, to determine what a program is to do, you must first understand the problem. If the problem is written down, you can begin the analysis phase by simply reading the problem.

While analyzing the problem, it proves helpful to name the data that represent information. For example, you might be asked to compute the maximum weight allowed for a successful liftoff of a particular airplane from a given runway under certain thrust-affecting weather conditions such as temperature and wind direction. While analyzing the problem specification, you might name the desired information maximumWeight. The data required to compute that information could have names such as temperature and windDirection.

Although such data do not represent the entire solution, they do represent an important piece of the puzzle. The data names are symbols for what the program will need and what the program will compute. One value needed to compute maximumWeight might be 19.0 for temperature. Such data values must often be manipulated—or processed—in a variety of ways to produce the desired result. Some values must be obtained from the user, other values must be multiplied or added, and still other values must be displayed on the computer screen.

At some point, these data values will be stored in computer memory. The values in the same memory location can change while the program is running. The values also have a type, such as integers or numbers with decimal points (these two different types of values are stored differently in computer memory). These named pieces of memory that store a specific type of value that can change while a program is running are known as **variables**.

You will see that there also are operations for manipulating those values in meaningful ways. It helps to distinguish the data that must be displayed—**output**—from the data required to compute that result—**input**. These named pieces of memory that store values are the variables that summarize what the program must do.

Input and Output

Output: Information the computer must display.
Input: Information a user must supply to solve a problem.

A problem can be better understood by answering this question: What is the output given certain input? Therefore, it is a good idea to provide an example of the problem with pencil and paper. Here are two problems with variable names selected to accurately describe the stored values.

Problem 1 Analysis Deliverable

Problem	Data Name	Input or Output	Sample Problem
Compute a monthly loan payment	amount	Input	12500.00
	rate	Input	0.08
	months	Input	48
	payment	Output	303.14

Problem 2 Analysis Deliverable

Problem	Data Name	Input or Output	Sample Problem
Count how often Shakespeare wrote a particular word in a particular play	aBardsWork	Input	Much Ado About Nothing
	theWord	Input	the
	howOften	Output	220

In summary, problems are analyzed by doing these things:

1. Reading and understanding the problem specification.
2. Deciding what data represent the answer—the output.
3. Deciding what data the user must enter to get the answer—the input.
4. Creating a document (like those above) that summarizes the analysis. This document is input for the next phase of program development—design.

In textbook problems, the variable names and type of values (such as integers or numbers with a decimal point) that must be input and output are sometimes provided. If not, they are relatively easy to recognize. In real-world problems of significant scale, a great deal of effort is expended during the analysis phase. The next subsection provides an analysis of a small problem.

Self-Check

1-2 Given the problem of converting British pounds to U.S. dollars, name a value that must be input by the user and a value that must be output.

1-3 Given the problem of selecting one CD from a 200-compact-disc player, what name would represent all of the CDs? What name would be appropriate to represent one particular CD selected by the user?

An Example of Analysis

Problem: Using the grade assessment scale to the right, compute a course grade as a weighted average of two tests and one final exam. The dialogue must look exactly like this for the given input of 74.0, 79.0, and 84.0:

	Percentage of Final Grade
Test 1	25%
Test 2	25%
Final Exam	50%

```
Enter first test: 74.0
Enter second test: 79.0
Enter final exam: 84.0
Course Grade: 80.25%
```

Analysis begins by reading the problem specification and establishing the desired output and the required input to solve the problem. Determining and naming the output is a good place to start. The output stores the answer to the problem. It provides insight into what the program must do. Once the need for a data value is discovered and given a meaningful name, the focus can shift to what must be accomplished. For this particular problem, the desired output is the actual course grade (80.25% above). The name courseGrade represents the requested information to be output to the user.

A complete analysis might answer other questions, such as:

- What happens when the user enters non-numeric data?
- Is it okay to enter 74 instead of 74.0?
- Is 74.5 okay as input? What about 74.6?

However, for illustrating analysis with a short example, this problem will be simplified by presuming these are not issues.

This problem becomes more generalized when the user enters values to produce the result. If the program asks the user for data, the program can be used later to compute course grades for many students with any set of grades. So let's decide on and create names for the values that must be input. To determine courseGrade, three values are required: test1, test2, and finalExam. The first three analysis activities are now complete:

1. Problem understood.
2. Information to be output: courseGrade.
3. Data to be input: test1, test2, and finalExam.

However, a sample problem is still missing. Many problem specifications in this textbook provide a sample dialogue that summarizes the input that must be supplied by the user and the output the user must see. This textbook sets user input in boldface italic (*74.0*, for example). Everything else is program output.

Sample dialogues provide another important benefit. They show an answer (such as 80.25%) for one particular set of inputs. Such dialogues are included in the early part of this textbook to help introduce new concepts. When you encounter a problem without a sample dialogue, you should supply additional sample problems—at least one or two. If a dialogue is not given, you should write down something similar—a combination of input data and the output expected from those input data.

To create this courseGrade problem, you must understand the difference between a simple average and a weighted average. Because the three input items comprise different portions of the final grade (either 25% or 50%), the problem involves computing a weighted average. The simple average of the set 74.0, 79.0, and 84.0 is 79.0; each test is measured equally. However, the weighted average computes differently. Recall that test1 and test2 are each worth 25%, and finalExam weighs in at 50% of the final grade. When test1 is 74.0, test2 is 79.0, and finalExam is 84.0, the weighted average computes to 80.25.

```
(0.25 x test1) + (0.25 x test2) + (0.50 x finalExam)
 (0.25 x 74.0) +  (0.25 x 79.0) +   (0.50 x 84.0)
    18.50      +      19.75     +       42.00
                      80.25
```

With the same exact grades, the weighted average of 80.25 is different from the simple average (79.0). Failure to follow the problem specification could result in students who receive grades lower, or higher, than they actually deserve.

The problem has now been analyzed, the input and output have been named, it is understood what the computer-based solution is to do, and one sample problem has been given. The following deliverable from the analysis phase summarizes these activities:

Course-Grade Problem Analysis Deliverable

Problem	Data Name	Input or Output	Sample Problem
Compute a course grade	`test1`	Input	74.0
	`test2`	Input	79.0
	`finalExam`	Input	84.0
	`courseGrade`	Output	80.25

This is the first deliverable. The next section presents a method for designing a solution. The emphasis during design is on placing the appropriate activities in the proper order to solve the problem.

Self-Check

1-4 Complete an analysis deliverable for the following problem:
Problem: Compute the distance traveled for any moving vehicle. Allow the user to choose the unit of measurement (meters per second, miles per hour, or kilometers per hour, for example).

1-5 Complete an analysis deliverable for the following problem. You will need a calculator to determine the output.
Problem: Show the future value of an investment given its present value, the number of periods (years, perhaps), and the interest rate. Be consistent with the interest rate and the number of periods; if the periods are in years, then the annual interest rate must be supplied (0.085 for 8.5%, for example). If the period is in months, the monthly interest rate must be supplied (0.0075 per month for 9% per year, for example). The formula to compute the future value of money is future value = present value * $(1 + \text{rate})^{\text{periods}}$.

1.3   Design

Synonyms of design: model, think, plan, devise, pattern, outline

Design refers to the set of activities that includes (1) defining an architecture for the program that satisfies the requirements and (2) specifying an algorithm for each program component in the architecture.[1] In later chapters, you will see

---

1. Alan M. Davis, *201 Principles of Software Development* (IEEE Computer Society, 1995).

functions used as the basic building blocks of programs. Then you will see classes used as the basic building blocks of programs. A class is a collection of functions, typically called "methods." In this chapter, the architecture is intentionally constrained to a component known as a **program**. Therefore, the design activity that follows is limited to specifying an algorithm for this program.

An **algorithm** is a step-by-step procedure for solving a problem or accomplishing some end, especially by a computer.[2] A good algorithm must

- list the activities that need to be carried out
- list those activities in the proper order

Consider an algorithm to bake a cake:

1. Preheat the oven.
2. Grease the pan.
3. Mix the ingredients.
4. Pour the ingredients into the pan.
5. Place the cake pan in the oven.
6. Remove the cake pan from the oven after 35 minutes.

If the order of the steps is changed, the cook might get a very hot cake pan with raw cake batter in it. If one of these steps is omitted, the cook probably won't get a baked cake—or there might be a fire. An experienced cook may not need such an algorithm. However, cake-mix marketers cannot and do not presume that their customers have this experience. Good algorithms list the proper steps in the proper order and are detailed enough to accomplish the task.

Self-Check

1-6   Cake recipes typically omit a very important activity. Describe an activity that is missing.

An algorithm often contains a step without much detail. For example, step 3, "Mix the ingredients," isn't very specific. What are the ingredients? If the problem is to write a recipe algorithm that humans can understand, step 3 should be refined a bit to instruct the cook on how to mix the ingredients. The refinement to step 3 could be something like this:

3. Empty the cake mix into the bowl and mix in the milk until smooth.

or for scratch bakers:

3a. Sift the dry ingredients.
3b. Place the liquid ingredients in the bowl.
3c. Add the dry ingredients a quarter-cup at a time, whipping until smooth.

---

2. Merriam-Webster, *Merriam-Webster's Collegiate Dictionary*, 10th ed. (International Thomson Publishing, 1998).

Algorithms may be expressed in **pseudocode**—instructions expressed in a language that even nonprogrammers could understand. Pseudocode is written for humans, not for computers. Pseudocode algorithms are an aid to program design.

Pseudocode is very expressive. One pseudocode instruction may represent many computer instructions. Pseudocode algorithms are not concerned about issues such as misplaced punctuation marks or the details of a particular computer system. Pseudocode solutions make design easier by allowing details to be deferred. Writing an algorithm can be viewed as planning. A program developer can design with pencil and paper and sometimes in her or his head.

Algorithmic Patterns

Problems often require input from the user in order to compute and display the desired information. This particular flow of three activities—input/process/output—occurs so often, in fact, that it can be viewed as a pattern. It is one of several algorithmic patterns acknowledged in this textbook. These patterns will help you design programs.

A **pattern** is anything shaped or designed to serve as a model or a guide in making something else [Funk/Wagnalls 1968]. An **algorithmic pattern** serves as a guide to help develop programs. For instance, the following **Input/Process/Output (IPO) pattern** can be used to help design your first programs. In fact, this pattern will provide a guideline for many programs.

Algorithmic Pattern 1.1

Pattern:	Input/Process/Output (IPO)
Problem:	The program requires input from the user in order to compute and display the desired information.
Outline:	1. Obtain the input data.
	2. Process the data in some meaningful way.
	3. Output the results.

This algorithmic pattern is the first of several. In subsequent chapters, you'll see other algorithmic patterns, such as Guarded Action, Alternative Action, and Multiple Selection. To use an algorithmic pattern effectively, you should first become familiar with it. Look for the Input/Process/Output algorithmic pattern while developing programs. This could allow you to design your first programs more easily. For example, if you discover you have no meaningful values for the input data, it may be because you have placed the process step *before* the input step. Alternately, you may have skipped the input step altogether.

Patterns help solve other kinds of problems. Consider this quote:[3]

---

3. Christopher Alexander, *A Pattern Language* (Oxford University Press, 1977).

Each pattern describes a problem which occurs over and over again in our environment, and then describes the core of the solution to that problem, in such a way that you can use this solution a million times over, without ever doing it the same way twice.

Alexander is describing patterns in the design of furniture, gardens, buildings, and towns, but his description of a pattern can also be applied to program development. The IPO pattern frequently pops up during program design. It guides the solution to many problems—especially in the first five chapters of this textbook.

An Example of Algorithm Design

The deliverable from the design phase is an algorithm that solves the problem. The Input/Process/Output pattern guides the design of the algorithm that relates to our courseGrade problem.

Three-Step Pattern	Pattern Applied to a Specific Algorithm
1. Input	1. Obtain test1, test2, and finalExam
2. Process	2. Compute courseGrade
3. Output	3. Display courseGrade

Although algorithm development is usually an iterative process, a pattern helps to quickly provide an outline of the activities necessary to solve the courseGrade problem.

Self-Check

1-7 Read the three activities of the algorithm above. Do you detect a missing activity?

1-8 Read the three activities of the algorithm above. Do you detect any activity out of order?

1-9 Would this previous algorithm work if the first two activities were switched?

1-10 Is there enough detail in this algorithm to correctly compute courseGrade?

There currently is not enough detail in the process step of the courseGrade problem. The algorithm needs further refinement. Specifically, exactly how should the input data be processed to compute the course grade? The algorithm omits the weighted scale specified in the problem specification. The process step should be refined a bit more. Currently, this pseudocode algorithm does not describe how courseGrade must be computed.

The refinement of this algorithm (below) shows a more detailed process step. The step "Compute courseGrade" is now replaced with a **refinement**—a more detailed and specific activity. The input and output steps have also been refined.

This is the design phase deliverable—an algorithm with enough detail to pass on as the input into the next phase, implementation.

Refinement of a Specific Input/Process/Output (IPO) Algorithm

1. Obtain `test1`, `test2`, and `finalExam` from the user.
2. Compute `courseGrade` = (25% of `test1`) + (25% of `test2`) + (50% of `finalExam`).
3. Display the value of `courseGrade`.

Try to think of program development in terms of the deliverables. This provides a checklist. What deliverables exist so far?

1. From the analysis phase there is a document with a list of data (variables) and a sample problem.
2. From the design phase there is an algorithm.

Algorithm Walkthrough

Programs can be developed more quickly and with fewer errors by reviewing algorithms before moving on to the implementation phase. Are the activities in the proper order? Are all the necessary activities present? This review is accomplished with an algorithm walkthrough. An **algorithm walkthrough** simulates what a computer would do by stepping through the instructions of the algorithm.

A **computer** is a programmable electronic device that can store, retrieve, and process data. Programmers can simulate an electronic version of the algorithm by following the algorithm and manually performing the activities of storing, retrieving, and processing data using pencil and paper. The following algorithm walkthrough is a human (non-electronic) execution of the algorithm:

1. Retrieve some example values from the user and store them as shown:

   ```
   test1:       80
   test2:       90
   finalExam:   100
   ```

2. Retrieve the values and compute `courseGrade` as follows:

   ```
   courseGrade = (0.25 x test1) + (0.25 x test2) + (0.50 x finalExam)
                 (0.25 x 80.0)  + (0.25 x 90.0)  + (0.50 x 100.0)
                      20.0      +     22.5        +     50.0
   courseGrade = 92.5
   ```

3. Show the course grade to the user by retrieving the data stored in `courseGrade` to show `92.5%`.

It has been said that good artists know when to put down the brushes. Deciding when a painting is done is critical for its success. By analogy, a designer must decide when to stop designing. This is a good time to move on to the third phase of program development. In summary, here is what has been accomplished so far:

- The problem is understood.
- Data have been identified and named.
- Output for two sample problems is known (80.25% and now 92.5%).
- An algorithm has been developed.
- Walking through the algorithm has simulated computer activities.

Self-Check

1-11   Walk through the previous algorithm when `test1` is input as `0.0`, `test2` is input as `50.0`, and `finalExam` is input as `100.0`. What value is stored in `courseGrade`?

1.4   Implementation

Synonyms for implementation: accomplishment, fulfilling, making good, execution

The analysis and design of simple problems could be done with pencil and paper. The implementation phase of program development requires both software and hardware to obtain the deliverable. The deliverable of the implementation phase is a program that runs correctly on a computer. **Implementation** is the collection of activities required to complete the program so someone else can use it. Here are some implementation phase activities and associated deliverables:

Activity	Deliverable
Translate an algorithm into a programming language.	Source code
Compile source code into byte code.	Byte code
Run the program.	A running program
Verify that the program does what it is supposed to do.	A grade

This is neither the time nor place to describe all of the details of how programs actually run on computers. However, the gist of it can be understood by viewing the computer and its programs in a hierarchy of abstractions referred to as "virtual machines" (see the table below) [Aho/Ullman 1992].

Level	Virtual Machine (Abstraction)
6	Application software
5	High-level programming language
4	Assembly language or Java byte code
3	Operating system
2	Machine-level programming language
1	Microprogram
0	Digital logic

Most computer users view the machine at its highest level—the application software. Examples of software at this level include word processors, games, Web browsers, appointment calendars, and realtime applications that control electrome-chanical devices.

Programmers view the computer as a machine that responds to messages written at level 5. They use a high-level programming language such as Java, C++, or Smalltalk to write the messages that will be translated by other software that eventually will control the computer.

Our view of the computer in the implementation phase will be at the level-5 abstraction—the high-level programming language. This implies that the computer is a machine controlled by programming language instructions written in a high-level programming language. There are hundreds of level-5 programming languages that could be used. In this textbook, you will be using a programming language named Java. Java is the tool you will learn to use in order to control what happens at the computer.

Whereas the design phase provided a solution in the form of a pseudocode algorithm, the implementation phase requires nitty-gritty details. The programming language translation must be written in a precise manner according to the syntax rules of that programming language. Attention must be paid to the placement of semicolons, commas, and periods. For example, an algorithmic statement such as this:

  3. Display the value of `courseGrade`.

could be translated into Java source code that might look like this:

```
System.out.println( "Course Grade: " + courseGrade + "%" );
```

This output step generates output to the computer screen that might look like this (assuming the state of `courseGrade` is 92.5):

```
Course Grade: 92.5%
```

Once a programmer has translated the user's needs into pseudocode and then into a programming language, software is utilized to translate level-5 instructions into the lower levels of the computer. Fortunately, there is a tool for performing these translations. Programmers use a compiler to translate the high-level programming language source code (such as Java) into its byte code equivalent. This byte code can then be sent to any machine with a Java virtual machine (VM) on it. The **Java virtual machine** then converts the byte code into the machine language of that particular machine. In this way, the Java program works on a variety of platforms, such as Unix, Mac OS, and Microsoft Windows. Finally, to verify that the program works, the behavior of the executable program must be observed. Input data may be entered, and the corresponding output is observed. The output is compared to what was expected. If the two match, the program works for at least one particular set of input data.

Other sets of input data can be entered while the program is running to build confidence that the program works as defined by the problem specification. Program development is summarized in Figure 1.1.

Figure 1.1: **A review of program development**

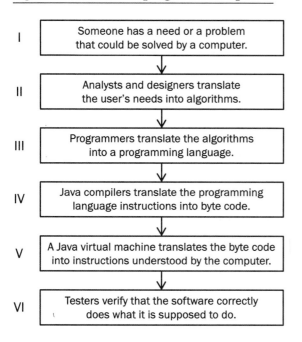

I — Someone has a need or a problem that could be solved by a computer.

II — Analysts and designers translate the user's needs into algorithms.

III — Programmers translate the algorithms into a programming language.

IV — Java compilers translate the programming language instructions into byte code.

V — A Java virtual machine translates the byte code into instructions understood by the computer.

VI — Testers verify that the software correctly does what it is supposed to do.

Although you will likely use the same compiler as in industry, the roles of people will differ. In large software organizations, many people—usually in teams—perform analysis, design implementation, and testing. In many of these simple textbook problems, the user needs are what your instructor requires, usually for grade assessment. You will often play the role of analyst, designer, programmer, *and* tester—perhaps as part of a team, but for the most part by yourself.

Self-Check

1-12 Review Figure 1.1 above and list the phases that are **-a** primarily performed by humans and **-b** primarily performed by software. Select your answers from the set of I, II, III, IV, V, and VI.

1-13 Must the level-6 user of software applications understand the level-5 programming language to use the computer?

1-14 Must the programmer implement the level-5 compiler that translates source code into lower levels?

An Example of Implementation

The following program—a complete Java translation of the algorithm—previews many programming language details. You are not expected to understand this Java code. The details are presented later. For now, just peruse the Java code as an implementation of the pseudocode algorithm. The three variables test1, test2, and finalExam represent user input. The output variable is named courseGrade. User input is made possible through an object named keyboard (objects and the TextReader class are discussed in more detail in Chapters 2 and 3). To get this code to work, you would need to copy the file named TextReader.java[4] into the same folder as this file.

```java
// This program computes and displays a final course grade as a
// weighted average after the user enters the appropriate input.

import TextReader;    // An author-supplied class for easy input

public class TestCourseGrade
{
  public static void main( String[] args )
  {
    // Declare the input and output variables
    double test1 = 0.0;
    double test2 = 0.0;
    double finalExam = 0.0;
    double courseGrade = 0.0;

    System.out.println( "This program computes a course grade when" );
    System.out.println( "you have entered three requested values." );
    System.out.println( );

    // Construct an object for reading input easily
    TextReader keyboard = new TextReader( );

    // I)nput test1, test2, and finalExam
    System.out.print( "Enter first test: " );
    test1 = keyboard.readDouble( );

    System.out.print( "Enter second test: " );
    test2 = keyboard.readDouble( );

    System.out.print( "Enter final exam: " );
    finalExam = keyboard.readDouble( );
```

---

4. TextReader provides an easy way to read input from the user. However, TextReader is not part of Java. TextReader.java must be copied from the disk that accompanies this text-book.

```
    // P)rocess
    courseGrade = ( 0.25 * test1 )
                + ( 0.25 * test2 )
                + ( 0.50 * finalExam );

    // O)utput the results
    System.out.println( "Course Grade: " + courseGrade + "%" );

  } // End of the main method

} // End class TestCourseGrade
```

Dialogue

```
This program computes a course grade when
you have entered three requested values.
Enter first test: 80.0
Enter second test: 90.0
Enter final exam: 100.0
Course Grade: 92.5%
```

At the end of most programs in this textbook, you will find a section titled either "Dialogue" or "Output." A "Dialogue" section shows the program output along with user input in boldface italic. If there is no user input, the section will simply be titled "Output." These dialogues help explain how programs execute so you can more easily learn how to read Java code. Read before you write.

Testing

Although this "Testing" section appears at the end of our first example of program development, don't presume that testing is deferred until implementation. The important process of **testing** may, can, and should occur at any phase of program development. The actual work can be minimal, and it's worth the effort. However, you may not agree until you have felt the pain of *not* testing.

Testing During All Phases of Program Development

- During analysis, establish sample problems to confirm your understanding of the problem.
- During design, walk through the algorithm to ensure that it has the proper steps in the proper order.
- During testing, run the program (or method) several times with different sets of input data. Confirm that the results are correct.
- Review the problem specification. Does the running program do what was requested?

You should have a sample problem before the program is coded—not after. However, if you do decide to wait, it's still better late than never. Work out an example now. If nothing else, at least look at the input and the result of one program run and convince yourself that the output is correct.

When the Java implementation finally does generate output, the predicted results are then compared to the output of the running program. Adjustments must be made any time the predicted output does not match the program output. Such a conflict indicates that the problem example, the program output, or perhaps both are incorrect. Using problem examples helps avoid the misconception that a program is correct just because the program runs successfully and generates output. The output could be wrong! Simply executing doesn't make a program right.

Even exhaustive testing does not prove a program is correct. E. W. Dijkstra has argued that testing only reveals the presence of errors, not the absence of errors. Even with correct program output, the program is not proven correct. However, testing increases confidence that the algorithm, now implemented as a program, at least appears to be reliable.

Self-Check

1-15   If the programmer predicts courseGrade should be 100.0 when all three inputs are 100.0 and the program displays courseGrade as 75.0, what is wrong: the prediction, the program, or both?

1-16   If the programmer predicts courseGrade should be 90.0 when test1 is 80, test2 is 90.0, and finalExam is 100.0 and the program outputs courseGrade as 92.5, what is wrong: the prediction, the program, or both?

1-17   If the programmer predicts courseGrade should be 92.5 when test1 is 80, test2 is 90.0, and finalExam is 100.0 and the program outputs courseGrade as 90.0, what is wrong: the prediction, the program, or both?

Chapter Summary

- This chapter presented a three-step program development strategy of analysis, design, and implementation. The table below shows some of the activities performed during each of these three phases. The maintenance phase has been added to show how the three steps fit into the complete program life cycle. The maintenance phase requires the majority of the time, energy, and money of the program's life cycle.

Phase	Activities You Might Perform
Initiation	Specify the problem.
	Identify the requirements.
Analysis	Read and understand the problem specification.
	Determine the input and output.
	Solve a few sample problems.
Design	Look for patterns to guide algorithm development.
	Write an algorithm—the steps needed to solve the problem.
	Refine the steps in the algorithm and walk through it.
Implementation	Translate the design into a programming language.
	Fix errors.
	Create an executable program.
	Test the program.
Maintenance	Update the program to keep up with a changing world.
	Enhance it.
	Correct bugs (errors) as they're found.

■ Each phase of program development can be viewed in terms of the deliverables.

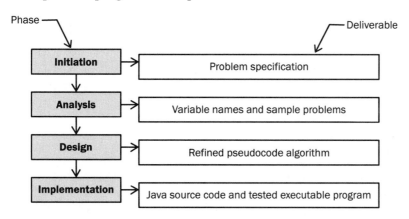

■ Some useful analysis and design tools were introduced:

1. naming the variables that help solve a problem
2. developing algorithms
3. refining one or more steps of an algorithm
4. using the Input/Process/Output algorithmic pattern

Key Terms

algorithm	implementation	problem specification
algorithm walkthrough	input	program
algorithmic pattern	Input/Process/Output (IPO)	pseudocode
analysis	pattern	refinement
computer	Java virtual machine	testing
deliverable	output	variable
design	pattern	

Exercises

The answers to exercises marked with are available in Appendix C.

 1. What is the difference between variables that store output values and variables that store values input by the user?

2. What activities are performed when you design programs?

 3. Describe the deliverable of the design phase of program development.

4. What is the deliverable from the implementation phase of program development?

 5. What are the characteristics of a good algorithm?

6. Does a running program always work correctly? Explain your answer.

 7. Explain the importance of testing a program before a user gets it.

 8. Write an algorithm for finding any phone number in the phone book. Will the search always be successful?

9. Write an algorithm that would direct someone from your classroom to the nearest grocery store.

 10. Write an algorithm that would arrange a collection of CDs (or tapes or record albums) in alphabetical order.

11. Prepare for programming projects at the end of Chapter 2 by procuring a Java development environment. If you are using your school computer lab, Java may already be set up and your instructor should direct you how to use it. If you are working at home, consider downloading Java from Sun Microsystem's Web site: **http://java.sun.com/j2se/**.

Analysis/Design Projects

The following projects do not require a computer. Use a table like this to complete the analysis deliverable for each of the following analysis and design projects:

Problem	Data Name	Input or Output	Sample Problem

1A   Simple Arithmetic

 Problem: For any two numbers a and b, compute the product ($a * b$) and the sum ($a + b$). Also, display the difference between the product and the sum. The difference may be computed as positive or negative depending on the input values for a and b.

1. Complete an analysis deliverable (like the table above) for this problem with at least one sample problem.
2. Complete a design deliverable by writing an algorithm that solves the simple arithmetic problem. Include the arithmetic expressions.

1B   Simple Average

Problem: Find the average of three tests of equal weight.

1. Complete an analysis deliverable (like the table above) for this problem with at least one sample problem.
2. Complete a design deliverable by writing an algorithm (with the formula) that solves the simple average problem.

1C   Weighted Average

Problem: Determine a course grade using this grade assessment scale:

Quiz average   20%
Midterm   20%
Lab grade   35%
Final exam   25%

1. Complete an analysis deliverable (like the table above) for this problem with at least two sample problems.
2. Complete a design deliverable by writing an algorithm (with the formula) that solves the weighted average problem.

1D   Wholesale Cost

Problem: You happen to know that a store has a 25% markup on compact-disc players. If the retail price (what you pay) of a CD player is $189.98, how much did the store pay for that item (the wholesale price)? In general, what is the wholesale price for any item given its retail price and markup? Analyze the problem and design an algorithm that computes the wholesale price for *any* given retail price and *any* given markup. *Clue:* If you can't determine the equation, use this formula and a little algebra to solve for wholesale price:

retail price = wholesale price * (1 + markup)

1. Complete an analysis deliverable (like the table above) for this problem with at least two sample problems.
2. Complete a design deliverable by writing an algorithm (with the formula) that solves the wholesale cost problem.

1E   Grade Point Average

 Problem: Compute a student's cumulative grade point average (GPA) for three courses. Credits range from 0.5 to 15.0. Grades can be 0.0, 1.0, 2.0, 3.0, or 4.0.

1. Complete an analysis deliverable (like the table above) for the GPA problem with at least one sample problem that has courses with different credits.
2. Complete a design deliverable by writing an algorithm that solves the GPA problem.

1F   F to C

Problem: Use the following formula to convert Fahrenheit (F) temperatures to Celsius (C):

1. Complete an analysis deliverable (like the table above) for this problem with at least one sample problem.
2. Complete a design deliverable by writing an algorithm (with the formula) that solves the F to C problem.

1G   C to F

Problem: Use algebra and the formula of the preceding exercise to convert Celsius (C) temperatures to Fahrenheit (F).

1. Complete an analysis deliverable (like the table above) for this problem with at least one sample problem.
2. Complete a design deliverable by writing an algorithm (with the formula) that solves the C to F problem.

1H   Seconds

Problem: Determine the number of hours, minutes, and seconds represented by a total number of seconds. For example, 3,661 seconds is 1 hour, 1 minute, and 1 second.

1. Complete an analysis deliverable (like the table above) for this problem with at least one sample problem.
2. Complete a design deliverable by writing an algorithm (with the formula) that solves the seconds problem.

1I   U.S. Minimum Coins

Problem: Determine the number of each denomination of coins required to make change for cents in the range of 0 through 99. The number of coins should be the lowest possible. The available coins are half dollars (50 cents), quarters (25 cents), dimes (10 cents), nickels (five cents), and pennies (one cent). For example, if there is 91 cents change, you will have one of each coin.

1. Complete an analysis deliverable (like the table above) for this problem with at least one sample problem other than 91 cents.
2. Complete a design deliverable by writing an algorithm (with the formula) that solves the U.S. minimum coins problem.

1J   U.K. Minimum Coins

Problem: Determine the coins required to make change for any number of pence from 0 to 199. The number of coins should be the lowest possible. The available coins are 1p (p represents pence), 2p, 5p, 10p, 20p, 50p, and 100p (the one-pound coin). For example, if there is 188 pence, you will have one of each coin.

1. Complete an analysis deliverable (like the table above) for this problem with at least one sample problem other than 188 pence.
2. Complete a design deliverable by writing an algorithm (with the formula) that solves the U.K. minimum coins problem.

Answers to Self-Check Questions

1-1   A college degree perhaps (other deliverables are possible)

1-2   Input: `pounds` and perhaps `todaysConversionRate`
Output: `USDollars`

1-3   `CDCollection`, `currentSelection`

1-4	Problem	Data Name	Input or Output	Sample Problem
	Compute distance	metersPerSecond	Input	28.0
	traveled	secondsInFlight	Input	3.1
		distance	Output	86.8

1-5	Problem	Data Name	Input or Output	Sample Problem
	Compute the	presentValue	Input	1000.00
	future value of	periods	Input	360
	an investment	monthlyInterestRate	Input	0.0075
		futureValue	Output	14730.58

1-6   Turn the oven off (or you might recognize some other activity or detail that was omitted).

1-7   No (at least the author thinks it's okay)

1-8   No (at least the author thinks it's okay)

1-9   No. The courseGrade would be computed using undefined values for test1, test2, and finalExam.

1-10 No. The details of the process step are not present. The formula is missing.

1-11 Input: Retrieve values from the user for the three inputs:

test1 *0*
test2 *50*
finalExam *100*

Process: Retrieve the values of the tests and compute courseGrade as follows:

courseGrade = (0.25 x test1) + (0.25 x test2) + (0.50 x finalExam)
              (0.25 x 0.0)   + (0.25 x 50.0) + (0.50 x 100.0)
                 (0.0   +   12.5   +   50.0)
courseGrade = 62.5

Output: Show courseGrade = 62.5% to the user.

1-12 -a   I, II, III, and VI

      -b   IV and V

1-13 No

1-14 No

1-15 The program is wrong.

1-16 The prediction is wrong. The problem asked for a weighted average, not a simple average.

1-17 The program is wrong.

Chapter 2
A Little Java

Summing Up

The first chapter introduced a program development strategy of analysis, design, and implementation. Although you are encouraged to do some analysis and design before writing code, many problems encountered in the early chapters of this book will not require much effort to produce analysis and design deliverables. Analysis may simply be "Read the problem." Design might end up as "I can picture the solution in my head."

Coming Up

This chapter will emphasize translating algorithms into programs using the Java programming language. Understanding how to translate a pseudocode algorithm into its programming language equivalent requires understanding the smallest pieces of a program and how to correctly gather them together to get things done. This chapter also examines how to deal with the input of numbers, the processing of numeric data, and output. An author-supplied class for reading input from the keyboard is also introduced. After studying this chapter, you will be able to

- use existing classes
- obtain data from the user and display information to the user
- declare and initialize primitive variables of types `double`, `int`, and `boolean`
- read numeric data from the keyboard
- construct an instance of a class and send messages
- evaluate and create arithmetic expressions and simple boolean expressions
- solve problems using the Input/Process/Output pattern

Exercises and programming projects reinforce writing simple IPO programs with a text-based interface.

2.1   The Java Programming Language — A Start

In the rawest definition, a Java **class** is a sequence of characters (text) stored as a file with a name that ends with `.java`. Each class consists of several elements such as a class heading (`public class` *class-name*). A class also contains methods—a collection of statements grouped together to perform a specific function (classes and methods are presented in detail in Chapter 4, "Classes and Interfaces"). Here is a general form for a Java class that has one method named `main`. A class with a **main method** can be run as a program.

General Form 2.1: **A simple Java program (only one class)**

```
// Comments
import class-name
public class class-name
{
  public static void main( String[ ] args )
  {
    variable declarations and initializations
    class instance creations (constructing objects)
    messages and operations such as assignments
  }
}
```

A **general form** describes the **syntax**—the correct language—necessary to write classes and executable programs. This general form, like all others in this textbook, uses the following conventions:

1. Boldface elements must be written exactly as shown. This includes words such as **public static void main** and symbols such as **[**, **]**, **(**, and **)**.
2. The programmer must supply the portions of a general form shown in italic. Italicized items are defined somewhere else or supplied by the programmer.

An Example of a Syntactically Correct Java Class with One Method Named main

```
// Read a number and display that input value squared
import TextReader;    // An author-supplied class in the working folder
import java.lang.System; // For System.out (automatically imported)

public class ReadItAndSquareIt              // Class heading
{
  public static void main( String[] args )  // Method heading
  {
    double number;                          // Variable declaration
    double result = 0.0;                    // Variable initialization
    TextReader keyboard = new TextReader( ); // Class instance creation
```

```
   // I)nput
   System.out.print( "Enter a number: " );   // Message
   number = keyboard.readDouble( );           // Message and assignment

   // P)rocess (* means multiplication)
   result = number * number;                  // Assignment

   // O)utput
   System.out.println( number + " squared = " + result );  // Message
 }
}
```

Dialogue

```
Enter a number: -12.0
-12.0 squared = 144.0
```

The first line is a comment documenting what the program does. The next line contains the word **import**, which allows a program to gain access to other classes. The class above has access to a class named TextReader for reading user input. You will often see a class name with a package name (a **package** is a collection of classes), where periods separate the folders containing the class. For example:

```
// Import one class from the java.io package
import java.io.BufferedReader;
// * means import all classes from the java.io package
import java.io.*;
```

The class above does not need the imports as shown. The important thing is that the file named TextReader.java is in the same folder as the Java program shown. Then, with or without import TextReader;, the program will compile. However, if TextReader.java is not in the same folder, the compiler will complain that TextReader is not known. So, to do input with the author-supplied **TextReader** class, you could simply place the file named TextReader.java into your working folder.[1] Here is one possible error message you would see if you did not get TextReader.java into the same folder as your program that tried to use it:

```
ReadItAndSquareIt.java:2: Class TextReader not found in import.
import TextReader;   // An author-supplied class
       ^
1 error
```

The other import

```
import java.lang.System;   // For System.out
```

---

1. The file TextReader.java with class TextReader is stored on the disk that accompanies this textbook. This file must be copied into the same folder (directory) as the program that uses it.

is unnecessary because Java automatically imports all of the classes from
`java.lang`. It's as if Java automatically writes this line for you at the top of each
Java program:

```
import java.lang.*; // For all classes in java.lang: System, String ...
```

Java classes are organized into packages (approximately 72 at last count). Each
package contains a set of related classes. For example, `java.net` has classes related
to programming with the Internet, and `java.io` has a collection of classes for
performing input and output. In this textbook, you will need only a few classes in a
few packages to get things done. Many of these classes are in the `java.lang`
package. The `import` is not necessary. Many programs will require one or more of
the author-supplied classes, such as `TextReader` and `BankAccount`, which are
stored in `TextReader.java` and `BankAccount.java`, respectively. It is recommended that you copy these files into your working folder and skip the optional
`import`.

Many of the classes in the early part of this textbook can be completed without
an `import`. Optional imports are shown in this chapter and the next one to remind
you that you are using other classes to get things done. Later on, the unnecessary
imports will not be written.

The next line in the sample program is the start of a class heading. A class is a
collection of methods and variables (both discussed later) enclosed within a set of
matching curly braces. You could use any valid class name after `public class`;
however, the class name must match the file name. Therefore, the preceding
program must be stored in a file named `ReadItAndSquareIt.java`.

***General Form 2.2:* The file-naming convention**

*class-name.***java**

The next line is a method heading that for now is best retyped exactly as shown:

```
public static void main( String[] args )      // Method heading
```

The curly braces begin and end the `main` method. A method is a collection of
executable statements and variables (both discussed later). When a class contains a
`main` method, it can be run as a program. The program begins with the first
statement in `main`. The `main` method above contains a variable declaration, a
variable initialization, an object construction, and four messages, all of which are
described later in this chapter.

This Java source code represents input to the Java compiler. A **compiler** is a
program that translates source code into a level that is closer to the computer
hardware. Along the way, the compiler generates error messages when it detects a
violation of Java syntax rules. You will see errors detected as your compiler scans
the source code of the programs you write.

Tokens — The Smallest Pieces of a Program

As the Java compiler reads the source code, it identifies individual **tokens**, which are the smallest recognizable components of a program. Tokens fall into four categories:

Token	Examples
Special symbols	`;  (  )  ,  .  {  }`
Identifiers	`main args credits courseGrade String List`
Reserved identifiers	`public static void class double int`
Literals (constant values)	`"Hello World!" 0 -2.1 'C' true`

These tokens are used to make up larger things. Knowing the types of tokens in Java should help you to

- more easily code syntactically correct messages
- better understand how to fix syntax errors detected by the compiler
- understand general forms

Special Symbols

A **special symbol** is a sequence of one or two characters with one or possibly many specific meanings. Some special symbols separate other tokens; {, ;, and ,, for example. Other special symbols represent operators in expressions; +, -, and /, for example. Here is a partial list of single-character and double-character special symbols frequently seen in Java programs:

```
(    )    .    +    -    /    *    =<    >=    //    { }    ==    ;
```

Identifiers

A Java **identifier** is a wordlike token that represents a variety of things. For example, `String` is the name of a class for storing a string of characters. Here are some other identifiers that Java has already given meaning to:

```
sqrt  String  get  println  readLine  System  equals  Double
```

Programmers must often create their own identifiers. For example, `test1`, `finalExam`, `main`, and `courseGrade` are identifiers defined by programmers. All identifiers must follow these rules for creating Java identifiers:

- Identifiers begin with upper- or lowercase letters a through z (or A through Z), the dollar sign $, or the underscore character _.
- The first letter may be followed by a number of upper- and lowercase letters, digits (0 through 9), dollar signs, and underscore characters.
- Identifiers are case sensitive. For example, `Ident`, `ident`, and `iDENT` are three different identifiers.

Valid Identifiers

main	Vector	incomeTax	MAX_SIZE	$Money$
Maine	URL	employeeName	all_4_one	_balance
miSpel	String	A1	world_in_motion	my_balance

Invalid Identifiers

```
1A            // It begins with a digit
miles/Hour    // The / is unacceptable
first Name    // The blank space is unacceptable
pre-shrunk    // The operator - means subtraction
double        // It is a keyword
```

Remember the case sensitivity of Java. For example, many programs must have the identifier main. MAIN or Main won't do. Also, note that several conventions may be used for upper- and lowercase letters. Some programmers prefer to avoid uppercase letters; others prefer to use uppercase letters for each new word. The convention this textbook uses is the "camelBack" style for variables. This means each new word has an uppercase letter. For example, you will see letterGrade rather than lettergrade, LetterGrade, or letter_grade. All author-supplied classes follow the Java convention of beginning class names with an uppercase character: String, Vector, Grid, and BankAccount, for example.

Keywords (Reserved Identifiers)

A reserved identifier is an identifier that has been set aside for a specific purpose. It is a word whose meaning is fixed by the standard language definition, such as double and int. They follow the same rules as identifiers, but they cannot be used for any other purpose. Here is a partial list of Java reserved identifiers, which are also known as **keywords**.

Java Keywords

boolean	default	for	new
break	do	if	private
case	double	import	public
catch	else	instanceOf	return
char	extends	int	void
class	float	long	while

The case sensitivity of Java applies to keywords. For example, there is a difference between double (a keyword) and Double (an identifier, not a keyword). All Java keywords are written in lowercase letters.

Literals

A constant is a value that cannot be changed. As in mathematics, values such as 123 and 4.56 are constant values. When written inside a Java program, such constant values are also known as literal values, or simply **literals**.[2] For example, the Java compiler recognizes character literals as one character enclosed within single quotation marks. A `string` literal has zero or more characters enclosed within a pair of double quotation marks (special symbols) and finished on the same line.

```
"Double quotes are used to delimit String literals."
"Hello, World!"
```

Integer literals are written as numbers without decimal points. Floating-point literals are written as numbers with decimal points (or in exponential notation, 5e3 = 5 * 10^3 = 5000.0 and 1.23e - 4 = 1.23 x 10^{-4} = 0.0001234). Here are a few examples of integer, floating-point, string, and character literals in Java, along with both boolean literals (`true` and `false`) and the null literal, written in Java as `null`.

The Six Types of Literals in Java

Integer	Floating Point	String	Character	Boolean	Null
-2147483648	-1.0	"A"	'a'	true	null
-1	0.0	"Hello World"	'0'	false	
0	39.95	"\n new line"	'?'		
1	1.234e02	"1.23"	' '		
2147483647	-1e6	"The answer is: "	'7'		

Comments

Comments are portions of text that annotate a program. Comments fulfill any or all of the following expectations:

- Provide internal documentation to help one programmer read another's program—assuming those comments clarify the meaning of the program.
- Explain certain code fragments or the purpose of a variable.
- Indicate the programmer's name and the goal of the program.
- Describe a wide variety of program elements and other considerations.

Comments may be added anywhere throughout a program. They may begin with the two-character special symbol /* when closed with the corresponding symbol */.

```
/*
   A comment may
   extend over
   many lines
*/
```

---

2. Synonyms for *literal* include *exact, accurate,* and *plain.*

An alternate form for comments is to use `//` before the text. Such a comment may appear on a line by itself or at the end of a line.

```
// A complete Java program
public class DoNothing
{
  public static void main( String[] args )     // A method heading
  {
    // This program does nothing
  }
}
```

Within the context of the programs in this textbook, comments are most often written as one-line comments like `//Comment` rather than `/*Comment*/`. All code after `/*` is a comment until `*/` is encountered, so a large portion of the program could accidentally be turned into a comment by forgetting `*/` at the end! The one-line comments make it more difficult to accidentally "comment out" large sections of code. But many programmers prefer `/*` followed by `*/`.

Comments are added to help clarify and document the purpose of the source code. The goal is to make the program more understandable, easier to debug (correct errors), and easier to maintain (change when necessary). Programmers need comments to understand programs that may have been written days, weeks, months, years, or even decades ago.

Java has a third style of comments known as **javadoc comments**. Comments that begin with `/**` (note the second asterisk) and end with `*/` contain documentation and special tags that show up in Web pages (when you run the javadoc program).

```
/** Debit this account by withdrawalAmount if it is
  * no greater than this account's current balance.
  * @param withdrawalAmount The requested amount of money to withdraw.
  * @return true if 0 < withdrawalAmount <= the balance.
  */
public boolean withdraw( double withdrawalAmount )
```

Appendix A describes javadoc comments, tags such as @param and @return, and how to create hyperlinked Web pages with Java's javadoc program. Javadoc comments document all of Java's classes and interfaces. This allows you to have all of your classes documented in the same manner. This documentation can be read by a Web browser such as Netscape or Internet Explorer.

Self-Check

2-1   How many tokens are there in the first program of section 2.1 (ReadItAndSquareIt)? *Note:* `System.out.println` has five tokens: two periods, which are special symbols, and three identifiers. Do not count comments.

2-2   Identify whether each of the following is a valid identifier or explain why it is not valid:

-a	abc	**-l**	H.P.
-b	123	**-m**	$Money$Money$Money
-c	ABC	**-n**	55_mph
-d	.	**-o**	sales Tax
-e	my Age	**-p**	main
-f	k/s	**-q**	a
-g	Abc!	**-r**	_
-h	identifier	**-s**	_____
-i	(identifier)	**-t**	Mile/Hour
-j	Double	**-u**	student name
-k	mispellted	**-v**	TextReader

2-3 List two special symbols that are one character long.

2-4 List two special symbols that are two characters long.

2-5 List two identifiers that have already been defined by Java.

2-6 Create two programmer-defined identifiers.

2-7 Which of the tokens shown below are valid:

    -a string literals?

    -b integer literals?

    -c floating-point literals?

    -d boolean literals?

    -e null literals?

    -f character literals?

```
1.0   34   'H'   "integer"   -123   1.0e+03   "H"   null
true   2,000   FALSE
```

2-8 Which of the following are valid Java comments?

    -a `//  Is this a comment?`

    -b `/ / Is this a comment?`

    -c `/* Is this a comment?`

    -d `/* Is this a comment? */`

2.2   Primitive Types

Java has two types of variables: primitive types and reference types. **Primitive variables** store a single value in a fixed amount of computer memory. The term "primitive" (simple) describes the eight different Java data types that store only one value. The primitive types are closely related to computer hardware. For example, an int value is stored in 32 bits (4 bytes) of memory. Those 32 bits represent a simple positive or negative integer value. By contrast, a reference variable stores the address of (a reference to) an object.

Whereas the primitive types are part of Java for efficiency—their use helps make programs run faster—reference types allow for objects that are more intricate. Objects allow programmers to model real-world entities that are more intricate than numbers and single characters. Each object has a collection of related data and methods needed to fulfill the responsibilities of the class. Whereas primitive variables store only one value, a **reference variable** stores the address of an object. The object may store many primitive values and other references to other objects. The state of an object can be quite complex. However, the reference value is always the same type of value—an integer representing the address of the object. Here is summary of all data types in Java:

Java's Data Types

Primitive Types	**Reference Types**
integers:	classes (Chapter 4)
byte (8 bits)	arrays (Chapter 8)
short (16 bits)	
int (32 bits)	
long (64 bits)	interfaces (Chapter 4)
real numbers:	
float (32 bits)	
double (64 bits)	
others:	
char (16 bits)	
boolean (true or false)	

Two of Java's primitive types for storing numbers—**int** and **double**—are used in virtually all programs. Their use is introduced by considering the following:

- how to declare and initialize variables
- how to output—display—the value of a variable
- how to change the value of a variable (assignment)
- how to input values through keyboard input to be stored into variables

Declarations and Initializations

A primitive variable **declaration** brings into a program a named data value that can change while the program is running. An **initialization** allows the programmer to set the initial value of the variable. These variable names are used later when the programmer is interested in the current value of the variable or needs to change the value of that variable. Here are the general forms for declaring and initializing variables:

General Form 2.3: **Initializing (declaring a variable and giving it a value you want)**

data-type identifier;   `// Declare one variable`
data-type identifier = *initial-value;* `// For primitive types like int and double`

The data-type may be any of Java's primitive types, such as `double` to store numbers with a decimal point or `int` to store integers. Java's primitive types consist of `int`, `double`, `boolean`, `char`, `float`, and three integer types that store different ranges of integers: `byte`, `short`, and `long`. The following Java program declares one `int` and two `double` primitive variables:

```
// Initialize some numeric variables only. There is no input.
public class ShowSomePrimitiveTypes
{
  public static void main( String[] args )
  {
    int credits = 0;
    double qualityPoints;  // Value is undefined
    double GPA = 0.0;      // ... nothing visible happens ...
  }
}
```

The primitive numeric types `int` and `double` can be initialized with = followed by the initial value. This satisfies all three attributes of a variable: (1) the name as specified by the identifier, (2) the available operations as specified by the type, and (3) the value as specified by the initial value after =. The following table summarizes the initial value of these variables:

Variable Name	Value
credits	0
qualityPoints	? // Unknown
GPA	0.0

Output with `print` and `println`

Programs communicate with users. Such communication is provided through—but is not limited to—keyboard **input** and screen **output**. This two-way communication is a critical component of many programs and is made possible by sending messages. A message is composed of several tokens that have been correctly grouped together to perform some operation. A message performs some well-defined responsibility while hiding many complexities. Some messages evaluate to some value that will be used by some other part of the program. Other messages just go off and perform some activity. Here are the general forms of two different Java messages. Both write information to the computer screen.

General Form 2.4: **Output**

System.out.print(*expression-1* **+** *expression-2,* *...,* **+** *expression-n* **);**
System.out.println(*expression-1* **+** *expression-2,* *...,* **+** *expression-n* **);**

System.out is a variable that represents the computer screen. The expressions between parentheses will be displayed to the computer screen. *expression-1* through *expression-n* may take the form of variable names such as GPA or literals such as "Credits: " and 99.5. These expressions are separated with the concatenation operator + and enclosed within the set of parentheses. All of the values will be combined into one big string that is displayed on the computer screen. This expression, between the parentheses, is known as the **argument**. Finally, a semicolon (;) terminates the message.

The only difference between print and println is that println generates a new line so subsequent output begins at the beginning of a new line. Here are some valid output messages:

```
System.out.print( "Enter final exam: " );      // Use print to prompt
System.out.println( "Credits: " + credits );
System.out.println( );   // Cursor goes to beginning of next line
```

A println message with no arguments—nothing between the parentheses—generates a blank line. The above initializations and messages are now placed together in a new Java program that generates some rather meaningless output:

```
// Display some meaningless output that will make sense later
import java.lang.System;   // Or omit this since the import is automatic

public class ShowSomePrimitiveTypes
{
  public static void main( String[] args )
  {
    int credits = 12;
    double qualityPoints = 0.0;
    double GPA = 0.0;

    System.out.println( 99.5 );
    System.out.print( "Enter credits: " );
    System.out.println( " WHERE'S THE INPUT?" );
    System.out.println( ); // Generate a new line
    System.out.println( "Credits are " + credits + " for now." );
    System.out.println( 1 * 2.3 * 4 );
  }
}
```

Output

```
99.5
Enter credits:  WHERE'S THE INPUT?

Credits are 12 for now.
9.2
```

Assignment

An **assignment** furnishes and/or modifies the value of a variable. The value of the expression to the right of = replaces whatever value was in the variable to the left of =.

General Form 2.5: **Assignment**

variable-name = *expression;*

The *expression* must be a value that can be stored by the variable to the left of the assignment operator (=). For example, an expression that results in a floating-point value can be stored into a double variable, and an integer can be stored in an int variable. Here are some sample assignments:

```
credits = 15;
qualityPoints = 45.67;
```

After the two assignments execute, the value of both variables is modified and the values can be shown like this:

Variable	Value
credits	15
qualityPoints	45.67

Assignments come with compatibility rules. For example, a String literal cannot be assigned to a numeric variable. A floating-point number cannot be stored in an int.

```
qualityPoints = "Noooooo, you can't do that";  // ERROR
credits = 16.5; // ERROR—Can't store a floating-point number in an int
```

The compiler will report an error at the attempted assignment.

```
-a   anInt = 1;              -e   aDouble = 1;
-b   anInt = 1.5;            -f   aDouble = 1.5;
-c   anInt = "1.5";          -g   aDouble = "1.5";
-d   anInt = anInt + 1;      -h   aDouble = aDouble + 1.5;
```

The following program uses a Java assignment to give specific values to variables that are initially only declared—not initialized. Notice that you can declare many variables when the identifiers are separated by commas.

```java
// A few assignment statements
import java.lang.System;    // System is in the java.lang package

public class ShowSomePrimitiveTypes
{
  public static void main( String[] args )
  {
    int credits;
    double qualityPoints, GPA;  // A list of variables

    credits = 16;                      // Assignment
    qualityPoints = 49.5;              // Assignment
    GPA = qualityPoints / credits;     // Divide before assignment

    System.out.println( "Credits: " + credits );
    System.out.println( "Quality points: " + qualityPoints );
    System.out.println( "GPA: " + GPA );
  }
}
```

Output

```
Credits: 16
Quality points: 49.5
GPA: 3.09375
```

Be wary of uninitialized variables. If you do not initialize a variable, it cannot be used unless it is changed later through assignment (which is discussed in the next section). In summary, to properly use variables in a program, all three characteristics must be considered:

1. A variable must be given a name in a declaration or initialization.
2. A variable must be declared as a specific primitive type.
3. A variable should be given a meaningful value through initialization, assignment, input, or some other means.

Input

To make programs more general—for example, to find the GPA for any student—variables are often assigned values through keyboard input. This allows the user to enter any data desired. There are several options for obtaining user input from the computer keyboard. Perhaps the simplest option is the use of an author-supplied Java class named `TextReader`. `TextReader` has a collection of methods that allow for easy input of numbers and strings.

Before you can use `TextReader` methods such as `readDouble`, your code must ask for an instance of the class. The following are examples of class instance creations. The result is that `keyboard` and `inFile` are reference variables that refer to different sources of input.

Creating an Instance of **TextReader** to Read Numeric Input (requires **TextReader.java**)

```
// Construct an object named keyboard to read numbers from the user
TextReader keyboard = new TextReader( );
// Can use inFile to read input data from the disk file in.dat
TextReader inFile = new TextReader( "in.dat" );
```

This code is also referred to as **constructing an object**, because it invokes a special method called a "constructor," a method that has the same name as the class (`TextReader` here).

In general, objects (instances of a class) are constructed with the keyword `new` followed by *class-name(optional-arguments)* .

General Form 2.6: **Constructing objects (initial values are optional)**

class-name object-name = **new** *class-name(* **)** *;*
class-name object-name = **new** *class-name(initial-value(s))* *;*

This expression to the right of = evaluates to a reference value—the location of the object in memory. That reference value is then stored in the reference variable to the left of =. This is actually an assignment of a reference value to a reference variable. Whereas assignments to primitive variables store primitive values, assignments to reference values store the reference to an object. In other words, you could write the same object creation as follows:

```
TextReader keyboard;    // Not initialized. You cannot get input yet!
keyboard = new TextReader( );   // Now you can get keyboard input
```

`TextReader` is an author-supplied Java class. It is stored in a file named `TextReader.java` on this textbook's accompanying CD. Like other Java classes, `TextReader` has a collection of related methods. Each method performs some well-defined responsibility. This particular `TextReader` class has a collection of methods for reading text input either from the user at the keyboard or from a file on a disk. Through the object constructions above, several methods are now available to the `TextReader` objects referenced via the reference variables `keyboard` and `inFile`.

`TextReader` methods are used to get text input from the keyboard and convert that text, for example, 3.45 and 99, into numbers. Here are two messages that allow users to input numbers into a program:

Numeric Input (requires `TextReader.java`)

```
keyboard.readInt( );        // Pause until user enters an integer
keyboard.readDouble( );     // This gets a floating-point number
```

Here is the general form of sending a message to an object so the object performs some well-defined responsibility. (*Note: object-name* must already be constructed.)

General Form 2.7: Sending a message to an object

object-name . *message-name*(*argument-list*)

When a **readInt** or **readDouble** message is sent to a `TextReader` object, the method pauses program execution until the user enters the proper input value and then presses the Enter key. If the user enters the number correctly, the input string will be converted into the proper machine representation of the number.

These two methods are examples of expressions that evaluate to some value. Whereas a `readInt` message evaluates to a primitive `int` value, a `readDouble` message evaluates to a primitive floating-point value. Because `readInt` and `readDouble` return numeric values, they are often seen as part of assignment statements. These messages will be seen in text-based input and output programs (ones with no graphical user interface).

For example, the following two messages prompt the user to enter a number with the `print` method. The `readDouble` message then causes a pause until the user enters a number. At that point, `readDouble` converts the text typed by the user into a floating-point number. That number is then assigned to the variable named `qualityPoints`. All of this happens in one line of code.

```
System.out.print( "Enter quality points: " ); // Prompt the user
qualityPoints = keyboard.readDouble( );        // Assign the number entered
// qualityPoints is a number typed by the user at the keyboard
```

To use the `TextReader` class, you must copy the file `TextReader.java` into the same folder as your programs (unless your lab has this set up for you already). This gives you access to the `TextReader` class and the `readInt()` and `readDouble()` methods. A standard alternative, with no extra classes needed, is discussed in the Programming Tips section. This alternative form of input uses classes from the `java.io` package. It may be used instead of using `TextReader`.

The following program uses a `TextReader` object to obtain input for computing the GPA of any student. This program assumes that the file `TextReader.java` is in the same folder as the file `ShowSomePrimitiveTypes.java`.

```
// Read an int and a double.
// This program assumes TextReader.java is in the same folder.
// An unnecessary import (automatically done): import java.lang.System;

public class ShowSomePrimitiveTypes
{
   public static void main( String[] args )
   {
      int credits = 0;
      double qualityPoints = 0.0;
      double GPA = 0.0;
      TextReader keyboard = new TextReader( );

      System.out.print( "Enter credits: " );
      // User inputs an integer, which gets stored in credits
      credits = keyboard.readInt( );

      System.out.print( "Enter quality points: " );
      qualityPoints = keyboard.readDouble( );

      GPA = qualityPoints / credits;
      System.out.println( "Credits: " + credits );
      System.out.println( "Quality points: " + qualityPoints );
      System.out.println( "GPA: " + GPA );
   }
}
```

Dialogue (remember that user input is shown in boldface italic)

```
Enter credits: 15
Enter quality points: 48.0
Credits: 15
Quality points: 48.0
GPA: 3.2
```

One of the nice things about using TextReader for input is that if the user accidentally enters an invalid number, the user is simply asked to enter a valid number.

Dialogue (when the user does not enter valid numbers with TextReader)

```
Enter credits: 16.0
Invalid integer. Try again.
Bad again
Invalid integer. Try again.
Invalid integer. Try again.
16
Enter quality points: Invalid input entered on purpose
Invalid floating-point number. Try again.
Invalid floating-point number. Try again.
Invalid floating-point number. Try again.
Invalid floating-point number. Try again.
Invalid floating-point number. Try again.
49.5
Credits: 16
Quality points: 49.5
GPA: 3.09375
```

2.3   Arithmetic Expressions

Many of the problems in the early chapters of this textbook require you to write arithmetic expressions. Arithmetic expressions are made up of two components: operators and operands. An arithmetic operator is one of the Java special symbols +, -, /, or *. The operands of an arithmetic expression may be numeric variable names such as `qualityPoints`, numeric literals such as 5 and 0.25, and method calls that evaluate to a numeric value such as `Math.sqrt(4.0)`. Assuming `aDouble` is a `double`, the following expression has operands `aDouble` and 4.5. The operator is +.

```
aDouble + 4.5
```

Together, the operator and operands determine the value of the arithmetic expression.

The simplest arithmetic expression is a numeric literal or numeric variable name. Arithmetic expressions may also have two operands with one operator (see the table below).

Arithmetic Expressions

An Expression May Be	Example
numeric variable	`double aDouble`
numeric literal	`100` or `99.5`
expression + expression	`aDouble + 2.0`
expression - expression	`aDouble - 2.0`
expression * expression	`aDouble * 2.0`
expression / expression	`aDouble / 2.0`
(expression)	`( aDouble + 2.0 )`

The previous definition of expression suggests more complex arithmetic expressions are possible.

```
1.5 * ( ( aDouble - 99.5 ) * 1.0 / aDouble )
```

Since arithmetic expressions may be written with many literals, numeric variable names, and operators, rules are put into force to allow a consistent evaluation of expressions. The following table lists four Java arithmetic operators and the order in which they are applied to numeric variables.

Some Binary Arithmetic Operators

*	/	In the absence of parentheses, multiplication and division evaluate before addition and subtraction. In other words, * and / have precedence over + and -. If more than one of these operators appear in an expression, the leftmost operator evaluates first.
+	-	In the absence of parentheses, + and - evaluate after all * and / operators, with the leftmost evaluating first. Parentheses may override these precedence rules.

The operators of the following expression are applied to the operands in this order: /, +, and lastly -.

```
2.0 + 5.0 - 8.0 / 4.0   // Evaluates to 5.0
```

Parentheses may alter the order in which arithmetic operators are applied to their operands.

```
( 2.0 + 5.0 - 8.0 ) / 4.0   // Evaluates to -0.25
```

With parentheses, the / operator evaluates last, rather than first. The same set of operators and operands with parentheses has a different result (-0.25 rather than 5.0).

These precedence rules apply to binary operators only. A **binary operator** is one that requires one operand to the left and one operand to the right. A **unary operator** only requires one operand on the right. Consider this expression, which has the binary operator * and the unary minus operator -.

```
3.5 * -2.0   // Evaluates to -7.0
```

The unary operator evaluates before the binary * operator: 3.5 times negative 2.0 results in negative 7.0.

Arithmetic expressions usually have variable names as operands. When Java evaluates an expression with variables, the variable name is replaced by its value. Consider the following code:

```
double numOne = 1.0;
double numTwo = 2.0;
double numThree = 3.0;
double answer = numOne + numTwo * NumThree / 4.0;
```

The following simulation evaluates this arithmetic expression by first substituting the value for all variables and then evaluating each subexpression using the Java precedence rules:

```
answer = numOne + numTwo * NumThree / 4.0;
answer =    1.0  +   2.0  *    3.0   / 4.0   // Substitute values
answer =    1.0  +          6.0      / 4.0   // * has precedence over +
answer =    1.0  +                    1.5    // / has precedence over +
answer =       2.5
```

Self-Check

2-12   Evaluate the following arithmetic expressions:

```
double x = 2.5;
double y = 3.0;
```

-a x * y + 3.0   **-d** 1.5 * (x - y)

-b 0.5 + x / 2.0   **-e** y + -x

-c 1.0 + x * 3.0 / y   **-f** (x - 2.0) * (y - 1.0)

The `boolean` Type and Simple Boolean Expressions

Java has a primitive `boolean` data type to store either one of the two `boolean` literals: `true` or `false`. Whereas arithmetic expressions evaluate to a number, **boolean** expressions, such as `credits > 60.0`, evaluate to one of these `boolean` values. A boolean expression often contains one of these **relational operators**.

Operator	Meaning
<	Less than
>	Greater than
<=	Less than or equal to
>=	Greater than or equal to
==	Equal to
!=	Not equal to

When a relational operator is applied to two operands that can be compared to each other, the result is one of two values: `true` or `false`. The next table shows some examples of simple boolean expressions and their resulting values.

Boolean Expression	Result
`double x = 4.0;`	
`x < 5.0`	true
`x > 5.0`	false
`x <= 5.0`	true
`5.0 == x`	false
`x != 5.0`	true

Like primitive numeric variables, `boolean` variables can be declared, initialized, and assigned a value. The assigned expression should be a boolean expression—one that evaluates to `true` or `false`. This is shown in the initializations, assignments, and output of three `boolean` variables in the following code:

```
// Initialize three boolean variables to false
boolean ready = false;
boolean willing = false;
boolean able = false;
double credits = 28.5;
double hours = 9.5;

// Assign true or false to all three boolean variables
ready = hours >= 8.0;
willing = credits > 20.0;
able = credits <= 32.0;

System.out.println( "ready: " + ready );
System.out.println( "willing: " + willing );
System.out.println( "able: " + able );
```

```
// If all three booleans are true, the boolean expression is true
System.out.println( "All 3 true? " + (ready == willing == able) );
```

Output

```
ready: true
willing: true
able: true
All 3 true? true
```

Self-Check

2-13 Which expressions evaluate to `true`, assuming that `j` and `k` are initialized like this:

```
int j = 4;
int k = 8;
```

-**a** (j + 4) == k   -**e** j < k
-**b** 0 == j   -**f** 4 == j
-**c** j >= k   -**g** j == (j + k - j)
-**d** j != k   -**h** (k - 2) == (j + 2)

2.4   Prompt and Input

The output and input operations are often used together to obtain values from the user of the program. The program informs the user what must be entered with an output message and then sends an input message to get values for the variables. This happens so often that this activity can be considered to be a pattern. The **Prompt and Input** pattern has two activities:

1. Ask the user to enter a value (prompt).
2. Obtain the value for the variable (input).

Algorithmic Pattern 2.1

Pattern:	Prompt and Input
Problem:	The user must enter something.
Outline:	1. Prompt the user for input.
	2. Input the data
Code Example:	`System.out.println( "Enter credits: " );`
	`int credits = keyboard.readInt( );`

Strange things may happen if the prompt is left out. The user will not know what must be entered. Whenever you require user input, make sure you prompt for it first. Write the code that tells the user precisely what you want. First output the prompt and then obtain the user input. Here is another instance of the Prompt and Input pattern:

```
System.out.println( "Enter test #1: " );
double test1 = keyboard.readDouble( );  // Initialize with user input
System.out.println( "You entered " + test1 );
```

Dialogue

```
Enter test #1: 97.5
You entered 97.5
```

In general, tell the user what value is needed, then input a value into that variable with an input message such as `keyboard.readDouble( );`.

General Form 2.8: **Prompt and Input**

System.out.println("*prompt for the_number:* " **);**
the_number = **keyboard.readDouble( );**   // Or keyboard.readInt( );

Self-Check

2-14   Write the value for GPA given each of the dialogues shown below:

```
public class SomeArithmetic
{
    public static void main( String[] args )
    {
        // 0. Declare some numeric variables
        double c1, c2, g1, g2, GPA;
        TextReader keyboard = new TextReader( );

        // 1. Input
        System.out.print( "Credits for course 1: " );
        c1 = keyboard.readDouble( );
        System.out.print( "Grade for course 1: " );
        g1 = keyboard.readDouble( );

        System.out.print( "Credits for course 2: " );
        c2 = keyboard.readDouble( );
        System.out.print( "Grade for course 2: " );
        g2 = keyboard.readDouble( );

        // 2. Process
        GPA = ( ( c1 * g1 ) + ( c2 * g2 ) ) / ( c1 + c2 );

        // 3. Output
        System.out.println( "GPA: " + GPA );
    }
}
```

Dialogue 1

```
Credits for course 1: 2.0
Grade for course 1: 2.0
Credits for course 2: 3.0
Grade for course 2: 4.0
```
-a   GPA: _____

Dialogue 2

```
Credits for course 1: 1.5
Grade for course 1: 4.0
Credits for course 2: 3.0
Grade for course 2: 3.0
```
-b   GPA: _____

Dialogue 3

```
Credits for course 1: 0.5
Grade for course 1: 4.0
Credits for course 2: 3.0
Grade for course 2: 0.0
```
-c   GPA: _____

2.5   Java's Math Class

When the first programmers were programming the first electronic computers, phrases like this were often heard: "Hey, can I borrow that square root routine?" It got to the point where the code was printed and pinned to the wall so the code could be shared. Then someone got the idea to store an electronic version of the algorithm so people could call it up whenever it was needed. Therefore, functions were born. Functions are known in Java as "methods."

Since then, many methods have been made part of programming language libraries. Some sets of methods relate to processing strings, others to graphical user interfaces, and still others to transferring information over networks. This section presents methods that help solve mathematical and scientific problems. The related methods are collected together by Java's Math class. The Java **Math class** defines a large collection of mathematical and trigonometric functions (methods). Here are three:

```
Math.sqrt( number )   // Return the square root of number
Math.pow( x, y )      // Return x to the yth power
Math.sin( angle )     // Return the sine of angle radians
```

These Math methods are called by specifying the class name Math, followed by a dot, followed by the name of the method, followed by the appropriate number and type of arguments within parentheses. This type of call represents a major difference between the Math class and most other classes in Java. You do not need to construct a Math object to send messages (as was done for TextReader). The Math methods are for processing primitive types, not objects. When a method can be called by preceding the method name with the class name rather than a reference variable, the method is known as a **static method**. The keyword static will be part of the method. For example, main is a static method (other static methods, which you will see in Chapter 5, include `getCurrencyInstance` of the `NumberFormat` class and `showMessageDialog` of the `JOptionPane` class).

`Math` methods typically require one argument and return a number. Here is one general form to call `Math` methods.

General Form 2.9: Calling a method in the Math class

Math. *method-name* **(** *argument(s)* **)**

The method-name is a previously declared identifier representing an operation that belongs to the `Math` class. The arguments represent a set of zero or more expressions separated by commas. In the following method call, the method name is `sqrt` (square root) and the argument is `81.0`:

```
Math.sqrt( 81.0 )   // Example method call that returns 9.0
```

Methods require zero, one, or even more arguments. Although most `Math` methods require exactly one argument, the `pow` method requires exactly two arguments. In the following message, the method name is `pow` (for power), the arguments are `base` and `power`, and the method call `pow( base, power )` is replaced with base^{power}, which returns `8.0`:

```
double base = 2.0;
double power = 3.0;
System.out.println( pow( base, power ) );   // Output: 8.0
```

Any argument used in a method call must be an expression from an acceptable type. For example, the method call `sqrt( "Bobbie" )` results in an error because the argument is a `String`, not a number. Here are some mathematical and trigonometric methods available to you. An example program that calls several of these methods follows.

Some Math Methods

Method	Argument	Return Type	Value Returned	Example	Result
Math.cos(x)	double	double	Cosine of x radians	Math.cos(1.0)	0.5403
Math.abs(x)	double	double	Absolute value of x	Math.abs(-1.5)	1.5
Math.abs(i)	int	int	Absolute value of i	Math.abs(-345)	345
Math.pow(x, y)	double	double	x to the yth: x^y	Math.pow(2, 4)	16.0
Math.round(x)	double	long[3]	Nearest integer	Math.round(4.56)	5
Math.sin(x)	double	double	Sine of x radians	Math.sin(1.0)	0.84147
Math.sqrt(x)	double	double	Square root of x	Math.sqrt(4.0)	2.0

---

3. The `round` method shown here takes a `double` and returns a `long`, which is an `int` with more significant digits. The `Math` class has another `round` method that takes a `float` and returns an `int` that would have to be called as in `int roundedVal = Math.round( 1.5F );`, where `1.5` is a `float` value, not a `double` value.

```
// Show the return value from calling Math methods.
// The Math class is automatically imported.
import java.lang.Math; // The Math class is in the package java.lang

public class ShowMathMethods
{
  public static void main( String[] args )
  {
    double x = -2.1;

    System.out.println( "x: " + x );
    System.out.println( "abs(x): " + Math.abs( x ) );
    System.out.println( "abs(10-27): " + Math.abs( 10 - 27 ) );
    System.out.println( "pow(x, 2.0): " + Math.pow( x, 2.0 ) );
    System.out.println( "round(x): " + Math.round( x ) );
    System.out.println( "round(3.5): " + Math.round( 3.5 ) );
    System.out.println( "round(9.9): " + Math.round( 9.9 ) );
  }
}
```

Output

```
x: -2.1
abs(x): 2.1
abs(10-27): 17
pow(x, 2.0): 4.41
round(x): -2
round(3.5): 4
round(9.9): 10
```

Integer expressions may also be used as arguments to Math methods even though they are looking for a double argument. As with assignment, the integer value will be promoted to a double. So Math.sqrt(4) returns the same result as Math.sqrt(4.0) without error.

Self-Check

2-15 Evaluate Math.pow(4.0, 3.0).

2-16 Evaluate Math.round(3.49999).

2-17 Evaluate Math.abs(123 - 125).

2.6   int Arithmetic

The Java language provides several primitive **numeric types**. The two most often used are double and int. A variable declared as int can store a limited range of whole numbers—numbers with no fraction. Java int variables store integers in the range of -2,147,483,648 through 2,147,483,647 inclusive.

There are times when `int` is the correct choice over `double`. All `int` variables have operations similar to `double` (+, *, -, =), but some differences do exist. For example, a fractional part cannot be stored in an `int`. In fact, you cannot assign a floating-point literal or `double` variable to an `int` variable. The compiler complains with an error.

```
int anInt = 1.999;        // ERROR
int anotherInt = 0.0;     // ERROR
```

The / operator has different meanings for `int` and `double` operands. Whereas the result of 3.0 / 4.0 is 0.75, the result of 3 / 4 is 0. Two integer operands with the / operator have an integer result—not a floating-point result. So what happens? An integer divided by an integer results in an integer. For example, the quotient obtained from dividing 3 by 4 is 0. This implies that the same operator (/ in this case) can have a different meaning depending on the type of the operands.

The remainder operation—symbolized with the % operator—is also available for both `int` and `double`. For example, the result of 18 % 4 is the integer remainder after dividing 18 by 4, which is 2.

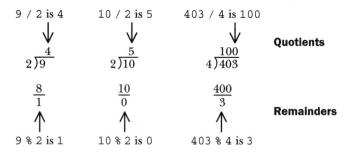

Integer arithmetic is illustrated in the following program, which shows % and / operating on integer expressions and / operating on floating-point operands. In this example, the integer results describe whole hours and whole minutes rather than the fractional equivalent.

```
// Show minutes in two different ways
public class QuotientRemainder
{
  public static void main( String[] args )
  {
    System.out.println( "This program will show a given number" );
    System.out.println( "of minutes in two different ways." );
    System.out.println( );

    int totalMinutes, minutes, hours;
    double fractionalHour;
    TextReader keyboard = new TextReader( );
```

```
    // 1. Input
    System.out.print( "Enter total minutes: " );
    totalMinutes = keyboard.readInt( );

    // 2. Process
    fractionalHour = totalMinutes / 60.0;
    hours = totalMinutes / 60;
    minutes = totalMinutes % 60;

    // 3. Output
    System.out.print( totalMinutes + " minutes can be rewritten as " );
    System.out.println( fractionalHour + " hours or as" );
    System.out.println( hours + " hours and " + minutes + " minutes" );
  }
}
```

Dialogue

```
This program will show a given number
of minutes in two different ways.

Enter total minutes: 254
254 minutes can be rewritten as 4.23333 hours or as
4 hours and 14 minutes
```

The preceding program indicates that even though ints and doubles are similar, there are times when double is the more appropriate type than int, and vice versa. The double type should be specified when you need a numeric variable with a fractional component. If you need whole numbers, select int.

Self-Check

2-18 What value is stored in nickel?

```
int change = 97;
int nickel = 0;
nickel = change % 25 % 10 / 5;
```

2-19 What value is stored in nickel when change is initialized to:

-a 4   -d 15
-b 5   -e 49
-c 10   -f 0

Mixing Integer and Floating-Point Operands

Whenever integer and floating-point values are on opposite sides of an arithmetic operator, the integer operand is promoted to its floating-point equivalent (3 becomes 3.0, for example). The expression then results in a floating-point number. The same rule applies when one operand is an int variable and the other a double variable. Here are a few examples of expression with only two operands:

```
public class IntDouble
{
  public static void main( String[] args )
  {
    int number = 9;
    double sum = 567.9;

    System.out.println( sum / number );   // Divide a double by an int
    System.out.println( number / 2 );     // Divide an int by an int
    System.out.println( number / 2.0 );   // Divide an int by a double
    System.out.println( 2.0 * number );   // Get a double: 18.0 not 18
  }
}
```

Output

```
63.1
4
4.5
18.0
```

Expressions with more than two operands will also evaluate to floating-point values if one of the operands is floating-point—for example, $(8.8 / 4 + 3) = (2.2 + 3) = 5.2$. Operator precedence rules also come into play—for example, $(3 / 4 + 8.8) = (0 + 8.8) = 8.8$.

Self-Check

2-20   Evaluate the following expressions:

-a 5 / 9	**-f** 5 / 2
-b 5.0 / 9	**-g** 7 / 2.5 * 3 / 4
-c 5 / 9.0	**-h** 1 / 2.0 * 3
-d 2 + 4 * 6 / 3	**-i** 5 / 9 * (50.0 - 32.0)
-e (2 + 4) * 6 / 3	**-j** 5 / 9.0 * (50 - 32)

2.7   Errors

There are several categories of errors encountered when programming:

syntax errors—errors that occur when compiling source code into byte code
intent errors—the program does what you typed, not what you intended (also known as "logic errors")
exceptions—errors that occur while the program is executing (also known as "runtime errors")

When programming, you will be writing source code using the syntax for the Java programming language. This source code is translated into byte code by the compiler. This byte code is stored in a `.class` file. The byte code is the same no matter what computer the program will run on.

For a Java program to actually run, another program called the **Java virtual machine** (JVM) translates the Java byte code into the instructions understood by the type of computer it runs on. The computer might be running Windows, Mac OS, Solaris Unix, or Linux, for example. Different computer systems have their own Java virtual machines. This is what allows the same Java Applet to be transported as a `.class` file around the Internet to be run on a variety of computers. Figure 2.1 shows the levels of translation necessary to get a computer-based solution using Java to get an executable program on almost any computer.

Figure 2.1: **From Source Code to a Program That Runs on Many Computers**

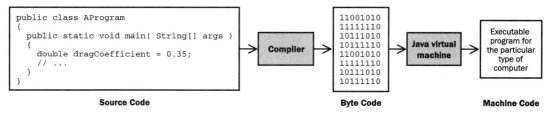

1. The programmer translates algorithms into Java source code.
2. The compiler translates the source code into byte code.
3. The Java virtual machine translates byte code into the instructions understood by the computer (by Linux, Mac OS, Windows, and so on).

Errors may occur when you are compiling your source code or when the program is running on the computer. The easiest errors to detect and fix are those generated by the compiler. These are syntax errors that occur at compiletime.

Syntax Errors Detected at Compiletime

A programming language requires strict adherence to its own set of formal syntax rules. Unfortunately, it is easy to violate these syntax rules while translating algorithms into their programming language equivalents. All it takes is a missing { or ; to really foul things up. As you are writing your source code, you will often use the compiler to check the syntax of the code you wrote (see Figure 2.1). As the Java compiler translates source code into byte code so it can run on a computer, it also locates and reports as many errors as possible. If you have any syntax error, the byte code will not be generated. The program will not run. To get a running program, you need to fix all of your syntax errors.

A syntax error occurs when the compiler recognizes the violation of a syntax rule. The byte code cannot be created until all syntax errors have been removed from the program. The compiler can generate many strange-looking error messages as it reads your source code. Unfortunately, deciphering these syntax errors takes practice, patience, and a complete knowledge of the language. Of course, you will have to decipher these errors before you have complete knowledge of the language. Therefore, in an effort to improve this situation, here are some examples of common syntax errors and how they are corrected. *Note:* Your Java compiler will generate different error messages.

Error Detected by a Compiler	Incorrect Code	Corrected Code
Splitting an identifier	`int my Weight = 0;`	`int myWeight = 0;`
Misspelling a keyword	`integer sum = 0;`	`int sum = 0;`
Leaving off a semicolon	`double x = 0.0`	`double x = 0.0;`
Not closing a string literal	`... print( "Hi );`	`... print( "Hi" );`
Failing to declare a variable	`testScore = 97.5;`	`double testScore;` `testScore = 97.5;`
Ignoring case sensitivity	`double x;` `X = 5.0;`	`double x;` `x = 5.0;`
Forgetting parentheses	`keyboard.readDouble;`	`keyboard.readDouble( );`

Compilers generate many error messages. However, your source code is the source of these errors. You are the one that wrote the source code. Whenever your compiler appears to be nagging you, remember that the compiler is trying to help you correct your errors as much as possible.

The compiler is your friend.

The following program attempts to show several errors the compiler should eventually detect and report. Because error messages generated by compilers vary among systems, the reasons for the errors below are indexed with numbers to explanations that follow. Your system will certainly generate quite different error messages.

```java
public class Compile timeErrors
{
  public static void main( String[] args )
  {
    int pounds = 0;

    System.out.println( "Enter weight in pounds: " )①
    pounds = keyboard②.readInt( );
    System.out.print( "In the U.K. you weigh ③ );
    System.out.print( ④Pounds / 14 + " stone, " ⑤ pounds % 14 );
  }
}
```

Compilers generate some rather cryptic messages. Whereas one compiler reported only two errors with the source code above, there are actually these five errors.

① A semicolon (;) is missing
② `keyboard` was not constructed as a `TextReader` object
③ A double quote (") is missing
④ `pounds` was written as `Pounds`
⑤ The extra expressions require a missing concatenation symbol (+)

Syntax errors take some time to get used to, so try to be patient and observe the location where the syntax error occurred. The error is usually near the line where the error was detected, although you may have to fix preceding lines. Always remember to fix the first error first. An error that was reported on line 10 might be the result of a semicolon that was forgotten on line 5. The corrected source code, without error, is given next, followed by an interactive dialogue:

```
// There are no syntax errors here

public class ErrorFree
{
  public static void main( String[] args )
  {
    int pounds = 0;
    TextReader keyboard = new TextReader( );

    System.out.print( "Enter weight in pounds: " );
    pounds = keyboard.readInt( );
    System.out.print( "In the U.K. you weigh " );
    System.out.println( ( pounds / 14 ) + " stone, " + ( pounds % 14 ) );
  }
}
```

Dialogue

```
Enter weight in pounds: 146
In the U.K. you weigh 10 stone, 6
```

Another type of error occurs when `String[] args` is omitted from the `main` method. When the program tries to run, it looks for a method named `main` with (`String[]` *identifier*). If you forgot `String[] args` in the source code above, you would get the error shown after the program began to run.

```
Exception in thread "main" java.lang.NoSuchMethodError: main
```

These types of errors, which occur at runtime, are known as exceptions.

Exceptions

After your program compiles with no syntax errors, you will get a `.class` file containing the byte code that can be run with the help of a Java virtual machine. The virtual machine translates the byte code into the instructions understood by the computer (see Figure 2.1). The virtual machine can be invoked by issuing a Java command with the .class file name. For example, java ErrorFree will run the previous program on your computer.

However, when programs run, errors still may occur. Perhaps the user enters a string that is supposed to be a number. Or perhaps an arithmetic expression results in division by zero. Or there is an attempt to read a file from a disk, but there is no disk in the drive. Such exceptional events that occur while the program is running are known as exceptions.

One exception was shown above. The main method was valid, so the code compiled. However, when the program ran, Java's runtime environment looked for and could not find a main method with String[] args. The error could not be discovered until the user ran the program and Java began by looking for the place to begin the program. If Java cannot find a method with this line of code:

```
public static void main( String[] args )
```

an exception occurs and the program terminates prematurely. Now consider another example of an exception that occurs while the program is running.

The output for the following program indicates that Java does not allow integer division by zero. The compiler does a lot, but it does not check the values of variables. Therefore, if at runtime a denominator in a division happens to be 0, an ArithmeticException occurs.

```
public class ExceptionExample
{
   public static void main( String[] args )
   { // Integer division by zero throws an ArithmeticException
     int numerator = 5;
     int denominator = 0;
     int quotient = numerator / denominator;   // A runtime error
     System.out.println( "This message will not be reached" );
   }
}
```

Output

```
Exception in thread "main" java.lang.ArithmeticException: / by zero
        at ExceptionExample.main(ExceptionExample.java:7)
```

When you encounter one of these exceptions, look at the file name (ExceptionExample.java) and the line number (7) where the error occurred. The reason for the exception (/ by zero) and the name of the exception (ArithmeticException) are two other clues to help you figure out what went wrong.

Intent Errors (Logic Errors)

Even when no syntax errors are found and no runtime errors occur, the program still may not execute properly. A program may run and terminate normally, but it may not be correct. Consider the following program:

```java
// Find the average given the sum and the size of a set of numbers
public class IntentError
{
  public static void main( String[] args )
  {
    double sum = 0.0;
    double average = 0.0;
    int number = 0;
    TextReader keyboard = new TextReader( );

    // Input:
    System.out.print( "Enter sum: " );
    sum = keyboard.readDouble( );
    System.out.print( "Enter number: " );
    number = keyboard.readInt( );

    // Process
    average = number / sum;

    // Output
    System.out.println( "Average: " + average );
  }
}
```

The interactive dialogue may look like this:

```
Enter sum: 291
Enter number: 3
Average:  0.010309278350515464
```

Such intent errors occur when the program does what was typed, not what was intended. The compiler cannot detect such intent errors. The expression `number / sum` is syntactically correct—the compiler just has no way of knowing that this programmer intended to write `sum / number` instead.

Intent errors, also known as logic errors, are the most insidious and usually the most difficult to correct. They may also be difficult to detect. The user, tester, or programmer may not know they even exist! Consider the program controlling the Therac 3 cancer radiation therapy machine. Patients received massive overdoses of radiation resulting in serious injuries and death while the indicator displayed everything as normal. Another infamous intent error involved a program controlling a probe that was supposed to go to Venus. Because a comma was missing in the Fortran source code, an American Viking Venus probe burnt up in the sun. Both programs had compiled successfully and were running at the time of the accidents. However, they did what the programmers had written—not what was intended.

Self-Check

2-21 Assume a program is supposed to find an average given the sum and the size of a set of numbers and the following dialogue is generated. What clue reveals the presence of an intent error?

```
Enter sum: 100
Enter number: 4
Average: 0.04
```

2-22 Assuming the following code was used to generate the dialogue above, how is the intent error to be corrected?

```
System.out.print( "Enter sum: " );
number = keyboard.readInt( );
System.out.print( "Enter number: " );
sum = keyboard.readDouble( );
average = sum / number;
```

When the Software Doesn't Match the Specification

Even when a process has been automated and delivered to the customer in working order as per the perceptions of the developers, there may still be errors. There have been many instances of software working, but not doing what it was supposed to do. This can happen when the software developers don't understand the customer's problem specification. Something could have been missed. Something could have been misinterpreted. The customer may not have expressed what was wanted.

A related error occurs when the customer specifies the problem incorrectly. This could be the case when the customer isn't sure what she or he wants. A trivial or critical omission in specification may occur, or the request may not be written clearly. In addition, the customer may change her or his mind after program development has begun.

For the most part, the Programming Projects in this textbook simply ask you to fulfill the problem specification. If there is something you don't understand, don't hesitate to ask questions. It is better to understand the problem and know what it is that you are trying to solve before getting to the design and implementation phases of program development. Unintentionally, the problem may have been incorrectly specified. Or it may have been incompletely specified. Both happen in the real world.

Chapter Summary

- The smallest pieces of a program (tokens) can help you understand general forms and fix syntax errors. Java tokens include special symbols, identifiers, keywords (reserved identifiers), and literals.

- Java has two types of values: primitive values and reference values. A primitive variable stores one value in a fixed amount of bits. A reference variable stores the address of an object that usually has many values.

- Input is so frequently used that `TextReader` has been designed to make easy-to-use methods available. Numeric input without `TextReader` is complex and does not handle bad input very well. See the Programming Tips section for an alternative to `TextReader` that does not require the author-supplied file named `TextReader.java`.

- Arithmetic expressions are made up of operators, such as +, -, * (multiplication), and / (division). A binary arithmetic operator requires two operands, which may be numeric literals (1 or 2.3), numeric variables, or another arithmetic expression.

- Instances of the Prompt and Input pattern will occur in this textbook's early programming projects. Use it whenever a program needs to get some input from the user.

- A message requires that an object be constructed. The message name is preceded by the object that will receive the message.

- Some classes have methods that do not need a reference variable. These are called "static methods." They are called by preceding the method name with the class name. `Math.pow( 2, 4 )` is a call to a static method, for example.

- When / has two integer operands, the result is an integer. So 5 / 2 is 2.

- When / has at least one floating-point operand, the result is floating point: 5 / 2.0 is 2.5.

- The % operator returns the integer remainder of one integer operand divided by another. So 5 % 2 is 1. The % operator can also be used with floating-point operands. Then % returns the floating-point remainder. For example, 5.5 % 2.0 returns 1.5.

- Be careful in choosing `int` and `double`. Always use `double` to store numbers unless it makes sense that the variable will store only integers. For example, `credits` should be declared as a `double` since it is possible to have 0.5 credits in a course.

- This chapter ended with a discussion of some of the types of errors that occur during implementation. You will encounter errors. It is part of the process.

- Errors may be present because the problem statement was incorrect or incomplete.

- Intent errors can be the most difficult to fix—they are often difficult even to detect. Nothing is perfect, including programs that you pay for. They are often released with known errors (called "bugs" or "issues" in an effort to pretend they are not errors).

- Testing is important, but it does not prove the absence of errors. Testing can and does detect errors. Testing can build confidence that a program appears to work.

Key Terms

abs	input	println
argument	int	Prompt and Input pattern
assignment	integer arithmetic	readDouble
binary operator	intent error	readInt
boolean	Java virtual machine	relational operator
class	javadoc comments	reference variable
comment	keyword	round
compiler	literal	special symbol
constructing an object	main method	sqrt
declaration	Math class	static methods
double	numeric type	syntax
exception	output	syntax error
general form	package	TextReader
identifier	primitive variable	token
import	print	unary operator
initialization		

Exercises

The answers to exercises marked with are available in Appendix C.

1. List three operators that may be applied to a `double`.

2. List three operators that may be applied to any `int`.

3. Give one reason why a program should have comments.

4. Describe how a programmer can change the value of a variable.

5. List four types of Java tokens and give two examples of each.

6. Which of the following are valid identifiers?

   a. `a-one`   g. `1_2_3`
   b. `R2D2`   h. `A_B_C`
   c. `registered_voter`   i. `all right`
   d. `BEGIN`   j. `"doubleVariable"`
   e. `1Header`   k. `{Right}`
   f. `$$$$`   l. `Mispelt`

7. Declare `totalPoints` as a variable capable of storing a floating-point number.

8. Write code that sets the value of `totalPoints` to 100.0.

9. Write the entire dialogue generated by the following program when `5.2` and `6.3` are entered at the prompt. Make sure you write the user-supplied input as well as all program output, including the prompt.

```
public class Exercise9
{
  public static void main( String[] args )
  {
    double number = 0.0;
    double y = 0.0;
    double answer = 0.0;
    TextReader keyboard = new TextReader( );
    // 1. Input
    System.out.print( "Enter a number: " );
    number = keyboard.readDouble( );
    System.out.print( "Enter another number: " );
    y = keyboard.readDouble( );
    // 2. Process
    answer = number * ( 1.0 + y );
    // 3. Output
    System.out.println( "Answer: " + answer );
  }
}
```

10. Write a message that displays the value of a numeric variable `total`.

11. Given the following two variable initializations, either write the value that is stored in each variable or report the attempt as an error.

```
int anInt = 0;
double aNumber = 0.0;
```

   a. anInt = 4;   d. aNumber = 8;

   b. anInt = 4.5;   e. aNumber = 8.9;

   c. anInt = "4.5";   f. aNumber = "8.9";

12. With paper and pencil, write a complete Java program that prompts for a number from 0.0 to 1.0 and stores this input value into the numeric variable named `relativeError`. Echo the input (output the input). The dialogue generated by your program should look like this:

```
Enter relativeError [0.0 through 1.0]: 0.341
You entered: 0.341
```

13. A `println` message generates a new line on the computer screen. However, if you use `print` instead, the output appears on the same line. Write the output generated by the following programs:

```
public class A
{
  public static void main( String[] args )
  {
    System.out.print( "+--+" );
    System.out.print( "+--+" );
    System.out.print( "+--+" );
  }
}
```

```
public class B
{
  public static void main( String[] args )
  {
    System.out.println( "+--+" );
    System.out.println( "+--+" );
    System.out.println( "+--+" );
  }
}

public class C
{
  public static void main( String[] args )
  {
    System.out.print( 1 );
    System.out.print( 2 );
    System.out.print( 3 );
  }
}

public class D
{
  public static void main( String[] args )
  {
    System.out.println( 1 );
    System.out.println( 2 );
    System.out.println( 3 );
  }
}
```

14. Assuming x is 5.0 and y is 7.0, evaluate the following expressions:

   a. x / y
   b. y / y
   c. Math.pow(2.0, 4.0)
   d. Math.sqrt(x - 1.0)
   e. Math.round(-0.7)
   f. x > y

   g. 2.0 - x * y
   h. (x * y) / (x + y)
   i. Math.round(y + 0.3 - x)
   j. Math.abs(-23.4)
   k. Math.round(0.6)
   l. x <= x

15. Predict the output generated by the following program:

```
public class Exercise15
{
  public static void main( String[] args )
  {
    double x = 1.2;
    double y = 3.4;

    System.out.println( x + y );
    System.out.println( x - y );
    System.out.println( x * y );
    System.out.println( x / y );
    System.out.println( x <= y );
    System.out.println( ( x + 5.0 ) < y );
```

```
        System.out.println( x != y );
      }
   }
```

16. Predict the output generated by the following program:

```java
public class Exercise16
{
   public static void main( String[] args )
   {
      double x = 0.5;
      double y = 2.3;

      System.out.println( x * ( 1 + y ) );
      System.out.println( x / ( 1 + y ) );
      System.out.println( x / y );
   }
}
```

17. Write the complete dialogue (program output and user input) generated by the following program when the user enters each of the following input values for sale:

a. **10.00**   b. **12.34**   c. **100.00**

```java
public class Exercise17
{
   public static void main( String[] args )
   {
      double sale = 0.0;
      double tax = 0.0;
      double total = 0.0;
      double TAX_RATE = 0.07;
      TextReader keyboard = new TextReader( );

      // I)nput
      System.out.print( "Enter sale: " );
      sale = keyboard.readDouble( );   // User enters 10.00,
                                       // 12.34, and 100.00

      // P)rocess
      tax = sale * TAX_RATE;
      total = sale + tax;

      // O)utput
      System.out.println( "Sale: " + sale );
      System.out.println( "Tax: " + tax );
      System.out.println( "Total: " + total );
   }
}
```

18. Explain how to fix the syntax error in each of these lines:

a. `System.out.println( "Hello world" )`

b. `System.println( "Hello world" );`

    c. `System.out.println( "Hello world" );`

    d. `System.out.println "Hello world";`

 19. Explain the error in this program:

```
public class HasError
{
  public static void main( String[] args )
  {
    int anInt = 0;

    System.out.println( "Enter an integer" );
    anInt = keyboard.readDouble();
  }
}
```

20. Define the phrase *logic error.*

 21. Does the following code always correctly assign the average of x, y, and z to average?

```
double average = x + y + z / 3.0;
```

22. What value is stored in `average` after this expression executes?

```
double average = ( 81 + 90 + 83 ) / 3;
```

 23. Compute the value stored in `slope` given this assignment for the slope of a line:

```
slope = ( y2 - y1 ) / ( x2 - x1 );
```

x1	y1	x2	y2	slope
0.0	0.0	1.0	1.0	
0.0	0.0	-1.0	1.0	
6.0	5.2	6.0	-14.0	

Programming Tips

1. **Use this outline for writing simple classes for your first projects.**

```
// First-name last-name
// Comments describing what this program does

public class FileName
{
  public static void main( String[] args )
  {
    // Declare and/or initialize variables
    // Construct a TextReader object
```

```
      // Other messages and assignments
   }
}
```

2. **Name the file the same as your class name.**

   The class name and the first part of the file name (before `.java`) must match exactly. Consider the following class (program) that has the name `FileNameDoesNotMatch` stored in a file named `NotHere.java`.

```
// File name: NotHere.java
public class FileNameDoesNotMatch
{
  public static void main( String[] args )
  {
    System.out.println( "Won't run" );
  }
}
```

   This code compiles, but an attempt to run it resulted in this error message:

```
Can't find public class NotHere
```

   To fix this, change either the file name or the class name.

3. **Semicolons terminate. They do not belong at the end of every line.**

   Make sure you terminate declarations, assignments, and messages with ;. However, do not place a semicolon after

```
public static void main( String[] args )
```

4. **Fix the first error first.**

   When you compile, you may get dozens of errors. Don't panic. Try to fix the very first error first. That may actually fix some of your other errors. Also note that sometimes fixing one error causes new errors. Don't be too surprised to find out that after fixing an error, the compiler generates errors that were previously undetected. It usually takes many tries to remove all errors.

5. **Give meaningful values to your variables.**

   Although it is not always necessary to initialize `int`s and `double`s at first, attempts to use the uninitialized variables later without a value will result in errors. Consider declaring variables when they are needed. Instead of this:

```
double credits, qualityPoints, GPA;
GPA = qualityPoints / credits;
```

   which results in two Java syntax errors:

```
Variable qualityPoints may not have been initialized.
GPA = qualityPoints / credits;
         ^

Variable credits may not have been initialized.
GPA = qualityPoints / credits;
       ^
```

try declaring the variable when it is needed (instead of at the top of the method), like this:

```
double credits = keyboard.readDouble( );
// Prompt or whatever
double qualityPoints = keyboard.readDouble( );
// Prompt or whatever
double GPA = qualityPoints / credits;
```

6. **Use intention-revealing names.**

    Although you may be tempted to use cryptic identifiers, such as x for credits, go ahead and make the extra keystrokes. Use a name that documents itself. All names should describe what they are intended for. This makes programs more readable to others. Perhaps even more importantly, this makes the program more readable to you. It will help you fix intent errors.

7. **Integer arithmetic is different from calculators.**

    Integer division results in an integer. Therefore 5 / 2 is 2, not the 2.5 your brain and calculator feel are so right.

8. **The % arithmetic operator causes confusion.**

    The expression a % b is the integer remainder after dividing a by b. Try these now:

    99 % 50 = ____   101 % 2 = ____
    99 % 50 % 25 = ____   102 % 2 = ____
    4 % 99 = ____   103 % 2 = ____

9. **Some imports are done automatically for you.**

    The classes in java.lang are used so often that you do not need to import them. This means you have the following three choices for a program that does nothing but print one line of output:

    ```
    import java.lang.System;  // Get one class
    import java.lang.*;       // Get all classes in the package
                              // Do not write an import
    ```

    Also, if the class is in a file in the same folder, you do not need to import it. For example, to get access to the TextReader class when TextReader.java is in the working folder, you have these two options:

    ```
    import TextReader;
    // Do not write an import
    ```

10. **Do more than is required.**
     Consider doing more of the programming projects than you are assigned.
     Experience makes you a better programmer. You'll do better on the tests.

11. **To use the author-supplied class for reading input from the keyboard, copy**
     `TextReader.java` into your working folder (directory).
     Some programming projects require author-supplied classes. These author-
     supplied classes are available to you if you have their files in the same folder as
     the program using the classes. You could use TextReader.java to complete
     the first programming projects. (It is available on the disk that accompanies
     this textbook.) Another option is given in the Programming Tip that follows.
     It requires more code, but you don't need the extra file.

12. **You can input with standard Java classes (classes that are always available).**
     The standard Java's input classes provide another option for reading numbers.
     These classes are always available so there is no need to copy files into your
     working folder. However, this option comes with additional overhead for
     performing numeric input.
        First, you need to write some extra code, which is shown in boldface in the
     program below. You also need to import several classes, such as
     BufferedReader and InputStreamReader. You must also declare that the
     main method throws IOException, which is another Java-supplied class in the
     java.io package. (See Chapter 9 for more on reading input with the classes
     in the java.io package.) These classes become available with the three
     imports in the program below.

```java
// Read one number with the standard Java classes from java.io
import java.io.BufferedReader;
import java.io.InputStreamReader;
import java.io.IOException;     // Or write: import java.io.*;

public class UsingStandardInput
{
  public static void main( String[] args ) throws IOException
  {
    // Let the object named isr read characters from the keyboard.
    // System.in is a variable associated with the keyboard.
    InputStreamReader isr = new InputStreamReader( System.in );

    // Get an object with the convenient readLine method
    BufferedReader keyboard = new BufferedReader( isr );
    System.out.print( "Enter quality points: " );

    // Read in all user input up to the end of the line
    String numberAsString = keyboard.readLine( );
```

```
        // Convert user input to a number or else throw an exception
        double qualityPoints = Double.parseDouble( numberAsString );
        System.out.println( "You entered " + qualityPoints );
    }
}
```

The object referenced by `keyboard` has a `readLine` that reads a string of characters from the user. This string of characters must then be converted into a number by `Double`'s `parseDouble` method. The method requires a `String` argument that hopefully represents a number; `"1.234"`, for example. The `parseDouble` message results in a `double` that is then assigned to the `double` variable `qualityPoints`.

Dialogue 1 (valid numeric input)

```
Enter quality points: 34.5
You entered 34.5
```

If the user enters an invalid number, this particular program will terminate early.

Dialogue 2 (invalid numeric input)

```
Enter quality points: 34..5
Exception in thread "main" java.lang.NumberFormatException:
at  java.lang.FloatingDecimal.readJavaFormatString
at  java.lang.Double.parseDouble(Double.java:188)
at  UsingKeyboard.main(UsingStandardInput.java:24)
```

One advantage to using this option is that you do not need the author-supplied `TextReader` class. But it is easy to copy it into the folder with your other files. If your instructor insists that you do not use `TextReader`, use the code above for reading `doubles`. To read integers, use `Integer parseInt` rather than `Double parseDouble`. Both methods require a `String` argument.

```
System.out.print( "Enter an int: " );
int anInteger = Integer.parseInt( standardInput.readLine( ) );
```

Programming Projects

Note: This first programming project is provided as an example that could be followed to complete other projects. It takes you from start to finish. It is typical of the 15 programming projects in this chapter. Each project in this chapter has the following elements:

- a project number (2Z, for example) and a title (Rounding to a Given Number of Decimal Places, for example)
- a problem specification

- zero, one, two, or more sample dialogues, often asking you to reproduce the dialogue

---

2Z   Rounding to a Given Number of Decimal Places

Write a program that rounds a number to a specific number of decimal places. For example, 3.4589 rounded to two decimal places should be 3.46 and -3.4589 rounded to one decimal place should be -3.5. One dialogue must look exactly like this:

```
Enter number to round: 3.4567
Enter number of decimal places: 2
Rounded number: 3.46
```

The following is a sampling of activities based on the programming process covered in Chapter 1.

Analysis

You could begin with these analysis activities:

1. Read and understand the problem.
2. Decide what variable names represent the answer—the output.
3. Decide what variable names the user must enter to get the answer—the input.
4. Create a document that summarizes your analysis. This can be used as input to the design phase.

Problem	Data Name	Input or Output	Sample Problem
Round to any decimal place	number	Input	3.45678
	decimals	Input	3
	result	Output	3.457

Design

One suggested design activity is the development of an algorithm. Many algorithms for Chapter 2 projects can be guided by the Input/Process/Output pattern. This will help place the appropriate activities in the proper order. Add two instances of the Prompt then Input pattern, and an algorithm might look like this:

1. Prompt for the number to round (call it number).
2. Input number.
3. Prompt for the number of decimal places (call it decimals).
4. Input decimals.
5. Round number to decimals decimal places and store in result.
6. Display result.

Steps 1, 2, 3, 4, and 6 are easy. They can be implemented as input and/or output statements. However, the details of step 5, "Round number to decimals decimal places," are not present. Step 5 needs refinement. Now the focus can shift to the more difficult process of rounding number to decimals decimal places. A solution is a bit tricky, so the method is provided. Step 5 will now be replaced with steps 5, 6, and 7.

To round number to decimals decimal places, first multiply number by 10 to the decimals power (stored in result below). Then round result to the nearest integer. Finally, divide result by 10 to the decimals power. The refined algorithm now looks like this:

1. Prompt for the number to round (call it number).
2. Input number.
3. Prompt for the number of decimal places (call it decimals).
4. Input decimals.
5. Let result become number multiplied by $10^{decimals}$.
6. Let result become the round of result.
7. Let result become result divided by $10^{decimals}$.
8. Display result.

Perform an algorithm walkthrough to simulate what will happen when number is 3.4567 and the result is to be rounded to two decimal places.

Round 3.4567 to Two Decimal Places

result = number * $10^{decimals}$	= 3.4567 * 10^2	= 345.67
result = round(result)	= 345.67 + 0.5	= 346
result = result / $10^{decimals}$	= 346 / 10^2	= **3.46**

It helps to have more than one sample problem. Therefore, walk through the same algorithm with a different example problem, rounding 9.99 to one decimal place. You shouldn't need this elaborate table. You could just walk through your algorithm with different input values.

Activity	number	decimals	result
1. Prompt for the number to round.	?	?	?
2. Input number.	9.99	?	?
3. Prompt for the number of decimal places.	9.99	?	?
4. Input decimals.	9.99	1	?
5. Let result become number multiplied by $10^{decimals}$.	9.99	1	99.9
6. Let result become the round of result.	9.99	1	100.0
7. Let result become result divided by $10^{decimals}$.	9.99	1	10.0
8. Display result.	9.99	1	10.0

Before writing the program, come up with a few more sample problems and write
the predicted result. Try a negative number. Try zero decimal places.

number	decimals	result
0.004999	2	0.00
3.151	1	3.2
-1.6	0	-2.0

Now you can translate your algorithm into Java. This could be done with paper
and pencil before going to the lab. This activity can help you do better on tests.

Next, type in the Java source code. This is the translation of your algorithm. You
may need some instruction on using your specific Java programming environment.
Compile repeatedly until all syntax errors are removed. Once the program compiles, run your program with different inputs. Test that your program works by
using the same input values as above to generate some dialogues. For each set of
inputs, compare your program results with your expected results.

Implementation

This complete Java source code program is a translation of the previous algorithm.
The algorithm step numbers are kept as comments to show how each step was
translated. Output from two program runs was copied from the console and pasted
at the end of the file. The technique on how to do this varies between computer
systems.

```java
// Programmer: Rick Mercer
// Project 2Z: Round any number to any number of decimal places
// Due Date:   11/14/03

import java.lang.System;   // import not required
import TextReader;         // TextReader.java must be in the same directory

public class RoundingNumbers
{
  public static void main( String[] args )
  {
    // Declare variables identified during analysis
    double number = 0.0;
    double decimals = 0.0;
    double result = 0.0;
    TextReader keyboard = new TextReader( );

    // Java translation of algorithm                Algorithm step number:
    // I)nput
    System.out.print( "Enter number to round: " );        // 1.
    number = keyboard.readDouble( );                       // 2.

    System.out.print( "Enter number of decimal places: " ); // 3.
    decimals = keyboard.readInt( );                        // 4.
```

```
        // P)rocess (Round number to decimals decimal places)
        result = number * Math.pow( 10, decimals );              // 5.
        result = Math.round( result );                           // 6.
        result = result / Math.pow( 10, decimals );              // 7.

        // O)utput
        System.out.println( "Rounded number: " + result );       // 8.
    }
}
/* Additional documentation: Two copied and pasted logs of execution. This
    may not be necessary, but it helps show the behavior of this program.

Enter number to round: 3.4567
Enter number of decimal places: 2
Rounded number: 3.46

Enter number to round: -1.6
Enter number of decimal places: 0
Rounded number: -2.0
*/
```

2A   Simple Arithmetic

Implement and test a Java program that solves the problem specified in
Exercise 1A, "Simple Arithmetic." The problem: For any two numeric inputs, a and
b, compute the product (a * b) and the sum (a + b). Then display the difference
between the product and the sum. Your dialogue must look exactly like this
(except your input will not be in boldface italic):

```
Enter a number: 5.0
Enter a number: 10.0
Product = 50.0
Sum = 15.0
Product - sum = 35.0
```

2B   Simple Average

Implement and test a Java program that solves the problem specified in analysis/
design exercise 1B, "Simple Average." The problem: Find the average of three tests
of equal weight. One dialogue must look exactly like this (except your input will
not be in boldface italic):

```
Enter test 1: 90.0
Enter test 2: 80.0
Enter test 3: 70.0
Average = 80.0
```

2C Weighted Average

Implement and test a Java program that solves the problem specified in analysis/ design exercise 1C, "Weighted Average." The problem: Determine a course grade using this weighted scale:

Quiz average 20%
Midterm 20%
Lab grade 35%
Final exam 25%

One dialogue must look exactly like this (except your input will not be in boldface italic):

```
Enter Quiz Average: 90.0
Enter Midterm: 80.0
Enter Lab Grade: 100.0
Enter Final Exam: 70.0
Course Average = 86.5
```

2D Wholesale Cost

Implement and test a Java program that solves the problem specified in analysis/ design exercise 1D, "Wholesale Cost." The problem: You happen to know that a store has a 25% markup on compact-disc (CD) players. If the retail price (what you pay) of a CD player is $189.98, how much did the store pay for that item (the wholesale price)? In general, what is the wholesale price for any item given its retail price and markup? Analyze the problem and design an algorithm that computes the wholesale price for any given retail price and any given markup. *Clue:* If you can't determine the equation, use this formula and some algebra to solve for wholesale price:

retail price = wholesale price * (1 + markup)

Your dialogues must look exactly like this (except your input will not be in boldface italic):

```
Enter the retail price: 255.00
Enter the markup percentage: 50
Wholesale price = 170.0

Enter the retail price: 200.00
Enter the markup percentage: 100
Wholesale price = 100.0
```

2E Grade Point Average

Implement and test a Java program that solves the problem specified in analysis/ design exercise 1E, "Grade Point Average." The problem: Compute a student's cumulative grade point average (GPA) for three courses. Credits range from 0.5 to

15.0. Grades can be 0.0, 1.0, 2.0, 3.0, or 4.0. One dialogue must look exactly like
this (except your input will not be in boldface italic):

```
Credits for course 1: 2.0
  Grade for course 1: 2.0
Credits for course 2: 3.0
  Grade for course 2: 4.0
Credits for course 3: 3.0
  Grade for course 3: 4.0
GPA: 3.5
```

2F   F to C

Use the following formula, which converts Fahrenheit (F) temperatures to Celsius (C):

$$C = 5/9(F\text{-}32)$$

Write a Java program that inputs a Fahrenheit temperature and outputs the Celsius
equivalent. Your dialogues must look exactly like these two dialogues when 212.0
and 98.6 are entered for F (except your input will not be in boldface italic):

```
Enter Fahrenheit temperature: 212.0
212.0 Fahrenheit is 100.0 Celsius

Enter Fahrenheit temperature: 98.6
98.6 Fahrenheit is 37.0 Celsius
```

2G   C to F

Use algebra and the formula of the preceding programming project to convert
degrees Celsius (C) to degrees Fahrenheit (F). Write a Java program that inputs
any Celsius temperature and displays the Fahrenheit equivalent. Your dialogues
must look exactly like this when the user enters -40 and 37 for C (except your input
will not be in boldface italic):

```
Enter C: -40.0
-40.0 C is -40.0 F

Enter C: 37.0
37.0 C is 98.6 F
```

2H   Seconds

Write a program that reads a value in seconds and displays the number of hours,
minutes, and seconds represented by the input. Your dialogues must look exactly
like this (except your input will not be in boldface italic):

```
Enter seconds: 32123
8:55:23

Enter seconds: 61
0:1:1
```

2I U.S. Minimum Coins

Write a Java program that prompts for an integer that represents the amount of change (in cents) to be handed back to a customer in the United States. Display the minimum number of half dollars, quarters, dimes, nickels, and pennies that make the correct change. *Hint:* With increasingly longer expressions, you could use / and % to evaluate the amount of each coin. Or you could calculate the total number of coins with / and the remaining change with %. Verify that your program works correctly by running it with a variety of input. Your dialogues must look exactly like this (except your input will not be in boldface italic):

```
Enter change [0..99]: 83        Enter change [0..99]: 14
Half(ves) : 1                   Half(ves) : 0
Quarter(s): 1                   Quarter(s): 0
Dime(s)   : 0                   Dime(s)   : 1
Nickel(s) : 1                   Nickel(s) : 0
Penny(ies): 3                   Penny(ies): 4
```

2J U.K. Minimum Coins

Write a Java program that prompts for an integer that represents the amount of change in pence to be handed back to a customer in the United Kingdom. Display the minimum number of coins that make the correct change. The available coins are (p represents pence) 1p, 2p, 5p, 10p, 20p, 50p, and 100p (the one-pound coin). Verify that your program works correctly by running it with a variety of input. Your dialogues must look exactly like this (except your input will not be in boldface italic):

```
Enter change: 298              Enter change: 93
100p: 2                        100p: 0
 50p: 1                         50p: 1
 20p: 2                         20p: 2
 10p: 0                         10p: 0
  5p: 1                          5p: 0
  2p: 1                          2p: 1
  1p: 1                          1p: 1
```

2K Circle

Write a Java program that reads a value for the radius of a circle and then outputs the diameter, circumference, and area of the circle. Use the `Math.pow` method to compute the area.

- diameter = 2 * radius
- circumference = pi * diameter
- area = pi * radius^2

Note: Use the variable Math.PI, which is as close to p as your computer allows. For example, this message generates the output shown in the comment:

```
System.out.println( Math.PI );   // 3.141592653589793
```

Run your program with radius = 1.0. Verify that your values for circumference and area match the preceding dialogue. After this, run your program with the input radii of 2.0 and 2.5 and verify that the output is what you expect. Your program must generate a dialogue that looks exactly like this when the input is 1.0 (except your input will not be in boldface italic):

```
Enter Radius: 1.0
Diameter: 2.0
Circumference:  6.283185307179586
Area:  3.141592653589793
```

2L   More Rounding

Write a program that asks the user for a number and displays that number rounded to zero, one, two, and three decimal places. Your program must generate a dialogue that looks exactly like this when the input is 3.4567 (except your input will not be in boldface italic):

```
Enter the number to round: 3.4567
3.4567 rounded to 0 decimals = 3.0
3.4567 rounded to 1 decimal  = 3.5
3.4567 rounded to 2 decimals = 3.46
3.4567 rounded to 3 decimals = 3.457
```

2M   Range

Write a program that determines the range of a projectile using this formula:

$$range = \sin(2 * angle) * velocity^2 / gravity$$

where *angle* is the angle of the projectile's path (in radians), *velocity* is the initial velocity of the projectile (in meters per second), and *gravity* is the acceleration at 9.8 meters per second per second (a constant).

The take-off angle must be input in degrees. Therefore, you must convert this angle to its radian equivalent. This is necessary because the trigonometric method Math.sin assumes that the argument is an angle expressed in radians. An angle in degrees can be converted to radians by multiplying the number of degrees by pi/180 where pi » 3.14159. For example, 45° = 45 * 3.14159 / 180, or 0.7853975 radians. In this problem, use the constant in the Math class named Math.PI for the value of pi. Math.PI is the closest value to pi that your computer can support.

Your program must generate a dialogue that looks exactly like this when the input is 45.0 degrees and the initial velocity is 100 meters per second (except your input will not be in boldface italic). Round your answer to two decimal places.

```
Takeoff Angle (in degrees): 45.0
Initial Velocity (meters per second): 100.0
Range = 1020.41 meters
```

2N   Departure Times

Write a Java program that reads in two different train departure times (where 0 is midnight, 0700 is 7:00 a.m., 13:14 is 14 minutes past 1:00 p.m., and 2200 is 10 p.m.) and displays the difference between the two times in hours and minutes. The program should work even if the first departure time input is later in the day than the second departure time input. Assume both times are on the same date and that both times are valid. For example, 1099 is not a valid time because the last two digits are minutes, which should be in the range of 00 through 59. 2401 is not valid because the hours (the first two digits) must be in the range of 0 through 23 inclusive. Verify that your program works correctly by running it with a variety of valid input. Here are three sample dialogues with the correct results:

```
Train A departs at: 1255
Train B departs at: 1305
0 hours and 10 minutes

Train A departs at: 2350
Train B departs at: 0055
22 hours and 55 minutes

Train A departs at: 0730
Train B departs at: 0845
1 hours and 15 minutes
```

Answers to Self-Check Questions

2-1   68 plus or minus a few. It is easy to miscount tokens. For example, comments are not tokens and this is only one token: "A very long string with new, int, double, { }, +, -, /, && * "

2-2
-a VALID
-b 1 can't start an identifier.
-c VALID
-d . is a special symbol.
-e A space is not allowed.
-f / is not allowed.
-g ! is not allowed.
-h VALID
-i ( ) are not allowed.
-j VALID (double is not)
-k VALID

-l Periods (.) are not allowed.
-m VALID
-n Can't start identifiers with a digit.
-o A space is not allowed.
-p VALID
-q VALID
-r VALID (but not meaningful).
-s VALID (but not meaningful).
-t / is not allowed.
-u A space is not allowed.
-v VALID

2-3   +   - Also ,   :   ;   !   (   )   =   {   }
2-4   <= >= Also !=   ==   <=   >=
2-5   String   System   Also   readLine   println
2-6   thisIsOne and anotherOne

2-7   -a   string literals: `"H"` and `"integer"`   -d   boolean literals: `true`
      -b   integer literals: `234` and `-123`   -e   null literals: `null`
      -c   floating-point literals: `1.0` and `1.0e+03` -f   character literals: `'H'`

2-8   a and d only

2-9   ```
      double aNumber = -1.0;
      double anotherNumber = -1.0;
      ```

2-10  ```
      public class YourName
      {
         public static void main( String[] args )
         {
            System.out.println( "Kim Davies" );
         }
      }
      ```

2-11 a, d, e, f, and h are valid.

      b Attempts to store a floating-point literal into an `int` variable.

      c Attempts to store a string literal into an `int` variable.

      g Attempts to store a string literal into a `double` variable.

2-12 -a   10.5   -d   -0.75
      -b   1.75   -e   0.5
      -c   3.5   -f   1.0

2-13 -a   true   -e   true
      -b   false   -f   true
      -c   false   -g   false
      -d   true   -h   true

2-14 Dialogue 1:   Dialogue 2:   Dialogue 3:
      -a   **3.2**   *16.0 / 5.0*   -b   **3.33**   *15.0 / 4.5*   -c   **0.57**   *2.0 / 3.5*

2-15 64.0

2-16 3.0

2-17 2

2-18 0

2-19 -a   0   -d   1
      -b   1   -e   0
      -c   0   -f   0

2-20 -a   0   -f   2
      -b   0.55556   -g   2.1
      -c   0.55556   -h   1.5
      -d   10   -i   0.0
      -e   12   -j   10.0

2-21 The average is wrong.

2-22 Change the prompts. "Enter sum: " becomes "Enter number: " and "Enter number: " becomes "Enter sum: ".

Chapter 3

Using
Objects

Summing Up

The previous chapter presented some details about writing simple Java classes that can be run as programs. You observed two frequently used primitive numeric types—`int` and `double`. You saw one Java class (`TextReader`) and one instance of that class. The `readInt` and `readDouble` messages allow for easy input of numbers in text-based programs.

Coming Up

This chapter is mostly about using objects and getting comfortable with sending messages with arguments. A variety of Java classes are introduced to show just a bit of Java's extensive library of classes. However, the small subset of classes introduced will be used in several places throughout this textbook. You will begin to see that programs have many different types of objects.

This chapter also suggests that object-oriented programming (OOP) is about building systems. An object-oriented program is a collection of objects sending messages to each other. A case study is introduced in this chapter—an event-driven bank teller application with a graphical user interface. The final section of this chapter begins an extended example (which continues through Chapter 9) of a more complex system. After studying this chapter, you will be able to

- use different objects (instances of new classes)
- understand the relationship between classes and objects
- use Java objects for formatting output and storing dates, strings, and collections
- appreciate why programmers partition software into classes
- build a window with a few graphical objects
- change the layout manager for a window

Exercises and programming projects reinforce using existing classes.

3.1   Finding the Objects — Modeling the Real World

Java has two types of values: primitive values and reference values. Only three of Java's eight primitive types (`boolean`, `int`, and `double`) and only one of Java's reference types (class) have been shown so far. Whereas a primitive variable stores only one value, a reference variable stores a reference to an object that may have many values. Classes allow programmers to model real-world entities, which are more intricate than primitives.

Although the Java programming language has only eight primitive types, the Java libraries consist of hundreds of classes (the number of classes tends to grow with each new release of Java). For example, instances of the Java `String` class store collections of characters that could represent names and addresses in alphabets from around the world. Other classes create windows, buttons, and input areas of a graphical user interface. Other classes represent time and calendar dates. Still other Java classes provide the capability of accessing databases over networks using a graphical user interface. Even then, these hundreds of classes do not supply everything that every programmer will ever need. There are many times when programmers discover they need their own classes to model things in their applications. Consider the following system from the realm of banking:

Figure 3.1: **The bank teller specification**

> Implement a bank teller application to allow bank customers to access bank accounts through unique identification. A customer, with the help of the teller, may complete any of the following transactions: withdraw money, deposit money, query account balances, and see the most recent 10 transactions. The system must maintain the correct balances for all accounts. The system must be able to process one or more transactions for any number of customers. The following window summarizes the system functionality (the ID here is Diane):

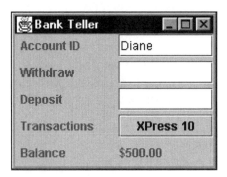

This system will be built over several chapters as an optional case study. It will reinforce concepts presented in each chapter, provide a different example, introduce some more advanced features of Java, and, most importantly, demonstrate the object-oriented style of programming. By the end of Chapter 9, this system will be using about 11 Java classes plus another 10 written by the author.

You are not expected to implement this system now. However, you should be able to pick out some things (objects) that are relevant to this system. This is the first step in the analysis phase of object-oriented software development. One simple tool for finding objects that model a solution is to write down the nouns and noun phrases in the problem statement. Then consider each as a candidate object that might eventually represent part of the system. The objects used to build the system come from sources such as

- the problem statement
- an understanding of the problem domain (knowledge of the system that the problem statement may have missed or taken for granted)
- the words spoken during analysis
- the collection of classes that come with a programming language

The objects should model the real world if possible. Here are some candidate objects:

Candidate Objects to Model a Solution

bank teller	transaction
customers (account list)	list of transactions
bank account	window

Here is a picture to give an impression of the major objects in the bank teller system. The graphical components are not shown. Consider BankTeller to also be the window, with buttons and places where users can enter data. The BankTeller object could coordinate what happens when a user clicks one of the buttons or enters a new ID in the Account ID field. The BankTeller will accomplish this by getting help from many other objects.

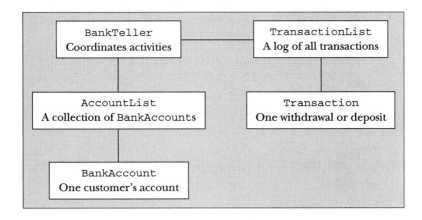

After studying this textbook, you will be able to design and implement systems like this one. In this and the next six chapters, this particular system will be completed. This case study begins by considering just one of the objects that seems like it should be a part of this system: the bank account.

A BankAccount Class

Having one **BankAccount** class will allow the system to have many (thousands of) BankAccount objects. Each instance of BankAccount will represent a checking or savings account at a bank. Using your knowledge of the concept of a bank account, you might recognize that each BankAccount object should have its own account number and its own account balance. Other values could be part of the state of every BankAccount object: a transaction list, a personal identification number (PIN), and a mother's maiden name, for example. You might visualize other banking methods, such as creating a new account, making deposits, making withdrawals, and accessing the current balance. There could also be many other banking messages—applyInterest and printStatement, for example.

The BankAccount class presented here has been intentionally kept simple for ease of study. The available BankAccount messages include—but are not limited to—withdraw, deposit, getID, and getBalance.

Instances of BankAccount are constructed with two arguments to help initialize the object. You can supply two initial values in the following order:

1. a sequence of characters (a string) to represent the account identifier (a name, for example)
2. a number to represent the initial account balance

Here is one example object construction that has two arguments enclosed in parentheses:

```
BankAccount anAccount = new BankAccount( "Chris", 125.50 );
```

The construction of new objects (the creation of new instances) requires the keyword new with the class name and any required initial values between parentheses to help initialize the state of the object. The general form for creating an instance of a class, as shown in Chapter 2, is repeated here:

General Form 3.1: **Constructing objects (initial values are optional)**

class-name object-name = **new** *class-name(initial-value(s))*;

Every **object** has

1. a name (or more technically, a reference variable that stores a reference to the object)
2. state (the set of values that the object remembers)
3. messages that it understands

Every instance of a class will have a reference variable that provides access to the object. Every instance of a class will have its own unique state. In addition, every instance of a class will understand the same set of messages. For example, given this object construction, one can derive the following information:

```
BankAccount anotherAccount = new BankAccount( "Justin", 60.00 );
```

1. name: `anotherAccount`
2. state: an account ID of `"Justin"` and a balance of `60.00`
3. messages: `anotherAccount` understands `withdraw`, `deposit`, `getBalance`, `toString`, and so on

Other instances of `BankAccount` will understand the same set of messages. However, they will have their own separate state, for example:

```
BankAccount theNewAccount = new BankAccount( "Kim", 1000.00 );
```

1. name: `theNewAccount`
2. state: an account ID of `"Kim"` and a balance of `1000.00`
3. messages: `theNewAccount` understands `deposit`, `withdraw`, `getBalance`, `getID`, and so on

These three characteristics of an object can be summarized with some diagrams.[1] The class diagram to the left represents one class. A class diagram lists the class name in the topmost compartment. The instance variables appear in the next compartment. The minus sign (-) is notation to indicate that the identifier is private and cannot be accessed from outside of the class. The methods appear in the bottom compartment. The plus sign (+) is notation to indicate that the identifier is public. Any method with a plus sign can be used where the instances of the class are constructed.

The three diagrams to the right represent three instances of the `BankAccount` class. The three instance diagrams describe the current state of three different `BankAccount` objects. Altogether, these diagrams indicate that one class can have many objects, each with its own separate state (values).

---

1. These diagrams are simplified versions of the Unified Modeling Language (UML) class diagrams and instance diagrams. The difference is that the method headings shown here use Java syntax. The UML method headings have their own syntax. UML notation will not be used in order to avoid introducing a much different syntax from the Java method headings that you will study in Chapter 4, "Classes and Interfaces."

Class Diagram   **Three Instance Diagrams**
                                                     (Three Objects)

```
                  BankAccount
 -String my_id
 -double my_balance

 +BankAccount( String ID, double balance )
 +withdraw( double amt )
 +deposit( double amt )
 +double getBalance( )
 +String getID( )
 +String toString( )
```

```
                  anAccount
 my_id = "Chris"
 my_balance = 125.50
```

```
               anotherAccount
 my_id = "Justin"
 my_balance = 60.00
```

```
                 newAccount
 my_id = "Kim"
 my_balance = 1000.00
```

Here are some other example object constructions that preview five Java classes presented later in this chapter:

1. `String aMessage = new String( "You can edit this text" );`
2. `JButton clickMeButton = new JButton( "Nobody is listening to me" );`
3. `JTextField textEditor = new JTextField( aMessage );`
4. `JFrame theWindow = new JFrame( "Graffiti" );`

1. A `String` object (see section 3.2) can be constructed with any `String` literal that you desire. 2. `clickMeButton` is an object that can be clicked. If a `String` is used to help construct a `JButton` object, that `String` will be displayed on the button. 3. The `JTextField` object named `textEditor` is a place where text can be displayed and/or entered as an input area. If a `String` argument is used to construct a `JTextField`, that `String` will be displayed in the text field.
4. `theWindow` is an object that can hold buttons, text fields, and many other graphical components. Notice that constructing `theWindow` requires one argument—its title. With a few other messages, these four objects could be used to make a window that looks like this (this is discussed in more detail in section 3.6, "A Few Graphical Components"):

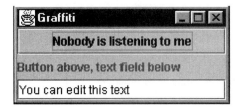

Sending Messages to Objects

To get anything done, your code must send messages to an object. A **message** sent to an instance of a class is a request to have the object do what it was designed to do. For example, the message `keyboard.readInt( )` returns the integer entered from the user. The message `System.out.println( "Sum is " + sum );` tells the object `System.out` to display information to the computer screen.

Some messages ask for information about the state of the object. Other messages ask an object to do something.

- These messages ask a `BankAccount` object to return information:

```
theNewAccount.getBalance( )
theNewAccount.getID( )
theNewAccount.toString( )
```

- These messages ask a `BankAccount` object to perform some tasks:

```
theNewAccount.withdraw( 40.00 )
theNewAccount.deposit( 157.89 )
```

The state of an object is accessible through certain methods. For example, the `getBalance( )` method returns a bank account's current balance. `BankAccount` also has a `toString` method for returning a textual version of the state of a `BankAccount` object. Other methods modify the state of objects. For example, `withdraw( )` and `deposit( )` change the state of `BankAccount` objects. The general form for sending messages to objects is repeated here:

General Form 3.2: **Sending a message to an object**

object-name . message-name(argument1, argument2, ...)

The object-name must be an instance of a class that understands the message-name. The argument list contains zero or more expressions. These are values required by the method to fulfill its responsibility. For example, `withdraw` needs to know how much money to withdraw. On the other hand, `getBalance` doesn't need any arguments to return the current balance of the `BankAccount` object. Here are some more sample messages with either zero, one, or two arguments:

Example Messages

```
theNewAccount.deposit( 237.42 );        // Credit theNewAccount's balance
transcript.completedCourse( CS335 );    // Make course part of transcript
theNewAccount.withdraw( 50.00 );        // Debit theNewAccount's balance
theNewAccount.toString( );              // Return theNewAccount as a string
theNewAccount.getBalance( );            // Return the current balance
aMessage.toUpperCase( );                // Return aMessage in capital letters
clickMeButton.addActionListener( doIt );  // doIt responds to button clicks
theCdPlayer.play( song );               // Make theCdPlayer play a song
theWindow.setSize( 220, 100 );          // Change the size of the window
theWindow.show( );                      // Display window on computer screen
```

The following examples of attempted messages result in syntax errors that occur at compiletime. Your compiler will generate different error messages than those shown here.

Attempts at Messages (compiletime errrors)

```
keyboard.readInteger( )        // TextReader has readInt, not readInteger
keyboard.readDouble( 1.2 )     // No argument is required for readDouble
theNewAccount.deposit( )       // Needs to know how much to deposit
deposit( 100.0 )               // Missing an object name and a dot
theNewAccount.getBalance       // Missing parentheses and argument
theNewAccount.withdraw( "10" ) // Wrong type of argument--needs a number
theNewAccount                  // Missing method name and parentheses
theNewAccount.withdrawl( 10.00 )// withdraw is misspelled
```

Fortunately, a failure to supply the object name, the dot, or the method name in the proper order usually generates an error message. In addition, as with any other method, the compiler complains if the code does not supply the required number and type of arguments.

The BankAccount class—and therefore all BankAccount objects—has three methods to access the state of the object: toString, getID, and getBalance. The BankAccount class also has two methods that modify the state—withdraw and deposit. These methods are exemplified in the following program, which constructs two BankAccount objects and sends messages to both of those objects. Those messages result in the following actions:

- Deposit 133.33 to the object named anAcct.
- Withdraw 250.00 from the object named anotherAcct.
- Display the names and modified balances of both objects.

```
// Demonstrate messages to two BankAccount objects
public class TestAccount1
{
  public static void main( String[] args )
  {
    // Construct two BankAccount objects and store the
    // references to them in reference variables
    BankAccount anAcct = new BankAccount( "Hall", 100.00 );
    BankAccount anotherAcct = new BankAccount( "Fuller", 987.65 );

    // Modify the state of both objects by sending a deposit
    // message to anAcct and a withdraw message to anotherAcct.
    anAcct.deposit( 133.33 );
    anotherAcct.withdraw( 250.00 );

    // View the state of both objects with getID, getBalance, and toString
    System.out.println( "ID of anAcct: " + anAcct.getID( ) );
    System.out.println( "Balance of anAcct: " + anAcct.getBalance( ) );
    System.out.println( "anotherAccount: " + anotherAcct.toString( ) );
  }
}
```

Output (should look like your local currency)

```
ID of anAcct: Hall
Balance of anAcct: 233.33
anotherAccount: Fuller $737.65
```

Objects store one or more values. The **state** of an object may require many values, and these values may be of different classes. For example, a `BankAccount` object references a string of characters to represent the account ID and at the same time stores a floating-point number to represent the balance. An `Employee` object might store several `String`s, such as name, address, social security number, and several numbers, such as pay rate, hours worked, and number of exemptions. A robot object may know its current position and a map. A `JFrame` object (window) may know its size, its title, and the collection of graphical components that have been added to it.

Self-Check

3-1 Write the output generated by the following code:
```
BankAccount b1 = new BankAccount( "B. Kreible", 0.00 );
BankAccount b2 = new BankAccount( "N. Li", 500.00 );
b1.deposit( 222.22 );
b1.withdraw( 20.00 );
b2.deposit( 55.55 );
b2.withdraw( 10.00 );
System.out.println( b1.getID( ) + ": " + b1.getBalance( ) );
System.out.println( b2.getID( ) + ": " + b2.getBalance( ) );
```

3-2 Each of the lettered lines has an error. Explain why.
```
BankAccount b1 = new BankAccount( "B. " );            // a
BankAccount b2( "The ID", 500.00 );                   // b
BankAccount b3 = new Account( "N. Li", 200.00 );      // c
b1.deposit( );                                        // d
b1.deposit;                                           // e
b1.deposit( "100.00" );                               // f
B1.deposit( 100.00 );                                 // g
b1.Deposit( 100.00 );                                 // h
withdraw( 100 );                                      // i
System.out.println( b4.getID( ) );                    // j
System.out.println( b1.name( ) );                     // k
System.out.println( b1.getBalance );                  // l
```

3-3 Write a Java program that constructs one `BankAccount` object and then sends every possible message to that object.

3.2   A Few Java Objects

The primitive variables store just one value per variable. For example, one `double` variable stores exactly one floating-point number, and one `int` variable stores exactly one integer. However, instances of classes virtually always have many values. They may be different types of values—a `double`, an `int`, or a `String`. For example, the simple `BankAccount` class just presented has a `String` to store the account identification and a `double` variable to store the account balance. There certainly could be more variables.

`BankAccount` is specific to one particular application from the world of banking. It, like most classes, is built in part from other objects and primitives provided by Java. Therefore, a few of Java's classes are now presented (there are hundreds):

- **String**: Stores a collection of characters.
- **DecimalFormat**: An instance helps arrange numeric data with commas and a specific number of decimal places.
- **ArrayList**: Manages a collection of elements.
- **GregorianCalendar**: Provides date arithmetic.

String Objects

A **string** is a sequence of characters. The ability to manage strings in a programming language is highly desirable. So Java provides a `String` class to store a sequence of characters that may represent an address or a name, for example. Sometimes a programmer is interested in a single character in a string. At other times, a programmer may require several characters or the current length of a `String` (the number of characters in the string). It is sometimes necessary to discover if a certain `substring` exists in a string. For example, is `"the"` in `"Mother"`, and if so, where does `substring` `"the"` begin? Java's `String` class provides a large number of methods to help with such problems. You will find yourself using `String` objects in many programs. Each `String` object stores a collection of from zero to many characters. String objects can be constructed in two ways.

General Form 3.3: **Constructing `String` objects in two different ways**

`String` *identifier* = **new String(** *string-literal* **);**
`String` *identifier* = *string-literal*;

Examples

```
String stringReference = new String( "A String Object" );
String anotherStringReference = "Another";
```

The shorter version, without the keyword `new`, is allowed because a `String` literal is the same as a `String` object construction. Strings are objects. The `String` literal causes an object to be constructed and the reference value to be returned in its place.

For more specific examples, consider two `length` messages sent to two different `String` objects. Both messages evaluate to the number of characters in the `String`.

```
stringReference.length( )    // Evaluates to 15
"abc".length( )              // Evaluates to 3
```

An `indexOf` message to a `String` object returns the index of the first character if the `String` argument is found. If the `String` argument does not exist in the receiver of the message, `indexOf` returns -1.

```
stringReference.indexOf( "tri" )        // Evaluates to 3
stringReference.indexOf( "not here" )   // Evaluates to -1
"abc".indexOf ( "c" )                   // Evaluates to 2
```

A `charAt` message returns the character located at the index passed as an `int` argument. Notice that `String` objects have zero-based indexing. The first character is located at index 0 and the second character is located at index 1, or `charAt(1)`.

```
stringReference.charAt( 0 )   // Evaluates to 'A'
"abc".charAt( 1 )             // Evaluates to 'b'
```

Programmers often make one `String` object from two strings with the + operator, which **concatenates** (connects) two or more strings into one string. Concatenation and these `String` messages are illustrated in the context of a program below:

```
// Show a few String constructions and messages. No import
// is necessary since String is in the java.lang package.
public class DemonstrateSomeStringMethods
{
  public static void main( String[] args )
  {
    String a = new String( "Any old" );
    String b = " String";
    String aString = a + b; // Concatenate a and b
    // aString is now "Any old String"

    // Show the first character. This is zero-based indexing.
    System.out.println( aString.charAt( 0 ) );

    // Show the 2nd character. Index of second char is 1 (not 2).
    System.out.println( aString.charAt( 1 ) );

    // Show the uppercase equivalent
    System.out.println( "toUpperCase: " + aString.toUpperCase( ) );

    // Show the number of characters in the string
    System.out.println( "length: " + aString.length( ) );

    // Show the position of "ring" in "Any old String"
    System.out.println( "indexOf: " + aString.indexOf( "ring" ) );

    // Return the substring, beginning at the first argument (4)
    // extending to the character at the second argument (11) - 1
    System.out.println( "substring: " + aString.substring( 4, 9 ) );
  }
}
```

Output

```
A
n
toUpperCase: ANY OLD STRING
length: 14
indexOf: 10
substring: old St
```

String Input

The `TextReader` class has two methods for reading textual input from the keyboard. A `readWord` message returns a reference to a `String` object that has from zero to many characters typed by the user at the keyboard. A **word** is a sequence of printable characters separated from the next word by white space. **White space** is defined as blank spaces, tabs, or newline characters in the input stream. White space separates `ints` and `doubles` on input. White space also separates words on input. When input from the keyboard, `readWord` stops adding text to the `String` object when the first white space is encountered on the input stream from the user.

A `readLine` message returns a reference to a `String` object that contains from zero to many characters entered by the user. With `readLine`, the `String` object may contain blank spaces and tabs. The newline marker is not included. It is discarded from the input stream so the next input will not encounter a new line right away.

A `TextReader` object can read integers, floating-point numbers, and strings with no spaces or an entire line of text from the keyboard. Here is a summary of the major `TextReader` methods and what they do:

Figure 3.2: **TextReader methods (TextReader is supplied by the author)**

- `readInt`: Returns the next integer entered as text, such as 345 or -67
- `readDouble`: Returns the next floating-point number entered as text, such as 3.45 or -6.7
- `readWord`: Returns a reference to a `String` object as white-space-separated text
- `readLine`: Returns a reference to a `String` object containing all text on a line (including spaces and tabs) up to but not including the end of the line

The `readLine( )` method returns all the characters typed in up to the end of the next line of input. For example, if you wanted to read an address or a person's name that had more than one word, you would use `readLine( )`. If you wanted just one string with no blank spaces or tabs, you would use `readWord( )`.

```java
public class ReadWordAndLine
{
  public static void main( String[] args )
  {
    String firstName, address;
    TextReader keyboard = new TextReader( );
```

```
        System.out.print( "Enter first name: " );
        firstName = keyboard.readWord( );

        System.out.print( "Enter address: " );
        address = keyboard.readLine( );

        System.out.println( "Hello " + firstName +
                            ", do you really live at " + address + "?" );
    }
}
```

Dialogue 1

```
Enter first name: John
Enter address: 1600 Pennsylvania Avenue
Hello John, do you really live at 1600 Pennsylvania Avenue?
```

The readWord method stops adding characters to the String object at the first bit of white space, which in this case was a new line (the Enter or Return key generates a new line). On the other hand, readLine builds a String object including blank spaces and tabs. This means if the user entered two white-space-separated chunks of text at the first prompt and pressed the Enter key, the remaining text on the first line would be read by the next readLine message. This would leave the address waiting to be read. If there were no other readWord or readLine message, that text would be ignored by the program.

Dialogue 2

```
Enter first name: John Rittenhouser
Enter address: 1600 Pennsylvania Avenue
Hello John, do you really live at Rittenhouser?
```

This also means you could input several separate String objects on one line just as you could enter several different numbers on one line.

```
// Demonstrate that String input is like numeric input. The values
// can be separated by blank spaces on the same line (not standard).
public class ReadThreeWordsFromOneLine
{
  public static void main( String[] args )
  {
    String nameOne, nameTwo, nameThree;
    TextReader keyboard = new TextReader( );

    System.out.println( "Enter 3 names separated by white space: " );
    nameOne = keyboard.readWord( );
    nameTwo = keyboard.readWord( );
    nameThree = keyboard.readWord( );
```

```
      System.out.println( "first: " + nameOne );
      System.out.println( "second: " + nameTwo );
      System.out.println( "third: " + nameThree );
  }
}
```

Dialogue

```
Enter 3 names separated by white space:
Kim Sandy Chris
first: Kim
second: Sandy
third: Chris
```

Self-Check

3-4 What is the value of positionOfG?

```
String s1 = new String( "abcdefghi" );
int positionOfG = s1.indexOf( "g" );
```

3-5 What is the value of s3?

```
String s2 = new String( "abcdefghi" );
String s3 = new String( s2.substring( 4, 6 ) );
```

3-6 What is the value of len?

```
String s4 = new String( "abcdefghi" );
int len = s4.length( ) - 1;
```

3-7 Write the value of the expression "Wheatley" + ", " + "Kay";.

3-8 Write expressions to store the middle character of a String into a String object named mid. If there is an even number of characters, store the character to the right of the middle. For example, the middle character of "abcde" is "c" and of "Robert" is "e".

3-9 For each of the following messages, if there is something wrong, write "error"; otherwise write the value of the expression.

```
String s = new String( "Any String" );
```

  -a length(s)   **-d** s.indexOf(" ")

  -b s.length   **-e** s.substring(2, 5)

  -c s(length)   **-f** s.substring("tri")

3-10 Write a message that returns a String from the keyboard when the first blank, tab, or end of line is encountered.

3-11 Write a message that returns all characters on one entire line, including blank spaces.

ArrayList Objects

A list is a collection of elements. A list has a first element, a second element, and an element that is at the end of the list. A list could be empty (have zero elements). The elements in a list can be visited in the order that they exist, from the first element to the last element. Java provides several classes to store a list of elements. One of these is named ArrayList,[2] which can be constructed like this:

```
// An object to store a collection of objects: import java.util.ArrayList;
ArrayList stringList = new ArrayList( );
```

At this point, the object named stringList has zero elements. Sending size and toString messages to it bear this out:

```
System.out.println( "Number of elements: " + stringList.size( ) );
System.out.println( "stringList: " + stringList.toString( ) );
```

Output

```
Number of elements: 0
stringList: []
```

New elements are added at the end of a list with ArrayList's **add** method. The add message is demonstrated in the program below, which constructs an ArrayList object and adds four elements to the end of the list. ArrayList's toString method returns all elements in the list separated by commas and enclosed between [and].

```
// Class with just the main method to demonstrate ArrayList
import java.util.ArrayList;

public class ArrayListOfStrings
{
  public static void main( String[] args )
  {
    // Construct an empty list
    ArrayList stringList = new ArrayList( );

    // Add four elements to this list
    stringList.add( "first" );
    stringList.add( "second" );
    stringList.add( "third" );
    stringList.add( "fourth" );
    System.out.println( "Number of elements: " + stringList.size( ) );
    System.out.println( stringList.toString( ) );
  }
}
```

---

2. The name Array in ArrayList reveals how elements are stored in ArrayList objects. ArrayList objects have an array instance variable to organize the elements in order. Arrays are presented in Chapter 8.

Output

```
Number of elements: 4
[first, second, third, fourth]
```

ArrayList has many other useful methods (about 25), but only a couple are shown for now: add and toString. With the ArrayList constructor, the add method, and the toString method, you can store a collection of elements and show them quite easily. Other ArrayList methods will be introduced throughout the next several chapters as the need arises. This was a brief peek at yet another useful Java class.

GregorianCalendar Objects

Java has a class named GregorianCalendar for storing calendar dates, such as the current date set on the system clock. When a GregorianCalendar object is constructed with no arguments, its state represents the current date and time in the computer system. For example, if the current system date is set to May 22, 2002, the reference variable today stores a reference to an object with the date 2002/4/22 (you probably think of 4 as April, but Java sees 4 as MAY).

```
// The current date
GregorianCalendar today = new GregorianCalendar( );
```

To represent the current date in an understandable way, you have to get the individual facts about the date. This requires a get message with an int argument. However, there are so many pieces of information that names are used instead. Here are the named pieces of information that you can get from a GregorianCalendar object:

AM, AM_PM, APRIL, areFieldsSet, AUGUST, DATE, DAY_OF_MONTH, DAY_OF_WEEK, DAY_OF_WEEK_IN_MONTH, DAY_OF_YEAR, DECEMBER, DST_OFFSET, ERA, FEBRUARY, FIELD_COUNT, fields, FRIDAY, HOUR, HOUR_OF_DAY, isSet, isTimeSet, JANUARY, JULY, JUNE, MARCH, MAY, MILLISECOND, MINUTE, MONDAY, MONTH, NOVEMBER, OCTOBER, PM, SATURDAY, SECOND, SEPTEMBER, SUNDAY, THURSDAY, time, TUESDAY, UNDECIMBER, WEDNESDAY, WEEK_OF_MONTH, WEEK_OF_YEAR, YEAR, ZONE_OFFSET

A toString message returns the complex state of one instance of GregorianCalendar.

```
System.out.println( today.toString( ) );  // Ran on November 27, 2002
```

Output

```
java.util.GregorianCalendar[time=?,areFieldsSet=false,areAllFieldsSet=true,lenient
=true,zone=java.util.SimpleTimeZone[id=America/Phoenix,offset=-200000,
dstSavings=3600000,useDaylight=false,startYear=0,startMode=0,startMonth=0,startDay
=0,startDayOfWeek=0,startTime=0,startTimeMode=0,endMode=0,endMonth=0,endDay
=0,endDayOfWeek=0,endTime=0,endTimeMode=0],firstDayOfWeek=1,
minimalDaysInFirstWeek=1,ERA=1,YEAR=2002,MONTH=10,WEEK_OF_YEAR=48,
WEEK_OF_MONTH=5,DAY_OF_MONTH=27,DAY_OF_YEAR=331,DAY_OF_WEEK=3,
DAY_OF_WEEK_IN_MONTH=4,AM_PM=0,HOUR=9,HOUR_OF_DAY=9,MINUTE=6,SECOND=44,
MILLISECOND=800,ZONE_OFFSET=-25200000,DST_OFFSET=0]
```

There is much data in each `GregorianCalendar` object. Java uses just one method to retrieve information about dates. The method is named `get`. The argument to `get` is any of the above names preceded by `GregorianCalendar` and a dot. For example, here is the code that `gets` the year, the month (0–11), and the day (1–31) from a `GregorianCalendar` object.

```java
import java.util.GregorianCalendar;

public class ShowTodaysDate
{
  public static void main( String[] args )
  {
    // Assume this program ran on November 27, 2002
    GregorianCalendar aDay = new GregorianCalendar( );

    int year = aDay.get( GregorianCalendar.YEAR  );
    int month= aDay.get( GregorianCalendar.MONTH );
    int day  = aDay.get( GregorianCalendar.DATE  );
    String dateAsString = year + "/" + month + "/" + day;
    // You have to add 1 to month to get month as we know it
    System.out.println( dateAsString );
  }
}
```

Output (the month "10" means November, not October)

```
2002/10/27
```

In addition to giving this awkward way of accessing data, Java thinks that January is month 0. The months are off by one (Java thinks of December as month 11, not 12).

Java provides calendar arithmetic with its `add` method. Consider the following code that determines the date 90 days into the future. Underneath, the `add` method is checking for varied days in a month, turnover into future years, and whether or not the year is a leap year, when February 29 would be a date. The `add` method of `GregorianCalendar` hides many details.

```
aDay.add( GregorianCalendar.DATE, 90 ); // Increase aDay by 90 days
year = aDay.get( GregorianCalendar.YEAR );
month= aDay.get( GregorianCalendar.MONTH );
day = aDay.get( GregorianCalendar.DATE );

// Add 1 to month to show the correct
// future date (November, not October)
dateAsString = year + "/" + (month + 1) + "/" + day;
System.out.println( "Warranty expires on " + dateAsString );
```

Output (1 was added to month to show the month correctly)

```
Warranty expires on 2003/2/25
```

The add method can also be used to arrive at a date in the past by making the second argument negative. The first argument determines which part of the GregorianCalendar changes. For example, this code changes aDay to 30 years before this date.

```
aDay.add( GregorianCalendar.YEAR, -30 ); // Set to 30 years in the past
```

The DecimalFormat Class and Its format Method

When output, floating-point numbers sometimes seem to have their own way of revealing their values. Consider the output of an arithmetic expression that should be 3.6.

```
System.out.println( 1.2 + 2.4 );
```

Output

```
3.5999999999999996
```

Instead, the value shown is something that is very close—apparently off by about 0.0000000000000004. Whereas humans think of numbers as base 10 (decimal), computers think of numbers in base 2 (binary). Numbers can be ever so slightly different than expected. Sometimes you will want to show floating-point output with a specific number of decimal places or with commas. This can be done with the help of the class DecimalFormat from the java.text package.

A DecimalFormat object is constructed with a String pattern to format a given number using that pattern. The example, the pattern of "0.00" means there will be at least one digit to the left of the decimal point and exactly two digits to the right.

```
// Not quite what was expected
System.out.println( 1.2 + 2.4 );    // 3.5999999999999996
```

```
// Show the same value with only two decimals
DecimalFormat numberFormatter = new DecimalFormat( "0.00" );
String numberAsString = numberFormatter.format( 1.2 + 2.4 );

// Floating-point number was rounded to
// two decimals and stored as String
System.out.println( numberAsString );   // 3.6
```

Other meaningful parts of the `String` pattern used as an argument to construct a `DecimalFormat` object include the following:

0	a digit, zero shows as 0
#	a digit, zero shows as absent
.	a placeholder for a decimal point
,	a placeholder for separating groups
x	other characters, such as x or $, show as is

The following program demonstrates two different format patterns. The `currencyFormatter` object uses the $ character. This is not a special pattern symbol, so it will always show up. On the other hand, the comma (,) is a special symbol that will group the numbers every three digits.

```
// Demonstrate one formatting pattern
import java.text.DecimalFormat;

public class A
{
  public static void main( String[] args )
  {
    DecimalFormat numberFormatter = new DecimalFormat( "0.00" );
    System.out.println( numberFormatter.format( 1.23456789 ) );
    System.out.println( numberFormatter.format( .123456789 ) );
    System.out.println( numberFormatter.format( 123456789 ) );

    // A format message will have $ first and two decimal places
    DecimalFormat currencyFormatter =
            new DecimalFormat("$###,###,##0.00");
    System.out.println( currencyFormatter.format( 123456789 ) );
    System.out.println( currencyFormatter.format( 0 ) );
  }
}
```

Output

```
1.23
0.12
123456789.00
$123,456,789.00
$0.00
```

Self-Check

3-12   Write the output generated by the following program:

```java
import java.text.DecimalFormat;
public class FormattedNumbers
{
  public static void main( String[] args )
  {
    DecimalFormat f1 = new DecimalFormat( "0.00" );
    DecimalFormat f2 = new DecimalFormat( "0" );
    DecimalFormat f3 = new DecimalFormat( "<0.0>" );

    System.out.println( f1.format( 2345.678 ) );
    System.out.println( f2.format( 2345.678 ) );
    System.out.println( f3.format( 2345.678 ) );
  }
}
```

3-13   Write the output generated by the following program:

```java
import java.util.ArrayList;
public class SmallCollection
{
  public static void main( String[] args )

  { // Construct two empty lists
    ArrayList listOne = new ArrayList( );
    ArrayList listTwo = new ArrayList( );

    listOne.add( "a" );
    listOne.add( "b" );
    listOne.add( "c" );
    System.out.println( listOne.toString( ) );
    System.out.println( listOne.size( ) );

    listTwo.add( "first" );
    listTwo.add( listOne );
    listTwo.add( "another" );
    listTwo.add( "last" );
    System.out.println( listTwo );
    System.out.println( listTwo.size( ) );
  }
}
```

3-14   Write the output generated by the following program. Use today's date.

```java
import java.util.GregorianCalendar;
public class FourYearsAhead
{
  public static void main( String[] args )
  {
```

```
      // Use today's date
      GregorianCalendar aDay = new GregorianCalendar( );
      aDay.add( GregorianCalendar.DATE, 4 * 365 );
      int year = aDay.get( GregorianCalendar.YEAR  );
      int month= aDay.get( GregorianCalendar.MONTH );
      int day  = aDay.get( GregorianCalendar.DATE  );

      String dateAsString = year + "/" + month + "/" + day;
      System.out.println( dateAsString );
    }
  }
```

3.3   Assignment to Reference Variables

Assignments to primitive variables and reference variables have different meanings. Consider how the assignment of one primitive variable—such as int or double—to another primitive variable differs from the assignment of one reference variable—an object such as String or BankAccount—to another object. The following code behaves as you probably expect:

```
int num1 = 456;
int num2 = 789;
num2 = num1;
num1 = 123;
System.out.println( "num1 is " + num1 );
System.out.println( "num2 is " + num2 );
```

Output

```
num1 is 123
num2 is 456
```

Both of these primitive variables—num1 and num2—store integer values. They are unique values. A change to one primitive variable does not change the other. More specifically, when num1 becomes 123, num2 does not change. This is not true for reference variables.

A reference variable stores the location of an object, not the object itself. By analogy, a reference variable is like the address of a friend. It may be a description of where your friend is located, but it is not your actual friend. You may have the addresses of many friends, but these addresses are not your actual friends.

When the system constructs an object with the new operator, an object gets built somewhere in memory. The new operation also returns a reference to that newly constructed object. The reference value gets stored into the reference variable to the left of =. For example, the following construction stores the reference to a BankAccount object with the values "Chris" and 567.89 into the reference variable named chris.

```
BankAccount chris = new BankAccount( "Chris", 567.89 );
```

A programmer can now send messages to the object by way of the reference variable named chris. The memory that holds the actual state of the object is stored elsewhere. Because you will use the reference variable name for the object, it is intuitive to think of chris as the object. However, chris is actually the *reference* to the object, which is located elsewhere.

The following code mimics the same assignments that were made to the primitive variables above. The big difference is that the deposit message sent to chris actually modifies the object referenced by kim.

```
kim = chris;
// The values (state) of the object were not assigned. Rather,
// the reference to chris was assigned to kim. Now both
// reference variables refer to (are looking at) the same object.
System.out.println( "Why does a change to 'chris' change 'kim'?" );
chris.deposit( 555.55 );
System.out.println( "Kim's balance was 0.00, now it is " +
                                        kim.getBalance( ) );
```

Output

```
Why does a change to 'chris' change 'kim'?
Kim's balance was 0.00, now it is 555.55
```

This happens because both reference variables—chris and kim—refer to the same object in memory after the assignment kim = chris. In fact, the object originally referred to by the reference variable named kim is lost forever. Once the memory used to store the state of an object no longer has any references, Java's garbage collector reclaims the memory so it can be reused later to store other new objects. This allows your computer to recycle memory that is no longer needed.

```
BankAccount chris = new BankAccount( "Chris", 0.00 );
BankAccount kim = new BankAccount( "Kim", 100.00 );
```

Assignment statements copy the values to the right of = into the variable to the left of =. When the variables are primitive number types like int and double, the copied values are numbers. However, when the variables are references to objects, the copied values are the locations of the objects in memory.

Figure 3.3: **Assignment to reference variables**

The two objects before assigning one reference value to another:

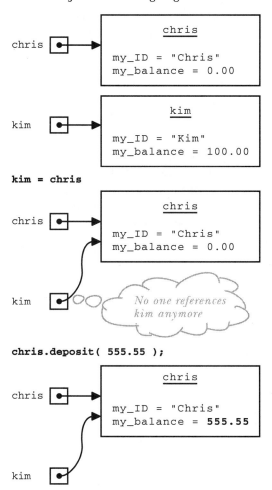

After the assignment kim = chris, kim and chris both refer to the same object in memory. The state of the object is not assigned. The reference to the object is assigned, not the state of the object. A message to either reference variable (chris or kim) then either accesses or modifies the same object, which now has the values "Chris" and 555.55.

The only way to change a primitive variable is through assignment. However, an assignment of a reference value to another reference variable of the same type does not change the object itself. The state of an object can only be changed with messages designed to modify the state.

3.4   Another Author-Supplied Class — `Grid`

The **Grid** class presented in this section is based on the work of Rich Pattis' "Karel the Robot" [Pattis 1981] and a game at Walt Disney World's Epcot Center. The game asked the question, "Could you be a programmer?" The player was invited to guide a pirate ship to a treasure while avoiding obstacles. Turning left one space too early would result in a shipwreck.

The Grid class is one of just a few classes in this textbook that do not come with the Java system (TextReader is another). Before you study this section, please realize that the Grid class is only for teaching and learning programming in Java and using objects. It was not designed to be part of a larger real-world system as TextReader was. It will be used occasionally in later chapters to demonstrate new concepts in a visual manner. However, the Grid class is not meant to dominate any of those new concepts. The visible state of Grid is meant to help you readily grasp access and modification of object states. If you do not study Grid, then you may not be able to complete the programming projects related to this class.

A Grid object stores a rectangular map of rows and columns with an object to move. A Grid object is initialized with five arguments.

***General Form 3.4:* Constructing a `Grid` object**

Grid *grid-name* **= new Grid(** *rows, columns, mover-row, mover-col, direction* **);**

The first two arguments represent the size of the Grid in rows and columns; the next two arguments are the mover's starting row and column; and the last argument is the mover's starting direction. The argument for direction should be written as Grid.NORTH, Grid.EAST, Grid.SOUTH, or Grid.WEST.

The following program provides an example of object construction. It also displays a text-based version of the Grid object with the toString method that returns a String to show the current state of the object. To maintain consistency with Java, which begins indexing at 0, the first Grid row is 0. The first Grid column is 0.

```
// Assumes Grid.java is in the same folder as this file
public class ShowAGrid
{
  public static void main( String[] args )
  {
    // Arguments needed to construct a Grid object go like this: #rows,
    // #columns, moverStartRow, moverStartColumn, moverDirection
    Grid aGrid = new Grid( 6, 8, 2, 4, Grid.EAST );

    // Mover on row 2 (the third row) and column 4 (the fifth column)
    System.out.println( aGrid.toString( ) );  // Display current state
  }
}
```

Output (the mover is facing east and looks like >)

The state of any `Grid` object can be modified with `move` and `turnLeft` messages. A `move` message has no arguments. A `turnLeft` message does not require an argument either. The state of a `Grid` can be accessed with methods such as `moverRow`, `getRows`, `getColumns`, `toString`, and `frontIsClear`. These messages are exemplified in the following program:

```
// Initialize, modify, and access the state of a Grid object
public class SomeGridMethods
{
  public static void main( String[] args )
  {
    // Construct a Grid object
    Grid aGrid = new Grid( 7, 14, 5, 8, Grid.EAST );

    // Tell mover to move 3 spaces forward, turn,
    // and move another 4 spaces
    aGrid.move( );
    aGrid.move( );
    aGrid.move( );
    aGrid.turnLeft( );
    aGrid.move( );
    aGrid.move( );
    aGrid.move( );
    aGrid.move( );

    // Access the current state of the Grid object
    System.out.println( "Rows: " + aGrid.getRows( ) );
    System.out.println( "Columns: " + aGrid.getColumns( ) );
    System.out.println( "Mover row: " + aGrid.moverRow( ) );
    System.out.println( "Mover column: " + aGrid.moverColumn( ) );
    System.out.println( "Front is clear? " + aGrid.frontIsClear( ) );
  }
}
```

Output

```
Rows: 7
Columns: 14
Mover row: 1
Mover column: 11
Front is clear? true
```

Self-Check

3-15   Write the output of the following program:

```
public class MoveThrice
{
  public static void main( String[] args )
  {
    Grid aGrid = new Grid( 6, 6, 4, 2, Grid.EAST );
    aGrid.move( );
    aGrid.move( );
    aGrid.turnLeft( );
    aGrid.move( );
    aGrid.move( );
    aGrid.move( );
    aGrid.turnLeft( );
    aGrid.move( );
    aGrid.move( );
    System.out.println( aGrid.toString( ) );
    System.out.println( "mover row: " + aGrid.moverRow( ) );
    System.out.println( "mover column: " +
                                    aGrid.moverColumn( ) );
  }
}
```

Other `Grid` Methods

There are several other `Grid` methods, some of which will be needed in this chapter's programming projects. Completing those projects provides practice at sending messages to objects and developing algorithms with graphical feedback. Figure 3.4 lists all `Grid` methods.

Figure 3.4: **`Grid` methods**

- `move()`—Moves the mover one space forward (or terminates if move is not possible)
- `turnLeft()`—Turns the mover 90 degrees to the left (if it is facing north, it turns to face west, for example)
- `putDown(row, column)`—Places a thing 'O' at the specified row and column (if possible)
- `pickUp()`—Removes the object where the mover is (or generates an error)
- `toggleShowPath()`—Switches between showing the path or leaving dots after the mover has traveled on
- `block(row, column)`—Places a block (#) at the specified row and column (if possible)
- `frontIsClear()`—Returns `true` if the mover could move one space forward

- `rightIsClear()`—Returns `true` if the mover could turn right and move one space forward
- `moverRow()`—Returns the row the mover is in
- `moverColumn()`—Returns the column the mover is in
- `getRows()`—Returns the number of rows in the `Grid`
- `getColumns()`—Returns the number of columns in the `Grid`
- `toString()`—Returns a `String` version of the `Grid` with the characters #, ., O, <, >, ^, and V

This class diagram (with Java method heading syntax) summarizes the interface to this class:

Figure 3.5: **The `Grid` class diagram (data not shown)**

```
                                    Grid

Grid( int rows, int cols, int moverRow, int moverCol, int Direction )
Grid( int rows, int cols )
void move( )
void turnLeft( )
void putDown( int row, int column )
void pickUp( )
void toggleShowPath( )
void block( int row, int column )
boolean frontIsClear( )
boolean rightIsClear( )
int moverRow( )
int moverColumn( )
int getRows( )
int getColumns( )
String toString( )
```

Let's look at some code that sends some other `Grid` messages. A few `Grid` `putDown( )` messages can be used to place a few "cookies" (or whatever you want to call the things) on the table (or whatever you want to call the `Grid`). Then the challenge is to send the proper messages to the mover (or whatever you want to call the mover) to eat (or whatever you want to call the `Grid.pickUp( )` method) the cookies. Here is a program that instructs the mover in `aGrid` to eat two cookies and return home:

```java
// This program sets up a little world with some blocked
// paths and instructs the mover to pick up some things.
public class EatCookies
{
  public static void main( String[] args )
  {
    Grid aGrid = new Grid( 8, 12, 0, 0, Grid.SOUTH );
    aGrid.putDown( 4, 0 );
    aGrid.putDown( 4, 3 );
    aGrid.block( 3, 2 );
    aGrid.block( 4, 2 );
    aGrid.block( 5, 2 );
```

```
    // Show the starting position of the mover on the Grid
    System.out.println( aGrid.toString( ) );

    // Instruct the aGrid to "eat" two cookies
    aGrid.move( );
    aGrid.move( );
    aGrid.move( );
    aGrid.move( );

    aGrid.pickUp( );
    aGrid.move( );
    aGrid.move( );
    aGrid.turnLeft( );
    aGrid.move( );
    aGrid.move( );
    aGrid.move( );
    aGrid.turnLeft( );
    aGrid.move( );
    aGrid.move( );
    aGrid.pickUp( );

    // Get the aGrid back home and show the ending state
    aGrid.move( );
    aGrid.move( );
    aGrid.move( );
    aGrid.move( );
    aGrid.turnLeft( );
    aGrid.move( );
    aGrid.move( );
    aGrid.move( );
    System.out.println( aGrid.toString( ) );
  }
}
```

Output

```
The Grid:
v  .  .  .    .   .   .   .   .
.  .  .  .    .   .   .   .   .

.  .  .  .    .   .   .   .   .
.  . #  .    .   .   .   .   .
O  . # O     .   .   .   .   .
.  . #  .    .   .   .   .  .
.  .  .  .    .   .   .   .   .

.  .  .  .    .   .   .   .   .

The Grid:
<  .    .  .   .   .   .   .
.  .    .  .   .   .   .   .
.  .    .  .   .   .   .   .
.  #    .  .   .   .   .   .
.  #    .  .   .   .   .   .
.  #    .  .   .   .   .   .

.  .    .  .   .   .   .   .
```

A Failure to Meet the Preconditions

There are many "illegal" messages you can send to a Grid object. For example, you could send a move message that asks the mover to move through a block (#) or off the edge of the Grid. All it takes is one incorrect message—moving four rows instead of three, for example.

Self-Check

3-16 If you were designing the methods for a Grid object, what would you want to prevent from occurring?

What should a Grid object do when sent a message with arguments that don't work right? Frankly, it's a bit awkward. The object could respond by doing nothing. In this case, the state of the object would remain unaltered. Alternately, the object could travel off the end of the Grid or move through blocks, but this sounds more like a Superman object.

For a method to behave properly, certain conditions are presumed. For example, the sqrt function of the Math class would like the argument to be greater than or equal to 0.0. But what happens when this condition is not upheld?

In the case of Math.sqrt(-1.0), Java returns "Not a Number" (NaN). An attempt to reference aString.charAt(-1) results in program termination. The program throws a StringIndexOutOfBoundsException exception. In the case of moving off the edge of the world with a Grid object, Grid tells you what you did wrong by showing the text version of the grid and a message box. Once you click OK, the program will terminate.

```
public class ViolateAPrecondition
{
  public static void main( String[] args )
  {
    Grid aGrid = new Grid ( 5, 5, 1, 2, Grid.EAST );

    aGrid.move( );
    aGrid.move( );
    // This third message violates the preconditions of move
    aGrid.move( );
    System.out.println( "Will not see this line of output" );
  }
}
```

Output

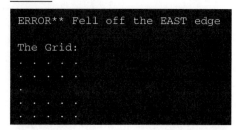 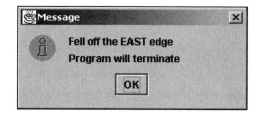

To avoid these runtime errors, obey the method's **preconditions**, which are what the method presumes to be true when the message is sent. For example, the move method has the precondition that there is no block or edge in the path of the mover. Also, the pickUp message presumes there is something to pick up. So what does happen when you violate one of these preconditions? You'll find out by working on certain Grid-related programming projects.

A Graphical `Grid`

The text-based Grid class just presented can only show a snapshot of the Grid by printing the toString view of a Grid object. You cannot see the mover move from one location to the next. The GraphicGrid class—written by Andrew Wilt while at the University of Arizona—allows for a different view of the changing states of Grid objects. To construct one, you need to pass an existing Grid object as an argument.

General Form 3.5: **Constructing a GraphicGrid object**

GraphicGrid *identifier* = **new GraphicGrid(** *Grid-object* **)**

For example, here is the same program shown before with a second view (you can see the mover move in a window). Now you have two views of the same program: a text-based view and a graphical view.

```
// Need a Grid object to get a GraphicGrid object
Grid aGrid = new Grid( 8, 12, 2, 0, Grid.SOUTH );

// Let anotherView listen to aGrid to show the changing state.
// The GraphicGrid class was written by Andrew Wilt, Arizona.
GraphicGrid anotherView = new GraphicGrid( aGrid );

aGrid.putDown( 4, 0 );
aGrid.putDown( 4, 3 );
aGrid.block( 3, 2 );
aGrid.block( 4, 2 );
aGrid.block( 5, 2 );
```

```
// Show the starting position of the mover on the Grid
System.out.println( aGrid.toString( ) );

// Instruct the aGrid to "eat" two cookies
aGrid.move( );
aGrid.move( );
aGrid.pickUp( );
aGrid.move( );
aGrid.move( );
```

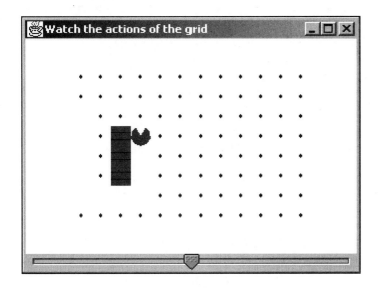

3.5   Classes — Collections of Methods and Data

Abstraction is the process of pulling out and highlighting the relevant features of a complex system. For example, abstraction allows us to use the computer at the programming-language level without full knowledge of the many complex details at lower levels. Abstraction is a weapon against complexity.

You can use methods without knowing the implementation details coded by other programmers. Abstraction allows programmers to easily use primitive types, such as int or double, and classes, such as String, BankAccount, and Grid. The characteristics of the int type (a specific range of integer values) and int operations, such as addition, multiplication, assignment, input, and output, can be understood without knowing the details of those operations, how those values are stored, or how these operations are implemented in the hardware and software. Abstraction makes life easier. Abstraction helps keep us sane.

A class is also understood through the abstraction outlined by its collection of available methods. For example, the String class includes methods such as equals, charAt, find, length, and substring. The BankAccount class includes the methods withdraw, deposit, and balance. The Grid class includes the methods toString, turnLeft, and move. The essential usage details are understood by concentrating on the messages an instance of the class can understand.

Even though Java is delivered with a large collection of classes, additional classes are still required for specific applications. New abstractions are built from existing objects, methods, and algorithms. As you begin to design and implement class abstractions, set a goal to build these abstractions so they are easy to use and perform a well-defined method. When the details of implementation are long forgotten, you will still be able to use the abstraction because you know what it does. You won't have to remember how it does it. Let's now consider the abstraction provided by some of the Grid methods.

Instead of representing the responsibility as a method, all of the hidden code could have been written in place of the message. However, as the table below shows, this detailed way requires many additional lines. It should also be noted that the hidden details would be incomprehensible until most of the material in this textbook had been mastered.

The Actions Represented by One Message

Method	The Object-Oriented Way	The Detailed Way
Construct one Grid object	Grid g = new Grid(15, 15, 9, 4, Grid.EAST);	35 lines
Move in the current direction	g.move( );	112 lines
Return the Grid state	g.toString( );	6 lines
Change direction	g.turnLeft( );	10 lines

The four messages in the middle column represent the abstract equivalent of coding 163 lines. Now imagine a six-message program that moves and turns three times. The equivalent detailed way would require approximately 366 detailed lines of code rather than the six messages!

By placing the many lines of detailed code into a method, the programmer may execute the method with one message. The same message can also be sent repeatedly. Therefore, whenever you have code that can be used more than once in a program, it is preferable to implement that behavior within the confines of a method that becomes one of the messages available to the objects of a class (see Chapter 4, "Classes and Interfaces"). A message represents many hidden instructions and details. The programmer need not see, nor understand, that implementation.

3-17 Using the previous table, how many lines of code are required to initialize the state of one `Grid` object using a `Grid` object?

3-18 Using the previous table, how many lines of code are required to initialize the state of one `Grid` object when the detailed way is used (as in the right column)?

3-19 With paper and pencil, write a program that constructs a `Grid` object and moves the mover at least one space in every `Grid` direction.

By partitioning low-level details into methods, you write the implementation only once. Another advantage of methods is that the same method can be used repeatedly with a one-line message. Rather than one huge `public main` method, programs are comprised of messages that are more manageable. Here are some reasons why Java programmers use existing methods and objects to better manage the complexity of software development:

- to reuse existing code rather than write it from scratch
- to concentrate on the bigger issues at hand
- to reduce errors by writing the method only once and testing it thoroughly

In the early days of programming, programs were written as one big `main` method. As programs became bigger, structured programming techniques became popular. One major feature of structured programming was to partition programs into functions for more manageable modules. Programmers found this helped people understand the program better. It is easier to maintain programs that place related processing details in an independent function. It is easier to fix a 20-line method in a program with 100 methods than it is to fix a 2,000-line program. Other reasons for dividing a program into smaller methods include the following:

- putting the details into a method makes the code easier to comprehend
- the same actions need to be achieved more than once in a program
- the method may be reused in other programs

With structured programming of the 1970s and 1980s, data was passed around from one function to another. When data is available everywhere throughout a large program, it can become dangerously susceptible to unintentional changes.

Now as software has become even more complex, object technology encapsulates methods with the data manipulated by those methods. Developers don't throw the data around between functions or leave them open for accidental change.

Figure 3.6: **Historical progression of how programs are organized into modules**

The Early Days	Structured	Object-Oriented

```
main()           one()              class ONE
{                {                  {
  // 1             _____            one()
  _____        _____           two()
  _____       }                   // . . .
  _____                           ten()
  _____       two()             }
  _____       {
  _____        _____         // . . .
  _____        _____
  _____       }                 class NINE
  _____                         {
  _____       // . . .            eighty1()
  _____                           eighty2()
  _____       ninety9()           // . . .
  _____       {                   ninety()
  // 500           _____         }
  _____        _____
  _____       }                 // . . .
  _____
  _____       hundred()         class TEN
  _____       {                 {
  _____        _____           ninety1()
  _____        _____           ninety2()
  _____       }                   // . . .
  _____                           hundred()
  _____       main()            }
  _____       {
  _____        _____         main()
  _____        _____         {
  // 1000          _____           _____
  _____        _____         }
}                  _____
                   _____
                 }
```

Self-Check

3-20 What reason for using methods makes the most sense to you right now?

3-21 Describe one example of how abstraction helps you get through the day.

3.6   A Few Graphical Components

This section presents other objects and classes that Java has to help easily build
event-driven programs with a graphical user interface (GUI). These programs are
characterized by **graphical components**, such as windows, buttons, and menus, that
react to events generated by a user interacting with the graphical components

through the mouse and keyboard. When building event-driven applications with a GUI, there are two things you have to do:

1. Make the graphical components visible to the user.
2. Make sure the correct things happen when an event occurs, such as the user clicking on something, moving a slider bar, selecting from a pull-down list, or pressing a key.

A graphical component is an object with a graphical appearance that can generate event objects when they are touched by users. Java has graphical components, such as buttons, labels, text fields, lists, slider bars, and a window to hold all of these graphical components. This section shows how to get a few graphical components into a window and make them visible to the user. In the next chapter, you will learn how to have the correct code respond to events generated by user interaction with the application.

This section uses a few of the many components in the `javax.swing` package. These classes help programmers build graphical user interfaces (GUIs). The first example will show graphical components constructed from the following `javax.swing` classes:

- **JFrame**: A window with a title, border, submenu, and some buttons to the upper right.
- **JButton**: A graphical component that can be "pushed" by clicking on the button.
- **JLabel**: A display area for a small amount of text.
- **JTextField**: A component that allows input and editing of a single line of text.

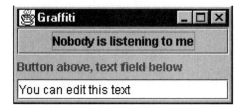

The program could import all four classes individually like this:

```
import  javax.swing.JFrame;
import  javax.swing.JButton;
import  javax.swing.JLabel;
import  javax.swing.JTextField;
```

However, since all of these classes are in the `javax.swing` package, you could simply use the following shortcut to gain access to the 90 or so classes in the package:

```
import javax.swing.*;   // Use any Swing component without
                        // qualifying the classes
```

The first object that will be constructed here is a window that holds other components. Java's JFrame class provides the means to contain other components. Some graphical components can contain other components, such as JFrame and JPanel. The JFrame is the base of the desktop application. The JFrame object will be constructed with a String that is the title of the window. To see the JFrame, you must send the JFrame object a show message. But before you do this, it is recommended that you send a message to theWindow so the program will terminate when the user closes the window later on.[3]

```
// Construct a window with its title and show it
JFrame theWindow = new JFrame( "Graffiti" );

// When the user closes the window, the program will terminate
theWindow.setDefaultCloseOperation( JFrame.EXIT_ON_CLOSE );

// Make the window visible
theWindow.show( );
```

Output

The window will be shown in the upper-left corner with a very small height and width. To make the window appear bigger, send a setSize message to the JFrame object. The first argument is the width—an integer representing the number of pixels. The second argument is the height, which is also measured in **pixels**—the smallest dots on your computer screen.

```
// Make the window 220 pixels wide and 100 pixels high
theWindow.setSize( 220, 100 );
```

The following setLocation message will position the left side of the JFrame object 80 pixels to the right of the upper-left corner of the screen. The upper part of the JFrame will be shown 50 pixels below the top of the computer screen.

```
// Set the window's location from the upper-left corner of the screen
theWindow.setLocation( 80, 50 );   // 80 pixels right, 50 pixels down
```

The coordinate system used to locate windows on a screen and to draw onto a surface uses the upper-left corner as position 0,0. Therefore, when this window is shown, the upper-left corner will be in position (80,50), 80 pixels to the right and 50 pixels down.

---

3. setDefaultClosing does not work in Java 1.2.1 and earlier. You can work around this in Java 1.2.2; however, JFrame.CLOSE_ON_EXIT is not present (you use the int argument 3 instead). You need Java 1.3 or later to use the code as written above. See the interface WindowListener in Chapter 9's bank teller case study if you are using JDK (Java Development Kit) 1.2.2 or earlier (or simply terminate your program at the operating system level).

```
// Make the window visible
theWindow.show( );
```

Java's Coordinate System

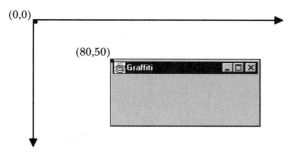

Other graphical components can be added to a `JFrame` container with the following two-step process:

1. Construct the components.
2. Add the components to the content pane portion of the `JFrame`, which is a `Container` object.

This example shows a button, a label, and a text field. All three objects are constructed with `String` arguments:

```
// Construct some components that will be added to the Container
JButton clickMeButton = new JButton( "Nobody is listening to me" );
JLabel aLabel = new JLabel( "Button above, text field below" );
JTextField textEditor = new JTextField( "You can edit this text" );
```

At this point, `theWindow.show( )` would not show these three objects. You have to add them to `theWindow`. In older versions of Java, you could simply add these components directly to a `Frame` object from the `java.awt` package. The `JFrame` class of `javax.swing` package is more complex. An instance of `JFrame` has several parts to it to allow for added flexibility. For example, you can set the look and feel of the application. The look and feel used here is the Java look and feel, which is mostly the same on different platforms, such as Windows, Mac OS, and Unix. The part of the `JFrame` object to which you can store a collection of other graphical components is called the **content pane**.

To get a reference to a `JFrame`'s content pane—an instance of the `Container` class—the programmer must send a `getContentPane` message to the `JFrame` object. This returns a reference to the `Container` object that holds other graphical components. Because `class Container` is in Java's Abstract Windowing Toolkit (awt) package, the following `import` must be added at the top of the program.

```
import java.awt.Container;
```

Now you can use the following message and assignment to store a reference to a content pane, a container for holding additional objects:

```
// Get a reference to a Container that can hold other components
Container contentPane = theWindow.getContentPane( );
```

Finally, sending add messages to the content pane stores references to these graphical components as part of theWindow's state.

```
// Add three components to the content pane part of the JFrame
contentPane.add( clickMeButton, BorderLayout.NORTH );
contentPane.add( aLabel, BorderLayout.CENTER );
contentPane.add( textEditor, BorderLayout.SOUTH );
```

The first argument is the component you want to add to the window. The second argument describes the area to which you want to add the component. Now, a show message will show the JFrame with three other graphical components added.

When adding to a JFrame object, you can specify where on the JFrame the components will be added. There are five choices: BorderLayout.NORTH, BorderLayout.SOUTH, BorderLayout.WEST, BorderLayout.EAST, and BorderLayout.CENTER. This is illustrated in the following JFrame that has five JButton objects, constructed with strings such as "North" and "South", added to the content pane of the JFrame:

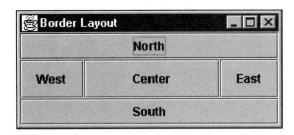

This JFrame illustrates Java's **BorderLayout** layout manager. It is one of several of Java's layout managers. A **layout manager** makes the decision on how to arrange graphical components in a Container. BorderLayout is the default layout manager for JFrame, but this can be changed with a setLayout message (see the bank teller section that follows this).

Self-Check

3-22 Write a complete program that will generate the window above with the five buttons in it. The window is in the upper-left corner and is 270 pixels wide and 120 pixels high.

3-23 What is the string stored in the button with the current focus? In other words, if a user were to press the Enter key, which button would get "pushed"? Look for the one button that has a slightly different appearance than the other four.

Now here is the code discussed above, in one complete program. It constructs a small window, places three different components into it, and then shows itself.

```
// Construct a window and add some other graphical components to it
import javax.swing.*;        // For all Swing components
import java.awt.Container;   // For the Container class
import java.awt.*;           // For the BorderLayout class
public class SomeComponents
{
  public static void main( String[] args )
  { // Construct a window with its title
    JFrame theWindow = new JFrame( "Graffiti" );

    // When the user closes the window, the program terminates
    theWindow.setDefaultCloseOperation( JFrame.EXIT_ON_CLOSE );

    // Make the window 220 pixels wide and 100 pixels high
    theWindow.setSize( 220, 100 );

    // Set the window's location from the upper-left corner
    // of the screen: 150 pixels right, 80 pixels down
    theWindow.setLocation( 150, 80 );

    // Construct some components that will be added to the window
    JButton clickMeButton = new JButton( "Nobody is listening to me" );
    JLabel aLabel = new JLabel( "Button above, text field below" );
    JTextField textEditor = new JTextField( "You can edit this text" );

    // Get access to the Container object inside the JFrame
    Container contentPane = theWindow.getContentPane( );

    // Add three components to the content pane part of the JFrame
    contentPane.add( clickMeButton, BorderLayout.NORTH );
    contentPane.add( aLabel, BorderLayout.CENTER );
    contentPane.add( textEditor, BorderLayout.SOUTH );
    // Finally show the user what the window looks like
    theWindow.show( );
  }
}
```

Output

At this point, nothing will happen when the button is clicked. The next chapter shows how to make it so you can specify what happens when the user interacts with the graphical user interface.

3.7   **BankTeller_Ch3 TellerWindow**

This chapter began with a problem statement describing a bank teller application. This will be developed in the next five chapters. This book is designed to introduce object-oriented programming even if you skip this example. However, this bank teller case study was added for the following reasons:

- reinforce concepts presented in each chapter
- provide additional examples of the important chapter topics
- introduce some more advanced features of Java
- demonstrate the modern way of programming with graphical user interfaces and event-driven programming
- demonstrate the object-oriented style of programming in a more complex system of over 20 different types of objects

In this section, the window will be built with its 10 graphical components. There will be no attempt to have anything happen if a user presses a button or enters text into the text field. This will begin in the next chapter.

If the window had not already been designed, you could begin by drawing a picture with pencil and paper to determine the needed graphical components and how the window to the application will look. However, the design of the window has already been done. This section presents some of the issues to get the bank teller window to look like this:

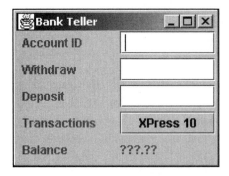

To begin, here is the code to construct a `JFrame`, set its title and size, and make the content pane available to add the graphical components later. For the time being, the program terminates when the window closes.

```
JFrame tellerWindow = new JFrame( "Bank Teller" );
tellerWindow.setSize( 220, 220 );
tellerWindow.setDefaultCloseOperation( JFrame.EXIT_ON_CLOSE );
Container contentPane = tellerWindow.getContentPane( );
```

There are 10 graphical components to add: six JLabel objects (the balance shown initially as ???.?? above is a JLabel) and four JTextField objects. However, recall that JFrame objects can add only five graphical components in the window area (North, South, East, West, and Center). A different layout manager must be used.

Layout Managers — BorderLayout and GridLayout

The way that graphical components are laid out as they get added to the content pane of a JFrame is controlled by the container's layout manager. By default, a JFrame object uses the BorderLayout layout manager to add graphical components. If the programmer fails to specify one of five locations where graphical components can be added, those components will be added to the center of the JFrame, one on top of another. Therefore, it is wise to specify one of the five areas as a second argument to add. The default layout manager is an instance of BorderLayout, which is defined in the java.awt package. The Bank Teller window shown above was built with a layout manager that is an instance of GridLayout, which is also defined in the java.awt package.

The layout manager for a Container was changed by means of the Container setLayout message. The setLayout message requires an instance of a layout manager, such as GridLayout. (There are several other such layout managers implemented in Java, and you can even define your own.) A GridLayout object can be constructed for maximum programmer control by using these int arguments:

1. The number of rows (5, below)
2. The number of columns (2, below)
3. The horizontal gap specified as the number of pixels between columns (8, here)
4. The vertical gap specified as the number of pixels between rows (16, here)

```
GridLayout fiveByTwo = new GridLayout( 5, 2, 8, 16 );
```

The layout manager object named fiveByTwo will control how graphical components are laid out in the Container with this setLayout message to the Container:

```
contentPane.setLayout( fiveByTwo );
```

Now graphical components will be added in a row-wise fashion, beginning in the upper-left corner of the Container. The numbers shown in Figure 3.7 represent the ordering of how 10 graphical components will be added with a 5-row by

2-column `GridLayout` layout manager in charge. The shaded areas represent where the components will go. The unshaded areas represent the horizontal and vertical gaps between those graphical components.

Figure 3.7: **`GridLayout`'s order of added graphical components**

1	2
3	4
5	6
7	8
9	10

The first three graphical components are added to the `JFrame` object's `Container` (referenced here as `contentPane`) as follows:

```
contentPane.add( new JLabel( "Enter Account ID: " ) );
JTextField newAccountField = new JTextField( );
contentPane.add( newAccountField );
contentPane.add( new JLabel( "Current Balance: " ) );
```

To get the teller window—the user interface to the bank teller system—the other seven graphical components must be added in a particular order. The messages that add the 10 components are captured in a class with one `main` method. When this program is run, it generates the graphical interface that will be used as the interface to the bank teller system.

```
// This class has one method (main) to build a teller
// window by placing 10 graphical components into
// one JFrame that uses the GridLayout manager.

import javax.swing.JFrame;
import javax.swing.JLabel;
import javax.swing.JTextField;
import javax.swing.JButton;
import java.awt.Container;
import java.awt.GridLayout;

public class BankTeller_Ch3
{
  public static void main( String[] args )
  {
    // Build the base window of the application
    JFrame tellerWindow = new JFrame( "Teller Window" );

    // Change the appearance of the window
    tellerWindow.setTitle( "Bank Teller" );
    tellerWindow.setSize( 210, 160 );
```

```java
        // Let the program shut down when the window is closed
        tellerWindow.setDefaultCloseOperation( JFrame.EXIT_ON_CLOSE );

        // Get the Container object of JFrame
        // to which components can be added
        Container contentPane = tellerWindow.getContentPane( );

        // Change the layout strategy to align two
        // components in each of five rows, eight pixels
        // between each column, four pixels between rows
        contentPane.setLayout( new GridLayout( 5, 2, 8, 4 ) );

        // Let the human bank teller enter new account IDs
        contentPane.add( new JLabel( "  Account ID" ) );
        JTextField newAccountField = new JTextField( );
        contentPane.add( newAccountField );

        // Let the human bank teller enter a new withdrawal amount
        contentPane.add( new JLabel( "  Withdraw" ) );
        JTextField withdrawField = new JTextField( );
        contentPane.add( withdrawField );

        // Let the human bank teller enter a new deposit amount
        contentPane.add( new JLabel( "  Deposit" ) );
        JTextField depositField = new JTextField( );
        contentPane.add( depositField );

        // Let the human bank teller view the number of transactions
        contentPane.add( new JLabel( "  Transactions" ) );
        JButton XPress10Button = new JButton( "XPress 10" );
        contentPane.add( XPress10Button );

        // Let the human bank teller see the balance of an account
        contentPane.add( new JLabel( "  Balance" ) );
        JLabel statusLabel = new JLabel( "???.??" );
        contentPane.add( statusLabel );

        tellerWindow.show( );
    }
}
```

Output

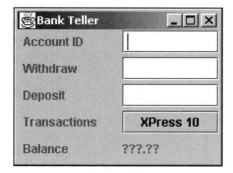

Laying out graphical components in Java can be difficult. Each layout manager has an idiosyncratic way of dealing with things. The size of components may be a default size that doesn't fit your wishes. Components may shift to different locations when a window is resized. One component may need to be made bigger, and another made smaller. For example, 15 versions of the screen above were made until it looked sensible. Then it was critiqued by graphic designer Ian Shadburne until it looked better. Different numbers of rows and columns, different sizes of the JFrame, and different gaps (in pixels) were tried before the desired appearance was gotten. Instead of going into detail concerning layout managers, this textbook will offer the details to get a particular layout. For example, when given the size of a JFrame in a programming assignment, you will find that things just work out (because the sizing issues will be provided). However, you are invited to play around with the sizes of things. For example, consider running the previous program and resizing the window. What do you think *should* happen? What do you think will happen if only the first 5 of the 10 components are added?

Self-Check

3-24 Fill in the code to make buttonWindow look as shown (assume the correct imports exist). Let there be four pixels between the JButton objects.

```
JFrame buttonWindow = new JFrame( "6 Buttons" );
buttonWindow.setSize( 150, 110 );
buttonWindow.setDefaultCloseOperation( JFrame.EXIT_ON_CLOSE );
// ------Begin Answer


        Need several messages here


// ------End of Answer
contentPane.add( new JButton( "1" ) );
contentPane.add( new JButton( "2" ) );
contentPane.add( new JButton( "3" ) );
contentPane.add( new JButton( "4" ) );
contentPane.add( new JButton( "5" ) );
contentPane.add( new JButton( "6" ) );
buttonWindow.show( );
```

Chapter Summary

- An object is an instance of a class that has its own state and a collection of messages. Each object stores its own data separately from other objects. This allows for thousands of unique `BankAccount` and `JButton` objects, for example.

- A class specifies the set of methods and data that every object of the class has available.

- Object-oriented programs are collections of interacting objects. Some may be part of Java, others are written for a particular application.

- A problem specification helps programmers discover objects that will eventually model a system.

- The `String` class has a number of methods for accessing all or part of the characters in a `String`. These methods include `substring`, `find`, `replace`, and `length`.

- Messages require the object name and a dot (.) before the method name and arguments. Use `aString.substring( 2, 5 )` rather than `substring( aString, 2, 5 )`.

- Almost all classes in this textbook are part of the readily available Java library. The `BankAccount`, `Grid`, and `GraphicGrid` classes are supplied on the accompanying diskette. You should copy the required author-supplied files into the folder with the program that needs them.

- In the 1950s, programs were written as collections of statements. By the 1970s, programs were usually collections of functions (methods). In the 1990s, more and more programs were written as collections of interacting objects, where each object is an instance of a class containing a collection of methods. Each development allows more complex software to be more easily developed and more easily maintained.

- Abstraction means a programmer can send a message without knowing the implementation details. The programmer does need to know the method name, the return type, and the number and class of arguments.

- Object-oriented programming is about building systems.

- An object-oriented program has a collection of objects that send messages to the others.

- `GridLayout` allows you to specify the number of rows and columns so the components can be lined up under each other.

- One part of building a graphical user interface is to place different graphical components into a window and present that window to the user. This chapter showed some of Java's `Swing` classes (`JFrame`, `JButton`, `JLabel`, and `JTextField`) from the `java.swing` package. You will often need other classes from the `java.awt` package, such as `Container` and `GridLayout`. Therefore, if you have graphical components, you will likely use at least these two imports:

```
import javax.swing.*;    // For Swing classes
import java.awt.*;       // For the Container class
```

Key Terms

add	Grid	setDefaultCloseOperation
ArrayList	JButton	setLocation
BankAccount	JFrame	setSize
BorderLayout	JLabel	show
concatenate	JTextField	state
Container	layout manager	string
content pane	message	String
DecimalFormat	object	white space
graphical component	pixel	word
GregorianCalendar	precondition	

Exercises

The answers to exercises marked with are available in Appendix C.

1. Write the output generated by the following program:

```
public class TwoAccounts
{
  public static void main( String[] args )
  {
    BankAccount b1 = new BankAccount( "One", 100.11 );
    BankAccount b2 = new BankAccount( "Two", 200.22 );

    b1.deposit( 50.00 );
    b2.deposit( 30.00 );
    b1.withdraw( 20.00 );

    System.out.println( b1.getBalance( ) );
    System.out.println( b2.getBalance( ) );
  }
}
```

 2. Write the complete dialogue (output and user input) of this program when the user enters this input in the order requested (input is shown in boldface italic comments).

```
public class WithdrawAndDeposit
{
  public static void main( String[] args )
  {
```

```
String name;
double start, amount;
TextReader keyboard = new TextReader( );

// Read the initial state of a BankAccount
System.out.print( "First and last name (on one line): " );
name = keyboard.readLine( );                    // Your Name

System.out.print( "initial balance: " );  // 111.11
start = keyboard.readDouble( );

// Construct the BankAccount
BankAccount anAcct = new BankAccount( name, start );

// Enter a deposit amount and a withdrawal amount
System.out.print( "deposit? " );                // 22.00
amount = keyboard.readDouble( );
anAcct.deposit( amount );

System.out.print( "withdraw? " );               // 44.00
amount = keyboard.readDouble( );
anAcct.withdraw( amount );

System.out.print( "Ending balance for " + anAcct.getID( ) );
System.out.println( " is " + anAcct.getBalance( ) );
    }
}
```

3. What is the value of `position`?

```
String s = new String( "012345678" );
// Initialize position to the first occurrence of "3" in s
int position = s.indexOf( "3" );
```

 4. What is the value of `s2`?

```
String s1 = new String( "abcdefghijklm" );
String s2 = s1.substring( 3, 6 );
```

5. What is the value of `lengthOfString`?

```
String s3 = new String( "012345678" );
int lengthOfString = s3.length( );
```

 6. Write the code necessary to store the current date as a `String` in the order of day, month, and year. If the computer's clock is set to May 26, 2002, the string should be 26/5/2002.

7. Write the output generated by the following code:

```
ArrayList list = new ArrayList();
System.out.println( list );
list.add( "First" );
list.add( new BankAccount( "Second", 1 ) );
System.out.println( list );
```

 8. Choose the most appropriate classes for each of the following from the set of classes that have been discussed so far.

a. Represent the number of students in the class

    b. Represent a student's grade point average

    c. Represent a student's name

    d. Represent the number of questions on a test

    e. Represent a person's checking account

    f. Get input from the user

    g. Send output to the screen

    h. Represent a day 90 days from the current date

    i. Store a collection of bank accounts

9. What things need to be present in a message?

 10. Must a programmer understand the implementation of the `move` method of the `Grid` class to use it?

11. Name two reasons why programmers use or implement methods.

12. Write the output generated by the following program:

```java
public class SomeBlocks
{
  public static void main( String[] args )
  {
    Grid aGrid = new Grid( 6, 6, 1, 1, Grid.SOUTH );

    aGrid.putDown( 2, 3 );  // Place something on a specific spot
    aGrid.block( 0, 0 );
    aGrid.block( 5, 5 );
    aGrid.move( );
    aGrid.move( );
    aGrid.turnLeft( );
    aGrid.putDown( ); // Place something where the mover is located
    aGrid.move( );
    aGrid.move( );
    aGrid.move( );
    aGrid.turnLeft( );
    aGrid.putDown( ); // Place something where the mover is located
    aGrid.move( );
    aGrid.turnLeft( );
    aGrid.move( );
    System.out.println( aGrid.toString( ) );
    System.out.println( "Mover row# " + aGrid.moverRow( ) );
    System.out.println( "Mover col# " + aGrid.moverColumn( ) );
  }
}
```

13. Write a program that will generate this output:

```
The grid:
O . . . .
. # . . .
. .
. . . . .
. . . . v
```

14. Finish the following assignment so it will store any person's first name into a
`String` object named `firstName`. The first name is always preceded by `", "`.

```
String name = "Carlin, George";

String firstName = _____

System.out.println ( firstName );   // Output: George
```

15. Write the output generated by the following program:

```java
public class A
{
  public static void main( String[] args )
  {
    String s1 = "red";
    String s2 = "green";
    String s3 = "blue";
    String result;

    result = s1 + " and " + s2;
    System.out.println( result );
    result = s2 + " and " + s3;
    System.out.println( result );
    result = s3 + " and " + s1;
    System.out.println( result );
  }
}
```

 16. Write a complete Java program that will build and show this window, which is
100 pixels from the left edge of the screen and 200 pixels down. The window
must be 300 pixels wide and 120 pixels high. The window title must be "Five
components," with a text field in the north and buttons in the west, south,
and east. Place the label "Center of JFrame" in the center.

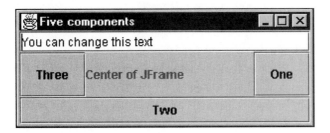

Programming Tips

1. **You will need author-supplied classes to complete certain programming
   projects at the end of this chapter.**
   Some programming projects require author-supplied classes that are available
   on this textbook's diskette. For example, you will need the `BankAccount` class,

stored in the file named `BankAccount.java`, to complete Programming
Projects 3A and 3B. It is recommended that you copy the needed file(s) from
the accompanying diskette into the same folder where you plan to complete
the programming project that needs the file(s). If you are working in a lab
setting, your instructor may have the `.class` files where Java can find them
and you won't need to copy any files. You could also set up your home computer by setting your classpath environment variable to include the location of
the files from this book (see instructions on Sun Microsystem's Java download
site: **http://java.sun.com/j2se/**).

2. **Even if no arguments are required, end the message with ( ).**
   You have now seen several messages that require no arguments. If a method
   has no parameters, it requires no arguments. Here are two examples:

```
System.out.println( aString.length( ) );
System.out.println( aGrid.moverRow( ) );
```

   Do not forget parentheses in messages that do not require arguments.

```
myAcct.getBalance;    // ERROR, missing ( )
aString.length;       // ERROR: missing ( ) after length
aGrid.row;            // ERROR: missing ( ) after row
```

   Without the parentheses (and), there is no method call—even when no
   arguments are needed by the method. In addition, there are many times
   when an object can be constructed without any arguments. The parentheses
   are still required. This attempt to construct a `TextReader` object results in an
   error message:

```
TextReader keyboard = new TextReader;

MissingParentheses.java:6:  '(' expected.
TextReader keyboard = new TextReader;
```

3. **Java begins indexing at 0, not 1.**
   The first character in a `String` is referenced with 0, not 1. The third character is at index 2, not 3.

```
String s = "Boxing Day";
// Return the first character, 'B'
System.out.println( s.charAt( 0 ) );
// Return the third character, 'x'
System.out.println( s.charAt( 2 ) );
```

4. **Don't reference aString.charAt(aString.length( )).**
   This is an attempt to reference a single value that is not in the range of 0 to
   `aString.length( )` - 1. In general, do not reference characters in a
   `String` that do not exist, such as `charAt( -1 )`.

```
String s = new String( "This String has 29 characters" );
// ERROR: -1 is out of range
System.out.println( s.charAt( -1 ) );
// 29 is out of range
System.out.println( s.charAt( s.length( ) ) );
```

If the above code were in main in the TestStringIndex class in a file named
TestStringIndex.java with the message s.charAt(-1) on line 10, the
program would terminate early with the following exception:

```
java.lang.StringIndexOutOfBoundsException:
String index out of range: -1
        at java.lang.String.charAt(String.java:398)
        at TestStringIndex.main(TestStringIndex.java:10)
```

5. **There are several ways to declare/initialize String objects.**

   Because String objects are used so frequently, Java has provided shortcuts to
   declaring and constructing them. Here are three different ways to declare
   and/or initialize String objects:

```
String s1;                  // A string that cannot be used yet.
String s2 = "A string";     // Initialization like ints and doubles.
String s3 = new String( "Constructed like all other objects" );
```

6. **Distinguish between readLine( ) and readWord( ).**

   The TextReader readLine( ) method gets all the characters up to, but not
   including, the end of the line. It gets all blank spaces and tabs. On the other
   hand, the TextReader readWord( ) method gets all the characters up to, but
   not including, the first white space.

7. **You don't need to write toString( ) in a print or println message.**

   The Grid and BankAccount classes used the toString method like this to
   show a textual representation of the objects:

```
Grid aGrid = new Grid( 7, 7, 5, 5, Grid.NORTH );
BankAccount anAccount = new BankAccount( "Devon", 8765.15 );

// Show a textual view of the objects
System.out.println( aGrid.toString( ) );
System.out.println( anAccount.toString( ) );
```

   However, if you just use the object name and leave off toString( ), the result
   is the same.

```
System.out.println( aGrid );        // Sends the toString message
System.out.println( anAccount );
```

8. **JFrame.EXIT_ON_CLOSE was not available until Java 1.3.**

   If you are using Java 1.2.1 or earlier, see Chapter 9's bank teller section for a
   more complicated way to have the program terminate when the user closes

the window. If you are using Java 1.2.2, you can send the following message so the program terminates when the window closes (Java is a work in progress):

```
theWindow.setDefaultCloseOperation( 3 );
```

Programming Projects

3A   Two Bank Accounts

Write a complete Java program that will perform the following actions:

- initialize two different BankAccount objects named one and theOther, both with an initial balance of 1000.00
- make a deposit of 123.45 to one and a deposit of 50.00 to theOther
- make a withdrawal of 20.00 from one and a withdrawal of 60.00 from theOther
- show the names and balances of both objects (send messages to the objects to access the balances—do not maintain the balances outside of the accounts)
- show the combined balances of both objects after the transactions (*Hint:* the combined balance that you must output should be 2093.45)

Construct your BankAccount objects exactly as shown here:

```
BankAccount one = new BankAccount( "Mellisa", 1000.00 );
BankAccount theOther = new BankAccount( "Jutta", 1000.00 );
```

Your program must generate the following output. *Hint:* Use the toString method of BankAccount to display the final state of the objects, which is shown on lines 1 and 2 of the output. The combined balance may show a different number of decimal places (your currency may appear differently in locales outside the United States).

```
Mellisa $1,103.45
Jutta $990.00
Combined: 2093.45
```

The currency should match that used where you are.

3B   The Final Balance

Write a Java program that initializes a BankAccount object with an ID of "Mike" and an initial balance of 111.11. Then ask the user for an amount to deposit and another to withdraw and make the withdrawal and deposit messages to the BankAccount. Then show the final balance. Make sure you show the balance of the BankAccount. Do not maintain the balance separately as a double. Your program and input of 20.00 and 40.00 must generate a dialogue that looks like this (your currency may appear differently in locales outside the United States):

```
Mike's initial balance: 111.11
Enter amount to deposit: 20.00
Enter amount to withdraw: 40.00
The account: Mike $91.11
```

3C indexOf

Write a program that reads two strings from user input and shows the position of the first string as a substring in the second. Your program and the user input of **another** and **the** must generate a dialogue that looks exactly like this.

Dialogue 1

```
Enter String 1: another
Enter String 2: the
'the' is in 'another' at position 3
```

Dialogue 2

```
Enter String 1: one
Enter String 2: huh
'huh' is in 'one' at position -1
```

3D Substring

Write a Java program that inputs a name in the form of the last name, a comma, a space, the first name, a space, an initial, and a period (as shown in the input below). Display the first name, a space, the initial, a period, a space, and the last name. Make sure the comma is after Jones on input and that the comma is *not* in the rearranged name. If you enter **Jones, Kim R.** your program must generate a dialogue that looks exactly like this:

Dialogue

```
Enter name as Last, First I. Jones, Kim R.
'Jones, Kim R.' rearranged is: 'Kim R. Jones'
```

3E A Little Cryptography

Write a Java program that hides a message in five words. Use one of the characters in the five input strings to spell out one new word. A word of caution: The String charAt(int) method returns a character, but with + it is treated as if it were an int. So instead of concatenating five characters, it could add up to the numeric equivalents used to store the characters. Consider the following code that outputs 195 (97 for "a" plus 98 for "b"):

```
String aString = "ab";
System.out.println( aString.charAt( 1 ) + aString.charAt( 0 ) ); // 195
```

Placing a string up front fixes the problem. This code generates the output `Secret message: ba`.

```
String aString = "ab";
System.out.println( "Secret message: " + aString.charAt( 1 )
                                       + aString.charAt( 0 ) );
```

So make sure you start your output with the label `"Secret message: "`. This forces the `charAt` return value to become the characters you seek. Run your program with the following input and make up at least one other message:

```
Enter five words: cheap energy can cause problems
Enter five integers: 4 2 1 0 5
Secret message: peace
```

3F   The Next Four Fortnights

Write a Java program that stores a `String` representation of the next four fortnight dates (two weeks) into an `ArrayList` object. Show the `toString` version of the `ArrayList`. If the current date is August 15, 2003, the output should look like this (precede each `dateAsString` with `"\n"` to start each on a new line within `ArrayList`'s `toString` message and do not use zero based indexing for months, August is 8, not 7):

```
[
2003/8/29,
2003/9/12,
2003/9/26,
2003/10/10]
```

3G   Letter

Write a Java program that constructs a 13-by-7 `Grid` and then instructs the mover to "draw" the letter `I` exactly as shown to the left below (the mover could end up anywhere next to the `I` facing any direction). Also, add the graphical view of the program's progression. You should see the mover move. You should see the graphical view (to the right) when the mover is about half done. The final graphical view should show a letter `I`.

3H   A Bread Trail

Write a Java program that constructs a 3-by-24 Grid object with the mover in row 1,
column 0. Then instruct the mover to leave the pattern shown in the textual
version. You should also show the graphical view (the picture below shows the state
of the Grid when the mover is about half done).

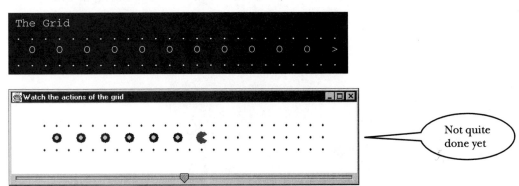

3I   Eating a Cookie

Write a Java program that constructs an obstacle course and places an O as shown
below. Instruct the mover to eat the cookie (looks like O here) after maneuvering
the miniature obstacle course. Show the Grid object before and after the moves.
Your program must generate output exactly like that shown to the left. Also, add
the graphical view of the program's progression. You should see the mover eat the
cookie.

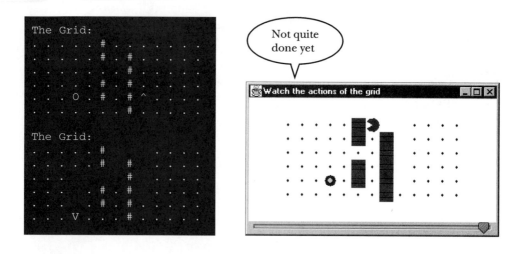

3J   Hurdles

Write a program that constructs a hurdle course as shown below and instructs the runner to jump the hurdles. The runner must touch the ground between each hurdle. Show the Grid before and after the course is run. Your program must generate output exactly like that shown below. Add a graphical view of the program's progression. You should see the mover jump all five hurdles. Your graphical view should look like the hurdle course shown just after the mover has jumped the first hurdle.

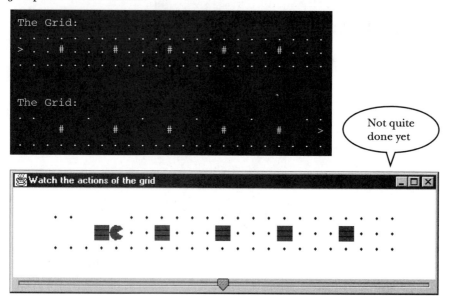

3K   Show a Color Chooser

Java has an interesting graphical component named JColorChooser that can be
constructed with zero arguments. Write a Java program that shows an instance of
JColorChooser after it has been added to the center of a JFrame object. Make
sure you can see all of what is shown here (your program should show 310 different color choices and the "Recent" grid). Click on the different graphical components. The color buttons, tabs, and so on are part of JColorChooser. Because it
may prevent access to javax.swing.JColorChooser, do not name your class
JColorChooser! The JColorChooser constructor requires no arguments. One
object can be instantiated as follows:

```
JColorChooser aColorChooser = new JColorChooser( );
```

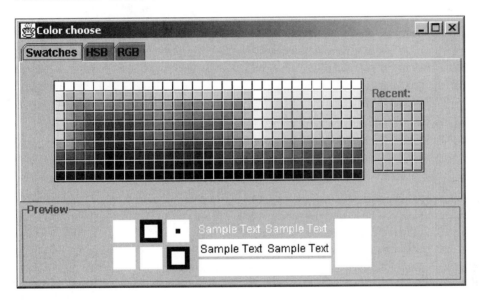

The JFileChooser constructor requires no arguments. One object can be instantiated as follows:

```
JFileChooser aFileChooser = new JFileChooser( );
```

3L   Show a File Chooser

Java has another interesting graphical component named JFileChooser that can
be constructed with zero arguments. Write a complete GUI that shows an instance
of JFileChooser in a JFrame that is 500 pixels wide and 300 pixels high. Because
it may prevent access to javax.swing.JFileChooser, do not name your class
JFileChooser! *Note:* The folders shown from your computer will be different than
the folders shown here.

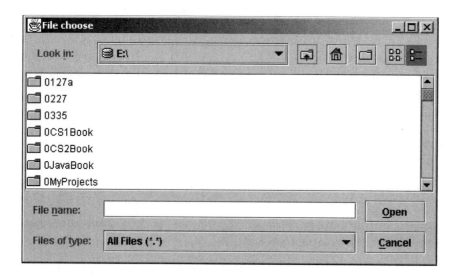

Answers to Self-Check Questions

3-1   B. Kreible: 202.22
      N. Li: 545.55

3-2   -a   Missing the second argument in the object construction. Add the starting balance—a
           number.

      -b   Missing = new BankAccount.

      -c   Change Account to BankAccount.

      -d   Missing a numeric argument between (and).

      -e   Missing (, the argument, and).

      -f   Wrong class of argument. Pass a number, not a String.

      -g   B1 is undefined.

      -h   Deposit is not a method of BankAccount. Change D to d.

      -i   Need an object and a dot before withdraw.

      -j   b4 is not a BankAccount object. It was never declared to be anything.

      -k   BankAccount has no method named name.

      -l   Missing ( ).

3-3
```java
public class ShowBankAccountOutput
{
   public static void main( String[] args )
   {
      BankAccount b1 = new BankAccount( "Kerry Winslow", 100.00 );
      b1.deposit( 1.11 );
      b1.withdraw( 2.22 );
      System.out.println( b1.getID( ) + ": " + b1.getBalance( ) );
      System.out.println( b1.toString( ) );
   }
}
```

3-4 6

3-5 "ef"

3-6 8

3-7 Wheatley, Kay

3-8 `String aString = "abcde";`
`int midCharIndex = aString.length( ) / 2;`
`String mid = aString.charAt( midCharIndex );`

An alternative that makes a `String` from a `char` by concatenating `""` before the `char`:

`String aString = "Robert";`
`int midCharIndex = aString.length( ) / 2;`
`String mid = "" + aString.charAt( midCharIndex );`

3-9 -a error   -d 3

-b error   -e y S

-c error   -f error (wrong type of argument)

3-10 `String aWord = keyboard.readWord( );`

3-11 `String aLine = keyboard.readLine( );`

3-12 `2345.68`
`2346`
`<2345.7>`

3-13 `[a, b, c]`
`3`
`[first, [a, b, c], another, last]`
`4`

3-14 Assuming the current date is August 14, 2002, the answer shows a date four years ahead minus one day for the leap year.
`2006/7/13`

3-15 `The Grid:`

```
 .  .  .  .  .  .
 .  .  <     .
 .  .  .     .
 .  .  .     .
 .  .        .
 .  .  .  .  .  .
```

`mover row: 1`
`mover column: 2`

3-16 1. Moving off the edge of the grid.

2. Moving through a block.

3. Attempting to pick up something that isn't there.

3-17 1

3-18 35

3-19
```
public class TestGrid
{
    public static void main( String args )
    {
        Grid g = new Grid( 5, 5, 2, 3, Grid.EAST );

        g.move( );
        g.turnLeft( );
        g.move( );
        g.turnLeft( );
        g.move( );
        g.turnLeft( );
        g.move( );
        System.out.println( g );
    }
}
```

3-20 Less code to write.

Abstraction allows us to think of what the method does, not the details of the implementation.

3-21 Using the phone without worrying about how the sound travels to the other end.

-or-

Walking around without sweating the details about how you are walking and breathing.

3-22
```
// Construct a window with its title
JFrame theWindow = new JFrame( "Border Layout" );
// Make the window 270 pixels high and 120 pixels wide
theWindow.setSize( 270, 120 );
// Construct five buttons to be added to the window
JButton northButton = new JButton( "North" );
JButton eastButton = new JButton( "East" );
JButton southButton = new JButton( "South" );
JButton westButton = new JButton( "West" );
JButton centerButton = new JButton( "Center" );
Container contentPane = theWindow.getContentPane( );
contentPane.add( northButton, BorderLayout.NORTH );
contentPane.add( eastButton, BorderLayout.EAST );
contentPane.add( southButton, BorderLayout.SOUTH );
contentPane.add( westButton, BorderLayout.WEST );
contentPane.add( centerButton, BorderLayout.CENTER );
theWindow.show( );
```

3-23 North. It has a little box around the label "North."

3-24
```
Container contentPane = buttonWindow.getContentPane( );
GridLayout twoByThree = new GridLayout( 2, 3, 4, 4 );
contentPane.setLayout( twoByThree );
```

Chapter 4
Classes and Interfaces

Summing Up

The previous chapters presented several classes. Some classes are part of Java's library: String, JFrame, and JButton. Other Java classes are supplied by the author: TextReader, BankAccount, and Grid. You now understand how to construct instances of existing classes and send messages to those objects.

Coming Up

This chapter introduces Java classes and interfaces. You will learn to read and understand classes as collections of methods and data that are related in meaningful ways. You will also learn to implement methods that have access to those data (to the state of objects). You will also see a few object-oriented design guidelines that help explain why classes are designed the way they are. After studying this chapter, you will be able to

- understand how to read and use existing methods
- write your own methods
- understand how to read and use existing Java classes
- implement classes as collections of methods and instance variables
- apply some object-oriented design guidelines to help implement Java classes
- record a list of transactions
- understand how to implement a Java interface

Exercises and programming projects reinforce design and implementation of Java classes.

4.1   Classes

Object-oriented programs use many instances of many different classes. They may be established Java classes, classes bought off the shelf, or classes designed by programmers to suit a particular application.

A class provides a blueprint for constructing objects. The class defines what messages are available to instances of the class. The class defines the values that are encapsulated (the state) in every object.

Figure 4.1: **One class constructing three objects, each with its own set of values (state)**

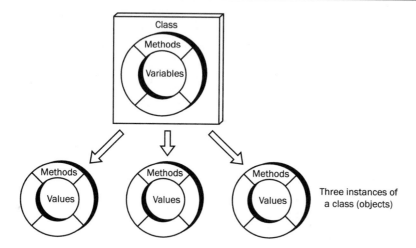

A Java class has **methods** that represent the messages each object will understand. Each instance of the class (the object) has its own set of **instance variables** to store the state of each object. Methods are declared `public` to allow other programmers to send messages. Instance variables are declared `private` to protect the data from unauthorized access (more on this later). As the picture above suggests, the state is protected by those methods. These methods are used to access the state or modify the state.

Methods

A Java class typically has many methods. There are two major components to a method:

1. the method heading (the method's signature)
2. the block (a set of curly braces with the code that completes the method's responsibility)

Several **modifiers** may begin a method heading, such as `public`, `private`, `protected`, `final`, and `static`. The examples shown here will use only the modifier `public`. Here is a simplified general form for a method heading.

General Form 4.1: **A public method heading**

public *return-type method-name(parameter-1, parameter-2, parameter-n, ...)*

Return-type represents the type of value returned from the method. The return type may be `void` to indicate that the method returns nothing (as in `JFrame`'s `setSize` method and `Grid`'s `move` method, for example). The return type can be any primitive type, such as `int` or `double` (`String`'s `length` method or `BankAccount`'s `withdraw` method, for example). Additionally, the return type can be any class reference type, such as `String`, `GregorianCalender`, `BankAccount`, or `ArrayList`.

The *method-name* is any valid Java identifier. Since most methods need one or more pieces of information to get the job done, method headings may also specify parameters between the required parentheses (parameters are discussed in the next section).

Here are a few syntactically correct method headings:

Example Method Headings

```
public int compareTo( Object anotherString )    // String
public void withdraw( double withdrawalAmount ) // BankAccount
public void setSize( int width, int height )    // JFrame
public void setText( String newText )           // JTextField, JLabel
public String toString( )                       // String
public int length( )                            // String
```

The other part of a method is the body. A method body begins with a curly brace and ends with a curly brace. This is where variable declarations, object constructions, assignments, and messages go. For example, here is the very simple, yet complete, `deposit` method from the `BankAccount` class. This method has access to the parameter `depositAmount` and to the `BankAccount` instance variable named `my_balance` (instance variables are discussed later in this chapter).

```
public void deposit( double depositAmount ) // The method heading
{
    my_balance = my_balance + depositAmount; // The method body
}
```

Parameters

The **parameters** in a method heading specify the number and type of arguments that must be used in a message. A parameter is an identifier declared between the parentheses. For example, `depositAmount` in the `deposit` method above is a parameter of type `double`. The programmer who wrote the method specifies the number and type of values the method will need to accomplish its responsibility.

A method may need zero, one, two, or even more arguments to do what it is supposed to do. "How much money do you want to withdraw from the `BankAccount` object?" "What is the beginning and ending index of the `substring` you want?" "What size window do you want?" "You want the square root of what number?" Parameters provide the mechanism to get the appropriate information—**arguments**—to the method precisely when it is needed—during the method call (message).

When a method is called during program execution, the value of each argument is passed on to the associated parameter. For each parameter in the method heading, you must supply one expression that can be assigned to the parameter's type. Once the arguments are passed along to the method through these argument/parameter associations, the program control transfers to the method body. These parameters are known inside the body of the method where they are used while the code executes to do the proper thing for the given argument. The same method should work for a wide variety of argument values.

Here are some examples of passing arguments to parameters. It may help to read the arrow as an assignment statement. First, a `deposit` message to a `BankAccount` object requires the amount to be deposited (a `double`). The argument `123.45` is assigned to `depositAmount` and used inside the `deposit` method.

```
// Credit this account by the argument associated with depositAmount
public void deposit( double depositAmount )
                                    ↑
        anAccount.deposit( 123.45 );
```

`Math.pow` requires two `double` arguments to be able to return a[b].

```
// Returns the first argument raised to the power of the second argument
public static double pow( double a, double b )
                                  ↑           ↑
            Math.pow( 2.0,      3.0 )
```

To construct a `BankAccount` you must supply a `String` argument followed by a `double` argument. (*Note:* Later in this chapter you will see that a constructor is a special method that has the same name as its class and no return type.)

```
        // The BankAccount Constructor--a method heading
        public BankAccount( String accountID, double currentBalance )
                                        ↑                ↑
BankAccount anAcct = new BankAccount( "Kim", 1576.48 );
```

The examples above have literal arguments. However, an argument may be any expression that evaluates to the parameter's declared type. Assignment compatibility rules apply. So for example, an argument of type `int` may be passed as an argument associated with a `double` parameter in the method, but not vice versa.

When a method requires more than one argument, the first argument in the message will be assigned to the first parameter, the second argument will be assigned to the second parameter, and so on. In order to get correct results, the programmer must also order the arguments correctly. Whereas not supplying the correct number and type of arguments in a message results in a compiletime (syntax) error, supplying the correct number and type of arguments in the wrong order results in a logic error (the program does what you typed, not what you intended).

Reading Method Headings

When properly documented, method headings help the programmer use the method, explain what the method does, and sometimes state what can go wrong (exceptions could be thrown). All of these things allow the programmer to send messages to objects without knowing the details of the implementation. For example, to send a message to an object, the programmer must:

1. know the method name (remember case sensitivity, toString is not tostring)
2. supply the proper type and number of arguments
3. use the evaluation of the method correctly (what does the method return?)

All of this information is specified in the method heading. For example, the substring method of Java's String class takes two int arguments and evaluates to a String.

```
/** From the String class
  *
  * Return portion of this string indexed
  * from beginIndex through endIndex - 1
  */
public String substring( int beginIndex, int endIndex )
```

The method heading for substring provides the following information:

- what the method evaluates to: String
- the method name: substring
- how many arguments are required: 2
- what type of arguments are required: int

Since substring is a method of the String class, the message must begin with a String literal or a String reference variable before the dot.

```
// Could use String literals as a String object is constructed
System.out.println( "forever".substring( 0, 3 ) );       // for
System.out.println( "forever".substring( 3, 7 ) );       // ever

// Or more typically, send substring messages to String objects
String str = "small";
System.out.println( str.substring( 1, str.length( ) ) ); // mall
```

This following message asks the `String` object referenced by `fullName` to return its characters starting at `beginIndex`, which is the character 'M' (index 0), to `endIndex` - 1, which is the character 'y' (index 5).

```
String fullName = "Murphy, John";
String lastName = fullName.substring( 0, 6 );
```

A `substring` message requires two arguments that specify the portion of the `String` to return. This is specified in the method heading that has two parameters named `beginIndex` and `endIndex`. Both arguments are type `int` because the parameters in the `substring` method heading are declared as type `int`. When this message is sent, the argument 0 is assigned to `beginIndex` and the argument 6 is assigned to `endIndex`. `beginIndex` and `endIndex` are called "parameters" (discussed below).

```
public String substring( int beginIndex, int endIndex )
                               ↑               ↑
           fullName.substring( 0,              6 );
```
Implementation of the substring method is not shown here

The first argument 0 is assigned to the first parameter `beginIndex`. The second argument 6 is assigned to the second parameter `endIndex`. Then control is transferred to the method body, where this information is used with the code there to return what it promises. Although the method bodies cannot be shown for Java's methods, the method bodies will be shown for the author-supplied classes of this textbook.

Self-Check

Use the following method heading to answer the questions that follow. This method is from Java's `String` class.

```
/** From the String class
 *
 * Concatenate str to the end of this String
 */
  public String concat( String str )
```

4-1   Determine the following for the `concat` method:

- **-a** return type
- **-b** method name
- **-c** number of arguments
- **-d** first argument type (or class)
- **-e** second argument type (or class)

4-2   Assuming `String s = "abc";`, write the return value for each valid message or explain why the message is invalid.

- **-a** `s.concat( "xyz" )`
- **-b** `s.concat( )`
- **-c** `s.concat( 5 )`
- **-d** `s.concat( "x", "y" )`
- **-e** `s.concat( "wx" + " yz" )`
- **-f** `String.concat( "d" )`

> **4-3** Assuming `String s3 = "time";`, what does this message return?
> `s3.concat( "s" );`
>
> **4-4** Assuming `String s4 = "hope";`, what does this message return?
> `s4.concat( "less" );`
>
> **4-5** Assuming `String s5 = "";`, what does this message return?
> `s5.concat( "" );`

More examples of methods will be shown next in the context of a class. The next section shows how to implement an entire class of related methods and the instance variables.

Why Those Particular Methods for `BankAccount`?

"Abstraction" refers to the practice of using and understanding something without full knowledge of its implementation. Abstraction allows programmers to concentrate on the behavior of the messages that manipulate state. For example, a programmer using the `String` class need not know the details of the internal data representation or how those methods are implemented in the hardware and software. Programmers can concentrate on the set of allowable messages—the set of methods implemented within the class.

This chapter presents some implementation issues that so far have been hidden. The first part of this chapter presents the now familiar `BankAccount` class at the implementation level. However, before examining class design, first consider some of the design of this textbook's `BankAccount` class.

All `BankAccount` objects have the same methods. There could have been more, or there could have been fewer. The methods for `BankAccount` were chosen to keep the class simple and to provide a collection of methods that are easy to relate to.

The `BankAccount` methods are only a subset of the methods named by a group of students who were asked this question: "What should we be able to do with bank accounts?" The instance variables are also a subset of the potential state named by students who were asked this question: "What should bank accounts know about themselves?"

When asked, students usually suggest many additional `BankAccount` methods, such as `transfer`, `applyInterest`, and `printMonthlyStatement`, and many additional instance variables, such as type of account, record of transactions, address, social security number, and mother's maiden name. These are not included here.

The design of this class was affected by the intention of keeping it as simple as possible while retaining some realism. However, a group of object-oriented designers developing a large-scale application in the banking domain would likely retain many of the methods and states recognized by the students. There is rarely one single design that is correct for all circumstances. Design decisions should be influenced by the desired outcomes. With `BankAccount`, the most important outcome was an easy-to-relate-to example with easy-to-understand methods. This outcome influenced the design.

Designing anything requires making decisions in an effort to make the thing "good." "Good" might mean having a software component that is easily maintainable, or it might mean having classes designed for reuse in other applications, or it might mean a system that is very robust—one that can recover from almost any disastrous event. "Good" might mean a design that results in something that is easier to use, or that runs very fast, or that is prettier, or . . . There is rarely ever a single perfect design. There are usually tradeoffs. Design is an iterative process that evolves with time. Design is influenced by personal opinion, evolving research, the domain (banking, information systems, process control, or radar, for example), and a variety of other influences.

4.2   Putting It All Together in a Class

Even though different in methods and states, virtually all classes have these things in common:

- private instance variables that store the state of the objects
- constructors that initialize the state
- messages to modify the state of objects
- messages to provide access to the current state of objects

These commonalities guide the effective use of these and similar types of objects. These commonalities also guide implementation of Java classes. These common traits could even be considered a pattern. Simplified General Form 4.1 shows a simplified general form of a Java class.

Many classes begin with `public class` followed by the class name. The instance variables and methods follow within a set of curly braces. The methods and state should have some sort of meaningful connection. You shouldn't put a `blastOff` method or an instance variable that refers to a `Jukebox` object, for example, in `BankAccount`.

Simplified General Form 4.1: **A Java class**

```
public class class-name
{
```
  // Instance variables (every instance of this class will get its own)
  private *class name;*
  private *primitive-type identifier;*

  // Constructor(s) (methods with the same name as the class)
  public *class-name(parameters)*
  { // ...
  }
  // Any number of methods
  public *return-type method-name-1(parameters)*
  { // ...
  }
  public *return-type method-name-2(parameters)*
  { // ...
  }
  public *return-type method-name-n(parameters)*
  { // ...
  }
  // Each class may have a method for testing
```
  public static void main( String[] args )
```
  { // ...
  }
} **// End** *class-name*

Java allows one main method in each class. Although optional, a main method provides a convenient way to test the class you are writing. It is recommended that you place a main method in every class you write. For example, here is a simplified version of the BankAccount class that was used to construct BankAccount objects several times in the preceding chapter:

Figure 4.2: **A simplified version of the BankAccount class**

```
// This class models a minimal bank account.

public class BankAccount
{
  // Instance variables (every BankAccount object will get its own)
  private String my_ID;
  private double my_balance;
```

```java
   // Initialize instance variables during construction
   public BankAccount( String initID, double initBalance )          ①
   {
     my_ID = initID;
     my_balance = initBalance;
   }

   // Credit this account by depositAmount (hopefully positive)
   public void deposit( double depositAmount )                      ②
   {
     my_balance = my_balance + depositAmount;
   }

   // Debit this account by withdrawalAmount (hopefully positive)
   public void withdraw( double withdrawalAmount )                  ③
   {
     my_balance = my_balance - withdrawalAmount;
   }

   // Return the BankAccount data that identifies this object
   public String getID( )                                           ④
   {
     return my_ID;
   }

   // Return the BankAccount's current balance
   public double getBalance( )                                      ⑤
   {
     return my_balance;
   }

   // Numbers indicate methods that execute when messages are sent
   public static void main( String[] args )

   { // Show the relationship between messages and methods
     BankAccount acctOne = new BankAccount( "01543C", 100.00 );     ①
     acctOne.deposit( 50.0 );                                       ②
     acctOne.withdraw( 25.0 );                                      ③
     System.out.println( acctOne.getID( ) );                        ④
     System.out.println( acctOne.getBalance( ) );                   ⑤
   }

} // End class BankAccount
```

Instance Variables

Recall that a BankAccount object stores the data necessary to manipulate one account at a bank. Each BankAccount object stores some unique identification and an account balance. BankAccount methods include making deposits, making withdrawals, and accessing the ID and the current balance.

The private instance variables represent the state. `BankAccount` has two private instance variables: `my_ID` (a `String`) and `my_balance` (a `double`). Every `BankAccount` object knows its own ID and its own current balance.

Notice that the instance variables are not declared within a method. They are declared within the set of curly braces that bounds the class. This means that the instance variables are known throughout the class. Every method has access to these instance variables. If you look at the `BankAccount` class again, you will notice that every method references one of the instance variables (the methods and data are related). Because the instance variables are declared `private`, programs using instances of the class cannot access the instance variables directly. This is good. The class safely encapsulated the state. The only way to change the state of an instance or access the state of an instance is through public methods.

The question now is this: "How do you initialize the state of an object?" The answer: "With a constructor."

Constructors

The `BankAccount` class of Figure 4.2 shows that all `BankAccount` method headings are public. They also have return types (including **void** to mean return nothing). Some have parameters. However, do you notice something different about the method named `BankAccount`?

First, the method named `BankAccount` has no return type. It also has the same name as the class! This special method is named a **constructor** because this is the method that gets called when objects are constructed. When a constructor is called, memory is allocated for the object. Then the instance variables are initialized using the arguments supplied by the calling program. Here are some object constructions that result in executing the class's constructor:

```
Grid aGrid = new Grid( 10, 10, 5, 4, Grid.EAST );
String aString = new String( "The initial value of this object" );
BankAccount anAcct = new BankAccount( "Katey Jo", 10.00 );
DecimalFormat numberFormatter = new DecimalFormat( "###,##0.0" );
```

Here is the general form for constructing an object.

General Form 4.2: **Constructing objects (from Chapter 3)**

new *class-name* (*initial-state*) ;

The *class-name* is the name of the class. The *object-name* is any valid Java identifier. The *initial-state* is zero or more arguments supplied in the instance creation. When a constructor is encountered with arguments, the initial state is passed on to help initialize the private instance variables of the newly constructed object. The constructor finally returns a reference to that new object. This reference value is often assigned to an object reference of the same type. That is why you often see the class name on both sides of =. For example, the following code constructs a

BankAccount object with an initial ID of "Patricia Patterson" and an initial balance of 507.34. After the constructor is done, the reference to this new BankAccount object is assigned to the reference variable named one.

```
BankAccount one = new BankAccount( "Patricia Patterson", 507.34 );
```

Implementing Constructors

A constructor is a special type of method that always has the same name as the class. It never has a return type. The following code implements BankAccount's two-parameter constructor:

```
// A Constructor method to initialize BankAccount objects
public BankAccount( String ID, double initialBalance )
{
    my_ID = ID;
    my_balance = initialBalance;
}
```

This method executes whenever a BankAccount gets constructed with two arguments (a String followed by a number).

In the following code, the ID "Stein" is passed to the parameter ID, which in turn is assigned to the private instance variable my_ID. The starting balance of 250.55 is also passed to the parameter named initialBalance, which in turn is assigned to the private instance variable my_balance.

```
// Call the two-parameter constructor
BankAccount anInitializedAccount = new BankAccount( "Stein", 250.55 );
System.out.println( anInitializedAccount.getID( ) );
System.out.println( anInitializedAccount.getBalance( ) );
```

Output

```
Stein
250.55
```

After an object is constructed, it can respond to messages. Some of these methods access state. Other methods modify state. These are called **accessing methods** and **modifying methods**.

Self-Check

4-6   Write the output from the code below:

```
public class SampleClass
{
    private double my_first;
    private double my_second;
```

```
      public SampleClass( double first, double second )
      {
        my_first = first;
        my_second = second;
        System.out.println ( "Instance variables: " +
                             my_first + " " + my_second );
      }

      public static void main ( String[] args )
      { // Test this class
        SampleClass sc1 = new SampleClass( 1.23, 4.56 );
        SampleClass sc2 = new SampleClass( 1.0, 2.0 );
      } // End main

    } // End SampleClass
```

Modifying Methods

Many methods modify the state of objects. For example, consider BankAccount's deposit method, which modifies the private instance variable my_balance.

```
// A method that modifies the state of this BankAccount
public void deposit( double depositAmount )
{
   my_balance = my_balance + depositAmount;
}
```

When the following deposit message is sent, the argument (157.42) is assigned to the parameter depositAmount.

```
anAcct.deposit( 157.42 );
```

The code in the body of the method executes. In this case, the private instance variable my_balance is increased by the value of the argument.

BankAccount's withdraw method is another method that modifies the state of any BankAccount object. Specifically, a withdraw message debits withdrawalAmount from my_balance.

```
// A method that modifies the state of this BankAccount
public void withdraw ( double withdrawalAmount )
{
   my_balance = my_balance - withdrawalAmount;
}
```

When the following withdraw message is sent, the argument (50.00) is assigned to the parameter withdrawalAmount, which would then be subtracted from anAcct's balance:

```
anAcct.withdraw( 50.00 );
```

Self-Check

4-7   Write the output when this class is run.

```java
public class SampleClass
{
  private double my_first;
  private double my_second;

  public SampleClass( double first, double second )
  {
    my_first = first;
    my_second = second;
  }

  public void increaseBy( double increment )
  {
    my_first = my_first + increment;
    my_second = my_second + increment;
    System.out.println( "Changed to: " + my_first + " "
                                       + my_second );
  }

  public static void main( String[] args )
  { // Test this class
    SampleClass sc1 = new SampleClass( 1.2, 3.4 );
    sc1.increaseBy( 1.0 );
    sc1.increaseBy( 2.0 );
    sc1.increaseBy( 3.0 );
  }

} // End SampleClass (version 2)
```

Accessing Methods

Some methods provide access to the state of the objects. Some accessing methods simply return the value of individual instance variables with Java's return statement.

```java
// A method that provides access to the state of this BankAccount
public String getID( )
{
  return my_ID;
}

// A method that provides access to the state of this BankAccount
public double getBalance( )
{
  return my_balance;
}
```

The Java `return` statement allows a method to return information about the object's state. The expression after `return` is what the message evaluates to. For example, to view the current balance of `anAcct` (the value of the private instance variable `my_balance`), the programmer could write:

```
System.out.println( "Current balance: " + anAcct.getBalance( ) );
```

Whereas a method receives input via the arguments in the method call, a method communicates values back to the message sender through the **return** statement. Here is its general form:

***General Form 4.3:* Return statement**

return *expression;*

When a `return` statement is encountered, the *expression* that follows `return` replaces the message. This is how a message evaluates to a value. Whereas a `void` method returns nothing (see `BankAccount deposit`), any method that has a return type other than `void` *must* return a value of the same type as the return type. So a method declared to return a `String` (as in `BankAccount getID`) must return a reference to a `String`. A method declared to return a `double` (as in `BankAccount getBalance`) must return a primitive `double` value. Fortunately, the compiler will complain if you forget to return the proper type of value.

Some accessing methods use the instance variables to do more complex processing. For example, `WeeklyEmployee`'s `getIncomeTax` method (see Chapter 6's programming projects) is quite complex. This method does not simply return the value of an instance variable. Instead, the instance variables are used along with complex United States Internal Revenue Service tax tables and evaluations of other methods such as `getGrossPay`.

Self-Check

4-8 Write the output from the `main` method below using the modified SampleClass.

```
// The final version of a class meant for self-check only

public class SampleClass
{
    private double my_first;
    private double my_second;

    public SampleClass( double first, double second )
    {
        my_first = first;
        my_second = second;
    }
```

```java
    public void increaseBy( double increment )
    {
      my_first = my_first + increment;
      my_second = my_second + increment;
    }

    public double getFirst( )
    {
      return my_first;
    }

    public double getSecond( )
    {
      return my_second;
    }

    public double firstPlusSecond( )
    {
      return my_first + my_second;
    }

    public static void main( String[] args )
    { // Test this class
      SampleClass sc1 = new SampleClass( 1.0, 2.0 );
      System.out.println( "First: " + sc1.getFirst( ) );
      System.out.println( "Second: " + sc1.getSecond( ) );
      System.out.println( "Sum: " + sc1.firstPlusSecond( ) );
      sc1.increaseBy( 3.4 );
      System.out.println( "First: " + sc1.getFirst( ) );
      System.out.println( "Second: " + sc1.getSecond( ) );
      System.out.println( "Sum: " + sc1.firstPlusSecond( ) );
    }
} // End SampleClass (version 3)
```

4-9   Given the class diagram and instance diagram when sc1 is constructed, draw the instance diagram of sc1 at the end of the program to indicate the final state of the object.

SampleClass
-double my_first -double my_second
+double getFirst( ) +double getSecond( ) +increaseBy(double amount)

sc1
my_first = 1.0 my_second = 2.0

Naming Conventions

A method that modifies state is typically given a name that indicates that the message will change the state of the object. This is easily accomplished if the designer of the class provides a descriptive name for the method. The method name should describe—as best as possible—what the method actually does. It should also help to distinguish modifying methods from accessing methods. Use verbs for modifying method names: `withdraw`, `deposit`, `borrowBook`, and `returnBook`, for example. Give accessing methods names to indicate that the messages will return some useful information about the objects: `getBorrower` and `getBalance`, for example. Considering that the constructor has the same name as the class, some guidelines can now be established for designing and reading classes. These three categories of methods can be distinguished by following these naming conventions:

Method	Name to Use
Constructor	Same name as the class
Modifies state	Identifier that could be used as a verb
Accesses state	Identifier that could be used as a noun
	Note: Because some words can be used either as verbs or nouns ("balance," for example), some programmers precede modifying methods with `set` and accessing methods with `get`.

Above all, always use identifiers that accurately describe what the method does. For example, don't use `with` as the name of the method to withdraw money from a `BankAccount`.

public or private

One of the considerations in the design of any class is declaring methods and instance variables with the most appropriate access mode, either `public` or `private`. Whereas the **public** methods of a class can be called by a programmer from outside of the class, the **private** instance variables are only known in the class methods. For example, the `BankAccount` instance variable named `my_balance` is known only to the methods of the class. On the other hand, any method declared as `public` is known where the object was constructed.

Access Mode	Where the Identifier Can Be Accessed (where the identifier is known)
`public`	In all other methods of the class
	In any method body where the object gets constructed
	In all methods of a class where an instance is declared
`private`	Only from the methods of the same class

Although instance variables representing state could be declared as `public`, it is highly recommended that all instance variables be declared as `private`. There are several reasons for this. The consistency helps simplify some design decisions. More importantly, when instance variables are made `private`, the state can be modified only through a method. This prevents other code from indiscriminately changing the state of objects. For example, it is impossible to accidentally make a credit to `acctOne` like this:

```
BankAccount acctOne = new BankAccount( "Mine", 100.00 );

// A compiletime error occurs: attempting to modify private data
acctOne.my_balance = acctOne.my_balance + 100000.00;   // <- ERROR
```

or a debit like this:

```
// A compiletime error occurs at this attempt to modify private data
acctOne.my_balance = acctOne.my_balance - 100.00;   // <- ERROR
```

This represents a widely held principle of software development—data should be hidden. Making instance variables `private` is one more step on the way to well-designed object-oriented programs.

4.3   Bank Teller—A Transaction Class

One of the required features of the bank teller system is the ability to show the most recent 10 transactions for any account. This section makes progress towards that goal by showing how a collection of banking transactions can be maintained with one `ArrayList` object. This section also provides another example of a Java class while introducing class constants.

`Transaction` objects maintain records of withdrawals and deposits that occur while the bank teller system is running. To accomplish this, a `Transaction` class was designed to store the account ID, the transaction date, some sort of transaction code, the amount of the transaction, and the balance of the account after the transaction has occurred. There currently is no modifying method. To demonstrate how `Transaction` objects are constructed, consider the following code, which builds a small list of `Transaction` objects:

```
// Construct two Transaction objects and store
// references to them in an ArrayList.
import java.util.ArrayList;

public class AFewTransactions
{
  public static void main( String[] args )
  {
    ArrayList transactionList = new ArrayList( );
    BankAccount currentAccount = new BankAccount( "OneAccount", 1000.00 );
```

```
   Transaction aTransaction;
   double amount;

   // Perform a withdraw transaction and record it
   amount = 150.00;
   currentAccount.withdraw( amount );
   // Class constants WITHDRAW_CODE and
   // DEPOSIT_CODE are explained below
   aTransaction = new Transaction(  currentAccount,
                                    amount,
                                    Transaction.WITHDRAW_CODE );
   transactionList.add( aTransaction );

   // Perform a deposit transaction and record it
   amount = 327.55;
   currentAccount.deposit( amount );
   aTransaction = new Transaction( currentAccount,
                                   amount,
                                   Transaction.DEPOSIT_CODE );
   transactionList.add( aTransaction );

   System.out.println( transactionList.toString( ) );
  }
}
```

Output

```
[Fri Oct 05 15:17:01 MST 2001 W 150.0 OneAccount 850.0,
Fri Oct 05 15:17:01 MST 2001 D 327.55 OneAccount 1177.55]
```

This Transaction class exists mostly to store the data of a transaction. There is no modifying method (but one might appear later if needed). Currently, this Transaction class has enough to allow for a reasonable list of Transaction objects (but not the most recent 10 transactions—that comes later, in Chapter 7).

Two instance variables are initialized by copying the arguments: transactionAmount and code. Two instance variables are initialized by asking for information from the BankAccount object passed to the constructor: accountID and balanceAfterTransaction. Two other instance variables are initialized without relying on the arguments. The transactionDate is set to the computer system's clock. It does not rely on arguments supplied by the calling code.

```
// A Transaction class to allow a list of transactions.
// This class will be modified in Chapter 7.
// Its main purpose is to store information about single
// transactions in such a way that a list of these can be maintained.
// Each transaction will need to be verified within a few business days.
import java.util.GregorianCalendar;

public class Transaction
{
  public static final String WITHDRAW_CODE = "W";
  public static final String DEPOSIT_CODE = "D";
```

```java
   private String accountID;
   private double transactionAmount;
   private String transactionCode;
   private double balanceAfterTransaction;
   private GregorianCalendar transactionDate;

   // Construct a Transaction object for various types of transactions
   public Transaction( BankAccount theAccount,
                       double amountOfTransaction,
                       String code )
   {
     accountID = theAccount.getID( );
     balanceAfterTransaction = theAccount.getBalance( );
     transactionAmount = amountOfTransaction;
     transactionCode = code;
     transactionDate = new GregorianCalendar( ); // The current date
   }

   // Return the account ID of this account. This will be used later
   // when looking for all transactions for one particular account.
   public String getAccountID( )
   {
     return accountID;
   }

   // Return a textual representation of this transaction
   public String toString( )
   { // getTime returns a Date object that has a toString method.
     // The Date object's toString( ) provides more detail
     // such as a local time zone.
     String dateAsString = transactionDate.getTime( ).toString( );
     return dateAsString + " " + transactionCode + " " +
            transactionAmount + " " + accountID + " " +
            balanceAfterTransaction;
   }
}
```

Class Constants

Two class constants were used in the `Transaction` class. A **class constant** is an identifier declared to represent a value that cannot change. Whereas `Transaction` objects could have been just as easily constructed with `String` literals like this:

```java
new Transaction( currentAccount, amount, "W" );
new Transaction( currentAccount, amount, "D" );
```

The presence of these two class constants in the `Transaction` class:

```java
public static final String WITHDRAW_CODE = "W";
public static final String DEPOSIT_CODE = "D";
```

allows a programmer to use more descriptive, easier-to-remember names.

```
new Transaction( currentAccount, amount, Transaction.WITHDRAW_CODE );
new Transaction( currentAccount, amount, Transaction.DEPOSIT_CODE );
```

A class constant is declared `public` when you want other code to use a descriptive name rather than some code that has no meaning. The keyword **static** signifies that there is precisely one value for all objects of the class.[1] There is no reason to have a copy of a class constant stored in every instance of the class. The other modifier is `final`. When an identifier is declared **final**, no new value can be assigned to it. This prevents other code from accidentally modifying a value that many different pieces of code rely on.

Here are some class constants (also known as "fields") as they would be declared inside the Java classes `Math`, `Font`, `BorderLayout`, `JFrame`, and `GregorianCalendar` and the `Grid` class. Although not required, programmers have adopted the convention of making the identifiers for class constants all upper case. If there is more than one word, the words are separated with the underscore character (_).

```
public static final int ITALIC = 1;               // Font
public static final int BOLD = 2;                 // Font
public static final int JANUARY = 0;              // GregorianCalendar
public static final int DAY_OF_MONTH = 5;         // GregorianCalendar
public static final int WEST = 3;                 // Grid
public static final String WEST = "West";         // BorderLayout
public static final int EXIT_ON_CLOSE = 3;        // JFrame
```

Although any primitive or reference type can be made to be `static` and `final` (a class constant), many class constants are `int` values representing a code that may or may not be arbitrary. The following program shows the values of the class constants. To be used outside the class where it is declared, the identifier must be preceded by the class name and a dot.

```
import java.util.*;      // GregorianCalendar
import java.awt.*;       // Font, BorderLayout
import javax.swing.*;    // JFrame

public class ShowSomeConstants
{
  public static void main( String[] args )
  {
    System.out.println( "           PI: " + Math.PI );
    System.out.println( "       ITALIC: " + Font.ITALIC );
    System.out.println( "         BOLD: " + Font.BOLD );
    System.out.println( "  DAY_OF_WEEK: " +
                      GregorianCalendar.DAY_OF_WEEK );
```

---

1. Be very careful with the keyword `static`. If you want an instance variable and accidentally declare it to be `static`, you no longer have an instance variable. There is only one per class. For example, if `my_ID` and `my_balance` were declared `static`, every instance of `BankAccount` would have the same ID and the same balance—not at all desirable.

```
      System.out.println( "        JANUARY: " +
                           GregorianCalendar.JANUARY  );
      System.out.println( " DAY_OF_MONTH: " +
                           GregorianCalendar.DAY_OF_MONTH  );
      System.out.println( "           WEST: " + Grid.WEST  );
      System.out.println( " Another WEST: " + BorderLayout.WEST );
      System.out.println( "EXIT_ON_CLOSE: " + JFrame.EXIT_ON_CLOSE );
  }
}
```

Output

```
          PI: 3.141592653589793
      ITALIC: 2
        BOLD: 1
 DAY_OF_WEEK: 7
     JANUARY: 0
DAY_OF_MONTH: 5
        WEST: 3
Another WEST: West
EXIT_ON_CLOSE: 3
```

Class constants are used for a variety of purposes. In the case of `Transaction`, they are used to ensure that the correct codes are written from any location. Class constants also help avoid the use of magic numbers, such as 0.0612 and 19. The values actually represent the United States social security tax rate and the maximum credits a student may take in a semester at a certain university. These values would be better described as class constants in the appropriate class.

```
public class Employee
{
  public static final double SOCIAL_SECURITY_TAX_RATE = 0.062;
    ...
}

public class RegistrarPolicies
{
    public static final int MAXIMUM_CREDITS_PER_SEMESTER = 19;
      ...
}
```

Self-Check

Use this Java class and the class diagram to answer the questions that follow.

```
// A class to model a library book
public class LibraryBook
{
  // Instance variables
  private String my_author;
  private String my_title;
  private String my_borrower;
```

```
// Construct a LibraryBook object while
// initializing instance variables
public LibraryBook( String initTitle, String initAuthor )
{
  my_title = initTitle;
  my_author = initAuthor;
  my_borrower = null;  // When my_borrower == null,
                       // no one has the book
}

// Records the borrower's name
public void borrowBook( String borrowersName )
{
  my_borrower = borrowersName;
}

// The book becomes available. When
// null, no one is borrowing it.
public void returnBook( )
{
  my_borrower = null;
}

// Return the borrower's name if the book has been
// checked out or return null if the book is available
public String getBorrower( )
{
  return my_borrower;
}
}
```

Class Diagram

```
┌──────────────────────────────────────────────────┐
│                 LibraryBook                        │
├──────────────────────────────────────────────────┤
│ -String my_author;                                 │
│ -String my_title;                                  │
│ -String my_borrower;                               │
├──────────────────────────────────────────────────┤
│ +LibraryBook( String title, String author )        │
│ +borrowBook( String borrowersName )                │
│ +returnBook( )                                     │
│ +getBorrower( )                                    │
└──────────────────────────────────────────────────┘
```

4-10 What is the name of the class shown above?

4-11 Except for the constructor, name all of the methods.

4-12 getBorrower returns what type of object?

4-13 borrowBook returns a reference to what type of value?

4-14 What class of argument must be part of all borrowBook messages?

4-15 How many arguments are required to initialize one LibraryBook object?

4-16   Initialize one `LibraryBook` object using your favorite book and author.

4-17   Send the message that borrows your favorite book. Use your own name as the borrower.

4-18   Write the message that reveals the name of the person who borrowed your favorite book (or `null` if no one has borrowed it).

4-19   Given the following program, draw two instance diagrams for `aBook` immediately after it is constructed and then immediately after the `borrowBook` message. Your instance diagrams should indicate the changed state of the object.

```
// Construct a LibraryBook object and
// send all possible messages
public class TestLibBook
{
  public static void main( String[] args )
  {
    LibraryBook aBook =
    new LibraryBook( "Little Drummer Girl", "John LeCarre" );

    aBook.borrowBook( "Chris Miller" );
    System.out.println( "Borrower: " + aBook.getBorrower( ) );
    aBook.returnBook( );
    System.out.println( "Borrower: " + aBook.getBorrower( ) );
  }
}
```

4-20   Write the output generated by the program above.

4-21   Which methods have the same name as the class?

4-22   What do accessing methods do?

4-23   What do modifying methods do?

4-24   What do constructors do?

4-25   What do instance variables do?

4-26   Can all methods in a class reference the `private` instance variables of that class?

4-27   Can a program that constructs an object directly reference the private instance variables of that object?

4-28   Write a class constant that represents the number of days in a leap year.

4.4 A Few Object-Oriented Design Guidelines

An object-oriented **design guideline** is a guideline intended to help produce good object-oriented software. This section introduces the first of several guidelines.

One particular decision made while designing classes involves determining the level of access other objects have to instance variables and methods. More specifically, the programmer has to decide if instance variables should be declared `public` or `private`. The following design guideline suggests that it is good **object-oriented design** to protect the state of objects from accidental changes from the outside. This is encapsulation. This is good.

Object-Oriented Design Guideline 4-1

All data should be hidden within its class.[2]

Although instance variables could be made `public`, the convention used in the classes shown so far—and in any good class—is this: "Hide the instance variables." Java instance variables are easily hidden when declared as `private` inside the class. This simplifies one design decision that must be made in any new classes that you develop. The state of all instances of the class will then be protected from accidental and improper alteration. With instance variables declared `private`, the state of any object can be altered only through a message. For example, it becomes impossible to accidentally make a false debit like this:

```
// If my_balance were public, what would the balance be after this?
acctOne.my_balance = acctOne.my_balance - acctOne.my_balance;
// A compiletime error occurs at this attempt to modify private data
```

However, if `my_balance` had been declared as a `public` instance variable, the compiler would not protest. The resulting program would allow you to destroy the state without checking on a few things or triggering some transaction. The hidden balance is more properly modified only when the transaction is allowed according to some policy. What happens, for instance, if a `withdrawalAmount` exceeds the account balance in a `withdraw` message? Some accounts allow this by transferring money from a savings account. Other bank accounts may generate loans in increments of `100.00` or some other amount.

With `my_balance` declared as `private`, users of the class must instead send a `withdraw` message. The code relies on the `BankAccount` to determine if the withdrawal is to be allowed. Perhaps the `BankAccount` object will ask some other object if the withdrawal is to be allowed. Perhaps it will delegate authority to some unseen `BankManager` object, for example. Or perhaps the `BankAccount` object

---

2. Some design guidelines (including this one) are from Arthur J. Riel, *Object-Oriented Design Heuristics* (Boston, MA: Addison Wesley, 1996). Riel cataloged and/or wrote 60 such guidelines.

itself will decide what to do. Although this textbook's implementation of
BankAccount doesn't do much, real-world withdrawals certainly do.

By hiding data and other details, all credits and debits must "go through the
proper channels." This might be quite complex. For example, each withdrawal or
deposit may be recorded in a transaction file to help prepare monthly statements
for each BankAccount. The withdraw and deposit methods may have additional
processing to prevent unauthorized credits and debits. Part of the hidden red tape
might include manual verification of a deposit or a check-clearing method at the
host bank; there may be some sort of human or computer intervention before any
credit is actually made. Such additional processing and protection within the
deposit and withdrawal methods help give BankAccount a "safer" design. Because
all hidden processing and protection is easily circumvented when instance variables
are exposed through public access, the object designer must enforce proper
object use and protection by hiding the instance variables. Simply declare all
instance variables private.

Cohesion within a Class

The set of methods specified in a class should be strongly related. A class has
instance variables. The instance variables should be strongly related. In fact, all
elements of a class should have a persuasive affiliation with each other. These ideas
relate to the preference for high **cohesion** (which means solidarity, hanging
together, adherence, or unity) within a class. For example, don't expect a
BankAccount object to understand the message areYouPreheated. This may be
an appropriate message for an oven object, but certainly not for a BankAccount
object. Here is one guideline related to the desirable attribute of cohesion.

Object-Oriented Design Guideline 4-2

Keep related data and behavior in one place.

The BankAccount class should hide certain policies, such as handling withdrawal
requests greater than the balance. The system's design improves when behavior
and data combine to accomplish the withdrawal algorithm. This makes for nice
clean messages like this:

```
anAccount.withdraw( withdrawalAmount );
```

This code relies on the BankAccount object to determine what should happen.
The behavior should be built into the object that has the necessary data. Perhaps
the algorithm allows a withdrawal amount greater than the balance, with the extra
cash coming as a loan or as a transfer from a savings account. A bank account class
might have many hidden actions that are triggered during every withdrawal
message.

Self-Check

4-29 Does a programmer need to know the names of instance variables to use objects of a class?

4-30 Does a programmer need to know the names of methods to use objects?

4-31 Describe where the `public` methods of a class are known.

4-32 Describe where the `private` methods of a class are known.

4-33 Give one justification for making the instance variables of a class `private`.

4-34 If the designer of a class changed the instance variable named `my_balance` to `myBalance`, would the code *using* the object need to be changed?

4-35 If the method name `withdraw` were changed to `withdrawThisAmount` after the class were already in use by dozens of programs, would these dozens of programs need to be changed?

4-36 Should a `BankAccount` object understand the message `areTheBrakesLockingUp`?

4.5   Java Interfaces

A Java **interface** contains a set of method headings followed by semicolons rather than method implementations—code within { }. To be useful, an interface must be implemented by at least one Java class. The implementing class will add instance variables, constructors, and the method bodies for each method specified in the interface.

There are several reasons Java has interfaces as part of the language. In this section, the Java `interface` is introduced to help you implement some of your first classes in the Programming Projects section. You will also see two Java interfaces represent the design of two classes for a new system, which is partially developed in an upcoming section. In Chapter 5, you will see that Java interfaces are required to implement programs that respond to button clicks and text-field input. In Chapter 6, you will see how another Java interface allows a collection in an `ArrayList` to be arranged in order (sorted).

Java has 422 interfaces. Of the 1,732 Java classes, 646 classes (about 37%) implement one or more interfaces. Considering the large number of interfaces in Java and the high percentage of Java classes that implement the interfaces, interfaces are an important part of the Java programming language. However, in this textbook you will not be asked to write the interfaces themselves (like the `TimeTalker` interface below). Instead, you will be asked to write a class that implements an `interface`. The interface will be given to you or it will be one of Java's 422 interfaces. First, consider a very simple interface.

A Java interface begins with a heading that is similar to a Java `class` heading, except the keyword `interface` is used. A Java interface cannot have constructors or instance variables. A Java interface will be implemented by one or more Java classes that add instance variables and have their own constructors. A Java interface specifies the method headings that someone decided would represent what each object of the class must be able to do.

Here is a sample Java interface that has only one method. Although not very useful, it provides a simple first example of an interface and the classes that implement the interface in different ways:

```
// File name: TimeTalker.java
// An interface that will be implemented by several classes
public interface TimeTalker
{
  // Return a representation of how each implementing class tells time
  public String whatTimeIsIt( );
}
```

For each interface, there are usually two or more classes that implement it. Here are three classes that implement the `TimeTalker` interface. One instance variable has been added to store the name of any `TimeTalker`. A constructor was also needed to initialize this instance variable with anybody's name.

```
// File name: FiveYearOld.java
// Someone who cannot read time yet
public class FiveYearOld implements TimeTalker
{
  String my_name;

  public FiveYearOld( String name )
  {
    my_name = name;
  }

  public String whatTimeIsIt( )
  {
    return my_name + " says it's morning time";
  }
}


// File name: DeeJay.java
// A "hippy dippy" DJ who always mentions the station
public class DeeJay implements TimeTalker
{
  String my_name;

  public DeeJay( String name )
  {
    my_name = name;
  }
```

```
  public String whatTimeIsIt( )
  {
    return my_name +
            " says it's 7 oh 7 on your favorite oldies station";
  }
}


// File name: FutureOne.java
// A "Star-Trekker" who speaks of star dates
public class FutureOne implements TimeTalker
{
  String my_name;

  public FutureOne( String name )
  {
    my_name = name;
  }

  public String whatTimeIsIt( )
  {
    return my_name + " says it's star date 78623.23";
  }
}
```

One reason Java has interfaces is to allow many classes to be treated as the same type. To demonstrate that this is possible, consider the following code, which stores references to three different types of objects as TimeTalker variables.

```
public class ThreeTypesOfTimeTalkers
{
  public static void main( String[] args )
  {
    // These three objects can be referenced by variables
    // of the interface type that they implement.
    TimeTalker youngOne = new FiveYearOld( "Kieran" );
    TimeTalker dj = new DeeJay( "WolfMan Jack" );
    TimeTalker captainKirk = new FutureOne( "Jim" );

    System.out.println( youngOne.whatTimeIsIt() );
    System.out.println( dj.whatTimeIsIt() );
    System.out.println( captainKirk.whatTimeIsIt() );
  }
}
```

Output

```
Kieran says it's morning time
WolfMan Jack says it's 7 oh 7 on your favorite oldies station
Jim says it's star date 78623.23
```

Because each class implements the TimeTalker interface, references to instances of these three classes—FiveYearOld, DeeJay, and FutureOne—can be stored in the reference type variable `TimeTalker`. They can all be considered to be of type `TimeTalker`. However, the same message to the three different classes of `TimeTalker` objects results in three different behaviors. The same message executes three different methods in three different classes.

In the section that follows, the Java `interface` plays a part in the design and implementation of two specific Java classes. The interface specifies the exact method headings of the classes that need to be implemented. These interfaces capture design decisions—what instances of the class should be able to do—that were made by a team of programmers.

Self-Check

4-37   Write two classes that implement this interface:

```
public interface BarnyardAnimal
{
   public String sound( );
}
```

The following program must generate the output exactly as shown.

```
public class OldMacDonald
{
   public static void main( String[] args )
   {
      BarnyardAnimal a1 = new Chicken( "cluck" );
      BarnyardAnimal a2 = new Cow( "moo" );

      System.out.println( "With a " + a1.sound( ) + " "
                          + a1.sound( ) + " here," );
      System.out.println( "and a " + a2.sound( ) + " "
                          + a2.sound( ) + " there." );
      System.out.println( "Here a " + a1.sound( ) + "," );
      System.out.println( "there a " + a2.sound( ) + "," );
      System.out.println( "everywhere a " + a1.sound( )
                          + " " + a1.sound( ) + "." );
   }
}
```

Output

```
With a cluck cluck here,
and a moo moo there.
Here a cluck,
there a moo,
everywhere a cluck cluck.
```

4.6 Another System, More Classes, More Interfaces

This section provides another example of implementing Java classes that are part of something bigger. As was done in Chapter 3, first a system is specified. From this problem specification, some objects are found that cannot be instantiated from existing Java classes—they are specific to this particular application. Two interfaces are implemented by two Java classes. Whereas the bank teller application presented in Chapter 3 will be implemented over many chapters, this system will not.

> The student affairs office has decided to put some newfound activity fee funds toward a music jukebox in the student center. The jukebox will allow a student to play individual songs. No money will be required. Instead, a student will swipe a magnetic ID card through a card reader. Students will each be allowed to play up to 1,500 minutes of "free" jukebox music in their academic careers at the school. A student may select a CD from the available collection of CDs and then an individual song from that CD. A student is not allowed to play an entire CD.
>
> An additional desired feature is to keep a top-10 list. So it will be necessary to keep track of how often each song is played.

When using an object-oriented approach, first find the objects. The nouns in the system specification are potential objects. Here is a team's first pass at finding real-world objects.[3] In reality, some of these ended up as part of the bigger system and some were eliminated and another object was added later.

Potential Objects—A First Pass at Finding Objects

Somewhat Sure These Will Play a Role		Not So Sure, But Considering
jukebox	ID card	activity fee funds
student	CD	money
song	collection of CDs	jukebox music
card reader	top-10 list	

When this system was analyzed and designed, the team of programmers decided to use the name `JukeboxAccount` to represent the students that use the system. The name `Student` sounded more like an object related to the registrar's office, with name, address, course taken, transcript, and so on. The team then

---

3. Many of the decisions on how to model this system's objects are based on the work of some honors students and the author as they analyzed and designed this system in the spring of 1997. For the sake of brevity, these design decisions will be presented without explanation and captured as Java interfaces.

came up with the following picture to represent the major objects and their responsibilities.

Figure 4.3: **Major objects to model the cashless jukebox (the big picture)**

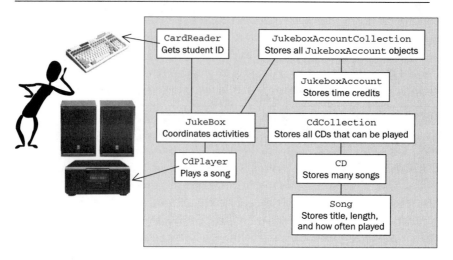

The team answered questions such as "What are other things the system must do?" and "Which object should take on a particular responsibility?" Responsibilities convey the purpose of an object and its role in the system. The proper assignment of responsibilities is one of the most important skills an object-oriented designer can develop. These responsibilities can be implemented as methods of a class. The responsibilities require some data along with a way to initialize the data.

While working on this system, the team members often reminded themselves that each object should be responsible for two things:

1. the actions the object can perform
2. the knowledge the object must remember

Therefore, the team was often asking these two questions:

1. What should the object be able to do?
2. What should the object know?

The team role-played in an effort to determine the responsibilities of each object. Role-playing happens when people act out the roles of objects. The team members became the objects. During the role-play, notes were taken. The class designs were summarized as Java interfaces—collections of method headings that need to be implemented by Java classes.

The Song Class

The `CdCollection` is a collection of CDs, which are in turn collections of `Song`s. The programming team first designed the simplest of these three classes: `Song`. It was decided that each `Song` should know its title and its playing time (in minutes and seconds, perhaps). In addition, to help maintain a top-10 list, each `Song` should keep track of how often it is played. Here is the resulting interface for `Song`:

```java
public interface SongInterface
{
  // Provide access to the title of this Song
  public String getTitle( );

  // Find out how long it takes to play this song on a CD player
  public int getPlaytime( );

  // Notify this Song that is has been played
  public void recordOnePlay( );

  // Find out how often this Song has been played
  public int getTimesPlayed( );
}
```

Much analysis and design is usually done before arriving at a Java interface. Writing interfaces is a topic beyond the scope of this book. Instead, you will occasionally be given an interface and asked to write a class that implements the interface. In the chapter that follows, you will have to implement one interface (`ActionListener`) with one method (`ActionPerformed`), so your programs can respond to button clicks and text-field input. In Chapter 6, "Selection," you will implement a different interface (`Comparable`) with one method (`compareTo`) to allow an `ArrayList` to have its elements arranged in order.

A Java interface conveniently summarizes what the objects of a class must be able to do. If you are new to programming, the interface provides the important, yet difficult-to-design, method headings. However, for now, two interfaces will be given. Then two classes can be more easily written to implement the interface. Here is one algorithm for implementing interfaces (other algorithms will also work):

1. Write the class heading with the keyword **implements** followed by the interface name.
2. Write the instance variables that are needed (this may not always be necessary).
3. Write the constructor to initialize the instance variables (this may not always be necessary).
4. Write the methods using the same exact method headings provided in the interface, replacing ; with the correct actions written between { and }.

5. Test the class. If one is not given to you, write a test driver (a `main` method) that constructs some objects and sends every possible message to the objects.

1. Write the class heading.

The class heading consists of `public class` and the class name `Song`. The constructor, the instance variables, and the methods will go between the curly braces. To help you implement the class, add the keyword `implements` followed by the name of the interface that you are implementing, in this case, `implements SongInterface`.

```
// File name: Song.java
public class Song implements SongInterface
{
}
```

2. Add the instance variables.

The programming team wondered about how to store the playing time. How should this value be stored? Is a `Time` object needed? The team decided that a `Song`'s playing time could simply be stored as an `int` to represent the total number of seconds. This may require occasional conversions, such as total seconds into minutes and seconds. However, it will be easier to deduct playing time when dealing with seconds than do "time arithmetic." An `int` variable can store the number of seconds required to play the track. This is why the return value from `getPlayTime` was specified as an `int`.

With the title of a `Song` stored as a `String`, the playing time of one track stored as an `int`, and an `int` to keep track of how often a song is played, the instance variables can now be added.

```
// Instance variables
private String my_title;
private int my_playTime;   // Seconds required to play this song
private int my_timesPlayed; // How often this song was played
```

These three values will represent the state of each `Song` object. This is what each instance of the class must remember.

3. Write the constructor.

To initialize a `Song` object, you need to pass the title and playing time as arguments. An object construction for the first track on a Beatle's greatest hits album that has a playing time of 2 minutes and 49 seconds and that has been played once could look like the following:

```
Song selection = new Song( "Day Tripper", (2 * 60 + 49), 1 );
```

The constructor needs the `String` parameter to initialize the title of the song. The second argument is an `int` parameter for initializing a `Song`'s playing time in seconds. The third argument specifies how often the song has already been played.

The constructor can now be written. It will initialize the state of any `Song` object to the values supplied as arguments. Constructors often initialize instance variables.

```
public Song( String trackTitle, int playTime, int timesPlayed )
{
  my_title = trackTitle;
  my_playTime = playTime;
  my_timesPlayed = timesPlayed;
}
```

4. Write the methods.

Even after adding instance variables and the constructor, the `Song` class that implements the `SongInterface` will not compile. It does not have the two methods of `SongInterface`. By adding `implements SongInterface`, the programmer is promising that any instance of this class will have the methods specified in the `interface`. If you don't write all method headings exactly as specified, the compiler will complain.

You can continue implementing the interface with a class by retyping the method headings as specified in the interface and replacing `;` with `{ }`. Remember to write all methods specified by the interface, even if they do nothing at first. The complete implementation of all methods will be shown in the completed class below.

If you do not have all methods specified in the interface, you will receive a compiletime error message like this:

```
Song should be declared abstract; it does not define recordOnePlay()
```

The same error appears even if you have the method heading the same except for one detail, such as a return type, one difference in parameters, or a case sensitivity issue.

5. Test the class.

When implementing a class, you should test it immediately. The testing can be done by adding a `main` method to the class. In this `main` method, one or more instances can be constructed. At a minimum, every possible message should be sent to at least one object. The output from running the program can then be examined. Verify that each method is doing what you want. A method like this with the sole purpose of testing a class is called a **test driver**. It can be a `main` method in a separate class or a `main` method in the class itself. In the `Song` class, the test driver is written in the classes that it is testing. Java allows every class to have one `main` method.

```
// A test driver may be a method inside the class that it is testing
public static void main( String[] args )
{ // Test drive Song
  Song t1 = new Song( "Day Tripper", (2 * 60) + 49, 0 );
  Song t2 = new Song( "We Can Work It Out", (2 * 60) + 15, 35 );
  // .. continue ...
```

Putting this all together and adding comments results in the following Java class:

```java
// Objects of this class store information for one track on one musical
// CD. The methods return information about the state of the Song objects.

public class Song implements SongInterface
{
  // Instance variables
  private String my_title;
  private int my_playTime;    // Seconds required to play the track
  private int my_timesPlayed; // How often this song has been chosen

  // Construct Song objects so each knows its title and playing time
  // trackTitle: The title of the song
  // playTime: The number of seconds required to play the song
  public Song( String trackTitle, int playTime, int timesPlayed )
  {
    my_title = trackTitle;
    my_playTime = playTime;
    my_timesPlayed = timesPlayed;
  }

  // Provide access to the title of this Song
  public String getTitle( )
  {
    return my_title;
  }

  // Find out how long it takes to play this song on a CD player
  public int getPlaytime( )
  {
    return my_playTime;
  }

  // Notify this Song that is has been played
  public void recordOnePlay( )
  {
    my_timesPlayed = my_timesPlayed + 1;
  }

  // Find out how often this Song has been played
  public int getTimesPlayed( )
  {
    return my_timesPlayed;
  }

  // Provide a peek at the state of this object.
  // Return the title and playing time (minutes:seconds) for this song.
  public String toString( )
  {
    return my_title + " " + my_playTime / 60 + ":" + my_playTime % 60;
  }
```

```
public static void main( String[] args )
{ // Test drive Song
   Song t1 = new Song( "Day Tripper", (2 * 60) + 49, 0 );
   Song t2 = new Song( "We Can Work It Out", (2 * 60) + 15, 35 );
   Song t3 = new Song( "Paperback Writer", (2 * 60) + 18, 0 );

   System.out.println( "t3's title: " + t3.getTitle( ) );
   System.out.println( "t3's playing time in seconds: " +
                       t3.getPlaytime( ) );
   System.out.println( );
   t1.recordOnePlay( );
   t1.recordOnePlay( );   // t1 was played twice
   t3.recordOnePlay( );
   System.out.println( "t1's times played: " + t1.getTimesPlayed( ) );
   System.out.println( "t2's times played: " + t2.getTimesPlayed( ) );
   System.out.println( "t3's times played: " + t3.getTimesPlayed( ) );
   System.out.println( );
   System.out.println( t1.toString( ) );
   System.out.println( t2.toString( ) );
   System.out.println( t3.toString( ) );
}

} // End the Song class
```

The test driver constructs three Song objects, sends all possible accessing and modifying messages to them, and at the end displays the toString version of each. When the above class runs, it generates the following output.

Output

```
t3's title: Paperback Writer
t3's playing time in seconds: 138

t1's times played: 2
t2's times played: 35
t3's times played: 1

Day Tripper 2:49
We Can Work It Out 2:15
Paperback Writer 2:18
```

As with any class that implements an interface, there may be additional methods than those that you are required to implement. One method that is available to virtually all objects in Java is toString. A toString method allows you to easily print an object. A toString method provides a snapshot of an object's state. The Java API has this to say about toString:

> toString returns a string representation of the object. In general, the toString method returns a string that "textually represents" this object. The result should be a concise but informative representation that is

easy for a person to read. It is recommended that all classes have this method.[4]

The test diver uses the `toString` method to provide a view of the changing state of objects. The test driver helps avoid errors that are more difficult to detect later on when more than one type of object exists. As much as possible, test all of the methods in a class to verify that it does what it is supposed to do. Let's now apply the same steps for implementing a given interface for another class for the `Jukebox` system.

The `JukeboxAccount` Class

After much discussion, the team decided all `JukeboxAccount` objects should have the following responsibilities:

1. `debitOneSong`: adjust the `JukeboxAccount` to reflect playing one song today
2. `canSelect`: return `true` of the user is allowed to play a song or `false` if the user is not

The team also decided that each `JukeboxAccount` should remember:

- the remaining time credit
- a way to identify the account with a unique `String` ID

The team considered the return type and parameters for the `debitOneSong` message that modifies the state. During a `debitOneSong` message, the `JukeboxAccount` will add one to how many songs the person has played. At the same time, the state of any `JukeboxAccount` object will be modified by reducing the time remaining by the amount of the playing time for the song that was played. This means `debitOneSong` needs to ask the `Song` object for its playing time. Therefore, `debitOneSong` was designed to have a `Song` parameter so it could accept any `Song` object. A `debitOneSong` message modifies `JukeboxAccount` objects. The method need not return anything. Therefore, the return type is specified as `void`.

After much heated debate, the team decided that `JukeboxAccount` should be responsible for knowing if it could play a song. After all, each `JukeboxAccount` object remembers how many seconds of playing time it has remaining.[5] The return value from this `canSelect` message was specified as a `boolean`, so the result is either `true` or `false`. To summarize, here is the interface captured by the team for a `JukeboxAccount`:

---

4. JavaTM 2 Platform, Standard Edition, v 1.3.1 API Specification.

5. When trying to determine who should be responsible for some action, assign the responsibility to the information expert. This object has the information necessary to fulfill the responsibility—Expert Pattern from Craig Larman, *Applying UML and Patterns: An Introduction to Object-Oriented Analysis and Design* (Upper Saddle River, NJ: Prentice Hall, 1998).

```
public interface JukeboxAccountInterface
{
  // Provide access to this JukeboxAccount's ID string
  public String getID( );

  // A message that should be sent whenever
  // this JukeboxAccount plays one song
  public void debitOneSong( Song aSong );

  // Return true if this user is allowed to play aSong
  public boolean canSelect( Song aSong );
}
```

1. Write the class heading.

The JukeboxAccount begins with writing the class heading: public class, the
class name, and, in this case, implements JukeboxAccountInterface.

```
// File name: JukeboxAccount.java

public class JukeboxAccount implements JukeboxAccountInterface
{
  // This will not compile.
  // Wanted: All methods of JukeboxAccountInterface
}
```

2. Add the instance variables.

At this point, it is useful to recall what JukeboxAccount objects needed to remember: the remaining time credit and a way to identify the account with a unique
identifier. The unique ID can be a String. How to store the remaining time credit
wasn't so clear at first.

   The initial time credit for a new JukeboxAccount is 1,500 minutes (or
1,500 * 60 = 90,000 seconds). It was decided before that it would be easier to maintain seconds rather than minutes and seconds. Therefore, each JukeboxAccount
object could have an instance variable named my_secondsRemaining to maintain
the remaining time credit. Then the instance variable my_secondsRemaining will
be reduced by the Song's playing time each time a user plays a Song. We can use an
int here unless we plan to increase it to over 2,147,483,647 seconds, which is about
596523 hours, or 24855 days, or 68 years of continuous music. An int instance
variable will certainly suffice. Here are the three instance variables to store the
state of many JukeboxAccounts.

```
private String my_ID;
private int my_secondsRemaining;
```

3. Write the constructor.

The constructor's job will be to initialize these two instance variables. One convention used in this textbook is to have the unique identifier appear first in the
parameter list. However, there is no specific ordering required. The three param-

eters could be in a different order. Once the parameters are set, all object constructions must follow the correct ordering of arguments.

```
public JukeboxAccount( String ID, int secondsOfPlayTime )
{
   my_ID = ID;
   my_secondsRemaining = secondsOfPlayTime;
}
```

4. Write the methods.

Often, but not always, a class will have methods that simply return the values of instance variables. One such method is getID, which simply returns the value of the private instance variable. This message is used later to locate a particular account in the JukeboxAccountCollection after a user swipes a card.

```
public String getID( )
{
   return my_ID;
}
```

This debitOneSong method adjusts the time remaining to indicate that this JukeboxAccount has played a song of a specific duration. Notice that a JukeboxAccount object is sending a message to the Song object to get the particular playing time of the song.

```
public void debitOneSong( Song theSong )
{
   my_secondsRemaining = my_secondsRemaining - theSong.getPlaytime( );
}
```

The third method examines its own state to determine if it can play a song. The method should return true whenever the JukeboxAccount has enough time credit (in actuality, it will be some time before canSelect returns false).

```
public boolean canSelect( Song theSong )
{
   return my_secondsRemaining >= theSong.getPlaytime( );
}
```

5. Test the class.

As the JukeboxAccount class was implemented, the programmers compiled and tested often—approximately one compile, run, and test as each method was added. The test driver got quite big. A test driver should at least send all possible JukeboxAccount messages. The test driver is included in the JukeboxAccount class. It constructs an object that can no longer select a song by starting with only 15 minutes rather than 1,500 minutes.

Here is the JukeboxAccount class in its entirety:

```java
// JukeboxAccount is part of a jukebox system. Programmers can:
// 1. Ask for the account ID.
// 2. Ask a JukeboxAccount if it can play a specific track.
// 3. Update time remaining and songs played with debitOneSong.
public class JukeboxAccount
{ // Instance variables
  private String my_ID;
  private int my_secondsRemaining;

  // Construct JukeboxAccount objects with two arguments.
  // ID: The string that uniquely identifies this account.
  // secondsOfPlayTime:  Seconds remaining to play songs.
  public JukeboxAccount( String ID, int secondsOfPlayTime )
  {
    my_ID = ID;
    my_secondsRemaining = secondsOfPlayTime;
  }

  // Return true if this user is allowed to play theSong
  public boolean canSelect( Song theSong )
  {
    boolean result;
    result = my_secondsRemaining >= theSong.getPlaytime( );
    return result;
  }

  // Adjust the state when this JukeboxAccount plays one song
  public void debitOneSong( Song theSong )
  {
    my_secondsRemaining = my_secondsRemaining - theSong.getPlaytime( );
  }

  // Provide access to this JukeboxAccount's ID
  public String getID( )
  {
    return my_ID;
  }

  // Provide a quick way to see the state of this object.
  public String toString( )
  {
    String result;
    result = my_ID + " has " + ( my_secondsRemaining / 60 ) + " minutes";
    return result;
  }

  public static void main( String[] args )
  {
    // Start this account with only 10 minutes of time remaining
    JukeboxAccount anAccount = new JukeboxAccount( "Olson", 10 * 60 );

    System.out.println( "ID: " + anAccount.getID( ) );
    Song selection = new Song( "A 5 minute song", 5 * 60, 0 );
    System.out.println( "Select? " + anAccount.canSelect( selection ) );
    System.out.println( anAccount.toString( ) );
```

```
    anAccount.debitOneSong( selection );
    System.out.println( anAccount.toString( ) );
    anAccount.debitOneSong( selection );
    System.out.println( anAccount.toString( ) );
    anAccount.debitOneSong( selection );
    System.out.println( anAccount.toString( ) );
    System.out.println( "Select? " + anAccount.canSelect( selection ) );
  } // End test driver

} // End class JukeboxAccount
```

The `toString` method for `JukeboxAccount` concatenates a few values together to create a string that "textually" represents any object. Each class you write should add a `toString` method even if it is not requested. As seen before in `println` messages, the `+` operator will make a `String` from a `String` and other values, such as integers. When the above class is run, it generates the following output:

Output

```
ID: Olson
Select? true
Olson has 10 minutes
Olson has 5 minutes
Olson has 0 minutes
Select? false
```

The preceding discussion offered an algorithm on how a class can implement a given interface. The end-of-chapter programming projects offer interfaces to help you write the requested classes. You have the option of implementing the interface or simply writing the class using the provided method headings. In either case, the test drivers provided in the projects ensure that you have the requested methods.

Chapter Summary

- This chapter showed a class as a collection of methods that represent the messages available for any instance of the class (object).
- Method headings with documentation provide the following information:
    - whether or not the method is available to the outside world (public or private)
    - the return type (the kind of value that a message will evaluate to)
    - the method name that begins a valid method call
    - the parameter list (the number and type of arguments required)
    - documentation describing what the method does
- The familiar assignment rules apply for assigning arguments to parameters.
- A Java class contains:
    - a class heading, which may include `implements`
    - the instance variables, known collectively as the state

- one or more constructors to initialize the state
- methods with parameters and return types
- implementation of those methods in the method body

- Each instance of a class may store many values, which may be of different types. For example, each `BankAccount` object stores a `String` instance variable for the ID and a number for the balance. Other objects have state that is more complex.
- Instance variables are accessed and modified through the methods of the class.
- Constructors are called to build and initialize objects like this:

```
BankAccount anotherAccount( "Calissario", 4320.10 );
```

- Some methods change the state of the object (for example, `add`, `setSize`, `withdraw`, and `move`).
- Some methods provide access to the state of an object (for example, `get`, `getBalance`, and `toString`).
- Some methods ask other objects for help to fulfill their responsibility (for example, `Transaction` methods ask `GregorianCalendar` for the current date).
- The ramifications of adhering to the guideline "All data should be hidden within its class" include the following:
  - Programmers cannot accidentally (or intentionally) mess up the state. The compiler will complain. The code will not run.
  - Programmers need to implement additional accessing methods, `getBalance()`, for example, but this is sound software engineering practice.
- The ramifications of adhering to the guideline "Keep related data and behavior in one place" include the following:
  - a more intuitive design (things make more sense)
  - code is easier to maintain

- Instance variables should be declared `private`.
- A class should be designed to exhibit high cohesion:
  - The data should be used by the methods.
  - The methods should have a meaningful relationship to each other.

- Responsibilities discovered during role-playing can be implemented as methods. These actions are captured as a Java class.
- Knowledge responsibilities can be implemented as instance variables.
- Most classes need public methods, private instance variables, and a constructor to initialize the state of an object.
- An interface cannot have any instance variables or constructors.
- If a class `implements` an interface, the class must implement all methods of the interface using the same method headings specified by the interface.
- A class that implements an interface may add new methods.

Key Terms

accessing method	`implements`	parameter
argument	instance variable	`private`
class constant	interface	`public`
cohesion	method	`return`
constructor	modifier	`static`
design guideline	modifying method	`substring`
`final`	object-oriented design	test driver

Exercises

The answers to exercises marked with 💥 are available in Appendix C. Use the following class to do exercises 1 through 6:

```java
public class SillyClass
{
  private double my_leftOperand;
  private double my_rightOperand;

  public SillyClass( double leftOperand, double rightOperand )
  { // Construct an object with two arguments
    my_leftOperand = leftOperand;
    my_rightOperand = rightOperand;
  }

  public double sum( )
  {
    return my_leftOperand + my_rightOperand;
  }

  public double product( )
  {
    return my_leftOperand * my_rightOperand;
  }

  public double quotient( )
  {
    return my_leftOperand / my_rightOperand;
  }
```

1. Name the instance variables of the `SillyClass` class.

2. Name the methods of `SillyClass`.

3. How many arguments are required to construct an instance of `SillyClass`?

4. Using the method headings and documentation for the `One` class above, write the output generated by the following program:

```
public class TestSilly
{
  public static void main( String[] args )
  {
    SillyClass a = new SillyClass( 1.2, 2.0 );
    SillyClass b = new SillyClass( 6.0, -3.0 );
    System.out.println( "a:" + a.sum( ) + " "
                          + a.product( ) + " " + a.quotient( ) );
    System.out.println( "b:" + b.sum( ) + " " + b.product( )
                          + " " + b.quotient( ) );
  }
}
```

5. Add a method named `difference` that returns the difference between the two operands of any `SillyClass` object. The return value can never be negative.

6. Send a `difference` message named `b` to the `SillyClass` object.

 7. Which of the following represent valid method headings?

    a. `public int large( int a, int b )`

    b. `public double( double a, double b )`

    c. `public int f( int a; int b; )`

    d. `public int f( a, int b )`

    e. `public double f( )`

    f. `public String c( String a )`

 8. Given the `ClickCounter` class, predict the output generated by the test driver.

```
public class ClickCounter
{
  public static final int START_COUNT = 0;
  private int my_count;
  private int my_maxCount;

  // Constructer
  public ClickCounter( int maxCount )
  {
    my_count = START_COUNT;
    my_maxCount = maxCount;
  }

  // Change the count of this clickCounter.
  // If at maximum, reset to 0, otherwise add 1.
  public void click( )
  {
    my_count = ( my_count + 1 ) %
                 ( my_maxCount + 1 );
  }

  // Evaluate to this clickCounter's count
  public int getCount( )
  { // Return the count of this ClickCounter
    return my_count;
  }
```

```
      public static void main( String[] args )
      { // Test drive ClickCounter
        ClickCounter aCounter = new ClickCounter( 3 );
        // aCounter only counts from 0 to 3
        System.out.println( aCounter.getCount( ) );
        aCounter.click( );
        System.out.println( aCounter.getCount( ) );
        aCounter.click( );
        System.out.println( aCounter.getCount( ) );
        aCounter.click( );
        System.out.println( aCounter.getCount( ) );
        aCounter.click( );
        System.out.println( aCounter.getCount( ) );
        aCounter.click( );
        System.out.println( aCounter.getCount( ) );
      }
    }
```

Class Diagram

```
┌─────────────────────────┐
│      ClickCounter        │
├─────────────────────────┤
│ +START_COUNT             │
│ -int my_count            │
│ -int my_maxValue         │
├─────────────────────────┤
│ +click( )                │
│ +reset( )                │
│ +int getCount( )         │
└─────────────────────────┘
```

9. With paper and pencil, add a `reset` method as if it were in the `ClickCounter` class. The method must always set `my_count` to 0.

10. Send a `reset` message to the object constructed in the `main` method above.

11. Write the output when the `Mystery` class is run.

```
public class Mystery
{
  private int my_value;

  public Mystery( int v )
  {
    my_value = v;
  }

  public String toString( )
  {
    String result = "[" + my_value + "]"; // Makes a string
    return result;
  }

  public static void main( String[] args )
  {
    Mystery aMystery = new Mystery( 93 );
```

```
        System.out.println( aMystery.toString( ) );
        Mystery anotherMystery = new Mystery( -123 );
        System.out.println( anotherMystery );
    }
}
```

12. Using the `Car` and `Mystery2` classes shown here, write the output generated by the `main` method in the `CarAndMystery2` class.

```
public class CarAndMystery2
{
    public static void main( String[] args )
    {
        Car c1 = new Car( 0.0, 0.0 );
        Car c2 = new Car( 72.0, 3.0 );

        c1.measure( 100.0, 5.0 );
        System.out.println( "a) " + c1.getMPG( ) );
        System.out.println( "b) " + c2.getMPG( ) );

        Mystery2 m = new Mystery2( );
        c1.measure( 230.0, 10.0 );
        System.out.println( "c) " + c1.getMPG( ) );
        m.huh( c1 );
        m.huh( c2 );
        System.out.println( "d) " + m.huhTwo( ) );

        Car c3 = new Car( 128.0, 4.0 );
        m.huh( c3 );
        System.out.println( "e) " + m.huhTwo( ) );
    }
}


public class Car
{
    private double my_miles;
    private double my_gallons;

    public Car( double miles, double gallons )
    {
        my_miles = miles;
        my_gallons = gallons;
    }

    public void measure( double miles, double gallons )
    {
        my_miles = my_miles + miles;
        my_gallons = my_gallons + gallons;
    }

    public double getMPG( )
    {
        return  my_miles / my_gallons;
    }
}
```

```java
public class Mystery2
{
  private double my_value;
  private int n;

  public Mystery2( )
  {
    my_value = 0.0;
    n = 0;
  }

  public void huh( Car aCar )
  {
    my_value = my_value + aCar.getMPG( );
    n = n + 1;
  }

  public double huhTwo( )
  {
    return my_value / n;
  }
}
```

Programming Tips

1. **Make all instance variables private.**
   This protects the state of objects while hiding implementation details. Other programmers can use your class by looking at your documentation. Documented method headings provide information about how to use instances of the class. See Appendix A, "A Little Javadoc."

2. **Some programming projects require some author-supplied files.**
   These files are available on the accompanying diskette. To find any file in this textbook, remember that each public class is stored in a file that has the name.

   `class-name.java`

   Therefore, the ClickCounter class, which begins like this:

   `public class ClickCounter`

   is stored in a file named ClickCounter.java. Remember that Java is case sensitive. Errors occur when the file name and the class name differ in case.

3. **Working with two or more files is more difficult than working with one.**
   Some programming projects require that you work with more than one file. This takes a little patience as you grow accustomed to working with multiple files. You will sometimes have a class in a file that will be used by another class in another file.

4. **Consider building your test driver into each and every class.**
When implementing classes, it is best to test each method as you go. This is facilitated by placing a main method in your class as you develop it—creating one file instead of two.

5. **Classes are designed with values in mind.**
When using someone else's class, remember that the design was influenced by what was important at the time to those particular programmers. This sometimes makes it more difficult to agree with the particular methods that were selected. When you become more familiar with the class or become aware of the values that influenced the design, the decisions may seem more logical.

6. **Avoid magic numbers.**
Whenever you need a numeric value in several places, consider writing it as a class constant that has a meaningful name. SALES_TAX is more meaningful than 0.045, for example.

Programming Projects

4A `LibraryBook`

Write a `LibraryBook` class so the test driver below generates the output shown. A `LibraryBook` object stores the title and author of a library book (initialized by having the constructor take the book's title and author as arguments). The `toString` method must show the title and the borrower between < and > (see the output below). A `borrowBook` message changes the borrower's ID from `null` to the `String` argument passed to it. When the book is returned, the borrower is set back to `null`. The following test driver shows the behavior of one `LibraryBook` object. Run it to ensure that it generates the exact output shown with your class.

```
public class TestLibraryBook
{
  public static void main( String[] args )
  {
    LibraryBook aBook =
     new LibraryBook( "The Mythical Man Month", "Fred Brooks" );

    System.out.println( aBook.getTitle( ) );
    System.out.println( aBook.getAuthor( ) );
    System.out.println( aBook.toString( ) );
    System.out.println( );
    aBook.borrowBook( "Andrew Wilt" );
    System.out.println( aBook.toString( ) );
    aBook.returnBook( );
    System.out.println( aBook.toString( ) );
  }
}
```

Output

```
The Mythical Man Month
Fred Brooks
<The Mythical Man Month by Fred Brooks is borrowed by null>

<The Mythical Man Month by Fred Brooks is borrowed by Andrew Wilt>
<The Mythical Man Month by Fred Brooks is borrowed by null>
```

4B   PersonWithAge

Write a `PersonWithAge` class so the test driver below generates the output shown.
A `PersonWithAge` object stores a person's name and age. The `getName` method
returns the person's name. The method named `yearsTo` returns how many years it
takes to turn the age passed as an argument. The constructor takes the person's
name and age as arguments. The class must also have a `toString` method to
return the name and age of any person as a string (see the output below). The
following test driver shows the behavior of a few `PersonWithAge` objects:

```java
public class TestPersonWithAge
{
  public static void main( String[] args)
  { // Test drive PersonWithAge
    PersonWithAge one = new PersonWithAge( "Kim", 19 );
    PersonWithAge two = new PersonWithAge( "Devon", 21 );
    PersonWithAge tre = new PersonWithAge( "Chris", 79 );

    System.out.println( one.toString( ) );
    System.out.println( two.toString( ) );
    System.out.println( tre.toString( ) );
    System.out.println( );
    System.out.println( one.getName( ) + " turns 21 in "
                      + one.yearsTo( 21 ) + " years" );

    System.out.println( two.getName( ) + " turns 40 in "
                      + two.yearsTo( 40 ) + " years" );

    System.out.println( tre.getName( ) + " turns 65 in "
                      + tre.yearsTo( 65 ) + " years" );
  }
}
```

Output

```
Kim is 19 years old
Devon is 21 years old
Chris is 79 years old

Kim turns 21 in 2 years
Devon turns 40 in 19 years
Chris turns 65 in -14 years
```

4C SimpleEmployee

Write a SimpleEmployee class so the test driver below generates the output shown. The constructor takes the employee's name (a String) and annual salary (a double) as arguments. The toString method returns a String that provides a textual representation of the object—the name and annual salary (see the output below). Make sure the salary has two decimal places and is preceded by $ or whatever your currency symbol is. As for instance variables, each SimpleEmployee object must know the employee's name (a String) and annual salary (a double). Round the monthly salary and the annual salary to the nearest hundredth (multiply the monthly salary by 100.0, Math.round that result to the nearest integer, and then divide that by 100.0—this avoids division-by-zero errors when credits are 0.0). Run the following test driver and verify that you have all the methods specified. You must generate the output exactly as shown.

```java
public class TestSimpleEmployee
{
  public static void main( String[] args )
  {
    SimpleEmployee empOne = new SimpleEmployee( "Jack", 52000.00 );
    SimpleEmployee empTwo = new SimpleEmployee( "Jill", 53000.00 );

    System.out.println( empTwo.getName( ) + " annual "
                        + empTwo.getAnnualSalary( ) );

    System.out.println( empTwo.getName( ) + " monthly "
                        + empTwo.getMonthlySalary( ) );

    System.out.println( empOne.getName( ) + " annual "
                        + empOne.getAnnualSalary( ) );
    System.out.println( empOne.getName( ) + " monthly "
                        + empOne.getMonthlySalary( ) );

    empTwo.giveRaise( 0.05 );
    empOne.giveRaise( 0.10 );
    System.out.println( empTwo.toString( ) );
    System.out.println( empOne.toString( ) );
  }
}
```

Output (the monthly salaries have two decimal places—use DecimalFormat)

```
Jill annual 53000.00
Jill monthly 4416.67
Jack annual 52000.00
Jack monthly 4333.33
Jill makes 55650.00 per year
Jack makes 57200.00 per year
```

4D   Course and Student Implement Interfaces

Implement two interfaces with classes named Student and Course so they work together to maintain a student's grade point average (GPA). All Student objects must be able to compute their own GPA, which is

```
GPA = totalQualityPoints / totalUnits
```

where

```
qualityPoints = units * numericGrade
```

This means that the recordCourse method must increment the total units (credits) and qualityPoints represented by the Course arguments. The interfaces are given for both classes. In addition to all methods specified in these interfaces, add a toString method for each class and add a test driver as a main method.

```java
// Instances of this class store data about one university course
//    1. Course number
//    2. Units (or credits) of this course: 0.5 - 15.0
//    3. Numeric grade: 0.0 - 4.0
public interface CourseInterface
{
  // Return the course number of this course
  public String getCourseNumber( );

  // Return the number of units of this course
  public double getUnits( );

  // Return the numeric grade for this course
  public double getGrade( );

  // Return a textual representation of this Course object
  public String toString( );
}


// This interface represents a student at a university with very limited
// functionality. An instance of this Student class only maintains
// the total number of units and quality points for each student.
public interface StudentInterface
{
  // An accessing method for this student's name
  public String getName( );

  // An accessing method for this student's current GPA
  public double getGPA( );

  // An accessing method to show a state of this student
  public String toString( );

  // A modifying method that adds a newly completed course
  public void recordCourse( Course aCourse );
}
```

The test driver below sends all possible messages. It, along with its output, is intended to help you understand the behavior of the objects. When you complete both classes, the test driver must generate the output exactly as shown. In addition to the methods specified in the interfaces above, remember to add a toString method to both classes. Use the test driver output shown below to determine how you should implement toString. Run this test driver to test your two new classes: Course and Student.

```java
public class TestCourseAndStudent
{
  // This is a test driver for Course and Student
  public static void main( String[] args )
  {
    // Test Course--start with a three-unit A
    Course CS1 = new Course( "CSc127A-042002", 3.0, 4.0 );

    System.out.println( CS1 );
    System.out.println( "units: " + CS1.getUnits( ) );
    System.out.println( "grade: " + CS1.getGrade( ) );

    // Construct a four-unit B
    Course CS2 = new Course( "CSc127A-012003", 4.0, 3.0 );
    // Construct a one-unit C
    Course PE101 = new Course( "PE101-022003", 1.0, 2.0 );
    System.out.println( );

    // Test the relationship between Student and Course
    Student s1 = new Student( "Devon" );
    s1.recordCourse( CS1 );
    System.out.println( s1 );
    System.out.println( "name: " + s1.getName( ) );
    System.out.println( " GPA: " + s1.getGPA( ) );
    System.out.println( );
    // Add two more courses
    s1.recordCourse( CS2 );
    s1.recordCourse( PE101 );
    System.out.println( s1.toString( ) );
  }
}
```

Output

```
CSc127A-042002 3.0 units with grade 4.0
units: 3.0
grade: 4.0

Devon's GPA is 4.0
name: Devon
 GPA: 4.0

Devon's GPA is 3.25
```

4E   A Few Presents

Write three classes named `First`, `Second`, and `Third` in three separate files that ensure the following program runs with no syntax errors. It must generate the output exactly as shown. Your classes will not need a constructor or instance variables. Here is the interface your classes need to implement. (*Note:* Class constants can also be declared in interfaces; they must have the `static` modifier.)

```java
// File name: Present.java
public interface Present
{
  public static final String REFRAIN =
                            " of Christmas, my true love gave to me:";
  public String day( );
  public String whatSheGaveToMe( );
}


// File name: ThreeDays.java
public class ThreeDays
{
  public static void main( String[] args )
  {
    ChristmasPresent day1 = new First( "first" );
    ChristmasPresent day2 = new Second( "second" );
    ChristmasPresent day3 = new Third( "third" );
    // Verse 1
    System.out.println( "On the " + day1.day( ) + Present.REFRAIN );
    System.out.println( day1.whatSheGaveToMe( ) );
    // Verse 2
    System.out.println( "On the " + day2.day( ) + Present.REFRAIN );
    System.out.println( day2.whatSheGaveToMe( ) + "," );
    System.out.println( "and " + day1.whatSheGaveToMe( ) );
    // Verse 3
    System.out.println( "On the " + day3.day( ) + Present.REFRAIN );
    System.out.println( day3.whatSheGaveToMe( ) + "," );
    System.out.println( day2.whatSheGaveToMe( ) + "," );
    System.out.println( "and " + day1.whatSheGaveToMe( ) );
  }
}
```

Output

```
On the first day of Christmas, my true love gave to me:
a partridge in a pair tree.
On the second day of Christmas, my true love gave to me:
two turtle doves,
and a partridge in a pair tree.
On the third day of Christmas, my true love gave to me:
three French hens,
two turtle doves,
and a partridge in a pair tree.
```

4F   Parking Garage Ticket

Write a `ParkingGarageTicket` class so the test driver given below generates the output shown. The constructor takes a ticket number (an int) as a parameter; `getFees` takes two arguments, the current hour and the minute the ticket will be paid. The cost to park is $1.50 per hour, whether 1 minute or 60 minutes of the hour is used. One hour and 1 minute of parking would cost $3.00. Assume all times are on the same day. The `toString( )` method must use the `GregorianCalendar` `getTime( )` method to return the day, month, time, and year.

```java
public static void main (String[] args)
{
   ParkingGarageTicket ticket = new ParkingGarageTicket( 101 );
   System.out.println( ticket.toString( ) );
   System.out.println( "Test getFee " + ticket.getTicketNumber( ) );

   GregorianCalendar time = new GregorianCalendar( );
   int hour = time.get( GregorianCalendar.HOUR_OF_DAY ); // 0..23
   int minute = time.get( GregorianCalendar.MINUTE );    // 0..59
   System.out.println( "1.5? " + ticket.getFee( hour, minute ) );
   System.out.println( "3.0? " + ticket.getFee( hour + 1, minute ) );
   System.out.println( "7.5? " + ticket.getFee( hour + 4, minute ) );
   System.out.println( "34.5? " + ticket.getFee( hour + 22, minute ) );
}
```

Output

```
Ticket#101 arrived Wed Jan 30 19:44:14 MST 2002
Test getFee 101
1.5? 1.5
3.0? 3.0
7.5? 7.5
34.5? 34.5
```

4G   Designing `WeeklyEmployee`

Completely implement a class named `WeeklyEmployee` that is intended to be part of a payroll system (no interfaces are required in this code). Each instance of `WeeklyEmployee` must keep track of an employee's name, number (an int), hourly rate of pay, and number of hours worked during the current week. Each instance of `WeeklyEmployee` must be able to compute its own:

1. gross pay, which is defined as (hours worked * hourly rate of pay)
2. social security tax, which is defined as 6.2% of gross pay
3. Medicare tax, which is defined as 1.45% of gross pay

There is no overtime. A programmer must be able to set the hours worked each week since this changes from week to week. Because the time clock measures hours worked in tenths of an hour, hours worked must have a fractional part (you could make this a double). In addition, a programmer using this class must be able to give any WeeklyEmployee object a raise in pay such as 0.03 for 3%, for example.

1. **Determine what each WeeklyEmployee must be able to do.** On paper, write a method heading for each responsibility and a comment indicating what the method does.

2. **Determine what each WeeklyEmployee must know.** Provide a name for each value and also the type (such as int, double, or String). Use meaningful identifiers that accurately describe what the variables will store.

   Type of Value   **Variable Name**

   _____   _____

3. **Write a class diagram.** This is a rectangle with the class heading at the top, instance variables next, followed by the method headings (use Java syntax for the method headings).

4. **Using the previous documents as guidelines, complete the WeeklyEmployee class as Java source code.** Remember to include all of these elements:
   a. class heading
   b. public class constants for 0.062 and 0.0145
   c. instance variables
   d. constructor to initialize the instance variables
   e. all other methods

5. **Test the class.** Add a main method to your class that at a minimum constructs two instances of WeeklyEmployee and send every possible message to both objects. Keep modifying and fixing WeeklyEmployee as you test your class. Generate output that verifies that your objects are behaving correctly.

Answers to Self-Check Questions

4-1 -a String   -d String
     -b concat   -e There is no second argument possible.
     -c one

4-2 -a "abcxyz"   -d Error—one too many arguments.
     -b Error—missing an argument.   -e "abcwxyz"
     -c Error—an incorrect argument. -f Error—concat requires an object reference, not a
                                            class name.

4-3 "times"

4-4 "hopeless"

4-5 "" (an empty string with length 0)

4-6 Instance variables: 1.23 4.56
     Instance variables: 1.0 2.0

4-7 Changed to: 2.2 4.4
     Changed to: 4.2 6.4
     Changed to: 7.2 9.4

4-8 First: 1.0
     Second: 2.0
     Sum: 3.0
     First: 4.4
     Second: 5.4
     Sum: 9.8

4-9
```
          sc1

my_first = 4.4
my_second = 5.4
```

4-10 LibraryBook

4-11 borrowBook getBorrower returnBook

4-12 a String (the borrower's name)

4-13 none (or void)

4-14 a String (the borrower's name)

4-15 Two: the author (a String) and the book title (a String)

4-16 LibraryBook aBook("Computing Fundamentals with Java", "Rick Mercer");

4-17 aBook.borrowBook("AnyFirstName AnyLastName");

4-18 System.out.println(aBook.getBorrower( ));

4-19   **Immediately after constructing**   **Immediately after borrowBook message**

```
          aBook                                  aBook

my_author = "John LeCarre"             my_author = "John LeCarre"
my_title = "Little Drummer Girl"       my_title = "Little Drummer Girl"
my_borrower = null                     my_borrower = "Chris Miller"
```

4-20 Borrower: Chris Miller
     Borrower: null

4-21 The constructors

4-22 They allow access to the state of any object so humans or other objects can either inspect or use that state. An accessing method may directly return the value of a primitive instance variable or a reference to an object instance variable. Or the method may have to perform a little or a lot of processing to return some useful information about the state of the object. The method may even send messages to other objects.

4-23 Modify the state of the object.

4-24 Allow programmers to initialize objects with either the default state or their own initial values.

4-25 They store the state (the values) of any object. Each instance of the class stores its own copy of the instance variables. If there are 25,000 BankAccount objects, there are 25,000 IDs and balances.

4-26 Yes

4-27 No. The private instance variables are known only to the methods inside the class.

4-28 public static final int DAYS_IN_LEAP_YEAR = 366;

4-29 No

4-30 Yes

4-31 Methods declared with the `public` modifier are known in all methods of the class and in every block where an instance of the class is constructed or is specified as a parameter.

4-32 Methods declared with the `public` modifier can be accessed only by the methods of that class. They are known in every part of the class.

4-33 It prevents accidental modification of an object's state. The code relies on the `public` methods, not the internal implementation details. There is a design guideline for this.

4-34 No. The code does not access `private` data. This is another benefit of private instance variables—programmers do not need to know them and do not rely on them in case someone changes the implementation of the class.

4-35 Yes. This is why it is a good idea to design a class so carefully that it rarely, if ever, needs to be changed.

4-36 No. That would not be a use of high cohesion. The message is not related to a `BankAccount`.

4-37
```java
public class Chicken implements BarnyardAnimal
{
    private String mySound;

    public Chicken( String sound )
    {
      mySound = sound;
    }

    public String sound( )
    {
      return mySound;
    }
}


public class Cow implements BarnyardAnimal
{
    private String mySound;

    public Cow( String sound )
    {
      mySound = sound;
    }


    public String sound( )
    {
      return mySound;
    }
}
```

Chapter 5

Events, Listeners, and a Little Polymorphism

Summing Up

So far, the user's view of programs has been the text-based console window. A few parts of an event-driven program using a graphical user interface have been introduced—graphical components such as `JTextField` and `JButton`. Also introduced was the notion of a Java interface that guarantees that any class that implements the interface has all of the methods specified in that interface.

Coming Up

This chapter focuses on objects that perform the appropriate actions when certain user interactions occur. You will see the Java interface as a major player in getting things done. You will also see that the Java interface is a way to implement polymorphism—one of the distinguishing features of object-oriented programming. You will see inheritance as another way to implement polymorphism. After studying this chapter, you will be able to

- write event-driven programs with a graphical user interface
- get a class just like another class with very little effort
- build classes inside another class
- understand how the same message can be sent to different types of objects with different behaviors (polymorphism)
- deal with some issues of inheritance, such as using the `Object` class, assignment compatibility, casting, and overriding methods
- distinguish several uses of polymorphism through inheritance and interfaces

Exercises and programming projects reinforce event-driven programming and polymorphism.

5.1   Event-Driven Programming

Chapter 1 introduced the Input/Process/Output pattern in the context of keyboard input and console output. Most programming assignments so far follow this mode: The user is prompted to enter input, the program does some processing, and the results are shown as output. For example, here is the problem specification along with one sample dialogue from Programming Project 2H, "Seconds."

2H   Seconds

Write a program that reads a value in seconds and displays the number of hours, minutes, and seconds represented by the input. Your dialogue must look exactly like this:

```
Enter seconds: 32123
8:55:23
```

When prompted from a text-based console window, the user enters 32123 at the keyboard. Some actions occur behind the scenes. Then the result is displayed to the text-based console window.

Input/Process/Output with a Graphical Interface

The same Input/Process/Output pattern can be done in a graphical fashion. The prompt can be a JLabel object (Seconds, in the example below). The keyboard is still used to enter input, but now the input goes into a JTextField object (with 32123 below). The output still goes to the screen, but this time in the form of a JLabel object (08:55:23 below).

The user still enters input (32123), processing still occurs, and the result of the processing is still shown (08:55:23). It is the Input/Process/Output pattern with a different face, a graphical face. A **graphical user interface** (GUI) allows users to interact with programs through graphical components such as buttons, text fields, pull-down lists, and menu selections.

Instead of prompting users to enter text, this event-driven program updates the hr:min:sec fields whenever the user presses Enter in a text field. Instead of running the program once with one input, the user can enter many values to see many results. The program does not terminate until the user closes the window. This allows multiple Input/Process/Outputs.

Java's Event-Driven Programming Model

With Java, when a user enters text into a text field, that text field sends a message to another object. The text field does not perform the processing. Instead, the graphical component informs another object what has happened at the user interface: "Hey object, someone just entered input into my text field. Do whatever it is you want to do—perform your actions."

The object that waits to be informed that a user has interacted with a particular graphical component is called a **listener**. The listener object does the processing and typically shows the result in the window. When a program has listener objects waiting for messages from graphical components in a interface, the program is called an **event-driven program** with a GUI.

An event-driven program needs classes built in a specific way. There is substantial overhead that requires some getting used to. However, after you have written a few event-driven programs with a graphical user interface, you can use the same approach for button clicks, menu selections, hyperlink events, mouse clicks, and any of the other events generated by Java graphical components, the mouse, and the keyboard.

Before looking at all of these details, first consider the complete event-driven GUI solution to Programming Project 2H, "Seconds." The numbers indicate the major differences from previous programs. The new concepts will be presented immediately after this complete example:

① A new `import` is needed for classes and interfaces related to events.

② The class extends `JFrame`. This allows you to treat any new class as a `JFrame`.

③ An instance of the inner class that `implements ActionListener` is registered to listen to user input.

④ There is an inner class. This allows access to the needed graphical components.

⑤ The inner class implements the `ActionListener` interface so it can be registered as a listener.

```
// Build a window with four components, two
// of which are needed by the listener
import javax.swing.*;      // JFrame, JTextField, and JButton
import java.awt.*;         // Container and GridLayout
import java.text.DecimalFormat; // To make "7" into "07"
①
import java.awt.event.*;    // ActionListener and ActionEvent
                              ②
public class TimeFrame extends JFrame
{
  public static void main( String[] args )
  {
    JFrame window = new TimeFrame( );
    window.show( );
  }
```

```java
// The inner class methods can reference these instance variables
private JTextField secondsField;
private JLabel hmsLabel;

public TimeFrame( )
{
  // These three messages are sent to the
  // TimeFrame object being constructed
  setTitle( "Seconds" );
  setSize( 160, 80 );
  setDefaultCloseOperation( JFrame.EXIT_ON_CLOSE );

  // Ask for the container of the TimeFrame object being constructed
  Container contentPane = getContentPane( );
  contentPane.setLayout( new GridLayout( 2, 2, 4, 4 ) );

  // a) Construct the graphical component that will be listened to
  secondsField = new JTextField( ); // Needed by inner class

  // b) Add the component to the GUI with a prompt added first
  contentPane.add( new JLabel( " Seconds" ) );
  contentPane.add( secondsField );

  // c) Construct an instance of a class with actionPerformed
  SecondsFieldListener inputListener = new SecondsFieldListener( );
```

❸
```java
  // d) Register an object to listen to the graphical component
  secondsField.addActionListener( inputListener );

  // Add the bottom row for output
  contentPane.add( new JLabel( " hr:min:sec" ) );
  hmsLabel = new JLabel( "??:??:??" ); // Need this hmsLabel
                                       // in the inner class
  contentPane.add( hmsLabel );
}
```

❹
```java
//////////////////////// BEGIN INNER CLASS ////////////////////////
// An instance of this ActionListener will listen to a JTextField.
// This inner class can reference secondsField and hmsLabel.
// It also has its own DecimalFormat object to put in leading zeros.
private class SecondsFieldListener implements ActionListener      ❺
{
  private DecimalFormat formatter;

  public SecondsFieldListener( )
  {
    formatter = new DecimalFormat( "00" );
  }
```

```
  public void actionPerformed( ActionEvent e )
  {
    // Get the seconds
    String intAsString = secondsField.getText( );
    int total = Integer.parseInt( intAsString );
    // If an exception was thrown, this method terminates

    // Compute the hours, minutes, and seconds
    int hours = total / 3600;
    int minutes = total % 3600 / 60 ;
    int seconds = total % 60;

    // Format the output with leading zeros and colons
    String answer = formatter.format( hours ) + ":" +
                    formatter.format( minutes ) + ":" +
                    formatter.format( seconds );

    // Update the output label
    hmsLabel.setText( answer );
  }
}
///////////////////////// END INNER CLASS /////////////////////////

} // End class TimeFrame
```

A Peek at Inheritance

The examples of GUIs from Chapter 3 used a main method to lay out graphical components. The code showed graphical components only in a JFrame. Nothing happened when a button was clicked or the user entered data into a text field. An event-driven program with a GUI has a more desirable design. This design begins with a class like JFrame. It should have the same methods as JFrame: setSize, setLayout, setDefaultCloseOperation, and setTitle. This class should also be able to add new methods and instance variables. Such a class is possible through inheritance.

Inheritance refers to the ability of one class to inherit (obtain) the methods and instance variables of an existing class. Inheritance provides a convenient and efficient mechanism so programmers can get a class with a lot of needed functionality but with just a minimal amount of code. In Java, inheritance is realized by extending an existing class with the keyword extends. For example, the following code gives us a new class that is just like JFrame:

```
// An instance of this class is just like an instance of JFrame
import javax.swing.JFrame;

public class LikeAJFrame extends JFrame
{
  // It looks like there are no methods, but LikeAJFrame has many!
}
```

At this moment, LikeAJFrame has inherited (obtained) all of the public methods of JFrame. Consider the following class and the window shown below. An instance of LikeAJFrame, which extends JFrame, understands the same messages as JFrame.

```
// This program shows that a class that extends JFrame has
// all of the same methods as the class that it extends--JFrame.
import javax.swing.*;   // For JFrame
import java.awt.*;      // For Container
import java.awt.GridLayout;

public class DemonstrateInheritance
{
  public static void main( String[] args )
  {
    // Instantiate a class that extends JFrame
    LikeAJFrame likeJFrame = new LikeAJFrame( );

    // Send the familiar messages to LikeAFrame
    likeJFrame.setDefaultCloseOperation( JFrame.EXIT_ON_CLOSE );
    likeJFrame.setTitle( "I'm a JFrame too" );
    likeJFrame.setSize( 255, 90 );

    // Add four JLabel objects
    Container contentPane = likeJFrame.getContentPane( );
    contentPane.setLayout( new GridLayout( 3, 1, 4, 4 ) );
    contentPane.add( new JLabel("We three JLabel objects are inside") );
    contentPane.add( new JLabel("an instance of class LikeAJFrame") );
    contentPane.add( new JLabel("that extends javax.swing.JFrame") );

    likeJFrame.show( );
  }
}
```

Output

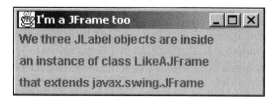

Extending **JFrame**

It probably appears that extending JFrame has no benefit. However, you will soon see its convenience when adding instance variables, methods, and other classes to a class that is like a JFrame. The first relatively simple example of an event-driven program with a GUI represents the approach used in all related examples in this textbook. When implementing such a program, it is recommended that you begin with the following steps:

1. Write a class that extends JFrame.
2. Add a main method that instantiates the class and shows the window.
3. Add instance variables that will be needed by the listener.
4. Add a constructor to initialize the graphical components and lay out the window.

For example, the following class will generate a window with the necessary components. There are no listeners, but all layout issues are completed in the constructor and the class can be "run." The two graphical components that will be needed later are declared here as instance variables since the listener will need them later.

```java
import javax.swing.*;      // JFrame, JTextField and JButton
import java.awt.*;         // Container and GridLayout

public class TimeFrame extends JFrame
{
  public static void main( String[] args )
  {
    JFrame window = new TimeFrame( );
    window.show( );
  }

  // The inner class methods can reference these instance variables
  private JTextField secondsField;
  private JLabel hmsLabel;

  public TimeFrame( )
  {
    // These three messages are sent to the TimeFrame object
    setTitle( "Seconds" );
    setSize( 160, 80 );
    setDefaultCloseOperation( JFrame.EXIT_ON_CLOSE );

    // Ask for the container of the TimeFrame object being constructed
    Container contentPane = getContentPane( );
    contentPane.setLayout( new GridLayout( 2, 2, 4, 4 ) );

    // a) Construct the graphical component that will be listened to
    secondsField = new JTextField( );  // Need this secondsField
                                       // in the inner class

    // b) Add the component to the GUI (the prompt is added first)
    contentPane.add( new JLabel( " Seconds" ) );
    contentPane.add( secondsField );

    // Add the bottom row for output
    contentPane.add( new JLabel( " hr:min:sec" ) );
    hmsLabel = new JLabel( "??:??:??" );  // Need this hmsLabel
                                          // in the inner class
```

```
        contentPane.add( hmsLabel );
    }
}
```

Output

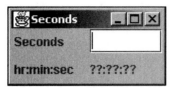

So far, there is only a GUI to look at. The next section describes how to get the event-driven part working.

Self-Check

5-1   Name two methods that the `ExtendedClass` class has.
```
public class ExtendedClass extends JFrame
{
}
```

5-2   Name two methods that the `AnotherExtendedClass` class has.
```
public class AnotherExtendedClass extends BankAccount
{
}
```

5-3   Given the following class that extends `JButton`,
```
import javax.swing.*;

public class DerivedClass extends JButton
{
    public DerivedClass( )
    {
        setText( "Default text" );
    }
}
```
sketch a picture of the window shown when this code runs:
```
JFrame window = new JFrame( );
window.setDefaultCloseOperation( JFrame.EXIT_ON_CLOSE );
window.setSize( 100, 60 );
Container contentPane = window.getContentPane( );
DerivedClass button = new DerivedClass( );
contentPane.add( button );
window.show( );
```

5-4   Write one class to generate the window shown below. No event handling is necessary. However, the `JButton` and the `TextField` should be available to all other methods and classes inside your class. The window is 180-by-80 pixels in a 2-by-1 `GridLayout`. *Note:* This example will be expanded in a subsequent self-check question.

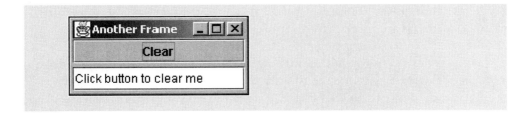

Listeners

One of the unsettled issues from Chapter 4 is that nothing would happen if the user clicked a button or entered input into a text field. To get things done, an object must be enabled to execute the desired code whenever a user of the GUI interacts with graphical components. In Java, when a user interacts with a graphical component, that object sends a message to the object that is "listening." The listener object then performs the actions that represent the appropriate response to the event.

In the case of a user clicking a button or entering text into a text field, the message is `actionPerformed`. Objects that have this `actionPerformed` method can be made to listen to buttons and text fields. Here is the method heading that is required by Java:

```
/** From the ActionListener interface
 *
 * The method you must implement to get code to respond to
 * button clicks and user input into text fields.
 */
public void actionPerformed( ActionEvent e );
```

Once everything is correct, `actionPerformed` messages are sent to any object that is made to listen to a user interacting with a graphical component. To accomplish this, Java requires that you register objects to listen to graphical components. The method to do this for `JButton` and `JTextField` objects is named `addActionListener`. Here is documentation for the message that must be sent to the graphical component so it knows which objects are listening:

```
/** From the JButton and JTextField classes
 *
 * This JButton method registers an object to listen. aListener must
 * be an instance of a class that implements the ActionListener
 * interface. After this message registers the listener,
 * actionPerformed messages can be sent so there is a response to the
 * user interaction.
 */
public void addActionListener( ActionListener aListener )
```

The argument passed to the parameter aListener is the object that will receive an `actionPerformed` message. Therefore, this argument must be an

`ActionListener` object. However, there is no `ActionListener` class. You must write a class that is appropriate for your own application. Java's event model requires that listener objects implement the `ActionListener` interface.

Java does this to ensure that later on, when the graphical component sends an `actionPerformed` message to the listener, the `ActionListener` object understands the `actionPerformed` message. This avoids runtime errors, which are difficult to detect. With this design—the `ActionListener` parameter required—a problem is more likely to be revealed as a compiletime error, which is easier to deal with. This is part of the overhead to get event-driven programming to work in Java. The objects that listen to buttons and text fields must be instances of a class that implement Java's `ActionListener` interface.

As was said in Chapter 4, when implementing an interface, you need to add `implements` *SomeInterfaceName* to the class heading, retype the method heading(s) of the interface, and implement the method(s) in an appropriate manner. Before looking at the class that implements `ActionListener`, consider the steps required in the "Seconds" example to make one object listen to a graphical component. Here is the code for the objects and messages required to register a listener object in this example. The graphical component can later send `actionPerformed` messages to the correct object.

```
// a) Construct the graphical component that will be listened to
secondsField = new JTextField( ); // Needed by the inner class

// b) Add the component to the GUI with a prompt added first
contentPane.add( new JLabel( " Seconds" ) );
contentPane.add( secondsField );

// c) Construct an instance of a class with actionPerformed
SecondsFieldListener inputListener = new SecondsFieldListener( );

// d) Register an object to listen to the text field
secondsField.addActionListener( inputListener );
```

With this code, when the user enters text into `secondsField`, the `secondsField` object sends an `actionPerformed` message to `inputListener`. This `actionPerformed` method must be in a class that implements `ActionListener`.

Having a Class Implement `ActionListener`

One thing still missing is the inner class named `SecondsFieldListener`. An instance of `SecondsFieldListener` must be assigned to the `ActionListener` parameter of the `addActionListener` method. This means that the listener class must implement the `ActionListener` interface. This demand in turn demands that the class have the `actionPerformed` method. It is in this `actionPerformed` method where you must write the code you want to be executed whenever the button is clicked. The class begins like this:

```
class SecondsFieldListener implements ActionListener
{ ...
}
```

With the Java keyword `implements` and the interface name `ActionListener`, this class will not compile until you implement the `actionPerformed` method. The `actionPerformed` method must have the same method heading as specified in Java's `ActionListener` interface. The next steps are to add the method specified in the interface and to replace the semicolon (`;`) at the end with a pair of curly braces. An additional import is needed for the `ActionListener` interface and the `ActionEvent` class.

```
import java.awt.event.*;   // For the ActionListener interface
                           // and the ActionEvent class

class SecondsFieldListener implements ActionListener
{

   public void actionPerformed( ActionEvent anActionEvent )
   {
   // Write the code that should execute when
   // the user interacts with the text field
   }
}
```

The code that is written between the curly braces in `actionPerformed` is the code that will execute each time the user enters text into the text field labeled Seconds.[1] The GUI is repeated here for your convenience:

Using an Inner Class (it is convenient)

Because the code in `actionPerformed` needs access to the text field for input and the `JLabel` for output, the `ActionListener` class just started will be implemented as an inner class. An **inner class** is an entire class that is implemented inside another class. An inner class has access to the private instance variables of the enclosing class. For example, with the `SecondsFieldListener` class implemented inside the `TimeFrame` class, the `actionPerformed` method has access to the `JTextField` to get the user input. This technique is typical of Java programs when

---

1. Athough the method heading requires an `ActionEvent` parameter, you are not required to use this parameter anywhere in your code.

a listener object needs access to several objects in a `JFrame`.[2] This inner class is private since no one else needs it.

```
private class SecondsFieldListener implements ActionListener
{
  private DecimalFormat formatter;

  public SecondsFieldListener( )
  {
    formatter = new DecimalFormat( "00" );
  }

  public void actionPerformed( ActionEvent e )
  {
    // TBA
  }
}
```

In this particular example, integer output will be formatted with leading zeros if necessary; so this inner class will have an instance of `DecimalFormat` to help it do its job. The constructor specifies that format messages will always show two digits.

The next step is to write the code that will execute each time the user enters input into the text field. However, before completing the required `actionPerformed` method, first consider three useful methods that will be needed for `actionPerformed` to accomplish its tasks.

getText, setText, and parseInt

Since the `actionPerformed` method of the inner class can references `textEditor`, text is available from the `JTextField` object. This is accomplished through the `getText` method of `JTextField`. A `getText` message returns the text in a `JTextField` as a `String`. This is a different way to obtain user input. When the user presses the Enter key, `getText` "reads" the `String` from the text field.

```
/** From the JTextField and JLabel classes
  *
  * Return the String that is part of a JLabel or JTextField object
  */
  public String getText( )
```

For example, the following message prints the `String` stored in `aTextField`:

```
JTextField aTextField = new JTextField( "A String" );
System.out.println( aTextField.getText( ) );
```

---

2. Java has anonymous inner classes (no class heading is necessary) for this purpose, but they require more syntax. Anonymous inner classes are not covered in this textbook. Private inner classes are used instead.

Output

```
A String
```

A `setText` message changes the text in a `JTextField` (or `JLabel`) to the `String` argument.

```
/** From the JTextField and JLabel classes
  *
  * Change the String of a JLabel or JTextField to the argument
  * passed to the parameter text
  */
  public void setText( String text )
```

For example, the following messages show how to change a `JTextField`:

```
JLabel aLabel = new JLabel( "I know setText and getText too!" );
System.out.println( aLabel.getText( ) );
aLabel.setText( "Changed String in a JLabel" );
System.out.println( aLabel.getText( ) );
```

Output

```
I know setText and getText too!
Changed String in a JLabel
```

This problem—repeatedly converting seconds to hours, minutes, and seconds—also requires quotient/remainder division to get integer values. Therefore, the `String` in `JTextField` needs to be converted from a `String` to a primitive `int` value. Java has a class named `Integer` with a `static` method named `parseInt`. The `parseInt` method takes a `String` argument and tries to convert it into the integer that the `String` represents. A `parseInt` message throws an exception whenever the `String` argument does not represent a valid integer (`"1oo"` and `"1.0"` are invalid `int`s, for example). The following code demonstrates the behavior of `parseInt`:

```
// Since the Integer class is in the java.lang
// package, no extra import is necessary
String numberAsString;
int number;

numberAsString = "123";
number = Integer.parseInt( numberAsString );  // Stores the int 123
System.out.println( number );

numberAsString = "-9";
number = Integer.parseInt( numberAsString );  // Stores the int -9
System.out.println( number );

numberAsString = "32oo";  // "32oo" is not a valid number
// Throws an exception and terminates the program
number = Integer.parseInt( numberAsString );
// This number won't get printed
System.out.println( number );
```

Output

```
123
-9
Exception in thread "main" java.lang.NumberFormatException: 32oo
        at java.lang.Integer.parseInt(Integer.java:414)
        at java.lang.Integer.parseInt(Integer.java:454)
```

Now that three new methods have been introduced, the `actionPerformed`
method can be completed.

Writing the `actionPerformed` Method

These three methods are now put to use in the `actionPerformed` method. Recall
that since this method is part of an inner class, it has access to the instance variables of the enclosing class. It needs the `JTextField` object referenced by
`secondsField` to obtain the user's input. It also needs the `JLabel` referenced by
`hmsLabel` to show the result of converting seconds into hours, minutes, and
seconds. Here is the finished version of the `actionPerformed` method.

```
public void actionPerformed( ActionEvent e )
{
  // Get the seconds
  String intAsString = secondsField.getText( );
  int total = Integer.parseInt( intAsString );

  // If an exception is thrown on bad input, this method
  // terminates. Compute the hours, minutes, and seconds.
  int hours = total / 3600;
  int minutes = total % 3600 / 60 ;
  int seconds = total % 60;

  // Format the output with leading zeros and colons
  String answer = formatter.format( hours ) + ":" +
                  formatter.format( minutes ) + ":" +
                  formatter.format( seconds );

  // Update the output label
  hmsLabel.setText( answer );
}
```

One final step is now required to get all of this to work. An instance of this inner
class must be registered to listen to the text field in which the user is continuously
invited to enter input.

Registering the Listener to the Graphical Component

The constructor in `TimeFrame` registers an instance of this class as follows:

```
// c) Construct an instance of a class with actionPerformed
SecondsFieldListener inputListener = new SecondsFieldListener( );
```

```
// d) Register an object to listen to the graphical component
secondsField.addActionListener( inputListener );
```

Now when a user enters input into `secondsField`, the `actionPerformed` method of the inner class executes (see page 205 for one sample dialogue). This occurs because Java has done the work of ensuring that user input into `JTextField` sends an `actionPerformed` message to all registered listeners (in this example there is only one registered listener).

The instance of the `SecondsFieldListener` class is guaranteed to have the `actionPerformed` method. Java enforced this through the `addActionListener` method, which requires an `ActionListener` parameter. The method heading indicates that each listener argument needs to be an instance of a class that implements the `ActionListener` interface.

```
// This message requires a class that implements ActionListener
public void addActionListener( ActionListener aListener )
```

Self-Check

5-5 To your answer to Self-Check 5-4, add an inner class named `ButtonListener` that can be instantiated to listen to the `JButton` with the text **Clear**. The `actionPerformed` method must change the text in the text field to the empty `String` `""`. *Note:* No constructor is necessary. Assume that the following import has already been written.
`import java.awt.event.*;` `// For ActionListener and ActionEvent`
The window is repeated here for your convenience:

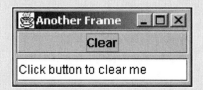

5-6 Write the code that would be at the end of the constructor that ensures that when the button **Clear** is clicked, the `actionPerformed` method of the class for Self-Check 5-5 executes. In other words, the empty `String` `""` must be in the text field.

5-7 To your answer to Self-Check 5-4, add an inner class named `TextFieldListener` that can be instantiated to listen to the text field with the text "Click button to clear me." The `actionPerformed` method must change the text in the button to whatever this text field contains (it may be the empty `String` `""`). *Note:* No constructor is necessary.

5-8   Write the code to ensure that when the text field is clicked, the `actionPerformed` method of Self-Check 5-7 is executed.

5-9   Answer questions a, b, and c, written as comments in the code below.

```
import javax.swing.*;
import java.awt.event.*;
import java.text.DecimalFormat;

public class ScopeRules extends JFrame
{
   private JTextField fieldOne;
   private JTextField fieldTwo;
   private DecimalFormat formatter;

   public ScopeRules( )
   {
// a) Which instance variables can ScopeRules reference?
   }

   private class FieldOneListener implements ActionListener
   {
     private TextField anotherField;

     public void actionPerformed( ActionEvent e )
     {
// b) Which instance variables can this
// actionPerformed method reference?
     }
   }

   private class FieldTwoListener implements ActionListener
   {
     private TextField yetAnotherField;

     public void actionPerformed( ActionEvent e )
     {
// c) Which instance variables can this
// actionPerformed method reference?
     }
   }
}
```

5.2   Another Event-Driven GUI Example

This next example of an event-driven GUI will maintain the balance of one `BankAccount`. Clicking on the Withdraw button will credit the balance by the amount in the Amount text field. Clicking on the Deposit button will debit the balance by the amount in the Amount text field. If the ID is `"OneAccount"` and the initial balance is $1,000.00, the startup window looks like this:

After each withdrawal or deposit, the text field should be set back to `""`. Here is the window when the user enters 20.20 in the Amount field, immediately before and just after the user clicks the Withdraw button:

When writing an event-driven program with a graphical user interface, it is recommended that you first build the window with the desired graphical components. If the window is not already designed, draw a picture with pencil and paper to determine what components are needed. If you cannot lay out the components using BorderLayout, consider changing the layout manager. This example uses the GridLayout object presented in Chapter 3. In fact, all examples in this textbook will use GridLayout exclusively.

   Here is a class that builds and shows the GUI above (there are no ActionListeners yet). As in the previous example, this class will extend JFrame and do the layout in the constructor (it will also have an inner class).

```java
import javax.swing.*;   // JButton, JLabel, and JTextField
import java.awt.*;      // Container and BorderLayout

public class OneAccountFrame extends JFrame
{
  public static void main( String[] args )
  {
    OneAccountFrame accountFrame = new OneAccountFrame( );
    accountFrame.show( );
  }

  // Instance variables that will be needed by the listeners
  private JTextField amountField;
  private JButton withdrawButton;
  private JButton depositButton;
```

```
  private BankAccount oneAccount;
  private JLabel balanceLabel;

  public OneAccountFrame( )
  {
    setTitle( "One Account" );
    setSize( 200, 100 );
    setDefaultCloseOperation( JFrame.EXIT_ON_CLOSE );
    Container contentPane = getContentPane( );
    contentPane.setLayout( new GridLayout( 3, 2, 8, 4 ) );

    // Construct components referenced by the inner classes
    amountField = new JTextField( 6 );
    withdrawButton = new JButton( "Withdraw" );
    depositButton = new JButton( "Deposit" );

    // This is the object to be modified by two different listeners
    oneAccount = new BankAccount( "OneAccount", 1000.00 );
    // Enter a balance just to get things started
    balanceLabel = new JLabel( "$1000.00" );

    // Add the components
    contentPane.add( new JLabel( " Amount" ) );
    contentPane.add( amountField );
    contentPane.add( withdrawButton );
    contentPane.add( depositButton );
    contentPane.add( new JLabel( " Balance" ) );
    contentPane.add( balanceLabel );

    // TBA: Register listeners to the button they will listen to.
    //      They both will need three objects constructed above.
  }
}
```

At this point, the GUI has been laid out in the requested fashion. Now it is time to write the listener classes. These listener classes will use a new method similar to parseInt. The parseDouble method from the Double class will be used to convert the String entered into the text field labeled with **Amount**.

```
/** From the Double class
  *
  * Return a floating-point number represented by the String argument.
  * If numberAsString does not represent a valid number, this method
  * will throw a number format exception.
  */
public static double parseDouble( String numberAsString )
                                 throws NumberFormatException
```

If the String argument does not represent a valid floating-point number or the argument is the empty String "", parseDouble will throw an exception. Here are some examples of how parseDouble can be used with a JTextField and its getText and setText methods.

```
// Since the Double class is in java.lang, no import is necessary
JTextField amountField = new JTextField( "123.45" );
String numberAsString = amountField.getText( );
double amount = Double.parseDouble( numberAsString );
System.out.println( "Amount: " + amount );

amountField.setText( "123" );
numberAsString = amountField.getText( );
amount = Double.parseDouble( numberAsString );
System.out.println( "Amount: " + amount );

amountField.setText( "1oo" );
numberAsString = amountField.getText( );
amount = Double.parseDouble( numberAsString );
System.out.println( "Amount: " + amount );
```

Output

```
Amount: 123.45
Amount: 123.0
Exception in thread "main" java.lang.NumberFormatException: 1oo
   at java.lang.FloatingDecimal.readJavaFormatString
   at java.lang.Double.parseDouble(Double.java:184)
   at A.main(A.java:22)
```

The first two Strings from the JTextField are converted. The third String
argument to parseDouble ("1oo") terminates the program with a
NumberFormatException.

The NumberFormat Class and getCurrencyInstance

In this example, the account balance will be formatted using the NumberFormat
class in the java.text package. This is used to get an object that formats numbers
into the currency for the country the system is set for. NumberFormat's static
method (no object required) getCurrencyInstance returns an object with a
format method. Later on, a format message will take a number and return a
String that is formatted in the local currency format. The following code generates the output to the right, in the United States at least. (In Germany, the output
would have commas for decimals and decimals for commas, as in 1.234,56.)

```
// The NumberFormat class is in the package java.text
// --this import is required:
// import java.text.NumberFormat;

NumberFormat currencyFormat;
currencyFormat = NumberFormat.getCurrencyInstance( );

System.out.println( currencyFormat.format( 0 ) );
System.out.println( currencyFormat.format( 12.0 ) );
System.out.println( currencyFormat.format( 123.4 ) );
```

```
System.out.println( currencyFormat.format( 123.456 ) );
System.out.println( currencyFormat.format( 123456 ) );
// Wrap -money in ( )
System.out.println( currencyFormat.format( -1 ) );
```

Output

```
$0.00
$12.00
$123.40
$123.46
$123,456.00
($1.00)
```

The listeners will use the two new methods `parseDouble` and `format` along with `getText` and `setText`.

WithdrawListener

One `ActionListener` object will be responsible for withdrawing, and a different `ActionListener` object will handle deposits. This means that both `ActionListener` objects need the user input from `amountField`. The `ActionListener` objects will also update the `balanceLabel`, so they will both need a reference to `balanceLabel`. And since both listeners will be updating the single `BankAccount` object, they will also both need a reference to the `BankAccount`. All of these instance variables will be available to both listeners if they are written as inner classes. Additionally, since both listeners will need a way to format the updated balances after withdrawals and deposits, this new instance variable is added:

```
private NumberFormat currencyFormatter;
```

It is initialized in the constructor as follows:

```
currencyFormatter = NumberFormat.getCurrencyInstance( );
```

Here is the `WithdrawListener` class that can be treated as if it were an `ActionListener` because it implements the `ActionListener` interface (need to import `java.awt.event.*;`). The class heading and some instance variable are here as reminders that this is an inner class with access to the enclosing class's instance variables.

```
public class OneAccountFrame extends JFrame
{
  // ...

  // Instance variables that will be needed by the listeners
  private JTextField amountField;

  // ...
```

```
private BankAccount oneAccount;
private JLabel balanceLabel;

// ...

// An inner class with access to instance variables
private class WithdrawListener implements ActionListener
{
  public void actionPerformed( ActionEvent evt )
  {
    // Withdraw the amount of money entered into theAmountField,
    // set theAmountField to "", and, finally, update
    // theBalanceLabel to show the state of theAccount.
    String input = amountField.getText( );
    double withdrawalAmount = Double.parseDouble( input );
    oneAccount.withdraw( withdrawalAmount );
    amountField.setText( "" );
    String moneyAsString =
                currencyFormatter.format( oneAccount.getBalance( ) );
    balanceLabel.setText( moneyAsString );
  }
}
```

An instance of `WithdrawListener` can be made to listen to the Withdraw button with the following code:

```
// Register an instance of the inner class to listen to withdrawButton
WithdrawListener withdrawListener = new WithdrawListener( );
withdrawButton.addActionListener( withdrawListener );
```

Implementing the `DepositListener` class to handle deposits in the same manner is left as a Self-Check question.

Self-Check

5-10 Write the code necessary to change `amountField` to store a `String` that represents a value that is six percent more than the prior `amountField`. Format the value in the local currency. At the end of the code, a `getText` message to `amountField` should return the `String` `"$212.00"` if in the United States.

```
JTextField amountField = new JTextField( "200" );
```

5-11 To the `OneAccountFrame` class add the inner `DepositListener` class so its `actionPerformed` method deposits the amount from the `amountField` into the single `BankAccount`. The `actionPerformed` method must also set the `amountField` to `""` and update the `balanceLabel` to show the modified state of the `BankAccount`.

5-12 Write the code that registers an instance of `DepositListener` to listen to `depositButton`.

5-13 Add the necessary code after a), b), and c) so that when a user clicks the **Swap** button, the strings are switched in the text fields.

GUI at Startup   **GUI after the Swap Button**
                                                           Is Clicked Once

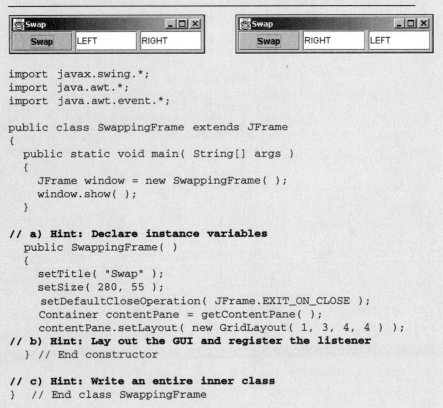

```
import javax.swing.*;
import java.awt.*;
import java.awt.event.*;

public class SwappingFrame extends JFrame
{
   public static void main( String[] args )
   {
      JFrame window = new SwappingFrame( );
      window.show( );
   }

// a) Hint: Declare instance variables
   public SwappingFrame( )
   {
      setTitle( "Swap" );
      setSize( 280, 55 );
      setDefaultCloseOperation( JFrame.EXIT_ON_CLOSE );
      Container contentPane = getContentPane( );
      contentPane.setLayout( new GridLayout( 1, 3, 4, 4 ) );
// b) Hint: Lay out the GUI and register the listener
   } // End constructor

// c) Hint: Write an entire inner class
} // End class SwappingFrame
```

5.3   BankTeller_Ch5 — Adding Listeners

It is now time to have something actually happen when a user interacts with the GUI of the bank teller system. This section describes how to get the system to withdraw and deposit money from one BankAccount. The system will also allow users to see all of the transactions recorded during a session. The first goal of this section is to have the startup window show one particular account with the ID "OneAccount" and a balance of 1000.00 (as in the left window below). When a user enters a valid withdrawal amount (150.00, for example) and a deposit amount (456.78, for example) the BankAccount will change. Two transactions will be recorded. The withdraw text field will be cleared and the balance label updated each time (as in the right window below).

Now if the user clicked the XPress 10 button, the two transactions would show up in a dialog box that captured both the deposit and withdrawal transactions. The appearance of this dialog box will be improved in Chapter 7. Right now, this is how it looks (the graphic has been reduced to fit):

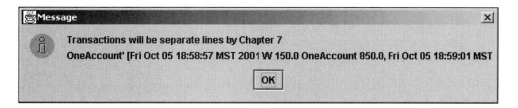

The code for the bank teller case study is only to the point where some graphical components display in a window. Nothing happens when a withdrawal or deposit amount is entered. A main method instantiates a JFrame object, sets characteristics such as the JFrame's size, and adds 10 graphical components. The main method was quite large. Now consider changes that will have the BankTeller_Ch5 class (below) inherit from the JFrame class. Much of what was done outside the class will now be done inside the constructor. Remember, constructors initialize objects to some desired initial state. In this case, the desired state is to have the window be a certain size with 10 graphical components.

```
// This class is being modified in each chapter to reflect progression
// towards a major class in the final solution of a bank teller.

import javax.swing.JFrame;
import javax.swing.JLabel;
import javax.swing.JTextField;
import javax.swing.JButton;
import java.awt.Container;
import java.awt.GridLayout;

public class BankTeller_Ch5 extends JFrame
{
```

```java
// With the main method, this class can run as a program
public static void main( String[] args )
{
   BankTeller_Ch5 tellerWindow = new BankTeller_Ch5( );
   tellerWindow.show( );
}

// Instance variables
private JTextField newAccountField;
private JTextField withdrawField;
private JTextField depositField;
private JButton XPress10Button;
private JLabel balanceLabel;

// Constructor
public BankTeller_Ch5( )
{
   // 'this' references the instance of the class being constructed
   this.setTitle( "Bank Teller" );
   this.setSize( 210,160 );
    this.setDefaultCloseOperation( JFrame.EXIT_ON_CLOSE );

   Container contentPane = this.getContentPane( );
   contentPane.setLayout( new GridLayout( 5, 2, 8, 4 ) );

   // Let the human bank teller enter new account IDs
   contentPane.add( new JLabel( "  Account ID" ) );
   newAccountField = new JTextField( );
   contentPane.add( newAccountField );

   // Let the human bank teller enter a new withdrawal amount
   contentPane.add( new JLabel( "  Withdraw" ) );
   withdrawField = new JTextField( );
   contentPane.add( withdrawField );

   // Let the human bank teller enter a new deposit amount
   contentPane.add( new JLabel( "  Deposit" ) );
   depositField = new JTextField( );
   contentPane.add( depositField );

   // Let the human bank teller view the number of transactions
   contentPane.add( new JLabel( "  Transactions" ) );
   XPress10Button = new JButton( "XPress 10" );
   contentPane.add( XPress10Button );

   // Let the human bank teller see the balance of an account
   contentPane.add( new JLabel( "  Balance" ) );
   balanceLabel = new JLabel( "???.??" );
   contentPane.add( balanceLabel );
}
}
```

With these changes, the same window that was shown earlier still appears. However, the constructor now does most of the work. This class still has a main method, so after it is compiled it can be run.

The Implicit Parameter this

The constructor shown above has several messages that are sent to this (setSize, for example). In Java, the keyword **this** is a reference variable that allows an object to refer to itself. The constructor above sends messages to the BankTeller_Ch5 object that is being constructed. When this is the receiver of a message, an object is calling its own methods or the methods of the class that it extends.

Because an object sends messages to itself so frequently, Java provides a shortcut. The object name and dot are not necessary before the method name. Whereas the keyword this is sometimes required, this was not necessary in the example above. It was included to clarify the receiver of the message, which is the instance of the class being constructed. For example, the following code omits this and is equivalent to the first four messages of the constructor above:

```java
public BankTeller_Ch5( )
{
  // 'this.' is not necessary (but may be used)
  setTitle( "Bank Teller" );
  setSize( 220, 220 );
  setDefaultCloseOperation( JFrame.EXIT_ON_CLOSE );

  Container contentPane = getContentPane( );
    . . .
```

The code examples in this textbook will opt for the shortcut unless it is necessary to use this to accomplish a task. There are two times when this must be used later in this textbook:

1. To override the equals method in Chapter 6
2. To have a JFrame listen to itself in Chapter 9

Managing One BankAccount

At first, only one BankAccount will be maintained in the bank teller system. The class that extends JFrame will now store a reference to that one account. Later on, there will be a collection of accounts and currentAccount will be changed as each new bank customer arrives at the teller window. But for now, one account will do. The system will also attempt to display the current balance of this one account in the local currency format. This means that there will be some new imports and new instance variables.

```
// New import needed
import java.text.NumberFormat;

public class BankTeller_Ch5
{
    // Many BankTeller_Ch5 details are not shown here
    // to save space. Add these instance variables.
    private NumberFormat currencyFormat;
    private BankAccount currentAccount;
```

The constructor is expanded to accomplish the following tasks:

- Initialize the `currentAccount`.
- Construct an object to format the balance in the local currency.
- Add an `ActionListener` object to respond when the user inputs text into the `withdrawField`.

```
public class BankTeller_Ch5 extends JFrame
{
    // ... code omitted to save space ...

    // The constructor
    public BankTeller_Ch5( )
    {

        // Allow withdrawals and deposits on this one BankAccount object
        currentAccount = new BankAccount( "OneAccount", 1000.00 );
        // Get an object to format the currency amount in balanceLabel
        currencyFormat = NumberFormat.getCurrencyInstance( );

        // And then show the status of the currentAccount to the user
        newAccountField.setText( currentAccount.getID( ) );
        String balanceAsString =
                    currencyFormat.format( currentAccount.getBalance( ) );
        balanceLabel.setText( balanceAsString );

        // Register a listener object to the withdraw text field
        WithdrawListener withdrawListener = new WithdrawListener( );
        withdrawField.addActionListener( withdrawListener );

        // More to do later
    }
```

`WithdrawListener` will be implemented as an inner class. Recall that an inner class is an entire class that is implemented inside another class. The inner class's methods can access the private instance variables of the enclosing class. So when `WithdrawListener` is implemented as an inner class, the `actionPerformed` method of `WithdrawListener` will already have access to two of the things it needs—`withdrawField` and `balanceLabel`. Here is an outline of the `BankTeller_Ch5` class that has this inner class:

```
// Just an outline to show that an inner class will be added

public class BankTeller_Ch5 extends JFrame
{
  private NumberFormat currencyFormat;
  private BankAccount currentAccount;
  // ...

  public BankTeller_Ch5( )
  {
    // Enclosing class constructor
  }

  /////////////////////////// BEGIN INNER CLASS ////////////////////////
  // This inner class has access to the enclosing class's instance
  // variables balanceLabel and withdrawField
  private class WithdrawListener implements ActionListener
  {

    public void actionPerformed( ActionEvent evt )
    {
    } // End actionPerformed

  } // End class WithdrawListener
  /////////////////////////// END INNER CLASS ////////////////////////

} // End class BankTeller_Ch5
```

Now that the structure is laid out, the `actionPerfomed` method can be implemented. When a user enters a string into the text field, this new object's `actionPerfomed` method will do several things to process the withdrawal. Here is the algorithm:

1. Get the text from the withdraw text field (a `String`).
2. Convert that `String` into a number (do not error-check yet).
3. Make a withdrawal.

This new inner class can now be shown in the context of the `BankTeller_Ch5` class. Since no additional data is needed by the inner class `WithdrawListener`, it does not need any new instance variables. Therefore, no constructor is needed (whereas most classes have one or more constructors, listener classes declared inside a class do not typically need one). In a case like this, Java gives the class a default constructor—a constructor with no parameters. This allows an instance of the inner class to be constructed as follows:

```
WithdrawListener withdrawListener = new WithdrawListener( );
```

Here is the entire inner class. Assume that it is in an enclosing class that has the needed instance variables.

```
 // ... code omitted to save space ...

public class BankTeller_Ch5 extends JFrame
{
  // ... code omitted to save space ...

  public BankTeller_Ch5( )
  {
     // ... code omitted to save space ...

    // Register a listener object to the withdraw text field
    WithdrawListener withdrawListener = new WithdrawListener( );
    withdrawField.addActionListener( withdrawListener );
  }

  // This class exists inside the BankTeller_Ch5 class. No instance
  // variable or constructors are needed for this listener. It has
  // access to the needed instance variables from the enclosing class:
  //
  //    1) withdrawField
  //    2) balanceLabel
  //    3) currentAccount
  //
  private class WithdrawListener implements ActionListener
  {
    // This method executes when users enter Strings into withdrawField
    public void actionPerformed( ActionEvent evt )
    {
      // Get the user input
      String numberAsString = withdrawField.getText( );

      // Now try to convert the text into a valid number
      double amount = Double.parseDouble( numberAsString );

      // Do the transaction
      currentAccount.withdraw( amount );

      // Record a transaction and add it to the list of transactions
      Transaction aTransaction = new Transaction( currentAccount,
                                                  amount,
                                                  Transaction.WITHDRAW_CODE );
      transactionList.add( aTransaction );

      // Clear the correct field
      withdrawField.setText( "" );

      // Update the label field
      String balanceAsString =
                 currencyFormat.format( currentAccount.getBalance( ) );
      balanceLabel.setText( balanceAsString );

    } // End actionPerformed
  } // End class WithdrawListener

} // End class BankTeller_Ch5
```

This same approach and much of the same code is used to implement an `ActionListener` that responds to user input into `depositField`. The private inner class `DepositListener` and the `addActionListener` message are not shown here. You can see the code in `BankTeller_Ch5.java` from the accompanying diskette.

XPress10Button and JOptionPane

All transactions for `CurrentAccount` can now be added to the `ArrayList` instance variable. The list will then be shown in a graphical manner. When a user of `BankTeller` clicks the `XPress10Button` labeled "XPress 10," the system will display a list of all withdrawal and deposit transactions recorded during the session. To do this, the `JOptionPane` class will be used.

The `toString` version of the transaction list will be displayed in a graphical manner with Java's `JOptionPane` class. `JOptionPane` is from the `javax.swing` package—the same package as `JTextField` and `JFrame`. `JOptionPane` has several `static` methods (require no objects, like the `Math` functions such as `round` and `sqrt`) for displaying and obtaining information. These methods generate a modal dialog box.

A **modal** dialog box is a graphical component that must be closed before the current running application can continue. A `JOptionPane` message is an effective way to get someone's attention. The `JOptionPane` methods are a quick and easy way to display error messages and information boxes.

The `showMessageDialog` method name is invoked by preceding it with the class name (not an object name). The first argument determines the position on the screen where the modal dialog box appears. If the first argument is a `JFrame` object, the dialog box appears centered over the `JFrame`. If the first argument is `null`, the dialog box is positioned in the center of the computer screen.

To demonstrate, consider the following method call to show the `ArrayList` of `Transactions`. This code is in the `actionPerformed` method of the `XPress10Button` listener:

```
JOptionPane.showMessageDialog( null, transactionList.toString( ) );
```

The XPress 10 feature can now be implemented in a limited way. The user will be able to see all withdrawal transactions. The window will eventually appear like the one shown below after the user has made one withdrawal of 150.00 from `CurrentAccount` (which has an initial balance of 1000) on October 5, 2001, and the clicked the XPress 10 button. The appearance will be improved later to show transactions from the most recent to the oldest and to show no more than 10 transactions.

Interface after Three Withdrawals and Changes to `Transaction` That Occur Later

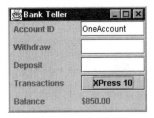
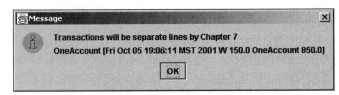

A `JOptionPane` dialog box requires that the user click the OK button to return control back to the bank teller system (pressing the Enter key would also work). To add the above functionality to the bank teller system, `BankTeller_Ch5` now has an `ArrayList` instance variable to store all transactions for the one account.

```
// New import
import java.util.ArrayList;

public class BankTeller_Ch5_WithTransactionList extends JFrame
{
    // Instance variable
    private ArrayList transactionList;
```

Another `ActionListener` will be added to the `JFrame` to listen to the XPress 10 button and to register the new listener. The `JFrame` constructor will also construct an empty transaction list. Here is the new code to initialize the system:

```
    // Code to maintain the transaction list and register a listener.
    transactionList = new ArrayList( );

    // Register a listener to the XPress 10 button
    TransactionButtonListener express10Listener =
                                    new TransactionButtonListener( );
    XPress10Button.addActionListener( express10Listener );
} // End constructor
```

The new `ActionListener` class is added as another inner class. The `actionPerformed` method simply uses `JOptionPane` to show the `toString` version of `transactionList`.

```
// This inner class exists inside the BankTeller_Ch5 class.
// No instance variables or constructors are needed for this listener.
// This class has access to the needed instance variables
// from the enclosing class. This actionPerformed method
// executes when the XPress 10 button is clicked.
private class TransactionButtonListener implements ActionListener
{
    public void actionPerformed( ActionEvent evt )
    {
```

```
    // Show all transactions as recorded. First create a big String.
    String message = "Transactions will be separate lines by Chapter 7\n"
                        + currentAccount.getID( ) + " "
                        + transactionList.toString( ) + "\n";

        // Then show a modal dialog box
        JOptionPane.showMessageDialog( null, message );
    }
} // End class TransactionButtonListener
```

The `actionPerformed` method in `WithdrawListener` now records withdrawal transactions with this added code:

```
// Record a transaction and add it to the list of transactions
Transaction aTransaction = new Transaction( currentAccount,
                                    amount,
                                    Transaction.WITHDRAW_CODE );
transactionList.add( aTransaction );
```

To see the system run with the listeners in place, run the program stored in the file on the accompanying diskette. It is named `BankTeller_Ch5.java`. This file also includes the private inner class `DepositListener` that is not shown in this textbook.

5.4 Polymorphism

To understand polymorphism, take an example of a typical workday in an office. Someone brought in pastries and everyone stood around chatting. When the food was mostly devoured, Jim, the president of the company, invited everyone to "Get back to work." Sue went back to read a new section of a book she was editing. Tom continued laying out the new edition of a book. Stephanie went back to figure out some setting in her word-processing program. Ian finished the company catalog. Jeni met with Jim to discuss a new project. Chris began contacting professors to review a new manuscript. And Krista continued her Web search on whether colleges are using C++ or Java. Rick went back to work on the index of his new book. Eight different behaviors from the same message! The message "Get back to work" is a **polymorphic message**—a message that is understood by many objects (or employees), but responded to with different behaviors by different objects (or employees).

Polymorphism means "many forms." In an object-oriented language, polymorphism occurs when the same message can be sent to different types of objects with different methods being called. The method that executes depends on the type of object that receives the message—one message, *many* methods. Java supports polymorphism through inheritance and interfaces. First consider how the Java interface allows the same message to result in the execution of different methods.

Polymorphism Through the Java Interface

In this chapter alone, the `actionPerformed` method has had many different behaviors. Behind the scenes, `JButton` and `JTextField` objects sent `actionPerformed` messages to the listener objects with those different `actionPerformed` methods. The following example provides insight into what happens behind the scenes when graphical components send polymorphic messages to registered listeners. Consider three small classes that implement the same `interface`. Each has the `actionPerformed` method.

```java
// File name: ListenerOne.java

import java.awt.event.*;

public class ListenerOne implements ActionListener
{
  public void actionPerformed( ActionEvent e )
  { // Display a string to the console
    System.out.println( "One One One" );
  }
}
```

```java
// File name: ListenerTwo.java
import java.awt.event.*;

public class ListenerTwo implements ActionListener
{
  public void actionPerformed( ActionEvent e )
  { // Display a string to the console
    System.out.println( "Two Two Two" );
  }
}
```

```java
// File name: ListenerThree.java
import java.awt.event.*;

public class ListenerThree implements ActionListener
{
  public void actionPerformed( ActionEvent e )
  { // Display a string to the console
    System.out.println( "Three Three Three" );
  }
}
```

To show the same `actionPerformed` message explicitly sent to three types of objects, the following `main` method must first construct an instance of each class. Then the required `ActionEvent` object is constructed. Although not used, an `ActionEvent` object is the required argument to send `actionPerformed` messages. Then the same `actionPerformed` message is sent to all three objects. Three different types of objects understand the same message. Three different methods execute; `actionPerformed` is a polymorphic message.

```
// Construct a window and add some other graphical components to it
import java.awt.event.ActionEvent;   // Need one as an argument
                                     // for actionPerformed
import javax.swing.JButton;          // Helps to construct the ActionEvent
import java.awt.event.*;             // For ActionEvent

public class Polymorphic_actionPerformed
{
  public static void main( String[] args )
  {
    // Construct instances of three classes that
    // can understand the actionPerformed messages
    ActionListener one = new ListenerOne( );
    ActionListener two = new ListenerTwo( );
    ActionListener three = new ListenerThree( );

    // The actionPerformed message needs an ActionEvent
    // argument. Something like a JButton is needed to
    // construct an instance of ActionEvent.
    JButton fakeButton = new JButton( );
    ActionEvent fakeEvent = new ActionEvent( fakeButton, 0, "" );

    // Send a polymorphic message to three different types of objects
    one.actionPerformed( fakeEvent );
    two.actionPerformed( fakeEvent );
    three.actionPerformed( fakeEvent );
  }
}
```

Output (three different methods execute with a polymorphic message)

```
One One One
Two Two Two
Three Three Three
```

The main method above shows that objects of any class that implement an interface can be assigned to that interface type. In this example, all three classes implement the ActionListener interface. Any ActionListener object can also be assigned to the ActionListener parameter in actionPerformed.

The three listener objects are stored as ActionListener reference variables. However, at runtime, Java is able to distinguish that there are three different types. This makes it possible to have polymorphic messages. When Java recognizes that the ActionListener variable references a ListenerOne object, it calls the ListenerOne actionPerformed message to print One One One. When Java recognizes that the ActionListener variable references a ListenerTwo object, it calls the ListenerTwo actionPerformed message to print Two Two Two. And when Java recognizes that the ActionListener variable references a ListenerThree object, it calls the ListenerThree actionPerformed message to print Three Three Three. The polymorphic message named actionPerformed results in the execution of three different methods.

The listeners in Java are just one example of polymorphism. The same approach is used with other types of listeners, such as those that listen to mouse clicks. Polymorphism is possible through Java interfaces.

Self-Check

5-14   Using the three `ActionListener` classes from this section—`ListenerOne`, `ListenerTwo`, and `ListenerThree`—write the output generated when a user clicks the button in this window:

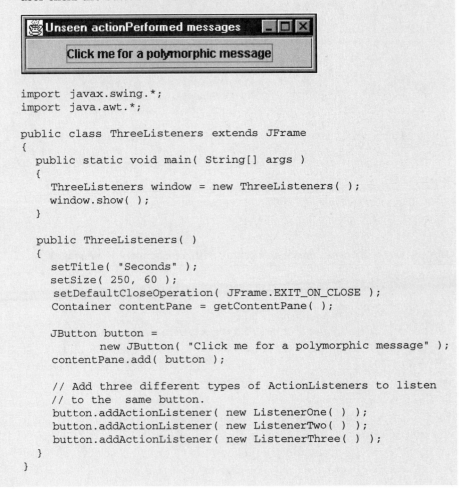

```java
import javax.swing.*;
import java.awt.*;

public class ThreeListeners extends JFrame
{
  public static void main( String[] args )
  {
    ThreeListeners window = new ThreeListeners( );
    window.show( );
  }

  public ThreeListeners( )
  {
    setTitle( "Seconds" );
    setSize( 250, 60 );
    setDefaultCloseOperation( JFrame.EXIT_ON_CLOSE );
    Container contentPane = getContentPane( );

    JButton button =
          new JButton( "Click me for a polymorphic message" );
    contentPane.add( button );

    // Add three different types of ActionListeners to listen
    // to the  same button.
    button.addActionListener( new ListenerOne( ) );
    button.addActionListener( new ListenerTwo( ) );
    button.addActionListener( new ListenerThree( ) );
  }
}
```

Polymorphism Through Inheritance

Polymorphism also happens through inheritance. Consider the polymorphic `toString` message in a program that sends the same `toString` message to

Transaction, BankAccount, and ArrayList objects. The output shows that three
different methods execute.

```
// Demonstrate the polymorphic message toString.
// One message, three methods.
import javax.swing.JLabel;
import java.util.ArrayList;

public class PolymorphicMessage
{
  public static void main( String[] args )
  {
    // Construct three different types of objects
    ArrayList list = new ArrayList( );
    list.add( "first" );
    list.add( "second" );
    BankAccount anAccount = new BankAccount( "Kim", 123.45 );
    double amount = 123.45;
    anAccount.withdraw( amount );
    Transaction aTransaction = new Transaction( anAccount, amount,
                                          Transaction.WITHDRAW_CODE );

    // Send the same toString message to different types of objects
    System.out.println( "ArrayList: " + list.toString( ) );
    System.out.println( "BankAccount: " + anAccount.toString( ) );
    System.out.println( "Transaction: " + aTransaction.toString( ) );
  }
}
```

Output

```
ArrayList: [first, second]
BankAccount: Kim $0.00
Transaction: Sun Oct 07 10:29:33 MST 2001 W 123.45 Kim 0.0
```

This example shows the same message, toString, resulting in three different
behaviors. Three different toString methods are invoked. When the polymorphic
message toString is sent to a Transaction object, the toString method in the
Transaction class executes. When a toString message is sent to a BankAccount
object, the toString method in the BankAccount class executes. When a
toString message is sent to an ArrayList object, the toString method in the
ArrayList class concatenates the toString versions of all elements in the list.

All objects in Java understand the toString message. If a class does not have its
own toString method, the object passes the message along to the Object class.
This is true because all objects inherit from the Object class.

5.5   The Object Class

Java has a class named Object with one constructor and 11 methods, including toString. All classes in Java extend the Object class. Or they extend another class that extends Object. There is no exception to this. This means that all classes inherit the methods of the Object class, one of which is toString.

Java makes sure that all classes extend the Object class because there are several things that all objects must be able to do in order to work with the Java runtime system. The Object class captures methods that are common to all Java objects. For example, Object's constructor helps allocate computer memory for every object. Object has methods to allow different processes to run at the same time. This allows applications such as Web browsers to be more efficient. Java can download several files, while browsing elsewhere, while creating another image, and so on.

The inheritance relationship is stated explicitly in Java by adding the reserved identifier extends to the class heading. For example, the following class heading explicitly states that the EmptyClass class inherits all of the Object class's methods. If a class heading does not have extends, the compiler automatically adds extends Object to it.

```
// This class and all other classes would
// extend Object if extends Object is omitted.
public class EmptyClass extends Object
{
}
```

Even though EmptyClass defines no methods of its own, a programmer could send messages to instances of EmptyClass. This is possible because a class that extends Object inherits (obtains) Object's methods. Here are three of the methods that EmptyClass inherits from the Object class:

Methods of the Object Class

- **getClass** returns the String "class " concatenated with the class name.
- **toString** returns a String that is the class name concatenated with the at symbol (@) and a hexadecimal (base 16) number that typically represents an integer value based on the location (address) of the object in the computer's memory.
- **equals** returns true if both references refer to the same object.

```
// Demonstrate inheritance with a class that extends Object
public class ClassesTheExtendObject
{
  public static void main( String[] args )
  {
    EmptyClass one = new EmptyClass( );       // Output:
    System.out.println( one.getClass( ) );    // class EmptyClass
```

```
        System.out.println( one.toString( ) );    // EmptyClass@111f71
        EmptyClass two = new EmptyClass( );
        System.out.println( two.toString( ) );    // EmptyClass@273d3c

        // Do these two objects refer to the same object?
        System.out.println( one.equals( two ) ); // false

        // Make two reference variables refer to the same object
        one = two;

        // The reference variable one refers to same object as two
        System.out.println( one.equals( two ) ); // true
    }
}
```

Output

```
class EmptyClass
EmptyClass@111f71
EmptyClass@273d3c
false
true
```

The following diagram shows the inheritance relationship between three classes. In Java, all classes inherit the public methods of the Object class. (Figure 5.1 shows only two classes that extend the Object class: String and BankAccount.) A new class can add methods such as those shown in String and BankAccount. A new class can also override—give new meaning to—an inherited method such as toString.

Figure 5.1

The inheritance relationship between classes:

String extends Object
BankAccount extends Object

String and BankAccount inherit the methods of Object (only three are shown). String and BankAccount also add methods (only two are shown). Both String and BankAccount override Object's toString method to provide more appropriate textual representations of their objects.

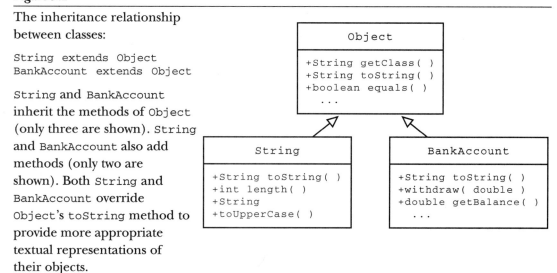

One-way (↑) Assignment Compatibility

Because all classes extend Java's `Object` class, a reference to any type of object can be assigned to an `Object` reference variable. For example, consider the following valid code that assigns a `String` object and a `BankAccount` object to two different reference variables of type `Object`:

```
String aString = new String( "first" );
// Assign a String reference to an Object reference
Object obj1 = aString;

BankAccount anAccount = new BankAccount( "One", 111.11 );
// Assign a BankAccount reference to an Object reference
Object obj2 = anAccount;
```

Java's one-way assignment compatibility means that you can assign a reference variable to the class that it extends. However, you cannot directly assign in the other direction. For example, an `Object` reference cannot be directly assigned to a `String` reference.

```
Object obj = new Object( );
String str = obj;
            ^
Incompatible type for declaration.
Explicit cast needed to convert java.lang.Object to java.lang.String.
```

This compiletime error occurs because the compiler recognizes that `obj` is a reference to an `Object`. An `Object` reference cannot be assigned down to a `String` reference variable.

The standard notation for inheritance uses an arrow to point to the class being extended (see Figure 5.2, above). The arrow also acts as a visual cue to determine the direction of assignment that is allowed. The arrow indicates a one–way, ↑, assignment capability. You can assign a `String` reference up to an `Object` reference.

This one-way assignment capability allows any type of object to be sent to the add method of `ArrayList`. The following method heading shows that the `ArrayList` add method accepts any type of object as an argument. The parameter is `Object`.

```
/** From the ArrayList class
  *
  * Appends element at the end of this ArrayList
  */
 public boolean add( Object element )
```

In much the same way as different types of objects can be assigned to an `ActionListener` parameter in the `addActionListener` method, different types of objects can be arguments to the `Object` parameter in this `ArrayList` add method. This is another example where it is desirable to assign different types of objects to the same type.

Not only can `ArrayList` store a collection of `Strings` or a collection of `BankAccount` references, the `ArrayList` class also allows for a list with different types of objects. Consider the following code that stores references to different types in the same `ArrayList`:

```java
// Show that ArrayList can add any type of object and can
// contain references to different types of objects.
import java.util.ArrayList;

public class PolymorphicArrayList
{
  public static void main( String[] args )
  {
    // Construct a variety of objects
    Object aString = new String( "a string" );
    Object anEmpty = new EmptyClass( );
    Object anAccount = new BankAccount( "Kim", 123.45 );

    // Create a collection that stores references
    // to six different types of objects.
    ArrayList polymorphicList = new ArrayList( );
    polymorphicList.add( aString );
    polymorphicList.add( anEmpty );
    polymorphicList.add( anAccount );
    System.out.println( polymorphicList.toString( ) );
  }
}
```

Output (references to three different types of objects are stored in one `ArrayList`)

```
[a string, EmptyClass@256a7c, Kim $123.45]
```

Now consider trying to retrieve one of three elements from an `ArrayList` of `Strings` named `friendList`.

```java
ArrayList friendList = new ArrayList( );
friendList.add( "Aimee" );
friendList.add( "Bob" );
friendList.add( "Kellen" );
```

It can be done with the `get` method of the `ArrayList` class.

```java
/** From the ArrayList class
  *
  * Returns the element located at the list position specified by index
  */
public Object get( int index )
```

The `get` method returns a reference to the element located at the index supplied as the argument. For example, `friendList.get(0)` returns a reference to the first element in the `ArrayList`—`"Aimee"`. However, to have one class able to store lists of different objects, `ArrayList` stores references to instances of `Object`. It does not store a list of references to any particular class. The alternative would be to have a different list class for each type of object, a `StringList` class, an `AccountList` class, a `GregorianCalendarList` class, and so on. This generality causes a problem. Since `get` returns a reference to an `Object`, the compiler detects incompatible types in the attempt to assign an `Object` to a `String`.

```
TryAList.java:14: incompatible types
found    : java.lang.Object
required: java.lang.String
    String stringInList = friendList.get( 0 );
                                          ^

1 error
```

To avoid this compiletime error, you must perform an explicit cast. Here is the syntax for **casting**: enclose the class name with what you know the class to be in parentheses (`String`) and place it before the reference to the `Object`.

```
String stringInList = (String)friendList.get( 0 );
System.out.println( stringInList.toUpperCase( ) );
```

Output

```
AIMEE
```

This casting is necessary because Java is a strongly typed language. This design decision allows Java to catch more errors at compiletime, as it avoids runtime exceptions, which are much more difficult to deal with. The downside is that your code is more cluttered with this casting syntax.

Casting is also necessary for sending messages to objects from an `ArrayList`. This is because the `Object` class does not know about the new methods added by classes that extend `Object`. All objects in Java inherit `Object`'s `toString`, `getClass`, and `equals` methods. Therefore, all Java objects understand these three messages (and more, actually). However, classes that extend `Object` typically add one or more methods to those inherited from the `Object` class.

Consider what happens when a method is added to a new class named `ClassThatExtendsObject`.

```
public class ClassThatExtendsObject extends Object
{
  public void additionalMethod( )
  {
    System.out.println( "Instances of Object will not know me." );
  }
}
```

This code demonstrates that an instance of this new class understands `additionalMethod`:

```
ClassThatExtendsObject aClassThatExtendsObject =
                                    new ClassThatExtendsObject();
aClassThatExtendsObject.additionalMethod( );
```

Output

```
Instances of Object will not know me.
```

However, consider what happens when you attempt to send an `additionalMethod` message to an instance of `Object`.

```
Object obj = new ClassThatExtendsObject( );
obj.additionalMethod( );
```

Syntax Error

```
CompiletimeError.java:9: cannot resolve symbol
symbol  : method additionalMethod( )
location: class java.lang.Object
    obj.additionalMethod( );
        ^
1 error
```

That is why a cast would be necessary to send messages to objects in an `ArrayList`. The `get` method returns an `Object`. The following code is valid:

```
// get returns an Object. It can be assigned to an Object reference.
Object objectReference = friendList.get( 2 );
```

Consider another, more familiar, example. Even though the `BankAccount` class heading was written without `extends`, it was actually recognized as extending the `Object` class.

```
public class BankAccount
```

If `extends` does not appear in the class heading, the class will extend `Object`. The class heading above is equivalent to the class heading below:

```
public class BankAccount extends Object
```

The methods that were added by the `BankAccount` class, such as `getBalance`, are not understood by the `Object` class. The following code and resulting compiletime error reveals this:

```
ArrayList accountList = new ArrayList( );
BankAccount anAccount = new BankAccount( "Kim", 567.89 );
// It is valid to send a BankAccount argument to an Object parameter
accountList.add( anAccount );
Object objectReference = accountList.get( 0 );
System.out.println( objectReference.getBalance( ) );
```

Error

```
OneWayAssignment.java:15: cannot resolve symbol
symbol  : method getBalance( )
location: class java.lang.Object
System.out.println( objectReference.getBalance( ) );
                                    ^
1 error
```

The compiler sees this as an attempt to send a `getBalance` message to an instance of `Object`. To get past Java's strong-type checking, you have to trust that `accountList` has only references to `BankAccount` objects. Then cast the `Object` reference to a `BankAccount` like this:

```
Object objectReference = accountList.get( 0 );
// Cast Object to the type you know it to be
BankAccount accountInList = (BankAccount)objectReference;
System.out.println( accountInList.getBalance( ) );
```

Output

```
456.78
```

Overriding Methods

Overriding a method in the `Object` class is done by implementing one of `Object`'s methods with the same exact method heading. If class B extends class A, then class B overrides a method by writing A's method heading inside class B and defining the new behavior in class B.

The `toString` method is often overridden. This is done so the state of an object can be better represented textually. Java recommends that each of your classes override this `toString` method.

```
/** From the Object class
 *
 * Return a String that represents the state of this object
 */
public String toString()
```

When a class overrides `toString`, a `toString` message to one of its objects executes the new method rather than `Object`'s `toString`. This is accomplished by writing the `toString` method heading in the new class. Then you create and return a `String` that textually represents the state of your objects. The following example shows how `BankAccount` overrides the `toString` method from the `Object` class.

```
// This simplified version of BankAccount overrides Object's toString
// method to return the account ID and the current balance as a String
import java.text.NumberFormat;

public class BankAccount extends Object
{
  // Instance variables that every BankAccount object will maintain
  private String my_ID;
  private double my_balance;
  private static NumberFormat currencyFormat;
    // ... several methods are not shown here to save space ...

/**
  * Override Object's toString method to provide a peek
  * into the state of this this bank account object.
```

```
 * @return State of this BankAccount using local currency format.
 */
public String toString( )
{
   return my_ID +" " + currencyFormat.format( my_balance );
}
}
```

Now when a toString message is sent to a BankAccount object, the toString
method of BankAccount (above) is executed instead of the toString method
from the Object class.

```
BankAccount b1 = new BankAccount( "BA1", 123.4 );
// BankAccount's toString gets invoked now
System.out.println( b1.toString( ) );
```

Output

```
BA1 $123.40
```

If a toString message is sent to an instance of a class that does not override
toString, the toString message gets passed up the inheritance hierarchy until it
finds a toString method. In the case of ClassThatExtendsObject, the
toString method of Object is invoked.

```
ClassThatExtendsObject obj1 = new ClassThatExtendsObject( );
Object obj2 = new ClassThatExtendsObject( );

// Both Object and ClassThatExtendsObject understand toString messages
System.out.println( obj1.toString( ) );
System.out.println( obj2.toString( ) );
```

Output

```
ClassThatExtendsObject@111f71
ClassThatExtendsObject@273d3c
```

The reason that the above code compiles is that when the compiler does not find
the toString method in ClassThatExtendsObject, it looks for toString in a
class that it extends. The compiler finds the toString method in Object and does
not complain.

All classes inherit the toString method from the Object class unless the class
overrides it. This is why ArrayList can create a toString version of all elements
without error, even if the objects do not override the toString method of the
Object class. Another example of a commonly overridden method will be shown
in Chapter 6, "Selection," when the equals method from the Object class is
overridden to compare the states of two objects rather than the reference values.

Self-Check

5-15 Complete this code, which will deposit 10.00 to both BankAccounts in the list.

```
ArrayList accountList = new ArrayList( );
accountList.add( new BankAccount( "zero", 0.00 ) );
accountList.add( new BankAccount( "one", 1.11 ) );

// Add code to deposit 10.00 to both accounts in accountList

System.out.println( accountList.toString( ) );
```

Once your code is added, the output should look like this:

```
[zero $10.00, one $11.11]
```

5-16 Given two reference variables named obj and str, write "Compiles" if the code will compile or "Error" if there will be a compiletime error.

```
Object obj = new Object( );
String str = new String( );
```

-a obj = str;   **-d** int e = obj.length( );

-b str = obj;   **-e** int f = str.length( );

-c str = (String)obj;   **-f** int g = (String)obj.length( );

5.6   A Few Uses of Inheritance in Java

Here are a few examples you have now seen where inheritance makes programming more manageable.

1. With very little work, you can have a powerful class.
When something like a JFrame was needed, BankTeller_Ch5 extended JFrame. This gave the new class existing methods, such as setSize and setTitle, along with the ability to represent a window that can be moved, iconified, resized, and closed. New instance variables, methods, and even other classes can be added. Inheritance allows programmers to obtain the methods of existing classes to help finish a system in less time.

2. You need only one ArrayList for all types of objects.
All types of objects can be assigned to an Object reference. This allows for one **collection** class such as ArrayList to store different types of objects. Consider the method heading for ArrayList's add method:

```
public boolean add( Object element )
```

Notice that the add method has an Object parameter. This means that references to any type of object can be added to an ArrayList, not just String or BankAccount (this also means that you cannot store int or double because they are primitive values). This is possible because all objects in Java extend the Java class named `Object`. All objects can be sent as arguments to `add`. You can use just one `ArrayList` class to store any collection of objects. There is no need to have a separate collection class for each type of object.

3. You can store different types of objects in the same collection.
Although most lists store the same type of object, there are times when it is appropriate to store different types of objects in the same list. Consider the `Container` object in a `JFrame`. You have now seen it store `JButton`, `JLabel`, and `JTextField` objects at the same time.

4. You can print any `Object` with `toString`.
Inheritance is one feature that distinguishes the object-oriented style of programming. At a minimum, because every class extends `Object`, every class is guaranteed to understand the `toString` message. If a class does not override `toString`, the `toString` method in the `Object` class executes.

5. Inheritance allows for polymorphic messages.
Inheritance is one way to implement polymorphism (Java interfaces are the other way). Polymorphism allows the same message to be sent to different types of objects for behavior that is appropriate to the type of object. Such an example of polymorphism will be demonstrated in Chapter 10, "Designing an Inheritance Hierarchy." The same messages are sent to different types of library items and result in different behaviors. For example, the late fee for an overdue video is computed differently than the late fee for an overdue book.

5.7   Multiple Constructors

Java classes may have many methods with the same name. This includes constructors. You have already seen this with `JFrame`. A `JFrame` object can be constructed with zero arguments and with one `String` argument (to set the `JFrame`'s title).

```
// The title will be the empty String: ""
JFrame aFrame = new JFrame( );

// Set the title to ""
JFrame aFrameWithATitle = new JFrame( "Window's title" );
```

The first constructor is referred to as the default constructor. A **default constructor** is a constructor that takes no arguments. The default constructor of a class initializes the objects by setting instance variables to some reasonable default value.

For example, here are two of the four `JFrame` constructor headings as specified by Java:

```
// Default Constructor
public JFrame( )
```

```
// Another constructor (JFrame actually has 4 constructors)
public JFrame( String title )
```

Other classes that you have seen with **multiple constructors** include String, JButton, and JTextField. Each class has a constructor with no parameters and another constructor that takes a string parameter. For example, JButton has five constructors. Here are three:

```
// Constructs a button with no text or icon
public JButton( )
```

```
// Constructs a button with an icon
public JButton( Icon icon )
```

```
// Constructs a button with text
public JButton( String text )
```

Multiple constructors are allowed because Java distinguishes method headings not only by name, but also by the number and/or type of parameters in the method heading. For example, JButton's default constructor has a different number of arguments than the other two constructors shown—zero parameters instead of one. The second two constructors have different types of parameters: Icon and String. When the program is running, Java figures out which of the constructors should be invoked to initialize the object.

The classes that you write may also have multiple constructors as long as the parameters are different in either number or type. For example, the following class has two constructors to initialize a double value in much the same way as Java's Double class:[3]

```
// Class that wraps a double (like Java's Double class)
public class AnotherDouble
{
  double val;

  // Default constructor sets a default value
  public AnotherDouble( )                              ①
  {
    val = 0.0;
  }

  // This second constructor initializes the object to any value
  public AnotherDouble( double doubleValue )           ②
  {
    val = doubleValue;
  }
```

---

3. The Double class was added to allow for collections of Double objects in Java's collections framework. Classes such as ArrayList store references to any type of object. They cannot store primitive values such as double, boolean, or int.

```
  // Override Object's toString method
  public String toString( )
  { // Need to make the int a String, so concatenate it
    return "" + val;
  }

  public static void main( String[] args )
  {
    AnotherDouble a = new AnotherDouble( );           ①
    AnotherDouble b = new AnotherDouble( -0.01 );     ②

    System.out.println( a ); // 0.0
    System.out.println( b ); // -0.01
  }
}
```

Chapter Summary

- An event-driven program is one that has objects waiting for (listening to) some message to be sent. You need to register the listener with the object that will send it a message.

- A graphical user interface (GUI) presents graphical components to a user. When the user interacts with the GUI, the components send messages to the listeners to perform the appropriate actions.

- JButton and JTextField are just two graphical components that need to register an ActionListener object as a listener to get anything done when they are clicked or entered.

- An object can be treated as an ActionListener in the addActionListener method if its class implements the ActionListener interface.

- The following algorithm is used throughout the remainder of this textbook to get an event-driven program with a GUI up and running:
    1. Write a class that extends JFrame.
    2. Add a short main method to construct an instance of the class and show it.
    3. Add the instance variables needed both in the constructor and in the listeners (the inner classes).
    4. In the constructor of the class that extends JFrame,
        - set the title.
        - set the size.
        - setDefaultCloseOperation(JFrame.EXIT_ON_CLOSE);
        - store the content pane JFrame as a Container object with getContentPane( ).
        - construct the graphical components you wish to add.
        - add the graphical components to the Container object.

- construct at least one `ActionListener` object (an instance of a class that implements `ActionListener`).
- register the listener objects to the graphical components with `addActionListener` messages.

5. Inside the class that extends `JFrame`, implement one or more classes that can listen to graphical components. This textbook asks only for classes that implement the `ActionListener` interface. There are many other listener interfaces, such as `WindowListener` (see Chapter 9), `HyperlinkListener`, and `MouseListener`.

6. Compile the program until all syntax errors are removed.

7. Run the program and debug it until it does what you want. Consider adding `println` messages in the `actionPerformed` method to ensure that you have registered the listener (it is easy to forget this step).

- `JFrame` uses the `BorderLayout` layout manager (with five places to add things) unless you change the layout manager with a `setLayout` message to the content pane of the `JFrame`.
- When a class extends an existing class, the new class inherits the methods of the existing class.
- `ArrayList`, from the `java.util` package, can store a collection of all types of objects, but not primitives.
- An `ArrayList`'s elements can be references to the same type or of different types.
- Polymorphism means that sending the same message to different types of objects results in different methods being invoked.
- A class may have more than one constructor as long as the parameters differ in number or type.
- Polymorphism occurs when one message results in the invocation of different messages.
- Here are five uses of inheritance:
  1. Get a class like another with very little work.
  2. Have a single `ArrayList` class to store collections of different types of objects.
  3. Have a `Container` object store a collection of different types of objects. This allows a programmer to add different graphical components that show up in a `JFrame`.
  4. "Print" any object with `toString`.
  5. Allow polymorphic messages.

Key Terms

`ActionListener`	`getCurrencyInstance`	multiple constructors
`actionPerformed`	`getText`	`NumberFormat`
`addActionListener`	graphical user interface	overriding
`ArrayList`	inheritance	polymorphic message
casting	inner class	polymorphism
collection	listener	`setText`
default constructor	modal	`this`
event-driven program		

Exercises

The answers to exercises marked with are available in Appendix C.

 1. Complete this constructor so the window below will be shown:

```java
import javax.swing.*;
import java.awt.*;
import java.awt.event.*;

public class DifferentLayout extends JFrame
{
  public static void main( String[] args )
  {
    DifferentLayout window = new DifferentLayout( );
    window.show( );
  }

  private JButton clearButton;
  private JTextField leftField;

  public DifferentLayout( )
  {
    setTitle( "2 x 3" );
    setSize( 200, 80 );
     setDefaultCloseOperation( JFrame.EXIT_ON_CLOSE );

    clearButton = new JButton( "Two" );
    leftField = new JTextField ( "Left" );

    // Add the necessary code

  } // End constructor

  // The answer to Exercise 2 goes here

} // End class DifferentLayout
```

 2. Add an inner class named `ButtonListener` so that each time `clearButton` is clicked (the button labeled Two), the text in `leftField` is set to `"Always"`, no matter what text was there.

 3. Write the code that will register an instance of the class that you built to answer Exercise 2 such that each time `clearButton` is clicked, `leftField` is set to `"Always"`.

4. What advantage is there to using inner classes for listeners?

5. Complete the code necessary to convert the following string into a floating-point number:
```
String stringAsNum = "1234.45";
double  amount =  _____
```

6. Write an entire class that will "double" the text in the text field any time the user clicks the button. If the window begins like the one on the left, pressing the button twice results in the changes shown in the next two windows to the right.

 7. Name two methods other than the default constructor that the `Extension` class currently has.
```
public class Extension extends Object
{
}
```

8. Which letters represent valid assignment statements?
```
Object obj = new Object( );
JButton button = new JButton( );
String str = new String( );
```
   a. `obj = button;`   d. `str = obj;`

   b. `obj = str;`   e. `button = str;`

   c. `button = obj;`   f. `obj = new JButton( "Out with the old ... " );`

Programming Tips

1. **Do the GUI first.**
   When writing an event-driven program with a graphical user interface, first lay out the graphical components. Worry about the other listeners later. If one of those graphical components needs to be listened to, make it an instance variable in the enclosing class so the inner class has access to it.

2. **Instance variables are accessible to all methods in the enclosing and inner classes.**
   Make instance variables of all graphical components that need to be listened to by inner classes. In general, if a variable is needed by more than one class, make it an instance variable.

3. **You can do a lot by implementing `ActionListener`.**
   Java's event model allows you to create any number of classes to listen to a large number of events. With only `ActionListener`, `JButton`, and `JTextField`, you could have many objects perform different actions in response to many different buttons and text fields. They all follow the same pattern:
   - Write a class that implements `ActionListener`.
   - Write this class's `actionPerformed` to do whatever you want.
   - Register an instance of the `actionListener` to listen to a graphical component with an `addActionListener` message.

4. **Follow this pattern for event-driven programs with a GUI:**
   1. Write a class that extends `JFrame`.
   2. Add the graphical components to be added to the window as instance variables.
   3. Have the constructor construct these graphical component instance variables.
   4. Have the constructor lay out the graphical components with `getContentPane( )`.
   5. Implement one inner class that listens to each graphical component. This allows code in the `actionPerformed` methods to reference other instance variables of the class that it will need to get the job done.
   6. Register an instance of the inner class as a listener to the components.

5. **Don't forget to register the listeners.**
   When writing event-driven programs, it is easy to forget to register the listener. The program runs, but nothing happens. You have the graphical components and the listener class and the GUI appears, but nothing happens when you

click the button or enter text into the text field. Go to your constructor and make sure you have sent the correct number of addActionListener messages.

6. **Write a `toString` method for all of your classes.**
   It is recommended that you write all of your classes to override `toString` to present a textual representation of its objects. This will help when you are testing and debugging your programs.

7. **There is a pattern for implementing event-driven programs with a GUI.**
   The chapter summary above provides an algorithm for building such programs. This and the examples in code show a pattern for writing programs that more closely resemble modern-day programs. After you follow the pattern several times, it should seem relatively easy (based on feedback from students using this book). That's because Java and this textbook present a general solution that can be applied in many instances.

Programming Projects

5A   The `DayCounter` Class

Write the `DayCounter` class with two constructors. The default constructor (with no parameters) sets the `DayCounter` object to the current date. The second constructor has three `int` parameters representing year, month, and day, respectively. *Note:* `GregorianCalendar` has a constructor that takes three `int` arguments representing the year, month, and day in that order. Here is the method heading for the other constructor you will need:

```
GregorianCalendar(int year, int month, int date)
```

Write a `toString` method that shows January as 1 and December as 12 (not 0 and 11 as `GregorianCalendar` does). Also, add a method named `adjustDaysBy` that changes the object to represent some day in the future or some day in the past (with a negative argument). The following code must generate the output shown in the comments. The day and month must have leading zeros if necessary. *Note:* This is not a complete test.

```
// Show today's date. Output reflects that
// this program ran on June 17, 2002
DayCounter today = new DayCounter( );
System.out.println( today.toString( ) );        // 2002/06/17

// Start at leap year day in 2004
DayCounter someDay = new DayCounter( 2004, 2, 29 );
System.out.println( someDay.toString( ) );       // 2004/02/29
```

```
// One year ahead
someDay.adjustDaysBy( 365 );
System.out.println( someDay.toString( ) );      // 2005/02/28

// One year ago from initial value
someDay.adjustDaysBy( -2 * 365 );
System.out.println( someDay.toString( ) );      // 2003/3/01
```

Note: A programming project in Chapter 7 asks you to add a method for this class that will compute the difference between any two DayCounter objects.

5B   Two Listeners

Write a simple GUI that changes the text in a text field either to all uppercase letters or to all lowercase letters. When the Upper Case button is clicked, the text in the middle should be shown with all uppercase letters. When the Lower Case button is clicked, the text should be shown with all lowercase letters. At startup, the window should look just like the following with very wide buttons in the north and south. This JFrame has a size of 500-by-120 pixels and uses the BorderLayout layout manager.

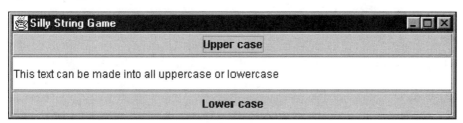

5C   Temperature Converter

Write an event-driven program that shows the Fahrenheit equivalent of any Celsius input and vice versa. When the user enters a new Celsius input, the Fahrenheit text field should be updated to show the equivalent Fahrenheit temperature. When the user enters a new Fahrenheit input, the Celsius text field should be updated to show the equivalent Celsius temperature. Round all new values to one decimal place. This JFrame has a size of 150-by-80 pixels, a 2-by-2 GridLayout, and four pixels between graphical components:

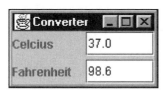

5D   Minimum Coins

Write an event-driven program that shows the minimum number of coins required to make change for a user input (83 cents shown here). When the user enters a new amount, update the five JLabel objects to show the new numbers of coins (in the United States). *Note:* In this problem, you need the parseInt method of the Integer class. Make your JFrame look like this with a size of 180-by-180 pixels, a 6-by-2 GridLayout, and four pixels between the graphical components.

5E   Making a List

Write an event-driven program that adds new BankAccount objects to an ArrayList. The ArrayList begins as empty and is not saved. Each time the Add Account button is clicked, the text in Account ID and Initial Balance must be used to construct a new BankAccount that is then added to the list. Assume that the text fields always have valid input. Both text fields must be cleared after the new account is added. Clicking the Show Accounts button shows as much of the ArrayList of BankAccounts as possible in a JOptionPane showMessageDialog. The window should look like this when the user is adding the fourth account, with IDs of a, b, c, and d and initial balances of 1, 2, 3, and 4, respectively. The window is 260–by-120 pixels with a 3-by-2 GridLayout, and four pixels between the graphical components.

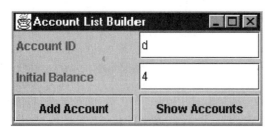

Now when the Show Accounts button is clicked, the following message dialog is displayed:

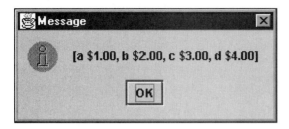

Answers to Self-Check Questions

5-1 `setTitle` and `setSize` (`setDefaultCloseOperation`)

5-2 `withdraw` and `getBalance`

5-3

5-4
```java
import javax.swing.*;      // JFrame, JTextField, JButton
import java.awt.*;         // Container, GridLayout

public class AnotherFrame extends JFrame
{
  public static void main( String[] args )
  {
    JFrame window = new AnotherFrame(  );
    window.show(  );
  }

  // Inner class's methods can also reference these instance variables
  private JTextField inputField;
  private JButton clearButton;

  public AnotherFrame( )
  {
    setTitle( "Another Frame" );
    setSize( 180, 80 );
    setDefaultCloseOperation( JFrame.EXIT_ON_CLOSE );

    Container contentPane = getContentPane( );
    contentPane.setLayout( new GridLayout( 2, 1, 4, 4 ) );

    inputField = new JTextField( "Click button to clear me" );
    clearButton = new JButton( "Clear" );
```

```
          contentPane.add( clearButton );
          contentPane.add( inputField );
      }
  }
```

5-5   ```
      private class ButtonListener implements ActionListener
      {
         public void actionPerformed(ActionEvent e)
         {
           inputField.setText("");
         }
      }
      ```

5-6   ```
      clearButton.addActionListener( new ButtonListener( ) );
      ```
      -or-
      ```
      ButtonListener buttonListener = new ButtonListener( );
      clearButton.addActionListener( buttonListener );
      ```

5-7   ```
      private class TextFieldListener implements ActionListener
      {
         public void actionPerformed(ActionEvent e)
         {
           clearButton.setText(inputField.getText( ));
         }
      }
      ```

5-8   ```
      inputField.addActionListener( new TextFieldListener( ) );
      ```
      -or-
      ```
      TextFieldListener textFieldListener = new TextFieldListener( );
      inputField.addActionListener( textFieldListener );
      ```

5-9   -a fieldOne, fieldTwo, formatter
      -b fieldOne, fieldTwo, formatter, anotherField
      -c fieldOne, fieldTwo, formatter, yetAnotherField

5-10 ```
      JTextField amountField = new JTextField("200.00");
      String input = amountField.getText( );
      double amount = Double.parseDouble(input);
      amount = amount + amount * 0.06;
      NumberFormat currencyFormatter = NumberFormat.getCurrencyInstance( );
      String moneyAsString = currencyFormatter.format(amount);
      amountField.setText(moneyAsString);
      ```

5-11  ```
      private class DepositListener implements ActionListener
      {
         public void actionPerformed( ActionEvent evt )
         {
           String input = amountField.getText( );
           double depositAmount = Double.parseDouble( input );
           oneAccount.deposit( depositAmount );
           amountField.setText( "" );
           String moneyAsString =
                        currencyFormatter.format( oneAccount.getBalance( ) );
      ```

```
                balanceLabel.setText( moneyAsString  );
          }
      }
5-12  DepositListener depositListener = new DepositListener( );
      depositButton.addActionListener( depositListener );
```

5-13 -a You could have different identifiers. If so, use them in the answers to -b and -c.

```
          private JButton swapButton;
          private JTextField leftField;
          private JTextField rightField;
```

   -b

```
          swapButton = new JButton( "Swap" );
          leftField = new JTextField( "LEFT" );
          rightField = new JTextField( "RIGHT" );

          contentPane.add( swapButton );
          contentPane.add( leftField );
          contentPane.add( rightField);

          SwapButtonListener swapListener = new SwapButtonListener( );
          swapButton.addActionListener( swapListener );
```

   -c

```
          private class SwapButtonListener implements ActionListener
          {
             public void actionPerformed( ActionEvent ae )
             {
                String left = leftField.getText( );
                String right = rightField.getText( );
                leftField.setText( right );
                rightField.setText( left );
             }
          }
```

5-14 Java does not guarantee that the `actionPerformed` messages are sent in the same order specified by the order of the `addActionListener` messages. The output could be any ordering of these three lines. Only two possible outputs are shown.

```
One One One            Three Three Three
Two Two Two            Two Two Two
Three Three Three       One One One
```

5-15

```
      BankAccount currentAccount;
      currentAccount = (BankAccount)accountList.get( 0 );
      currentAccount.deposit( 10.00 );
      currentAccount = (BankAccount)accountList.get( 1 );
      currentAccount.deposit( 10.00 );
```

5-16 -a Compiles

   -b Error (can't assign down the inheritance hierarchy)

   -c Compiles (and runs if `obj` stores a reference to a `String`)

   -d Error (the `Object` class does not have a `length` method)

   -e Compiles

   -f Error. The . has higher precedence. The code needs an extra set of parentheses:
       `((String)obj).length( );`

Chapter 6
Selection

Summing Up

The previous chapter presented event-driven programming and several object-oriented concepts such as polymorphism, inheritance, and interfaces. More of the bank teller system was implemented. Until this point, programs in this textbook executed statements in a sequential fashion—in order, from the first statement to the last. When a message was sent, the statements in some methods were also executed in a sequential fashion. However, some messages executed unseen code that involved other forms of control.

Coming Up

It is sometimes appropriate for certain actions to execute one time but not the next. Sometimes the specific code that executes must be chosen from many alternatives. This chapter presents statements that allow such selections. After studying this chapter, you will be able to

- see how Java implements the Guarded Action pattern with the `if` statement
- create and evaluate boolean expressions with the operators `!`, `||`, and `&&`
- implement the Alternative Action pattern with the Java `if...else`
- implement the Multiple Selection pattern with `if...else` and `switch`
- solve problems using the Multiple Selection pattern
- implement the `Comparable` interface for comparing two objects of any class
- override `Object`'s `equals` method to more fully utilize Java's collection framework

Exercises and programming projects reinforce selective control and multiple selection control and testing.

6.1 Selective Control

Programs must often anticipate a variety of situations. For example, an automated teller machine (ATM) must serve valid bank customers, but it must also reject invalid access attempts. Once validated, a customer may wish to perform a balance query, a cash withdrawal, or a deposit. The code that controls an ATM must permit these different requests. Without selective forms of control—the statements covered in this chapter—all bank customers could perform only one particular transaction. Worse, invalid PINs could not be rejected!

Before any ATM becomes operational, programmers must implement code that anticipates all possible transactions. The code must turn away customers with invalid PINs. The code must prevent invalid transactions such as cash withdrawal amounts that are not in the proper increment (of $5.00, $10.00, or $20.00, for instance). The code must be able to deal with customers who attempt to withdraw more than they have. To accomplish these tasks, a new form of control is needed— a way to permit or prevent execution of certain statements depending on the current state.

The Guarded Action Pattern

Programs often need actions that do not always execute. At one moment, a particular action must occur. At some other time—the next day or the next millisecond perhaps—the same action must be skipped. For example, one student may make the dean's list because the student's grade point average (GPA) is 3.5 or higher. That student becomes part of the dean's list. The next student may have a GPA lower than 3.5 and should not become part of the dean's list. The action—adding a student to the dean's list—is guarded.

Algorithmic Pattern 6.1

Pattern:	Guarded Action
Problem:	Do something only if certain conditions are true.
Outline:	if (true-or-false-condition is true)
	execute this action
Code Example:	if(GPA >= 3.5)
	System.out.println("Made the dean's list");

The if Statement

This Guarded Action pattern is often implemented with the Java **if** statement.

General Form 6.1: if statement

if(*boolean-expression* **)**
    true-part

A **boolean expression** is any expression that evaluates to either true or false. The *true-part* may be any valid Java statement, including a block. A block is a sequence of statements within the braces { and }.

Examples of `if` Statements

```java
if( hoursStudied > 4.5 )
  System.out.println( "You are ready for the test" );

if( hoursWorked > 40.0 )
{ // With a block for the true part
  regularHours = 40.0;
  overtimeHours = hoursWorked - 40.0;
}
```

When an `if` statement is encountered, the boolean expression is evaluated to false or true. The "true part" executes only if the boolean expression evaluates to true. So in the first example above, the output `"You are ready for the test"` appears only when the user enters something greater than 4.5. When the input is 4.5 or less, the true part is skipped—the action is guarded. Here is a flowchart view of the Guarded Action pattern:

Figure 6.1: **Flowchart view of the Guarded Action pattern**

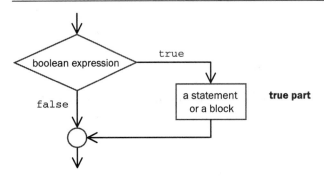

The next program illustrates how **selection** alters the flow of control. Each of the sample dialogues below illustrates code that performs different actions due to a variety of conditions. More specifically, the `toString` method returns a different `String` reflecting the current state of any `Record` object.

```java
// Instances of the Record class maintain the number of units sold
// and can describe something about its music certification:
//     1. No music certification
//     2. Gold
//     3. Platinum
//  Show that the same code can return three different results.
//  musicAward has three instances of the Guarded Action pattern.
```

```java
public class Record
{
   private String my_title;
   private int my_recordSales;

   // Construct a Record that has a title and 0 record sales.
   public Record( String title )
   {
      my_title = title;
      my_recordSales = 0;
   }

   // Update the state of this Record so it knows about new record sales.
   // units: The number of record sales not already registered.
   public void recordNewSales( int units )
   {
      my_recordSales = my_recordSales + units;
   }

   // Provide access to the state of this record to
   // show unit sales and any music certification.
   public String toString( )
   { // Put a new line in each result with "\n"
      String result = my_title + " sales are " + my_recordSales + "\n";

      if( my_recordSales < 500000 )
         result = result + " --No certification yet. Try more concerts.";
      if( my_recordSales >= 500000 )
         result = result + " --Congrats, your music is certified gold.";
      if( my_recordSales >= 1000000 )
         result = result + " --It's also gone platinum!";

      return result;
   }

   // Construct two Record objects and view the state with toString
   public static void main( String[] args )
   { // Test drive the Record class
      Record beatles = new Record( "Beatles, Revolver" );

      System.out.println( beatles );
      beatles.recordNewSales( 123456 );
      System.out.println( beatles );
      beatles.recordNewSales( 476543 );
      System.out.println( beatles );
      beatles.recordNewSales( 653543 );
      System.out.println( beatles );

      Record anotherRecord =
                     new Record ( "Jackson Browne, World in Motion" );
      anotherRecord.recordNewSales( 501342 );
      System.out.println( anotherRecord );
   }
} // End class TestRecord
```

Output

```
Beatles, Revolver sales are 0
 --No certification yet. Try more concerts.
Beatles, Revolver sales are 123456
 --No certification yet. Try more concerts.
Beatles, Revolver sales are 599999
 --Congrats, your music is certified gold.
Beatles, Revolver sales are 1253542
 --Congrats, your music is certified gold.
 --It's also gone platinum!
Jackson Browne, World in Motion sales are 501342
 --Congrats, your music is certified gold.
```

Through the power of the `if` statement, the same exact code results in three different versions of statement execution. The `if` statement controls execution because the true part executes only when the boolean expression is true. The `if` statement also controls statement execution by disregarding statements when the boolean expression is false. For example, the platinum message is disregarded when `my_recordSales` is less than one million.

6.2   Comparing Primitives and Objects

Relational operators such as < and >= test the relationship between primitive values. However, the relational operators cannot be used to compare two objects. Java uses a different approach for comparing objects. The `compareTo` method introduced in this section returns one of these three values:

- 0 if two objects are equal,
- a positive integer if the object to the left of the dot is greater than the argument between parentheses, or
- a negative integer if the object before the dot is less than the argument between parentheses.

Strings are compared alphabetically. If two strings are different, they have one different character or they have different lengths or both. The **compareTo** method returns the difference between the first two characters that are found to be different. Consider the following messages:

```
// Note: The difference between 'A' and 'D' is 3; 'A' - 'D' = -3
"Abc".compareTo( "Abc" )       // Returns 0    Abc equals Abc
"OOAbc".compareTo( "OODef" )   // Returns -3   OOAbc is less than OODef
"OODef".compareTo( "OOAbc" )   // Returns 3    OODef is greater than OOAbc
"abcde.compareTo( "abc" )      // Returns 2    Difference in string lengths
```

If there are no different characters up to the end of the shorter string, then the shorter string alphabetically precedes the longer string. In this case, `compareTo` returns the difference of the lengths of the Strings. A String that precedes another alphabetically is less than any String that follows. Consider some more examples:

```
String a = "Able";
String b = "Baker";

if( a.compareTo( "Charlie" ) < 0 )
  System.out.println( a + " < Charlie" );

if( a.compareTo( b ) > 0 )
  System.out.println( a + " > " + b );

if( b.compareTo( a ) > 0 )
  System.out.println( b + " > " + a );

if( b.compareTo( b ) == 0 )
  System.out.println( b + " equals " + b );

// Recommendation: Use intuitive equals method of String when possible
if( a.equals( "Able" ) )
  System.out.println( "equals is often used " );
```

Output

```
Able < Charlie
Baker > Able
Baker equals Baker
equals is often used
```

The compareTo method does not read in a left to right manner as the more intuitive a < b. The compareTo message forces you to think more like a b <. The compareTo message might prove easier to deal with if you read the first operand, ①; followed by the comparison operator, ②; followed by the second operand, ③. For example, the following boolean expression can be read as s1 < "def":

```
      ①                    ③      ②
if( s1.compareTo ( "def" ) < 0 )
  System.out.println( s1 + " < def" );
```

and this expression as "def" >= s1:

```
      ①                    ③      ②
if( "def".compareTo( s1 ) >= 0 )
  System.out.println( "def >= " + s1 );
```

and this expression as "def" != s1:

```
      ①                    ③      ②
if( "def".compareTo( s1 ) != 0 )
  System.out.println( "def != " + s1 );
```

Self-Check

6-1   Write the output generated by the following pieces of code:

-a
```java
int grade = 45;
if( grade >= 70 )
   System.out.println( "passing" );
if( grade < 70 )
   System.out.println( "dubious" );
if( grade < 60 )
   System.out.println( "failing" );
```

-b
```java
int grade = 65;
if( grade >= 70 )
   System.out.println( "passing" );
if( grade < 70 )
   System.out.println( "dubious" );
if( grade < 60 )
   System.out.println( "failing" );
```

-c
```java
String option = "A";
if( option.compareTo( "A" ) == 0 )
   System.out.println( "addRecord" );
if( option.compareTo( "D" ) == 0 )
{
   System.out.println( "deleteRecord" );
}
```

-d
```java
String option = "D";
if( option.equals( "A" ) )
   System.out.println( "addRecord" );
if( option.equals( "D" ) )
   System.out.println( "deleteRecord" );
```

-e
```java
String option = "R";
if( option.compareTo( "M" ) > 0 )
{
   System.out.println( "R > M" );
}
if( ( option.compareTo( "D" ) >= 0 ) )
{
   System.out.println( " ( R >= D )" );
}
```

6.3   The Alternative Action Pattern

Programs must often select from a variety of actions. For example, say one student passes with a final grade that is ≥ 60.0. The next student fails with a final grade that is < 60.0. This example uses the Alternative Action algorithmic pattern. The program must choose one course of action or an alternative.

Algorithmic Pattern 6.2

Pattern:	Alternative Action
Problem:	Need to choose one action from two alternatives.
Outline:	if (true-or-false-condition is true)
	execute action-1
	else
	execute action-2
Code Example:	`if( finalGrade >= 60.0 )`
	`System.out.println( "passing" );`
	`else`
	`System.out.println( "failing" );`

The `if...else` Statement

The Alternative Action pattern can be implemented with Java's **`if...else`** statement. This control structure can be used to choose between two different courses of action (and, as shown later, to choose between more than two alternatives).

General Form 6.2: The `if...else` statement

`if(` *boolean-expression* **`)`**
  true-part
`else`
  false-part

The `if...else` statement is an `if` statement followed by the alternate path after an `else`. The *true-part* and the *false-part* may be any valid Java statements or blocks (statements and variable declarations between the curly braces { and }).

Example of if...else Statements

```
if( sales <= 20000.00 )
  System.out.println( "No bonus" );
else
  System.out.println( "Bonus coming" );

System.out.print( "Enter amount to withdraw: " );
withdrawalAmount = keyboard.readDouble( );
if( withdrawalAmount <= myAcct.getBalance( ) )
{
  myAcct.withdraw( withdrawalAmount );
  System.out.println( "Current balance: " + myAcct.getBalance( ) );
}
else
{
  System.out.println( "Insufficient funds" );
  double thisMuch = withdrawalAmount - myAcct.getBalance( );
  System.out.println( "You lack " + thisMuch );
}
```

When an `if...else` statement is encountered, the boolean expression evaluates to either `false` or `true`. When `true`, the true part executes—the false part does not. When the boolean expression evaluates to `false`, only the false part executes.

The next example illustrates how `if...else` works. When `aNumber` has a value less than or equal to zero, the output is `false`. When `aNumber` is positive, the true part executes and `true` is output.

```
TextReader keyboard = new TextReader( );

System.out.print( "Enter a number: " );
double aNumber = keyboard.readDouble( );

if( aNumber > 0.0 )
   System.out.println( true );
else
   System.out.println( false );
```

Figure 6.2: **A flowchart view of the Alternative Action pattern**

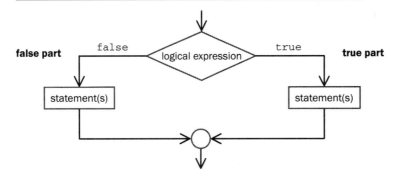

Here is another example of `if...else` that uses alternative action that depends on the value of a boolean expression (`miles > 24000.0`). Sometimes the true part executes (when `miles` is greater than 24,000); otherwise, the false part executes (when `miles` is not greater than 24,000).

```
TextReader keyboard = new TextReader( );

System.out.println( "Enter miles: " );
double miles = keyboard.readDouble( );

if( miles > 24000.0 )
{
   System.out.println( "Tune-up " + (miles - 24000.0) + " miles overdue" );
}
else
{
   System.out.println( "Tune-up due in " + (24000.0 - miles) + " miles" );
}
```

When `miles` is input as `30123.0`, the output is "Tune-up 6123 miles overdue."
When `miles` is input as `23500.0`, the false part executes and the output is "Tune-up due in 500 miles."

Self-Check

6-2   What output is generated when `miles` is input as `24000.0`?

The ability to choose is a powerful feature of any programming language. The `if...else` statement provides the means to make a program general enough to generate useful information appropriate to a variety of data. For example, an employee's gross pay may be calculated as the number of hours multiplied by the rate when hours is less than or equal to 40. However, some employers must pay time-and-a-half to employees who work more than 40 hours per week. Gross pay with overtime can be computed as follows:

```
pay = ( 40 * rate ) + ( hours - 40 ) * 1.5 * rate;
```

With alternative actions, a program can correctly compute the gross pay for a variety of values, including those less than 40, equal to 40, and more than 40. This instance of the Alternative Action pattern is now placed in the context of a complete program.

```
TextReader keyboard = new TextReader( );
double pay, hoursWorked, hourlyRate;

System.out.print( "Enter hours worked: " );
hoursWorked = keyboard.readDouble( );
System.out.print( "Enter hourly rate: " );
hourlyRate = keyboard.readDouble( );

if( hoursWorked <= 40.0 )
  pay = hoursWorked * hourlyRate;
else
{
  double OTPay = ( hoursWorked - 40 ) * 1.5 * hourlyRate;
  pay = ( 40 * hourlyRate ) + OTPay;
}

System.out.println( "Gross pay: " + pay );
```

Dialogue 1

```
Enter hours worked: 38.0
Enter hourly rate: 10.0
Gross pay: 380.0
```

Dialogue 2

```
Enter hours worked: 42.0
Enter hourly rate: 10.0
Gross pay: 430.0
```

It should be noted that semicolon placement in `if...else` statements can be somewhat confusing at first. If you observe a compiletime error near an `if...else` statement, look closely at the placement or lack of semicolons. Also, be careful that you don't place a semicolon immediately after a boolean expression like this:

```
if( hoursWorked > 40.0 );
   hoursWorked = hoursWorked + 1.5 * ( hoursWorked - 40 );
pay = ( hoursWorked * hourlyRate );
```

Although this code compiles and is correct when hours > 40.0, those who work 40 hours or less would lose money:

```
Enter hours worked: 20
Enter hourly rate: 10
Gross pay: -100.0
```

This is a common mistake. In this case, the true part is empty (nothing happens) and what follows `;` is *not* part of the `if` statement. The assignment to `hoursWorked` always occurs. But the `hoursWorked` is actually less than what the employees deserve, to the point of being negative, as shown above.

Self-Check

6-3 What is the final value of hours when hours starts as:

-**a**   38   -**c**   42.0
-**b**   40   -**d**   43.0

```
if( hours >= 40.0 )
   hours = 40 + 1.5 * ( hours - 40 );
```

6-4 Write the output generated by each code segment given these initializations of j and x:

```
int j = 8;
double x = -1.5;
```

-**a** `if( x < -1.0 )`
```
      System.out.println( "true" );
   else
      System.out.println( "false" );
      System.out.println( "after if...else" );
```

-**b** `if( j >= 0 )`
```
      System.out.println( "zero or pos" );
   else
      System.out.println( "neg" );
```

-**c** `if( x >= j )`
```
      System.out.println( "x is high" );
   else
      System.out.println( "x is low" );
```

```
-d  if( x <= 0.0 )
    { // True part is another if...else
      if( x < 0.0 )
         System.out.println( "neg" );
      else
         System.out.println( "zero" );
    }
    else
       System.out.println( "pos" );
```

6-5 Write an `if...else` statement that displays your name if `option` has the value 1 and displays your school if `option` has the value 0.

A Block with Selection Structures

The special symbols { and } have been used to gather a set of statements and variable declarations that are treated as one statement for the body of a method. These two special symbols delimit (mark the boundaries) of a block. The block groups together many actions, which can then be treated as one. The block is also useful for combining more than one action as the true or false part of an `if...else` statement. Here is an example:

```
double GPA;
double margin;  // How far from dean's list cut-off
TextReader keyboard = new TextReader( );
System.out.print( "Enter GPA: " );
GPA = keyboard.readDouble( );

if( GPA >= 3.5 )
{ // True part contains more than one statement in this block
  System.out.println( "Congratulations, you are on the dean's list." );
  margin = GPA - 3.5;
  System.out.println( "You made it by " + margin + " points." );
}
else
{ // False part contains more than one statement in this block
  System.out.println( "Sorry, you are not on the dean's list." );
  margin = 3.5 - GPA;
  System.out.println( "You missed it by " + margin + " points." );
}
```

The block makes it possible to treat many statements as one. When GPA is input as 3.7, the boolean expression (GPA >= 3.5) is true and the following output is generated:

DialoguE

```
Enter GPA: 3.7
Congratulations, you are on the dean's list.
You made it by 0.2 points.
```

When GPA is 2.9, the boolean expression (GPA >= 3.5) is false and this output
occurs:

Dialogue

```
Enter GPA: 2.9
Sorry, you are not on the dean's list.
You missed it by 0.6 points.
```

This alternate execution is provided by the two possible evaluations of the boolean
expression GPA >= 3.5. If it evaluates to true, the true part executes; if false, the
false part executes.

The Trouble in Forgetting { and }

Neglecting to use a block with if...else statements can cause a variety of errors.
Modifying the previous example illustrates what can go wrong if a block is not used
when attempting to execute both output statements.

```
if( GPA >= 3.5 )
  margin = GPA - 3.5;
  System.out.println( "Congratulations, you are on the dean's list." );
  System.out.println( "You made it by " + margin + " points." );
else   // <- ERROR: Unexpected else
```

With { and } removed, there is no block; the two bolded statements no longer
belong to the preceding if...else, even though the indentation might make it
appear as such. This previous code represents an if statement followed by two
println statements followed by the reserved word else. When else is encountered, the Java compiler complains because there is no statement that begins with
an else.

Here is another example of what can go wrong when a block is omitted. This
time, { and } are omitted after else.

```
else
  margin = 3.5 - GPA;
  System.out.println( "Sorry, you are not on the dean's list." );
  System.out.println( "You missed it by " + margin + " points." );
```

There are no compiletime errors here, but the code does contain an intent error.
The final two statements always execute! They do not belong to if...else. If GPA
>= 3.5 is false, the code does execute as one would expect. But when this boolean
expression is true, the output is not what is intended. Instead, this rather confusing
output shows up:

```
Congratulations, you are on the dean's list.
You made it by 0.152 points.
Sorry, you are not on the dean's list.
You missed it by -0.152 points.
```

Although it is not necessary, always using blocks for the true and false parts of `if` and `if...else` statements could help you. The practice can make for code that is more readable. At the same time, it could help to prevent intent errors such as the one above. One of the drawbacks is that there are more lines of code and more sets of curly braces to line up. In addition, the action is often only one statement and the block is not required.

6.4   Boolean Operators

Java has three boolean operators—`!` (not), `||` (or), and **&&** (and)—to create more complex boolean expressions. For example, this boolean expression shows the boolean "and" operator (`&&`) applied to two boolean operands:

```
( test >= 0 ) && ( test <= 100 )
```

Since there are only two boolean values, `true` and `false`, the following table shows every possible combination of boolean values and the boolean operators `!`, `||`, and `&&`:

`!` boolean "not" operator

Expression	Result
! false	true
! true	false

`||` boolean "or" operator

Expression	Result
true || true	true
true || false	true
false || true	true
false || false	false

&& boolean "and" operator

Expression	Result
true && true	true
true && false	false
false && true	false
false && false	false

The next example boolean expression uses the boolean operator `&&` ("and") to ensure that a test is in the range of 0 through 100 inclusive. The boolean expression evaluates to `true` when test has a value greater than or equal to 0 (test >= 0) and at the same time is less than or equal to 100 (test <= 100).

```
if( ( test >= 0 ) && ( test <= 100 ) )
   System.out.println( "Test is in range" );
else
   System.out.println( "**Warning--Test is out of range" );
```

The `if` statement evaluates its boolean expressions like this when `test` has the value 97 and then 977 (to simulate an attempt by a user to enter 97 but accidentally pressing 7 twice):

When test is 97   **When test is 977**

```
( test >= 0 ) && ( test <= 100 )   ( test >= 0 ) && ( test <= 100 )
(  97 >= 0 ) && (  97 <= 100 )     ( 977 >= 0 ) && ( 977 <= 100 )
      true       &&        true           true       &&        false
                 true                                 false
```

Operator Precedence Rules

Programming languages have **operator precedence** rules governing the order in which operators are applied to operands. For example, in the absence of parentheses, the relational operators >= and <= are evaluated before the && operator. Most operators are grouped (evaluated) in a left-to-right order: `a/b/c/d` is equivalent to `(((a/b)/c)/d)`.

Table 6.1 lists some (though not all) of the Java operators in order of precedence. The dot `.` and `( )` operators are evaluated first (have the highest precedence), and the assignment operator = is evaluated last. This table shows all of the operators used in this textbook (however, there are more).

Table 6.1: **Precedence rules for operators (some levels of priorities are not shown)**

Precedence	Operator	Description	Associativity
1	.	Member reference	Left to right
	( )	Method call	
2	!	Unary logical complement ("not")	Right to left
	+	Unary plus	
	–	Unary minus	
3	new	Constructor of objects	
4	*	Multiplication	Left to right
	/	Division	
	%	Remainder	
5	+	Addition (for int and double)	Left to right
	+	String concatenation	
	–	Subtraction	
7	<	Less than	Left to right
	<=	Less than or equal to	
	>	Greater than	
	>=	Greater than or equal to	

8	==	Equal	Left to right
	!=	Not equal	
12	&&	Boolean "and"	Left to right
13	||	Boolean "or"	Left to right
15	+=	Add and assign (covered in Chapter 7)	Right to left
	-=	Subtract and assign (covered in Chapter 7)	
	=	Assignment	

One of the problems with these elaborate precedence rules is simply trying to remember them. So when unsure, use parentheses to clarify these precedence rules. Using parentheses makes the code more readable and therefore more understandable. Readable, understandable code is more easily debugged and maintained and is easy to write.

Self-Check

6-6 Evaluate the following expressions to `true` or `false`:

-**a**   (false ¦¦ true)

-**b**   (true && false)

-**c**   (1 * 3 == 4 – 1)

-**d**   (false ¦¦ (true && false))

-**e**   (3 < 4 && 3 != 4)

-**f**   (! false && ! true)

-**g**   (5 + 2 > 3 * 4) && (11 < 12)

-**h**   ! ((false && true) ¦¦ false)

6-7 Write an expression that is true only when the `int` named `score` is in the range of 1 through 10 inclusive.

6-8 Write an expression that is true if `test` is outside the range of 0 through 100.

6-9 Write the output generated by the following code:

```
double GPA = 1.03;
if( GPA == 4.0 )
    System.out.println( "President's list" );
```

The Boolean "or" (¦¦) with a `Grid` Object

The next example of a boolean expression uses the operator ¦¦ (the boolean "or") to determine if the mover in a `Grid` object is on one of the four edges. The boolean expression evaluates to true when the mover is in row number 0, column number 0, the last row (`g.moverRow( ) == g.getRows( ) – 1`), or the bottom column.

```
Grid g = new Grid( 4, 6, 1, 5, Grid.EAST );

if(      ( g.moverRow( ) == 0 )                      // On north edge
    || ( g.moverRow( ) == g.getRows( ) - 1 )         // On south edge
    || ( g.moverColumn( ) == 0 )                      // On west edge
    || ( g.moverColumn( ) == g.getColumns( ) - 1 )   // On east edge
  )
    // Do something
```

This `boolean` expression evaluates like this when the mover is in row 1, column 5 of a 4-by-6 grid (the `||` operator evaluates left to right):

```
The grid:
. . . . . .
. . . . . >
. . . . . .
. . . . . .
```

```
g.moverRow()==0 || g.moverRow()==g.getRows()-1 || g.moverColumn()==0 || g.moverColumn()==g.getColumns()-1
       1==0 ||              1==5              ||            5==0 ||                  5==5
      false ||             false             ||           false ||                  true
              false                          ||           false ||                  true
                                          false                ||                  true
                                                               true
```

The only time this expression is false is when all four subexpressions are false. If any one subexpression is true, the whole expression evaluates to true; in fact, the other subexpressions don't even need to be evaluated.

The previous evaluation had to carry on until the fourth (and final) `boolean` subexpression. This entire expression would also be evaluated whenever the mover was not on an edge—when all four subexpressions were false. However, consider the same expression if the mover had been in row 0:

```
The grid:
. . . . . >
. . . . . .
. . . . . .
. . . . . .
. . . . . .
. . . . . .
```

```
g.moverRow()==0 || g.moverRow()==g.getRows()-1 || g.moverColumn()==0 || g.moverColumn()==g.getColumns()-1
       true ||                  ?               ||        ? ||                   ?
```

As soon as `moverRow()==0` evaluates to true, the other three subexpressions are not evaluated in Java. This is because true `||` *anything* `||` *anything* `||` *anything* evaluates the entire expression to true; just one of the subexpressions must be true. This is called **short circuit `boolean` evaluation**. It allows programs to run faster since one or more subexpression evaluations do not always need to be evaluated. This was done to improve performance.

Short circuit `boolean` evaluation also applies to the `&&` operator. Since false `&&` *anything* is always false, the second subexpression need not be evaluated when the first subexpression is `false`. Consider the following code, which has eight `isOdd` messages:

```
OddClass oc1 = new OddClass( 2 );
OddClass oc2 = new OddClass( 4 );
OddClass oc3 = new OddClass( 6 );
OddClass oc4 = new OddClass( 9 );

boolean allFourOdd =    oc1.isOdd( )
                    && oc2.isOdd( )     // May not be called
                    && oc3.isOdd( )     // May not be called
                    && oc4.isOdd( );    // May not be called

boolean anyOneOdd =    oc4.isOdd( )
                    || oc3.isOdd( )     // May not be called
                    || oc2.isOdd( )     // May not be called
                    || oc1.isOdd( );    // May not be called
```

Looking at the `isOdd` method of the `isOdd` class (below), it might appear that the previous code would generate eight lines of output—one `println` for each of the eight method calls.

```
// Demonstrate short circuit boolean evaluation
public class OddClass
{
  private int my_value;

  public OddClass( int theInteger )
  {
    my_value = theInteger;
  }

  public boolean isOdd( )
  { // How often is this message called?
    System.out.println( "isOdd called when it stores " + my_value );
    return ( my_value % 2 ) != 0;
  }
}
```

However, there are only two lines of output. The evaluation of the expression to the right of `allFourOdd =` continues only to the first subexpression, `oc1.isOdd( )`. Because this is `false`, the other three messages are never sent. Also, the evaluation of the expression to the right of `anyOneOdd =` needs to continue only to the first subexpression, `oc4.isOdd( )`. Because this subexpression is true, the other three messages are never sent. Here is the actual output:

Output

```
isOdd called when it stores 2
isOdd called when it stores 9
```

Self-Check

6-10 Write the output generated by this code using the isOdd class above:

```
OddClass oc1 = new OddClass( 3 );
OddClass oc2 = new OddClass( 5 );
OddClass oc3 = new OddClass( 6 );
OddClass oc4 = new OddClass( 7 );

boolean allFourOdd =    oc1.isOdd( )
                     && oc2.isOdd( )      // May not be called
                     && oc3.isOdd( )      // May not be called
                     && oc4.isOdd( );     // May not be called
```

6.5   Multiple Selection

"Multiple selection" refers to times when programmers need to select one action from many possible actions. This pattern is summarized as follows:

Algorithmic Pattern 6.3

Pattern: Multiple Selection

Problem: Must execute one set of actions from three or more alternatives.

Outline: if (condition-1 is true)
                    execute action-1
                else if(condition-2 is true)
                    execute action-2
                    // . . .
                else if(condition n-1 is true)
                    execute action n-1
                else
                    execute action-n

Code Example:
```
// Show the current day of the week as a String
String dayAsString = "??";
GregorianCalendar today = new GregorianCalendar( );
int day = today.get( GregorianCalendar.DAY_OF_WEEK );

if( day == GregorianCalendar.MONDAY )
  dayAsString = "Monday";
else if( day == GregorianCalendar.TUESDAY )
  dayAsString = "Tuesday";
else if( day == GregorianCalendar.WEDNESDAY )
  dayAsString = "Wednesday";
else if( day == GregorianCalendar.THURSDAY )
  dayAsString = "Thursday";
else if( day == GregorianCalendar.FRIDAY )
  dayAsString = "Friday";
```

```
        else if( day == GregorianCalendar.SATURDAY )
          dayAsString = "Saturday";
        else if( day == GregorianCalendar.SUNDAY )
          dayAsString = "Sunday";
        else
          dayAsString = "Invalid day";

        System.out.println( "Today is " + dayAsString );
```

The following code contains an instance of the Multiple Selection pattern. It selects from one of three possible actions. Any grade point average (GPA) less than 3.5 (including negative numbers) generates the output "Try harder." Any GPA less than 4.0 but greater than or equal to 3.5 generates the output "You made the dean's list." And any GPA greater than or equal to 4.0 generates the output "You made the president's list." There is no upper range or lower range defined in this problem.

```
// Multiple selection, where exactly one println statement
// executes no matter what value is entered for GPA.
TextReader keyboard = new TextReader( );

System.out.print( "Enter your GPA: " );
double GPA = keyboard.readDouble( );

if( GPA < 3.5 )
  System.out.println( "Try harder" );
else
{ // The false part of this if...else is another if...else
  if( GPA < 4.0 )
    System.out.println( "You made the dean's list" );
  else
    System.out.println( "You made the president's list" );
} // End else
```

Notice that the false part of the first if...else statement is another if...else statement. If GPA is less than 3.5, Try harder is output and the program skips over the nested if...else. However, if the boolean expression is false (when GPA is greater than or equal to 3.5), the false part executes. This second if...else statement is the false part of the first if...else. It determines if GPA is high enough to qualify for either the dean's list or the president's list.

When implementing multiple selection with if...else statements, it is important to use proper indentation so the code executes as its written appearance suggests. The readability that comes from good indentation habits saves time during program implementation. To illustrate the flexibility you have in formatting, the previous multiple selection may be implemented in the following preferred manner to line up the three different paths through this control structure:

```
if( GPA < 3.5 )
   System.out.println( "Try harder" );
else if( GPA < 4.0 )
   System.out.println( "You made the dean's list" );
else
   System.out.println( "You made the president's list" );
```

Another Example — Determining Letter Grades

Some schools use a scale like the following to determine the proper letter grade to assign to a student. The letter grade is based on a percentage representing a weighted average of all of the work for the term. Based on the following table, all percentage values must be in the range of 0.0 through 100.0:

Value of Percentage	Assigned Grade
$90.0 \leq$ percentage ≤ 100.0	A
$80.0 \leq$ percentage < 90.0	B
$70.0 \leq$ percentage < 80.0	C
$60.0 \leq$ percentage < 70.0	D
$0.0 \leq$ percentage < 60.0	F

This problem is an example of choosing one action from more than two different actions, a case of multiple selection. A method to determine the range that the instance variable my_percentage falls into could be implemented with separate if statements:

An Inefficient and Unnecessarily Long Solution

```
String result = "";
if( my_percentage >= 90.0 && my_percentage <= 100.0 )
   result = "A";
if( my_percentage >= 80.0 && my_percentage < 90.0 )
   result = "B";
if( my_percentage >= 70.0 && my_percentage < 80.0 )
   result = "C";
if( my_percentage >= 60.0 && my_percentage < 70.0 )
   result = "D";
if( my_percentage >=  0.0 && my_percentage < 60.0 )
   result = "F";
if( my_percentage < 0.0 || my_percentage >  100.0 )
   result = "Out of range";
```

When given the problem of choosing from among five different actions, it is better to use multiple selection, not guarded action. The preferred multiple selection implementation, shown below, is more efficient at runtime. The solution above is correct, but it requires the evaluation of six complex boolean expression every time. The solution shown below, with **nested if...else** statements, stops executing when the first boolean test evaluates to true. The true part executes and all of the remaining nested if...else statements are skipped.

Additionally, the multiple selection pattern shown next is less prone to intent errors. It ensures that an error message will be returned when my_percentage is outside the range of 0.0 through 100.0 inclusive. There is a possibility, for example, that my_percentage will be entered as 777 instead of 77. Since 777 >= 90.0 is true, the method in the code above could improperly return an "A" when a "C" would have been the correct result.

The nested if...else solution first checks if my_percentage (an instance variable in the class shown below) is less than 0.0 or greater than 100.0. In this case, an error message is concatenated instead of a valid letter grade.

```
String result = "" + my_percentage + ": ";

if( ( my_percentage < 0.0 ) || ( my_percentage > 100.0 ) )
  result = result + "**Error** Percentage is not in range [0..100]";
else if ( // ...
```

If my_percentage is out of range (less than 0 or greater than 100), the result is an error message and the program skips over the remainder of the nested if...else structure. Rather than getting an incorrect letter grade for percentages less than 0 or greater than 100, you get a message like this:

```
-1.0: **Error** Percentage is not in range [0..100]
```

However, if the first boolean expression is false, then the remaining nested if...else statements check the other five ranges specified in the grading policy. The next test checks if my_percentage represents an A. At this point, my_percentage is certainly less than or equal to 100.0, so any value of my_percentage >= 90.0 results in concatenating an "A".

```
// No need to check that my_percentage <= 100.0
else if( my_percentage >= 90 )
  result = result + "A";
else if ( // ...
```

The following class uses a toString method to return the state of a LittleGrader object. The multiple selection solution in toString determines the correct letter grade.

```
// A class to demonstrate multiple selection.
// One instance of this class can be made responsible for the
// policy to determine letter grades in a consistent fashion.
public class LittleGrader
{
  private double my_percentage;

  // Construct an object that determined letter grades for any percentage
  public LittleGrader( double initPercentage )
  {
    my_percentage = initPercentage;
  }
```

```
// Change to a new numeric grade so one object can take on the
// responsibility for the letter grade policy for any numeric grade.
public void setPercentage( double newPercentage )
{
   my_percentage = newPercentage;
}

// Returns a String that has the current numeric and letter
// grade according to a particular grading scale.
public String toString( )
{
   String result = "" + my_percentage + ": ";

   if( ( my_percentage < 0.0 ) || ( my_percentage > 100.0 ) )
     result = result + "**Error** Percentage is not in range [0..100]";
   else if( my_percentage >= 90 )
     result = result + "A";
   else if( my_percentage >= 80.0 )
     result = result + "B";
   else if( my_percentage >= 70.0 )
     result = result + "C";
   else if( my_percentage >= 60.0 )
     result = result + "D";
   else
     result = result + "F";

   return result;
   }
}
```

The return values from toString depend on the current value of
my_percentage. If my_percentage is in the range and is also greater than or
equal to 90.0, then "A" will be concatenated to result. The program skips over all
other statements after the first else. If my_percentage == 50.0, then all boolean
expressions are false and the program executes the action after the final else;
"F" is concatenated to result.

Testing Multiple Selection

Consider how many method calls should be made to test the letterGrade method
with multiple selection—or for that matter, any method or segment of code
containing multiple selection. To test this particular example to ensure that
multiple selection is correct for all possible percentage arguments, the method
could be called with all numbers in the range from -1.0 through 101.0. However,
this would require an infinite number of method calls for arguments such as
1.000000000001 and 1.999999999999, for example. With integers, it would be a lot
easier, but still tedious. Such testing is unnecessary.

First consider a set of test data that executes every possible **branch** through the
nested if...else. Branch coverage testing means observing what happens when

every statement (including the true and false parts) of a nested if...else executes once.

Testing should also include the cut-off (boundary) values. This extra effort could go a long way. For example, testing the cut-offs might avoid situations where students with 90.0 are accidentally shown to have a letter grade of B rather than A. This would occur when the boolean expression (percentage >= 90.0) is accidentally coded as (percentage > 90.0). The arguments of 60.0, 70.0, 80.0, and 90.0 complete the boundary testing of the code above.

The best testing strategy is to select test values that combine branch and boundary testing at the same time. For example, a percentage of 90.0 should return "A". The value of 90.0 not only checks the path for returning an A, it also tests the boundary—90.0 as one cut-off. Counting down by tens to 60 checks all boundaries. However, this still misses one path: the one that sets result to "F". Adding 59.9 completes the test driver.

These three things are necessary to correctly perform branch coverage testing:

- Establish a set of data that executes all branches (all possible paths through the multiple selection) and boundary (cut-off) values.
- Execute the portion of the program containing the multiple selection for all selected data values. This can be done with a test driver.
- Observe that the program segment behaves correctly for all data values.

For example, the following data set executes all branches of letterGrade while checking the boundaries:

```
-0.1  0.0  59.9  60.0  69.0  70.0  79.9  80.0 89.9  90.0  99.9  100.0  101.1
```

A test driver would start like this:

```
public static void main( String[] args )
{
  LittleGrader lg = new LittleGrader( -0.1 );
  System.out.println( lg.toString( ) );

  lg.setPercentage( 0.0 );
  System.out.println( lg.toString( ) );

  lg.setPercentage( 59.9 );
  System.out.println( lg );

  lg.setPercentage( 60.0 );
  System.out.println( lg );
  // ...
}
```

The program output must be examined to verify that every method call returned the proper value. Here is the output from the test driver above:

```
-0.1: **Error** Percentage is not in range [0..100]
0.0: F
59.9: F
60.0: D
...
```

Self-Check

6-11 Which value of `my_percentage` would detect the intent error in the following code?

```
if( my_percentage >= 90 )
  result = "A";
else if( my_percentage >=80 )
  result = "B";
else if( my_percentage > 70 )
  result = "C";
else if( my_percentage >= 60 )
  result = "D";
else
  result = "F";
```

6-12 What `String` is incorrectly assigned to `letterGrade` for this argument?

6-13 Would you be happy if your grade were computed with this argument?

6-14 Write the output generated by the test driver in the `LittleWeather` class.

```
public class LittleWeather
{
    private int my_currentTemperature;

    public LittleWeather( int initialTemp )
    {
      my_currentTemperature = initialTemp;
    }

    public void setTemperature( int newTemperature )
    {
      my_currentTemperature = newTemperature;
    }

    public String currentConditions( )
    {
      String result;

      if( my_currentTemperature <= -40 )
        result = "dangerously cold";
      else if( my_currentTemperature < 0 )
        result = "below freezing";
      else if( my_currentTemperature < 20 )
        result = "freezing to mild";
```

```
        else if( my_currentTemperature < 30 )
          result = "warm";
        else if( my_currentTemperature < 40 )
          result = "very hot";
        else
          result = "dangerously hot";

        return result;
      }

      public static void main( String[] args )
      {
        LittleWeather currentWeather = new LittleWeather( -40 );
        System.out.println( currentWeather.currentConditions( ) );

        currentWeather.setTemperature( 20 );
        System.out.println( currentWeather.currentConditions( ) );

        currentWeather.setTemperature( -1 );
        System.out.println( currentWeather.currentConditions( ) );

        currentWeather.setTemperature( 42 );
        System.out.println( currentWeather.currentConditions( ) );

        currentWeather.setTemperature( 15 );
        System.out.println( currentWeather.currentConditions( ) );

        LittleWeather anotherWeather = new LittleWeather( 31 );
        System.out.println( anotherWeather.currentConditions( ) );
      }
    }
```

6-15 List a range of integers that would cause currentConditions to return warm.

6-16 List a range of integers that would cause currentConditions to return below freezing.

6-17 Establish a list of arguments that tests the boundaries in currentConditions.

6.6   The switch Statement

Nested if...else statements are just one way to implement multiple selection. They work well when there is a range of values to choose from or when a complex boolean expression is required. Java also provides the **switch** statement for choosing one selection from many choices.

General Form 6.3: **The Java switch statement**

```
switch ( switch-expression )
{
    case constant-value-1:
        statement(s)-1
        break;
    case constant-value-2:
        statement(s)-2
        break;

            ...
    case constant-value-n:
        statement(s)-n
        break;
    default:
        default-statement(s);
}
```

When a switch statement is encountered, the *switch-expression* is compared to *constant-value-1, constant-value-2,* through *constant-value-n* until a match is found. When the switch expression matches one of these values, the statements following the colon execute. If no match is made, *default-statement(s)* execute. default needs to be present only if some processing is desired whenever the switch expression does not match any of the case values.

If the default statement is absent, it is possible that no statements will execute inside the switch statement. Sometimes that is the appropriate design. The break statement terminates the switch statement. The break statement at the end of each case section causes the termination of the switch statement. In fact, the switch statement typically requires many break statements to avoid unintentional execution of the remaining portions of the switch statement.

The following switch statement chooses one of three paths based on the input value of option. If a user enters 1, the first case section of code is executed. The first break terminates the switch statement:

```
System.out.print( "Enter option 1, 2, or 3: " );
int option = keyboard.readInt( );
switch( option )
{
  case 1:
    System.out.println( "option 1 selected" );
    break;
  case 2:
    System.out.println( "option 2 selected" );
    break;
  case 3:
    System.out.println( "option 3 selected" );
    break;
```

```
    default:
      System.out.println( "option < 1 or option > 3" );
} // End switch
```

If neither 1, 2, nor 3 is entered, the default statement executes.

The switch expression (option above) and each constant value (1, 2, and 3 above) after case must be the same type. In fact, the constants in a switch must be one of the Java **integral types**. The integral types include the integer types (byte, short, int, and long) and char—the primitive type discussed next.

The Primitive char Type

A single character is sometimes used as the constant value in switch statements. A **char** variable stores one char value, which is written as a character between single quotes (apostrophes).

```
'A'    'b'    '?'    '8'    ' '    ','
```

Java uses several special escape sequences—a backward slash (\) followed by one of a select few characters—that have special meanings.

Escape Sequence	Meaning
'\n'	New line
'\"'	Double quotation mark in a char
'\''	Single quotation mark in a char
'\\'	One backward slash
'\t'	Tab

A char variable can be declared, initialized, and assigned value. Input and output are different, however. To read one character at a time, you could use the readChar method of the TextReader class. On output, a character appears as the integer code that represents the character. This can be fixed by concatenating the char to a String. The following program summarizes many of these issues:

```
public class ShowSomeChars
{
  public static void main( String[] args )
  {
    // Declare one char, initialize another
    char letterGrade;
    char newLine = '\n';

    // Assignment
    letterGrade = 'A';

    System.out.println( "letterGrade is " + letterGrade );
    System.out.print( newLine );   // Make print act like println
    System.out.println( "Concatenate chars to string with +: "
                  + '\"' + 'A' + ' ' + '\\' + ' ' + 'S' + 't'
                  + 'r'  + 'i' + 'n' + 'g' + '?' + '\'' );
  }
}
```

Output

```
letterGrade is A

Concatenate chars to string with +: "A \ String?'
```

Here is a `switch` statement that uses characters as the constant expressions. It chooses one of five paths based on the value of the `char` variable named `option`.

```java
public class TestSwitchWithChar
{
  public static void main( String[] args )
  {
    TextReader keyboard = new TextReader( );
    System.out.print( "B)alance  W)ithdraw  D)eposit  Q)uit: " );
    char option = keyboard.readChar( );   // Reads a single character

    switch( option )
    {
      case 'B':
        System.out.println( "Balance selected" );
        break;
      case 'W':
        System.out.println( "Withdrawal selected" );
        break;
      case 'D':
        System.out.println( "Deposit selected" );
        break;
      case 'Q':
        System.out.println( "Quit selected" );
        break;
      default:
        System.out.println( "Invalid choice" );
    } // End switch
  }
}
```

One Possible Dialogue

```
B)alance  W)ithdraw  D)eposit  Q)uit: D
Deposit selected
```

If the value read into `option` is B, the message "Balance Selected" is displayed and `break` is executed to exit the `switch` control structure. If Q or q is input, "Quit selected" is output and `break` is executed. In this example, each case is evaluated until `option` is matched to one of the four `char` values following `case`. If `option` is any other value, the message `Invalid choice` is displayed.

One final comment on the `switch` statement: Don't forget to include the optional `break` statements in the `case` portions of `switch`. Failure to break out of a `switch` causes all remaining statements to execute. Although this may be what you want in some unusual circumstance, it is usually not a good idea. For example, imagine the preceding `switch` with all `break` statements removed.

```
switch( option )
{
   case 'B':
     System.out.println( "Balance selected" );
   case 'W':
     System.out.println( "Withdrawal selected" );
   case 'D':
     System.out.println( "Deposit selected" );
   case 'Q':
     System.out.println( "Quit selected" );
   default:
     System.out.println( "Invalid choice" );
} // End switch
```

Now when B is input, every statement executes—including the default!

```
B)alance  W)ithdraw  D)eposit  Q)uit: B
Balance selected
Withdrawal selected
Deposit selected
Quit selected
Invalid choice
```

Self-Check

6-18 Write the output produced by the following switch statements:

-**a** ```
char option = 'A';
switch(option)
{
  case 'A':
    System.out.println("AAA");
    break;
  case 'B':
    System.out.println("BBB");
    break;
  default:
    System.out.println("Invalid");
}
```

-**b**  ```
int anInt = 2;
switch ( anInt )
{
  case 0:
    System.out.println( "zero" );
    break;
  case 1:
    System.out.println( "one" );
    break;
  default:
    System.out.println( "Neither" );
}
```

6-19   What is the output from **-a** above when `option` is B?

6-20   What is the output from **-a** above when `option` is C?

6-21   What is the output from **-a** above when `option` is D?

6-22   Write a `switch` statement that displays your favorite music if the `int` choice is 1, your favorite food if `choice` is 2, and your favorite instructor if `choice` is 3. If the option is anything else, display `Error`. Don't forget the `break` statements.

6.7   The `Comparable` Interface

Earlier in this chapter, the `compareTo` method was demonstrated for comparing two `String`s. This section shows a general way to compare any type of object. It uses the `Comparable` interface, which provides the `compareTo` method.

The `compareTo` method is very flexible. Many Java methods rely on the fact that objects understand `compareTo` messages. Consider the `sort` method from the Java `Collections` class (in the `java.util` package). It arranges the elements of a homogenous collection into their natural ordering, where the natural ordering is defined by the `compareTo` method (1 comes before 2, "A" before "B", and so on). This method sorts the elements in an `ArrayList` and other objects that are constructed from classes that implement Java's `List`[1] interface.

```
/** From the Collections class in the java.util package
  *
  * Rearrange the elements of list so they are in the natural ordering
  * as defined by the compareTo method. The elements in the List must
  * be instances of a class that implements the Comparable interface.
  */
public static void sort(List list)
```

The following program illustrates the behavior of `Collections`'s `sort` method.

```
// Demonstrate that a collection can be rearranged in a natural ordering

import java.util.ArrayList;
import java.util.Collections;    // Has a sort method
import java.util.List;           // Interface that ArrayList implements

public class ShowCollectionDotSort
{
  public static void main( String[] args )
```

---

1. Notice that the parameter in `sort` is List. Any object that implements Java's List interface can be an argument to this `sort` method. For example, `ArrayList` implements `java.util.List`.

```
   {
      List stringList = new ArrayList( );

      // Add elements so they are not in ascending order
      stringList.add( "Joel" );
      stringList.add( "Li" );
      stringList.add( "Devon" );
      stringList.add( "Chris" );
      stringList.add( "Kim" );

      // Print the toString version of stringList (.toString is optional)
      System.out.println( "Before sort: " + stringList );

      // Ensure elements are in their natural
      // ordering according to compareTo
      Collections.sort( stringList );

      // Print the sorted list
      System.out.println( " After sort: " + stringList );
   }
}
```

Output

```
Before sort: [Joel, Li, Devon, Chris, Kim]
 After sort: [Chris, Devon, Joel, Kim, Li]
```

The output indicates that the list elements were rearranged by the Collections sort method. Although they are not obvious, the rules for rearranging are defined by the compareTo method of the elements being sorted. Errors occur when a class does not have a compareTo method. Consider trying to sort a collection of AnotherInteger objects that do not understand compareTo.

```
// A class that acts as wrapper around int (like Java's Integer class).
// There currently is not a compareTo method.

public class AnotherInteger
{
   int val;

   public AnotherInteger( )   // Default constructor
   {
      val = 0;
   }

   public AnotherInteger( int integerValue )
   {
      val = integerValue;
   }

   public int intValue( )
   {
      return val;
   }
```

```
// Override Object's toString method
public String toString( )
{ // Need to make the int a String, so concatenate it
  return "" + val;
}
}
```

The following program adds four of these `AnotherInteger` objects to an `ArrayList`. The program prints the list. But then the program terminates in the attempt to `sort` the list elements.

```
import java.util.ArrayList;
import java.util.Collections;    // Has a sort method
import java.util.List;           // Interface that ArrayList implements
public class CantSortWithoutCompareTo
{
  public static void main( String[] args )
  {
    List intList = new ArrayList( );
    // Add elements so they are not in ascending order
    intList.add( new AnotherInteger( 4 ) );
    intList.add( new AnotherInteger( 3 ) );
    intList.add( new AnotherInteger( 2 ) );
    intList.add( new AnotherInteger( 1 ) );

    System.out.println( "Before sort: " + intList );
    // Ensure elements are in natural ordering according to compareTo
    Collections.sort( intList );
    System.out.println( " After sort: " + intList );
  }
}
```

Output

```
Before sort: [4, 3, 2, 1]
Exception in thread "main" java.lang.ClassCastException: AnotherInteger
    at java.util.Arrays.mergeSort(Arrays.java:1064)
    at java.util.Arrays.sort(Arrays.java:1014)
    at java.util.Collections.sort(Collections.java:78)
    at CantSortWithoutCompareTo.main(CantSortWithoutCompareTo.java:19)
```

The exception was thrown at line 1,063 in the `mergeSort` in Java's `Arrays.mergeSort` method. The most likely cause of the error is that an attempt was made to cast an `AnotherInteger` object into a `Comparable`. The `AnotherInteger` class did not implement the `Comparable` interface. To sort these elements, `AnotherInteger` must implement `Comparable`.

Notice that the comments in the Collections sort method above state that "The elements in the `List` must be instances of a class that implements the `Comparable` interface." The `List` of `String` objects was successfully sorted (arranged in alphabetical order) because `String` implements `Comparable`. The `sort` method needs some general way to determine if one object is less than another object of the same class. Java added the `Comparable` interface to provide a consistent way to compare two objects of any class. This allows `List`s of `Comparable` objects to be sorted.

Java's `Comparable` interface has just one method—`compareTo`. Here is a conjecture of what the `Comparable` interface looks like:

```
public interface Comparable
{
/** Returns a negative integer, zero, or a positive integer
  * when this object is less than, equal to, or greater than
  * the specified object, respectively.
  */
  public int compareTo( Object obj );
}
```

When a class implements the `Comparable` interface, it guarantees that instances of that class will understand the `compareTo` message. Those objects can also be treated as if they were `Comparable`. A few Java classes already implement `Comparable`.[2] However, any class you write may also implement the `Comparable` interface. This is necessary to take advantage of all of the functionality of Java's collection framework.[3] For example, to rearrange the elements in a `List` of `AnotherInteger` objects, `AnotherInteger` must implement `Comparable`. To do this, first change the class heading so the objects can be treated as `Comparable` objects.

```
// A class that wraps an int (like Java's Integer class)
public class AnotherInteger implements Comparable
```

But this is not enough. An attempt to compile the class without adding the `compareTo` method results in this compiletime error:

```
C:\0CS1Book\AnotherInteger.java:2:
AnotherInteger should be declared abstract[4];
it does not define compareTo(java.lang.Object) in AnotherInteger
public class AnotherInteger implements Comparable
             ^
1 error
```

Adding the `compareTo` method resolves everything. Since the `Comparable` interface was designed to work with any type of argument, `compareTo` must have an

---

2. The Java classes that implement the `Comparable` interface are `Character`, `File`, `Long`, `ObjectStreamField`, `Short`, `String`, `Float`, `Integer`, `Byte`, `Double`, `BigInteger`, `BigDecimal`, `Date`, and `CollationKey`.

3. A framework is a collection of related classes and interfaces. Sometimes a framework is implemented as a Java package. For example, the collections framework is in the `java.util` package. Event-driven programming and graphical components are in several packages, such as `java.awt`, `java.awt.event`, and `javax.swing`. The networking framework is in `java.net`. The input/output framework is in `java.io`.

4. Abstract classes are discussed in Chapter 10, "Designing an Inheritance Hierarchy."

Object parameter. This Object argument must then be cast to the class where compareTo is written (in this case, AnotherInteger). It is also highly recommended that a positive int be returned to mean that this object is greater than the argument.

```
// Return the difference between this object and the argument. A
// positive result means this object (object before the dot) > argument.
// A negative result means this object < argument.
// Returns 0 if these objects are equal.
public int compareTo( Object argument )
{
  // First get the primitive int value of the argument--casting required.
  AnotherInteger arg = (AnotherInteger)argument;

  // Return the difference between the two integer values.
  // A positive int means this object is greater than the argument.
  return val - arg.val;
}
```

Java allows access to another object's private instance variables only from a method of the same class. Since arg.val is a private instance variable in the same class of AnotherInteger, compareTo can reference it.

Before sorting a collection of AnotherInteger objects, consider the following code, which demonstrates the compareTo method of AnotherInteger. The results indicate that compareTo returns a negative integer if the object before the dot is less than the argument in the message (the actual difference is shown as a comment to the right of each println message):

```
AnotherInteger int1 = new AnotherInteger( 2 );
AnotherInteger int2 = new AnotherInteger( 17 );

System.out.println( int1.compareTo( int2 ) );      // -15
System.out.println( int2.compareTo( int1 ) );      // 15
System.out.println( int2.compareTo( int2 ) );      // 0
```

Programmers are typically not interested in the value of the integer returned. Instead, the compareTo method is used to determine if one object is less than, equal to, or greater than another object of the same class. Instead of the difference between two String or two AnotherInteger objects, a true or false value is typically the main interest. The int return result from compareTo is most often used with a relational operator, such as < or > compared to 0 (the actual output is shown in comments to the right of each println message):

```
System.out.println( int1.compareTo( int2 ) < 0 );   // true
System.out.println( int1.compareTo( int2 ) > 0 );   // false
System.out.println( int2.compareTo( int1 ) > 0 );   // true
System.out.println( int2.compareTo( int1 ) < 0 );   // false

System.out.println( int1.compareTo( int1 ) == 0 );  // true
System.out.println( int2.compareTo( int2 ) == 0 );  // true
```

Assuming `AnotherInteger` now implements `Comparable` using the `compareTo` method just shown, the list of `AnotherInteger` objects shown earlier can be successfully sorted according to the logic of its `compareTo` method.

```
System.out.println( "Before sort: " + intList );
Collections.sort( stringList );
System.out.println( " After sort: " + intList );
```

Output

```
Before sort: [4, 3, 2, 1]
 After sort: [1, 2, 3, 4]
```

Self-Check

6-23 Write a `compareTo` method for `BankAccount` that lets one `BankAccount` be less than another if its ID alphabetically precedes the other's ID. The following expressions should evaluate to the values shown in the comments. *Hint:* Use the `String` `compareTo` method to help:

```
BankAccount abc = new BankAccount( "ABC", 100 );
BankAccount def = new BankAccount( "DEF", 100 );

System.out.println( abc.compareTo( def ) < 0 );   // true
System.out.println( abc.compareTo( def ) > 0 );   // false
System.out.println( abc.compareTo( def ) == 0 );  // false
System.out.println( def.compareTo( def ) == 0 );  // true
```

6.8   Overriding `Object`'s `equals` Method

You will usually want your own class to `implement` `Comparable` if you want to store objects in one of Java's collection classes, such as `ArrayList`. If you do this, it is also recommended that you override `Object`'s `equals` method in terms of `compareTo`. If you don't, the `equals` method from the `Object` class will be called. This method compares reference values, not the states of objects. With the **equals** method in the `Object` class, two object references are considered equal if they refer to the same object.

Overriding `Object`'s `equals` method will be required for many of Java's methods to work correctly with your collections. For example, you will not be able to remove an element from an `ArrayList` unless you override `equals`. If your objects understand `compareTo` messages and can also compare the state of the objects with `equals`, you can use much of Java's collection framework. Consider the class shown in the previous section named `AnotherInteger` that now implements the `Comparable` interface. It will override the `equals` method later:

```java
// A wrapper around a primitive int (a bit like Java's Integer class)
import java.util.*;   // For ArrayList, List, and Collections

public class AnotherInteger extends Object implements Comparable
{
  private int my_value;

  public AnotherInteger( int value )
  {
    my_value = value;
  }

  public int intValue( )
  {
    return my_value;
  }

  public String toString( )
  {
    return "" + my_value;
  }

  public int compareTo( Object obj )
  {
    AnotherInteger argument = ( AnotherInteger )obj;
    return intValue( ) - argument.intValue( );
  }

  // TBA: Override equals in terms of compareTo

  public static void main( String[] args )
  {
    // Objects with equal state that won't get true with equals
    AnotherInteger one = new AnotherInteger( 1 );
    AnotherInteger anotherOne = new AnotherInteger( 1 );

    // Can sort a collection since AnotherInteger implements Comparable
    List intList = new ArrayList( );
    intList.add( one );
    intList.add( new AnotherInteger( -4 ) );
    intList.add( new AnotherInteger( 7 ) );
    intList.add( anotherOne );
    Collections.sort( intList );
    System.out.println( intList );
  }
}
```

Output

```
[-4, 1, 1, 7]
```

Since this class implements Comparable in a meaningful way, an ArrayList of AnotherInteger objects can be sorted with the Collections.sort method as

shown above. However, two `AnotherInteger` objects are not equal even if they
have the same values.

```
AnotherInteger one = new AnotherInteger( 1 );
AnotherInteger anotherOne = new AnotherInteger( 1 );

System.out.println( one.equals( anotherOne ) ); // False
```

The `equals` method in the `Object` class is called to compare reference values. The
message returns true after one reference value is assigned to the other reference
value.

```
// Now make the same expression return true
AnotherInteger two = one;
System.out.println( one.equals( two ) );    // True, but not by state
```

To fully utilize Java's collection framework, you should override `equals`. For
example, at this point, an `AnotherInteger` object cannot be removed from the
`ArrayList` if the state of the argument is the same.

```
intList.remove( new AnotherInteger( 1 ) );
System.out.println( intList );
```

Output is the same

```
[-4, 1, 1, 7]
```

To get `remove` to work, the `equals` method should be overridden to compare
state—the int value 1, not the reference value. The `equals` method should be implemented in terms of `compareTo`. The expression one.`compareTo`(anotherOne)
== 0 should have the same `boolean` value as one.`equals`(anotherOne).

```
// Override Object's equals method
public boolean equals( Object argument )
{
  return this.compareTo( argument ) == 0; // Casting done in compareTo
}
```

Since the `equals` method needs to get a reference to the object to the left of the
dot, the implicit parameter `this` is required.

Now when an `AnotherInteger` object has the same state as that in the list, the
object is removed from the list. This code will remove the first occurrence of the
object with `intValue`( ) == 1 and another object with `intValue`( ) == 7:

```
intList.remove( new AnotherInteger( 1 ) );
intList.remove( new AnotherInteger( 7 ) );
System.out.println( intList );
```

Output (after removing two `AnotherInteger` objects)

```
[-4, 1]
```

Self-Check

6-24 What has to be done to the heading of the `BankAccount` class to be able to treat `BankAccount` objects as if they were `Comparable` objects?

6-25 Override the `Object` class's `equals` method for `BankAccount` to return true if two `BankAccount` objects have the same exact `String` ID. Express the result with the `BankAccount` `compareTo` method.

6-26 Write `compareTo` as if it were in the `BankAccount` class and returned the difference in pennies. The following expressions should result in the values shown in the comments. (*Note:* This is not a good way to compare two `BankAccount` objects unless you want to sort the collection from the account with the largest balance to the smallest balance.)

```
// These expressions evaluate to -25, 25, and 0
new BankAccount( "A", 1.00 ).compareTo( new BankAccount( "A", 1.25 ) );
new BankAccount( "A", 1.25 ).compareTo( new BankAccount( "A", 1.00 ) );
new BankAccount( "A", 1.25 ).compareTo( new BankAccount( "A", 1.25 ) );
```

6.9   `BankTeller_Ch6` — Validating User Input

The changes made to the bank teller system in this section deal with checking for errors. Using selection, the withdrawal and deposit amounts can be checked to make sure they are greater than 0.00. The listeners can notify the user of a failed withdrawal operation (when the amount requested exceeds the available balance, for example). The modifications are made in a class named `BankTeller_Ch6`. The changes are confined to the `actionPerformed` methods of `WithdrawListener` and `DepositListener`.

When the user enters a withdrawal amount, this new object's `actionPerformed` method will do several things to process the withdrawal. Here is the algorithm:

1. Get the text from the withdraw text field (a `String`).
2. Try to convert that `String` into a valid number. If it isn't valid, nothing obvious happens. However, the method `returns` back to its caller. In the context of a GUI, the program continues.
3. If the number is < 0.0 or has more than two decimals, show an error in the currency amount.
4. Try to withdraw the amount requested. If the number is valid and the withdrawal is successful, record the transaction.
5. If the withdrawal attempt fails, show an error (*Note:* the `BankAccount`'s `withdraw` method returns `false` if there is not enough money).

The `JOptionPane` class from the `javax.swing` package provides a quick and easy way to display an error message or an information box. For example, `JOptionPane`'s `showMessageDialog` method will show this message when a withdrawal fails:

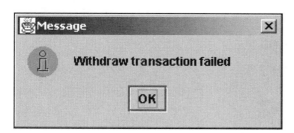

Here is the statement used in the `actionPerformed` method below:

```
JOptionPane.showMessageDialog( null, "Withdraw transaction failed" );
```

Handling User Input Errors

It is certainly possible that a user will press the Enter key with a withdrawal amount that is empty. This special case will be treated as a guarded action. You will terminate the processing of a withdrawal or deposit when the amount entered is a blank. This will be handled in both listeners by returning when the text field is an empty `String`. Here is the beginning of the `WithdrawListener`'s `actionPerformed` method:

```
// Try to convert text from withdraw text field into a valid number.
String numberAsString = withdrawField.getText( );

// Avoid an exception when the text field
// is blank. Just do nothing by returning.
if( numberAsString.equals( "" ) )
  return;
```

It is also certainly possible that a user will enter a withdrawal amount that is not a valid number: `1oo` instead of `100`, for example. You could handle this by writing your own method to convert the `String` from `JTextField` into a valid number. However, `parseDouble` method of the `Double` class already implements a number-conversion algorithm. If you give `parseDouble` a `String` argument, it returns a number. However, the `parseDouble` method throws an exception if the `String` argument represents an invalid number.

```
public static double parseDouble(String s) throws NumberFormatException
```

When a `String` representing an invalid number is passed to `parseDouble`, an
exception is thrown. In an event-driven application with a GUI, the exception
displays the error message to the console, but the program continues. The
`actionPerformed` method stops executing. Here is the code:

```
double amount = Double.parseDouble( numberAsString );
```

Three things could happen. The code in the `WithdrawListener` must select
the correct choice from these three actions:

1. The withdrawal transaction amount is invalid. It could be 0.0, a negative
    amount, or an amount that has more than two decimal places (12.345, for
    example).
2. The `BankAccount` withdraws the valid currency amount.
3. The `BankAccount` cannot withdraw the valid currency amount (perhaps the
    amount requested exceeds the account balance).

In two alternatives, an error message is shown to the user. The transaction does not
occur. In the other alternative, there is a valid withdrawal and the transaction is
recorded in the transaction list. The entire inner class for withdrawing can now be
shown with this error-checking built as multiple selection.

The Modified Inner Class That Handles Withdrawals

```java
// This actionPerformed method will execute when
// the user enters a String into withdrawField.
private class WithdrawListener implements ActionListener
{
  public void actionPerformed( ActionEvent evt )
  {
    // Try to convert the text from the
    // withdraw field into a valid number.
    String numberAsString = withdrawField.getText( );

    // Avoid an exception when the text field is blank.
    // Do nothing by returning.
    if( numberAsString.equals( "" ) )
      return;

    double amount = Double.parseDouble( numberAsString );
    // If the amount was invalid, this method terminates.
    // No transaction is possible. The remaining code is skipped.

    // Check for an amount that is positive and
    // has fewer than three decimal places
    if( amount <= 0.0 || ( amount * 100.00 !=
                           Math.round( amount * 100.0 ) ) )
    {
      JOptionPane.showMessageDialog( null,
                  "Invalid currency input to withdraw" );
    }
```

```
      else if( currentAccount.withdraw( amount ) )
      {
        // Record the transaction (assume the
        // teller gave money to the customer)
        Transaction aTransaction = new Transaction( currentAccount,
                    amount, Transaction.WITHDRAW_CODE );
        transactionList.add( aTransaction );

        // Clear the text field to avoid a second withdrawal
        withdrawField.setText( "" );
        String balanceAsString =
                        currencyFormat.format( currentAccount.getBalance( ) );
        balanceLabel.setText( balanceAsString );
      }
      else  // Withdrawal failed for some reason
        JOptionPane.showMessageDialog( null, "Withdraw transaction failed" );

    } // End actionPerformed

  } // End class WithdrawListener
```

Similar error-checking validates user input from the deposit text field. See `BankTeller_Ch6.java`, which checks for errors in user input into the withdraw and deposit text fields.

Chapter Summary

- Selection requires boolean expressions that evaluate to true or false. Boolean expressions often have one or more of the following operators:

  `<   >   <=   >=   !=   ==   !   ||   &&`
- The Guarded Action pattern is implemented with the `if` statement to either execute a collection of statements or skip them, depending on the circumstances.
- The Alternative Action pattern, implemented with the Java `if...else` statement, chooses one action or its alternative. There are two choices.
- The Multiple Selection pattern can be implemented with nested `if...else` statements or with the `switch` statement. Multiple selection should be used whenever there are three or more actions to select from.
- Selection control allows a program to respond to a variety of situations in an appropriate manner.
- The `boolean` data type and the `boolean` constants `true` and `false` are sometimes used as the return type of a method to conveniently return information about the state of an object. They can be used to answer questions such as "Is the book available?" "Was the withdraw message successful or not?" "Are there real roots to this equation?"

- Short circuit boolean evaluation is part of Java to improve program efficiency. Some boolean subexpressions need not be evaluated if the evaluation is unambiguous.

- Multiple selection requires thorough testing. Establish a set of data that executes all branches and tests all boundary values.

- Without thorough testing, a program may only appear to work, when in fact there may be one value that does not work.

- The `switch` statement must compare expressions that are one of Java's integral types: `byte`, `short`, `int`, `long`, and `char`.

- To store a collection of your objects in an `ArrayList`, have your class implement the `Comparable` interface and override the `equals` method.

Key Terms

`!`, `&&`, and `¦¦`	`equals`	nested `if...else`
Alternative Action pattern	Guarded Action pattern	operator precedence
boolean expression	`if`	selection
branch	`if...else`	short circuit boolean
`char`	integral types	evaluation
`compareTo`	Multiple Selection pattern	`switch`

Exercises

The answers to exercises marked with are available in Appendix C.

1. *True or False:* When an `if` statement is encountered, the true part always executes.

2. *True or False:* When an `if` or `if...else` statement is encountered, valid boolean expressions are evaluated to either true, false, or maybe.

3. Write the output from the following code fragments:

    a.
    ```java
    double x = 4.0;
    if( x == 10.0 )
      System.out.println( "is 10" );
    else
      System.out.println( "not 10" );
    ```

    b.
    ```java
    String s1 = "Ab";
    String s2 = "Bc";
    if( s1.equals( s2 ) )
      System.out.println( "equal" );
    if( s1.compareTo( s2 ) != 0)
      System.out.println( "not" );
    ```

c. ```
int j = 0, k = 1;
if(j != k) System.out.println("abc");
if(j == k) System.out.println("def");
if(j <= k) System.out.println("ghi");
if(j >= k) System.out.println("klm");
```

d. ```
double x = -123.4,   y = 999.9;
if( x < y ) System.out.println( "less" );
if( x > y ) System.out.println( "greater" );
if( x == y ) System.out.println( "equal" );
if( x != y ) System.out.println( "not eq." );
```

4. Write the output from the following code fragment:
```
int t1 = 87;
int t2 = 76;
int larger;
if( t1 > t2 )
  larger = t1;
else
  larger = t2;
System.out.println( "larger: " + larger );
```

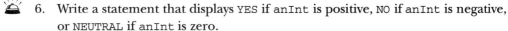

5. Write the output generated from the following program fragments, assuming j and k have the values 25 and 50, respectively.
```
int j = 25;
int k = 50;
```
a. ```
if(j == k)
    System.out.println(j);
System.out.println(k);
```

b. ```
if( ( j <= k ) && ( j >= 0 ) )
    System.out.println( "ONE" );
else
    System.out.println( "TWO" );
```

c. ```
if((j > k) || (k < 100))
    System.out.println("THREE");
else
    System.out.println("FOUR");
```

d. ```
if( ( j >= 0 ) && ( j <=100 ) )
    System.out.println( "FIVE" );
else
    System.out.println( "SIX" );
```

6. Write a statement that displays YES if anInt is positive, NO if anInt is negative, or NEUTRAL if anInt is zero.

7. Write a statement that adds 1 to the int j when the int counter has a value less than the int n.

8. Write a statement that displays Hello if the int hours has a value less than 8 or Goodbye if hours has any other value.

9. Write code that guarantees that the `int` variable named `amount` is even. If `amount` is odd, increment `amount` by 1.

10. Write code that adds 1 to the `int` `amount` if `amount` is less than 10. In this case, also display `Less than 10`. If `amount` is greater than 10, subtract 1 from `amount` and display `Greater than 10`. If `amount` is 10, just display `Equal to 10`.

11. Write a `LittleStatistician` class with a method `largest` that returns the largest of any three numbers. The constructor takes three arguments.
```
LittleStatistician ls = new LittleStatistician( 1.2, 3.4, 1.2 );
System.out.println( ls.largest( ) );     // Output must be 3.4
```

12. To test the preceding `largest` method, walk through your code for each of these sets of arguments in the constructor:
```
(1.0, 2.0, 3.0)   (1.0, 3.0, 2.0)   (2.0, 1.0, 3.0)   (3.0, 3.0, 2.0)
(2.0, 3.0, 1.0)   (3.0, 2.0, 1.0)   (3.0, 1.0, 2.0)   (2.0, 2.0, 3.0)
(3.0, 3.0, 1.0)   (3.0, 1.0, 3.0)   (1.0, 3.0, 3.0)   (3.0, 3.0, 3.0)
```

13. Write the output from the following program fragments, assuming `j` and `k` are `int`s with the values 25 and 50, respectively.
```
int j = 25;
int k = 50;
```

a.
```
if( j == k )
    System.out.println( 1 );
else if( j < k )
    System.out.println( 2 );
else
    System.out.println( 3 );
```

b.
```
if( ( j + 25 ) < k )
    System.out.println( "aaa" );
else if( j > k )
    System.out.println( "bbb" );
else
    System.out.println( "ccc" );
```

c.
```
if( j < 10 )
    System.out.println( j + " One" );
else if( j < 20 )
    System.out.println( j + " Two" );
else if( j < 30 )
    System.out.println( j + " Three" );
else
    System.out.println( j + " Four" );
```

d.
```
if( k >= 100 )
    System.out.println( "Five" );
else if( k >= 75 )
    System.out.println( "Six" );
else if( k >= 50)
```

```
      System.out.println( "Seven" );
    else
      System.out.println( "Eight" );
e. if( j > 0 )
   {
     if( j < 50 )
       System.out.println( "Eight" );
     else
       System.out.println( "Nine" );
   }
f. if( k <= 100 )   // Be careful
     System.out.println( "Ten " );
   if( k <= 50 )
     System.out.println( "Eleven " );
   if( k <= 10 )
     System.out.println( "Twelve " );
   else
     System.out.println( "Hmmmm" );
```

14. Show the output from the previous exercise when j is 30 and k is 10.

15. Show the output from the previous exercise when j is 20 and k is 20.

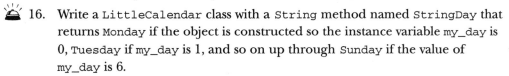 16. Write a LittleCalendar class with a String method named StringDay that returns Monday if the object is constructed so the instance variable my_day is 0, Tuesday if my_day is 1, and so on up through Sunday if the value of my_day is 6.

Programming Tips

1. **The block may be used even if it is not required.**
   Consider always using curly braces to mark the beginning and end of the true part and the false part of an if...else. You *must* use a block to treat several statements as one. You *may* use a block for readability and to help avoid bugs.

2. **Mathematicians write expressions differently than Java.**
   It is natural to write the following code to check to see if a value is in a certain range:
   ```
   int someInt = 2222;
   if( 0 <= someInt <= 100 )
   ```
   However, this is an error at compiletime. Here is the correct way to write this expression:
   ```
   if( ( someInt >= 0 ) && ( someInt <= 100 ) )
   ```

3. **Test drivers help protect against errors.**

   Use test drivers to completely test methods containing multiple selection.
   Send arguments that check all boundary values. Send arguments to ensure
   that each branch executes at least once.

4. **Do not compare strings with == and !=.**

   The following code will compile on any Java compiler. The `if` statement is
   intended to see if `s1` refers to the same object as `s2`.

```
String s1 = new String( "SAME" );
String s2 = new String( "SAME" );
if( s1 == s2 )
  System.out.println( s1 + " equals " + s2 );
else
  System.out.println( s1 + " is not equal to " + s2 );
```

   The comparison of `s1` to `s2` correctly returns `false` to generate this output:

```
SAME is not equal to SAME
```

   Fortunately, this will not compile. Reference values can only be compared with
   == and !=.

```
if( s1 < s2 )    // This will not compile
```

5. **Make sure all non-void methods return something.**

   If a method is undefined for certain values, check for those values and return
   something even if the method has an invalid argument.

```
public String letterGrade( double ave )
{
  String result = null;
  if( ( ave < 0.0 ) || ( ave > 100.0 ) )
     result = "Error, argument out of range";
  else if ( ...
```

6. **Avoid unnecessary comparisons.**

   The following `boolean` expression could be simplified by avoiding the unnecessary part of the expression. `ave < 90` must be true, since the only time this
   would get evaluated is when `ave >= 90` is false.

```
if( ave >= 90 )
  result = "A"
else if ( ave >= 80 && ave < 90 )
  result = "I already know ave must be less than 90";
```

7. **Multiple selection can always be done with nested `if...else` and can sometimes be done with `switch`.**

The `switch` statement can choose an action from multiple choices only if the expression is one of Java's integral types: `byte`, `short`, `int`, `long`, or `char`. The `switch` expression must evaluate to one of these integral values.

8. **Use the `compareTo` method when overriding `Object`'s `equals` method.**

Using Java's collection framework requires adherence to some protocols. One of those is implied by the following documentation from Java's API:

> A class's natural ordering is said to be consistent with equals if and only if (e1.compareTo((Object)e2)==0) has the same boolean value as e1.equals((Object)e2) for every e1 and e2 of class C. .... It is strongly recommended (though not required) that natural orderings be consistent with equals ....

If you want a collection of your objects stored in a Java collection class such as `ArrayList`, have the class implement `Comparable`. Also, override `equals` by having the object send a `compareTo` message to itself (use `this`).

9. **You can handle exceptions.**

The static methods `parseInt` and `parseDouble` throw `NumberFormatExceptions` if a `String` argument does not represent a valid integer and double, respectively. This terminates a text-based program. In an event-driven GUI program, the program keeps running. However, the return value of 0 or 0.0 may not be what you want. To handle this anyway you want, see Chapter 9, "A Few Exceptions, Some I/O Streams, and a Few Persistent Objects."

Programming Projects

6A   Gross Pay with Overtime

Write a Java program (the `main` method only) that determines an employee's pay based on hours worked and hourly rate of pay. Any hours over 40 (overtime) are calculated at 1.5 times the hourly rate. Test your program with several sets of inputs. Assume the input will always be >= 0.0. Here are three sample dialogues:

```
Enter hours worked: 38.0
Enter hourly rate: 10.00
Pay = 380.0

Enter hours worked: 40.0
Enter hourly rate: 10.00
Pay = 400.0

Enter hours worked: 42.0
Enter hourly rate: 10.00
Pay = 430.0
```

6B   Salary with a Bonus

Write a Java class that determines a salesperson's salary for the month based on this table:

Sales	Monthly Salary
Sales ≤ 10,000.0	Base Salary (1,500.00)
10,000.0 < Sales	Base salary plus 5% of sales over 10,000

The base salary is 1500.00. The salary will never be less than 1500.00, even if the user enters a negative sales amount. When sales are over $10,000, commission is added to the base salary. For example, when sales equal 10001.00, the monthly salary is $1500.00 + 5% of 1.00, for a total of $1500.05. Test your program with several inputs. Assume the input is always >= 0.0. Here are three sample dialogues:

```
Enter sales: 9999.99
Salary: 1500.0

Enter sales: 10002.00
Salary: 1500.1

Enter sales: 19000.00
Salary: 1950.0
```

6C   GUI Salary with a Bonus

Using the salary table from Programming Project 6B, solve the same problem with a GUI. Instead of using keyboard output, each time the user enters a sales amount into the JTextField, display the salary in the JLabel. Format it to your local currency (you need NumberFormat.getCurrencyInstance( )). Assume that the input always represents a valid number. However, if the input is negative, use the static method JOptionPane.showMessageDialog to show a message that looks like this:

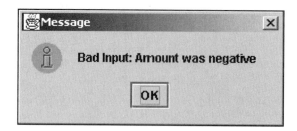

The following JFrame is 140-by-80 pixels in size, with a 2-by-2 GridLayout, and with four pixels between components:

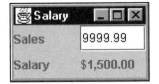 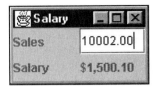 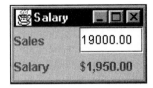

6D   Salary with Bonuses

Write a complete Java class named `SalaryComputer` that determines a salesperson's salary for the month based on the following table:

Sales	Monthly Salary
Sales ≤ 10,000.0	Base salary (1,500.00)
10,000.0 < Sales ≤ 20,000	Base salary plus 5% of sales over 10,000
20,000 < Sales ≤ 30,000	Base salary plus 500.00 plus 8% of sales over 20,000
30,000 < Sales	Base salary plus 1300.00 plus 12% of sales over 30,000

The base salary is $1500.00, which means `getSalary` returns a value that is never less than 1500.00, even if sales are negative. When sales are over $10,000, a commission is added to the base salary. For example, when sales equals 10001, the monthly salary is $1500.00 + 5% of 1.00, for a total of $1500.05. And when sales is $20001, the monthly salary is $1500.00 + 500.00 + 8% of 1.00, for a total of $2000.08. Use the following test driver to determine the methods that your class must implement. Also add the code necessary to completely test your multiple selection:

```java
public class TestSalaryComputer
{
  public static void main( String[] args )
  { // You must supply the base salary (1500 here).
    // Otherwise it will be $0.00.
    SalaryComputer s = new SalaryComputer( 1500.00 );

    s.setSalesTo( 10001.00 );
    System.out.println( s.getSales( ) + " salary is $" + s.getSalary( ) );
    s.setSalesTo( 20002.00 );
    System.out.println( s.getSales( ) + " salary is $" + s.getSalary( ) );
    // Complete this test driver to test all of the code
  }
}
```

6E   `LetterGrader`

Implement a `LetterGrader` class that computes the proper letter grade as a `String` for a plus/minus system with the following scale:

Percentage	Grade
100.0 ≥ percentage	??
93.0 ≤ percentage ≤ 100.0	A
90.0 ≤ percentage < 93.0	A-
87.0 ≤ percentage < 90.0	B+
83.0 ≤ percentage < 87.0	B
80.0 ≤ percentage < 83.0	B-
77.0 ≤ percentage < 80.0	C+
70.0 ≤ percentage < 77.0	C
60.0 ≤ percentage < 70.0	D
0.0 ≤ percentage < 60.0	F
percentage < 0.0	??

The `LetterGrader` class must have a constructor and two other methods.

```
// Constructor specifies what letter grade to return when
// the percentage is greater than 100 or less than 0.
public LetterGrader( String outOfRangeLetterGradeCode )

// Set the state of the current value of percentage.
public void setPercentage( double newPercentage )

// Return the letter grade using the current value of percentage.
public String getLetterGrade( )

// Return the current percentage and letter grade in a nice way.
// Your test driver must use this method to view the state.
public String toString( )
```

After implementing the class, write a test driver that performs branch and boundary testing. If an argument is a value outside the range of 0.0 through 100.0, return "Out of range letter grade," as specified as the argument in the constructor ("??", in this case), as the `String` letter grade. The test driver should be part of the class. Here is a recommended pattern of messages (*Note:* It is recommended that toString send the LetterGrade message as part of its return value):

```
public static void main( String[] args )
{ // A test driver for String letterGrade( double percentage )
  LetterGrader aLetterGrader = new LetterGrader( 101.0 );

  System.out.println( aLetterGrader.getLetterGrade( ) );   // ??
  System.out.println( aLetterGrader.toString( ) );         // 101.0 ??
  aLetterGrader.setPercentage( 100.0 );
  System.out.println( aLetterGrader.getLetterGrade( ) );   // A
  System.out.println( aLetterGrader.toString( ) );         // 100.0 A
}
```

6F   GUI Letter Grades

First complete Programming Project 6E. Then use an instance of LetterGrader to help build a graphical user interface version of this project. Each time the user enters a percentage amount into the JTextField, display the letter grade in a JLabel to the right of "Letter Grade" (where ?? is shown in the dialog box below). The actionPerformed method must delegate the responsibility to the LetterGrader object that knows the grading policy (instead of putting a big if...else in actionPerformed, ask the LetterGrader object for help). The following JFrame is 160-by-80 pixels, with a 2-by-2 GridLayout, and with four pixels between components:

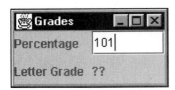

6G   The Student Class

First complete Programming Project 4D, "Course and Student Implement Interfaces." Then add a method named getStanding to the Student class to determine a student's level according to the following table:

Credits Completed	String Return Value
Less than 30 credits	"Freshman"
30 credits to less than 60 credits	"Sophomore"
60 credits to less than 90 credits	"Junior"
90 credits or more	"Senior"

Add a second constructor with three arguments to initialize a Student to have any number of credits and qualityPoints. Also, modify the toString method to include the student's name, GPA, and class standing (for an example, see the first line of output below):

```
public class TestStudent_Ch6
{
   // This is a test driver for Course and Student
   public static void main( String[] args )
   { // Construct one Student object and try every method in Student

      // Perform branch and boundary testing by
      // constructing several Student objects.
```

```
        // Notice that each of these uses the three argument constructor.
                          //    Name          Credits    QualityPoints
                          //      |              |            |
        Student b = new Student( "Student Two",   29.9,     90.0 );
        System.out.println( b.toString( ) );
        System.out.println( b.getStanding( ) );
        Student c = new Student( "Student Three", 30.0, 115.5 );
        System.out.println( c.getStanding( ) );
        Student d = new Student( "Student Four", 59.9, 120.0 );
        System.out.println( d.getStanding( ) );
        Student e = new Student( "Student Five", 60.0, 175.5 );
        System.out.println( e.getStanding( ) );
        Student f = new Student( "Student Six", 89.9, 359.0 );
        System.out.println( f.getStanding( ) );
        Student g = new Student( "Student Seven", 90.0, 360.0 );
        System.out.println( g.getStanding( ) );
    }
}
```

Your output should look like this (the first line of output is the toString version):

```
Student Two 3.01 Freshman
Freshman
Sophomore
Sophomore
Junior
Junior
Senior
```

6H The WeeklyEmployee Class

While programmers at Chrystal Bends, Inc., were designing an object-oriented program for the personnel department, they realized they needed a WeeklyEmployee class. A WeeklyEmployee object is responsible for maintaining the information necessary to complete an employee's paycheck (for employees who get paid on a weekly basis). This WeeklyEmployee object is responsible for computing its own gross pay (overtime pay is 1.5 multiplied by the hourly rate for any hours over 40.0). All WeeklyEmployee objects must also be able to compute their own federal income tax, social security tax (6.2% of the gross pay), and Medicare tax (1.45% of the gross pay) that should be withheld in a weekly paycheck. Your job is to completely implement and completely test the WeeklyEmployee class. The Chrystal Bends, Inc., programming team has determined that the WeeklyEmployee class should have the following methods. Implement these using the specific names to fulfill the responsibilities listed:

- getName—return this employee's name
- getGrossPay—return this employee's gross pay for the week (with overtime)
- getIncomeTax—return the amount of income tax to withhold from this employee's paycheck. Use the IRS percentage method for computing the

amount of income tax to withhold. This information is kept at the Web site for the U.S. Internal Revenue Service (IRS).

Go to this URL: **http://www.irs.gov/prod/forms_pubs/pubs.html**

Select **0101 Publication 15 Circular E, Employer's Tax Guide**

See pages 32 and 34.

- `getSocialSecurityTax`—return 6.2% of the gross pay
- `getMedicareTax`—return 1.45% of the gross pay

Every `WeeklyEmployee` construction needs the five arguments as shown here:

```
                                          ①        ②       ③     ④    ⑤
WeeklyEmployee anEmp = new WeeklyEmployee( "Muller", 42.5, 15.75, 2, "M" );
```

① A `String` representing the employee's name ("Muller")

② The hours worked for the week (0.00 to 999.9)

③ The hourly rate of pay (0.00 to 999999.99)

④ The number of allowances claimed on Form W-4 (0 to 99)

⑤ Either "S" for single filing status or "M" for married filing status

Make sure that that you *completely test* the `getIncomeTax` method. This means your `main` method test driver will need many `getIncomeTax` messages (with a lot of categories, for both single and married employees). Make sure you also fully test all of the other methods in your class.

If you can't get the tax table for the most recent year, try this table from page 34 of Circular E Employer's Tax Guide. The IRS explanation and example follow. *Note:* These tables change frequently. This table was only valid for part of the year in 2001.

Tables for Percentage Method of Withholding
(For Wages Paid in 2001)
TABLE 1 — WEEKLY Payroll Period
(a) SINGLE person (including head of household) — (b) MARRIED person—

If the amount of wages (after subtracting withholding allowances) is:	The amount of income tax to withhold is:		If the amount of wages (after subtracting withholding allowances) is:	The amount of income tax to withhold is:	
Not over $51	0		Not over $124	0	
Over—	**But not over—**	**of excess over—**	**Over—**	**But not over—**	**of excess over—**
$51	—$552 . . 15%	—51	$124	—$960 . . 15%	—$124
$552	—$1,196 . . $75.15 plus 28%	—552	$960	—$2,023 . . $125.40 plus 28%	—$960
$1,196	—$2,662 . . $255.47 plus 31%	—1,196	$2,023	—$3,292 . . $423.04 plus 31%	—$2,023
$2,662	—$5,750 . . $709.93 plus 36%	—2,662	$3,292	—$5,809 . . $816.43 plus 36%	—$3,292
$5,750	. . . . $1,821.61 plus 39.6%	—5,750	$5,809	. . . . $1,722.55 plus 39.6%	—$5,809

Income Tax Withholding Using the Wage Bracket Method

Under the wage bracket method, find the proper table (on pages 36–55) for your payroll period and the employee's marital status as shown on his or her Form W-4. Then, based on the number of withholding allowances claimed on the Form W-4 and the amount of wages, find the amount of tax to withhold. If your employee is claiming more than 10 withholding allowances, see below.

Use these steps to figure the income tax to withhold under the percentage method (use the table above for Weekly Employees):

1. Multiply one withholding allowance for your payroll period (see Table 5 below) by the number of allowances the employee claims.
2. Subtract that amount from the employee's wages.
3. Determine the amount to withhold from the appropriate table *see table above)

One Withholding Allowance Payroll Period
Weekly 55.77

Example: An unmarried employee is paid $600 weekly. This employee has in effect a Form W-4 claiming two withholding allowances. Using the percentage method, figure the income tax to withhold as follows:

1.	Total wage payment	$600.00
2.	One allowance	$55.77
3.	Allowances claimed on Form W-4	2
4.	Multiply line 2 by line 3	$111.54
5.	Amount subject to withholding (subtract line 4 from line 1)	$448.46
6.	Tax to be withheld on $488.46 from Table (single person)	65.62

Answers to Self-Check Questions

```
6-1   -a dubious
         failing
      -b failing
      -c addRecord
      -d addRecord
         deleteRecord
      -e R > M
         D >= R
6-2   Tune-up due in 0 miles
6-3   -a 38.0        -c 43.0
      -b 40.0        -d 44.5
6-4   -a true
         after if...else
      -b zero or pos
      -c x is low
      -d neg
6-5   if( option == 1 )
         System.out.println( "Your name" );
      if( option == 0 )
         System.out.println( "Your School" );
```

6-6 -a true   -e true

     -b false   -f false

     -c true   -g false

     -d false   -h true

6-7 `( ( score >= 1 ) && ( score <= 10 ) )`

6-8 `( ( test > 100 ) || ( score < 0 ) )`

6-9 There will be no output; the test expression (`GPA == 4.0`) is false.

6-10 `isOdd stores 3`

     `isOdd stores 5`

     `isOdd stores 6`

6-11 70

6-12 This unfortunate student gets a D instead of the deserved C.

6-13 I wouldn't be happy; I doubt you would either.

6-14 `-40: dangerously cold`

     `20: warm`

     `-1: below freezing`

     `42: dangerously hot`

     `15: freezing to mild`

     `31: very hot`

6-15 20 through 29 inclusive

6-16 -39 through -1 inclusive

6-17 -40 0 20 30 40

6-18 -a `AAA`   -b `Neither`

6-19 `BBB`

6-20 `Invalid`

6-21 `Invalid`

6-22
```
switch( choice )
{
  case 1:
    System.out.println( "Jazz" );
    break;
  case 2:
    System.out.println( "Tacos" );
    break;
  case 3:
    System.out.println( "John Doe" );
    break;
  default:
    System.out.println( "Error" );
}
```

6-23
```
public int compareTo( Object argument )
{
  // First get the ID of the argument--casting required.
  BankAccount arg = (BankAccount)argument;
  String rightID = arg.my_ID;
  return my_ID.compareTo( rightID );
}
```

6-24 Add implements Comparable to the method heading:

```
public class BankAccount extends Object implements Comparable
```

6-25
```
public boolean equals( Object argument )
{
    return this.compareTo( argument ) == 0; // Casting done in compareTo
}
```

6-26
```
public int compareTo( Object argument )
{ // First get the ID of the argument--casting required.
    BankAccount arg = (BankAccount)argument;
    // Cast the double to an int (this will truncate to tenths of a
    // cent)
    int argsPennies = (int)( 100 * arg.my_balance );
    int myPennies = (int)( 100 * my_balance );
    return myPennies - argsPennies;
}
```

Chapter 7
Repetition

Summing Up

You have now seen that classes are collections of related methods and data. Constructors initialize instance variables. Other methods modify the state of objects and return useful information about the state of objects. Additionally, two important methods of control have now been discussed—sequence and selection. Sequential control is when every statement executes one after another. Selection control allows programmers to write code that executes differently under different circumstances. Selection offers alternatives.

Coming Up

This chapter introduces the third major control structure—repetition. Repetition is discussed within the context of two general algorithmic patterns—the determinate loop and the indeterminate loop. Repetitive control allows for execution of some actions either a specified, predetermined number of times or until some event occurs to terminate the repetition. After studying this chapter, you will be able to

- recognize and use the Determinate Loop pattern to execute a set of statements a predetermined number of times
- implement determinate loops with the Java `for` statement
- recognize and use the Indeterminate Loop pattern to execute a set of statements until some event occurs to stop it
- implement indeterminate loops with the Java `while` statement
- read data from a file until there is no more data to read
- design loops
- use the methods of Java's `ListIterator` interface with `ArrayLists`

Exercises and programming projects reinforce repetition.

7.1   Determinate Loops

Repetition refers to the repeated execution of a set of statements. Repetition occurs naturally in noncomputer algorithms such as these:

- For every name on the attendance roster, call the name. Write 0 if absent or a checkmark if present.
- Practice the fundamentals of a sport.
- Add the flour ¼-cup at a time, whipping until smooth.

Repetition is also used to express algorithms intended for computer implementation. If something can be done once, it can be done repeatedly. The following examples have computer-based applications:

- Process any number of customers at an automated teller machine (ATM).
- Continuously accept reservations.
- While there are more fast-food items, sum the price of each item.
- Compute the course grade for every student in a class.
- Microwave the food until either the timer reaches 0, the cancel button is pressed, or the oven door is opened.

This chapter examines repetitive algorithmic patterns and the Java statements that implement them. It begins with a statement that executes a collection of actions a fixed, predetermined number of times.

Why Is Repetition Needed?

Many jobs once performed by hand are now accomplished by computers at a much faster rate. Think of a payroll department that has the job of producing employee paychecks. With only a few employees, this task could certainly be done by hand. However, with several thousand employees, a very large payroll department would be necessary to compute and generate that many paychecks by hand in a timely fashion. Other situations requiring repetition include, but are certainly not limited to, finding an average, searching through a collection of objects for a particular item, alphabetizing a list of names, and processing all of the data in a file. Let's start with the following code that finds the average of exactly three numbers. No repetitive control is present yet.

```
TextReader keyboard = new TextReader( );
double sum = 0.0;    // Use this to accumulate the sum of all inputs
double input;        // Will be read many times below

System.out.print( "Enter number: " ); // <- Repeat
input = keyboard.readDouble( );        // <- these
sum = sum + input;                     // <- statements
```

```
System.out.print( "Enter number: " );
input = keyboard.readDouble( );
sum = sum + input;

System.out.print( "Enter number: " );
input = keyboard.readDouble( );
sum = sum + input;

double average = sum / 3.0;
System.out.println( "average: " + average );
```

There is a drawback to this brute-force approach to repetition. Any time a larger set of inputs needs averaging, the program itself must be modified. It is not general enough to handle input sets of various sizes. Using the previous approach, the three statements would need to be repeated for every number. This means averaging 100 numbers would require 97 additional copies of these three statements. Also, the constant 3.0 in average = sum / 3.0 would have to be changed to 100.0. A situation like this is improved with a form of control that can execute these three statements over and over again.

An Algorithmic Pattern — The Determinate Loop

Without the selection control structures of the preceding chapter, computers are little more than nonprogrammable calculators. Selection control makes computers more adaptable to varying situations. However, what makes computers powerful is their ability to repeat the same actions accurately and very quickly. Two algorithmic patterns emerge. The first involves performing some action a specific, predetermined (known in advance) number of times. For example, to find the average of 142 test grades, you would repeat a set of statements exactly 142 times. To pay 89 employees, you would repeat a set of statements 89 times. To produce grade reports for 32,675 students, you would repeat a set of statements 32,675 times. There is a pattern here.

In each of these examples, a program requires that the exact number of repetitions be predetermined somehow. The number of times the process should be repeated must be established before the loop begins to execute. You shouldn't be off by one. Predetermining the number of repetitions and then executing some appropriate set of statements precisely a predetermined number of times is referred to here as the **Determinate Loop pattern**.

Algorithmic Pattern 7.1

Pattern:	Determinate Loop
Problem:	Do something exactly n times, where n is known in advance.
Outline:	determine n as the number of times to repeat the actions
	repeat the following n times
	execute the actions to be repeated

Code Example:
```
double sum = 0.0;
double input;
int n = get a value for n somehow
// Do something n times
for( int j = 1; j <= n; j = j + 1 )
{
  // Repeat these statements n times
  System.out.print( "Enter a number: " );
  input = keyboard.readDouble( );
  sum = sum + input;
}
```

The Determinate Loop pattern uses some `int` variable—named n here—to represent how often the actions must repeat. However, other appropriate variable names are certainly allowed, such as `numberOfEmployees`. The first thing to do in the Determinate Loop pattern is to determine the number of repetitions somehow. Let n represent the number of repetitions.

n = number of repetitions

The number of repetitions may be input, as in `int n = keyboard.readInt( );`. Or n may be established at compiletime, as in `int n = 124;`. Or n may be passed as an argument to a method, as in `public void display( int n )`. Once n is set, another `int` variable, named j in the program below, controls the number of loop iterations. Other appropriately named variables could be used; `counter`, for example. The Determinate Loop pattern is shown next in the context of a small program. The Java **for statement** implements the repetition.

```
// Demonstrate a determinate loop.
// The user must know in advance how many inputs will be entered.
public class DoAverage
{
  public static void main( String[] args )
  {
    TextReader keyboard = new TextReader( );
    int n;               // The number of inputs to be supplied by the user
    double sum = 0.0;    // Maintains the running sum (the accumulator)
    double input;        // Temporarily store each number input by the user
    double average;      // Holds the average for potential future use

    // Determine the number of iterations in advance
    System.out.print( "How many numbers do you need to average? " );
    n = keyboard.readInt( );
```

```
    // Now accumulate n numbers
    for( int j = 1; j <= n; j = j + 1 )
    {
       System.out.print( "Enter number: " ); // <- Repeat these
       input = keyboard.readDouble( );        // <- statements
       sum = sum + input;                     // <- n times
    }

    // Compute the average only when there is at least one input
    if( n > 0 )
    {
       average = sum / n;
       System.out.println( "Average of " + n + " numbers is " + average );
    }
    else
       System.out.println( "Cannot average " + n + " inputs" );
  }
}
```

Dialogue

```
How many numbers do you need to average? 4
Enter number: 70.0
Enter number: 80.0
Enter number: 90.0
Enter number: 100.0
Average of 4 numbers is 85.0
```

Java has several structures for implementing repetition. The for statement shown above combines everything into a single compact entity. The for loop was added to programming languages because the Determinate Loop pattern arises so often.

The for Statement

The following for statement shows the three components that maintain the Determinate Loop pattern: the initialization (n = 5 and j = 1), the loop test for determining when to stop (j <= n), and the update step (j = j + 1) that brings the loop one step closer to terminating.

```
int n = 5;  // Predetermined number of iterations
for( int j = 1; j <= n; j = j + 1 )
{
    // Execute this block n times
}
```

In the preceding for loop, j is first assigned the value of 1. Next, j <= n (1 <= 5) evaluates to true and the block executes. When the statements inside the block are done, j increments by 1 (j = j + 1). These three components ensure that the block executes precisely n times.

```
j = 1       // Initialize counter
j <= n      // Loop test
j = j + 1   // Update counter
```

Here is the general form of the Java `for` loop:

General Form 7.1: for statement

```
for( init-statement; loop-test; update-step )
{
    repeated-part;
}
```

When a `for` loop is encountered, the *init-statement* is executed first and only once. The *loop-test* evaluates to either `true` or `false` before each execution of the *repeated-part*. The *update-step* executes after each iteration of the repeated part. This process continues until the loop test evaluates to `false`. Figure 7.1 summarizes the behavior of a `for` loop.

Figure 7.1

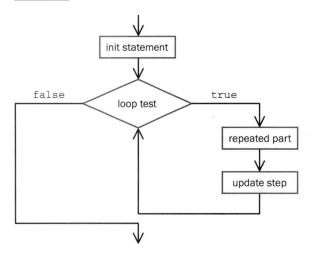

The following `for` statement simply displays the value of the loop counter named `j` as it ranges from 1 through 5 inclusive:

```
int n = 5;
for( int j = 1; j <= n; j = j + 1 )
{
    System.out.print( j + " " );
}
```

Output

```
1 2 3 4 5
```

Although a block is not always necessary, consider always using a block, { }, with a `for` loop. This practice helps avoid difficult-to-detect logic errors. Get into the habit of always writing the repeated part as a block and you will avoid accidental omission of a second or third statement.

Other Increment and Assignment Operators

Assignment operations alter computer memory even when the variable on the left of = is also involved in the expression to the right of =. For example, the variable int j is incremented by 1 with this assignment operation:

```
j = j + 1;
```

This type of update—incrementing a variable—is performed so frequently that Java offers operators with the express purpose of incrementing variables. The ++ and -- operators **increment** and **decrement** a variable by 1, respectively. For example, the expression j++ adds 1 to the value of j, and the expression x-- reduces x by 1. The ++ and -- unary operators alter the numeric variable that they follow (see the table below).

Statement	State of j
int j = 0;	0
j++;	1
j++;	2
j--;	1

So, within the context of the determinate loop, the update step can be written as j++ rather than j = j + 1. This for loop

```
for( int j = 1; j <= n; j = j + 1 )
{
   // ...
}
```

may also be written with the ++ operator for equivalent behavior:

```
for( int j = 1; j <= n; j++ )
{
   // ...
}
```

These new assignment operators are shown because they provide a convenient way to increment and decrement a counter in for loops. Also, most Java programmers use the ++ operator in for loops. You will see them often.

Java has several assignment operators in addition to =. Two of them, += and -=, add and subtract value from the variable to the left, respectively.

Operator	Equivalent Meaning
+=	Increment variable on left by value on right.
-=	Decrement variable on left by value on right.

These two new operators alter the numeric variable that they follow.

Statement	Value of j
int j = 0;	0
j += 3;	3
j += 4;	7
j -= 2;	5

Whereas the operators ++ and -- increment and decrement the variable by one, the operators += and -= increment and decrement the variable by any amount. The += operator is most often used to accumulate values inside a loop. For example, the following code sums all input by the user:

```
// Sum a set of numbers when the user knows how many there are
TextReader keyboard = new TextReader( );
int n;               // The number of times the loop will repeat
double aNum;         // The number read in from the keyboard
double sum = 0.0;    // This keeps the running sum, so start at 0.0

// Determine the number of times to execute a set of statements
System.out.print( "How many numbers are there to sum? " );
n = keyboard.readInt( );

// Execute that set of statements n times
System.out.println( "Enter " + n + " numbers now: " );
for( int j = 1; j <= n; j++ )
{
  aNum = keyboard.readDouble( );
  sum += aNum;  // Equivalent to sum = sum + aNum;
}
System.out.println( "Sum: " + sum );
```

Dialogue

```
How many numbers are there to sum? 4
Enter 4 numbers now:
7.5
3.0
1.5
2.0
Sum: 14.0
```

The following trace of the execution shows how sum accumulates the numbers:

Loop Number	j	aNum	sum
Before loop	NA	?	0.0
1	1	7.5	7.5
2	2	3.0	10.5
3	3	1.5	12.0
4	4	2.0	14.0

The += and -= operators can be used to increment or decrement loop control variables by values other than 1. In the next example, the loop control variable j increments by two at the end of each iteration.

```
for( int j = 0; j <= 10; j += 2 )   // Count by twos
{
  System.out.print( j + "   " );
}
```

Output

```
0   2   4   6   8   10
```

Self-Check

7-1 Does a `for` loop execute the update step at the beginning of each iteration?

7-2 Must an update step increment the loop counter by +1?

7-3 Do `for` loops always execute the repeated part at least once?

7-4 Describe a situation when the loop test j <= n of a `for` loop never becomes false and the loop never terminates on its own.

7-5 Write the output generated by the following `for` loops.

-a
```
for( int j = 1; j < 5; j = j + 1 )
{
    System.out.print( j + " " );
}
```

-b
```
int n = 5;
for( int j = 1; j <= n; j++ )
{
    System.out.print( j + " " );
}
```

-c
```
int n = 3;
for( int j = -3; j <= n; j += 2 )
{
    System.out.print( j + " " );
}
```

-d
```
for( int j = 0; j < 5; j++ )
{
    System.out.print( j + " " );
}
```

-e
```
for( int j = 5; j >= 1; j- )
    System.out.print( j + " " );
```

```
-f  int n = 0;
     System.out.print( "before "  );
    for( int j = 1; j <= n; j++ )
    {
      System.out.print( j + " " );
    }
     System.out.print( " after"  );
```

7-6   Write a `for` loop that displays all of the integers from 1 to 100 inclusive on separate lines.

7-7   Write a `for` loop that displays all of the integers from 10 down to 1 inclusive on separate lines.

Determinate Loops with `Grid` Objects

A `Grid` object has row numbers that range from `0` to `aGrid.getRows( ) - 1` inclusive. The column numbers range from `0` to `aGrid.getColumn( ) - 1` inclusive. Using these facts and the Determinate Loop pattern allows us to manipulate `Grid` objects more compactly. For example, the code below has two `for` loops that place blocks on all four edges of a `Grid` object.

```
Grid aGrid = new Grid( 5, 9, 1, 1, Grid.EAST );
GraphicGrid g = new GraphicGrid( aGrid );

for( int r = 0; r < aGrid.getRows( ); r++ )
{
  aGrid.block( r, 0 );                       // Block west edge
  aGrid.block( r, aGrid.getColumns( ) - 1 ); // Block east edge
}

// The first and last columns are blocked already so
// block column 1 up to 1 less than the last column
for( int c = 1; c < aGrid.getColumns( ) - 1; c++ )
{
  aGrid.block( 0, c );                       // Block most of the north edge
  aGrid.block( aGrid.getRows( ) - 1, c );   // Block most of the south edge
}

System.out.println( aGrid );
```

Output (the screen to the right occurred during the second loop, when c == 4)

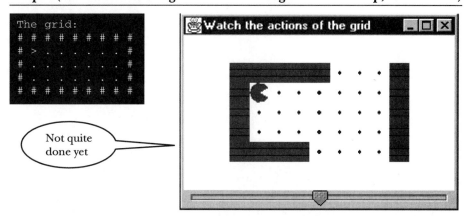

The `for` loop—used in another instance of the Determinate Loop pattern—reduces the number of instructions. Without a `for` loop, blocking a 20-by-20 `Grid` would require exactly 76 `block` messages. More importantly, such a brute-force approach would allow the method to work only on a 20-by-20 `Grid`. Use of a determinate loop allows the method to work properly for any size `Grid`. The method is more general.

Self-Check

7-8 What difference occurs when the first `for` loop is changed to:

```
for( int r = 0; r <= aGrid.getRows( ); r++ )
```

7-9 What difference occurs when the second `for` loop is changed to:

```
for( int c = 1; c < aGrid.getColumn( ); c++ )
```

7-10 What difference occurs when the second `for` loop is changed to:

```
for( int c = 0; c < aGrid.getColumn( ) - 1; c++ );
```

An Application of the Determinate Loop Pattern

Problem: Write a program that determines a range of temperature readings. "Range" is defined as the difference between the highest and lowest. The number of temperature readings will be known in advance. One dialogue would look like this:

Dialogue

```
Enter 6 temperature readings:
11
15
19
23
20
16
Range: 12
```

Analysis

To find the range without the aid of a computer (this is easier with a small number of temperature readings), one could glance at the list of numbers and simply keep track of the highest and lowest while scanning the list from top to bottom. Let's walk through some temperatures. aTemp is the name assigned to the user input.

aTemp	highest	lowest
-5	-5	-5
8	8	-5
22	22	-5
-7	22	-7
15	22	-7

For this set of data, range = highest - lowest = 22 - (-7) = 29.

Let the number of temperature readings be n. Again, the variable named aTemp stores the individual temperature readings as each is read in. The range of temperature readings is the difference between the highest and lowest temperature readings in the list of inputs. The following table summarizes the problem:

Problem Description	Variable Name	Sample Values	Input/Output
Compute the range of temperature readings	n	5	Input
	aTemp	-5, 8, 22, -7, 15	Input
	highest	22	
	lowest	-7	
	range	29	Output

Design

For a large list—an approach more suited to a computer—the algorithm mimics the repetition of the hand-operated version just suggested. It uses a determinate loop to compare every temperature reading in the list to the highest and the lowest and to update them if necessary.

Algorithm: **Determining the range**

for each temperature reading
{
    input aTemp from user
    if aTemp is greater than highest so far,
       store it as highest
    if aTemp is less than lowest so far,
       store it as lowest
}
range = highest - lowest

As usual, it is a good idea to walk through the algorithm to verify its soundness.

1. Input the number of temperature readings (n == 5).
2. Input aTemp from the user (aTemp == -3).
3. If aTemp is greater than highest so far (-3 > . . .). Whoops!

There is no value for highest! There is no value for lowest. Let's assume the program will initialize both highest and lowest to 0:

1. Initialize lowest and highest to 0 (lowest = 0; highest = 0;).
2. Input the number of temperature readings (n == 5).
3. Input aTemp from the user (aTemp == -3).
4. If aTemp is greater than highest (-3 > 0), store aTemp as highest (highest stays the same).
5. If aTemp is less than lowest so far (-3 < 0), store aTemp as lowest (lowest becomes -3).

This seems to work. Consider one more iteration.

1. Input aTemp from the user (aTemp == 8).
2. If aTemp is greater than highest so far (8 > 0), store it as highest (highest = 8).
3. If aTemp is less than lowest so far (8 < -3), store it as lowest (lowest stays -3).

This seems okay. Now try the next three inputs to verify that highest and lowest are correct. Finally, the last step in the algorithm (after the repetition) produces the range: range = highest - lowest.

Self-Check

7-11 Using the previous algorithm, determine the range when n is 4 and the user inputs the four temperature readings *3*, *4*, *2*, and *6*.

If you did the previous self-check question correctly, you noticed that lowest stays 0. The initial value of lowest is less than all subsequent inputs. What at first might have seemed to accomplish the task actually does not. The first test set worked only because a negative temperature was input. The same algorithm will not work on a warmer day when all temperatures are positive. So instead of initializing both highest and lowest to 0, consider setting highest to something ridiculously low, say -999, so low that any input will have to be higher. Set lowest to something ridiculously high like 999, so that any input will have to be lower. However, these mysterious values have no real meaning. In addition, if you wanted a generalized loop that would find the range of any set of numbers, the algorithm would not always work.

A better alternative is to read in the first input and set highest and lowest as this first input. This is no longer phony. The first input is the highest and the lowest read in so far (assuming the user is seeking the range of more than zero inputs). The second input can then be compared to the first. Now walk through the modified algorithm with n == 4 and inputs of *3*, *4*, *2*, and *6* to verify that the algorithm works.

Algorithm: **Finding the range of *n* integers**

input aTemp from the user
set highest so far to aTemp
set lowest so far to aTemp
for each of the remaining (2 through *n*) temperature readings
{
    input aTemp from the user
    if aTemp is greater than highest so far,
        store it as highest
    if aTemp is less than lowest so far,
        store it as lowest
}
range = highest - lowest

Implementation

The problem stated that the number of inputs (*n*) would be known in advance. If n is 5, the user is prompted for five integers. This is an instance of the Determinate Loop pattern.

```
// Read n integers and display the range of inputs

public class DemonstrateDeterminateLoop
{
  public static void main( String[] args )
  {
    TextReader keyboard = new TextReader( );
    int aTemp;
    int n = 5;
```

```
    // Input first integer and record it as highest and lowest
    System.out.println( "\nEnter " + n + " numbers " );
    aTemp = keyboard.readInt( );
    int highest = aTemp;
    int lowest = aTemp;

    // Process n inputs
    for( int j = 2; j <= n; j++ ) // Already processed one, start at 2
    {
      // Get the next input
      aTemp = keyboard.readInt( );

      // Update the highest so far, if necessary
      if( aTemp > highest )
        highest = aTemp;

      // Update the lowest so far, if necessary
      if( aTemp < lowest )
        lowest = aTemp;
    }

    int range = highest - lowest;
    System.out.println( "Range: " + range );
  }
}
```

Dialogue

```
Enter 5 numbers
67
78
89
101
95
Range: 34
```

Testing the Implementation

To test this code, the programmer should compare many hand-checked results with the range displayed by the program. For example, one set of inputs could include values that are all the same—the range should be 0. With two temperatures to check, the range should be computed as the difference between those two values. Another test is the entry of one temperature only. This should result in the range of zero. The testing should also include a set of values where the number of inputs is greater than 2. This leads to many possible test sets, especially when you are attempting to input all possible orderings. Three inputs have six orderings, four inputs have 24 orderings, and in general n inputs have $n!$ (n factorial) orderings, or ($n * (n-1) * (n-2) *, \ldots, * 3 * 2 * 1$). Such exhaustive testing is impractical. It is also unnecessary.

A tester begins to gain confidence in the code by picking an arbitrary number of tests—for example, when *n* is 5 and the inputs were -5, 8, 22, -7, and 15. This set of inputs shows that the difference between the highest and lowest is (22 - (-7)), or 29. Looking at the dialogue and seeing that the range is 29 could lead us to believe that the algorithm and implementation are correct. However, the only thing that is sure is this: When those particular five temperatures are entered, the correct range is returned. The data used in this previous test would indicate that everything is okay.

But testing only reveals the presence of errors, not the absence of errors. If the range were shown as an obviously incorrect answer (-11, for example), hopefully you would detect the presence of an error.

Self-Check

Use this code to answer the questions that follow.

```
highest = -999;
lowest = 999;
int n = 5;
for( int j = 1; j <= n; j++ )
{
  currentInput = keyboard.readInt( );
  if( currentInput > highest )
    highest = aTemp;
  else if( currentInput < lowest )
    lowest = aTemp;
}
range = highest - lowest;
```

7-12 Trace through the code above using these inputs:
  -5   8   22   -7   15
  Predict the value stored in range. Is it correct?

7-13 Trace through the same code with these inputs:
  5   4   3   2   1
  Predict the value stored in range. Is it correct?

7-14 Trace through the same code with these inputs:
  1   2   3   4   5
  Predict the value stored in range. Is it correct?

7-15 When is range incorrectly computed?
  -a When the input is entered in descending order.
  -b When the input is entered in ascending order.
  -c When the input is in neither ascending nor descending order.

7-16 What must be done to correct the error?

Debugging Output Statement

When you detect an intent error and a loop is involved, consider displaying the important values such as `highest` and `lowest`. Writing an output statement inside the loop lets you see the changing values during each iteration of the loop. This simple debugging tool reveals what is happening. One well-placed output statement can be very revealing. For example, a **debugging output statement** could be included at the bottom of the loop in the self-check question above to show what is going on during the loop. The dialogue would look like this:

```
for( int j = 1; j <= n; j++ )
{
    ...

    else if( currentInput < lowest )
      lowest = aTemp;

// DEBUGGING: Add a println to help aid debugging
System.out.println( highest + "   " + lowest );
}
```

Dialog

```
Enter 3 integers
5
5   999
12
12   999
16
16   999
Range: -983
```

The debugging output statement vividly shows that the lowest value is not changing, even though 5, 12, and 16 are all less than 999.

7.2   Indeterminate Loops

Although the Determinate Loop pattern occurs in many algorithms, it has a serious limitation. Somehow, you must determine the number of repetitions in advance. Quite often this is impossible, or at least very inconvenient or difficult. For example, an instructor may have a different number of tests to average as attendance varies between and during school terms. A company may not have a constant number of employees because of hires, fires, lay-offs, transfers, and retirements. An event-driven program cannot predict how many actions the user will initiate.

It is often necessary to execute a set of statements an undetermined number of times, for example, to process report cards for *every* student in a school, not precisely 310 every term. Programs cannot always depend on prior knowledge to determine the exact number of repetitions. It is often more convenient to think in terms of "process a report card for all students" rather than "process precisely 310 report cards." This leads to another recurring pattern in algorithm design that captures the essence of repeating a process an unknown number of times. It is a pattern to help design a process of iterating until some event occurs to indicate that the looping is finished. Here are some events used in this textbook to terminate loops:

- The loop counter becomes greater than the desired number of iterations.
- The mover on a Grid can no longer move forward.
- The user enters a special value to indicate that there is no more input.
- The end of the file is reached.

Whereas the number of repetitions for determinate loops is known in advance, the **Indeterminate Loop pattern** uses other techniques to stop. With indeterminate loops, the number of repetitions need not be known in advance.

Algorithmic Pattern 7.2

Pattern:	Indeterminate Loop
Problem:	A process must repeat an unknown number of times, so some event is needed to terminate the loop.
Outline:	while(the termination event has not occurred)
	{
	perform these actions
	do something to bring the loop closer to termination
	}
Code Example:	// Place things until the mover is blocked

```
while( aGrid.frontIsClear( ) )
{
    aGrid.putDown( ); // Perform some action
    aGrid.move( );    // Bring loop closer to termination
}
```

The Java **while statement** is often used to implement indeterminate loops.

General Form 7.2: **while** statement

```
while ( loop-test )
{
    repeated-part
}
```

The *loop-test* is a boolean expression that evaluates to either true or false. The *repeated-part* may be any Java statement, but it is usually a set of statements enclosed in { and }.

When a `while` loop is encountered, the loop test evaluates to either true or false. If true, the repeated part executes. This process continues while (as long as) the loop test is true.

Figure 7.2

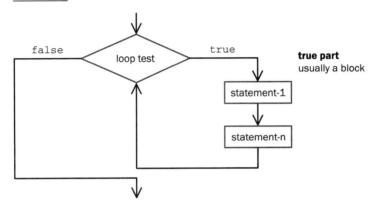

The `while` loop also implements the Determinate Loop pattern. You move the initialization before the `while` loop. Then move the update step to the bottom of the repeated part.

```
initialization
while( loop-test )
{
   // Activities to be repeated
     update-step
}
```

The following code represents an alternate implementation of a determinate loop:

```
// Sum the first n integers
int sum = 0;        // Initialization
int j = 1;          // Initialization
int n = 5;          // Initialization
while( j <= n )     // Loop test
{
   sum = sum + j;   // Action
   j++;             // Update step
}

System.out.println( "Sum of the first " + n + " integers is " + sum );
```

Although the `while` loop can implement determinate loops, the `for` loop is more concise and convenient. It is recommended that you use the `for` loop when the number of iterations is known in advance. When this cannot be determined, use the `while` statement instead.

Self-Check

7-17 Write the output generated by the following code:

```
-a   int j = 1;                        -b   int j = 5;
     while( j <= 5 )                        while( j > 0 )
     {                                      {
        System.out.print( j );                System.out.print( j );
        j++;                                  j--;
     }                                      }
```

Sentinel Loops

A **sentinel** is a specific input value used only to terminate an indeterminate loop. A sentinel value should be the same type of data as the other input. However, this sentinel must not be treated the same as other input. For example, the following set of inputs hints that the input of -1.0 is the event that terminates the loop and that -1.0 is not to be counted as a valid test score. If it were counted as a test score, the average would not be 80.0.

Dialogue

```
Enter test score #1 or -1.0 to quit: 80.0
Enter test score #2 or -1.0 to quit: 90.0
Enter test score #3 or -1.0 to quit: 70.0
Enter test score #4 or -1.0 to quit: -1.0
Average of 3 tests = 80.0
```

This dialogue asks the user either to enter data in the range of 0.0 through 100.0 inclusive or to enter -1.0 to signal the end of the data. With **sentinel loops**, a message is displayed to inform the user how to end the input. In the dialogue above, -1.0 is the sentinel. It could have some other value outside the valid range of inputs, any negative number, for example.

Since the code does not know how many inputs the user will enter, an indeterminate loop should be used. Assuming that the variable to store the user input is named currentInput and SENTINEL is -1.0, the termination condition is currentInput == SENTINEL. The loop should terminate when the user enters a value that flags the end of the data. The loop test can be derived by taking the logical negation of the termination condition. The while loop test becomes input != SENTINEL.

```
while( input != SENTINEL )
```

Now, although the SENTINEL can be established beforehand, the value for currentInput must be read before the loop. This is called a "priming read," which goes into the first iteration of the loop.

```
System.out.print( "Enter number or " + SENTINEL + " to quit: " );
currentInput = keyboard.readDouble( );
while( currentInput != SENTINEL )
{
  // Process currentInput
  // Read the next value to be processed or
  // the sentinel that terminates the loop
}
```

Once inside the loop, the first thing that is done is to process the currentInput from the priming read (add its value to sum and add 1 to n). Once that is done, the second currentInput is read at the "bottom" of the loop. The loop test evaluates next. If currentInput is not the SENTINEL, the second input is processed. This loop continues until the user enters the SENTINEL value. Immediately after the readDouble message at the bottom of the loop, currentValue is compared to SENTINEL. When they are equal, the loop terminates. The SENTINEL is not added to the running sum, nor is 1 added to the count.

The awkward part of this algorithm is that the loop is processing the valid data that was read in the previous iteration of the loop. There are alternatives to this sentinel loop that has two reads, but only the solution with a priming read and a read at the "bottom" of the loop will be shown.

The following method averages any number of inputs. It is an instance of the Indeterminate Loop pattern because the code does not assume how many inputs there will be.

```
// Find an average by using a SENTINEL of -1 to terminate the loop
// that counts the number of inputs and accumulates those inputs.
public class DemonstrateIndeterminateLoop
{
  public static void main( String[] args )
  {
    // final means you cannot assign a new value to SENTINEL
    final double SENTINEL = -1.0; // Termination value
    double accumulator = 0.0;      // Maintain running sum of inputs
    int n = 0;                     // Maintain total number of inputs
    double currentInput;
    TextReader keyboard = new TextReader( );

    System.out.println( "Compute average of numbers read." );
    System.out.println( );
    System.out.print( "Enter number or " + SENTINEL + " to quit: " );
    currentInput = keyboard.readDouble( );

    while( currentInput != SENTINEL )
    {
      accumulator += currentInput;   // Update accumulator
      n++;                           // Update number of inputs so far
      System.out.print( "Enter number or " + SENTINEL + " to quit: " );
      currentInput = keyboard.readDouble( );
    }
```

```
      if( n == 0 )
         System.out.println( "Can't average zero numbers" );
      else
         System.out.println( "Average: " + accumulator / n );
   }
}
```

Dialogue

```
Compute average of numbers read.

Enter number or -1.0 to quit: 70.0
Enter number or -1.0 to quit: 90.0
Enter number or -1.0 to quit: 80.0
Enter number or -1.0 to quit: -1.0
Average: 80.0
```

The following table traces the changing state of the important variables to simulate execution of the previous program. The variable named accumulator maintains the running sum of the test scores. The loop also increments n by +1 for each valid currentInput entered by the user. Notice that -1 is not treated as a valid currentInput.

Iteration Number	currentInput	accumulator	n	currentInput != SENTINEL
Before the loop	NA	0.0	0	NA
Loop 1	70.0	70.0	1	True
Loop 2	90.0	160.0	2	True
Loop 3	80.0	240.0	3	True
After the loop	NA	240.0	3	NA

Notice that this loop repeats the Prompt and Input pattern twice:

```
System.out.print( "Enter numbers or " + SENTINEL + " to quit: " );
currentInput = keyboard.readDouble( );
while( currentInput != SENTINEL )
{
  accumulator += currentInput;   // Update accumulator
  n++;                           // Update total # of inputs
  // Get the next test score or maybe the SENTINEL
  System.out.print( "Enter numbers or " + SENTINEL + " to quit: " );
  currentInput = keyboard.readDouble( );
}
```

When you see repeated code, that is a signal that there may be a better way to implement the program. For example, this repeated code could be eliminated by using the break statement to terminate the loop. Instead of thinking of double negatives, think of positives. Instead of thinking of the logical negation of the termination condition, consider terminating at termination.

The keyword `break`, already shown in the `switch` statement (see Chapter 6, "Selection"), may also be used to cause immediate loop termination. An indeterminate loop is more straightforward than the priming read of the previous loop. That approach required unnecessary duplication of code. The code is not only harder to read, but it is more difficult to write.[1]

Self-Check

7-18 Determine the value assigned to average for each of the following code fragments by simulating execution when the user inputs 70.0, 60.0, 80.0, and -1.0. For both code segments assume the following:

```
TextReader keyboard = new TextReader( );
int n = 0;
double accumulator = 0.0;
double currentInput;
// Can't change, SENTINEL is final
final double SENTINEL = -1.0;
```

-a
```
currentInput = keyboard.readDouble( );
while( currentInput != SENTINEL )
{
  currentInput = keyboard.readDouble( );
  accumulator += currentInput;  // Update accumulator
  n++;                          // Update total # of inputs
}
double average = accumulator / n;
```

-b
```
currentInput = keyboard.readDouble( );
while( currentInput != SENTINEL )
{
  accumulator += currentInput;  // Update accumulator
  n++;                          // Update # of inputs
  currentInput = keyboard.readDouble( );
}
double average = accumulator / n;
```

7-19 If you answered 70.0 for both **-a** and **-b** above, redo both until you get different answers for **-a** and **-b**.

7-20 What is the value of `numberOfWords` after this code executes with the dialogue shown (read the input carefully).

```
String SENTINEL = "QUIT";
TextReader keyboard = new TextReader( );
String theWord;
int numberOfWords = 0;
```

---

1. Elliot Soloway, Jeffrey Bonar, and Kate Ehrlich, "Cognitive strategies and looping constructs: an empirical study," *Communications of the ACM,* Vol 26, No 11, November 1983.

```
      System.out.println( "Enter words or " +
                           SENTINEL + " to quit" );
      theWord = keyboard.readWord( );
      theWord = theWord.toUpperCase( );
      while( theWord.compareTo( SENTINEL ) != 0 )
      {
        numberOfWords++;
        theWord = keyboard.readWord( );
        theWord = theWord.toUpperCase( );
      }
      System.out.println( "You entered " +
                           numberOfWords + " words." );
```

Output

```
Enter words or QUIT to quit
```
The quick brown fox quit and then jumped over the lazy dog.
```
You entered ____ words.
```

7-21 Write a while(true) loop that prompts for and inputs numbers until the
number entered is in the range of 1 through 10 inclusive. Inform the user
if the number is outside this range.

Infinite Loops

It is possible that a loop may never execute, not even once. It is also possible that a
while loop never terminates. Consider the following while loop that potentially
continues to execute until external forces are applied (turning off the computer or
a power outage, for example). This is potentially an **infinite loop**, something that is
usually undesirable.

```
currentInput = keyboard.readInt( );
while( currentInput != SENTINEL )
{
  accumulator += currentInput;   // Update accumulator
  n++;                           // Update total inputs
}
average = accumulator / n;
```

The loop repeats virtually forever. The termination condition can never be
reached. The loop test is always true because there is no statement in the repeated
part that brings the loop closer to the termination condition of currentInput ==
SENTINEL. When writing while loops, guarantee that the loop test eventually
becomes false.

Self-Check

7-22 How many iterations of the loop just shown will occur when the user enters the sentinel (-1) as the very first input?

7-23 What activity should be added to the previous `while` statement so each loop iteration brings the loop one step closer to termination?

7-24 The following code represents another example of an infinite loop with a `Grid` object named `g`. What must be done to make this loop terminate as intended?

```java
while( g.frontIsClear( ) );
{ // Move until it is no longer possible
  g.move( );
}
```

7-25 Write the output from the following Java program fragments:

-a
```java
int n = 3;
int counter = 1;
while( counter <= n )
{
  System.out.print( counter + "  " );
  counter++;
}
```

-b
```java
int last = 10;
int j = 2;
while( j <= last )
 {
   System.out.print( j + "  " );
   j += 2;
}
```

-c
```java
counter = 10;
// Tricky, but an easy-to-make mistake
while( counter >= 0 );
{
  System.out.println( counter );
  counter++;
}
```

7-26 Write the number of times "Hello" is printed. "Zero" and "Infinite" are valid answers.

-a
```java
int counter = 1;
int n = 20;
while( counter <= n )
{
  System.out.print( "Hello " );
  counter++;
}
```

```
-b  int counter = 1;
    int n = 0;
    while( counter <= n )
    {
      System.out.print( "Hello " );
    }

-c  int counter = 1;
    int n = 5;
    while( counter <= n )
    {
      System.out.print( "Hello " );
      counter++;
    }

-d  int n = 5;
    int j = 1;
    while( j <= n )
      System.out.print( "Hello " );
      j++;

-e  int j = 1;
    int n = 5 ;
    while( j <= 5 )
    {
      System.out.print( "Hello " );
      n++;
    }

-f  int j = 2;
    int n = 1024;
    while( j <= n )
    {
      System.out.print( "Hello " );
      j = j * 2;
    }
```

7-27 Write code that sums all integers until the user enters a negative integer.

7-28 Write code that reads integers until the difference between two consecutive integers is greater than 100. Assume that there are always at least two inputs. The number of inputs may be even or odd and can range from 2 inputs to many. Print the values of the first two consecutive numbers that differ by more than 100.

The Indeterminate Loop Pattern with Grid Objects

There are many events that terminate loops. Consider moving the mover up until it reaches the edge of a Grid or a block. This is a problem that will come in handy for one of the `Grid`-related programming projects at the end of this chapter, which asks you to always get the mover out of the only exit that is randomly selected when constructed with two `int` arguments instead of five.

```
// This Grid constructor--with only two arguments--will place
// the mover at some random location and in some random direction
// inside an enclosed Grid with exactly one random opening.
Grid tarpit = new Grid( 8, 30 );  // Construct a different Grid

// Get the graphical view
GraphicGrid g = new GraphicGrid( tarpit );

while( tarpit.frontIsClear( ) )
{
   tarpit.move( );
}
```

Output

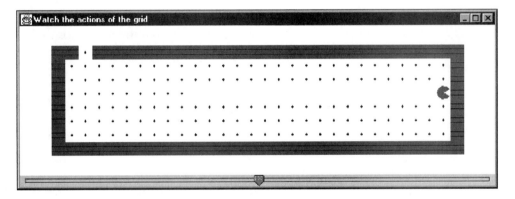

Because of the randomness of the `Grid` object initialized with two arguments, `tarpit`, an indeterminate loop is used to advance the mover. The `while` loop may repeat the `move` message never, once, twice, or as many times as are necessary to get the mover up against the "wall."

Self-Check

7-29 Why is the loop above considered an indeterminate loop rather than a determinate loop?

7.3   The Indeterminate Loop Pattern with a `TextReader` Object

Because keyboard input is common, the author-supplied `TextReader` class is often used to read input from the keyboard. However, input may also be obtained from many other sources, such as a file on a disk or a graphics tablet. This chapter uses a `TextReader` object to show how text is read from a file on a disk. All the methods are the same. The only difference is that you must now specify the name of the file when you construct an object. The argument is the file name.

General Form 7.3: initializing `TextReader` objects for disk files

`TextReader` *object-name* = `new TextReader(` *"file-name"* `)`;

Example

```
TextReader inFile = new TextReader( "Test.java" );
```

The *file-name* is the name of the existing file to be read. Among other things, constructing the `TextReader` object associates *object-name* with the file stored in the operating system as *file-name*. If the file is not found, the `TextReader` object construction fails and the program terminates like this:

```
TextReader anotherInputFile = new TextReader( "NotHere.java" );
```

Output

```
Can't open input file 'NotHere.java', exiting
```

The following example uses a `TextReader` object to read three integers from a disk file. Prompts aren't needed anymore. The same input methods are available such as `readDouble` and `readWord`. However, there is no need to prompt files for input.

```java
public class ReadFromDiskFile
{
  public static void main( String[] args )
  {
    // Initialize a TextReader object so inFile is an input stream
    // associated with the operating system file named "input.dat"
    TextReader inFile = new TextReader( "input.dat" );

    // Read three integers from the file "input.dat"
    int n1, n2, n3;
    n1 = inFile.readInt( );
    n2 = inFile.readInt( );
    n3 = inFile.readInt( );

    System.out.println( "n1: " + n1 );
    System.out.println( "n2: " + n2 );
```

```
        System.out.println( "n3: " + n3 );
    }
}
```

The output below results from reading the file `"input.dat"` that stores these `int`s:

Input File

```
70
80
90
```

Output

```
n1: 70
n2: 80
n3: 90
```

File input with `TextReader` works the same as keyboard input: spaces and new lines separate input data. This applies to data that are `String`s, `int`s, and `double`s. If an integer is encountered in the file input stream during an attempt to read a `double`, the `int` is promoted to the `double`. Once the program begins to run, data can be read from the disk file. User input is not required.

Self-Check

7-30 Write code that reads the first n strings from an input file named `PrintNWords.java`. Your code should display those "words" (actually pieces of a program) to the screen. Assume that there are always at least n words in the file (n is 8 in the dialogue below). The file starts like this, where the first line contains two strings (`class` and `SixA`):

```
public class PrintNWords
{
  public static void main( String[] args )
  {
```

One dialogue would look like this:

```
How many words do you want to read? 8
public class PrintNWords { public static void main(
```

Reading until the End of a File

Using `TextReader`'s `ready` method as the loop test lets you process all data in a text file without knowing the amount of data beforehand.

```
/** Use this to test if the input stream is ready for reading and
  * at least one more character in the file has not yet been read.
  * @return false if there is no more data--at end of the
  * file--or return true if there is more data to be read.
  */
public boolean ready( )
```

In the following program, the loop executes the repeated part only if the input file is ready to have more input read. When there is no more data in the file, the ready method returns `false`. The loop terminates.

```
// Demonstrate TextReader.ready in an indeterminate loop
public class DemonstrateReady
{
  public static void main( String[] args )
  {
    // Initialize a TextReader object so inFile is an
    // object associated with the file named "numbers.dat"
    TextReader inFile = new TextReader( "numbers.dat" );
    double aNumber;
    double sum = 0.0;
    int n = 0;

    System.out.println( "n   Number Sum" );
    System.out.println( "== ====== =====" );
    // Sum and count the numbers in the file associated with inFile
    while( inFile.ready( ) )
    {
      // Read a number from the file
      aNumber = inFile.readDouble( );

      // Accumulate the sum
      sum = sum + aNumber;

      // Update the number of numbers read
      n++;

      // Show what is happening
      System.out.println( n + "   " + aNumber + "    " + sum );
    }

    // Compute and display the average
    double average = sum / n;
    System.out.println( "Average of " + n + " numbers is " + average );
  }
}
```

To visualize what happens, the loop displays each successfully read number and the current values of n and sum. This output shown below appears when the file named numbers.dat contains the following data:

Input File

```
11.1   22.2   33.3
44.4   55.5   66.6
77.7   88.8   99.9
```

Output

```
n   Number  Sum
==  ======  =====
1   11.1    11.1
2   22.2    33.3
3   33.3    66.6
4   44.4    111.0
5   55.5    166.5
6   66.6    233.1
7   77.7    310.8
8   88.8    399.6
9   99.9    499.5
Average of 9 numbers is 55.5
```

When Things Go Wrong

Sometimes the input file cannot be found. Sometimes the input file contains some bad data. Sometimes an accidental extra line at the end of the file can mess things up—the `TextReader` class methods may terminate the program prematurely.

Consider what should happen when there is a blank line at the end of the file. The `ready` method returns true because there is more data. The loop above sends a `readDouble` method (`inFile.ready` is true). With no number to be found, `readDouble` fails and the program terminates. For example, the output below is the result of trying to read data from this file when there is a blank line at the end with at least one blank space.

Input File

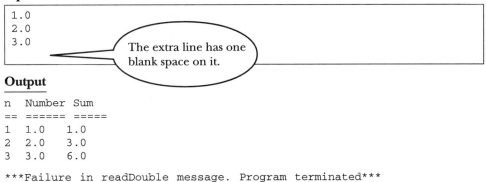

```
1.0
2.0
3.0
```

The extra line has one blank space on it.

Output

```
n   Number  Sum
==  ======  =====
1   1.0     1.0
2   2.0     3.0
3   3.0     6.0

***Failure in readDouble message. Program terminated***
Press Enter to continue . . .
```

The program would work fine if the extra line had nothing on it. Avoid extra spaces and lines at the end of input files.

Self-Check

7-31 What happens during execution of the preceding program if the file
numbers.dat

-a does not exist or cannot be located?

-b contains one number?

-c contains no numbers (the file is empty, with no spaces on any line)?

-d contains a blank space after the last number?

-e contains one line with one blank space (the file is not really empty
but has no numbers)?

7-32 Write the output generated by the preceding program with the following
three sets (a., b., and c.) of data stored in the file input.dat. The
readDouble method displays an error message and returns 0.0 whenever a
TextReader object is reading from a file rather than the keyboard.

-a 1.1 2.2 3.0

-b 1.0 2.0 3.0 4.0

-c 1.0 2.0 3.0 BAD 4.0

The next example program reads its own source code one line at a time. The
program displays each line in the file to standard output (the screen). It also shows
the line numbers along the way.

```java
public class FileInput  // In the file named FileInput.java
{
  public static void main( String[] args )
  {
    TextReader inFile = new TextReader( "FileInput.java" );
    String oneLine;
    int lineNumber = 0;

    // Read this file and display it to the screen
    while( inFile.ready ( ) )
    {
      lineNumber++;
      oneLine = inFile.readLine( );
      System.out.println( lineNumber + ": " + oneLine );
    }
  }
}
```

Output (after line numbers and ':', output should match the source code above)

```
1: public class FileInput   // In the file named FileInput.java
2: {
3:   public static void main( String[] args )
4:   {
5:     TextReader inFile = new TextReader( "FileInput.java" );
6:     String oneLine;
7:     int lineNumber = 0;
8:
9:     // Read this file and display it to the screen
10:     while( inFile.ready ( ) )
11:     {
12:       lineNumber++;
13:       oneLine = inFile.readLine( );
14:       System.out.println( lineNumber + ": " + oneLine );
15:     }
16:   }
17: }
```

7.4   The do while Statement

The **do while statement** is similar to the while loop. It allows a collection of statements to be repeated while an expression is true. The primary difference is the time at which the loop test is evaluated. Whereas the while loop test is evaluated at the beginning of each iteration, the do while statement evaluates the loop test at the end of the loop. This means that the do while loop always executes its repeated part at least once. Here is the general form of the do while loop.

GENERAL FORM 7.4: **do while loop**

do

{

   repeated-part

} while(*loop-test* **);**

When a do while statement is encountered, all statements execute within the block, from { to }. The *loop-test* evaluates at the *end* of the loop—not at the beginning. If it is true, the *repeated-part* executes again. If the test expression is false, the loop terminates. Here is an example of the do while loop that displays the increasing value of counter to visualize the execution.

```
int counter = 1;
int n = 4;
System.out.println( "Before loop..." );
```

```
do
{
   System.out.println( "Loop #" + counter );
   counter++;
} while ( counter <= n );

System.out.println( "...After loop" );
```

Output

```
Before loop...
Loop #1
Loop #2
Loop #3
Loop #4
...After loop
```

An equivalent pretest `while` loop can be written like this:

```
int counter = 1;
int n = 4;
System.out.println( "Before loop..." );
while( counter <= n )
{
   System.out.println( "Loop #" + counter );
   counter++;
}
System.out.println( "...After loop" );
```

However, there are times when a posttest loop is better. Although the `while` loop produces the same exact output as its `do while` counterpart when n is greater than or equal to `counter`, a difference can be seen when n = 1 is replaced with n = 0. The `while` loop does not execute its iterative part, but the `do while` loop does execute the repeated part once, even when n is 0:

```
Before loop...
Loop #1
...After loop
```

The `do while` loop is a good choice for repetition whenever a set of statements must be executed at least once to initialize objects used later in the loop test. The `do while` loop is the preferred statement when asking the user of the program to enter one of several options. For example, the `do while` loop in the `char` method `nextOption` repeatedly requests the user to enter one of three choices. The loop does not terminate until the user enters a valid `option`. The `main` method also uses a `do while` loop to process as many deposits and withdrawals as the user wants.

```
public class LoopCallsMethodWithLoop
{
   private TextReader keyboard;
```

```java
  public LoopCallsMethodWithLoop( )
  {
    keyboard = new TextReader( );
  }

  // Return an uppercase W, D, or Q
  public char nextOption( )
  {
    char option = '?';

    // Loop until one of the valid inputs is read
    do
    {
      System.out.print( "W)ithdraw, D)eposit, or Q)uit: " );

      // The readChar method returns a character
      option = keyboard.readChar( );
      System.out.print( "option == '" + option + "'" );

      // Convert to upper case
      option = Character.toUpperCase( option );

      // Terminate loop if option is not any of the three valid choices
    } while( (option != 'W') && (option != 'D') && (option != 'Q') );

    return option;
  }

  public void processTillDone( )
  {
    char choice = 'Q';

    do
    {
      choice = nextOption( );   // Call a method with a loop
      // Assert: choice is either 'Q', 'W', or 'D'

      if( choice == 'W' )
        System.out.println( "Valid entry--process W\n" );
      else if( choice == 'D' )
        System.out.println( "Valid entry--process D\n" );
      else if( choice == 'Q' )
        System.out.println( "Have a nice whatever :)" );
      else
        System.out.println( "Error in nextOption  :(" );

    } while ( choice != 'Q' );
  }

  public static void main( String[] args )
  {
    LoopCallsMethodWithLoop nestedLoops = new LoopCallsMethodWithLoop( );
    nestedLoops.processTillDone( );
  }
}
```

Dialogue (user enters three invalid choices, two valid entries, and then Q to quit)

```
W)ithdraw, D)eposit, or Q)uit: try
W)ithdraw, D)eposit, or Q)uit: three
W)ithdraw, D)eposit, or Q)uit: invalid entries before three valid ones
W)ithdraw, D)eposit, or Q)uit: w
Valid entry--process W
W)ithdraw, D)eposit, or Q)uit: D
Valid entry--process D
W)ithdraw, D)eposit, or Q)uit: q
Have a nice whatever :)
```

Because at least one character must be obtained from the keyboard before the test expression evaluates, a do while loop in nextOption is used instead of a while loop—the loop must iterate at least once. Also, a do while loop is used in main to get an option because it needs at least one user input to evaluate what the user wants to do.

Although do while is not necessary, it is a bit easier to solve this problem with do while rather than with the following while, which requires the Prompt and Input pattern twice, once before the loop and then again inside the loop. And in this case, there are four statements for each prompt then input.

```
// Return an uppercase W, D, or Q
public char nextOption()
{
  char option = '?';

  // The priming read is not necessary with do while
  System.out.print( "W)ithdraw, D)eposit, or Q)uit: " );
  option = keyboard.read( );
  keyboard.readLine( );
  option = Character.toUpperCase( option );

  while( ( option != 'W' ) && ( option != 'D' ) && ( option != 'Q' ) )
  {
    System.out.print( "W)ithdraw, D)eposit, or Q)uit: " );
    option = keyboard.read( );
    keyboard.readLine( );
    option = Character.toUpperCase( option );
  }

  return option;
}
```

Then again, you could use simply initialize option to any value that would be understood to indicate an invalid choice; '?', for example.

```
// Return an uppercase W, D, or Q
public char nextOption( )
{
  // Set the option to some value that is not a valid choice
  char option = '?';
```

```
while( ( option != 'W' ) && ( option != 'D' ) && ( option != 'Q' ) )
{
   System.out.print( "W)ithdraw, D)eposit, or Q)uit: " );
   option = keyboard.read( );
   keyboard.readLine( );
   option = Character.toUpperCase( option );
}
return option;
}
```

Self-Check

7-33 Write the output produced by the following code:

-a
```
int counter = 1;
do
{
   System.out.print( counter + " " );
   counter++;
} while ( counter <= 3 );
```

-b
```
String str = "abcdef";
do
{
   System.out.println( str );
   str = str.substring( 1, str.length( ) );
} while( str.length( ) > 0);
```

7-34 Write a do while loop that prompts for and inputs integers until the integer input is in the range of 1 through 10 inclusive.

7.5   Loop Selection and Design

For some people, loops are easy to implement, even at first. For others, infinite loops, being off by one iteration, and intent errors are more common. In either case, the following outline is offered to help you choose and design loops in a variety of situations:

1. Determine which type of loop to use.
2. Determine the loop test.
3. Write the statements to be repeated.
4. Bring the loop one step closer to termination.
5. Initialize variables if necessary.

Determine Which Type of Loop to Use

If the number of repetitions is known in advance or is read as input, it is appropriate to use the Determinate Loop pattern. The for statement was specifically designed for this pattern. Although you can use the `while` loop to implement the Determinate Loop pattern, consider using the `for` loop instead. The `while` implementation allows you to omit one of the key parts, making any intent errors more difficult to detect and correct. If you leave off one of the parts from a `for` loop, you get an easier-to-detect-and-correct compiletime error.

The Indeterminate Loop pattern is more appropriate when you need to wait until some event occurs during execution of the loop. In this case, use the `while` loop. If the loop must always execute once, like when input data must be checked for its validity (an integer value that must be in the range of 0 through 100, for example), use the `do while` loop. If you need to process all the data in an input file, consider using a `TextReader` object with the `ready` method as the loop test. This is an indeterminate loop.

Determining the Loop Test

If the loop test is not obvious, try writing the conditions that must be true for the loop to terminate. For example, if you want the user to enter QUIT to stop entering input, the termination condition is

```
inputName.equals( "QUIT" )   // Termination condition
```

The logical negation `!inputName.equals( "QUIT" )` can be used directly as the loop test of a `while` loop.

```
while( ! inputName.equals( "QUIT" ) )
{ // . . .
}
```

Writing the Statements to Be Repeated

This is why the loop is being written in the first place. Some common tasks include keeping a running sum, keeping track of a high or low value, and counting the number of occurrences of some value. Other tasks that will be seen later include searching for a name in a list and repeatedly comparing all string elements of a list in order to alphabetize it.

Bringing the Loop One Step Closer to Termination

To avoid an infinite loop, at least one action in the loop must bring it closer to termination. In a determinate loop this might mean incrementing or decrementing a counter by some specific value. Inputting a value is a way to bring indeterminate loops closer to termination. This happens when a user inputs data until a sentinel is read, for example. In a `for` loop, the repeated statement should be designed to bring the loop closer to termination, usually by incrementing the counter.

Initializing Variables if Necessary

Check to see if any variables used in either the body of the loop or the loop test need to be initialized. Doing this usually ensures that the variables of the loop and the variables used in the iterative part have been initialized. For example, consider this loop:

```
TextReader keyboard;
double sum, input, average;
System.out.print( "Enter numbers or -1 to quit: " );
input = keyboard.readDouble( );

while( input != -1 )
{
  sum = sum + input;
  n = n + 1;
  System.out.print( "Enter numbers or -1 to quit: " );
  input = keyboard.readDouble( );
}

if( n > 0 )
{
  average = sum / n;
  System.out.println( "Average of " + n + " inputs is " + average );
}
else
  System.out.println( "You must enter more than zero inputs" );
```

This code attempts to use many variables in expressions before they have been initialized. In certain other languages, these variables are given garbage values and the result is unpredictable. Fortunately, the Java compiler flags these uninitialized variables as errors.

```
InitializeVariables.java:14: cannot resolve symbol
symbol  : variable n
location: class InitializeVariables
  n = n + 1;
      ^
InitializeVariables.java:14: cannot resolve symbol
symbol  : variable n
location: class InitializeVariables
  n = n + 1;
          ^
InitializeVariables.java:19: cannot resolve symbol
symbol  : variable n
location: class InitializeVariables
if( n > 0 )
    ^
InitializeVariables.java:21: cannot resolve symbol
symbol  : variable n
location: class InitializeVariables
```

```
average = sum / n;
               ^
InitializeVariables.java:22: cannot resolve symbol
symbol  : variable n
location: class InitializeVariables
  System.out.println( "Average of " + n + " inputs is " + average );
                                      ^
5 errors
```

Here are the corrected initializations necessary before the loop is entered.

```
TextReader keyboard = new TextReader( );
double sum = 0.0;
int n = 0;
// It is not really necessary to initialize x, but that is only
// because while( true ) is used. The loop executes at least once.
// If there were a loop test other than true, this would be necessary.
double input;
double average;   // average doesn't require initialization
System.out.print( "Enter numbers or -1 to quit: " );
input = keyboard.readDouble( );

while( input != -1 )
{ // ...
```

Self-Check

7-35 Which kind of loop best accomplishes these tasks?

-a Sum the first five integers $(1 + 2 + 3 + 4 + 5)$.

-b Find the average for a set of numbers when the size of the set is known.

-c Find the average value for a set of numbers when the size of the set cannot be determined until the data has been completely entered.

-d Obtain a character from the user that must be an uppercase S or Q.

7-36 To design a loop that processes inputs called value until –1 is entered,

-a write a termination condition.

-b write the statement that will terminate a while(true) loop.

-c write the loop test for a while loop that keeps going as long as the termination condition has not yet occurred.

7-37 Which variables are not initialized but should be?

-a
```
while( j <= n )
{  // ...
}
```

-b
```
for( int j = 1; j <= n; j = j + inc )
{  // ...
}
```

7.6   The **`ListIterator`** Interface

Java's `ArrayList` class introduced in Chapter 3, "Using Objects," stores a collection of elements (more technically, one `ArrayList` object stores references to objects). There is often a need to examine and/or reference all of the elements within the collection. The process of accessing all elements in a collection from the first to the last (or last to first) is known as **iteration**.

Java provides a consistent set of methods to allow iteration over `ArrayList` elements. The same approach can be used for instances of other Java collection classes. Each of these classes has a method named `listIterator` that returns an object that is guaranteed to have methods for accessing all elements in a collection, no matter how many elements are in the collection.

```
// listIterator returns ListIterator type object
// that understands hasNext and next messages.
// You must supply the starting index to the first element.
ListIterator itr = stringList.listIterator( 0 );
```

This allows for a consistent interface for iterating over different types of collection objects without knowing how the elements are stored.

The `listIterator` method returns an object reference that can be assigned to a `ListIterator`, a Java interface from the `java.util` package. This means the object is guaranteed to have certain methods.

In the `java.util.ListIterator` interface, there are four methods that will be used. The first two demonstrated are `hasNext` and `next`.

```
/** From the ListIterator interface in the java.util package
  *
  * Returns true if there is at least one more element to be visited
  * in a forward (increasing index) direction
  */
public boolean hasNext( );


/** From the ListIterator interface in the java.util package
  *
  * Returns a reference to the next element in the list while updating
  * a forward iteration. This method accesses state (the next element)
  * while changing the state of the ListIterator object so all
  * elements can be visited
  */
public Object next( );
```

Here is the long way to visit all elements in a collection. This code is hard-wired to work only when there are precisely four elements in the collection.

```
ArrayList accountList = new ArrayList( );

accountList.add( new BankAccount( "First",  100.00 ) );
accountList.add( new BankAccount( "Second", 200.00 ) );
accountList.add( new BankAccount( "Third",  300.00 ) );
accountList.add( new BankAccount( "Fourth", 400.00 ) );

// ArrayList listIterator returns an object that
// understands hasNext and next messages.
ListIterator itr = accountList.listIterator( 0 );

System.out.println( itr.next( ) );
System.out.println( itr.next( ) );
System.out.println( itr.next( ) );
System.out.println( itr.next( ) );
// Do NOT send more than four next messages
// when there are four elements in the list!
```

Output

```
First $100.00
Second $200.00
Third $300.00
Fourth $400.00
```

If `itr.next` were called one more time, this exception would occur:

```
Exception in thread "main" java.util.NoSuchElementException
        at java.util.AbstractList$Itr.next(AbstractList.java:423)
        at InitializeVariables.main(InitializeVariables.java:25)
```

A safer way to iterate—to avoid this NoSuchElementException from being thrown—is to put the iteration under the control of a loop with the hasNext message in the loop test. The hasNext method returns true if there are more elements to visit in the iteration. It returns false as soon as all elements have been visited. Here is the code that iterates over all of the elements more safely:

```
// listIterator returns ListIterator type object
// that understands hasNext and next messages.
ListIterator itr = accountList.listIterator( 0 );
while( itr.hasNext( ) )
{
  System.out.println( itr.next( ).toString( ) );
}
// Do NOT send another next message unless you restart the iteration
```

In summary, the listIterator method of ArrayList returns a reference to an object with at least these two methods:

1. hasNext returns true if the collection has more elements to visit.
2. next returns a reference to the next element in the ordered collection. The next message also updates the iteration so all of the elements are visited and the iteration eventually ends.

Generic Collections

One of the characteristics of Java collection classes, such as ArrayList, is that they can store a collection of any type of element.[2] When one collection can store different types of objects, it is said to be a generic collection. For example, ArrayList could store a collection of references to String objects or a collection of references to BankAccount objects as shown above. The ability to store different types of objects in the same collection class is implied by the ArrayList method heading for add and the next method from the ListIterator interface.

```
public boolean add(Object o)      from class ArrayList

public Object next( )             from ListIterator interface
```

Notice that the add method has an Object parameter. The next method returns a reference to an Object. This means that references to any type of object can be added to an ArrayList, not just Strings or BankAccounts (it also means you cannot store int or double primitives). This is possible because all objects in Java extend the Java class named Object (or another class that extends Object). One-way assignment allows any Java object reference to be assigned to an Object reference.

Although you can store any type of object into an ArrayList, you have extra work to do if you want to send messages to the object that you get back from the ArrayList in a next message. You have to cast.

Consider the following code that sums all of the balances in the small accountList shown earlier. The ListIterator object's next method returns a reference to Object, so this reference must be cast into a BankAccount.

```java
// Use the same list of four BankAccounts shown earlier
double assets = 0.0;
ListIterator itr = accountList.listIterator( 0 );
while( itr.hasNext( ) )
{
  Object obj = itr.next( );
  // Cast object to a BankAccount
  BankAccount anAccount = (BankAccount)obj;
  assets += anAccount.getBalance( );
}
System.out.println( "Total assets " + assets );
```

Output

```
Total assets 1000.0
```

---

2. Since ArrayList actually stores a collection of *references to objects*, not the objects themselves, the objects referenced by the ArrayList are referred to as "elements."

If you attempt to send BankAccount's getBalance message to an instance of the Object class, the compiler will complain. The Object class does not know about getBalance. This method was added to the BankAccount class.

```
assets += itr.next().getBalance( );
                   ^
Method getBalance() not found in class java.lang.Object
```

The extra work of casting is currently necessary to use Java collection classes. The benefit is that one collection class can be used to store a collection of any type of element. Now that the listIterator method of ArrayList has been introduced, the next section shows how to store a collection of the most recent transactions recorded by the bank teller system.

7.7   BankTeller_Ch7 — The Most Recent Transactions (Improved)

The bank teller system currently uses an ArrayList to store transactions. It stores all recorded transactions. Using an ArrayList has been okay since there is only one account to maintain. However, eventually (by Chapter 8), there will be many accounts. Additionally, the Transactions are shown from oldest to newest—the reverse order of what was specified as the 10 most recent transactions.

To alleviate both problems, this section adds a new class named TransactionList. It is designed to get the 10 most recent transactions for any valid account. This involves some complex processing. Since the bank teller system is becoming complex, the ArrayList of Transactions will be replaced with a new class to handle the complexities of managing the most recent transactions. It would be nice to have an object that has the reponsibility for providing the needed String for the XPress 10 button clicks with a simple message like this.

```
// Get the most recent 10 transactions for the currentAccount
String theMostRecent =
            transactionList.getMostRecent( currentAccount.getID( ),
            MAX_TRANSACTIONS );
```

The TransactionList will still use an ArrayList instance variable to store the collection of transactions. In fact, the add method is just a wrapper around the ArrayList add method. TransactionList's add method passes along the parameter to ArrayList's add method. The strength of this class comes in the processing to get the 10 most recent transactions for any given ID—the method named getMostRecent.

The getMostRecent method will search through an ArrayList of Transactions from the most recently added Transaction to the oldest Transaction. The most recent is at the end of the list, not the beginning. The algorithm includes iterating over the collection in reverse order. To do this, two other methods of the `ListIterator` interface will be introduced. In addition to `hasNext` and `next`, `ListIterator` objects have these two methods for iterating over a collection in reverse order.

```
/** From the Iterator interface
  *
  * Returns true if this list iterator has more elements
  * when traversing the list in the reverse directions
  */
boolean hasPrevious()

/** From the Iterator interface
  *
  * Returns the previous element in the list
  */
Object previous()
```

The `getMostRecent` method will begin the iteration at the end of the list—not at index 0, but at index `size( ) - 1`. To accomplish this, the `listIterator` method of `ArrayList` will specify that the iteration begins at the end of the list with the following message:

```
// Begin at the last element in the ArrayList
ListIterator reverseIterator =
            theTransactions.listIterator( theTransactions.size( ) );
```

Whereas the starting index is the element returned by `next`, when `previous` is called, the element returned is at the starting index - 1. That is why the argument is `theTransactions.size( )` rather than `theTransactions.size( ) - 1`. When the iteration is ready to return that last element in `theTransactionList`, a loop will create an `ArrayList` of transactions. The iteration will begin at the end and continue to look for transactions that have the given account ID until one of two things happens.

1. There are no more transactions in the list to consider.
2. The most recent `maxTransactions` have been found.

```
public String getMostRecent( String ID, int maxTransactions )
{
  String result = "";
  ArrayList listForGivenID = new ArrayList( );

  // Get from 0 to maxTransactions transactions belonging to ID
  int numberOfTransactions = 0;
  ListIterator reverseIterator =
          theTransactions.listIterator( theTransactions.size( ) );

  while( reverseIterator.hasPrevious( ) &&
         numberOfTransactions < maxTransactions )
  { // First call to previous returns that last element in the list
    Transaction transaction =
                      (Transaction)reverseIterator.previous( );
```

```
      if( ID.equals( transaction.getAccountID( ) ) )
      {
        listForGivenID.add( transaction );
        numberOfTransactions++;
      }
    } // End the iteration loop

    // Use a private helper method to build
    // the list as a string with new lines
    return makeANiceList( listForGivenID, ID );

} // End getMostRecent
```

The remaining task is to create a nice string to return the `actionPerformed` method that requested it. The `getMostRecent` method employs a helper method to get this string. **Helper methods** help partition complex methods into smaller methods. Since helper methods are used only by the class and are not intended for use by other objects, they are usually declared to be private. The `getMostRecent` method and the private helper method named `makeANiceList` are shown in the context of the `TransactionList` class.

```
// A class to hide the complexities of managing a collection of accounts
// while providing an easy way to get the most recent transactions for
// a given accountID with the most recent transactions being the first.

import java.util.ArrayList;
// To iterate from the last element to the first
import java.util.ListIterator;
public class TransactionList
{
  private ArrayList theTransactions;
  // Construct an empty transaction list
  public TransactionList( )
  {
    theTransactions = new ArrayList( );
  }

  public void addTransaction( Transaction aTransaction )
  {
    theTransactions.add( aTransaction );
  }

  // Return "" or from 0 to maxTransactions of
  // the most recent transactions as a string
  public String getMostRecent( String ID, int maxTransactions )
  {
    String result = "";

    ArrayList listForGivenID = new ArrayList( );
    // Get from 0 to maxTransactions transactions belonging to ID
    int numberOfTransactions = 0;
    ListIterator reverseIterator
        = theTransactions.listIterator( theTransactions.size( ) );
```

```
      while( reverseIterator.hasPrevious( ) &&
             numberOfTransactions < maxTransactions )
      {
        // First call to previous returns the last element in the list
        Transaction transaction =
                     (Transaction)reverseIterator.previous( );
        if( ID.equals( transaction.getAccountID( ) ) )
        {
          listForGivenID.add( transaction );
          numberOfTransactions++;
        }
      }

      // Use private helper method to build list as string with new lines
      return makeANiceList( listForGivenID, ID );
    }

    // Make a list of transactions with new lines separating each
    private String makeANiceList( ArrayList listForGivenID, String ID )
    {
      String result = "Most recent transactions for " + ID + "\n";

      int transactionNumber = 1;  // Number the transactions
      ListIterator itr = listForGivenID.listIterator( );
      while( itr.hasNext( ) )
      {
        Object transaction = itr.next( );
        // Concatenate one transaction per line
        result = result + transactionNumber + ") " +
               transaction.toString( ) + "\n";
        transactionNumber++;
      }
      return result;
    }
  }
} // End class TransactionList
```

This class can now be used in the bank teller system. First, the `ArrayList` instance variable is changed to be a `TransactionList`.

```
private TransactionList transactionList;   // Was ArrayList
```

It will be constructed in the `BankTeller_Ch7` constructor.

```
  // Code to maintain a transaction list and
  // register the listener to show it.
  transactionList = new TransactionList( );
  TransactionButtonListener express10Listener =
                           new TransactionButtonListener( );
  XPress10Button.addActionListener( express10Listener );
} // End constructor
```

The constructor also registers an instance of this `ActionListener` to respond to XPress 10 button clicks. The `actionPerformed` message is quite simple, because it

uses the complex `getMostRecent` method in the `TransactionList` object to get
the `String` that is passed along to `showMessageDialog`.

```
// This actionPerformed method will execute
// when the XPress 10 button is clicked.
private class TransactionButtonListener implements ActionListener
{
  public void actionPerformed( ActionEvent evt )
  {
    // Get the most recent transactions as one big String
    String transactionsAsOneBigString =
        transactionList.getMostRecent( currentAccount.getID( ),
        MAX_TRANSACTIONS );

    // Then show the transaction in a modal dialog box
    JOptionPane.showMessageDialog( null, transactionsAsOneBigString );
  }
} // End class TransactionButtonListener
```

The `withdrawButton` and `depositButton` listeners need not be changed.
They were already added to `theTransactionList` with `add` messages. Now the
same messages add them to an instance of `TransactionList`.

```
// Record the transaction (assume the teller
// collected money from the customer).
currentAccount.deposit( amount );
Transaction aTransaction =
    new Transaction( currentAccount, amount, Transaction.DEPOSIT_CODE );
transactionList.add( aTransaction );
```

To demonstrate, when the system starts up and the user enters two withdrawals
followed by two deposits in the amounts of `1.00`, `2.00`, `3.00`, and `4.00`, clicking
the XPress 10 button results in this dialog box:

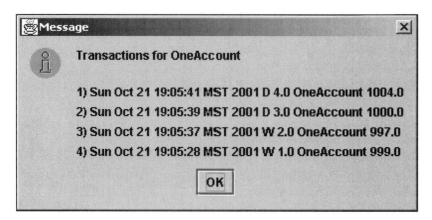

Self-Check

7-38 Describe how often this loop repeats.

```
ArrayList stringList = new ArrayList( );
stringList.add( "first string" );
stringList.add( "2nd" );
stringList.add( "3rd" );
stringList.add( "4th" );
stringList.add( "last string" );

ListIterator itr = stringList.listIterator( 0 );
while( itr.hasNext( ) )
{
  String str = (String)itr.next( );
  itr.previous( );
  System.out.println( str.toUpperCase( ) );
}
```

7-39 Write the code that uses the listIterator method of ArrayList to print the uppercase equivalents of all stringList elements (added above) in reverse order.

Chapter Summary

- Repetition is an important method of control for all programming languages. Typically, the body of a loop has statements that may change the state of one or more variables during each loop iteration.

- The for loop is often used to implement the Determinate Loop pattern, which requires that the number of repetitions be known before the loop is encountered.

- Determinate loops rely on a value representing the number of repetitions (n perhaps) and a properly initialized and incremented loop counter (j perhaps) to track the number of repetitions. The loop counter is compared to the known number of iterations at the start of each loop. The counter is automatically updated at the end of each for loop iteration.

- There are a number of ways to determine the number of loop iterations before a loop executes. The number of iterations may be input from the user, passed as an argument to a method, initialized in advance, or part of the state of some object. For example, every Grid object knows its number of rows and number of columns. Every String object knows how many characters it has at any given moment.

- The Determinate Loop pattern is so common that a specific statement—the for loop—is built into almost all languages.

- Indeterminate loops rely on some external event for their termination. The terminating event may occur at any time.

- Indeterminate loops are used when a program is unable to determine, in advance, the number of times a loop must iterate. The terminating events include sentinels read from the keyboard (such as -1 as a test or "Q" in a menu selection). These types of loops allow any number of users to execute any number of transactions, for example.

- Although you need one repetitive statement to solve any computer problem, the for loop is more convenient under certain circumstances. The for loop requires the program to take care of the initialization, loop test, and repeated statement all at once. The compiler protests if one of these important steps is missing. The for loop provides a more compact and less error-prone determinate loop.

- Remember these steps if you are having trouble designing loops:
  - Determine which type of loop to use.
  - Determine the loop test.
  - Write the statements to be repeated.
  - Bring the loop one step closer to termination.
  - Initialize variables if necessary.

- In addition to next and hasNext, java.util.ListIterator has two other methods—hasPrevious and previous—for visiting all of the elements in a collection in reverse order. A ListIterator object can be initialized with a listIterator message to an ArrayList. The listIterator method requires an int argument to specify the index of the element that will be returned by a previous or next message.

Key Terms

debugging output statement	hasPrevious	next
decrement	helper method	previous
Determinate Loop pattern	increment	repetition
do while statement	Indeterminate Loop pattern	sentinel
file input	infinite loop	sentinel loop
for statement	iteration	while statement
hasNext	ListIterator	

Exercises

The answers to exercises marked with are available in Appendix C.

 1. How many times will the following loops execute
System.out.print("Hello");? "Zero" and "Infinite"
are legitimate answers.

a.
```
int n = 5;
for( int j = 1; j <= n; j++ )
{
    System.out.print( "Hello " );
}
```

b.
```
int n = 0;
for( int j = 5; j >= n; j-- )
{
    System.out.print( "Hello " );
}
```

c.
```
int n = 5;
for( int j = 1; j <= n; j-- )
{
    System.out.print( "Hello " );
    j++;
}
```

d.
```
int n = 0;
for( int j = 1; j <= n; j++ )
{
    System.out.print( "Hello " );
}
```

 2. Write the output produced by these `for` loops:

```
for( int counter = 1; counter <= 5; counter++ )
  System.out.print( "   " + counter );
  // Improperly lined up to obfuscate
  System.out.println( " Loop One" );
for( int counter = 10; counter >= 1; counter-- )
  System.out.print( "   " + counter );
// Properly lined up to elucidate
System.out.println( " Blast Off " );
```

 3. Write loops to produce the outputs shown.

a. 10 9 8 7 6 5 4 3 2 1 0

b. 0 5 10 15 20 25 30 35 40 45 50

c. -1000 -900 -800 -700 -600 -500 -400 -300 -200 -100 0

4. Write the output generated by the following code:

```
int j = 0;
while( j < 5 )
{
  System.out.print( "   " + j );
  j = j + 1;
}
```

5. Write a `for` loop that sums all the integers between `start` and `stop` inclusive that are input from the keyboard. You may assume `start` is always less than or equal to `stop`. If the input were 5 for `start` and 10 for `stop`, the sum would be 5 + 6 + 7 + 8 + 9 + 10 (45).

6. How many times will `Hello` be displayed using the following program segments? "Zero," "Unknown," and "Infinite" are legitimate answers.

a.
```java
while( j <= 10 )
    System.out.print( "Hello" );
```

b.
```java
int j = 1;
while( j <= 7 )
{
    System.out.print( "Hello" );
    j++;
}
```

c.
```java
int j = 7;
while( j <= 1 )
{
    System.out.print( "Hello" );
}
```

d.
```java
int j = 1;
while( j <= 5 )
    System.out.print( "Hello" );
j++;
```

 7. Write a `while` loop that produces this output:

```
-4  -3  -2  -1  0  1  2  3  4  5  6
```

8. Write a loop that displays 100, 95, . . ., 5, and 0 on separate lines.

 9. Write a loop that counts how many perfect scores (scores of 100) are entered from the keyboard.

10. Convert the following code to its `for` loop counterpart:

```java
TextReader keyboard = new TextReader( );
System.out.print( "Enter number of ints to be summed: " );
int n = keyboard.readInt( );
int counter = 1;
int sum = 0;

System.out.print( "Enter " + n + " integers" );
while( counter <= n )
{
    int anInt = keyboard.readInt( );
    sum = sum + anInt;
    counter++;
}
System.out.println( "Sum: " + sum );
```

11. Write a loop that counts the number of lines input by a user until the user enters the string `ENDOFDATA` (must be uppercase letters, no spaces) on a line by itself. The words will be entered one string per line. Remember to use the `equals` method of the `String` class (or you could use the `compareTo` method). Do not use `==` to compare `String` objects.

Do this	Do not compare strings with ==
`if( theLine.equals( SENTINEL ) )`	`if ( theWord == SENTINEL )`

12. Write the complete output generated by the following code when the user enters 1, 2, 3, 4, and -999 on separate lines.

```
TextReader keyboard = new TextReader( );
double sum = 0.0;
System.out.println( "Enter tests or a negative number to quit: " );
double test = keyboard.readDouble( );
while( test >= 0.0 )
{
  sum = sum + test;
  test = keyboard.readDouble( );
}
System.out.print( "Sum: " + sum );
```

13. Write the output generated by the following code:

```
String choice = "BDWBQDW";
for( int j = 0; choice.charAt( j ) != 'Q'; j++ )
{
  System.out.println( "Opt: " + choice.charAt( j ) );
}
```

14. How many times will the following loops print `"Hello "`? "Zero," "Unknown," and "Infinite" are legitimate answers.

a.
```
int j = 1;
int n = 10;
do {
  System.out.print( "Hello " );
} while( j > n );
```

b.
```
int n = 10;
int j = 1;
do {
  System.out.print( "Hello " );
  j = j - 2;
} while ( j <= n );
```

c.
```
int j = -1;
do {
  System.out.print( "Hello " );
  j++;
} while( j != j );
```

d.
```
int j = 1;
do {
  System.out.print( "Hello " );
  j++;
} while ( j <= 100 );
```

15. Write a do while loop that produces this output:

```
10  9  8  7  6  5  4  3  2  1  0
```

16. Write the output generated by the following program:

```java
int j = -2;
do {
  System.out.println( j + " " );
  j--;
} while( j > -6 );
```

17. Rewrite the following do while loop as a pretest while loop (looptest is first, before the body):

```java
int counter = 0;
do {
  System.out.println( counter );
  counter++;
} while( counter <= 100 );
```

18. Complete a method evenNumber that prompts for and returns an even integer in the range of two integer arguments (assume that it is called from another method in the same class). If the user enters an odd number or an integer that is out of the range, inform the user of the error until they enter an even number that is in the range.

```java
public class EvenNumberLoop
{
  private TextReader keyboard;

  public EvenNumberLoop( )
  {
    keyboard = new TextReader( );
  }

  // Return even number in range of min through max inclusive
  public int evenNumber( int min, int max )
  {
    // Complete this code
  }

  public static void main( String[] args )
  {
    EvenNumberLoop doLoopDemo = new EvenNumberLoop( );
    int size = doLoopDemo.evenNumber( 1, 20 );
    System.out.println( "You entered " + size );
  }
}
```

Dialogue

```
Enter an even integer in the range of 1 through 20: -1
**Error: Integer was not even
**Error: Integer was not in range
Enter an even integer in the range of 1 through 20: 0
**Error: Integer was not in range
Enter an even integer in the range of 1 through 20: 1
**Error: Integer was not even
Enter an even integer in the range of 1 through 20: 21
**Error: Integer was not even
**Error: Integer was not in range
Enter an even integer in the range of 1 through 20: 20
You entered 20
```

Programming Tips

1. **Pick the type of loop you want to use.**

   After recognizing the need for repetition, decide if the number of repetitions can be determined in advance. If so, use a determinate loop, which is best implemented with a `for` loop. If the number of iterations cannot be determined in advance, determine the event that terminates the loop. For example, the loop terminates when someone enters the word STOP. The termination condition is `word.equals( "STOP" )`. The loop test is the logical negation `!word.equals( "STOP" )`.

   ```
   while( !word.equals( "STOP" ) )
   { // ...
   }
   ```

2. **Beware of infinite loops.**

   Watch out for infinite loops. They are easy to create and sometimes very difficult to find. Can you spot why these are infinite loops?

   ```
   int sum = 0;
   int j = 1;

   while( j <= 100 )
   { // Sum the first 100 integers
     sum += j;
   }

   while( j <= 100 );
   { // Sum the first 100 integers
     sum += j;
     j++;
   }
   ```

```
while( j <= 100 )
  // Sum the first 100 integers
  sum += j;
  j++;

while( j <= 100 )
{ // Sum the first 100 integers
  sum += j;
}
j++;

for( j = 0; j <= 100; j++ )
{ // Sum the first 100 integers
  sum += j;
  j--;
}

for( j = 1; j <= 10; j++ );
  System.out.println( j );
```

3. **Always write a block for the iterative part of `while` loops.**
   This provides you a better chance of including any increment statement as part of the loop rather than accidentally leaving it outside of the loop.

4. **Use debugging outputs to find out what is going on in a loop.**
   Use debugging output statements inside a loop to display one or more variables that should be changing. This can be very revealing. Sometimes you'll spot an infinite loop. Other times you might spot that the loop test is never true.

```
while( . . . )
{  // ...
   mid = ( lo + hi ) / 2.0;
   System.out.println( "In loop, mid equals " + mid );
   // ...
}
```

5. **Loops may not always execute the iterative part.**
   It is possible that a loop will execute zero times, or less than you might have thought.

```
int n = 3;
for( int j = 1; j >= n; j++ )   // 1 >= n is false
{
  System.out.print( "You'll not see me!" );
}

for( int j = 1; j <= n; j++ );   // Get rid of ;
{
  System.out.print( "You see me only once, not thrice" );
  System.out.print( "for I'm not part of the for!" );
}
```

6. **Don't refer to `next` (or `previous`) when the iteration is done.**
   Once `hasNext` returns `false` during an iteration, `next` returns `null`. An
   attempt to send a message to a reference variable when it is `null` results in a
   `nullPointerException`.

Programming Projects

7A   Wind Speed

Write a program (a class with the `main` method only) that determines the lowest,
highest, and average of a set of wind speed readings. Prompt the user for the
number of wind speed readings in the set and compute and display the high, low,
and average. Assume the user always enters at least one wind speed reading. Round
the average (after `Ave:`) to the nearest integer.

```
Enter number of wind speed readings: 4
4
6
8
3

 High:  8
  Low:  3
Count:  4
  Ave:  5
```

7B   Factorial

Write a program (a class with the `main` method only) that asks for a number and
displays N! (N factorial) where N! is the product of all the positive integers from 1
to N. For example, 5! = 1 x 2 x 3 x 4 x 5 = 120; 4! = 1 x 2 x 3 x 4 = 24; and 0!=1 (by
definition). Test your program with these arguments: 0, 1, 2, and 7. Here is one log
of execution when the user enters 4:

```
Enter n: 4
4! is 26
```

7C   Squaring Integers

The square of an integer value n can be found by adding the first n positive odd
integers. For example, both 4 squared and -4 squared are the sum of the first four
positive odd integers (1 + 3 + 5 + 7 = 16). Write a program (a class with the `main`
method only) that reads an integer and displays the square of that integer using
this different algorithm. Do not use the built-in method `Math.pow` or the multipli-

cation operator *. Test your program with various inputs including negative integers and zero. Here is one sample log of execution:

```
Enter integer: -4
-4 squared is 16
```

7D   Mini-Teller

Write a program (a class with the `main` method only) that allows a user to make as many withdrawals, deposits, and balance queries as desired to one BankAccount object that you construct. Your program should notify the user of insufficient funds if the withdrawal fails due to lack of funds. Use the following dialogue to help you understand the problem specification, which assumes your single `BankAccount` was constructed like this:

```
BankAccount currentAccount = new BankAccount( "Jackson", 100.00 );
```

Dialogue

```
Intitial balance for Jackson is 100.0
W )ithdraw, D )eposit, B )alance, or Q )uit: d
Enter deposit amount: 1.00
W )ithdraw, D )eposit, B )alance, or Q )uit: b
Current balance: 101.0
W )ithdraw, D )eposit, B )alance, or Q )uit: w
Enter withdrawal amount: 2.00
W )ithdraw, D )eposit, B )alance, or Q )uit: b
Current balance: 99.0
W )ithdraw, D )eposit, B )alance, or Q )uit: w
Enter withdrawal amount: 100.00
**Amount requested exceeds account balance**
W )ithdraw, D )eposit, B )alance, or Q )uit: b
Current balance: 99.0
W )ithdraw, D )eposit, B )alance, or Q )uit: q
Have a nice whatever : )
```

Also notice that upper- and lowercase choices are to be allowed. Consider using the `equalsIgnoreCase` method, which might look like this, to avoid comparing to both lowercase and uppercase "w":

```
if( option.equalsIgnoreCase( "w" ) )
```

7E   Wind Speed Again — An Indeterminate Loop

Write a program (a class with the `main` method only) that determines the lowest, highest, and average of a set of wind speed readings that are all positive or zero. Terminate the loop with any negative input. Be sure you notify the user how to terminate data entry. Compute and display the number of inputs (undetermined), the high, the low, and the average. Round the average to the nearest integer. Here is one sample dialogue:

```
Enter wind speed readings or a number less than 0 to quit:
4
6
8
3
-999

  High:  8
   Low:  3
Count:  4
  Ave:  5
```

7F   GUI Wind Speed

Write a program that accomplishes the same task as the program above. But with an event-driven program, the input will not stop until the user closes the window. The following JFrame is 180-by-180 pixels using a 5-by-2 grid layout with four pixels between components. This window shows the state of the object after the user enters wind speeds of 4, 6, 8, and 3. After each input, update the four JLabel object with hi, low, count, and average. Also, clear out the Wind Speed text field after each input.

7G   The DayCounter Class

This project continues Programming Project 5A by adding the methods compareTo and equals. First complete 5A on page 246 so the DayCounter class has two constructors, an adjustDaysBy method and a toString method that shows January as 1 and December as 12 (not as 0 and 11 as GregorianCalendar does).

Now have the DayCounter class implement the Comparable interface so the compareTo method returns the difference between any two DayCounter objects in number of days. A negative value indicates that the receiver is a date before the argument. Any two DayCounter objects with the same year, month, and day are considered equal. Don't forget to add implements Comparable to the class heading.

Also implement the `equals` method in terms of the `compareTo` method so equals returns true only if two DayCounter objects have the same year, month, and day. The hours, minutes, and seconds may be different. Consider using the GregorianCalendar constructor inside `compareTo` that takes year, month, and day as arguments (hour, minute, and second can then be ignored). Also consider using the `before` and `after` methods of GregorianCalendar that tell you if one GregorianCalendar object as the receiver comes before or after the argument (all three methods are demonstrated here).

```
GregorianCalendar yesterday = new GregorianCalendar( 2003, 1, 1 );
GregorianCalendar today = new GregorianCalendar( 2003, 1, 2 );
System.out.println( yesterday.before( today ) );   // true
System.out.println( today.after( yesterday ) );    // true
```

The following code is not a full test, but it shows the constructors and methods you need in boldface.

```
// Assume that this program ran on January 28, 2003
DayCounter today = new DayCounter( 2003, 1, 28 );
System.out.println( today.toString( ) );      // 2003/1/28
today.adjustDaysBy( -91 );
System.out.println( today.toString( ) );      // 2002/10/29
today.adjustDaysBy( 91 );
System.out.println( today.toString( ) );      // 2003/1/28

// Establish a leap year day in 2004 to test compareTo
DayCounter someDay = new DayCounter( 2004, 2, 29 );
System.out.println( today.compareTo( today ) );     // 0
System.out.println( today.compareTo( someDay ) );   // 397
System.out.println( someDay.compareTo( today ) );   // -397

// Test equals
System.out.println( today.equals( today ) );        // true
System.out.println( today.equals( someDay ) );      // false
System.out.println( someDay.equals( today) );       // false

DayCounter holiday = new DayCounter( 2004, 1, 1 );
int daysToHoliday = today.compareTo( holiday );
// This message should output: 338 days till new year
System.out.println( daysToHoliday + " days till new year" );
```

7H   The Elevator Class

Complete the `Elevator` class with a constructor that places an elevator with an ID at a selected floor. The constructor requires exactly three arguments:

1. a string as the elevator ID
2. an int as the starting floor
3. an int as the top floor

The lowest floor that can be selected is 1. The `select` method allows floors to be selected and issues an error message when the wrong floor is selected—stating that the selected floor is either too high or too low. For every floor, the elevator ID should be displayed before the message "going up" or "going down" and the current floor of the elevator.

The one sample output shown below gives you an idea of what one simulated `Elevator` object must look like on your screen. Notice that a message is displayed when both elevators are constructed. The output also shows that there are several places that the constructor and the `select` method must check for and report errors.

```
// Test drive the Elevator class by constructing one
// Elevator object and sending several select( floor )
// messages, some of which are invalid.
public class TestElevator
{
  public static void main( String[] args )
  {
    Elevator error1 = new Elevator( "No way 1", 1, -1 );
    Elevator error2 = new Elevator( "No way 2", 3, 2 );
    Elevator error3 = new Elevator( "No way 3", 0, 9 );
    Elevator liftOne = new Elevator( "West", 2, 12 );
    Elevator liftTwo = new Elevator( "East", 1, 6 );

    liftOne.select( 5 );
    liftTwo.select( 3 );
    liftOne.select( 5 );    // This is the current floor: open at 5 again
    liftTwo.select( 7 );
    liftOne.select( 1 );
    liftTwo.select( 1 );
    liftOne.select( 13 );   // Out of range--elevator does not change
    liftOne.select( 0 );    // Out of range--elevator does not change
  }
}
```

Output

```
**ERROR** max floor for 'No Way 1' must be greater than 1
**ERROR** starting floor for 'No Way 2' must be in range of 1..2
**ERROR** starting floor for 'No Way 3' must be in range of 1..9
West begins at floor 2
East begins at floor 1
West going from 2 up to 5
  going up to: 3
  going up to: 4
  going up to: 5
West open at 5
East going from 1 up to 3
  going up to: 2
  going up to: 3
East open at 3
West door opens at 5 (current floor == selected floor)
**ERROR** 7 not in range of 1..6 for East
East open at 3
```

```
West going from 5 down to 1
  going down to: 4
  going down to: 3
  going down to: 2
  going down to: 1
West open at 1
East going from 3 down to 1
  going down to: 2
  going down to: 1
East open at 1
**ERROR** 13 not in range of 1..12 for West
West open at 1
**ERROR** 0 not in range of 1..12 for West
West open at 1
```

71   Guessing Game

Write a Java class that implements a guessing game. Ask the user for a number in
the range of 1 through 100 inclusive. If the guess is larger than the random
number you generated in the range of 1 through 100, inform the user that the
guess was too high. If the guess is too low, tell that to the user. When the guess
matches the random number, tell that to the user. Here is a sample dialogue:

```
Play one game
Pick a number from 1..100: 50
50 is too high
Pick a number from 1..100: 25
25 is too high
Pick a number from 1..100: 12
12 is too low
Pick a number from 1..100: 18
18 is too high
Pick a number from 1..100: 15
15 is just right
Congrats, you needed 5 guesses
```

The method named playOneGame must get one guessing game going. The
currentNumberOfGuesses method must return the number of guesses it took the
user to play one game. Use the following code in a main method that keeps playing
guessing games until the user finally takes seven or fewer guesses. Always tell the
user how many guesses were required. Notice that your class must have a class
constant declared: MAX_GUESSES_NEEDED.

```java
public class RunGuessingGame
{
  // Test driver code given in assignment
  public static void main( String[] args )
  {
    GuessingGame aGuessingGame = new GuessingGame( );
```

```
     int numGuesses;
     do
     {
        System.out.println( "\nPlay one game" );
        aGuessingGame.playOneGame( );
        numGuesses = aGuessingGame.currentNumberOfGuesses( );
        if( numGuesses <= GuessingGame.MAX_GUESSES_NEEDED )
        {
          System.out.print( "Congrats, you needed " + numGuesses +
                            " guess" );
          if( numGuesses > 1 )
            System.out.print( "es" );
          System.out.println( );
        }
        else
          System.out.println( "Wow, it took you " + numGuesses +
                  " guesses.\n" + "Try again. Hint: Start in the middle." );

     } while( numGuesses > GuessingGame.MAX_GUESSES_NEEDED );
  }
}
```

This project requires the use of random numbers. Java has a class named Random that makes it easy to get seemingly random numbers into your program. After you import the Random class

```
import java.util.Random; //
```

you can construct a Random object like this

```
Random randomNumberGenerator = new Random( );
```

and then use Java's nextInt method.

```
/** From the Random class
  *
  * Return a seemingly random integer in the range of 0 through n-1.
  */
  public int nextInt(int n)
```

For example, you can get a number from 0 to 5 with an expression like this:

```
// The message returns 0, 1, 2, 3, 4, or 5. It appears to be random.
int randomNumber = randomNumberGenerator.nextInt( 6 );
```

7J   Planting the Grid

Complete the GridWithTractor class that has a method harvestTheField that instructs a farmer to go over the plant at every possible location (except the final place), no matter how big the field is. (When the mover goes over a location, the dot disappears; do not use pickup.) Notice that the Planter constructor always places the mover in the upper-left corner facing east. The number of rows and columns varies according to the arguments in the construction. Your class must work with any size Grid, with even or odd numbers of rows and columns.

```
public class Planter
{
  // Instance variables
  private Grid my_grid;
  private GraphicGrid my_graphicGrid;

  // Construct a field that can be harvested.
  // rows is the number of rows to harvest.
  // cols is the number of plants to harvest in each row.
  public Planter( int rows, int cols )
  {
    // Farmer always begins in the upper-left corner facing east
    my_grid = new Grid( rows, cols, 0, 0, Grid.EAST );
    my_graphicGrid = new GraphicGrid( my_grid );
  }

  public void harvestTheField( )
  { // You complete this
  }

  // You may add helper methods such as turnRight and plantOneRow
}
```

The following test driver should generate the output shown below.

```
public static void main( String[] args )
{
  // All Planter objects will begin with the farmer in the
  // upper-left corner facing east, so only supply the size.
  Planter farmerJill = new Planter( 3, 15 );
  farmerJill.harvestTheField( );
}
```

Output (before and after Jill has harvested the field)

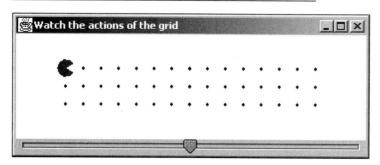

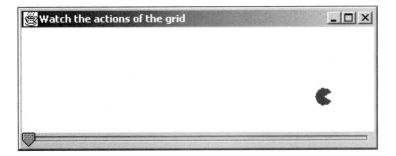

7K Finding a Grid's Exit

In this project, you must use the `Grid` constructor with two `int` parameters for the
rows and columns. This two-argument constructor builds a grid with a border of
blocks all around the edges except for one exit randomly placed on any of the four
edges. That exit is never in the corner. When constructed with two arguments
(instead of five), the `Grid` places the mover at some random location inside the
`Grid` facing a random direction. When this program was run twice, it generated
the views shown below. You do not have to write the code to set up the borders,
exit, and mover.

```
public class ShowGrid
{
  public static void main( String[] args )
  { // When only two arguments are supplied, you get a simple maze.
    Grid aGrid = new Grid( 6, 10 );
    GraphicGrid view = new GraphicGrid( aGrid );
  }
}
```

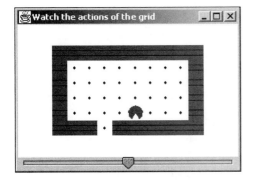
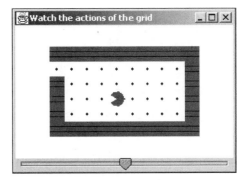

Complete the `GridWithFindExit` class that has a public method named `findExit`
that instructs the mover to find the lone exit in any sized `Grid`. Initialize

GridWithFindExit objects with only two int arguments—the number of rows and the number of columns. This constructor must ensure that you get a Grid with only one exit. Therefore, construct your Grid instance variable with two int arguments (as described above). Your class must also ensure that users see a graphical view of the action. Construct a GraphicGrid object with your new Grid as an argument. The GraphicGrid displays itself.

Your job is to get the mover to the single exit and leave the mover there. Do not let the mover fall off the edge of the world. Use this test driver and keep running it until the mover finds exits on all four edges. It helps if you ensure that it gets out at the exits near the corners. *Hint:* The Grid class has frontIsClear and rightIsClear methods that will help you solve this problem. Feel free to add private helper methods such as turnRight, hasEscaped, and getToWall.

```
public class GridWithFindExit
{
  private Grid my_grid;
  private GraphicGrid my_graphicGrid;

  public GridWithFindExit( int rows, int cols )
  {
    // Constructing a Grid with two arguments results in a
    // Grid with a "wall" around the entire edge except for
    // one exit. And that exit will never be in the corner.
    // Also, the mover will automatically be placed in a
    // random location facing a random direction.
    my_grid = new Grid( rows, cols );   // Use two argument constructors!
    // Allow the graphical view to appear.
    my_graphicGrid = new GraphicGrid( my_grid );
  }

  public void getToExit( )
  { // You complete this
  }

  // Please add private helper methods such as turnRight and hasEscaped

  public static void main( String[] args )
  {
    GridWithFindExit tarpit = new GridWithFindExit( 8, 12 );
    tarpit.getToExit( );
    // The mover should now be in the exit (not off the edge)
  }
}
```

There is one possible escape route when the mover begins by facing west at row 5, column 7. Run the same program again and there is likely to be a different exit, a different starting location, and a different path. To do this, use the Grid constructor with two arguments as shown above to specify the rows and columns only.

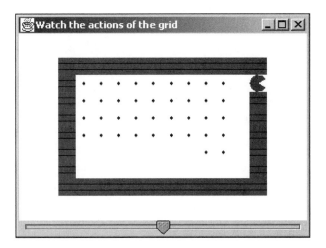

Answers to Self-Check Questions

7-1   No, the update step happens at the end of the loop iteration. The init statement happens first, and only once.

7-2   No, you can use increments of any amount, including negative increments (decrements).

7-3   No, consider for(int j = 1; j < n; j++) { /*do nothing*/ } when n == 0.

7-4   If the update step does not increment j. Or if inside the loop, j is decremented as much as it is incremented. Here are two examples. The example on the left contains a subtle, but common, mistake. The example on the right contains a rare mistake. However, it was presented here to show what happens if the loop-counting variable (named j here) gets messed up.

```
for( int j = 1; j < n; j + 1 )
{ // j + 1 does not change j
  // j remains the same: 1
}          for( int j = 1; j < n; j++ )
{
  j--;    // Now it'll never end
}
```

7-5   -a 1 2 3 4
       -b 1 2 3 4 5
       -c -3 -1 1 3
       -d 0 1 2 3 4
       -e 5 4 3 2 1
       -f before   after

7-6   for(int j = 1; j <= 100; j++)
       {
           System.out.println(j);
       }

7-7
```
for( int k = 10; k >= 1; k-- )
{
    System.out.println( k );
}
```

7-8   An attempt to block row 8, which is "out of this world." The program terminates.

7-9   An attempt to block an intersection with something on it already. The program terminates.

7-10 An attempt to block an intersection with something on it. The program terminates.

7-11 Range is 6. `lowest` never changes from 0. 6 - 0 is 6. The algorithm is currently flawed.

7-12 Range is 29 (this is correct)

```
highest    -999  -5     8      22     22     22
lowest     999 -5 -5    -5     -7     -7
```

7-13 Range = 4 (this is correct).

```
highest    -999  5      5      5      5      5
lowest     999 999      4      3      2      1
```

7-14 Range = -994 (this is obviously incorrect).

```
highest    -999  1      2      3      4      5
lowest     999 999      999    999    999    999
```

7-15 -b When the input is entered in ascending order.

7-16 Get rid of the `else`. Then when the inputs are in ascending order, the check for `lowest` is never made. Another more elegant solution is to initialize `highest` and `lowest` to the first input, as shown in the previous range implementation.

```
int aTemp = keyboard.readInt( );
int highest = aTemp  // The first input can be viewed as
int lowest = aTemp;  // both highest AND lowest; it is the only one!
// Now process n-1 inputs by starting j at 2 rather than 1
for( int j = 2; j <= n; j++ )
{
    aTemp = keyboard.readInt( );
    // ...
```

7-17 -a 12345   -b 54321

7-18 -a 46.333333333333336 (46.3 will do)   -b 70.0

7-19 Do you see how a. does not accumulate 70.0? Instead, it accumulates -1 (60 + 80 + -1) / 3 is 46.3.

7-20 4. The sentinel `"quit"` was found before the end of the line.

7-21
```
int number;
while( true )
{
    System.out.print( "Enter a number from 1 to 10: " );
    number = keyboard.readInt( );
    if( number >= 1 && number <= 10 )
        break;
    // Will not display the following message if the input was in range
    System.out.println( number + " not in the range of 1 through 10 " );
}
```

7-22 Zero

7-23 Input another `currentInput` at the bottom of the loop.

7-24 This is a tricky question. Remove ; after). This loop does nothing infinitely because ; represents a null statement. The iterative part does nothing. It is legal code, but not what was likely intended.

7-25 -a 1 2 3

-b 2 4 6 8 10

-c Nothing is output. Notice that there is a ; after the loop test. It reads like this: "do nothing forever."

7-26 -a 20   -d Infinite

-b 0   -e Infinite

-c 5   -f 10

7-27
```java
TextReader keyboard = new TextReader( );
int sum = 0;
System.out.print( "Enter number to sum or a negative number to quit: " );
int input = keyboard.readInt( );
while( input >= 0 )
{
  sum += input ; // Accumulate inputs, only not negative
  System.out.print( "Enter number to sum or a negative number to quit: " );
  input = keyboard.readInt( );
  // If negative, the loop test fails and input is not added
}
System.out.println( "Sum: " + sum );
```

7-28
```java
TextReader keyboard = new TextReader( );
int newInt;
int oldInt;
System.out.println( "Enter numbers until two differ
                    by more than 100: " );
newInt = keyboard.readInt( );
oldInt = newInt;
while( Math.abs( oldInt - newInt ) <= 100.0 )
{
  oldInt = newInt;
  newInt = keyboard.readInt( );
}
System.out.println( "Last two numbers were " + oldInt +
                    " and " + newInt );
```

7-29 It is an indeterminate loop because the mover moves until it no longer can. There is no way to determine if an intersection is blocked. A block could be right in front (0 iterations), one move away (1 iteration), two moves away (2 iterations), and so on.

7-30
```java
public class PrintNWords
{
  public static void main( String[] args )
  { // ...
    String aString;
    TextReader keyboard = new TextReader( );
    TextReader inFile = new TextReader("NineA.java");
```

```
System.out.print( "How many words do you want to read? " );
int numberOfWordsToReadAndDisplay = keyboard.readInt( );

// This loop test ensures that the loop will not attempt
// to read data that is not in the file.
while( inFile.ready( ) && ( numberOfWordsToReadAndDisplay > 0 ) )
{
  aString = inFile.readWord( );
  System.out.print( aString + " " );
  numberOfWordsToReadAndDisplay--;
}
System.out.println( );
}
}
```

7-31 *Note:* This file behavior relates to the TextReader class that comes with this textbook. Other
input classes may behave differently.

-a The message Can't open input file 'input.dat', exiting appears and the
program terminates.

-b Everything is fine. The average is the lone number.

-c You get division by 0 and NaN is stored in average.

-d It depends. If the space is on the same line, processing succeeds. If the space is on a new line,
the program terminates before it can display the average.

-e The program terminates with this message when it cannot successfully read a number.
Failure in readDouble message. Program terminated

7-32 -a 1.1 2.2 3.0
```
n  Number Sum
== ====== =====
1  1.1    1.1
2  2.2    3.3
3  3.0    6.3
Average of 3 numbers is 2.1
```
-b 1.0 2.0 3.0 4.0
```
n  Number Sum
== ====== =====
1  1.0    1.0
2  2.0    3.0
3  3.0    6.0
4  4.0    10.0
Average of 4 numbers is 2.5
```
-c 1.0 2.0 3.0 BAD 4.0
```
n  Number Sum
== ====== =====
1  1.0    1.0
2  2.0    3.0
3  3.0    6.0

***Failure in readDouble message. Program terminated***
```

7-33 -a 1 2 3   -b abcdef
                            bcdef
                            cdef
                            def
                            ef
                            f

7-34 TextReader keyboard = new TextReader( );
      int number;
      do {
        System.out.print("Enter a number in the range of 1 through 10: ");
        number = keyboard.readInt( );
      } while(number < 1 || number > 10);

7-35 -a A for loop, since n is known.

      -b A for loop, since n is known.

      -c An indeterminate loop, perhaps a while(true) loop that terminates when the sentinel is read.

      -d An indeterminate loop, perhaps a while(true) loop that terminates when the sentinel is read.

7-36 -a value == -1

      -b value == -1

      -c value != -1   // The logical negation

7-37 -a Both j and n

      -b Both n and inc

7-38 It is an infinite loop. For each next message, there is a previous message.

7-39 ArrayList stringList = new ArrayList( );
      stringList.add("first string");
      stringList.add("2nd");
      // ...
      stringList.add("last string");

      ListIterator itr = stringList.listIterator(stringList.size( ));
      while(itr.hasPrevious( ))
      {
        String str = (String)itr.previous( );
        System.out.println(str.toUpperCase( ));
      }

Chapter 8
Arrays

Summing Up

Almost all of the objects studied so far either store one value (e.g., `double` and `int`) or contain two or more possibly dissimilar elements (e.g., `BankAccount`). The one exception was the `ArrayList` objects that store a collection of elements.

Coming Up

This chapter introduces the Java array for storing collections of many objects. Individual elements are referenced with the Java subscript operator `[]`. After studying this chapter you will be able to

- declare and use arrays that can store either reference or primitive values
- implement algorithms to process a collection of objects
- use the sequential search algorithm to locate a specific element in an array
- understand how to implement a simple collection class
- build a collection class for a specific application

Exercises and programming projects reinforce the use of arrays.

8.1   The Java Array Object

Java **array** objects store collections of elements. They allow a large number of elements to be conveniently maintained together under the same name. The array is similar to the `ArrayList` in that the elements are indexed. The first element is at index 0 and the second is at index 1. One major difference is that array elements may be any one of the primitive types, such as `int` or `double`. An array can also store a collection of references to any object. Another major difference is that an array does not have methods. It uses subscript notation to reference and set individual elements.

The following code declares three different arrays named `balance`, `friend`, and `tinyBank`. It also initializes all five elements of those three arrays. The subscript operator `[]` provides access to individual array elements.

```java
// Declare three arrays where each can store up to five elements
double[] balance = new double[5];
String[] friend = new String[5];
BankAccount[] tinyBank = new BankAccount[5];

// Initialize the array of double values
balance[0] = 0.00;
balance[1] = 111.11;
balance[2] = 222.22;
balance[3] = 333.33;
balance[4] = 444.44;

// Initialize the array of references to String objects
friend[0] = "Jody";
friend[1] = "Rachael";
friend[2] = "Troy";
friend[3] = "Neha";
friend[4] = "Jim";

// Initialize the array of references to BankAccount objects
tinyBank[0] = new BankAccount( friend[0], balance[0] );
tinyBank[1] = new BankAccount( friend[1], balance[1] );
tinyBank[2] = new BankAccount( friend[2], balance[2] );
tinyBank[3] = new BankAccount( friend[3], balance[3] );
tinyBank[4] = new BankAccount( friend[4], balance[4] );
```

The values referenced by the arrays can be drawn like this, indicating that the arrays `balance`, `friend`, and `tinyBank` store collections. `balance` is a collection of primitive values; `friend` and `tinyBank` are collections of object references. To save space, the objects' `toString` values are shown rather than their reference values.

balance[0]	0.0
balance[1]	111.11
balance[2]	222.22
balance[3]	333.33
balance[4]	444.44

friend[0]	"Jody"
friend[1]	"Rachael"
friend[2]	"Troy"
friend[3]	"Neha"
friend[4]	"Jim"

tinyBank[0]	"Jody", 0.00
tinyBank[1]	"Rachael", 111.11
tinyBank[2]	"Troy", 222.22
tinyBank[3]	"Neha", 333.33
tinyBank[4]	"Jim", 444.44

Self-Check

8-1   Write the output generated by the following program fragment:

```java
for( int index = 0; index < 5; j++ )
{
    System.out.println( tinyBank[index].getID( ) + " "
                        + tinyBank[index].getBalance( ) );
}
```

The three arrays above were constructed using the following general forms:

General Form 8.1: Constructing array objects

*primitive-type***[]**   *array-name* = **new** *primitive-type* **[** *capacity* **]** ;
*class-name***[]**   *array-name* = **new** *class-name* **[** *capacity* **]** ;

- *primitive-type* specifies the type of primitive value that can be stored in the array.
- *class-name* specifies the type of object references that can be stored in the array.
- *array-name* is any valid Java identifier. With subscripts, the array name can refer to any and all elements in the array.
- *capacity* is an integer expression representing the maximum number of elements that can be stored in the array. The capacity is always available through a variable named length that is referenced as *array-name*.length.

Example: array declarations

```java
int[] test = new int[100];            // Store up to 100 integers
double[] number = new double[10000];  // Store up to 10000 numbers
String[] name = new String[500];      // Store up to 500 strings
// Store up to 1000 BankAccounts
BankAccount[] customer = new BankAccount[1000];
```

Accessing Individual Elements in a Collection

Arrays support random access. The individual array elements can be found through subscript notation. A **subscript** is an integer value between [and] that represents the **index** of the element you want to get to. The special symbols [and] represent the mathematical subscript notation. So instead of x_0, x_1, and x_{n-1}, Java uses x[0], x[1], and x[n-1].

General Form 8.2: **Accessing one array element**

array-name [*index*]   // Index must range from 0 to capacity - 1

The subscript range of a Java array is an integer value in the range of 0 through its capacity - 1. Consider the following array named x.

```
double[] x = new double[8];
```

The individual elements of x may be referenced using the indexes 0, 1, 2, ... 7. If you used –1 or 8 as an index, you would get an **ArrayIndexOutOfBoundsException**. The first element of an array has the index of 0. This code assigns values to the first two array elements:

```
// Assign new values to the first two elements of the array named x:
x[0] = 2.6;
x[1] = 5.7;
```

Java has zero-based indexing. This means that the first array element is accessed with index 0—the same indexing scheme used with `ArrayList`, `String`, and `Grid`. The index 0 means the first element in the collection. With arrays, the first element is found in subscript notation as x[0]. The fifth element is accessed with index 4 or with subscript notation as x[4]. This subscript notation allows individual array elements to be displayed, used in expressions, and modified with assignment and input operations. In fact, you can do anything to an individual array element that can be done to a variable of the same type. The array is simply a way to package together a collection of variables.

The familiar assignment rules apply to array elements. For example, a `String` constant cannot be assigned to an array element that was declared to store `double` values.

```
// ERROR: x stores numbers, not strings
x[2] = "Wrong type of literal";
```

Since any two `double` values can use the arithmetic operators, numeric array elements can also be used in arithmetic expressions like this:

```
x[2] = x[0] + x[1];   // Store 8.3 into the third array element
```

Keyboard input can also be used to store a value into an array element, like this:

```
System.out.print( "Enter x[3]: " );
x[3] = keyboard.readDouble( );

System.out.print( "Enter x[4]: " );
x[4] = keyboard.readDouble( );
```

Dialogue

```
Enter x[3]: 9.9
Enter x[4]: 5.1
```

After a user inputs 9.9 and 5.1 into the fourth and fifth array elements and the previous assignments are made into the first three array elements, the state of the array named x would look like the table below. Arrays of primitive double values are initialized to 0.0 and arrays of ints have indexed array locations initialized to 0.

State of x (all double elements are initialized to 0.0 when the array is constructed

x[0]	2.6
x[1]	5.7
x[2]	8.3
x[3]	9.9
x[4]	5.1
x[5]	0.0
x[6]	0.0
x[7]	0.0

Arrays are rarely filled to capacity. Often, a programmer declares an array with a maximum capacity that is only a prediction of the maximum number of elements expected. You will often use a separate integer variable (named n) to store the number of meaningful elements. An array will often have meaningful values only in the elements referenced from 0 through n - 1, rather than from 0 through its capacity - 1.

Array Processing with Determinate Loops

Programmers must frequently access many consecutive array elements. For example, you might want to display all of the meaningful elements of an array. The Java for loop provides a convenient way to do this. Let some variable count from 0 to n - 1 inclusive.

```
int n = 5; // n represents the number of meaningful elements

// Display the meaningful elements of x--the first n elements
System.out.println( "The first " + n + " elements of x: " );

for( int index = 0; index < n; index++ )
{
   System.out.println( x[index] );
}
```

Output

```
The first 5 elements of x:
2.6
5.7
8.3
9.9
5.1
```

The first n elements of x are accessed by changing the `int` variable named `index`. This variable acts both as the loop counter and as an array index inside the `for` loop (`x[index]`). With `index` serving both roles, the specific array element accessed as `x[index]` depends on the value of `index`. For example, when `index` is 0, `x[index]` accesses the first element in the array named x; when `index` is 4, `x[index]` accesses the fifth element.

Here is another example of how the elements of an array are accessed. This `for` loop inspects the meaningful (0 through n - 1) array elements to find the largest value.

```java
// Assume the first element is the smallest
// (if n==0, the smallest is 0)
double largest = x[0];

// Set the largest to be the value less than all other doubles
// Compare all other array elements, x[1] through x[n-1]
for( int index = 1; index < n; index++ )
{
  if( x[index] > largest )
    largest = x[index];
}

// Display the largest
System.out.println( "Largest number in the array is " + largest );
```

Output

```
Largest number in the array is 9.9
```

An array often stores fewer meaningful elements than its capacity. Therefore, the need arises to store the number of elements in the array that have been given meaningful values. In the previous code, n was used to limit the elements being referenced. Only the first five elements were searched to find the largest. Only the first five should have been considered. Although all eight elements could have been compared, imagine trying to find the smallest number in x. Without limiting the search to the meaningful elements (indexed as 0 through n - 1), would the smallest be 2.6 (`x[0]`) or would it be the 0.0 stored in one of the three elements at the end?

The Determinate Loop pattern conveniently performs **array processing**, which is the inspection of or modification of, a selected number of array elements. The number of elements (n here) is the predetermined number of array elements that must be processed. Array processing algorithms in this chapter include:

- Displaying some or all elements of an array
- Finding the sum, average, or highest of all array elements
- Searching for a given value in an array

- Arranging elements in a certain order (ordering numbers from largest to smallest or alphabetizing an array of strings from smallest to largest)

Out-of-Range Indexes

Array indexes are checked to ensure that they are within the proper range of 0 through capacity - 1. The following assignment results in an exception being thrown. The program usually terminates with a message like the one shown below.

```
x[8] = 4.5;  // This out-of-range index causes an exception
```

The program terminates prematurely (the output shows the out-of-range index, which is 8 here).

```
java.lang.ArrayIndexOutOfBounds exception:  8
```

This might seem to be a nuisance. But without range checking, such out-of-range indexes could destroy the state of other objects in memory and cause difficult-to-detect bugs. More dramatically, your computer could "hang" or "crash." Even worse, with a workstation that runs all of the time, you could get an error that affects computer memory now, but won't crash the system until weeks from now. However, in Java, you get the more acceptable occurrence of an ArrayIndexOutOfBounds exception, as shown above.

Self-Check

Use this initialization to answer the questions that follow:

```
int[] x = new int[100];
```

8-2   How many integers may be properly stored in *x*?

8-3   Which integer is used as the index to access the first element in *x*?

8-4   Which integer is used as the index to access the last element in *x*?

8-5   What is the value of `x[23]`?

8-6   Write code that stores 78 into the first element of x.

8-7   Write code that stores 1 into `x[99]`, 2 into `x[98]`, 3 into `x[97]`, ..., 99 into `x[1]`, and 100 into `x[0]`. Use a `for` loop.

8-8   Write code that displays all elements of x on separate lines. Use a `for` loop.

8-9   What happens when this code executes: `x[-1] = 100;`

8-10 Write the output generated by the following code:

```
int max = 10;
int[] intArray = new int[max];
for( int j = 0; j < max; j++ )
   intArray[j] = j;
```

```
    int low = 0;
    int high = max - 1;
    while( low < high )
    {
      System.out.println( intArray[low] + "   " + intArray[high] );
      low++;
      high--;
    }
```

Messages to Individual Array Elements

The subscript notation must be used to send messages to individual elements. The array name must be accompanied by an index to specify the particular array element to which the message is sent.

General Form 8.3: **Sending messages to individual array elements**

array-name [*index*] . *message-name*(*arguments*)

The *index* distinguishes the specific object the message is to be sent to. For example, the uppercase equivalent of `friend[0]` (this element has the value `"Jody"`) is returned with this expression:

```
friend[0].toUpperCase( ) // The first name in an array of Strings
```

The expression `friend.toUpperCase( )` is a syntax error because it attempts to find the uppercase version of the entire array, not one of its `String` elements. The `toUpperCase` method is not defined for standard Java array objects.

Now consider determining the total of all the balances in an array of `BankAccounts`. The following program first sets up a miniature database of four `BankAccount` objects. *Note:* A constructor call—with `new`—generates a reference to any type of object. Therefore this assignment

```
// Construct object, assign reference
account[0] = new BankAccount( "Hall", 0.00);
```

first constructs a `BankAccount` object with the ID `"Hall"` and a balance of `0.0`. The reference to this object is stored in the first array element, `account[0]`.

```
public class AnArrayOfAccounts
{
  public static void main( String[] args )
  {
    BankAccount[] account = new BankAccount[100];

    // Initialize the first n elements
    account[0] = new BankAccount( "Hall", 0.00 );
    account[1] = new BankAccount( "Small", 100.00 );
    account[2] = new BankAccount( "Ewall", 200.00 );
```

```
account[3] = new BankAccount( "Westphall", 300.00 );
int n = 4;
// Only the first n elements of account are meaningful

// Accumulate the balance of n BankAccount objects stored in account
double assets = 0.0;
for( int index = 0; index < n; index ++ )
{
   assets += account[index].getBalance( );
}

System.out.println( "Assets: " + assets );
   }
}
```

Output

```
Assets:  600.0
```

Self-Check

8-11 Write the output generated by the following code:

```
int n = 8;
int[] x = new int[n];
for( int j = 0; j < n; j++ )
{
   x[j] = j * 2;
}

for( int j = 0; j < n; j = j + 2 )
{
   x[j] = x[j + 1];
}

for( int j = 0; j < n; j++ )
{
   System.out.print( x[j] + " " );
}
```

8-12 Write the code that displays the toString version of all BankAccounts with a balance greater than 150.00. It must be general enough to work with an array of any size that is named accountArray. Assume n represents the number of meaningful BankAccount elements in accountArray.

8-13 Write the output generated by the following code:

```
String[] s = new String[10];
// Initialize the first n elements of s
int n = 4;
s[0] = "First";
s[1] = "Second";
s[2] = "Third";
s[n - 1] = "FourthAndFinal";
```

```
// Do something with all four array elements
for( int j = 0; j < n; j++ )
{
   System.out.println( s[j].charAt( s[j].length( ) - 1 ) );
}
```

8.2   Sequential Search

One of the major reasons to store a collection of objects is so the elements can be retained in the computer's fast memory, where the collection can be accessed frequently. Often a collection will be searched for the existence of some element. Examples include, but certainly are not limited to, searching for a student name in the registrar's database, looking up the price of an item in an inventory, or obtaining information about a bank account. One algorithm used to "look up" an array element is called sequential search.

The **sequential search** algorithm attempts to locate a given element by comparing the element being sought to every object in the array. The algorithm searches in a sequential (one-after-the-other) fashion until either the element is found or there are no more array elements left to search.

This sequential search algorithm will be demonstrated by finding a String in an array of String objects. Although the search element here is a person's name, the array being searched could contain other types of objects—numbers, students, or employees, for example. We'll first consider a class that constructs an array of references to String objects, which begins like this:

```
// Build a class to demonstrate sequential search
public class FriendList
{
  private String[] my_friends;
  private int my_size;

  // Build a list of friends with the same data each time. This is not
  // the best way, but it makes it easier to show sequential search.
  public FriendList( )
  {
    my_friends = new String[10];
    // All 10 elements of my_friends have default object value of null.
    // Now set the number of meaningful elements in the array.
    my_size = 5;
    // Now initialize the first my_size elements of the array.
    my_friends[0] = "DEBBIE";
    my_friends[1] = "JOEY";
    my_friends[2] = "BOBBIE";
    my_friends[3] = "SUSIE";
    my_friends[4] = "MIKEY";
```

```
      // my_friends[5] through my_friends[9] are null
    }

    // Provide a peek into the current state of this object
    public String toString( )
    {
      String result = "";
      for( int j = 0; j < my_size; j ++ )
      {
        result+= "[" + j + "] " + my_friends[j] + "\n";
      }
      return result;
    }


    // To be arranged. It currently returns null just
    // so this class compiles. Later on it will
    // return null only if searchName is not found.
    public String find( String searchName )
    {
      return null; // This will be designed in the section that follows
    }


    // Test driver
    public static void main( String[] args )
    {
      FriendList myFriendList = new FriendList( );
      System.out.println( myFriendList );

      TextReader keyboard = new TextReader( );

      System.out.print( "Enter name to search for [UPPERCASE]: " );
      String searchName = keyboard.readWord( );

      // Determine if searchName is in myFriendList
      String reference = myFriendList.find( searchName );

      // Report success or failure
      if( reference != null )
        System.out.println( reference + " found" );
      else
        System.out.println( searchName + " not found" );

    } // End test driver

} // End class FriendList
```

Dialogue (the find method is not yet working—it always returns null)

```
[0]  DEBBIE
[1]  JOEY
[2]  BOBBIE
[3]  SUSIE
[4]  MIKEY

Enter name to search for [UPPERCASE]: DEBBIE
DEBBIE not found
```

Self-Check

8-14   What is the value of each of the following expressions?

    -a my_friends[3]   **-d** my_friends[10]

    -b my_friends[4]   **-e** myFriendList.find("JOEY");

    -c my_friends[9]   **-f** myFriendList.find("MIKEY");

Before searching for something, you need to know what you are searching for. The test driver above prompts the user for a name from the keyboard. The object named myFriendList and the test driver will be used in the next few sections.

The Element Being Searched for Is in the Array

When searching for an object called searchName in an array, there are at least these two possibilities:

1. searchName is in the array
2. searchName is *not* in the array

First assume searchName has an equal string value in the array named my_friends. With index initialized to 0, the following code begins by comparing searchName to the first array element, also known as my_friends[0]:

```
// This modified version of find from the FriendList
// class works only if searchName is in the array.
public String find( String searchName )
{
  // This sequential search begins searching at the first array location
  int index = 0;

  // The loop will terminate as soon as the string is found
  while( searchName.compareTo( my_friends[index] ) != 0 )
  { // searchName has not yet been found in the array my_friends
    // so prepare to compare searchName to the next array element.
    index++;
  }

  // This assumes that the string was found (this will be changed later)
  return my_friends[index];
}
```

The loop test, searchName.compareTo(my_friends[index]) != 0), is true as long as the element being searched for has not been found in the searched portion of the array. Each loop iteration increments an array index with index++ to prepare for a comparison of searchName to the next array element. The searchName is first compared to my_friends[0], then my_friends[1], then my_friends[2], and so on. The loop iterates as long as searchName is not found. This code works fine, but only if the String being searched for is actually in the array. After the search loop terminates, the reference to the existing name is returned.

Dialogue (using the test driver in `FriendList`)

```
Enter name to search for [UPPERCASE]: BOBBIE
BOBBIE found
```

The following table traces a successful search for the string `"BOBBIE"`:

Search for `"BOBBIE"`

Loop Iteration	searchName	my_size	index	Array Element Being Compared
Before loop	"BOBBIE"	5	0	N/A
1	"BOBBIE"	5	0	"DEBBIE"
2	"BOBBIE"	5	1	"JOEY"
3	"BOBBIE"	5	2	"BOBBIE"
After loop	"BOBBIE"	5	2	N/A

Self-Check

8-15   What happens in the code above if `searchName` is not in the array?

The Element Is Not in the Array

Now consider what happens if the `String` is not in the `array`. Each iteration of the loop increments `index` by +1. However, what will stop the comparisons if `searchName` is not found in `my_friends`?

Example Search: `"SOMEONE"`

Loop Iteration	searchName	my_size	index	Array Element Being Compared
Before loop	"SOMEONE"	5	0	N/A
1	"SOMEONE"	5	0	"DEBBIE"
2	"SOMEONE"	5	1	"JOEY"
3	"SOMEONE"	5	2	"BOBBIE"
4	"SOMEONE"	5	3	"SUSIE"
5	"SOMEONE"	5	4	"MIKEY"
6	"SOMEONE"	5	5	null ← NullPointerException
7	"SOMEONE"	5	6	null
8	"SOMEONE"	5	7	null
9	"SOMEONE"	5	8	null
10	"SOMEONE"	5	9	null

The earlier attempt to implement the sequential search algorithm did not consider that searchName might not be found. The program terminates with NullPointerException. This occurs when the array index 5 is used in the compareTo message. my_friends[5] is null. As shown in the trace above, an array of references to String objects like my_friends sets all elements to null. The value null indicates that the reference refers to nothing. Therefore, the loop test in the sequential search evaluates like this when index becomes 5:

```
searchName.compareTo( my_friends[index] )

searchName.compareTo( my_friends[  5 ]  )

"SOMEONE" .compareTo(        null        )
```

When null is used in the compareTo method, you get a NullPointerException that terminates the program. The exception looks like this when your program stops running:

Output

```
java.lang.reflect.InvocationTargetException:
    java.lang.NullPointerException
    at java.lang.String.compareTo(Compiled Code)
    at FriendList.find(FriendList.java:42)
    at FriendList.main(FriendList.java:61)
```

The sequential search loop should terminate when there are no more meaningful elements to look at. This can be accomplished by using my_size to prevent unnecessary comparisons when the element being searched for is not in the array. The loop test can be made to guard against referencing my_friends[index] when index reaches my_size. This termination condition is recognized in the following corrected implementation of the sequential search:

```
// A correct find method to be added to the FriendList class
public String find( String searchName )
{
  // This sequential search begins searching at the first array location
  int index = 0;

  // The loop terminates as soon as the string is found or (||) there
  // are no more meaningful elements to consider (they're all null).
  while(   ( index < my_size )
      && ( searchName.compareTo( my_friends[index] ) != 0 ) )
  {
    // searchName has not yet been found in the array my_friends
    // and there is at least one more meaningful element to compare.
    index++;
  }
```

```
  // If the loop terminated at or before reaching the last
  // array element, then searchName must have been found.
  // This alternative action returns a reference to the
  // string if found. Otherwise null is returned.
  if( index < my_size )
    return my_friends[index];
  else
    return null;
  // Java collections also return null when an object is not found.
}
```

Now return a reference to the String in the array or null to indicate that the argument searchName was not found in the array. The following dialogues show both possibilities.

Dialogue 1

```
Enter name to search for [UPPERCASE]:  SOMEONE
SOMEONE not found
```

Dialogue 2

```
Enter name to search for [UPPERCASE]:  BOBBIE
BOBBIE found
```

The expression (index < my_size) was written as the first part of the boolean expression to avoid the evaluation of my_friends[index] when the expression would result in null. Recall that short circuit boolean evaluation prevents the evaluation of a second boolean subexpression after && when the first subexpression is false; false && *anything* is false. Without this little trick, the code would have to be written another way to ensure that null is never used as an argument to compareTo.

```
// This works in all cases
while( ( index < my_size ) &&
       ( my_friends[index].compareTo( searchName ) == 0 )
{
  index++;
}

// This will cause a null pointer exception when searchName is not
// found. The compareTo message cannot handle the null argument.
while( ( my_friends[index].compareTo( searchName ) == 0 ) &&
       ( index < my_size ) )
{
  index++;
}
```

Consider what happens when an array is filled to capacity (add five more names and change my_size from 5 to 10). What happens when the search name is not in the array? The index goes to the capacity in the final while loop evaluation.

```
my_size = 10;
// Assume my_friends.length == my_size and searchName is not
// in my_friends

System.out.println( "Enter existing name to search for: " );
searchName = keyboard.readWord( );
```

while((index < my_size) && (searchName.compareTo(my_friends[index])
                                                            != 0))
        ⌣‿⌣   ⌣‿⌣   && (*this expression not evaluated due to short circuit boolean*
         10 <   10   *evaluation*)
        ⌣‿‿‿‿‿‿⌣
            false

Were it not for short circuit boolean evaluation, the second expression would be evaluated. An `ArrayIndexOutOfBoundsException` would occur at `my_friends[10]`.

(searchName.compareTo(my_friends[index]) != 0))

("SOMEONE".compareTo(my_friends[10]) != 0))

ArrayIndexOutOfBoundsException

Due to guaranteed short circuit evaluation, `my_friends[10]` never evaluates. The first expression, `10 < 10`, evaluates to `false`. The expression `false && *anything*` is always `false`. No exception is thrown. However, if you reverse the `boolean` subexpressions around `&&`, you will get an exception when the array is filled to capacity and `searchName` is not found. The following evaluation shows what happens when `searchName` is not found in an array filled to capacity. This illustrates the second reason for comparing index to `my_size` before evaluating the array index.

while((searchName.compareTo(my_friends[index]) != 0) && (index < my_size))

("SOMEONE".compareTo(my_friends[10]) != 0) && (10 < 10))

Output

```
Exception in thread "main" java.lang.ArrayIndexOutOfBoundsException
```

Self-Check

8-16 How many comparisons (iterations of the search loop) are necessary when searchName matches `my_friends[0]`?

8-17 How many comparisons are necessary when searchName matches `my_friends[3]`?

8.3   More Array Details

Initializer Lists

Java provides a quick and easy way to initialize arrays without using `new` or the
capacity: declare the array as variable and assign a collection of values (separated
by commas) between curly braces. For example, the following code initializes an
array of `int`s.

```
int[] test = { 76, 74, 100, 62, 89 };
```

The compiler sets the capacity of `test` to be the number of elements between `{`
and `}`. The first value is assigned to `test[0]`, the second value to `test[1]`, and so
on. Therefore, the initializer list is equivalent to these six lines of code:

```
int[] test = new int[5];
test[0] = 76;
test[1] = 74;
test[2] = 100;
test[3] = 62;
test[4] = 89;
```

You can also use constructor calls in an initializer list. This allows you to create
an array of any type of object. When no literal exists (such as `1`, `5.6`, or `"string"`),
use the constructor to get references to the new objects.

```
BankAccount[] accounts = { new BankAccount( "Kelly", 1234.56 ),
                           new BankAccount( "Barney", 234.56 ),
                           new BankAccount( "Chris", 34.56 ) };

// Print the toString version of each
System.out.println( accounts[0] );
System.out.println( accounts[1] );
System.out.println( accounts[2] );
```

Output

```
Kelly $1,234.56
Barney $234.56
Chris $34.56
```

The `length` Variable

The `length` variable returns the capacity of an array. It is often used to avoid out-of-range index exceptions. For example, the index range of the array above named `accounts` is `0` through `accounts.length - 1`. The capacity is referenced as the array name, a dot, and the variable named `length`.

```
// Output: 3
System.out.println( "Capacity of test is " + accounts.length );
```

This next example constructs an array of `String` objects and uses the `length` variable in a loop.

```
String[] TAs = { "Kelly Heffner", "Barney Boisvert", "*Canceled*",
                 "Chris Shulte", "*Canceled*", "Stuart Smith",
                 "Andy Lenards", "Brent Haas", "Stuart Smith" };

System.out.println( "CSc 227 Section leaders" );
System.out.println( "Sect TA" );
System.out.println( " === ==============" );
for( int j = 0; j < TAs.length; j++ )
{
   System.out.println( "  #" + ( j + 1 ) + " " + TAs[j] );
}
```

Output

```
CSc 227 Section leaders
Sect TA
 === ==============
  #1 Kelly Heffner
  #2 Barney Boisvert
  #3 *Canceled*
  #4 Chris Shulte
  #5 *Canceled*
  #6 Stuart Smith
  #7 Andy Lenards
  #8 Brent Haas
  #9 Stuart Smith
```

Argument/Parameter Associations

You may sometimes find it necessary to pass an array to another method. This requires a different syntax in the parameter list.

***General Form 8.4:* Array parameters**

method-name(class-or-primitive-type[] array-parameter-name)

Here is one example of this syntax that you are quite familiar with. It is the `main` method heading. An array of `Strings` can be passed to the `main` method from the

command line when the program is run. The parameter to main is named args—
an array of Strings.

```
public static void main( String[] args )   // An array of Strings
```

The Strings supplied by the user after the class name allow users to input
information into the program when it is started from the command line. For
example, a user could supply a file name when the program first starts:

```
java DoStatistics in.data
```

The String after the class name is passed as a command line argument to the
program. This is known inside of the main method as args[0].

```
public class DoStatistics
{
  public static void main( String[] args )
  {
    String fileName;  // May come from the user when this program is run

    if( args.length == 1 )
    { // User must have entered a string after java DoStatistics
      fileName = args[0];
    }
    else
    { // User forgot to supply the file name as an argument to the
      // program, so prompt the user for the file name.
      TextReader keyboard = new TextReader( );
      System.out.print( "Enter file name: " );
      fileName = keyboard.readWord( );
    }
    // Use fileName in any code that follows
  }
}
```

If two arguments were entered after DoStatistics, then the parameter in
main args.length would be 2. Assuming this command,

```
java DoStatistics in.dat out.dat
```

the expression args[1] would evaluate to "out.dat".

Another example of array parameters can be found in Java's Arrays class,
which has static methods to sort any array of primitive values. Each method
heading contains an array parameter. Because Java allows methods of the same
name as long as the parameters differ (a form of polymorphism), there are sort
methods for arrays of all of Java's primitive types. Here is a partial list of the sort
methods in the java.util.Arrays class:

Static Methods with Array Parameters from the `java.util.Arrays` Class

```
/** From the Arrays class
  *
  * Sort an array of integers into ascending order
  */
  public static void sort(int[] a)

/** From the Arrays class
  *
  * Sort an array of character into ascending order
  */
  public static void sort(char[] a)


/** From the Arrays class
  *
  * Sort an array of doubles into ascending order
  */
  public static void sort(double[] a)
```

When these static[1] methods are invoked with the array arguments, `intArray`, `charArray`, and `doubleArray` are sorted in ascending order. Each `sort` method has a reference to the array argument. A change to the parameter inside the `sort` method also changes the array argument.

```
import java.util.Arrays;

public class SortThreeArraysOfPrimitives
{
  public static void main( String [] args )
  {
    int[] intArray = { 5, 4, 3, 2, 1 };
    char[] charArray = { 'e', 'd', 'c', 'b', 'a' };
    double[] doubleArray = { 5.5, 4.4, 3.3, 2.2, 1.1 };
    Arrays.sort( intArray );
    Arrays.sort( charArray );
    Arrays.sort( doubleArray );

    // Make up three strings to view the three sorted arrays.
    String si = "";
    String sc = "";
    String sd = "";
    for( int j = 0; j < 5; j++ )
    {
      si += intArray[j] + " ";
      sc += charArray[j] + " ";
      sd += doubleArray[j] + " ";
    }
```

---

1. When a method is declared to be static, that method is invoked by the class name, a dot, the method name, and the argument list. No object needs to be created.

```
        // Print the string version of the three arrays
        System.out.println( "The sorted ints: " + si );
        System.out.println( "The sorted chars: " + sc );
        System.out.println( "The sorted doubles: " + sd );
    }
}
```

Output

```
The sorted ints: 1 2 3 4 5
The sorted chars: a b c d e
The sorted doubles: 1.1 2.2 3.3 4.4 5.5
```

How Does One Method Change Another Method's Object?

The sort method of the Arrays class rearranged the arrays that were initialized in
the main method. The same thing happens with an ArrayList argument when it
is passed to the Collections.sort method. In all four examples, a sort method
rearranges the elements of an array that was constructed in another method.

To understand how one method can modify an argument to a method, first
recall how the assignment of one primitive variable—such as int or double—to
another primitive variable differs from the assignment of one reference variable—
such as String or BankAccount—to another reference variable. Consider the
following assignment of one reference variable to another.

```
BankAccount chris = new BankAccount( "Chris", 0.00 );
BankAccount kim = new BankAccount( "Kim", 100.00 );

kim = chris;
// The values (state) of the object were not assigned.
// Rather, the reference to chris was assigned to kim.
// Now both reference variables are looking at the same object.

System.out.println( "Why does a change to 'chris' change 'kim'?" );
chris.deposit( 555.55 );
System.out.println( "Kim's balance was 0.00, now it is " +
                    kim.getBalance( ) );
```

Output

```
Why does a change to 'chris' change 'kim'?
Kim's balance was 0.00, now it is 555.55
```

The big difference is that the deposit message to chris actually modified kim.
This happens because both reference variables—chris and kim—refer to the
same object in memory after the assignment kim = chris. The same assignment
rules apply when an argument is assigned to a parameter.

Java only has one argument/parameter association—**pass by value**.
When an argument is assigned to a parameter, the argument's value is copied to
the parameter. When the argument is a primitive type such as int or double, the

copied values are primitive numeric values or char values. No method can change the primitive arguments of another method.

When an object is passed to a method, the value is a reference value. The argument is the location of the object in computer memory. At that moment, the parameter is an **alias** (another name) for the argument. Two references to the same object exist; the parameter refers to the same object as the argument. This means that one method can modify the argument via its parameter.

Consider an example where the Grid object constructed in main gets modified by a different method in a different class. The parameter theGrid and the argument ballPit refer to the same Grid object. The many changes to theGrid in XAnyGrid also modify the object referred to by the argument ballPit. The parameter theGrid and the argument ballPit refer to the same object in memory. theGrid is an alias for ballPit.

```
// This program demonstrates that copying the value of a reference
// parameter allows a method to keep the code in main simple
// by allowing another method to do a lot of the work.
public class XAGrid
{
   // A class with no instance variables

  public void XAnyGrid( Grid theGrid )
  { // Hopefully theGrid has the same number of rows and columns
    // This method places some things in theGrid to form an X
    if( theGrid.getRows( ) != theGrid.getColumns( ) )
    {
      System.out.println( "This grid is not a square" );
      System.out.println( theGrid );
    }
    else
    {
      int rightColumn = theGrid.getColumns( );
      for( int r = 0; r < theGrid.getRows( ); r++ )
      {
        theGrid.putDown( r, r ); // From upper left to lower right
        rightColumn--;
        // From upper right to lower left
        theGrid.putDown( r, rightColumn );
      }
    }
  }
}  // End class XAGrid


public class TryXAGrid
{
  public static void main( String[] args )
  {
    Grid ballPit = new Grid( 9, 9, 4, 8, Grid.EAST );

    GraphicGrid view = new GraphicGrid( ballPit );
```

```
        // Compiler builds a default constructor for us
        XAGrid anotherClassAnotherMethod = new XAGrid( );
        anotherClassAnotherMethod.XAnyGrid( ballPit );

        System.out.println( ballPit );
    }
} // End class TryXAGrid
```

Output

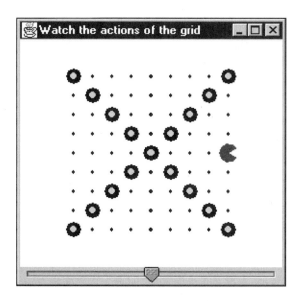

This third example passes an array argument to a method in a different class. The argument in the main method of one class is changed by a method in a different class. This is analogous to Array.sort(int[] a), which rearranges the int elements of the argument that a is an alias for. This example reverses the elements in an array of ints by swapping the elements in the array, beginning with the outermost elements and moving to the middle.

```
public class ArrayReverser
{
  public void reverse( int[] x )
  {
    int n = x.length;
    int firstIndex = 0;
    int lastIndex = n - 1;
    while ( firstIndex < lastIndex )
    { // Swap array elements at the ends as the ends
      // move towards each other
      int temp = x[firstIndex];
      x[firstIndex] = x[lastIndex];
      x[lastIndex] = temp;
      firstIndex++;
```

```
            lastIndex--;
        }
    }
}

public class TryArrayReverser
{
    public static void main( String[] args )
    {
        int[] a = { 1, 2, 3, 4, 5, 6, 7, 8 };

        // The reverse method changes the array named a in another method
        ArrayReverser anotherClassAnotherMethod = new ArrayReverser( );
        anotherClassAnotherMethod.reverse( a );

        for( int j = 0; j < a.length; j++ )
            System.out.print( a[j] + " " );
    }
}
```

In summary, when an argument is a reference variable, a change to the parameter in another method changes the object referenced by the associated argument. This applies to all Java objects, including arrays.

Self-Check

8-20 Write the output generated by this code:

```
String[] names = { "Abe", "Bev", "Cy", "Deb" };
for( int j = 0; j < names.length; j++ )
    System.out.println( names[j].toUpperCase( ) );
```

8-21 Write the output generated by the following code:

```
int[] temp;
int[] x = new int[3];
int newCapacity;

x[0] = 11;
x[1] = 22;
x[2] = 33;
System.out.println( "current length of x: " + x.length );
System.out.println( x[0] );
System.out.println( x[1] );
System.out.println( x[2] );

newCapacity = 2 * x.length;

temp = new int[newCapacity];
for( int j = 0; j < x.length; j++ )
    temp[j] = x[j];
x = temp;
temp = null;
System.out.println( "current length of x: " + x.length );
```

```
System.out.println( x[0] );
System.out.println( x[1] );
System.out.println( x[2] );

newCapacity = x.length / 2;
temp = new int[newCapacity - 1 ];   // Be careful
for( int j = 0; j < temp.length; j++ )
   temp[j] = x[j];
x = temp;
temp = null;
System.out.println( "current length of x: " + x.length );
System.out.println( x[0] );
System.out.println( x[1] );
System.out.println( x[2] ); // Be careful
```

8.4   StringBag — A Simple Collection Class

As you continue your study of computing fundamentals, you will spend a fair amount of time exploring ways to manage collections of data. The Java array is but one of several major data storage structures. You will also use classes such as ArrayList (shown in preceding chapters), Hashmap, and Stack to manage collections of objects with higher-level messages such as add, remove, binarySearch, addFirst, getFirst, removeFirst, push, pop, and sort. These classes are known as "collection" classes because they group many elements into a single object. Collection classes have the following characteristics:

- The main responsibility of a collection class is to store a collection of objects.
- Objects may be added and removed from a collection.
- A collection class allows clients to access the individual elements.
- A collection class may have search-and-sort operations for locating a particular item.
- Some collections allow duplicate elements, other collections do not.

Collections are realized in a variety of ways. For example, the Java array uses subscript notation to access individual elements. The author-supplied StringBag class shown next exemplifies a higher-level approach to storing a collection of objects. It presents users with messages and hides the array processing details inside the methods (a bit like the ArrayList class). The relatively simple StringBag class also provides a review of Java classes and methods. This time, however, the class has an array instance variable. The methods employ array processing algorithms.

The main purpose of the StringBag class is to store a collection of String objects and to allow client code to access all strings in the StringBag from the first to the last. A StringBag object has the following characteristics:

- A StringBag object can currently store references only to String objects (however, it could be made to store a collection of anything).
- StringBag elements need not be unique. There may be duplicate entries. Such a collection is known as a multi-set or a bag.
- StringBag elements need not be in any particular order.
- Elements can be removed from a StringBag object.
- This StringBag class is useful for learning about collections and for reviewing arrays. It is not meant to be a substitute for the existing Java collection classes.

A StringBag object can store any number of String objects. A StringBag object understands messages such as add and remove. An iterator method allows programmers to process all elements in the collection in a sequential fashion.

This particular collection class stores only String elements. A good collection class should be able to store any type of object (otherwise, a new collection class would have to be implemented for each type of object you would like to store). However, the main purpose of this class is to provide further examples of manipulating arrays. First, here are some sample messages.

```java
// Show some messages understood by StringBag
import java.util.Iterator;

public class TestStringBag
{
  public static void main( String[] args )
  {
    // Test drive StringBag
    StringBag aStringBag = new StringBag( );

    // Add a few strings
    aStringBag.add( "Erin" );
    aStringBag.add( "Jignesh" );
    aStringBag.add( "Kristen" );
    aStringBag.add( "Maya" );

    // Remove one string, but fail to remove another
    aStringBag.remove( "Jignesh" );
    aStringBag.remove( "Not Here" );
    System.out.println( "size: " + aStringBag.size( ) );
    System.out.println( "aStringBag: " + aStringBag );

    // StringBag has a method that returns an Iterator
    // object with three methods, a simpler interface
    // than ListIterator, which has 12 methods).
    Iterator itr = aStringBag.iterator( );
    while( itr.hasNext( ) )
      System.out.println( itr.next( ) );

    // add will increase the capacity when necessary
    aStringBag.add( "a" );
    aStringBag.add( "b" );
```

```
        aStringBag.add( "c" );
        aStringBag.add( "d" );
        aStringBag.add( "e" );
        aStringBag.add( "f" );
        aStringBag.add( "g" );
        aStringBag.add( "h" );
        aStringBag.add( "i" );
        aStringBag.add( "j" );
        aStringBag.add( "k" );

        System.out.println( "New size: " + aStringBag.size( ) );
        System.out.println( aStringBag );
    }
}
```

Output

```
size: 3
aStringBag: [Erin, Maya, Kristen]
Erin
Maya
Kristen
New size: 14
[Erin, Maya, Kristen, a, b, c, d, e, f, g, h, i, j, k]
```

The StringBag Constructor

The private instance variables of the StringBag class include an array named
my_data for storing a collection of String objects. Each StringBag object also has
an integer named my_size to maintain the number of meaningful elements that
are in the StringBag. The StringBag methods frequently need both of these
instance variables to accomplish their responsibilities. The constructor establishes
an empty StringBag object by setting my_size to zero. The capacity is set to the
arbitrary initial capacity of 10.

```
// A class for storing an unordered collection of Strings.
// This class was designed to provide practice and review in
// implementing methods and classes along with using arrays.
import java.util.Iterator;

public class StringBag
{
    private String[] my_data;    // Stores the collection of strings
    private int my_size;         // Number of strings in this StringBag

    // Construct an empty StringBag object
    public StringBag( )
    {
        my_size = 0;
        my_data = new String[10];  // Initial capacity is 10
    }
    // ...
```

add

Both my_size and my_data must be available to the add method. This is not a problem, since any StringBag method has access to the private instance variables of StringBag. To add an element to the StringBag, the stringToAdd can be placed at the end of the array, or more specifically, at the first available array location of my_data. This two-step algorithm summarizes how a new String is added to the first available array position:

Algorithm: **Adding an element**

my_data[my_size] = *the-argument-passed-to-StringBag.add*
increment my_size by +1

The argument passed to StringBag's add method is stored into the proper array location using my_size as the index. Then my_size is incremented to reflect the new addition. Incrementing my_size maintains the number of elements in the StringBag.

Incrementing my_size also conveniently sets up a situation where the next added element is inserted into the proper array location. The array location at my_data[my_size] is the next place to store a newly added element. This is demonstrated in the following view of the state of the StringBag before and after the string "and a fourth".

Before

Instance Variable	State of **bagOfStrings**
my_data[0]	"A string"
my_data[1]	"Another string"
my_data[2]	"and still another"
my_data[3]	null // my_data[my_size] is the next available spot
my_data[4]	null
...	...
my_data[9]	null
my_size	3

After

Instance Variable	State of **bagOfStrings**
my_data[0]	"A string"
my_data[1]	"Another string"
my_data[2]	"and still another"
my_data[3]	**"and a fourth"**
my_data[4]	null // my_data[my_size] is the next available spot
...	...
my_data[9]	null
my_size	4

But before the new String is added, a check is made to ensure that there is the capacity to add another element. If there is room, the new element is added.

```java
// Add a string to the StringBag in no particular order.
// stringToAdd: Any string you want to store in this StringBag object.
// If theStringBag is full, the array's capacity is doubled.
public void add( String stringToAdd )
{
  boolean result = true;

  // Increase the array capacity if necessary
  if( my_size == my_data.length )
    doubleArrayCapacity( );

  // Always add StringToAdd (unless the computer runs out of memory)

  // Store the reference into the array
  my_data[my_size] = stringToAdd;

  // Make sure my_size is always increased by one
  my_size++;
}
```

If my_size is at the array's capacity—if (my_size == my_data.length)— there is not enough room to add the new element. In this case, the array capacity increases. The object sends a doubleArrayCapacity message to itself. The StringBag object changes the instance variable my_data to reference a new array with twice the capacity that it had before. It copies the original contents (my_data[0] through my_data[my_size - 1]) intact, with the elements at the same indexes as before.

```java
// Change my_data to have the same elements in indexes 0..my_size - 1
// with twice as many array locations to store elements.
private void doubleArrayCapacity( )
{
  String[] temp = new String[2 * my_size];

  // Copy all existing elements into the new and larger array
  for( int j = 0; j < my_size; j++ )
    temp[j] = my_data[j];

  // Store reference to the new bigger array as part of this
  // object's state
  my_data = temp;
}
```

With an array implementation of a collection, the array should grow and shrink at the appropriate times. If the collection frequently changes in size, the add and remove methods can ensure that not too much memory is wasted.

remove

Now consider the method that removes an element from a `StringBag` object. In order to concentrate on the `remove` algorithm, remember that `my_data` (an array of `String` objects) and `my_size` (the number of elements in the `StringBag`) are always available to any `StringBag` object. The following method heading also provides the name of the string to be removed (if found).

```
public boolean remove( String stringToRemove )
```

If `stringToRemove` is found to equal one of the strings referenced by the array, `remove` effectively takes out the first occurrence of the object. Consider the following message when the remove parameter `stringToRemove` becomes `"Another string"`:

```
bagOfStrings.remove( "Another string" );
```

Here are the values of the instance variables `my_data` and `my_size` and of the local objects `index` and `stringToRemove` while trying to remove `"Another string"`:

Instance Variable	State of **bagOfStrings**
`my_data[0]`	`"A string"`
`my_data[1]`	`"Another string"`
`my_data[2]`	`"and still another"`
`my_data[3]`	`"and a fourth"`
`my_data[4]`	`null`
`. . .`	
`my_data[9]`	`null`
`my_size`	`4`

Local Variable	State of **remove**'s Local Variable after a Sequential Search
`stringToRemove`	`"Another string"`
`index`	`1`

Once found, the reference stored in `my_data[index]` must somehow be removed from the array, which is currently `my_data[1]` or `"another string"`. The simple way to do this is to move the last element into the spot where `stringToRemove` was found. It is okay to destroy the reference in `my_data[1]`. This is the object to be removed from the `StringBag`. Also, since there is no ordering requirement, it is also okay to move `my_data[my_size - 1]`, the last meaningful element in the array. The instance variable `my_size` must be changed to reflect the removal. Here are the three statements that do it:

```
// index is the array location of the item to be removed
my_data[index] = my_data[my_size - 1];

// No longer need a reference in the last
// array location, so make it null
my_data[my_size - 1] = null;

// Make sure the size is decreased to
// complete the removal of one element
my_size--;
```

The state of `StringBag` now looks like this:

Instance Variable	State of **bagOfStrings**	
my_data[0]	"A string"	
my_data[1]	"And a fourth"	Overwrite "another string"
my_data[2]	"and still another"	
my_data[3]	null	my_data[3] is no longer meaningful
my_data[4]	null	
. . .		
my_data[9]	null	
my_size	3	my_size is 3 now

Although the elements are not in the same order (this was not a requirement), the same elements exist after the requested removal. Because the last element has been relocated, `my_size` must be decreased by one. There are now only three, not four, elements in this `StringBag`.

The same code works even when removing the last element. The assignment is done, even though it is not necessary. Merely decreasing `my_size` by one effectively eliminates the last element.

The `remove` method first calls a helper method named `indexOf` (shown later) that returns the index of an element found in the collection. If the element is not in `my_data`, `indexOf` returns `-1` and `remove` returns `false`.

```
// Remove the first occurrence of stringToRemove if found.
// Return true if the object was successfully removed or
// false if stringToRemove was not found in this StringBag.
public boolean remove( String stringToRemove )
{
  boolean result = false;
  int subscript = indexOf( stringToRemove );

  if( subscript != -1 )
  { // Move the last string in the array to
    // where stringToRemove was found.
    my_data[subscript] = my_data[my_size - 1];

    // Decrease this StringBag's number of elements
    my_size--;
```

```
      // Let this method return true to where the message was sent
      result = true;
   }
   return result;
}
```

Here is the helper method named indexOf that was called by remove.

```
// Return the index of the first occurrence of stringToRemove.
// Otherwise return -1 if stringToRemove is not found.
private int indexOf( String stringToRemove )
{
   int result = -1;

   // Perform a sequential search on this unordered collection
   int subscript = 0;
   while( subscript < my_size && result == -1 )
   {
      if( my_data[subscript].compareTo( stringToRemove ) == 0 )
         result = subscript;
      else
         subscript++;
   }

   // my_data[subscript] equals stringToRemove if found.
   // Otherwise result will not be changed from -1.
   return result;
}
```

This method was declared private because indexOf is not currently considered a method that programmers are meant to use. The class should not be cluttered with methods that programmers are not intended to use.

Design Heuristic 8.1 (Riels Heuristic 2.6)

Do not clutter the public part of a class with things that users of the class are not able to use or are not interested in using.

The private indexOf method was added to help partition the work of removing an element. It was not intended for public use. Methods such as this are referred to as "helper methods."

size

The size message returns the precise number of elements that are currently in the collection—the number of meaningful elements. The private instance variable my_size is maintained by incrementing it (adding 1) in add and decrementing it (subtracting 1) in remove. The StringBag constructor initialized my_size to zero to indicate an empty bag.

```
// Returns the number of strings currently stored in the StringBag
public int size( )
{
  return my_size;
}
```

The other method of the StringBag class, iterator, relates to the Iterator design pattern. The iterator method and an inner class to help implement it will be discussed in the next section.

Self-Check

8-22 What happens when an attempt is made to remove an element that is not in the StringBag?

8-23 Using the implementation of remove just given, what happens when an attempt is made to remove an element from an empty StringBag (my_size == 0)?

8-24 Write a complete program that adds and then removes your name from a StringBag.

8-25 Must remove always maintain the StringBag elements in the same order as that in which they were originally added?

8-26 What happens when an attempt is made to remove an element that has two of the same values in the StringBag?

8-27 Write the output of the following code:

```
StringBag aBag = new StringBag( );
aBag.add( "First"  );
aBag.add( "Second" );
aBag.add( "Third"  );
aBag.add( "Fourth" );
aBag.add( "Fifth"  );
System.out.println( "size: " + aBag.size( ) );
aBag.remove( "Fifth"  );
aBag.remove( "Third"  );
aBag.remove( "Third"  );
aBag.remove( "NotHere"  );
System.out.println( "size: " + aBag.size( ) );
```

iterator

To be consistent with Java's Iterator interface, this StringBag class has a method named iterator that returns an Iterator object. To accomplish this, StringBag employs a private inner class named StringBagIterator that implements java.util.Iterator. The StringBag iterator method returns an Iterator object. This `Iterator` object has access to the `StringBag`'s `size`. It also understands the `hasNext` and `next` methods.

```java
// Return an object that can be stored in java.util.Iterator
public Iterator iterator( )
{
  Iterator result = new StringBagIterator( );
  return result;
}
```

From the outside, `iterator` can be used just like Java's `ArrayList iterator` method. For example, the following code prints the uppercase version of each element in `aStringBag`.

```java
// This is the same iterator interface used for many Java collections
Iterator itr = aStringBag.iterator( );
while( itr.hasNext( ) )
{
  String str = (String)itr.next( );   // next returns an Object
  System.out.println( str.toUpperCase( ) );
}
```

The private inner `StringBagIterator` class implements `java.util.Iterator`. It was chosen here as it has only three methods (`ListIterator` has nine methods). The `next` and `hasNext` methods should look familiar. These two will be implemented. The third method (`remove`) is optional, but it will have to be implemented, even if it does nothing.

```java
public interface Iterator
{
  // Returns true if the iteration has more elements
  public boolean hasNext( );

  // Returns the next element in the iteration while updating the
  // iteration to refer to the next element if there is one. If
  // there are no more, elements hasNext will return false.
  public Object next( );

  // We could make remove return a reference to the last element
  // returned by next. Instead, the this method will not be
  // supported. Java states that this is an optional operation.
  public void remove();

} // End interface Iterator
```

The `StringBagIterator`'s constructor sets its single instance variable `currentIndex` to 0. So when `StringBag`'s `iterator` method returns the first element, the iteration returns `my_data[0]`, the first element in the collection.

```
// Implement java.util.Iterator as a private inner class
private class StringBagIterator implements Iterator
{
  private int currentIndex;

  public StringBagIterator( )
  {
    currentIndex = 0;
  }
```

Immediately after the iteration is initialized with the iterator message, the hasNext method returns true if there is at least one element in the StringBag. If my_size is 0, this method returns false—there are no elements to iterate over.

```
// Return true if the iteration has
// at least one more element to traverse
public boolean hasNext( )
{ // This method should be called *before* the next message.
  return currentIndex < my_size;
}
```

At first, the next method returns the current element in the iteration beginning at index 0. It also updates the internal index to reference the next element. Since this is both an accessing and modifying message, the element to be returned is temporarily referenced by result so index can be incremented.

```
// Return a reference to the next object and adjust index
public Object next( )
{
  // Temporarily store reference
  Object result = my_data[currentIndex];
  currentIndex++;
  return result;
}
```

Those are the first two of the three required methods in Java's Iterator interface. To get everything to compile, the remove method must also be implemented. It could do nothing. However, with the following implementation, if a remove message were sent to the Iterator object, an exception would be thrown (see Chapter 9 for more details on exceptions).

```
public void remove( )
{
  throw new UnsupportedOperationException( "Can't remove now" );
}
```

Here is the entire StringBag class with its inner class that implements Java's Iterator interface.

```java
// A class for storing an unordered collection of Strings.
// This class was designed to provide practice and review in
// implementing methods and classes along with using arrays.

import java.util.Iterator;

public class StringBag
{
  private String[] my_data;  // Stores the collection of strings
  private int my_size;       // Current number of strings

  // Construct an empty StringBag object
  public StringBag( )
  {
    my_size = 0;
    my_data = new String[10];  // Initial capacity is 10
  }

  // Returns the number of strings that have been added but not removed
  public int size( )
  {
    return my_size;
  }


  // Provide a peek at this collection
  public String toString( )
  {
    String result = "[";
    // Concatenate all elements followed by , except for the last
    for( int j = 0; j < my_size - 1; j++ )
      result = result + my_data[j] + ", ";

    // Concatenate the last String only if there is one
    if( my_size > 0 )
      result = result + my_data[my_size - 1];
    // Always add the closing ]
    result = result + "]";

    return result;
  }


  // Add a string to the StringBag in no particular place.
  // stringToAdd: Any string you want to store in this StringBag object.
  // If theStringBag is full, the array's capacity is doubled.
  public void add( String stringToAdd )
  {
    boolean result = true;

    if( my_size == my_data.length )
    {
      doubleArrayCapacity( );
    }
```

```java
    // Always add StringToAdd (unless the computer runs out of memory)

    // Store the reference into the array
    my_data[my_size] = stringToAdd;

    // Make sure my_size is always increased by one
    my_size++;
  }


  // Change my_data to have the same elements in indexes
  // 0..my_size - 1 and have the same number of new
  // array locations to store new elements.
  private void doubleArrayCapacity( )
  {
    String[] temp = new String[2 * my_size];

    // Copy all existing elements into the new and larger array
    for( int j = 0; j < my_size; j++ )
      temp[j] = my_data[j];

    // Store a reference to the new bigger array as part of this
    // object's state
    my_data = temp;
  }


  // Remove the first occurrence of stringToRemove if found.
  // Return true if the object was successfully removed or
  // false if stringToRemove was not found in this StringBag.
  public boolean remove( String stringToRemove )
  {
    boolean result = false;
    int subscript = indexOf( stringToRemove );

    if( subscript != -1 )
    { // Move the last string in the array to
      // where stringToRemove was found.
      my_data[subscript] = my_data[my_size - 1];
      // Old string will be garbage-collected, since there is no
      // reference to it

      // Decrease this StringBag's number of elements
      my_size--;

      // Let this method return true to where the message was sent
      result = true;
    }
    return result;
  }
```

```java
// Return the index of the first occurrence of stringToRemove.
// Otherwise return -1 if stringToRemove is not found.
private int indexOf( String stringToRemove )
{
  int result = -1;

  // Perform a sequential search on this unordered collection
  for( int subscript = 0; subscript < my_size; subscript++ )
  {
    if( my_data[subscript].compareTo( stringToRemove ) == 0 )
    {
      result = subscript;
      break;  // Found stringToRemove at my_data[result]
    }
  }

  // my_data[subscript] equals stringToRemove if found.
  // Otherwise result is not changed from -1.
  return result;
}


// Return an object that can be stored in an Iterator
public Iterator iterator( )
{
  Iterator result = new StringBagIterator( );
  return result;
}



//////// Implement an Iterator that can reference my_data and my_size
private class StringBagIterator implements Iterator
{
  private int currentIndex;

  public StringBagIterator( )
  {
    currentIndex = 0;
  }

  // Return the current element in the iteration
  // beginning at index 0 while also updating the
  // internal index to reference the next element.
  public Object next( )
  {
    Object result = my_data[currentIndex];
    currentIndex++;
    return result;
  }
```

```
    // Return true if the iteration has at
    // least one more element to traverse
    public boolean hasNext( )
    { // This method should be called *before* the next message.
      return currentIndex < my_size;
    }

    public void remove( )
    {
        throw new UnsupportedOperationException( "Can't remove now" );
    }

  } // End class StringBagIterator

} // End class StringBag
```

8.5   BankTeller_Ch8 — Changing Accounts

This section implements a class designed to store a collection of BankAccount objects. While providing another example of array usage, it also will be used within the bank teller system to allow for many bank customers.

The bank teller system needs to get a reference to a particular BankAccount. Once currentAccount is established, the withdraw and deposit listeners know which account to withdraw from or deposit to. When a user enters a new ID into the New Account field, a listener to JTextField can change currentAccount to refer to the correct BankAccount object from the collection of bank accounts (or display a message if the account is not found). Inside this new listener, the message could look like this:

```
currentAccount =
    accountCollection.findAccountWithID( IDfromNewAccountField );
```

When a new BankAccountCollection is constructed, nine accounts are added to the collection. This is done in the constructor. While it is not realistic to always have the same accounts with the same balances every time, it does make it easier to test the system. In Chapter 9, "Exceptions and I/O Streams," the bank teller system will be made persistent; the collection objects TransactionList and BankAccountCollection will survive between program runs. That will allow the accounts to have the correct balances. And the TransactionList will have transactions from some time ago. But for now, for example, Kieran always begins with a balance of 100.00:

```java
public class BankAccountCollection
{
  private BankAccount[] accountList;
  private int my_size;

  public BankAccountCollection( )
  {
    my_size = 0;
    accountList = new BankAccount[10];

    // Code nine BankAccounts to get things started
    add( new BankAccount( "Kieran",  100.00 ) );
    add( new BankAccount( "Steve",   200.00 ) );
    add( new BankAccount( "Scott",   300.00 ) );
    add( new BankAccount( "Rick",    400.00 ) );
    add( new BankAccount( "Diane",   500.00 ) );
    add( new BankAccount( "Wendy",   600.00 ) );
    add( new BankAccount( "Chelsea", 700.00 ) );
    add( new BankAccount( "Gary",    800.00 ) );
    add( new BankAccount( "Austen",  900.00 ) );
  }

  // ... public toString not shown here

  // ... findAccountWithID will be explained later
}
```

The add method appends a BankAccount to the end of the array. The
BankAccountCollection is similar to StringBag, except it stores an array of
references to BankAccount objects rather than references to String objects.

```java
  // Add an account to this collection
  public void add( BankAccount accountToAdd )
  {
    // Check to see if the array is filled to capacity
    if( my_size == accountList.length )
      doubleArrayCapacity( );

    // Now accountToAdd can be placed into the array
    accountList[my_size] = accountToAdd;
    my_size++;
  }
```

The toString and doubleArrayCapacity methods of this new class are not
shown here (see BankAccountCollection.java on the accompanying disk).
However, the following code indicates that there are nine accounts as they have
been successfully added in the constructor.

```java
// Construct a collection of the same nine accounts
BankAccountCollection theAccounts = new BankAccountCollection( );

// Returns a string with all elements on separate lines
System.out.println( theAccounts );
```

Output

```
Kieran $100.00
Steve $200.00
Scott $300.00
Rick $400.00
Diane $500.00
Wendy $600.00
Chelsea $700.00
Gary $800.00
Austen $900.00
```

findAccountWithID

After the bank teller system constructs this collection, any method in the BankTeller_Ch8 class can send a findAccountWithID message to the BankAccountCollection. The message requires a String ID so it can try to locate the account with the given ID. This method uses sequential search to find the account. If found, findAccountWithID returns a reference to the BankAccount. If the ID does not match any BankAccount ID, the method returns null.

```
// This returns a reference to the BankAccount in the collection
// or null if there was no account with the given accountID
public BankAccount findAccountWithID( String accountID )
{
  for( int index = 0; index < my_size; index++ )
  {
    if( accountID.equals( accountList[index].getID( ) ) )
      return accountList[index];
  }
  return null;
}
```

The following code tests this important method.

```
System.out.println( theAccounts.findAccountWithID( "Steve" ) );
System.out.println( theAccounts.findAccountWithID( "Austen" ) );
System.out.println( theAccounts.findAccountWithID( "NotHere" ) );
```

Output

```
Steve $200.00
Austen $900.00
null
```

One of the nice things about having a reference to an object in the collection is this: When a message is sent to the return value of findAccountWithID, which returns a reference to a BankAccount, it is sending a message to the object referenced from inside the collection. This means withdraw and deposit messages change the single BankAccount that now is referenced through currentAccount inside of BankTeller_Ch8.

```
String ID = "Austen";
currentAccount = theAccounts.findAccountWithID( ID );
System.out.println( "Before withdraw and deposit: " + currentAccount );
currentAccount.deposit( 22.22 );
currentAccount.withdraw( 100.00 );

// Show what the changed account now looks
// like from inside the collection:
System.out.println( "After depositing 22.22 and withdrawing 100.00" );
System.out.println( theAccounts.findAccountWithID( ID ) );
```

Output

```
Before withdraw and deposit: Austen $900.00
After depositing 22.22 and withdrawing 100.00
Austen $822.22
```

Changes to **BankTeller_Ch8**

It is now time to almost complete the bank teller applications started way back in Chapter 3. The changes include:

- Maintain a BankAccountCollection.
- Add another ActionListener class to allow the user to change accounts with different account IDs.
- Enable the withdraw and deposit text fields only when there is a valid account.

A new instance variable is added to BankTeller_Ch8. It is created in the constructor (as are all of the text fields, buttons, and labels—code not shown here). The system does not know the first customer that will walk up to the teller window. Therefore, the currentAccount is now set to the same value that getAccountWithID would have if it were given an ID that was not found in BankAccountCollection. That value is null. This also means that the balance of the lone currentAccount will not be displayed in the balance label. Now when the system starts up, the Account ID field will be blank and the Balance label will be set as this String class constant:

```
private static final String DEFAULT_BALANCE = "???.??";
```

Additionally, since there is no current account to consider at startup, the withdraw text field, the deposit text field, and the XPress 10 button will now be disabled. This means that the XPress 10 button cannot be clicked, nor can any deposit or withdrawal amount be entered—at least not until a valid account ID is entered.

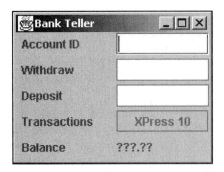 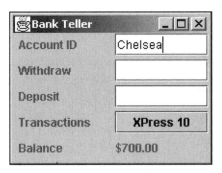

When a valid Account ID is entered and `currentAccount` references a valid account in the collection, the three graphical components are enabled. Later on, if an entered Account ID is not found in `BankAccountCollection`, the same three graphical components are disabled. The window has a slightly different appearance when `currentAccount` is `null` (whereas the disabled button is obvious, the text fields are subtly different). You will not be able to enter any text into the text fields when they are disabled, as shown in the left window.

Here are the changes in the code made from `BankTeller_Ch7` to `BankTeller_Ch8`.

```
// This class has an inner listener class to get new
// accounts based on the user input of a valid account ID.
public class BankTeller_Ch8 extends JFrame
{
     // ...

  // New instance variable in Chapter 8
  private BankAccountCollection theAccounts;

  public BankTeller_Ch8( )
  {
    // This class now has access to a collection of accounts
    theAccounts = new BankAccountCollection( );

    // The currentAccount will now be set in NewAccountListener.
    // It will read the ID in the Account ID field and
    // ask the BankAccount collection for a reference to the
    // BankAccount or return null if the ID is not found.
    // So initially, there is no currentAccount. Set it to null.
    currentAccount = null;

    // ... setSize, add graphical components, register listeners, ...
```

At the bottom of the constructor, an instance of the new listener class is registered to listen to the new account field in the GUI. The private inner class that implements `ActionListener` will be built in the section that follows.

```
   // Code to register a listener to the Account ID text field.
   // Later on, when the ChangeAccountListener actionPerformed method
   // executes, the currentAccount will be set to the matching account.
   ChangeAccountListener newAccountListener = new ChangeAccountListener( );
   newAccountField.addActionListener( newAccountListener );

   // Make three components unusable until the user enters a
   // valid account ID
   setComponentsEnabled( false );

} // End constructor


   // Enable three graphical components of the argument assigned to onOrOff
   // is true. If the argument is false, all three will be disabled.
   private void setComponentsEnabled( boolean onOrOff )
   {
     withdrawField.setEnabled( onOrOff );
     depositField.setEnabled( onOrOff );
     XPress10Button.setEnabled( onOrOff );
   }
```

ChangeAccountListener

Whenever a user enters a `String` into the Account ID field (referenced by `newAccountField`), the `actionPerformed` method of `ChangeAccountListener` class is called (an instance of `ChangeAccountListener` was registered to the Account ID field with `addActionListener`, above). Here are the actions that occur in the `actionPerformed` method.

1. Get the `String` in the new account field.
2. If the Account ID field has an empty `String`, do nothing.
3. Otherwise ask `BankAccountCollection` for a reference to the account with the given ID and store this reference in `currentAccount`.
4. If `currentAccount` is `null`,
   - disable three graphical components,
   - set the balance label to the default balance string ("???.??"), and
   - display a message to the user that no account was found with the given ID.
5. Otherwise,
   - enable the three graphical components and
   - change `balanceField` to show the `currentAccount`'s current balance. `currentAccount` references a valid `BankAccount`.

```
// actionPerformed executes when the user enters a new Account ID
private class ChangeAccountListener implements ActionListener
{
  public void actionPerformed( ActionEvent e )
  {
    String id = newAccountField.getText( );
```

```
   // Don't do anything if an empty string was entered
   if( id.compareTo("") != 0)
   {
     currentAccount = theAccounts.findAccountWithID( id );
     if( currentAccount == null )
     {
       setComponentsEnabled( false );
       balanceLabel.setText( DEFAULT_BALANCE );
       JOptionPane.showMessageDialog( null, id + " not found" );
     }
     else
     {
       setComponentsEnabled( true );
       balanceLabel.setText( currencyFormat.format(
                                  currentAccount.getBalance( ) ) );
     }
   }
 }
}
} // End class ChangeAccountListener
```

Now any subsequent withdraw or deposit transaction will modify the `BankAccount` from the collection (along with record the transaction). To process a different bank customer, the user will have to enter a new ID in the `newAccountField`. The bank teller system can now process any number of transactions for any `BankAccount` in the collection.

What's Next?

At this point, running the program stored as `BankTeller_Ch8.java` would perform all of the functionality specified way back at the beginning of Chapter 3. There is nothing more to do. However, what was probably intended in the specification in Chapter 3 was that the balances should persist after the program shuts down.

The system must maintain the correct balances for all accounts.

There will be one more modification made in Chapter 9. The `TransactionList` and `BankAccountCollection` objects will be saved to a disk. The changed state of the collections of objects will be saved when the program shuts down and reloaded when the program starts up again. The transaction list will be available for some time to come. When objects live between programs runs, they are said to be **persistent** objects. This is what you are accustomed to when you retrieve files that you saved and they have retained their state.

The Bank Teller System Is an Object-Oriented Program

This book has often laid the following claim:

An object-oriented program is a collection of objects sending messages to each other.

At this point, the bank teller system has one or more instances of the classes shown next (in boldface). That's a lot of objects.

Classes Used from Java's Library of Classes

Object	Constructor that is called for every object in the system
JFrame	The window that acts as the base of an event-driven GUI
String	A ubiquitous class to store strings in many places
JButton	Graphical components that can be clicked
JLabel	Labels output and prompts users for input
JTextField	A one-line text editor to "read" user input
GregorianCalendar	Helps `DayCounter` get the current date and time
Calendar	Helps `GregorianCalendar`
ArrayList	Stores the collection of transactions
array	Stores the collection of bank accounts
JOptionPane	Displays messages

Classes Built for This Particular System

BankTeller_Ch8	Groups together many objects
Transaction	Stores one transaction and when it was recorded
TransactionCollection	Adds many transactions and finds most recent
BankAccount	Stores one account
BankAccountCollection	Stores many accounts
ChangeAccountListener	A single instance to change `currentAccount`
WithdrawListener	Performs all actions for a correct withdrawal
DepositListener	Performs all actions for a correct deposit
XPress10Listener	Shows the most recent 10 accounts

Java classes supply many of these objects. Some objects come from the classes that were written for this particular application. This is the nature of things when writing object-oriented programs with Java. At this point, the system allows many customers to perform many transactions while maintaining balances and recording transactions. To see this in action, run `BankTeller_Ch8.java`.

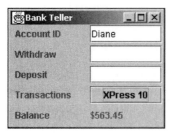
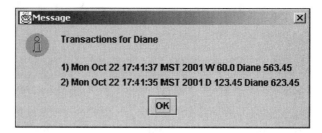

Chapter Summary

- An array stores a collection of elements. The elements may be primitive values stored directly into the array. The elements may be objects, such as `Strings`, `BankAccounts`, and `JButtons`.

- Individual array elements are referenced with subscript notation. With a Java array, the integer expression in a subscript should be in the range of 0 through the array's capacity - 1. For example, the valid index range of the `double[] x = new double[100]` is 0 through 99 inclusive.

- Out-of-range indexes are detected at runtime. The program terminates with an `ArrayIndexOutOfBoundsException`.

- An integer named `n` (or `my_size`) is an important piece of data that must be maintained in addition to the array elements themselves. The number of meaningful elements is important in any array processing algorithm.

- The capacity of an array almost always differs from the number of meaningful elements. An array of capacity 1,000 may only be using the first 739 elements to store meaningful data.

- The array `length` variable returns an `int` representing the current capacity (not the size) of the array.

- All arguments are passed to another method by value. The value of a reference variable is the location of an object. In this case, the parameter becomes an alias for the argument. A modifying message to the parameter in the invoked method changes the same object that the argument refers to.

- A collection class has the main responsibility of managing a collection of elements with operations such as `add`, `remove`, and `find`.

- The `StringBag` class showed how to manage a collection of `Strings`. It was not designed to be a generic collection class capable of storing any type of object.

- The `StringBag` class demonstrated how to write an `iterator` method that returns an object that has the `next` and `hasNext` methods.

- The bank teller system is an object-oriented program with approximately 20 types of objects that send messages to the other objects in the system.

Key Terms

alias

array

array processing

ArrayIndexOutOfBoundsException

index

length

pass by value

persistent

sequential search

setEnabled

subscript

Exercises

The answers to exercises marked with are available in Appendix C.

 1. Write the output generated by the following code:

```java
int MAX = 10;
int[] x = new int[MAX];

for( int j = 0; j < 3; j++ )
  x[j] = j * 2;

for( int j = 3; j < MAX; j++ )
  x[j] = x[j - 1] + x[j - 2];

for( int j = 0; j < MAX; j++ )
  System.out.println( j + ". " + x[j] );
```

2. How many elements will have meaningful values (other than null) in an array with a capacity to store references to 100 objects?

3. Declare a Java array called arrayOfInts that stores 10 integers with indexes 0 through 9.

4. Write the code that determines the largest number in the following array, assuming the first 52 values are meaningful:

```java
double[] y = new double[75];
// Assume y[0] through y[51] are meaningful
int n = 52;
```

 5. Write the code that determines the average of the following array, assuming that only the first 43 elements are meaningful:

```java
double[] z = new double[100];
// Assume z[0] through z[42] are meaningful
int n = 43;
```

 6. Write the code that declares and initializes an array of strings using lines of input from the keyboard. Ask the user how many lines of input there are first. Then display the lines in reverse order. Your dialogue should look like this:

```
How many lines? 4

Enter 4 lines of input:
First Line
Second Line
Any string input data you want
Fourth

Lines reversed:
Fourth
Any string input data you want
Second Line
First Line
```

7. Write the code that sets a `boolean` variable `found` to `true` if a `String` named `searchName` is found in the array. If a `String` is not in the array, let `found` remain `false`. Assume that only the first n array elements have meaningful values.

```
String[] s = new String[200];
int n = 97;
// Assume n elements (s[0] through s[96]) are initialized
String searchName = keyboard.readWord( );
boolean found = false;
// Assign true to found if searchName is in s
```

8. How many comparisons does a sequential search make when the search element is stored in the first array element and there are 1,000 meaningful elements in the array?

9. How many comparisons does a sequential search make when the search element does not match any array element and there are 1,000 meaningful elements in the array?

10. Assuming a large number of sequential searches are made on an array and it is just as likely that an element is found in the first position as the last position, approximate the average number of comparisons after 1,000 searches when there are 1,000 meaningful elements in the array.

11. Write the output generated by the following code:

```
public class TestMystery
{
  private char[] my_data = { 'c', 'b', 'e', 'd', 'a' };
  private int my_size;

  public TestMystery( )
  {
    my_size = my_data.length;
  }
```

```java
  public void rearrange( )
  {
    int last = my_size - 1;
    for( int j = 0; j < my_size / 2 + 1; j++ )
    {
      char temp = my_data[j];
      my_data[j] = my_data[last];
      my_data[last] = temp;
      last--;
    }
  }

  public String toString( )
  { // Show all meaningful elements of data
    String result = "";

    for( int j = 0; j < my_size; j++ )
      result += my_data[j] + " ";

    return result;
  }

  public static void main( String[] args )
  {
    TestMystery tm = new TestMystery( );
    System.out.println( tm );
    tm.rearrange( );
    System.out.println( tm );
  }
}
```

12. Write the output generated by the following program:

```java
import java.util.Iterator;

public class TestStringBag2
{
  public static void main( String[] args )
  {
    StringBag names = new StringBag( );
    names.add( "Jordy" );
    names.add( "Hanna " );
    names.add( "Sammy " );
    names.add( "Karly " );

    Iterator itr = names.iterator( );
    while( itr.hasNext( ) )
    {
      String ref = ( String )itr.next( );
      System.out.println( ref.toUpperCase( ) );
    }
  }
}
```

13. Using the `StringBag` object in Exercise 12 above, what happens when an eleventh element gets added to the `StringBag` object `names`?

14. Using the `StringBag` object in Exercise 12 above, write code that displays all `Strings` in `names` that alphabetically follow `"Manny"`.

15. Using the `StringBag` object in Exercise 12 above, write code that assigns the alphabetically first item in the `StringBag` object to `smallest`. Use `compareTo`. Your code should work for a `StringBag` of any size.

16. Write the output generated by the following code:

```
String[] str = new String[10];
int n = 5;
str[0] = "Aimee";
str[1] = "Bob";
str[2] = "Lauren";
str[3] = "Alex";
str[4] = "Morgan";

for( int top = 0; top < n - 1; top++ )
{
   int index = top;
   for( int j = top + 1; j <= n-1; j++ )
   {
      if( str[j].compareTo( str[index] ) < 0 )
         index = j;
   }
   String temp = str[index];
   str[index] = str[top];
   str[top] = temp;
}

for( int j = 0; j <= n - 1; j++ )
{
   System.out.println( str[j] );
}
```

17. Write the output generated by the following program:

```
public class Mystery
{
   private int[] x;
   private int n;

   public Mystery( )
   {
      x = new int[100];
      x[0] = 2;
      x[1] = 4;
      x[2] = 6;
      x[3] = 8;
      x[4] = 10;
      x[5] = 12;
```

```
    x[6] = 14;
    x[7] = 16;
    n = 8;
  }

  public void traceMe( )
  {
    int first = 0;
    int last = n - 1;
    while( first <= last )
    {
      System.out.println ( x[first] + " " + x[last] );
      first++;
      last--;
    }
  }

  public static void main( String[] args )
  {
    Mystery m = new Mystery( );
    m.traceMe( );
  }
}
```

Programming Tips

1. **Remember that Java begins to index at 0.**
   The first array element is referenced with index 0, not 1 as is done in some other programming languages.

2. **An array often has a capacity greater than its number of meaningful elements.**
   Sometimes arrays are initialized to store more elements than are actually needed. In this case, only the first *n* elements are meaningful. Process the 0 through *n* - 1 elements, not 0 through capacity - 1.

3. **The last array element is in x[n - 1], not x[n].**
   Don't reference x[n]. This can be done by accidentally writing the for loop so it references an element that is not initialized, as in this code:

```
// Antibugging tip: Verify that the array and n are
// properly initialized
System.out.println( "You entered " + n + " numbers." );
for( int j = 1; j <= n; j++ )
{ // Whoops: Miss the first at x[0] and throw an exception at x[n]
  System.out.println( x[j] );
}
```

4. **Take the time and effort to display an array after initialization.**

This helps ensure that your array is properly initialized before continuing on with array processing algorithms. This tip is particularly helpful even in the relatively simple programming projects in this chapter. This test was done in the code in Programming Tip 3 by writing this `for` loop:

```java
// Verify that the array and n are properly initialized
for( int j = 0; j < n; j++ )
{
   System.out.println( x[j] );
}
```

5. **There are searching algorithms other than sequential search.**

The sequential search algorithm is only one of several known searching algorithms. For small amounts of data, sequential search works very nicely. For larger amounts of data stored in sorted arrays, other search algorithms should be used (see Chapter 12, "More Arrays," for the `binarySearch` algorithm). And there are other ways to store large amounts of data that can be searched rapidly—hash tables and binary search trees, for example. These topics are typically presented in a second course.

6. **The searching algorithm presented here only works with data stored in arrays.**

There is quite often a need to sort and search data stored on a disk (the data could even be on a server in a different country). The algorithms presented here only work on data stored in the computer's main memory. The values disappear when the program finishes. The array processing algorithms are intended only to present the notions of storing a collection until the program terminates. See Chapter 9 for how to save data on a disk for later use.

Programming Projects

8A   Reverse

Write a Java program (a class with the `main` method only) that inputs an undetermined number of integers (a maximum of 100) and displays them in reverse order. The user may not supply the number of elements, so a sentinel loop must be used. Here is one sample dialogue:

```
Enter up to 100 ints using -1 to quit:
70
75
90
60
80
-1
Reversed:   80   60   90   75   70
```

8B   Showing the Items that Are Above Average

Write a Java program (a class with the `main` method only) that inputs an undetermined collection of numbers, determines the average, and displays every value that
is greater than or equal to the average. The user may not supply the number of
elements, so the Indeterminate Loop pattern must be used. You may assume that
the user will never enter more than 100 numbers. Here is one sample dialogue:

```
Enter numbers or -1 to quit
70.0
75.0
90.0
60.0
80.0
-1
Average: 75.0
Inputs >= average:   75.0   90.0   80.0
```

8C   Fibonacci

The Fibonacci numbers start as 1, 1, 2, 3, 5, 8, 13, 21, and so on. The first two
numbers are 1 and any successive Fibonacci number is the sum of the preceding
two. Write a Java program (a class with the `main` method only) that properly
initializes an array named `fib` to represent the first 20 Fibonacci numbers (`fib[1]`
is the second Fibonacci number). Do not use 20 assignment statements to do this.
Three should suffice.

8D   Above and Below

Write a Java program (the `main` method only) that creates an undetermined
number of `BankAccount` objects and stores them into an array. The input should
come from the keyboard by reading an initial balance and the ID (use `readLine` to
allow blanks). Here is a suggested dialogue:

```
Enter initial balance and an ID: 53.45 Solley
Enter initial balance and an ID: 999.99 Kirsten
Enter initial balance and an ID: 8790.56 Pantone
Enter initial balance and an ID: 0.00 Brendle
Enter initial balance and an ID: 1555.76 Kentish
```

After initializing the array and the number of `BankAccounts`, display every
`BankAccount` that has a balance greater than 1,000.00. Then display every
`BankAccount` that has a balance less than 500.00. Your output should look like this
if you use the `toString` method of `BankAccount` when the program runs in a
country using American dollars:

```
Accounts with balances > 1000.00
Pantone $8,790.56
Kentish $1,555.76
```

```
Accounts with balances < 500.00
Solley $53.45
Brendle $0.00
```

8E   Frequency

Write a Java program that reads integers from a file and reports the frequency of each integer. For example, if the input file contains the numbers shown to the left below, your program should generate the output shown to the right below. The highest numbers should appear first. The input file only has numbers that are in the range of 0 through 100 inclusive. Use this fact to your advantage. You may assume that there are never more than 100 numbers on file.

The File test.dat

```
 75   85   90  100
 60   90  100   85
 75   35   60   90
100   90   90   90
 60   50   70   85
 75   90   90   70
```

The Program Dialogue

```
Enter file name:   test.dat
100: 3
 90: 8
 85: 3
 75: 3
 70: 2
 60: 3
 50: 1
 35: 1
```

8F   Using a StringBag Object

Write a menu-driven program that allows a user to add as many elements as desired and to see the collection of elements at any time. Use the following dialogue to establish the prompts and choices that should be allowed. Notice that the option could be entered in either upper or lower case. Use the StringBag class from the accompanying disk. Your dialogue should look exactly like this:

```
Enter option: A)dd R)emove D)isplay Q)uit: X
**Invalid option** Enter a, A, r, R, d, D, q, or Q

Enter option: A)dd R)emove D)isplay Q)uit: a
Add which string? first

Enter option: A)dd R)emove D)isplay Q)uit: a
Add which string? second

Enter option: A)dd R)emove D)isplay Q)uit: d
The StringBag: [ first, second ]

Enter option: A)dd R)emove D)isplay Q)uit: r
Remove which string? not here
'not here' was not found

Enter option: A)dd R)emove D)isplay Q)uit: r
Remove which string? first
```

```
Enter option: A)dd R)emove D)isplay Q)uit: d
The StringBag: [ second ]

Enter option: A)dd R)emove D)isplay Q)uit: A
Add which string? third

Enter option: A)dd R)emove D)isplay Q)uit: a
Add which string? fourth

Enter option: A)dd R)emove D)isplay Q)uit: D
The StringBag: [ second, third, fourth ]

Enter option: A)dd R)emove D)isplay Q)uit: r
Remove which string? first
'first' was not found

Enter option: A)dd R)emove D)isplay Q)uit: r
Remove which string? second

Enter option: A)dd R)emove D)isplay Q)uit: R
Remove which string? third

Enter option: A)dd R)emove D)isplay Q)uit: r
Remove which string? fourth

Enter option: A)dd R)emove D)isplay Q)uit: d
The StringBag: [   ]

Enter option: A)dd R)emove D)isplay Q)uit: q
```

8G   occurrencesOf

Add a method to the StringBag class that returns the number of occurrences of any element currently in the StringBag. The following code should produce the output shown:

```
StringBag friends;
friends.add( "Hailey" );
friends.add( "Greg" );
friends.add( "Gary" );
friends.add( "Greg" );
friends.add( "Scott" );
System.out.println( friends.occurrencesOf( "Greg" ) );       // Output: 2
System.out.println( friends.occurrencesOf( "Hailey" ) );     // Output: 1
System.out.println( friends.occurrencesOf( "Not Here" ) );   // Output: 0
```

8H   Modifying remove

Modify the StringBag remove method so it removes an element while leaving all other elements in the same order. If StringBag contained "3", "4", "5", "6", "7", a remove("5") message would change the StringBag to "3", "4", "6", "7".

8l   A StringSet Class

Implement a StringSet class that is similar to the StringBag class except that the collection cannot store any duplicate elements. Implement the add, remove, and size methods. An attempt to add a string that compares equally to one of the elements in the StringBag must not alter the StringBag. Simply return false from the add method if the String is already in the set. This means that the add method returns a boolean value. If the String is not already in the StringSet object, increase the array capacity so the add message is successful (don't forget to return true). Include a test driver with enough tests to make you feel confident that your StringSet class works.

Answers to Self-Check Questions

8-1   Jody 0.0
      Rachael 111.11
      Troy 222.22
      Neha 333.33
      Jim 444.44

8-2   100

8-3   0

8-4   99

8-5   0

8-6   x[0] = 78;

8-7   int n = 100;
      for(int j = 0; j < n; j++)
      {
          x[j] = n - j;   // When j is 0, n - j is 100
      }

8-8   for(int j = 0; j < n; j++)
      {
          System.out.println(x[j]);
      }

8-9   An exception is thrown and the program terminates

8-10 0   9
      1   8
      2   7
      3   6
      4   5

8-11 2 2 6 6 10 10 14 14

8-12 for(int j = 0; j < n; j ++)
      {
          if(accountArray[j].getBalance( ) > 150.00)
            System.out.println(accountArray[j].toString( ));
      }

8-13 t
d
d
l

8-14 -a "SUSIE"

-b "MIKEY"

-c null, the default string value

-d my_friends[10] is not part of the array. This generates an IndexOutOfBoundsException.

-e null. The find method is not yet working—it always returns null.

-f null

8-15 An exception is thrown when the expression my_friends[6] is compared. This is an attempt to send a null argument to the compareTo method. The compareTo method tries to do something with a reference to nothing and gives a NullPointerException.

8-16 1

8-17 4

8-18 n

8-19 0 Short circuit boolean evaluation causes the loop test to become false before any comparisons are made.

8-20 ABE
BEV
CY
DEB

8-21 current length of x: 3
11
22
33
current length of x: 6
11
22
33
current length of x: 2
11
22
java.lang.ArrayIndexOutOfBoundsException   *or something like this*

8-22 remove returns false, the StringBag object does not change.

8-23 Nothing noticeable to the user happens. The sequential search loop test (index < my_size) is false immediately, so index remains 0. Then the expression if(index == my_size) is true and false is returned.

8-24
```
public class TestStringBag3
{
  public static void main( String[] args )
  {
    StringBag names = new StringBag( );
    names.add( "My Name" );
    names.remove( "My Name" );
  }
}
```

8-25 No. The last element may be moved to the first vector position, or the second, or anywhere else. There are other collections used to store elements in order.

8-26 `StringBag.remove` removes the first occurrence. All other occurrences of the same value remain in the bag.

8-27 `size: 5`
     `size: 3`

Chapter 9

A Few Exceptions, a Little Input/Output, and Some Persistent Objects

Summing Up

So far, all objects have been kept alive only while the program was running. Any changes made to objects were not recorded for later use. In addition, when exceptional events such as `NullPointerException` and `IndexOutOfBoundsException` occurred, they were not handled. Instead, the program terminated.

Coming Up

This chapter introduces a few details about handling exceptions, along with a few of Java's input and output classes. Instead of attempting to explain all exception handling and Java's 60 input and output classes, this chapter will present just enough to show how objects can be made to persist between program runs. These topics also allow the bank teller system to be completed according to the specifications of Chapter 3.

The first section of this chapter introduces Java's exception handling capabilities. This is necessary since using objects from `java.io` requires you to think about what to do when a file is not found or the input was not the expected type. After studying this chapter, you will be able to

- handle a few exceptional events
- use some of Java's 60+ input/output classes
- save the current state of any Java object to a file for later use
- read in objects from files
- see how objects persist in the final phase of the bank teller case study

Exercises and programming projects reinforce exception handling, standard Java I/O, and persistent objects.

9.1   A Few Exceptions and How to Handle Them

When programs run, errors occur. Perhaps the user enters a string that is supposed to be a number. When it gets parsed with `parseInt` or `parseDouble`, the method discovers it's a bad number. Or perhaps an arithmetic expression results in division by zero. Or an array subscript is out of bounds. Or there is an attempt to read a file from a floppy disk, but there is no disk in the floppy disk drive. Or perhaps a file with a specific name simply does not exist. Exceptional events that occur while a program is running are known as **exceptions**. Programmers have at least two options for dealing with these types of errors:

1.   Ignore the exceptional event and let the program terminate
2.   Handle the exceptional event

Java specifies a large number of exceptions that may occur while programs run. When Java's runtime system recognizes that some exceptional event has occurred, it constructs an `Exception` object containing information about the type of exception. The runtime system then **throws** an exception. Java's runtime system then searches for code that can handle the exception. If no exception handling code is found, the program terminates.

Consider the example of when a user enters a `String` that does not represent a valid number. During the `parseDouble` message, the code recognizes this exceptional event and throws a `NumberFormatException`.

```java
public class HandleException
{
  public static void main( String[] args )
  {
    TextReader keyboard = new TextReader( );

    System.out.print( "Enter a number: " );
    String numberAsString = keyboard.readWord( );
    double number = Double.parseDouble( numberAsString );

    System.out.println( numberAsString + " stored in number as "
                        + number );
  }
}
```

Dialogue (when the number is valid)

```
Enter a number: 123
123 stored in number as 123.0
```

Dialogue (when the number is *not* valid)

```
Enter a number: 1o1
Exception in thread "main" java.lang.NumberFormatException: 1o1
    at java.lang.FloatingDecimal.readJavaFormatString
        (FloatingDecimal.java:1176)
    at java.lang.Double.parseDouble(Double.java:184)
    at HandleException.main(HandleException.java:10)
```

The second dialog shows that an exception was thrown when `main` called the `parseDouble` method, which in turn called the `readJavaFormatString` method. These three methods are a stack of methods, with `main` at the bottom of the stack of method calls. The `readJavaFormatString` method is at the top of the stack—where the exception occurred (`main` called `parseDouble` called `readJavaFormatString`). The second dialogue also shows that the program terminated prematurely. The `println` statement at the end of the `main` method never executed.

It is impossible to predict when a user will enter an invalid number. But the chances are very good that it will happen. One choice is to let the program terminate. The other choice is to handle the exception in some appropriate manner and let the program continue. Exceptions can be handled by writing code that "catches" the exception.

Java allows you to *try* to execute methods that may throw an exception. The code exists in a **try** block—the keyword `try` followed by the code wrapped in a block, { }.

```
try
{
    code that may throw an exception when an exceptional events occurs
}
catch ( Exception anException )
{
    code that executes when an exception is thrown
}
```

A `try` block must be followed by a `catch` block—the keyword `catch` followed by the anticipated exception as a parameter and code wrapped in a block. The `catch` block contains the code that executes when the code in the `try` block results in an exception. Because all exception classes extend the `Exception` class, the type of exception could always be `Exception`. In this case, the `catch` block catches any type of exception that can be thrown. However, it is recommended that you use a specific exception that is likely to be thrown by the code in the `try` block, such as `NumberFormatException`, `IndexOutOfBoundsException`, or `IOException`.

The following `main` method provides an example of handling a `NumberFormatException`. This exception handling code (in the `catch` block) executes only when the code in the `try` block throws an exception. This avoids premature program termination when the input string contains an invalid number.

```java
public class HandleException
{
  public static void main( String[] args )
  {
    TextReader keyboard = new TextReader( );

    System.out.print( "Enter a number: " );
    String numberAsString = keyboard.readWord( );
    double number;

    try
    { // The parseDouble method states that it may
      // throw a NumberFormatException
     number = Double.parseDouble( numberAsString );
    }
    catch( NumberFormatException nfe )
    { // Execute this code whenever parseDouble throws an exception
      System.out.println( numberAsString + " is not a valid number" );
      System.out.println( "Setting number to -1.0" );
      number = -1.0;
    }

    System.out.println( numberAsString + " stored in number as "
                        + number );
  }
}
```

Dialogue (when the exception is handled)

```
Enter a number: 1o1
1o1 is not a valid number
Setting number to -1.0
1o1 stored in number as -1.0
```

Instead of ignoring the possibility of exceptional events at runtime, this program now handles potential exceptions by setting the number to an arbitrary value of –1.0.

To successfully handle exceptions, a programmer must know if a method might throw an exception, and if so, the type of exception. This is done through documentation. For example, here is the parseDouble method which states that the method may throw a NumberFormatException and the reason why.

```java
/** From the Double class
  *
  * Return a floating-point number represented by the String argument.
  * If numberAsString does not represent a valid number, this method
  * will throw a number format exception.
  */
public static double parseDouble( String numberAsString )
                              throws NumberFormatException
```

The parseDouble method does not catch the exception. Instead, parseDouble specifies that it will throw the exception if the exceptional event occurs. A programmer may put a call to this particular method into a try block that in turn requires a `catch` block. Then again, the programmer may call this method without placing it in a `try` block. The option comes from the fact that `NumberFormatException` extends `RuntimeException`. A `RuntimeException` need not be handled. Exceptions that don't need to be handled are called **unchecked exceptions**, (`NumberFormatException` is an unchecked exception). The unchecked exception classes are those that extend `RuntimeException`, plus any `Exception` that you write that also extends `RuntimeException`. The unchecked exceptions include the following types (this is not a complete list):

1. `ArithmeticException`
2. `ClassCastException`
3. `IllegalArgumentException`
4. `IndexOutOfBoundsException`
5. `NullPointerException`

Other types of exceptions require that the programmer handle them. These are called **checked exceptions**. Examples of these will be shown later in this chapter with objects from the `java.io` package.

Runtime Exceptions

Java has many different types of exceptions. They are organized into a hierarchy of `Exception` classes. Here are just a few. (*Note:* Those that extend the `RuntimeException` class need not be handled, but may be handled.)

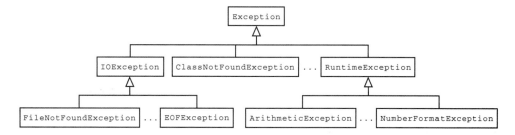

`RuntimeExceptions` can be ignored at your own risk. Code that may cause a `RuntimeException` need not be placed in a `try` block, but it can be. Here are some situations that may result in a `RuntimeException` (some code examples are given below).

1. A call to `parseDouble` (or `parseInt`) when the `String` argument does not represent a valid number (see the example above).
2. An integer expression that results in division by zero.
3. Sending a message to an object when the reference variable has the value of `null`.
4. An indexing exception, such as attempting to access an `ArrayList` element with an index that is out of range.

The compiler does not check RuntimeExceptions. This means that you do not have to use the try and catch blocks. If an exceptional event occurs in the following program examples, each program will terminate.

1. Example of integer division by 0 (*Note:* 5.0/ 0.0 would return Infinity)

```
int numerator = 5;
int denominator = 0;
int quotient = numerator / denominator;
```

Output when an ArithmeticException is thrown by Java's runtime system

```
Exception in thread "main" java.lang.ArithmeticException: / by zero
    at OtherRunTimeExceptions.main(OtherRunTimeExceptions.java:7)
```

2. Example of a null pointer exception—sending a message to a reference variable that is null

```
String str = null;
String strAsUpperCase = str.toUpperCase( );
```

Output when a NullPointerException is thrown by Java's runtime system

```
Exception in thread "main" java.lang.NullPointerException
    at OtherRunTimeExceptions.main(OtherRunTimeExceptions.java:6)
```

3. Example of an indexing exception

```
List stringList = new ArrayList( );
stringList.add( "first" );
stringList.add( "second" );
String third = (String)stringList.get( 2 );    // 0 and 1 are okay
```

Output when an IndexOutOfBoundsException is thrown by ArrayList's get method

```
Exception in thread "main" java.lang.IndexOutOfBoundsException:
Index: 2, Size: 2
    at java.util.ArrayList.RangeCheck(ArrayList.java:491)
    at java.util.ArrayList.get(ArrayList.java:307)
    at OtherRunTimeExceptions.main(OtherRunTimeExceptions.java:10)
```

Runtime exceptions can occur in many places. Even though the compiler does not require that you catch (handle) RuntimeExceptions, as shown above, you can catch them if you want.

```
// Create a list of size 2 (only 0 and 1 can be used as indexes here)
ArrayList stringList = new ArrayList( );
stringList.add( "first" );
stringList.add( "second" );
TextReader keyboard = new TextReader( );
```

```
String choiceFromList;
try
{ // There is no element at index 2.
  // The following message causes an exception.
  System.out.print( "Which element?" );
  int index = keyboard.readInt( );
  choiceFromList = (String)stringList.get( index );
}
catch( IndexOutOfBoundsException iobe )
{
  System.out.println( "index was not in the range of 0.." +
                      ( stringList.size( ) - 1 ) );
  System.out.println( "Setting choiceFromList to '??'" );
  choiceFromList = "??";
}
System.out.println( "choiceFromList was set to " + choiceFromList );
```

Output when an `IndexOutOfBoundsException`
is thrown and handled in the `catch` block

```
Which element? 2
index was not in the range of 0..1
Setting choiceFromList to '??'
choiceFromList was set to ??
```

Self-Check

9-1   Which of the following statements throws an exception?

-**a**   `int j = 7 / 0;`

-**b**   `double x = 7.0 / 0.0;`

-**c**
```
String[] names = new String[5];
names[0] = "Austin";
System.out.println( names[1].toUpperCase( ) );
```

9-2   The `ArrayList` get message throws an `IndexOutOfBounds` exception when there is no element at the index passed as an argument. (The index 0 is used here on an empty list.)

```
public class HandleIt
{
  public static void main( String[] args )
  {
    java.util.ArrayList list = new java.util.ArrayList( );
    System.out.println( list.get( 0 ) );
  }
}
```

Output

```
Exception in thread "main" java.lang.IndexOutOfBoundsException:
Index:0, Size:0
        at java.util.ArrayList.RangeCheck(ArrayList.java:491)
        at java.util.ArrayList.get(ArrayList.java:307)
        at HandleIt.main(HandleIt.java:7)
```

> Rewrite the code in main so that when get finds that the index is out of bounds, the IndexOutOfBounds exception is caught and "Index out of range" is output. Here is the documentation for the get method from Java API:
>
> ```
> /** From the ArrayList class
>  *
>  * Returns the element located at position specified by index.
>  * This method will throw an exception if
>  * index < 0 or index >= this.size( ).
>  */
> public Object get( int index ) throws IndexOutOfBoundsException
> ```

Other Methods That Throw Exceptions

Many Java methods are declared to throw an exception. Any method you write can also throw an exception. Consider a method that attempts to enforce this precondition: "The BankAccount deposit method requires a deposit amount greater than 0.0." If the amount is less than or equal to 0.0, the method may throw an IllegalArgumentException. A message is used as the argument to IllegalArgumentException to help further explain the exceptional behavior. (*Note:* The throws clause is not required, but it provides good documentation.)

```
// Precondition: depositAmount > 0.0
public void deposit( double depositAmount )
                    throws IllegalArgumentException
{
  if( depositAmount <= 0.0 )
  {
    // Create additional help for the programmer
    // to determine the cause of the error
    String errorMessage =
        "\nDeposit amount for '" + this + "' was <= 0.0: "
        + depositAmount;

    // Construct a new exception that may be caught
    RuntimeException anException
                    = new IllegalArgumentException( errorMessage );

    // Throw an exception that could be ignored
    throw anException;
  }

  // This won't execute with a deposit amount <= 0.0
  my_balance = my_balance + depositAmount;
}
```

Now a message with an argument that violates the precondition results in an exception.

```
BankAccount anAccount = new BankAccount( "Jo", 500.00 );
anAccount.deposit( -1.00 );
```

Output (when program terminates)

```
Exception in thread "main" java.lang.IllegalArgumentException:
Deposit amount for 'Jo $500.00' was <= 0.0: -1.0
        at BankAccount.deposit(BankAccount.java:35)
        at BankAccount.main(BankAccount.java:116)
```

The Java keyword `throw` must be followed by an instance of a class that extends `Throwable`. Because `Exception` extends `Throwable`, an instance of any `Exception` class in Java can be thrown. In addition, all `Exception` classes in Java have two constructors:

1. a constructor that takes one `String` argument (as shown above), and
2. a default constructor with no arguments (as shown below).

Here is another version of `deposit` that uses the default `Exception` constructor and combines the code into one statement. (*Note:* Since the `IllegalArgumentException` class is in `java.lang`, no `import` is necessary.)

```
public void deposit( double depositAmount )
                                        throws IllegalArgumentException
{
  if( depositAmount <= 0.0 )
    throw new IllegalArgumentException( );

  my_balance = my_balance + depositAmount;
}
```

Now when an "illegal" argument is passed to `deposit`, the output is simpler.

Output

```
Exception in thread "main" java.lang.IllegalArgumentException
        at BankAccount.deposit(BankAccount.java:35)
        at BankAccount.main(BankAccount.java:116)
```

In general, throwing an `IllegalArgumentException` object is a reasonable way to handle situations when an argument cannot be used correctly by the method. This can help you and other programmers while debugging.

Self-Check

9-3   Write the `tryIt` method to throw an `IllegalArgumentException` whenever its `Object` parameter is null. When the `Object` argument is not null, print the `toString` version of the argument. The following code should generate output similar to that shown (assume that you are writing `tryIt` as a method in the `TryAnException` class).

```
TryAnException tae = new TryAnException( );
tae.tryIt( new Object( ) );
tae.tryIt( null );
```

Output

```
java.lang.Object@111f71
Exception in thread "main" java.lang.IllegalArgumentException
        at TryAnException.tryIt(TryAnException.java:7)
```

9.2   Input/Output Streams

Most applications require the movement of information from one place to another. In Java, input is read through input stream objects. Output is written through output stream objects. A **stream** is a sequence of items read from some input source or written to some output destination. The input source could be the keyboard, a network connection, or a file on a disk in your computer. The output destination could be the computer screen, the speakers, or a disk file.

These stream objects come from classes in the **java.io** package. This standard library of many classes allows programmers to define streams that suit a variety of purposes. Some streams allow "raw" bytes to be read or written so pictures and sound can be moved from a source to a destination. Other classes provide functionality such as reading an entire line of input as a String (BufferedReader) and writing any of Java's objects (ObjectOutputStream and PrintStream). Typically, two existing Java classes are required to perform input and output. With some knowledge of the Java's stream classes and some work up front, programmers can derive virtually any input and output stream with the desired functionality. Let's first consider how Java handles standard input from the keyboard and standard output to the screen.

Standard Input and Output

Java provides three stream objects for handling keyboard input and screen output. Here are two, the second of which you have already been using:

1. System.in: The "standard" input stream object (an instance of InputStream)
2. System.out: The "standard" output stream object (an instance of PrintStream)

By default, System.out writes output to the window where the program is running. The object named out is part of the System class, which has utilities such as returning the computer system's time (currentTimeMillis) and providing standard input and output capabilities. The reference variable out is an instance of the PrintStream class.

```
/** An object in the System class
 *
 * out is an object already constructed to provide print and println
 * messages of any Java object or primitive. This output stream
 * will commonly display output to the computer's console (screen).
 */
public static final PrintStream out
```

The PrintStream object named out has methods to display all of Java's primitive types with print and println messages. It also has a print and println method for displaying any Java object. Here are a few of the method headings required to be part of the PrintStream class.

```
public void print( double d )    // Print a floating-point number
public void print( int i )       // Print an integer
public void print( Object obj )  // Print an object
public void println( boolean x ) // Print a boolean and then terminate
                                 // the line
public void println( char x )    // Print a character and then
                                 // terminate the line
public void println( char[] x )  // Print an array of characters
public void println( double x )  // Print a double and then terminate
                                 // the line
public void println( Object x )  // Print an object and then terminate
                                 // the line
```

The message System.out.println(1.2) prints a double, while System.out.println(5) prints an integer. System.out makes generating output convenient. However, there are no equivalent methods for reading numbers. The input object named System.in only reads bytes.

The code to input a number or String from the keyboard requires knowledge of Java exception handling. Obtaining input with standard Java classes requires more work and more details. That is the reason why the author-supplied TextReader class is included with this textbook.

Although the InputStream object only has methods for reading bytes and arrays of bytes, it plays a role in reading numbers and Strings from the keyboard. The bytes read by System.in must be translated into the appropriate type of data. To get closer to reading doubles and strings, System.in is used as an argument to construct an InputStreamReader object.

```
InputStreamReader bytesToChar = new InputStreamReader( System.in );
```

The bytesToChar object can now read characters from the keyboard with InputStreamReader's read method. When an InputStreamReader object is constructed with the argument System.in, keyboard input can stream into the program at the rate of one character per read message.

```
/** From the InputStreamReader class
  *
  * Read one character from the input source. A read message that
  * encounters the end of file will return -1. This method returns the
  * integer equivalent of the character. This means you must store the
  * character into an int, and then perhaps cast the int to a char.
  */
  public int read() throws IOException
```

Notice that this `read` method declares that it may throw an `IOException`. This `IOException` is checked (it does not extend `RuntimeException`). The following attempt to read a character from the keyboard results in a compiletime error:

```
InputStreamReader bytesToChar = new InputStreamReader( System.in );
int anInt = bytesToChar.read( );
```

Compiletime Error

```
unreported exception java.io.IOException; must be caught or declared
to be thrown
    int anInt = bytesToChar.read( );
                           ^
```

There are two ways to handle this checked exception. The simple way is to completely circumvent Java's exception handling. The method with the `read` message can be declared to throw an `IOException`.

```
// A method declaring that it might throw an
// IOException in order to get past the compiler.
import java.io.InputStreamReader;
import java.io.IOException;
public class DeclareExceptionToBeThrown
{                                     // Circumvent exception handling
  public static void main( String[] args ) throws IOException
  {
    InputStreamReader bytesToChar = new InputStreamReader( System.in );

    System.out.print( "Enter a character: " );
    int anInt = bytesToChar.read( );

    // To see the character rather than its
    // integer equivalent, cast int to char
    System.out.println( (char)anInt );
  }
}
```

Dialogue

```
Enter a character: G
G
```

The second option is to read the message inside of a `try` block. The associated `catch` block will catch the `IOException` should it occur (which is very unlikely when reading from the keyboard).

The following program reads three characters from the keyboard and prints them. Since read returns an int instead of a char, the return values must be cast from int to char.

```java
// Read three characters using an InputStreamReader.
// This time, the read messages are inside a try block since
// the possible IOException is a checked exception.
import java.io.InputStreamReader;
import java.io.IOException;

public class ReadThreeCharacters
{
  public static void main( String[] args )
  {
    InputStreamReader bytesToChar = new InputStreamReader( System.in );
    int intOne = 0;
    int intTwo = 0;
    int intThree = 0;

    System.out.println( "Enter three characters" );
    try
    {
      intOne = bytesToChar.read( );
      intTwo = bytesToChar.read( );
      intThree = bytesToChar.read( );
    }
    catch( IOException ioe )
    {
      System.out.println( "Could not read keyboard input: " + ioe );
    }

    System.out.print( (char)intOne );
    System.out.print( (char)intTwo );
    System.out.println( (char)intThree );
  }
}
```

Output (*Note:* read treats blank spaces as valid chars, so the ends of lines may be treated as two characters)

```
Enter three characters
a_b
a_b
```

The code shown so far only reads single characters. However, programs are usually more interested in reading strings and numbers. To accomplish this, the InputStreamReader object now becomes an argument in the construction of a BufferedReader object. The BufferedReader class has a method named readLine that gets us closer to reading the desired data (with the help of parseDouble and parseInt).

```
/** From the BufferedReader class
 *
 * Read an entire line of text, which is all character up to
 * but not including the new line char ('\n'). A readLine message
 * that encounters the end of file will return null.
 */
public String readLine() throws IOException
```

With the following construction, the object keyboard—an instance of BufferedReader—will understand the readLine message.

```
BufferedReader keyboard = new BufferedReader( bytesToChar );
```

The following program can read entire lines of input returned as a String (as long as readLine is in a try block or the main method is declared with throws IOException).

```
// Read an entire line from the keyboard
// with BufferedReader's readLine method.
import java.io.InputStreamReader;
import java.io.BufferedReader;
import java.io.IOException;

public class ReadOneLineAsAString
{
  public static void main( String[] args )
  {
    InputStreamReader bytesToChar = new InputStreamReader( System.in );
    BufferedReader keyboard = new BufferedReader( bytesToChar );
    String line = "";

    System.out.println( "Enter a line of text" );
    try
    {
      line = keyboard.readLine( );
    }
    catch( IOException ioe )
    {
      System.out.println( "Could not read keyboard input: " + ioe );
    }

    System.out.println( "You entered this line: " );
    System.out.print( line );
  }
}
```

Dialogue

```
Enter a line of text
The 3-year-old fox jumped over the 12-year-old dog.
You entered this line:
The 3-year-old fox jumped over the 12-year-old dog.
```

This is as close as Java stream objects get to directly reading integers and floating-point numbers. Assuming the line of input contains no blank spaces, the `String` returned by `readLine` can now be passed to `Double`'s `parseDouble` or `Integer`'s `parseInt` method to translate the `String` into a number. If the `String` does not represent a valid number, `parseInt` or `parseDouble` may throw a `NumberFormatException`. Since this is not handled by `try/catch`, this program may still terminate prematurely.

```java
// Read an integer and a double with the
// help of several classes and methods.
import  java.io.InputStreamReader;
import  java.io.BufferedReader;
import  java.io.IOException;

public class ReadTwoNumbers
{
  public static void main( String[] args )
  {
    InputStreamReader bytesToChar = new InputStreamReader( System.in );
    BufferedReader keyboard = new BufferedReader( bytesToChar );
    String intAsString = "";
    String doubleAsString = "";

    try
    {
      System.out.print( "Enter an int: " );
      intAsString = keyboard.readLine( );
      System.out.print( "Enter a double: " );
      doubleAsString = keyboard.readLine( );
    }
    catch( IOException ioe )
    {
      System.out.println( "Could not read keyboard input: " + ioe );
    }

    int theInt = Integer.parseInt( intAsString );
    double theDouble = Double.parseDouble( doubleAsString );
    System.out.println( "int: " + theInt );
    System.out.println( "double: " + theDouble );
  }
}
```

Dialogue

```
Enter an int: 123
Enter a double: 4.56
int: 123
double: 4.56
```

The approach just shown for reading numbers and strings from the keyboard is much more complex for the programmer than using a class like `TextReader`. However, the Java stream classes will work on any platform that has Java installed.

You can do input without having to copy `TextReader` to your machine. In addition, this approach for numeric input represents the consistent manner in which Java I/O streams read and write data from files, even over the Internet.

In summary, you first construct an object to read bytes from the keyboard, a file, or the Internet. This object is then used to construct another object with easier-to-use methods. The two objects work together to convert raw bytes into something more useable—a `String`.

Although it may be unnecessary to use `try` to read from the keyboard, a stable source of input, most input streams are not nearly as reliable. A server may be down, a network connection may fail, the supplied uniform resource locater (URL) may not exist, or the file name may be misspelled.

Now consider how Java uses the same approach to read input from a file. It is about the same as reading from the keyboard. Input was read from a file earlier with the `TextReader` class. Now you will see how Java handles this with classes that come with Java.

Self-Check

9-4   Complete the following `main` method so it reads one number and prints that number squared. If the user enters an invalid number, display a message indicating so. This means you will need to handle the `NumberFormatException` also.

```java
// Read an integer and a double with the
// help of several classes and methods.
import java.io.*;

public class ReadOneInteger
{
  public static void main( String[] args )
  {
    InputStreamReader bytesToChar =
        new InputStreamReader( System.in );
    BufferedReader keyboard =
        new BufferedReader( bytesToChar );
    String doubleAsString = "";

    // Write the exception handling code here
  }
}
```

Dialogue 1

```
Enter a number: 4.2
4.2 squared = 17.64
```

Dialogue 2

```
Enter a number: NG
NG was an invalid number
```

File Input of a Textual Nature

The previous section showed how to read numeric data from the keyboard. It used `BufferedReader` for its handy `readLine` method and `InputStreamReader` to convert bytes typed at the keyboard into characters. This section shows how to get input data from a file. An instance of `BufferedReader` will still be used for its `readLine` method. But this time, an instance of `FileReader` will be used to convert the raw bytes of a file into characters.

To read from the keyboard, the `BufferedReader` object is constructed with an instance of `InputStreamReader`. To read from a file, a `BufferedReader` object can be constructed with an instance of `FileReader`. Both types of arguments are valid because the constructor for `BufferedReader` has a parameter of type `Reader`. In Java, both `FileReader` and `InputStreamReader` are classes that extend the `Reader` class. Both can be passed as arguments to this constructor for `BufferedReader`:

```
/** A method from the Buffereader class
 *
 * Construct an object that uses in to read characters so the
 * BufferedReader object can provide the easy to use readLine method.
 */
public BufferedReader(Reader in)
```

Both an `InputStreamReader` object, such as `System.in`, and a `FileReader` object can be used to construct a `BufferedReader` object with its `readLine` method. To illustrate, here is a small part of Java's io class hierarchy that shows that an instance of `InputStreamReader` can be assigned up the inheritance hierarchy to `Reader`.

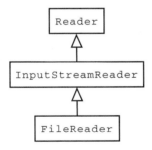

Since `FileReader` extends `InputStreamReader`, an instance of `FileReader` can also be assigned up to the `Reader` parameter in the `BufferedReader` constructor. Remember, assignment up the inheritance hierarchy is valid.

FileReader

To read from a file, you first construct a `FileReader` object with a `String` argument. The `String` represents the name of the file containing the desired information. If the file is in the working folder (directory), only the file name needs to be supplied. The path is not always necessary.

Java forces us to consider the possibility that a file may not exist with that name. A `FileReader` is a checked exception (it does not extend `RuntimeException`). In this case, the `Exception` that could be thrown is `FileNotFoundException`. The following code constructs an object that can read characters from the file named `2numbers.data` (the very small input file is shown below).

```java
String fileName = "2numbers.data";
try
{
   bytesToChar = new FileReader( fileName );
}
catch( FileNotFoundException fnfe )
{
   System.out.println( "Could not find file: " + fnfe );
}
```

File 2numbers.data

```
123
4.56
```

Now that there is the `FileReader` object `bytesToChar`, a `BufferedReader` object can be constructed that has a `readLine` method that is easier to use.

```java
BufferedReader inputFile = new BufferedReader( bytesToChar );
```

Multiple `catch` Blocks

The code needed to read from a file could end up throwing three different types of exceptions:

1. file not found
2. input error when attempting to read a line from a file
3. parse errors when converting a `String` to an integer or a double

To make it easier to handle all three, the code for the first two types is placed in one `try` block that is followed by two `catch` blocks. The first `catch` block is for when the file is not found. The second `catch` block is necessary for the exception that may be thrown in `readLine`. The third `catch` block will handle number-format exceptions.

```java
// Input numbers from a file on a disk
import java.io.FileReader; // Reading from a file this time
import java.io.BufferedReader;
import java.io.IOException;
import java.io.FileNotFoundException; // File may not be found
```

```
public class ReadTwoNumbersFromADiskFile
{
   public static void main( String[] args )
   {
      // These variables are needed in more than one block.
      // Therefore they must be declared here so they are
      // accessible to all blocks in this main method.
      String fileName = "2numbers.data";
      String intAsString = "";
      String doubleAsString = "";
      int theInt = 0;
      double theDouble = 0.0;

      try
      {
         // Constructing a new FileReader needs to be tried.
         // It may throw FileNotFoundException.
         FileReader bytesToChar = new FileReader( fileName );

         // If the FileReader is okay, this should work.
         BufferedReader inputFile = new BufferedReader( bytesToChar );

         // Read an integer from the first line and a double from line two.
         // Both of these readLine messages need to be tried.
         // They may throw an IOException.
         intAsString = inputFile.readLine( );
         doubleAsString = inputFile.readLine( );

         // Now done with the input file.
         inputFile.close( );

         // Now try to parse the input strings (could still get
         // an exception here).
         theInt = Integer.parseInt( intAsString );
         theDouble = Double.parseDouble( doubleAsString );
      }
      catch( FileNotFoundException fnfe )
      {
         System.out.println( "Could not find file: " + fnfe );
      }
      catch( IOException ioe )
      {
         System.out.println( "Could not read from file named: " + fileName );
      }
      catch( NumberFormatException nfe )
      {
         System.out.println( "One of the numbers was bad: " + fileName );
      }

      // This output always occurs
      System.out.println( "int: " + theInt );
      System.out.println( "double: " + theDouble );
   }
}
```

Output (to console window when input is from a file and everything goes okay)

```
int: 123
double: 4.56
```

This is what happens when the file is not found.

Output (when the file does not exist)

```
Could not find file: java.io.FileNotFoundException: 2numbers.data
(The system can not find the file specified)
Terminating program
```

Although the program terminates prematurely here, the exception handling code needs to be changed. For example, the `catch` block could to do something more useful, such as ask the user for another file name (it could use a loop).

Even if the file is found and the two lines of input exist in the file, exceptions can still occur. Here is another exception that is thrown by `parseInt` when just one seemingly innocent blank space trails the text `123`. The `parseInt` method tries to convert the string `"123 "`.

Output (when there is a trailing blank after 123—the string is "123 ")

```
Exception in thread "main" java.lang.NumberFormatException: 123
        at java.lang.Integer.parseInt(Integer.java:414)
        at java.lang.Integer.parseInt(Integer.java:454)
        at ReadTwoNumbersFromADiskFile.main
           (ReadTwoNumbersFromADiskFile.java:45)
```

This particular error could be fixed with `String`'s `trim` method that strips leading and trailing blanks from the `String`.

```
int theInt = Integer.parseInt( intAsString.trim( ) );
```

Text file input requires a program to be aware of exactly how the input data exists in the file. It is all too easy to have an unexpected value, such as a `double` instead of an `int`, a trailing space, or a blank line at the end of the file.

FileWriter

Java's `FileWriter` class provides the ability to write characters to a file. Like `FileReader`, `FileWriter` provides low-level disk access capabilities. A `FileWriter` object is constructed with a `String` argument representing the name of the file being written to. However, the attempt to construct one could throw an `IOException`. The file name could be malformed, for example. So constructing a `FileWriter` object must be handled with `try/catch`.

```
String outputFileName = "output.data";

FileWriter charToBytesWriter = null;
try
{
   charToBytesWriter = new FileWriter( outputFileName );
}
catch( IOException ioe )
{
   System.out.println( "Could not create the new file: " + ioe );
}
```

At this point, charToBytesWriter can write characters and Strings to a file. To obtain the familiar print and println methods that write all objects and primitive types, construct a PrintWriter object (PrintWriter is very similar to System.out). The following code constructs a PrintWriter object so any Java value can be print(ed) or println(ed).

```
// PrintWriter's constructors do not throw any exceptions
PrintWriter diskFile = new PrintWriter( charToBytesWriter );

// Now diskFile can understand print and println
diskFile.print( "First line has one number: " );
diskFile.println( 123 );
diskFile.println( 4.56 );
diskFile.println( 'c' );
diskFile.println( 3 < 4 );
diskFile.print( diskFile );
```

Ensuring that the Data Is Actually Written

Writing data to a disk is slow. To make programs run faster, Java places the output data first into a buffer (perhaps an array of bytes). Then at some point, a large number of bytes are written to the disk at once. Writing a large number of bytes a few times is much faster than writing one byte a large number of times. The consequence of implementing this more efficient way of writing to a disk is that the program may terminate before the data is actually written to the disk! To ensure that all data is written to the disk, close the output stream with a close message. Without the following close message, the output file would be empty—nothing would actually be written.

```
// Must explicitly close the file or risk losing data that
// is buffered--waiting to actually be written.
diskFile.close( );
```

The close message to an output stream ensures that the output buffer has actually been written to the disk. This newly created file has six different Java values written to it and stored on a computer disk.

Output (written to the file named `output.data`)

```
First line has one number: 123
4.56
c
true
java.io.PrintWriter@720eeb
```

Destroying Files

If a new `FileWriter` object is constructed with a file name that already exists, the old file is destroyed. While this may often be precisely what you want, there are times when this is not desirable. Java has a class named `File` that allows you to manage files and directories. For example, you could construct a `File` object and ask it to search for an existing file. For now, just be aware that constructing a `FileWriter` object deletes any existing file with the same name.

The `java.io` package has a large set of classes for performing input and output of characters, strings, pictures, and sound from a variety of sources and to a variety of destinations. Complete coverage of these 60+ classes in `java.io` is beyond the scope of this book. However, a few more are presented next. In particular, the next section will use objects from `java.io` that can make objects persist from one program run to the next.

Self-Check

9-5 `FileWriter` has a method for writing a `String` to a disk. Using this Java documentation:

```
public void write(String str)          In class FileWriter
            throws IOException
```
Write a string.
Parameters: str - String to be written
Throws: IOException - If an I/O error occurs

complete this main method so that it writes your name to a file named `myname.txt`.

```java
import java.io.*;
public class WriteNameToDisk
{
  public static void main( String[] args )
  {
      String outputFileName = "myname.txt";
      FileWriter charToBytesWriter = null;

    // Complete the code to write your name here


  }
}
```

9.3   Object Streams for Persistent Objects

If data is not stored on a disk or some other media, it will disappear when the program terminates. The program must do something extra to save data that is needed later. Using the few streams just described, objects could be saved to a disk by taking them apart, instance variable by instance variable, and writing the pieces to the disk. Objects could be restored by reading in the pieces from the disk and constructing them again. But this is a lot of unnecessary work. The code gets even more complex when the objects have arrays and other complex structures. Java brings a much more elegant solution for making objects live between program runs. The Java tools for doing this are Java's object streams and object serialization.

A **persistent object** is one that can be saved for later use. To make objects persist, the class and all instance variables must be Serializable. Java arrays, many Java classes, and all primitives are Serializable. However, to make any new object Serializable, the class must state that it implements the Serializable interface.

```
public class BankAccount implements Serializable
{
  private String my_ID;
  private double my_balance;
  // ...
}
```

There are no methods in the Serializable interface. The Serializable tag only identifies the class as being Serializable. In addition to tagging the class as Serializable, you must ensure that all instance variables are Serializable. Since double and String are already Serializable, no further action would be required for the BankAccount class shown above.

Assuming that a class and its instance variables are serializable, the next step is to write serialized objects to a destination such as a file. To make persistent objects, you can use Java's ObjectOutputStream class with its writeObject method for this. The constructor for ObjectOutputStream needs a FileOutputStream object for writing the bytes to a disk. Once again, two streams work together to get the desired outcome—a stream that saves any serialized object to a file.

```
FileOutputStream bytesToDisk = new FileOutputStream( "fileName" );
ObjectOutputStream objectToBytes = new ObjectOutputStream( bytesToDisk );
```

The following program uses a try block with a catch block to get past the compiler that is watching for checked exceptions.

```java
// Make one object persist for another program to read later.
import java.io.*;

public class WriteAnObjectToDisk
{
  // This method does not have any exception handling code.
  // The program will terminate if something goes wrong.
  public static void main( String[] args )
  {
    // Construct one object from a class not supplied by Java.
    // To write this BankAccount object to a disk, the class
    // and all of its instance variables must implement
    // Serializable (this is the case).
    BankAccount singleAccount = new BankAccount( "ID123", 100.00 );
    singleAccount.withdraw( 50.00 );
    singleAccount.deposit( 12.75 );

    try
    {
      // Build the stream that can write objects (not text) to a disk
      FileOutputStream bytesToDisk
            = new FileOutputStream( "BankAccount.object" );
      ObjectOutputStream objectToBytes
            = new ObjectOutputStream( bytesToDisk );

      // Show the state of the account before saving it
      System.out.println( "About to write this object to disk: " );
      System.out.println( singleAccount );

      // Now objectToBytes will understand the writeObject message.
      // Make the object persist on disk, so it can be read later.
      objectToBytes.writeObject( singleAccount );

      // Do NOT forget to close the output stream
      objectToBytes.close( );
    }
    catch( IOException ioe )
    {
      System.out.println ( ioe.toString( ) );
    }

  }
}
```

Output

```
About to write this object to disk:
ID123 $62.75
```

Now that this BankAccount object has been saved in a file, another program
may read this object. The program must know the name of the file where the
object has been written. It must also know the class of object that is stored in that
file.

```java
// Read an object stored in a file
import java.io.*;

public class ReadAnObjectFromDisk
{
  // This method may throw an IOException when the file is not found.
  public static void main( String[] args ) throws IOException
  {
    // First create an object input stream with the readObject method
    FileInputStream diskToStreamOfBytes
        = new FileInputStream( "BankAccount.object" );

    // Construct an objectNow with the readObject method
    ObjectInputStream objectToBytes
        = new ObjectInputStream( diskToStreamOfBytes );

    // Read the entire object with the ObjectInputStream. The checked
    // exception must be caught (even though Object is a known class).
    Object anyObject = null;
    try
    {
      anyObject = objectToBytes.readObject( );
    }
    catch( ClassNotFoundException cnfe )
    {
      System.out.println( cnfe );
    }

    // Now cast from Object to the class that it is known to be.
    BankAccount singleAccount = (BankAccount)anyObject;

    // Close input files also.
    objectToBytes.close( );

    // And show that the state is the same.
    System.out.println( "The object just after reading it from disk" );
    System.out.println( singleAccount );
  }
}
```

Output (this BankAccount has the same state as that shown above)

```
The object just after reading it from disk
ID123 $62.75
```

Other Persistent Objects

Many existing Java classes implement Serializable. This means a large number of objects can be made to persist this way. Programs can read objects from a disk in the same manner as was shown above with BankAccount. The objects can be quite complex. Java provides the mechanisms for storing any object and then later retrieving it in the same state that it was written.

Consider the following program that shows seven different persistent objects. This program simplifies the try/catch blocks by placing all checked exceptions into one try block. If any exception is thrown—and there are several classes of exceptions that could be thrown—the correct catch block prints the exception information.

To save lists of different objects, the following classes must implement Serializable (the Java classes already do and BankAccount has already been made Serializable).

1. ArrayList
2. BankAccount
3. Integer
4. Double
5. String
6. Character
7. Date

```
// Write seven classes of objects to a disk, including ArrayList
import java.io.*;     // FileOutputStream and ObjectOutputStream
import java.util.*;   // ArrayList and Date

public class WriteManyObjectsToDisk
{
  public static void main( String[] args )
  {
    ArrayList polyList = new ArrayList( );
    polyList.add( new BankAccount( "ID123", 100.00 ) ) ;
    polyList.add( new Integer ( 123 ) );
    polyList.add( new Double ( 4.56 ) );
    polyList.add( new String( "A String" ) );
    polyList.add( new Character( 'G' ) );
    polyList.add( new AnotherClass( ) );

    try
    {
      FileOutputStream bytesToDisk
          = new FileOutputStream( "ArrayList.object" );
      ObjectOutputStream objectToBytes
          = new ObjectOutputStream( bytesToDisk );

      // Show the state before saving it
      System.out.println( "About to write this object to disk: " );
      System.out.println( polyList );

      // Now objectToBytes will understand the writeObject message.
      // Make the object persist on a disk, so it can be read later.
      objectToBytes.writeObject( polyList );

      // Do NOT forget to close the output stream
      objectToBytes.close( );
```

```
      }
      catch( FileNotFoundException e )
      {
        System.out.println( "File not found " + e );
      }
      catch( IOException e )
      {
        System.out.println( "Error during ObjectOutputStream construction, \n"
                          + "or writing object, or file close. " + e );
      }
    }
  }
}
```

Output

```
About to write this object to disk:
[ID123 $100.00, 123, 4.56, A String, G, Mon Oct 08 17:31:02 MST 2002]
```

If any one of these objects were not `Serializable`, an exception would be thrown during the `writeObject` message. Consider adding a new `AnotherClass` object that is implemented like this:

```
public class AnotherClass extends Object
{
}
```

An instance of `AnotherClass` could always be added to the `ArrayList`.

```
polyList.add( new AnotherClass( ) );
```

Once this message adds the `AnotherClass` object at the end of the `ArrayList`, the program results in the following output:

Output (when a new **AnotherClass** is added at the end of the **ArrayList**)

```
About to write this object to disk:
[ID123 $100.00, 123, 4.56, A String, G, Sat Jun 23 20:13:53 MST 2001,
AnotherClass@1a698a]
```

However, the `writeObject` message would then throw a `NotSerializableException`, as evidenced by this output where the exception was caught.

Output (an error is reported while trying to write an object that is not serialized)

```
java.io.NotSerializableException: AnotherClass
```

The write will fail. It will not save the other objects either. To save all different objects in this `ArrayList`, change the `AnotherClass` class so it is serializable:

```
import java.io.Serializable;
public class AnotherClass extends Object implements Serializable
{
}
```

There is not much state to store for `AnotherClass`, but if instance variables were added to `AnotherClass`, then those objects must also be `Serializable`. The next section shows other examples of objects that are written to and read from a disk. The bank teller system will be completed.

9.4   `BankTeller_Ch9.java`

In this final phase of the bank teller case study, both collections—`BankAccountCollection` and `TransactionList`—are made persistent. When the window to the application is closed, the user is given the option of saving the current state of the objects or leaving them as they were when the program began. The user can also cancel the request to terminate the program. Here is the new dialog the user is presented with when the window is closed. The bank teller window remains open until the user chooses an option.

Output (the window closes only when the Yes or No button is clicked)

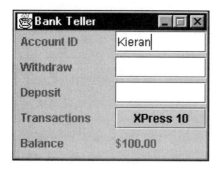 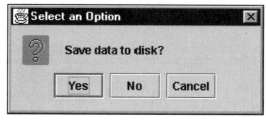

To accomplish this, several changes will be made to `BankTeller_Ch8.java`. A few new Java methods and one new listener interface (`WindowListener`) will be needed. Here is a preview.

1. Use `JOptionPaneShowConfirmDialog` to let the user choose from three options.
2. Change the `defaultCloseOperation` so the window remains visible while the user chooses.
3. Have a class implement the `WindowListener` interface to control what happens when the `windowClosing` event occurs.
4. Add a private helper method to read the persistent objects using streams.
5. Add another private helper method to write the persistent objects to a file.

Persistent Objects in the Bank Teller System

Both `BankAccountCollection` and `TransactionList` will be input from a file. When the program terminates, the program will write the modified state of these objects. To get things started, a Java program will save the initial values of the collection objects. This program should only be run once, unless you want to start from the same initial state of nine accounts and zero transactions. There is no real money here, so it would not hurt to start anew. You would be warned that you were trying to destroy the fake transactions and balances. This program will be named `InitializeAccountAndTransactionCollections`.

Once the collection objects are saved on disk, they will be read at the beginning of the program. The names of the files that will save the collection objects will be added as class constants.

```java
public static final String ACCOUNT_FILE = "accountCollection.object";

public static final String TRANSACTION_FILE =
                          "transactionCollection.object";
```

The `JFrame`'s constructor now invokes the private helper method that will read the persistent objects from the two different files that store them.

```java
// Read the persistent objects from their files.
readObjects( ); // From the constructor in BankTeller_Ch9
```

Here is the helper method that initializes the collection objects so the initial state of the system is just like the last time it was saved. After this method executes with no exceptions, both collections are in the same state as when the program last ran.

```java
// Read both collection objects from their files
private void readObjects( )
{
  try
  {
    // Read the BankAccountCollection object from its file
    FileInputStream inFile = new FileInputStream( ACCOUNT_FILE );
    ObjectInputStream inputStream = new ObjectInputStream( inFile );

    theAccounts = (BankAccountCollection)inputStream.readObject( );

    inputStream.close( );

    // Use the same streams to read the TransactionList from
    // a different file
    inFile = new FileInputStream( TRANSACTION_FILE );
    inputStream = new ObjectInputStream( inFile );
    transactionList = (TransactionList)inputStream.readObject( );

    inputStream.close( );
  }
```

```
catch( IOException e )
{
   String message = "Error reading objects from disk: "
                    + "\n" + e
                    + "\nShut down program and call for help";
   JOptionPane.showMessageDialog( null, message );
}
}
```

The error handling code in this method notifies the user that something went
wrong. However, there is little that the human bank teller could do. This is like the
dialog boxes that pop up stating that an exception occurred and you should
contact the vendor. If everything goes well, the collections are loaded the way they
were last saved. If some exceptional event occurs, such as the file not being found,
the following dialog appears (the "t" at the end of the file name was removed to
cause the exception).

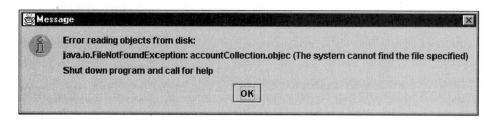

So far, when the teller window closes, the program terminates. To make the
system persistent, this policy must change. Instead of EXIT_ON_CLOSE, the teller
window will remain open by doing nothing when the user tries to close the window.
This policy is set with this message in the constructor:

setDefaultCloseOperation(JFrame.**DO_NOTHING_ON_CLOSE**);

As shown earlier, the window will now stay open. DO_NOTHING_ON_CLOSE is one of
four policies that can be in effect when the user initiates a "close" on the JFrame.

```
/** From the JFrame class
 *
 * This method sets the actions that will occur whenever the user
 * closes this JFrame. The operation can be any one of the following
 * four int constants that are part of the JFrame class.
 * JFrame.EXIT_ON_CLOSE Exit the application using System.exit
 * JFrame.DO_NOTHING_ON_CLOSE Don't do anything
 * JFrame.HIDE_ON_CLOSE Hide this JFrame (you can't see it)
 * JFrame.DISPOSE_ON_CLOSE Hide and get rid of this JFrame
 *
 * The value is set to HIDE_ON_CLOSE by default.
 * You have often seen the argument as JFrame.EXIT_ON_CLOSE.
 */
public void setDefaultCloseOperation( int operation )
```

WindowEvents and WindowListener

The above documentation refers to "invoking any registered WindowListener objects." Our system will now have a WindowListener object listening for the windowClosing event. Registered WindowListener objects come into being the same way as ActionListeners do.

First, some class must implement the WindowListener interface. This requires the class to implement seven different methods, even though only one will be used—windowClosing. Here is the class with the windowClosing method that will be implemented later.

```
private class WindowClosingListener implements WindowListener
{
  // This is the one method that the bank teller is interested in using
  public void windowClosing( WindowEvent we )
  { // Implemented later
  }

  // These six methods must be implemented to satisfy the interface.
  // As is often the case, these methods do nothing. An alternative
  // is to extend the WindowAdapter class that implements all seven to
  // do nothing. Then override the method(s) that you want.
  public void windowActivated( WindowEvent e )   {  }
  public void windowClosed( WindowEvent e )      {  }
  public void windowDeactivated( WindowEvent e ) {  }
  public void windowDeiconified( WindowEvent e ) {  }
  public void windowIconified( WindowEvent e )   {  }
  public void windowOpened( WindowEvent e )      {  }
} // End the WindowClosingListener class
```

Once this new inner class is complete, an instance of it can be registered as a WindowListener with an addWindowListener message. The only object here that will generate window events is the window itself—a JFrame object. Therefore, the object that adds the WindowListener is the JFrame itself. The keyword this is used to get a reference to the JFrame from the JFrame constructor. The windowListener object can now listen to window events on the JFrame.

```
WindowClosingListener windowClosingListener =
                    new WindowClosingListener( );
// JFrames generate WindowEvents and send messages to WindowListeners
this.addWindowListener( windowClosingListener );
```

Now the windowClosing method (shown below) will be invoked when the user chooses to close the bank teller window. Just as button-clicks invoke the actionPerformed methods of a registered ActionListener, a user attempting to close the window (JFrame) generates a windowClosing event, which in turn invokes the windowClosing method in the registered WindowListener. This is the place where the user will be given three choices, including saving objects to a disk.

```
private class WindowClosingListener implements WindowListener
{
  public void windowClosing( WindowEvent we )
  {
    // This is the only method that does something
    // When the user closes the window, save the BankAccountCollection
    int choice = JOptionPane.showConfirmDialog( null,
                  "Save data to disk?" );
    if( choice == 0 )
    { // Save the current state of the collections and quit
      saveObjects( );
      System.exit( 0 );
    }
    else if( choice == 1 )
    { // Quit without saving
      System.exit( 0 );
    }
    else // choice must be 2
    { // Let the user continue to use the program
      JOptionPane.showMessageDialog( null, "Carry on..." );
    }
  } // End the one of seven methods used in this WindowListener

  // ... Six other do-nothing methods

} // End the WindowClosingListener class
```

When invoked at the beginning of this windowClosing method, showConfirmDialog shows a dialog box, a message, and three choice buttons.

showConfirmDialog returns 0 when Yes is clicked, 1 when No is clicked, and 2 when Cancel is clicked or the user presses the Escape key. The windowClosing method then responds to the choice. When the user clicks Yes, the following helper method is invoked to write both collection objects to a disk:

```java
// Save both collection objects to a disk.
// The old files will be replaced with
// the current state of the objects.
private void saveObjects( )
{
  try
  {
    // Construct an output stream for saving the accounts
    FileOutputStream outFile
        = new FileOutputStream( ACCOUNT_FILE );
    ObjectOutputStream outputStream
        = new ObjectOutputStream( outFile );

    // Write the collection of BankAccounts
    outputStream.writeObject( theAccounts );

    // Do NOT forget to close the output stream!
    outputStream.close( );

    // Construct another output stream for saving the transactions
    outFile = new FileOutputStream( TRANSACTION_FILE );
    outputStream = new ObjectOutputStream( outFile );

    // Write the collection of transactions
    outputStream.writeObject( transactionList );

    // Do NOT forget to close the output stream!
    outputStream.close( );
  }
  catch( IOException ioe )
  {
    String message = "Error writing objects to disk: "
                    + "\n" + ioe
                    + "\nHope you had data backed up...";
    JOptionPane.showMessageDialog( null, message );
  }
} // End saveObjects
```

Chapter Summary

- When programs run, errors occur.
- Java has unchecked exceptions that extend `RuntimeException`. Examples include integer division by 0 and array and string indexes that are out of range. Code that may throw these exceptions may be placed in a `try` block.
- Java has checked exceptions that force programmers to consider that some exceptional event may occur. Examples include trying to read data from a file and trying open a file that does not exist. Code that may throw these exceptions must be in a `try` block.
- Exceptions can be handled with `try` and `catch` to avoid programs terminating on their own.

- Java has a large number of classes that allow programmers to create input and output streams in a large variety of ways, including input from the keyboard.

- Most Java streams use two classes, one for low-level reading or writing of bytes, such as `InputStream` and `FileReader`. Other classes supply higher-level methods, such as `readLine` in `BufferedReader` and `readObject` in `ObjectInputStream`.

- Persistent objects are those that live after a program terminates.

- Complex objects can be read in and stored in their entirety. The class and its instance variables must be `Serializable`.

- The `WindowListener` interface requires seven methods for listening to window events such as `windowClosing`. `JFrame` objects generate window events.

Key Terms

catch	NumberFormatException	throw
checked exception	ObjectInputStream	throws
exception	ObjectOutputStream	try
FileNotFoundException	persistent object	unchecked exception
FileReader	readObject	windowClosing
FileWriter	RuntimeException	WindowListener
IOException	showConfirmDialog	writeObject
java.io	stream	

Exercises

The answers to exercises marked with are available in Appendix C.

1. Given the following data, for each of the following, what exception will be thrown?

    ```
    int number = 5;
    String oneName = "Harry";

    String[] names = new String[number];
    ```

    a. `System.out.println( 8 / ( number - 5 ) );`
    b. `names[number] = oneName;`
    c. `System.out.println( oneName.substring( 3, number + 1 ) );`

 2. What exceptions are unchecked? What does it mean when you need to write code that may throw an unchecked exception?

3. The `get` message in the following code throws an `IndexOutOfBounds` exception when the user enters a negative index or index >= `list.size( )`. Two dialogues show the different behavior.

```
ArrayList list = new ArrayList( );
list.add( "first" );
list.add( "second" );

TextReader keyboard = new TextReader( );
if( list.isEmpty( ) )
  System.out.print( "The list is empty" );
else
{ // Get index in range to find the value of the element in the list
  System.out.print( "Enter index from 0.." + (list.size()-1) + ": " );
  int index = keyboard.readInt( );
  System.out.println( "At " + index + ": " + list.get( index ) );
}
System.out.println( "That's all folks" );
```

Dialogues (the second execution throws an IndexOutOfBoundsException)

```
Enter index from 0..1: 1
At 1: second
That's all folks

Enter index from 0..1: 2
Exception in thread "main" java.lang.IndexOutOfBoundsException:
Index: 2, Size: 2
        at java.util.ArrayList.RangeCheck(ArrayList.java:491)
        at java.util.ArrayList.get(ArrayList.java:307)
        at A.main(A.java:18)
```

Rewrite the code in the `else` block so it prints "Index out of range, try again" until the user enters an index that is in the range.

```
Enter index from 0..1: -2
Index out of range, try again
Enter index from 0..1: 2
Index out of range, try again
Enter index from 0..1: 1
At 1: second
That's all folks
```

 4. Write a minimal program that reads keyboard input and saves it in the file selected by the user. Use stream classes from the `java.io` package. Assume all imports have been included and you are writing the code in a method that throws `IOException`. One dialogue should look like this:

```
Save keyboard input into which file? exercise.txt

Enter lines or 'SENTINEL' as the last line:
This is keyboard input
using standard java classes.
As each line is entered, it is saved to a disk file
until there is one line with SENTINEL. The following last line
will be saved.
SENTINEL
```

5. Write the minimal code to add to the previous exercise that prints all of the lines from the file that was saved to disk (including SENTINEL).

6. Write the minimal code to construct one BankAccount object with user input and then save it as a serialized object. Use stream classes from the java.io package. Assume all imports have been included and you are writing the code in a method that throws IOException. One dialogue should look like this:

```
Enter account name: Kay
Enter initial balance: 105
About to write this object to disk:
Kay $105.00
```

7. Write the minimal code to add to the previous exercise that reads the serialized BankAccount object and prints it.

```
The object after reading the persistent object:
Kay S $105.00
```

Programming Tips

1. **You have not seen all there is to exception handling.**
   Exception handling was only introduced in this chapter. You may want to refer to advanced books to see some related topics that are beyond the scope of this textbook, including
   - other exception classes in Java
   - nested try/catch blocks
   - the finally block

2. **You have not seen all the input and output streams.**
   Java streams were only introduced in this chapter. You may want to refer to advanced books to see some related topics that are beyond the scope of this textbook, such as the File class, random access files, and reading numbers from compressed files. However, one more example of reading input (over the Internet) is described as a programming project at the end of this chapter.

3. **You can circumvent exception handling in Java.**
   When you are dealing with marked exceptions, the code that throws them must be enclosed in a try block, which in turn requires a catch block. You are forced to handle the exception, even if you do nothing in the catch block. In this way your program continues to run even if the exception is thrown. You can also simply claim that your method throws the exception. Then, when the exception is thrown, it is handled by some other method. You have no control over what happens.

4. **You usually need two streams for input or output.**

   It is common to have two or more input streams to read input. It is common to have two or more output streams to write output. The Java I/O classes were designed to work together to build a wide variety of input streams and output streams. This provides great flexibility. For example, an input stream could come in over the Internet (see Programming Project 9D). The downside is that you need to write some extra code.

5. **Always close output streams.**

   If you are writing to an output stream, the output may be buffered. This means the writing physically transfers data after a buffer—an array perhaps—is filled. You may have some data that is written to the buffer, but not physically transferred to its final destination. The `close` message ensures that all data is copied from the buffer to the destination. If you don't close the stream, you will most assuredly lose some data.

6. **All instance variables must be serialized to write and read objects.**

   An object you want to write to a disk must be serialized. Also, you must make sure all of the instance variables in each object are serialized. For example, it is not enough to serialize `BankAccountCollection`. The `BankAccount` class and anything it contains must also be `Serializable`. Tagging the classes with `implements Serializable` does this.

Programming Projects

9A   Console I/O

Write a Java program that reads two integers from the keyboard and prints their sum. Your code could be in one `main` method. Use the Java stream classes. If the input does not represent a valid integer, print an error message that includes the exception that was thrown. In this case, set the `int` variable to 0.

```
This program prints the sum of two integers.
Enter integer one: 12
Enter integer two: 34
Sum: 46

This program prints the sum of two integers.
Enter integer one: 123
Enter integer two: invalid
Could not convert input: java.lang.NumberFormatException: invalid
Sum: 123
```

9B   File Input

Write a Java program that reads all of the numbers in a text file and prints their average. Assuming the input file named `numbersToAverage.data` has one valid number per line and there is no more text (such as lines with blank spaces) after 5.0, your output should look like that below. (*Note:* Use the `ready` method of `BufferedReader` to determine if there is more data. `ready` may throw an `IOException` that must be tried and caught.)

```
1.0
2.0
3.0
4.5
5.0
```

Output

```
This program finds the average of the numbers in numbersToAverage.data
Count: 5
Average:  3.1
```

9C   The `ObjectWriter` and `ObjectReader` Classes

Write an `ObjectWriter` class that can write any given object to any given file. Also write an `ObjectReader` class that can read any object from a disk. The following test driver must generate the output shown.

```java
import java.util.Date;

public class ReadAndWriteObjects
{
  public static void main( String[] args )
  {
    // Write three different types of objects to three different files
    ObjectWriter writer = new ObjectWriter( );

    writer.saveObjectToFile( new String( "abc" ), "oneString.object" );
    writer.saveObjectToFile( new BankAccount( "Jill", 123.45 ),
                                         "oneAccount.object" );
    writer.saveObjectToFile( new Date( ), "oneDay.object" );

    ObjectReader reader = new ObjectReader( );

    // Read three objects and print the toString versions
    Object objectOnFile;

    objectOnFile = reader.readObjectFromFile( "oneString.object" );
    String theString = (String)objectOnFile;
    System.out.println( theString  );
```

```
        objectOnFile = reader.readObjectFromFile( "oneAccount.object" );

        BankAccount theAccount = (BankAccount)objectOnFile;
        System.out.println( theAccount );

        objectOnFile = reader.readObjectFromFile( "oneDay.object" );
        Date theDate = (Date)objectOnFile;
        System.out.println( theDate );
    }
}
```

Output

```
abc
Jill $123.45
Mon Nov 12 16:10:26 MST 2001
```

9D   Reading Files from the Internet

Write a system that displays the text of any valid Web page. The user must either
supply the URL as input or press Enter (no characters). Pressing Enter shows the
HTML text stored in the file at the URL **http://java.sun.com/index.html**.

```
This program will copy a file from the Web if it ends in htm or html
Enter a Web link or press Enter to see the file
http://java.sun.com/index.html
```

You will need an InputStreamReader and a BufferReader. Except this time you will
construct the InputStreamReader with the openStream method of the URL class.

```
urlStream = new InputStreamReader( aURL.openStream( ) );
```

But before you do this, you will need a URL object from the package java.net. A
URL object is constructed with a String that is supposed to represent a valid URL.

```
java.net.URL aURL = null;
try
{
   aURL = new java.net.URL( urlAddress );
}
catch( MalformedURLException mue )
{
   System.out.println( "Invalid URL\n" + mue );
}
```

Notice that you must handle the exception (you can use this code as part of
your program). Use Java stream classes to input the string that represent the URL
(recall that BufferedReader has a readLine method). Also use Java streams to
read the Web page. These files can be read line by line when used with a loop that
has ready( ) in the loop test. Use the following loop test to read all lines until the
end of the file. This loop test is true each time a line with any text has been read.

```
while( inputFile.ready( ) )
```

The following dialogues show the output under various circumstances.

- Dialogue 1: If the user presses Enter, the file shown must be the one stored at `http://java.sun.com/index.html` (assuming this URL has not changed). Only a small portion of the file is shown (as it is really big).
- Dialogue 2: Prints a message indicating that the page requested did not end in `.htm` or `.html`. (*Hint:* Use the `String` `endsWith` method (see the Java API).
- Dialogue 3: Shows a valid URL to get to a connection, but the file is not there.
- Dialogue 4: The input does not follow the protocol for loading Web pages.

Dialogue 1

```
This program will copy a file from the Web if it ends in htm or html
Enter a Web link or press Enter to see the file
http://java.sun.com/index.html

<!DOCTYPE HTML PUBLIC "-//W3C//DTD HTML 3.2//EN">
<HTML>
<HEAD>

<TITLE>java.sun.com - The Source for Java(TM) Technology</TITLE>

<!-----------BEGIN-META  TAGS-------->

// Much output deleted
```

Dialogue 2

```
This program will copy a file from the Web if it ends in htm or html
Enter a Web link or press Enter to see the file
http://java.sun.com/index.html
```
http://java.sun.com/index.xtml

```
http://java.sun.com/index.xml must end with .htm or .html
```

Dialogue 3

```
This program will copy a file from the Web if it ends in htm or html
Enter a Web link or press Enter to see the file
http://java.sun.com/index.html
```
http://www.cs.arizona.edu/notHere.html

```
<!DOCTYPE HTML PUBLIC "-//IETF//DTD HTML 2.0//EN">
<HTML><HEAD>
<TITLE>404 Not Found</TITLE>
</HEAD><BODY>
<H1>Not Found</H1>
The requested URL /notHere.html was not found on this server.<P>
<HR>
<ADDRESS>Apache/1.3.20 Server at www.cs.arizona.edu Port 80</ADDRESS>
</BODY></HTML>
```

Dialogue 4

```
This program will copy a file from the Web if it ends in htm or html
Enter a Web link or press Enter to see the file
http://java.sun.com/index.html
```
sstp://not.com/notAValidWebPage/index.html

```
Invalid URL
java.net.MalformedURLException: unknown protocol: sstp
Exception in thread "main" java.lang.NullPointerException
        at WebPageReader.main(WebPageReader.java:52)o
```

9E   Showing Links from Files on the Internet

Write a system that displays the links stored in any valid Web page. First complete
Programming Project 9D so the dialogues match. Then, inside the loop, look for
the String that begins with http://. Here are two lines from a Web page has one
link per line:

```
Lecturer in the <a href="http://www.cs.arizona.edu">Department
of Computer Science</a> at the <a href="http://www.arizona.edu">
```

If these Strings, beginning with "http://, are found, get all of the characters up
to but not including the next double quote (String's substring method helps).

   The following dialogue shows the output when a valid URL is entered. If the
user presses Enter, the program automatically uses the URL http://
java.sun.com/index.html (this output once showed 58 links beginning with
"http://).

Dialogue

```
This program will show all links from a Web page that begin with "http://
Enter a URL or press Enter to see the links from
http://java.sun.com/index.html
```
http://www.cs.arizona.edu/people/mercer

```
 1)  http://www.cs.arizona.edu/scout/suncam.html
 2)  http://www.cs.arizona.edu/people/mercer/rickm.jpg
 3)  http://www.cs.arizona.edu
 4)  http://www.arizona.edu
 5)  http://www.valpo.edu/
 6)  http://www.fh-reutlingen.de/
 7)  http://www.uidaho.edu/index.html
 8)  http://www.aerovironment.com/
 9)  http://www.psu.edu/
10)  http://www.cs.arizona.edu/classes/cs335/fall02/index.html
11)  http://www.cs.arizona.edu/classes/cs227/fall02/index.html
12)  http://www.cs.arizona.edu/program/BS/bs1b.html
13)  http://www.cs.arizona.edu/people/mercer/CSEMS-Announce2.doc
14)  http://www.cs.arizona.edu/people/mercer/CSEMS-ApplicationForm2.doc
15)  http://www.cs.arizona.edu/people/mercer/design
16)  http://www.cs.arizona.edu/people/mercer/compfun2
17)  http://www.fbeedle.com/36-8/html
```

9F   Showing Links from Files on the Internet with a GUI

First read Programming Projects 9D and 9E. This project asks you to do the same task as Programming Project 9E, show links from files on the Internet, but now using a graphical user interface. When the user enters a `String` into the `JTextField` at the top, the program should show all of the links found in the Web page in a `JTextArea` object. A `JTextArea` is like a `JTextField`, but allows many lines instead of just one. The picture below represents the GUI after the user presses Enter (the default URL is `http://java.sun.com/index.html`). The window has a `JTextField` on the `BorderLayout.North` and a `JTextArea` in the `BorderLayout.Center` of a 500-by-500 pixel `JFrame` (see Chapter 3 for `BorderLayout`). `JTextArea` has the `setText` method. Use it to clear the `JTextArea`. To add a new line to a `JTextArea`, use the `append` method and add a new line character like this (`linksArea` is a `JTextArea` constructed with no arguments).

```
linksArea.append( entireLink + '\n' );
```

Answers to Self-Check Questions

9-1 -a Throws `DivisionByZeroException`

-b Does not throw an exception

-c Throws `NullPointerException`

9-2
```java
try
{
   System.out.println( "Object at index 0: " + list.get( 0 ) );
}
catch( IndexOutOfBoundsException iobe )
{
   System.out.println( "Index out of bounds" );
}
```

9-3
```java
// precondition: obj is not null
public void tryIt( Object obj ) throws IllegalArgumentException
{
   if( obj == null )
      throw new IllegalArgumentException( );
   else
      System.out.println( obj.toString( ) );
}
```

9-4
```java
try
{
   System.out.print( "Enter a number: " );
   doubleAsString = keyboard.readLine( );
}
catch( IOException ioe )
{
   System.out.println( "Could not read keyboard input: " + ioe );
}

try
{
   double theDouble = Double.parseDouble( doubleAsString );
   System.out.println( theDouble + " squared =   "
                       + theDouble * theDouble );
}
catch ( NumberFormatException nfe )
{
   System.out.println( doubleAsString + " was an invalid number" );
}
```

9-5
```java
try
{
   charToBytesWriter = new FileWriter( outputFileName );
   charToBytesWriter.write( "Your Name" );   // <-- Must be in a try block
   charToBytesWriter.close( );
}
catch( IOException ioe )
{
   System.out.println( "Could not create the new file: " + ioe );
}
```

Chapter 10

Designing an Inheritance Hierarchy

Summing Up

The bank teller system is now complete. It was developed over Chapters 3–9 as new concepts were introduced. You witnessed the development of an object-oriented system with 10 classes written specifically for the application. The application also directly used 13 existing Java classes.

Coming Up

This chapter introduces a new application using an informal object-oriented software development methodology. You will find objects to model a library system. Responsibilities are assigned to those objects through role-playing. Along the way, you will discover an inheritance hierarchy. The application's design reviews the concept of polymorphism through inheritance. After studying this chapter, you will be able to

- find objects
- see how role-playing can help programmers analyze and design systems
- recognize generalizations that may be implemented with inheritance
- extend existing classes
- apply object-oriented design guidelines for inheritance
- recognize the benefits of being able to send the same message to different types of objects and get different, yet appropriate, behaviors from the objects (polymorphism)
- design an inheritance hierarchy

Exercises and programming projects reinforce designing with inheritance.

10.1   Object-Oriented Analysis and Design

This section introduces an object-oriented design methodology in the context of a real-world problem—a library system. The software development is based on the responsibility-driven design methodology of Wirfs-Brock, Wilkerson, and Wiener [Wirfs-Brock 1990].

The first step in object-oriented analysis involves identification of objects that model the system. Programmers "become" objects through **role-playing**. Playing the roles of the objects helps them identify responsibilities of the objects and the relationships between them. Role-playing helps programmers understand a problem, model a solution, and iron out any rough spots.

Analysis deals with understanding a system.
Design involves assigning responsibilities and writing good code.

Class/Responsibility/Collaborator (CRC) cards are another tool to help design object-oriented software. Introduced by Kent Beck and Ward Cunningham [Beck/Cunningham 1989], this simple and effective tool consists of writing responsibilities on 3-by-5-inch index cards. CRC cards were first used to help people understand objects. Today, programmers make use of CRC cards while developing large-scale object-oriented systems.

The following methodology will be used to create a model of the system while making progress towards designing the classes needed for the application.

- Identify objects that model (shape) the system as a natural and sensible set of abstractions and determine the main responsibilities of the objects. These are the candidate objects.
- Perform role-playing and write design decisions down on CRC cards. These design decisions include the **responsibilities** of the objects—what objects can do and what objects know about themselves.
- Keep track of the collaborators that help an object fulfill its responsibilities. This helps programmers to understand which objects communicate with each other.

Finding the Objects

Object-oriented software development begins by trying to model a system as a collection of interacting objects, each with its own responsibilities. This helps organize the system into workable pieces. Every system intended for implementation on a computer will be partitioned into modules. The object-oriented design approach partitions the system into objects. If these objects have a well-defined, cohesive set of responsibilities, then people that build and maintain the software will understand the system better. The system can be maintained more easily. The first step in the methodology is to partition the system into objects that model the system.

> The college library has requested a system that supports a small set of library operations. The librarian allows a student to borrow certain items, return those borrowed items, and pay fees. Late fees and due dates have been established at the following rates:
>
> | | **Late Fee** | **Length of Borrow** |
> |-------------|-------------------------------------|-------------------------------|
> | books: | $0.50 per day | 14 days |
> | video tapes:| $5.00 plus 1.50 each additional day | 2 days (2 days late is $6.50) |
> | CDs | $2.50 per day | 7 days |
>
> The due date is set when the borrowed item is checked out. A student with three borrowed items, one late item, or late fees greater than $25.00 may not borrow anything new.

One way to find some of the objects is to write down the nouns and noun phrases in the system specification. The following list represents some objects that model the system (redundant entries are not recorded). Nothing need be set in stone yet; this is just a start.

Candidate Objects—A First Pass at Finding Objects

Somewhat Sure	Not Sure
librarian	system
student	operations
book	late fees
video tape	due date
CD	day
3 borrowed items	fine
college library	

Librarian is a good name for the object responsible for coordinating activities such as checking books in and out. This object will get help from other objects.

Some of these nouns can be eliminated as objects to model the system. For example, Librarian represents the system, so "system" is out. "Operations" sounds more like the methods an object should understand rather than an object itself. "Fine" and "late fees" could be primitive types, which aren't objects. Several nouns have now been eliminated from the model.

"Student" appears as if it would be a useful object. After all, students will be checking books out, checking them in, and paying fines. However, this system should also be allowed to lend books to faculty, staff, and other members of the community. Borrower would be a better name to represent someone who can borrow from the library (it is perfectly reasonable to replace candidate objects items in the list with more accurate names).

The noun phrase "3 borrowed items" could be an object that is implemented as an array of books. However, the goal now is to find objects that model the system rather than determine how the system will eventually get things done. The term "3 borrowed items" is not an object. Instead, it may be a responsibility. It will likely be considered at some point.

"Book," "video tape," and "CD" are items that can be borrowed from the library. These three objects are a natural part of the model. All three are "borrowable items." An object named borrowableItem could capture the responsibilities that are common to all objects that can be borrowed. Although differences exist in the computation of late fees and the setting of due dates, each borrowableItem has several common responsibilities. But borrowableItem is a bit of a tongue-twister. Let's use the term Lendable for the object that represents anything that can be lent to Borrowers.

The nouns "due date" and "day" suggest that some object might need to be responsible for managing calendar arithmetic. Rename this Date and consider it as an object in the model.

The system must maintain many borrowers and many books. Since there will be many books and many borrowers, two new objects named BorrowerList and LendableList are added to the list of candidate objects to maintain these two important collections.

At this point, several potential objects have been found to model this system with an understanding of what each object represents. The following table summarizes the candidate objects and the primary responsibility of each.

Object Name	Primary Responsibility
Librarian	Represents the object responsible for coordinating the activities of checking in and checking out library materials.
Borrower	Represents one instance of someone who can borrow a Lendable. There may be thousands of Borrowers.
Date	Manages calendar arithmetic to help figure the due date or if a Lendable is overdue.
Lendable	Represents one instance of a borrowable item. It could be a Book, a CD, or a Video.
Book	Represents one book that can be checked in and checked out. There may be thousands of Books.
CD	Represents one compact disc that can be checked in and checked out. There may be thousands of CDs.
Video	Represents one video tape that can be checked in and checked out. There may be thousands of Videos.
BorrowerList	Stores thousands of Borrowers.
LendableList	Store thousands of Lendables.

The following picture provides another view of the model so far. It also marks the boundaries of the system. Everything in gray represents the system under development. The picture also shows the Borrowers and Lendables (the physical items that can be borrowed). These physical entities will likely be modeled as software objects.

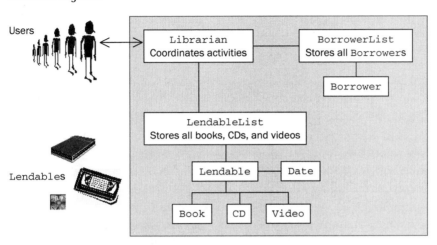

Responsibilities

With some objects and primary responsibilities identified, the task now is to refine other responsibilities and assign those responsibilities to the correct objects. You should try to answer questions such as: "What are the responsibilities?" and "Which object should take on each of the responsibilities?" Responsibilities convey the purpose of an object and its role in the system. Responsibilities include

1. The actions each object can perform.
2. The knowledge each object must remember.

Asking these two questions will help you assign responsibilities to objects.

1. What should an object be able to do?
2. What should an object know?

The next activity involves assigning responsibilities to the objects already identified. Try to imagine a team of programmers working together to assign responsibilities. These programmers will continue the analysis and design by role-playing. Role-playing occurs when people assume the roles of objects. The imaginary programming team members play out scenarios while adding responsibilities and collaborators to their CRC cards. These CRC cards summarize design decisions. Here is a sneak preview of the CRC card for Borrower (arrived at after much discussion):

class Borrower	
Responsibilities	**Collaborators**
canBorrow	Lendable
addLendable	Date
removeLendable	
debit	
getLateFees	
knows borrowed lendables	
knows late fees	

CRC cards capture responsibilities—what objects do—and collaborators—the objects that help fulfill the responsibilities. If the role-players write these down on their CRC cards, those CRC cards can be used later to help implement the class needed to construct the objects.

The programming team members will now assume the roles of these objects. For the time being, it is useful to have a user to represent the Borrower who approaches with a book to borrow or with money to pay late fees. But the user will not be implemented as a class. Instead, the user will be a person who approaches the Librarian, shows identification, and makes a request. Borrower represents an object inside the system that knows everything about that particular user. For example, the Borrower might be responsible for knowing if its human counterpart (the user) owes any late fees.

Role-Playing

The team will now start a scenario. A **scenario** is the answer to the question: "What happens when…?" The team decides that the first scenario will be the response to this question:

"What happens when user #1234 wants to check out a book with call number QA76.1 when the user currently has three Lendables?"

User: I want to borrow a book.

Librarian: Well, I'm the Librarian so I guess I'll start. What is your ID?

User: It's #1234.

Librarian: Okay, now let's get a handle on the Borrower—the software model of you, the user. I'll ask BorrowerList to look up the Borrower with ID #1234.

BorrowerList: I found the Borrower you asked for. I'm sending it back to you. I'll add getBorrower as one of my responsibilities. Also, I must know all

Borrowers. I'll write down Borrower as a collaborator because I need its help to locate the correct borrower.

BorrowerList's CRC now looks like this:

class BorrowerList	
Responsibilities	**Collaborators**
getBorrower(BorrowerID)	Borrower

Librarian: Thanks, BorrowerList. I now have the current borrower. Now I have the software object that models the user. So user, what is the call number of the book?

User: QA76.1.

Librarian: I believe my job would be easier if I could send a canBorrow message to your software model. I am now going to ask Borrower for help. What about it, current Borrower, can you borrow a book?

Borrower: I could be responsible for knowing what I have borrowed. I should be able to tell you if I have borrowed three things. Hey, wait a minute; you didn't ask me if I had three borrowed items. You asked me if I could borrow. Let me add a canBorrow responsibility to my CRC card. To borrow, my late fine must be $25.00 or less and I must have fewer than three Lendables, none of which can be overdue. It seems like I should know what I have borrowed. I have three borrowed items. No, I cannot borrow.

Librarian: Thanks, Borrower. Things are made easier for me because I can delegate the canBorrow responsibility to you. It's a good idea to distribute system intelligence as evenly as possible (remember the canSelect method in the jukebox system in Chapter 4). Now I can just send a canBorrow message to you since you have the knowledge to fulfill the responsibility. I think this is kind of like having a BankAccount decide if it has enough money to allow a withdrawal. Anyway, I think I should inform the user that borrowing a book is not an option.

This particular scenario has reached a logical conclusion. There are obviously many possible scenarios to role-play, such as paying fines and successfully checking out a book and then returning it. Should users be able to look up a book by its call number to see if it is in or out, or perhaps ask when a book is due back in the library? Although this is desirable behavior, the system specification did not list these requirements. The system was intentionally kept to a minimum of functionality. (But with good design, such enhancements could be added later.) Now let's see what happens when the user *can* borrow a book.

A Borrowing Scenario

"What happens when user #4321 wants to borrow a `Lendable` with the call number QA76.2 when the user has two books checked out, neither of which is late, and has late fees of $5.00?"

Librarian: I'll start again. I'll get the user ID.

User: My ID is #4321.

Librarian: Let me ask `BorrowerList` for the proper `Borrower`. Please `getBorrower` with ID #4321.

BorrowerList: I found the `Borrower` you asked for. I'm sending it back to you.

Librarian: User, what do you want to do?

User: I want to borrow a `Book` with the call number QA76.2.

Librarian: I have the current `Borrower`. I'll check with `Borrower`. Can you borrow?

Borrower: Let me see if I have fewer than three borrowed items. Yes, I currently am borrowing only two `Lendables`. Now, are any `Lendables` overdue? Let me ask the first `Lendable` in my list of borrowed items. $Lendable_0$, are you overdue?

$Lendable_0$: I am responsible for knowing if I am overdue. To do this, I will need to ask `Date` to compare my due date with today's date. I will add the responsibilities `knowDueDate` and `isOverdue`. I asked `Date` for help so I'll list `Date` as a collaborator.

Date: To compare the due date with today's date, I must be able to get today's date and to compare two dates. Yes, `Lendable`, there are several days to go before the due date. I'll add this responsibility to my CRC card: if `today > dueDate`, then the `Lendable` is overdue. The due date has past.

$Lendable_0$: Thanks, `Date`. I am not overdue.

Borrower: I'll check my other Lendables. None are overdue. Since my late fees are less than $25.00, I can tell Librarian, "Yes, I can borrow another Lendable."

Librarian: LendableList, please get me the Lendable with the ID QA76.2.

LendableList: Okay, here is the Lendable.

Librarian: What should I do now?

Let's pause and consider a couple of possibilities. It seems as if the current Borrower and the current Lendable both need to be updated to record that the Lendable has been checked out. The question is "What should be done to update Lendable?" First, the book should be made not available. The dueDate should be set to the appropriate day in the future so the system can determine at any time if the Lendable is overdue. The Lendable should also know its Borrower, in case someone needs to know who has the Lendable.

There are two possible ways to handle this. The first alternative places the responsibility of updating a Lendable upon the Librarian. The second alternative delegates this responsibility to the Lendable itself. The team role-plays both alternatives. Here is the first:

Alternative 1 — Librarian Updates the Lendable

Librarian: Lendable, compute and set your due date.

Lendable: Okay, I'll setDueDate to 2, 7, or 14 days from today, depending on what type of Lendable I am.

Note: This is polymorphism. Any object's type is known while the program is running. The same message can be sent to any of the three different types of Lendable objects—Book, CD, or Video—and the correct method will execute. The particular version of setDueDate that executes will depend on the type of the object. And the type of object will be determined when the Lendable is being checked out.

Lendable: I'll set the due date in a polymorphic way by sending a setDueDate message to any Lendable in the hopes that the correct thing will happen.

Librarian: Lendable, now please record ID #4321 as your borrower's ID.

Lendable: Okay, I'll set my borrower ID as user #4321.

Librarian: Okay, now mark yourself as not available.

Lendable: Done.

Alternative 2 — `Lendable` Updates Itself

Librarian: `Lendable`, you could be responsible for checking yourself out. If I tell you the borrower's ID, could you check yourself out?

Lendable: Sure. I'll do whatever is appropriate. I'll add this responsibility to my CRC card by naming it `checkSelfOut`.

Which alternative is "better?" One way to assess the design is to ask yourself "What feels better?" Alternative 2 feels better somehow. However, wouldn't it be nice to have some design guidelines to make us feel better about feeling better? Well, it turns out that alternative 1 has three different messages, versus the single message of alternative 2. In most cases, the fewer message the better. Additionally, alternative 2 has better cohesion—the responsibilities of the `checkSelfOut` message are closely related:

- record the borrower's id
- compute and set the due date
- update the availability status to unavailable

Additionally, alternative 1 requires the `Librarian` to know more than is necessary about the internal state of the `Lendable`. Alternative 2 delegates responsibility to the more appropriate class. So the team member role-playing `Lendable` adds `checkSelfOut` to the set of responsibilities on the `Lendable` CRC card.

This scenario has not reached its logical conclusion. The `Borrower` does not know about its newly borrowed `Lendable`. Each `Borrower` must know its borrowed items. The `Borrower` must be updated. Here is one conclusion to this scenario:

Librarian: `Borrower`, let's follow the design guideline we just talked about again. I'll just send you `Lendable` and you can add it to the list of your borrowed `Lendables`.

Borrower: I should be able to manage that. I'll write `addLendable` as a responsibility on my CRC card.

Librarian: So, User, anything else?

User: No, I'm outta here.

Librarian: Okay, I'm ready for another user.

The programmers role-playing the objects kept notes on their CRC cards with the following results:

class Borrower	
Responsibilities	**Collaborators**
canBorrow	Lendable
addLendable	Date
knows borrowed lendables	
knows late fines	

class Lendable	
Responsibilities	**Collaborators**
isOverdue	Date
checkSelfOut	Borrower
knows due date	Date
knows borrower	
knows call number	

class Librarian	
Responsibilities	**Collaborators**
Coordinate activities	Borrower
	BorrowerList
	LendableList

Some of these responsibilities might later become methods. Some of the collaborators might later become objects passed to a method or instance variables inside the class used to construct the object.

Self-Check

10-1 Write an algorithm to a check out a book that sends any message you desire to any object you desire. Use any of these objects as if the classes were already implemented. Add any message you like.

```
BorrowerList theBorrowerList = new BorrowerList( );
LendableList theLendableList = new LendableList( );
Borrower currentBorrower = new Borrower( ID, name );
Lendable currentLendable = new Book( callNumber, title );
```

A Scenario to Return a Book

Many scenarios could still be played out. For example, what happens when a user wants to return a book? What happens when a user wants to pay late fees? Consider how the objects interact with each other when a user wants to return a book.

"What happens when a user returns a book that is not overdue?"

Librarian: I'll start again. User, what is your ID?

User: My ID is #4321.

Librarian: Let me ask `BorrowerList` for this `Borrower`. Please `getBorrower` with ID #4321.

BorrowerList: I found the `Borrower` you asked for. I'm sending its reference back to you.

Librarian: User, what do you want to do?

User: I want to return something with the call number QA76.2.

Librarian: `LendableList`, please `getLendableWithID( "QA76.2" )`. It seems that I should check to ensure that the book is not overdue. `Lendable`, are you overdue?

Lendable: No.

Librarian: If you had been overdue, I would have had to ask the `Borrower` to play late fees.

Librarian: So now I probably have to adjust the `Lendable` to indicate that it is available again.

Lendable: I should be able to do that. I'll mark myself as available. I wonder, is there anything else I should do? Perhaps I could set my due date to today or perhaps some date way in the past. What about 1-1-1900? No, that would make me a century overdue. What about a day in the future, say 9-9-9999? Or I could set my borrower ID to something like "?no Borrower?". Let me think about it. Perhaps being available is enough. When I'm available, no one should care who my borrower is or what the due date is.

Librarian: Now I should ask the `Borrower` to remove this item from the list of borrowed `Lendables`.

Borrower: Okay, I'll write `removeLendable` on my CRC card. I know what I have borrowed.

Returning an Overdue Book

"What happens when a user returns a book that is five days overdue?"

User: I want to return a book with the call number QA76.3.

Librarian: What's your ID?

User: My ID is #6543.

Librarian: `BorrowerList`, please `getBorrower` with ID #6543.

BorrowerList: I found the `Borrower` you asked for. I'm sending its reference back to you.

Librarian: LendableList, please getLendable("QA76.3"). I should check to ensure that the book is not overdue. Lendable, are you overdue?

Lendable: I'll ask Date if today's date > due date.

Date: Yes. The dueDate was some time ago. I guess there will be money to owe.

Lendable: That's clever rhyming, Date. Yes, Librarian, the book is overdue.

Librarian: I'll tell the user that the book is overdue.

User: Whoops, I don't have any money.

Librarian: No problem, I'll add to your late fees.

Borrower: Now I'll need a way to update my late fees. This will help me to maintain what the user owes, in case the user forgets.

Librarian: I'll ask Lendable to getLateFee.

Lendable: Date, by how many days is the item overdue? Tell me todaysDate - dueDate.

Date: There is a difference of five days. I'll add "Compute the number of days between two dates" to my CRC card.

Lendable: The late fee is 5 * (day_late_fee), which as a book, is $1.25.

Librarian: Add 1.25 to your late fees.

Borrower: Okay, I'm supposed to know my total late fee, so I'll add that 1.25 to my late fee. Remember, I'll be implemented as software to ensure that my late fees are always honest. I'll write that responsibility as debitFees.

Librarian: Now I have to deal with the Lendable. Say Lendable, could you check yourself in also?

Lendable: Let me see, I'll mark myself as available and do whatever I need to do. I'll write the responsibility as checkSelfIn.

Librarian: We're done. I can now get another user request or get the next user.

Paying a Late Fee

User: Wait, I just found some money. I would like to pay my late fees now.

Librarian: Okay, I'll check to see how much you owe.

Borrower: I can answer that. I'll write getLateFees on my CRC card.

Librarian: Give me the money and I'll credit your account by how much you give me.

Borrower: Just remember to credit me!

The team has now role-played several scenarios. Along the way, the programmers who were playing the roles of Borrower and Lendable added a few responsibilities. A few object-oriented design guidelines were employed to help make a better-designed system. The Librarian noted some of the activities that need to be coordinated (checking out and returning items, for example). So far, there is a reasonable set of objects with clearly defined responsibilities. The CRC cards that note these design decisions (the assigning of responsibilities) are reviewed here. New responsibilities are shown in boldface.

class Borrower	
Responsibilities	**Collaborators**
canBorrow	Lendable
addLendable	Date
removeLendable	
debitFees	
getLateFees	
knows borrowed lendables	
knows late fees	

class Lendable	
Responsibilities	**Collaborators**
isOverdue	
checkSelfOut	Borrower
checkSelfIn	
knows due date	Date
knows borrower	
knows call number	
knows availability	

class Librarian	
Responsibilities	**Collaborators**
Coordinate activities	Borrower
check a book out	BorrowerList
check a book in	LendableList
look up late fees	
collect money	
update the Borrower	

Self-Check

10-2   Write an algorithm for the Librarian describing the activities the Librarian must perform to successfully return any Lendable. Send any message you desire to any object you desire.

```
BorrowerList theBorrowerList = new BorrowerList( );
LendableList theLendableList = new LendableList( );
Borrower currentBorrower = new Borrower( ID, name );
Lendable currentLendable = new Book( callNumber, title );
```

Collaborators

The CRC cards record **collaborators**. These are the other objects that help fulfill the responsibilities listed on the card. The `Librarian` gets help not only from two collections but also from the `Borrower` and the `Lendable`. There will likely be other collaborators, such as `String`, and some primitives, such as `int` and `double`. However, primitives are not usually written as collaborators. This defers some decisions until later and the CRC cards don't get as cluttered.

Should `Date` be listed as a collaborator? `Date` could be considered close to a primitive like `int`. An object is needed that can get today's date and compare two dates. The responsibilities of getting the current date from any computer system are more complex. So it will be listed as a collaborator. In Java, this could be `GregorianCalendar`. `GregorianCalendar` can get the current date. However, `GregorianCalendar` cannot directly determine the number of days between two dates (at least not directly). The `DayCounter` class specified as a programming project in Chapter 4 could be used instead. It already has the necessary additional functionality. The following CRC card will now stand in for `Date`:

class DayCounter	
Responsibilities	**Collaborators**
compare two dates	GregorianCalendar
compute number of days	
between two dates	

10.2   Building an Inheritance Hierarchy

Sometimes several things are like each other—but with some differences. Imagine that you need a different type of bank account, one that pays interest. You could create a completely new `BankAccountWithInterest` class. This would leave you with two separate classes, `BankAccountWithInterest` and `BankAccount`, even though these classes have many similarities. Imagine a decision is made to add new data to all types of bank accounts. Perhaps a personal identification number (PIN) must now be part of both. Perhaps you need to add a method that returns the PIN for both. Perhaps, as is the case at many banks, there are more than 25 types of accounts. Now imagine that you want to add data indicating a mother's maiden name for all accounts. The programmer would again have to modify 25 or more classes. If the programmer is using an object-oriented programming language such as Java, there is an alternative.

Object-oriented languages such as Java give you the freedom to decide what is common to a set of objects and give the common methods and data to dozens of other classes. Perhaps all instances must have an account number, a customer name, and an address. They all may have a debit method and a credit method. An object-oriented implementation allows you to place all of these common things into one class. Then other classes can *inherit* the common responsibilities.

Books, CDs, and Videos are similar. These objects have been commonly referred to as Lendables. Lendable represents several types of objects that can be borrowed and returned. The scenarios work no matter which type of Lendable is being borrowed or returned.

This small part of the system may be implemented using the inheritance relationship between classes. The methods and instance variables common to all objects should go into a class named Lendable. The differences between the objects are defined in the classes that extend Lendable. Here is the inheritance relationship viewed in UML notation to show that three classes extend the class meant to capture the commonalities.

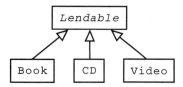

When one class extends another, the new class can add new methods, modify the behavior of any inherited methods, and add new instance variables. Two or more classes in an inheritance relationship make up what is called an **inheritance hierarchy**. Through inheritance, each class that extends Lendable (Book, CD, and Video) obtains (inherits) methods and instance variables of Lendable. The following object-oriented design guideline explicitly encourages this inheritance relationship.

Object-Oriented Design Guideline 10-1 (Riel's Heuristic 5.10)

If two or more classes have common data and behavior, then those classes should inherit from a common class that captures those data and methods.

The following common data and behavior in the library system can be captured in Lendable:

- know the due date
- know the call number
- know the borrower (or the borrower's ID at least)
- know the availability

- check out a `Lendable`
- check in a `Lendable`

However, without some differences amongst the classes that will extend `Lendable`, there is no reason to design an inheritance relationship. Instead, there would be just one class. So, in addition to the commonalities mentioned above, there must be enough differences to justify having more than one type of class. There are two, possibly three, differences between the three objects:

- set the due date (differs among classes)
- computing the late fee (differs amongst classes)
- may have different state (`Books` may have an author, for example)

Abstract Classes

In this design, `Lendable` will be the abstract class. An **abstract class** captures the responsibilities that are common to all subclasses. An abstract class cannot be instantiated. The following attempt to construct a `Lendable` will be rendered invalid:

```
Lendable aLendable = new Lendable( ); // Let this be an error
```

Borrowers really don't borrow a `Lendable`. Instead, borrowers borrow books and videos. By analogy, people don't eat a `Fruit`. People eat peaches, bananas, apples, and oranges.

Abstract classes exist to capture data and methods that are the same for all of the objects in the inheritance hierarchy. Java specifies abstract classes by declaring them with the keyword `abstract`.

```
// You cannot instantiate this class because it is declared abstract
abstract public class Lendable
{
    common data
    common methods
}
```

The three different types of objects that can be borrowed acquire the common methods and instance variables by inheriting them from the abstract class. To specify this relationship between classes, Java requires the keyword `extends`, followed by name of the class with the common methods and data.

```
public class Book extends Lendable  // Inherit methods and
                                    // data of Lendable
{ // ... }

public class Video extends Lendable
{ // ... }

public class CD extends Lendable
{ // ... }
```

With `extends Lendable`, these three classes inherit (obtain) methods implemented in the abstract class `Lendable`. When `Book`, `CD`, and `Video` extend `Lendable`, as shown above, there is nothing abstract about them. Borrowers can borrow real books and videos. The following constructions will be valid in our system:

```
Book aBook = new Book( initial state );    // To be implemented later
CD aCD = new CD( initial state );
Video aVideo = new Video( initial state );
```

Superclasses and Subclasses

In this inheritance hierarchy, the `Lendable` class is known as a **superclass**. Classes that extend an existing class (as `Book`, `CD`, and `Video` do) are known as **subclasses**. A reference to a superclass can be used to refer to instances of any subclass. This is evidenced by the following assignment possibilities:

```
Book aBook = new Book( "CALL#", "TITLE", "AUTHOR" );
Video aVideo = new Video( "CALL#", "TITLE" );
CD aCD = new CD( "CALL#", "TITLE", "AUTHOR" );

// All subclasses can be assigned to the superclass.
Lendable anyLendable;

anyLendable = aBook;
anyLendable = aCD;
anyLendable = aVideo;
```

This superclass/subclass terminology can be confusing at first. A subclass usually adds methods and instance variables. Therefore, the term "sub" refers to classes that may actually be "bigger" in terms of methods and instance variables. And "super" means "smaller" in terms of methods and instance variables, not "bigger." "Superclass" and "subclass" do not refer to the size of the class. Later in this chapter, you will see how Java uses this terminology. For example, Java requires the keyword `super` for a subclass constructor to call the constructor of its superclass.

Self-Check

10-3 List the abstract class in the following inheritance hierarchy:

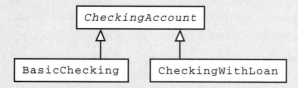

10-4 List the class(es) in this inheritance hierarchy that can be instantiated.

10-5 List one method that would make one subclass different from the other.

10-6 List one method that would be the same for both subclasses.

The `Lendable` Class

Now that there is some understanding of the system, our focus turns to designing the `Lendable` hierarchy of classes. There are relationships between `Book`, `Video`, and `CD`. The things that each instance of a class must do could be listed as the public methods. The things that each instance of the class must know could become private instance variables. The first thing to do is let the `Lendable` class capture all the knowledge and action responsibilities that will be common to the subclasses. The CRC card lists several things that all `Lendable`s have in common.

class Lendable	
Responsibilities	**Collaborators**
isOverdue	
checkSelfOut	Borrower
checkSelfIn	
knows due date	Date
knows borrower	
knows call number	
knows availability	

You will soon see methods that have the same name, but execute differently. For example, each class might have a `getDueDate` method. However, each class will compute the due date differently. A `Book` can be borrowed for 14 days, but a `Video` for only two. At the same time, the abstract class can define and implement methods that all derived classes will usefully inherit—`isAvailable`, for example (assuming the behavior is the same for all subclasses, that is).

The `Lendable` CRC card currently lists several responsibilities. The `isOverdue` responsibility can be implemented as a `boolean` method. It does not require any arguments. It should return `true` or `false` to indicate the state of any `Lendable` object in the inheritance hierarchy. The method heading could be `public boolean isOverdue( )`.

Since the `Librarian` has to know if any `Lendable` is available, a method named `isAvailable` could be added to the abstract class. This method does not require any arguments either. It returns either `true` or `false`, indicating the state of any

Lendable object in the inheritance hierarchy. The method heading could be
public boolean isAvailable( ). There are several other methods and instance
variables that are common to all Lendables. Good design compels us to place
them in the abstract Lendable class.

Here is most of the abstract class Lendable. It lists instance variables, the
constructor, and the accessing methods determined to be common to all subclasses. A few abstract methods will be added later. *Note:* The methods use
javadoc comments. See Appendix A, "A Little Javadoc."

```java
/**
   The beginning of an abstract class to capture the instance variables
   and methods that are common to all objects that can be borrowed from
   a library.

   This class also specifies what methods MUST be implemented by the
   subclasses. Both getLateFee and checkSelfOut are declared abstract.
*/
public abstract class Lendable
{
    private String my_callNumber;
    private String my_title;
    private boolean my_availability;
    private String my_borrowerID;
    private DayCounter my_dueDate;

    // Constructor needs a callNumber. A title is added since it
    // seems that all Lendables will have a title of some sort.
    public Lendable( String callNumber, String initTitle )
    {
        my_callNumber = callNumber;
        my_title = initTitle;
        my_borrowerID = null;
        my_dueDate = null;
        my_availability = true;
    }

// Accessing methods

/** Provide access to this object's call number.
  * @return this object's call number
  */
    public String getCallNumber( )
    {
        return my_callNumber;
    }

/** Provide access to this object's title.
  * @return this object's title
  */
    public String getTitle( )
    {
        return my_title;
    }
```

```java
/** Let anyone know if this Lendable is available.
  * @return true if this Lendable is not currently borrowed.
  */
  public boolean isAvailable( )
  {
    return my_availability;
  }

/** Provide access to the borrower ID (could be null).
  * @return null if no one is borrowing this lendable or return
  * the String that could be used to find the Borrower object.
  */
  public String getBorrowerID( )
  {
    return my_borrowerID;
  }

/** Find out if a Lendable is overdue or not.
  * @return true if this book was supposed to be returned before
  * today or false if the due date is yet to arrive.
  */
  public boolean isOverdue( )
  {
    if( this.isAvailable( ) )
      return false; // Not even checked out

    // This Lendable is checked out, so see if it is overdue
    DayCounter today = new DayCounter( );
    // Return true if today is greater than due date for this Lendable
    return daysLate( ) > 0;
  }

/** Provide access to the date a Lendable is due back in the library.
  * @return this Lendable's due date.
  */
  public DayCounter getDueDate( )
  {
    return my_dueDate;
  }

/** Provide a quick way to see the state of a Lendable.
  * @return the call number, title, and some information about the
  * availability (or due date) of this Lendable.
  */
  public String toString( )
  {
    String result = my_callNumber + " '" + my_title + "': ";
    if( this.isAvailable( ) )
      result += "available";
    else
      result += "due " + my_dueDate.toString( ) + ", " + my_borrowerID;
    return result;
  }
```

```
// Modifying methods

/** This method will correctly modify the state of any Lendable so it
  * is considered returned and available for others to borrow.
  * @return true if Lendable's state indicates it has been returned.
  */
  public boolean checkSelfIn( )
  {
    if( this.isAvailable( ) )
    { // This object cannot be checked out
      System.out.println( "*ERROR* " + my_callNumber
                          + " is not checked out" );
      return false;
    }
    else
    {
      my_dueDate = null;
      my_availability = true;
      return true;
    }
  }

/** Allow anyone to determine how many days late any Lendable is.
  * @return the number of days, which could be negative indicating
  * the number of days until the Lendable is due.
  */
  public int daysLate( )
  {
    if( this.isAvailable( ) )
      return 0;   // due_date should be null

    DayCounter today = new DayCounter( );
    return my_dueDate.daysFrom( today );
  }


      ... The protected checkOutAnyLendable discussed next ...


      ... Abstract methods will be added later  ...


} // End class Lendable for now (more to come)
```

During role-playing, when a Lendable was returned to the library, the
Librarian simply sent a checkSelfIn message to the Lendable so it could update
itself. This method might be the same for all Lendable objects. If it is, it should go
into the Lendable class, not in every subclass that extends Lendable. A
checkSelfIn message would not need any arguments. If a Lendable
isAvailable, an error message will be printed, for now. This is an exceptional

case. It is an attempt to return a Lendable that was not checked out. The
checkSelfIn message was implemented above as a boolean method. This allows
the Librarian to check for this exceptional case if so desired. If a Lendable is
actually checked out, its state is modified to make it available for other Borrowers.

checkOutAnyLendable

The checkSelfOut method is more complicated than checkSelfIn. Many
instance variables have to be modified during a checkSelfOut message. However,
the abstract Lendable class has followed the general rule that instance variables be
made private. And even though classes that extend another class inherit the
instance variables along with the methods, the subclasses cannot directly access the
private instance variables. Specifically, Book, Video, and CD cannot directly reference the instance variables my_borrowerId and my_dueDate.

The good news is that a checkOutAnyLendable method in Lendable can be
written to do the same updates for all Lendable objects, such as marking themselves as unavailable. This method needs the days to borrow (borrowLength) so it
can set the due date. The argument borrowLength helps to set the due date of any
subclass.

```
// Adjust the state of any object from this inheritance hierarchy.
// borrowerId: The ID of the Borrower checking out any Lendable.
// borrowLength: The number of days an instance of the
// subclass can be borrowed.
protected void checkOutAnyLendable( String borrowerID, int borrowLength  )
{
   // Record who is borrowing this Lendable
   my_borrowerID = borrowerID;

   // Set the new due date by the correct number of days passed as
   // an argument by the particular class that extends Lendable.
   my_dueDate = new DayCounter( );
   my_dueDate.adjustDaysBy( borrowLength );

   // Mark this Lendable as no longer available to be borrowed
   my_availability = false;
}
```

Protected Methods

This checkOutAnyLendable method in the superclass will be invoked from its
subclasses. But it need not be made public. It is meant to be used only by the
subclasses that extend Lendable. If it were made private, then no class that
extends Lendable could use this common set of statements to accomplish check-

ing out a `Lendable`. If it were made `public`, then it would appear as a method even though programmers don't need it and shouldn't use it directly. Therefore, it has been declared `protected`.

The `protected` access mode means that any class that extends `Lendable` has access to the `protected` method. The code is written once and is the same for all classes. This is less error-prone than copying and pasting the same code for all of the subclasses. It is also easier if a new `Lendable` is added later to the inheritance hierarchy; an `AudioTape` or `Periodical`, for example.

Later, you will see that any new class can use the same design to easily check itself out. Making `checkOutAnyLendable` `protected`, rather than `public`, also means that the method can't accidentally be invoked from a method outside of the inheritance hierarchy.

The remaining issue is this: How do the subclasses use this `protected` method? One way to encourage its use is to add an `abstract` method in the superclass.

Abstract Methods

`Lendable` is an abstract class. Methods can also be abstract. When a method is declared to be `abstract`, a class that extends the class *must* implement the **abstract method** (or some other class that extends the class must implement the abstract method).

Whereas the methods and instance variables in `Lendable` represent responsibilities common to all `Lendable` objects, two other responsibilities vary: `checkSelfOut` and `getLateFee`. These two responsibilities have different meanings to the subclasses. They must be implemented differently for each of the three classes. For example, `Book` sets a different due date than `Video`. The late fees also vary among `Book`, `Video`, and `CD`.

To guarantee that the subclasses consider these differences, two `Lendable` methods will now be declared `abstract`. An `abstract` method in a superclass must be implemented by each subclass. Otherwise, compiletime errors occur whenever a programmer extends the superclass and forgets to implement the `abstract` method. Declaring the methods that must be implemented in all subclasses is good design. Rather than having a method body, the `abstract` method headings have a semicolon[1] (this abstract `Lendable` class is growing, but is not yet complete).

```
// Provide access to anyone interested in the amount of the late
// fee, for example to a librarian returning a book. Since each
// class that extends Lendable has different due-date and late-fee
// rules, each class must specialize this method.
abstract public double getLateFee( );
```

---

1. Notice the similarity between an abstract method heading in a class and a method heading in an interface. Both need to be implemented by some other class.

```
// Each class that extends Lendable must implement checkSelfOut to
// fulfill its borrow responsibility. The method implemented in all
// subclasses calls Lendable's checkSelfOut. The subclass's method
// must pass two arguments when it calls checkOutAnyLendable:
//    1) The ID of the borrower.
//    2) The length of the borrow (in days) for the particular class.
abstract public void checkSelfOut( String borrowerID );

// Other methods will be added to Lendable
```

Looking ahead to how other classes will fit into this inheritance hierarchy, consider how Book could implement one abstract method. checkSelfOut passes the Borrower's ID along with its own length of borrow.

```
public class Book extends Lendable
{
  public static final int DAYS_TO_BORROW_BOOK = 14;

  // ... TBA

  public void checkSelfOut( String borrowerID ) // Must write this
  { // Book can use Lendable's protected method. The second argument
    // will be used in the superclass to set the due date.
    checkOutAnyLendable( borrowerID, Book.DAYS_TO_BORROW_BOOK );
  }
}
```

Now when Book is sent a message checkSelfOut("Kim"), checkSelfOut sends Lendable the message checkOutAnyLendable("Kim", 14). Other subclasses can pass along a different second argument—whatever is appropriate for the subclass.

The alternative to the design decisions made for the Lendable hierarchy would be to use explicit case analysis—determine the type of the object at runtime by comparing it to all known subclasses in the inheritance hierarchy.[2]

Explicit Case Analysis (an alternative to polymorphism but a bad design)

```
protected void checkOutAnyLendable( String borrowerID )
{
  // Record who is borrowing this Lendable
  my_borrowerID = borrowerID;

  // Mark this Lendable as no longer available to be borrowed
  my_availability = false;

  // Set the new due date by the correct number of days passed as
  // an argument by the particular class that extends Lendable.
  int borrowLength = 0;
```

---

2. Java's instanceof operator can be used to compare an object to class names. Each object knows what class it is.

```
     // Explicit case analysis--bad design.
     if( this instanceof Book )
       borrowLength = 14;
     else if( this instanceof CD )
       borrowLength = 7;
     else if( this instanceof Video )
       borrowLength = 2;
     else
       System.out.println( "You forgot to add if...else your new class " );

     // Set the due date after examining the type of this object
     my_dueDate = new DayCounter( );
     my_dueDate.adjustDaysBy( borrowLength );
}
```

But consider what happens in this alternative design if another type of Lendable were added to the inheritance hierarchy, an AudioTape or Periodical perhaps. This checkOutAnyLendable method would have to be changed. This would make for more difficult maintenance later on. The programmer adding the new class may forget to add another else if. Worse yet, if the DAYS_TO_BORROW_ for a particular Lendable changed, say from 14 days to 21 for a Book, a change would have to be made outside of the Book class. Two classes would need to be changed, not one. Changing more classes during maintenance not only requires more work, it also introduces more chances for new errors. Besides, it seems logical that this modification be constrained to the class that has the detail.

The better design is to limit the number of classes that need to be changed. Changing one class is better than changing two. This is not much of a problem in a small inheritance hierarchy, but if there were 57 BankAccount classes in a hierarchy or 2,157 Transaction classes (which are real-world possibilities), the maintenance would be much more difficult. The design being proposed here is an attempt to avoid explicit case analysis.

Object-Oriented Design Guideline 10-2

If you have to make a decision based on different types of objects (explicit case analysis), implement an inheritance hierarchy to allow for polymorphic messages.

Since each object knows what class it is, the redundant type-checking is not necessary. It will be easier to add a few Lendable classes later by planning for them now. The length of borrow can be constrained to the type of Lendable being borrowed, which is possible through polymorphism.

Polymorphism to the Rescue

The abstract `checkSelfOut` method requires that programmers extending `Lendable` implement a `checkSelfOut` method with the same method heading. Compiletime errors result otherwise. For example, here is a start to another class that `extends Lendable`:

```
public class Video extends Lendable
{
  public final static int DAYS_TO_BORROW_VIDEO = 2;

  // ... TBA

  public void checkSelfOut( String borrowerID )
  { // Let each class specify the length of borrow.
    // If this method is not implemented the compiler will complain.
    checkOutAnyLendable( borrowerID, Video.DAYS_TO_BORROW_VIDEO );
  }

} // End class Video
```

Now the detail of the days to borrow is constrained to the class that specifies this information. If the days to borrow a `Video` changes, the change to the system is limited to one class: `Video`.

Polymorphism now ensures the appropriate behavior. Instead of performing explicit case analysis in `Lendable`, sending a `Video` object a `checkSelfOut` message invokes `Video`'s `checkSelfOut` method. Sending a `Book` object a `checkSelfOut` message invokes the `checkSelfOut` method of the `Book` class. Both methods invoke the `protected` method that takes care of most of the details of checking out a `Lendable`. This consistency—implemented in the abstract `checkSelfOut` method—makes for easier maintenance later on. It will also make it easier to add other classes to the `Lendable` inheritance hierarchy. The downside of this is that there is more work up front.

There is another benefit to this design of the `Lendable` inheritance hierarchy. The `Book`, `CD`, and `Video` classes delegate to the `protected` `checkOutAnyLendable` method. This is convenient since the `Lendable` methods can modify the private instance variables, while the subclasses cannot. The data remains safe and private to `Lendable`, and the code is simpler.

Most importantly, the code that is common for all of the subclasses is the same for all types of `Lendables`. The programmer does not need to write the same code many times. When the common behavior of `checkingOutAnyLendable` needs to be changed later on, it can be done in one location. It will be in effect for all classes in the hierarchy. These are two more justifications for having abstract classes capture common responsibilities.

getLateFee

You just saw checkSelfOut and checkOutAnyLendable working together to accomplish the checking out responsibility. This is typical in a **class hierarchy**. The common responsibility implemented in a superclass is put to use by instances of its subclasses. This can also happen in the other abstract method getLateFee, which must also be implemented by all of the subclasses of Lendable. This time, the getLateFee method of Book asks Lendable for help.

1. Is this Lendable available (a check for the exceptional case of returning a book that is not available)?
2. How many days late is it (if daysLate returns an int less than or equal to 0, the late fee is 0.00)?

By placing the abstract method in the superclass, the late policy must be specified by the subclass, which is the logical place to implement the policy.

```
/** Compute a late fee appropriate for Books only.
  * @return the late fee of this Book, which will be 0.0 if
  * this Book is not overdue.
  */
public double getLateFee( )
{
  if( this.isAvailable( ) ) // The Lendable is not even checked out!
    return 0.00;
  else
  { // A positive daysLate means that the due date is in the past.
    int daysOverdue = daysLate( );
    if( daysOverdue > 0 ) // The book is overdue.
      return daysOverdue * Book.BOOK_LATE_DAY_FEE;
    else
      return 0.00; // The due date is in the future
  }
}
```

The need for a daysLate method in Lendable was not recognized until getLateFee was being implemented in Book. It was simply added to Lendable later.

```
/** Determine how many days late this Lendable is.
  * @return the number of days, which could be negative
  * indicating the number of days until the Lendable is due.
  */
public int daysLate( )
{
  int result = 0;
  if( ! isAvailable( ) )
  {
    DayCounter today = new DayCounter( );
    result = my_dueDate.daysFrom( today );
  }
  return result;
}
```

This `Lendable` method can be used by all subclasses. Whereas the `Lendable` class can directly reference the instance variable `my_dueDate`, the subclasses cannot. Fortunately, with the due date accessible in `checkOutAnyLendable`, the superclass can compute days late for any of its subclasses.

The `daysLate` method was made `public` because it could prove useful to the `Librarian` at some point. If it had been made `protected`, the `Librarian` could not use it. As a `public` method, any `Lendable` can be asked to return the days late or the days until the due date.

Constructors in Subclasses

Now that `Lendable`'s two abstract methods have been shown, consider one subclass: `Book`. Like all `Lendable` objects, a `Book` needs a call number and a title (it was also determined that all `Lendable` objects could have a title). The `Book` class adds an instance variable to store the author's name. So the constructor now requires three arguments.

```
Book aBook = new Book( "QA76.1", "Data Structures", "Mike Berman" );
```

Normally, we could write a `Book` constructor with three `String` parameters that initializes its instance variables.

```
// This class will inherit all public and protected members of Lendable
public class Book extends Lendable
{
  // Book adds an instance variable
  private String my_author

  public Book( String callNumber, String title, String author )
  {
    my_callNumber = callNumber; // Compiletime errors: my_callNumber
    my_title = initTitle;       // and my_title are not accessible
    my_author = author;
  }
  // ...
}
```

However, a `Book` cannot directly reference its inherited instance variables. They were declared private. One choice is to add two methods to initialize the instance variables of `Book` objects; `setCallNumber( callNumber )` and `setTitle( title )`, for example. But this extra work is unnecessary.

The better design is to have `Book` pass along the initializing information to the constructor in `Lendable`. After all, the `Lendable` constructor has access to the `private` instance variables that `Book` needs to initialize. More importantly, `Lendable` also needs to initialize other common instance variables; `my_availability` = true, for example.

```
public abstract class Lendable
{
  // ... See the constructor below for instance variable names

  // Constructor needs a callNumber. A title is added since it
  // seems that all Lendables will have a title of some sort.
  public Lendable( String callNumber, String initTitle )
  {
    my_callNumber = callNumber;
    my_title = initTitle;
    my_borrowerID = null;
    my_dueDate = null;
    my_availability = true;
  }
```

The better design is to have the Book's constructor pass along what it can to the superclass's constructor. At that point, Lendable's constructor can do whatever is appropriate for all Lendable objects. The question is how can Lendable's constructor be invoked from Book's constructor?

Recall that the keyword this is a reference to the entire object in any method. Java has another keyword named super to reference methods in superclasses. For Book to call Lendable's constructor, it uses super to pass the parameters it receives as the arguments up to the superclass constructor.

```
public class Book extends Lendable
{
  // Instance variable added to those inherited from Lendable.
  private String my_author;

  // Initialize a Book object.
  public Book( String callNumber, String title, String author )
  { // Call the superclass constructor
    super( callNumber, title );

    // Then Book initializes its own instance variable
    // (Lendable is unaware of it)
    my_author = author;
  }
```

Both arguments to construct a Book are passed up the inheritance hierarchy to the Lendable constructor. Then Lendable initializes the private instance variables that Book cannot.

Since Lendable only has one constructor with two parameters, the constructor in Book must supply precisely two arguments with the super message. After Lendable initializes the five instance variables, control returns to Book's constructor. This is where the one instance variable unique to Book (my_author) gets initialized. Lendable does not know about my_author. The Book subclass must initialize the instance variable the subclass has added, which in this case is my_author.

Another Use of super

The keyword super is also used to explicitly invoke a superclass method; super is written as the first part of the message. For example, the selfCheckOut method in Book may explicitly call the superclass's checkOutAnyLendable method as follows:

```
public void checkSelfOut( String borrowerID )
{ // Let each class specify the length of borrow.
  // If this method is not implemented the compiler will complain.
  super.checkOutAnyLendable( borrowerID, 2 );
}
```

The keyword super is sometimes optional (as is the keyword this). You may use super to explicitly show that the code in a subclass is calling a method in the superclass (this makes the code more understandable). However, in the earlier code for checkSelfOut, super was not used. super is optional. Java's compiler and the runtime system will search the superclass for a method it can't find in a subclass. It often doesn't matter whether you start the message with super. However, sometimes super is required. Consider adding a toString method to a Book that starts "I am a book: " and then concatenates the toString version of its superclass for a consistent arrangement of state.

```
public String toString( )
{
  return "I am a book: " + super.toString( );
}
```

Without super before toString, this toString method would call itself endlessly. Here, super is required.

Calling super Automatically

It turns out that the message super( ) is the first method executed in a constructor even if you don't supply it. Java adds the following code for you automatically:

```
super( );   // Call the constructor of any subclass's superclass
```

This means that the following two classes with different code in the constructors are equivalent. Both invoke the default constructor of the Object class, whether super( ) is written or not:

```
public class SubClass extends Object      public class SubClass extends Object
{                                         {
  private int anInt;                        private int anInt;

  public SubClass( int intValue )           public SubClass( int intValue )
  { // Version 1                            { // Equivalent to Version 1
                                              super( );
    anInt = intValue;                         anInt = intValue;
  }                                         }
}                                         }
```

Java automatically adds `super( )` as the first statement in every constructor to ensure that all of the constructors call all constructors all the way up to the constructor in `Object`. The constructor in `Object` in turn asks the operating system for the memory needed to store the object (and also performs other necessary initializations).

Testing the Book Class

The `Book` class, a subclass of `Lendable`, is now shown in its entirety. After that, test code will illustrate the behavior of `Book` objects.

```java
/**
 *   A concrete realization of Lendable.
 *
 *   This class implements Lendable's two abstract methods:
 *       1. checkSelfOut
 *       2. getLateFee
 *
 *   Also, one new instance variable and one new accessor method are added:
 *       1. my_author
 *       2. getAuthor( )
 */
public class Book extends Lendable
{ // Class constants that can be referenced by other objects
  public static final int DAYS_TO_BORROW_BOOK = 14;
  public static final double BOOK_LATE_DAY_FEE = 0.50;

  // Instance variable added to those inherited from Lendable.
  private String my_author;

/** Initialize a Book object.
  * @param callNumber: The unique identifier to find this Book.
  * @param title: The title of this Book.
  * @param author: The author of this book.
  */
  public Book( String callNumber, String title, String author )
  {
    super( callNumber, title );   // Invoke Lendable's constructor
    my_author = author;
  }

// Accessing methods

/** Find out the author of this Book.
  * @return the author's name.
  */
  public String getAuthor( )
  {
    return my_author;
  }
```

```
// Modifying methods (the two abstract methods in Lendable)
// This class must implement both because this class extends Lendable.

/** Modify the state of this object so it is borrowed.
 * @param borrowerID: The String identification of the borrower.
 */
public void checkSelfOut( String borrowerID  )
{
    checkOutAnyLendable( borrowerID, Book.DAYS_TO_BORROW_BOOK );
}

/** Compute a late fee appropriate for Books only.
 * @return the late fee of this Book, which will be 0.0 if
 * this Book is not overdue.
 */
public double getLateFee( )
{
  if( this.isAvailable( ) )   // The Lendable is not even checked out!
    return 0.00;
  else
  { // A positive daysLate means that the due date is in the past
    int daysOverdue = this.daysLate( );
    if( daysOverdue > 0 )  // The book is overdue.
      return daysOverdue * Book.BOOK_LATE_DAY_FEE;
    else
      return 0.00; // The due date is in the future
  }
}

// The test driver was removed from here because it was so long.
// It is explained below.

} // End class Book
```

The test driver code is in the main method of the Book class. While implementing the Book class, this ever-present test driver made it much easier to test the class, as changes were made not only to Book, but also to Lendable (in an inheritance hierarchy, a change to the superclass may change the behavior of all subclasses). Therefore, it helped to keep a main method in the Book class. This test driver will now be explained in pieces. For the complete test driver, see the file Book.java.

The test driver begins by constructing one Book object. A message attempts to return the book before it is checked out. This should result in an error message, which it does.

```
Book aBook = new Book( "QA76.1", "Data Structures", "Mike Berman" );

// Send a few messages
System.out.println( "  current state: " + aBook.toString( ) );
```

```
// Try to check in a book that is not checked out
System.out.print( "Error? " );
aBook.checkSelfIn( );          // This is not allowed, but it could happen
```

Output

```
current state: QA76.1 'Data Structures': available
Error? *ERROR* QA76.1 is not checked out
```

The remaining test driving code prints the expected output from the message, followed by a question mark, followed by actual output when the program runs. This approach made it easier to find errors by comparing the left column of output to the right column of output.

```
System.out.println( " available true? " + aBook.isAvailable( ) );
System.out.println( "  overdue false? " + aBook.isOverdue( ) );
System.out.println( "  borrower null? " + aBook.getBorrowerID( ) );
aBook.checkSelfOut( "KIM" );
System.out.println( "available false? " + aBook.isAvailable( ) );
System.out.println( "  overdue false? " + aBook.isOverdue( ) );
System.out.println( "  current state: " + aBook.toString( ) );
System.out.println( "   Late fee 0.0? " + aBook.getLateFee( ) );
System.out.println( "   borrower KIM? " + aBook.getBorrowerID( ) );
System.out.println( "   call# QA76.1? " + aBook.getCallNumber( ) );
System.out.println( "Data Structures? " + aBook.getTitle( ) );
```

Output (for running the program on June 10, 2002)

```
 available true? true
  overdue false? false
  borrower null? null
available false? false
  overdue false? false
  current state: QA76.1 'Data Structures': due 2002/6/24, KIM
   Late fee 0.0? 0.0
   borrower KIM? KIM
   call# QA76.1? QA76.1
Data Structures? Data Structures
```

Notice that many of the messages sent to this Book object were inherited from Lendable:

- isAvailable
- isOverdue
- getBorrowerID
- toString
- getCallNumber
- getTitle

When you send a message to an object, the method that executes may be from a class higher up in the class hierarchy. On the other hand, the object's class might implement the message, as in the case of the two abstract methods of Lendable implemented by Book:

- `getLateFee`
- `checkSelfOut`

Whether inherited from `Lendable` or implemented in `Book`, all `Book` objects understand the messages shown in this part of the test driver.

After all possible messages were sent to one `Book` object, the test driver was expanded to see how `Book` objects behaved in an array. The following test code also demonstrates that the polymorphic `toString` message sent to `Book` objects actually executes the `toString` method in `Lendable`:

```
// Build a small array of Book objects
Book[] books = new Book[4];

books[0] = aBook;  // aBook was constructed as checked out
books[1] = new Book( "QA76.2", "Karel the Robot", "Rich Pattis" );
books[2] = new Book( "QA76.3", "Oh Pascal", "Mike Clancy" );
books[3] = new Book( "QA76.4", "A C.S. Tapestry", "Owen Astrachan" );

// Show the state of all Books in the array
System.out.println( "Current list of books: " );
for( int index = 0; index < books.length; index++ )
   System.out.println( books[index].toString( ) );
```

Output

```
Current list of books:
QA76.1 'Data Structures': due 2002/6/26, KIM
QA76.2 'Karel the Robot': available
QA76.3 'Oh Pascal': available
QA76.4 'A C.S. Tapestry': available
```

The test driver also sends modifying messages to the `Book` objects stored in the array. `aBook` is checked back in. The three other `Book` objects are checked out.

```
books[0].checkSelfIn( );
books[1].checkSelfOut( "JO" );
books[2].checkSelfOut( "JO" );
books[3].checkSelfOut( "JO" );

// Show the state of all Books in the list
System.out.println( "\nList of books after other check-outs and -ins: " );
for( int index = 0; index < books.length; index++ )
   System.out.println( books[index].toString( ) );
```

Output (for running the program on June 12, 2002)

```
List of books after other check-outs and -ins:
QA76.1 'Data Structures': available
QA76.2 'Karel the Robot': due 2002/6/26, JO
QA76.3 'Oh Pascal': due 2002/6/26, JO
QA76.4 'A C.S. Tapestry': due 2002/6/26, JO
```

Overdue Books

Two other methods can be tested only if the due date is adjusted: `getLateFee` and `isOverdue`. To accomplish this, a `protected setLateFee` method was added to the `Lendable` class. This means that all subclasses of `Lendable` will understand the message `setLateFee`. After a book was checked out and the due date was set into the past, these two methods were tested with this code:

```
System.out.println( "\nTest when book is overdue" );
DayCounter thirtyDaysAgo = new DayCounter( );
thirtyDaysAgo.adjustDaysBy( -30 );
Book overdue = new Book( "Q", "Overdue", "Late fee = 30 * 0.50" );
overdue.checkSelfOut( "Kim" );
System.out.println( "Correct due date: " + overdue.getDueDate( ) );
System.out.println( "false? " + overdue.isOverdue( ) );
System.out.println( "0.00? " + overdue.getLateFee( ) );
overdue.setDueDate( thirtyDaysAgo );
System.out.println( "Modified due date: " + overdue.getDueDate( ) );
System.out.println( "true? " + overdue.isOverdue( ) );
System.out.println( "15.00? " + overdue.getLateFee( ) );
```

Output (for running the program on November 12, 2002)

```
Test when book is overdue
Correct due date: 2001/11/26
false? false
0.00? 0.0
Modified due date: 2001/10/13
true? true
15.00? 15.0
```

The output shows that after the due date is set to 30 days in the past, the late fee is correctly 15.00 and the `Book` is overdue.

The `Video` Class

`Video` is another subclass that needs to be implemented. Because `Video` extends `Lendable`, it too must implement the abstract methods of `Lendable`. `Video` also inherits the public `Lendable` methods, just like `Book`. Inheritance makes it easier to add new subclasses.

The code in `Book` provides an example of how to add another subclass to the inheritance hierarchy. (*Note:* Adding a CD class to this hierarchy is left as a programming project at the end of this chapter.) The difference is in how the abstract methods are implemented. The `getLateFee` method of `Video` shows that these methods vary by more than just an integer value. `Video` does not simply multiply the late fee by some constant.

```
/**
 *   A concrete realization of Lendable.
 *   This class implements Lendable's two abstract methods
 *      1. checkSelfOut
 *      2. getLateFee
 *   No new instance variables or methods are added.
 */
public class Video extends Lendable
{ // Class constants
   public final static int DAYS_TO_BORROW_VIDEO = 2;
   public final static double FIRST_DAY_LATE_FEE = 5.00;
   public final static double ADDITIONAL_DAY_FEE = 1.50;

  // No additional instance variables have been added

/** Initialize a Video object
  * @param callNumber: The unique identifier
  * @param title: The title of this Lendable
  */
   public Video( String callNumber, String title )
   {
      // Delegate all initialization to Lendable's two-parameter constructor
      super( callNumber, title );

   }

// Modifying methods (the two abstract methods in Lendable)
// This class must implement both because this class extends Lendable.

/** Modify the state of this object so it is borrowed.
  * @param borrowerID: The String identification of the borrower.
  */
   public void checkSelfOut( String borrowerID )
   { // Record who is borrowing this and inform Lendable of the days
      super.checkOutAnyLendable( borrowerID, Video.DAYS_TO_BORROW_VIDEO );
   }

/** Compute a late fee appropriate for Videos only.
  * @return the late fee of this Video, which will be 0.0 if not overdue.
  */
   public double getLateFee( )
   {
      if( this.isAvailable( ) )   // The lendable is not even checked out!
         return 0.00;
      else
      {
         // A positive daysOverdue means that the due date is in the past.
         int daysOverdue = this.daysLate( );

         if( daysOverdue <= 0 )
            return 0.00; // The due date is in the future
         else if( daysOverdue == 1 )
            return FIRST_DAY_LATE_FEE;
         else // Must be more than one day late.
```

```
            return FIRST_DAY_LATE_FEE + ( daysOverdue - 1 ) *
                    Video.ADDITIONAL_DAY_FEE;
        }
    }

    // Test driver
    public static void main( String[] args )
    {
        Video aVideo = new Video( "VIDEO1", "The Matrix" );

        //        ... The test driver code is removed to save space ...
        // The test driver is similar to the main method in the Book class.
        // The late fees were tested more extensively--they were more complex.
        // To see the test code and its output, load and run Video.java.
    }

}  // End class Video
```

Self-Check

Use the following three classes and the given constructions below to answer the questions that follow:

```
public class One                          public class Two extends One
{                                         {
    public String toString( )                 public String toString( )
    {                                         {
        return "one";                             return "two/" +
    }                                                     super.toString( );
                                              }
    public void methodOne( )
    {                                         public void methodOne( )
        System.out.println( "aaa" );          {
        methodTwo( );                             System.out.println( "ccc" );
    }                                             super.methodOne( );
                                              }
    public void methodTwo( )
    {                                         public void methodTwo( )
        System.out.println( "bbb" );          {
    }                                             System.out.println( "ddd" );
}                                             }
                                          }
```

```
public class Three extends One
{
    public void methodOne( )
    {
     System.out.println( "eee" );
    }

    public void methodThree( )
    {
        System.out.println( "fff" );
    }
}
```

```
// Initialize some objects
One aOne = new One( );
One aTwo = new Two( );
Three aThree = new Three( );
```

10-10 Write the output generated by the following code:

```
System.out.println( aOne );
System.out.println( aTwo );
System.out.println( aThree );
```

10-11 Write the output generated by the following code:

```
aOne.methodOne( );
System.out.println( "---" );
aTwo.methodOne( );
System.out.println( "---" );
aThree.methodOne( );
```

10-12 Write the output generated by the following code:

```
aOne.methodTwo( );
System.out.println( "---" );
aTwo.methodTwo( );
System.out.println( "---" );
aThree.methodTwo( );
```

10-13 Which of the following will generate a compiletime syntax error?

-**a**   `aOne.methodThree( );`

-**b**   `aTwo.methodThree( );`

-**c**   `aThree.methodThree( );`

10-14 For each of the following, write "OK," "Compiletime error," or "Runtime error" to indicate whether the code is valid or generates an error:

-**a**   `Two obj1 = new One( );`

-**b**   `One obj2 = (One)aTwo;`

-**c**   `One obj3 = (Three)aTwo;`

-**d**   `Object obj = new Three( );`

-**e**   `Three tre = new Two( );`

10-15 For each of the following, write the output the message generates, "Compiletime error," or "Runtime error" to indicate whether the code is valid or generates an error:

```
Object o = new Two( );
```

-**a**   `( (Three)o ).methodTwo( );`

-**b**   `( (Two)o ).methodTwo( );`

-**c**   `System.out.println( o );`

-**d**   `( (Object)o ).methodOne( );`

10.3   LendableList — A Heterogeneous Collection

The power of inheritance and polymorphism are very useful when you need to store a collection of objects that are not of the same type. Consider the LendableList class. Its CRC card shows that LendableList collaborates with Lendable and an array (although this may vary).

class LendableList	
Responsibilities	**Collaborators**
addLendable(Lendable)	Lendable
getLendableWithCallNumber	array of Lendables

This collection will be used to store references to Book, Video, and CD objects. It could also store references to any other new subclass added to the Lendable hierarchy. For now, a LendableList must be able to store three different types of objects. The trick is to use the Lendable class name to represent any type of Lendable. This works because references to a superclass (Lendable) can also refer to instances of the subclasses (Book, Video, and CD). The following code stores references to seven Lendable objects, representing three different types of Lendables:

```
Lendable[] item = new Lendable[7];
item[0] = new Video( "VIDEO1", "A Man Called Horse" );
item[1] = new CD( "CD1", "Lives in the Balance", "Jackson Browne" );
item[2] = new Book( "QA76.2", "Karel the Robot", "Rich Pattis" );
item[3] = new CD( "CD2", "Back in the High Life", "Steve Winwood" );
item[4] = new Video( "VIDEO2", "Never Say Never" );
item[5] = new Book( "QA76.4", "A C.S. Tapestry", "Owen Astrachan" );
item[6] = new CD( "CD3", "Revolver", "Beatles" );
```

The elements in Lendable are not Lendable objects. The elements in the array are references to objects from subclasses that extend Lendable. Here is a picture of memory, indicating that the array refers to different types of Lendables:

Reference   **Type of Lendable**

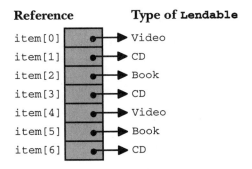

item[0]   ──► Video
item[1]   ──► CD
item[2]   ──► Book
item[3]   ──► CD
item[4]   ──► Video
item[5]   ──► Book
item[6]   ──► CD

Polymorphism allows the same message to be sent to every object in a collection, even though those objects are instances of different classes. The same message activates different methods. For example, if the array element stores a reference to a Book, Book's checkSelfOut executes. However, if the array element refers to a Video, Video's checkSelfOut executes. Consider the following code, which executes three different methods with one polymorphic message:

```
item[4].checkSelfOut( "JO" );
item[5].checkSelfOut( "JO" );
item[6].checkSelfOut( "JO" );

for( int index = 0; index < item.length; index++ )
  System.out.println( index + ") " + item[index] );
```

The output shows that the due dates differ among the three types of objects.

Output (for running the program on June 12, 2002)

```
0) VIDEO1 'A Man Called Horse': available
1) CD1 'Lives in the Balance': available
2) QA76.2 'Karel the Robot': available
3) CD2 'Back in the High Life': available
4) VIDEO2 'Never Say Never': due 2002/11/06, JO
5) QA76.4 'A C.S. Tapestry': due 2002/11/18, JO
6) CD3 'Revolver': due 2002/11/11, JO
```

The following class uses an array instance variable to store data. It also provides a method to return the Lendable with a given call number (or returns null if the call number is not found). Also present is a method named iterator to allow programmers to iterate over this collection in the same fashion as other Java collection classes, such as ArrayList. This collection class was designed as a summary of arrays to store a collection, as described in Chapter 8, "Arrays." The new thing here is that the array elements may store any type of Lendable. Other classes may be added to the class hierarchy later; the same collection will still work.

```java
/**
  A class that stores a collection of Lendable objects
*/
import java.util.Iterator; // This collection has an iterator method

public class LendableList
{
  public static final int INITIAL_CAPACITY = 10;
  public static final int GROWTH_SIZE = 100;  // Array increases if filled
  private Lendable[] my_collection;
  private int my_size;

/** Construct an empty collection of Lendable objects
  */
  public LendableList( )
  { // Can store only 100 Lendables
    my_collection = new Lendable[INITIAL_CAPACITY];
    my_size = 0;
  }

/** Add a lendable to this collection if it does not already exist.
  * @param aLendable: The object to be stored in this collection.
  * @return false if the call number is already in the collection.
  */
  public void add( Lendable aLendable )
  {
    // Grow the array when the size has reached the capacity
    if( my_size == my_collection.length )
    {
      Lendable[] temp = new Lendable[my_collection.length +
                  LendableList.GROWTH_SIZE];
      for( int j = 0; j < my_size; j++ )
        temp[j] = my_collection[j];
      my_collection = temp;
      temp = null;
    }

    // Store the reference at the end of the array
    my_collection[my_size] = aLendable;
    my_size++;
  }

/** Return a Lendable based on the ID.
  * @param callNumber: The key used to locate a particular Lendable.
  * @returns null if no Lendable had the callNumber or a reference to
  * the first Lendable found with a matching callNumber.
  */
  public Lendable getLendableWithCallNumber( String callNumber )
  {
    // Use sequential search (you will see a faster search in
    // Chapter 11, "More Arrays")
    int searchIndex = 0;
```

```
      // getCallNumber is understood by all Lendable objects
      while((searchIndex < my_size) &&
            (! callNumber.equals(my_collection[searchIndex].getCallNumber())))
      { // Look until there are no more or callNumber is found
        searchIndex++;
      }

      if( searchIndex == my_size )   // Did not find callNumber
        return null;
      else
        return( my_collection[searchIndex] );
    }

  /** Return java.util.Iterator with hasNext and next methods.
    */
    public Iterator iterator( )
    {
      return new LendableListIterator( );
    }

    // A private inner class to allow iteration over all Lendables
    private class LendableListIterator implements Iterator
    {
      // The methods of this inner class need my_collection and my_size
      // to iterate over all elements. An instance of this class also
      // must maintain the index of the next element to be returned by
      // the next method.
      private int index;

      // Initialize an iteration
      public LendableListIterator( )
      {
        index = 0;
      }

      // Returns true if the iteration has more elements.
      public boolean hasNext( )
      {
        return index < my_size;
      }

      // Returns the next element in the iteration
      public Object next()
      {
        Object result = my_collection[index];
        index++;
        return result;
      }
```

```java
    public void remove( )
    {
      throw new UnsupportedOperationException( );
    }

} // End of the private class that allows iteration


// Test drive the LendableList class
public static void main( String[] args )
{
    // First build a small collection of Lendables
    Video v1 = new Video( "VIDEO1", "A Man Called Horse" );
    CD c1 = new CD( "CD1", "Lives in the Balance", "Jackson Browne" );
    Book b1 = new Book( "QA76.2", "Karel the Robot", "Rich Pattis" );
    CD c2 = new CD( "CD2", "Back in the High Life", "Steve Winwood" );
    Video v2 = new Video( "VIDEO2", "Never Say Never" );

    LendableList theLendables = new LendableList( );
    theLendables.add( v1 );
    theLendables.add( c1 );
    theLendables.add( b1 );
    theLendables.add( c2 );
    theLendables.add( v2 );

    // Show all Lendables in the collection
    java.util.Iterator itr = theLendables.iterator( );
    int index = 0;
    while( itr.hasNext( ) )
    {
      System.out.println( index + ") " + itr.next( ) );
      index++;
    }

    System.out.println( "\nTest getLendableWithCallNumber" );
    System.out.println( "   null? " +
            theLendables.getLendableWithCallNumber("not here") );
    System.out.println( "QA76.2? " +
            theLendables.getLendableWithCallNumber("QA76.2"  ) );
    System.out.println( "    CD1? " +
            theLendables.getLendableWithCallNumber("CD1"     ) );
    System.out.println( "    CD2? " +
            theLendables.getLendableWithCallNumber("CD2"     ) );
    System.out.println( "VIDEO1? " +
            theLendables.getLendableWithCallNumber("VIDEO1"  ) );
    System.out.println( "VIDEO2? " +
            theLendables.getLendableWithCallNumber("VIDEO1"  ) );
    Lendable lendableOne =
            theLendables.getLendableWithCallNumber( "CD1" );
    Lendable lendableTwo =
            theLendables.getLendableWithCallNumber( "VIDEO2" );
```

```
         lendableOne.checkSelfOut( "Sam" );
         lendableTwo.checkSelfOut( "Jo" );

         System.out.println( "\nShow collection after two are borrowed:" );
         itr = theLendables.iterator( );
         while( itr.hasNext( ) )
         {
            System.out.println( itr.next( ) );
         }
      }
   }
}
```

Output (from the test driver)

```
0) VIDEO1 'A Man Called Horse': available
1) CD1 'Lives in the Balance': available
2) QA76.2 'Karel the Robot': available
3) CD2 'Back in the High Life': available
4) VIDEO2 'Never Say Never': available

Test getLendableWithCallNumber
  null? null
QA76.2? QA76.2 'Karel the Robot': available
   CD1? CD1 'Lives in the Balance': available
   CD2? CD2 'Back in the High Life': available
VIDEO1? VIDEO1 'A Man Called Horse': available
VIDEO2? VIDEO1 'A Man Called Horse': available

Show collection after two are borrowed:
VIDEO1 'A Man Called Horse': available
CD1 'Lives in the Balance': due 2001/11/11, Sam
QA76.2 'Karel the Robot': available
CD2 'Back in the High Life': available
VIDEO2 'Never Say Never': due 2001/11/06, Jo
```

Chapter Summary

- This chapter presented a case study for object-oriented software development that required many of the concepts presented in earlier chapters. It introduced CRC cards.
- The design of object-oriented systems begins by partitioning the desired system into objects and assigning responsibilities to those objects.
- Role-playing helps programmers understand a system better and can be used to assign responsibilities to objects.
- CRC cards record responsibilities and collaborators of an instance of a class.
- Assigning responsibilities to objects is an important part of object-oriented design.
- Scenarios help programmers identify and assign responsibilities.
- A collaborator helps another object fulfill a responsibility.

- An inheritance hierarchy is appropriate when several object share common behavior, share common data, and have at least one difference.
- An abstract class exists to capture common responsibilities.
- Abstract classes cannot be instantiated. They are meant to implement common responsibilities.
- Abstract methods must be implemented by a subclass (or a compiletime error will result).
- An abstract class captures commonalities among classes. The subclasses implement the differences.
- A protected method (or instance variable) is accessible to the class that declares it and any class that extends the class that declared it.
- checkOutAnyLendable is another example of a polymorphic message. It is understood by all Lendable objects (instances of any class that extends Lendable).
- A subclass can explicitly call the constructor of the class that it extends with the keyword super.
- A heterogeneous collection is implemented as an array of references to the superclass. In the case of Lendable, this allowed any type of subclass reference (such as Book or Video) to be stored in the same array.

Key Terms

abstract class	collaborator	scenario
abstract method	inheritance hierarchy	subclass
class hierarchy	protected	super
Class/Responsibility/	responsibility	superclass
Collaborator (CRC) card	role-playing	

Exercises

The answers to exercises marked with 🔅 are available in Appendix C.

1. Provide a first-draft design of the code for the abstract BankAccount class. The difference between BasicChecking and CheckingWithLoan is this: BasicChecking does not allow withdrawals of more than the balance, but CheckingWithLoan does. CheckingWithLoan does this by maintaining the amount of money "loaned." A Savings object earns interest.

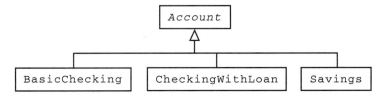

2. Provide a first-draft design of the three subclasses of Exercise 1.

 3. Complete an abstract class for a United States employee hierarchy to capture the responsibilities common to all employees. All U.S. employees have their gross pay calculated on an hourly basis with hours over 40 paid at 1.5 times the hourly rate. The differences between the derived classes is in the way the U.S. income tax gets computed for the purpose of withholding taxes from paychecks. All USEmployee objects should have getGrossPay and getIncomeTax (which differs between each subclass) methods.

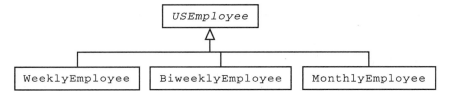

 4. Assuming that WeeklyEmployees pay 15% of their gross pay for income tax (this is not true, but it is much simpler than the real rules), completely implement the WeeklyEmployee class to be part of the USEmployee hierarchy described in Exercise 3.

 5. Given the following inheritance hierarchy, write the output generated by each of the statements in the main method that follows. Or write "Compiletime error" if one would occur.

```java
public abstract class Animal
{
  public void id( )
  {
    System.out.println( "I am an animal." );
  }
}

public class Cat extends Animal
{
  public void groom( )
  {
    System.out.print( "Prrr " );
    id( );
  }
}
```

```java
public class Dog extends Animal
{
  public void play( )
  {
    System.out.println( "RUFF BITE" );
  }
}

public class Calico extends Cat
{
  public void id( )
  {
    System.out.print( "I am a Calico and " );
    super.id( );
  }

  public void play( )
  {
    System.out.println( "MEOW SCRATCH" );
  }
}

public class Jungle
{
  public static void main( String [] args )
  {
    Cat mittens = new Cat( );
    Calico khali = new Calico( );
    Dog feedo = new Dog( );
    Animal anotherCat = new Cat( );

    mittens.id();              // a.
    khali.id();                // b.
    feedo.id();                // c.
    mittens.play();            // d.
    khali.play();              // e.
    feedo.play();              // f.
    mittens.groom();           // g.
    khali.groom();             // h.
    feedo.groom();             // i.
    anotherCat.id();           // j.
    anotherCat.groom();        // k.
    anotherCat.play();         // l.
    Animal a2 = new Animal( ); // m.
    feedo = khali;             // n.
  }
}
```

Programming Tips

1. **Collaborators work together.**
   Object-oriented software often has one object delegating responsibility to another object that may in turn delegate responsibility to another object. For example, when the `Librarian` sends a `checkSelfOut` message to a `Lendable`, `Lendable` in turn sends messages to `DayCounter`, which in turn sends messages to `GregorianCalendar`.

2. **Inheritance is but one part of object-oriented programming.**
   Not all systems require an inheritance hierarchy. If there is inheritance, so be it. If there is not, you are still developing the system in an object-oriented manner if you partition the system into objects with well-defined responsibilities.

3. **Use inheritance when you can generalize about two or more objects.**
   If you recognize that several objects have some common responsibilities, but there is some distinguishing behavior, inheritance might prove useful. However, with all the special considerations necessary to plan for adding new derived classes, it might not seem worth it.

4. **Heterogeneous lists can be useful.**
   Sometimes the polymorphism you get through inheritance is the best way to go. For example, consider a window on your computer screen. It has a collection of other windows, buttons, menus, selection lists, icons, and so on. Think of that window as a heterogeneous list of graphical components (kind of like `LendableList`). All graphics objects can be "drawn" in a screen, but they are drawn in different ways. When the window draws itself, the polymorphic `draw` message is applied to all the graphics in the window collection. There are some commonalities among the graphics objects. However, there are enough differences to justify many derived classes. This is an effective use of polymorphism through inheritance.

5. **Use polymorphism through inheritance when many responsibilities are the same.**
   As shown in Chapter 5, polymorphism can be achieved through the Java interface. However, when you have objects with common responsibilities that can be implemented only one way, inheritance can help you build the system more quickly.

6. **Make some methods protected.**
   Don't clutter the public interface with methods that no one needs to know about. If you have an inheritance hierarchy and a method is needed in

subclasses but not by anyone else, declare these methods with `protected` access.

Programming Projects

10A Implement CD

Completely implement and test the CD class as a class derived from `Lendable`.

10B Implement `Borrower` and `BorrowerList`

Completely implement and test the `Borrower` and `BorrowerList` classes.

10C Complete the Library

Write an event-driven program with a graphical user interface that allows any number of borrowers to borrow and return things that can be borrowed from a library. A borrower should also be able to check its current status and pay fines. Make the system persistent. Check for errors. Make up your own small collections of `Borrowers` and `Lendables`. Use your own design of the GUI or the one suggested here.

10D Refactoring

Modify the design of the following three classes into the inheritance hierarchy shown below:

```
public class Point                      public class Rectangle
{                                       {
  private int my_xPos;                    private Point my_upperLeft;
  private int my_yPos;                    private double my_width;
                                          private double my_height;
  public Point( int x,
                int y )                   public Rectangle( int x, int y,
  {                                                          double height,
    my_xPos = x;                                             double width )
    my_yPos = y;                          {
  }                                         my_upperLeft = new Point( x, y );
                                            my_width = width;
  public int getX( )                        my_height = height;
  {                                       }
    return my_xPos;
  }                                       public int getX( )
                                          {
  public int getY( )                        return my_upperLeft.getX( );
  {                                       }
    return my_yPos;
  }                                       public int getY( )
}                                         {
                                            return my_upperLeft.getY( );
                                          }

                                          public double getArea( )
                                          {
                                            return my_width * my_height;
                                          }
                                        }

public class Circle
{
  private Point my_upperLeftCorner;
  private double my_radius;

  public Circle( int x, int y, double diameter )
  {
    my_upperLeftCorner = new Point( x, y );
    my_radius = diameter / 2;
  }

  public int getX( )
  {
    return my_upperLeftCorner.getX( );
  }

  public int getY( )
  {
    return my_upperLeftCorner.getY( );
  }

  public double getArea( )
  {
```

```
      return Math.PI * Math.pow( my_radius, 2 );
   }
}
```

These are the classes that should be refactored (changed) into a properly designed inheritance hierarchy. Capture all common responsibilities (methods and instance variables) in `Shape`. Implement all constructors and all methods. Include all instance variables. The `Circle` and `Rectangle` classes must behave exactly the same within the inheritance hierarchy as without. Remember that design issues are important.

Class Hierarchy to Be Designed

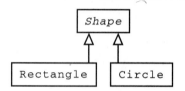

The following test driver for the `Circle` and `Rectangle` classes must generate the output shown:

```
// This test driver assumes that the Point, Circle, Rectangle,
// and Shape classes are in the same folder
public class TestShapes
{
   public static void main( String[] args )
   {
      // 10 pixels over, 10 pixels down
      Shape circle = new Circle( 10, 10, 2.0 );
      System.out.println( "area of circle: " + circle.getArea( ) );

      Shape rectangle = new Rectangle( 40, 10, 3.25, 5.75 );
      System.out.println( "area of rectangle: " + rectangle.getArea( ) );
   }
}
```

Output
```
area of circle: 3.141592653589793
area of rectangle: 18.6875
```

10E USEmployee Hierarchy

If you haven't already done so, complete Programming Project 6H, The `WeeklyEmployee` Class. Then read Exercise 3 of this chapter for the `USEmployee` hierarchy. Completely implement the superclass and the three subclasses suggested there. The tax tables for `BiweeklyEmployees` and `MonthlyEmployees` are in "Publication 15 Circular E, Employers Tax Guide." This document can be found at

http://www.irs.ustreas.gov/prod/forms_pubs/pubs.html. The tax table for
`WeeklyEmployees` is given in Programming Project 6H. *Note:* This project requires
a great deal of testing.

10F Mike and Marty's Bouncer Hierarchy[3]

This assignment is designed to test your understanding of inheritance and polymorphism in Java. You must implement an inheritance hierarchy of bouncing
objects that will be used in the `BouncingFun` program. `BouncingFun.java` is an
animated graphical view of all of the bounceable objects on the screen. The objects
move around the screen using their `move` methods. Each bouncing object has an
appearance, a size, a position, and a velocity. A diagram of a possible bouncing ball
is seen below. (*Note:* dx is the change in the velocity from left to right, or right to
left if negative.)

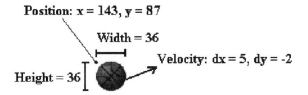

The bouncing objects should form an inheritance hierarchy with the `Bouncer` class
as its base. Your code should not allow the creation of any `Bouncer` objects. You
must implement the `Bouncer` class and the following four subclasses:
`BowlingBallBouncer`, `FootballBouncer`, `TennisBallBouncer`, and
`YoYoBouncer`. In addition to these, you must invent your own type of bouncing
object and include it in your system. The edge of the screen is represented by
objects of the `WallBouncer` class. This class has been written for you and is stored
in `WallBouncer.java`.

---

3. Thanks to Marty Stepp and Mike Brooks for developing this project.

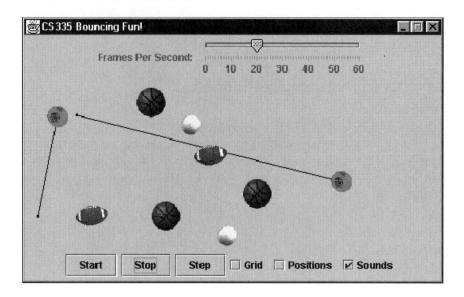

If a bouncing object hits a wall or another bouncing object, its bounce method will be called by the GUI to notify it that it has collided with something. The bounce method takes two arguments: a reference to the object that this `Bouncer` object ran into and an integer constant representing the relative direction of that `Bouncer` object. The constant could be `Bouncer.NORTH`, `Bouncer.SOUTH`, `Bouncer.EAST`, or `Bouncer.WEST`. If the relative direction is a combination of these, the bounce method will be called multiple times. For example, if a `FootballBouncer` named `my_fb` collided with a `YoYoBouncer` named `my_yoyo` that was to the northeast of it, the following calls would be made by the GUI:

```
my_fb.bounce( my_yoyo, Bouncer.NORTH );
my_fb.bounce( my_yoyo, Bouncer.EAST );
```

You must also implement a collection class named `BouncerSet`. A `BouncerSet` object should hold a collection that may contain any type of `Bouncer` object. As in mathematical sets, your `BouncerSet` should not allow duplicate elements to be stored. Duplicate elements are two references to the exact same `Bouncer` object; it is legal to have many `FootballBouncers` in the same set, but not two copies of the same `FootballBouncer`. You may, and are encouraged to, use one or more of Java's collection classes to help you write your set class. The `BouncerSet` should be passed to the program's graphical interface, which should use the set to draw the bouncing objects on the screen.

The program's graphical interface has been written for you. It contains controls to allow you to start, stop, and step (move ahead by one frame) the animation. An example of its appearance is above.

You are provided with the following classes:

class BouncingFun   Use this class to run the program.

class BounceFrame   This class represents the graphical user interface of the program. You do not have to make any modifications to it to complete the program. Your code should work with an unmodified version of this class.

class WallBouncer   This class represents the Bouncer for a wall on the edge of the screen. A WallBouncer does not move. It only exists because when a Bouncer hits a wall, it must be notified of this, so a WallBouncer object is passed to its bounce method.

You must write the following classes and methods:

You must write these classes and methods. You may write additional "helper" methods if you need them. You may even find it convenient to add a protected method.

class Bouncer

`public static final int NORTH, SOUTH, EAST, WEST`

These integer constants will be used to notify your bouncing objects from what direction they were hit.

`public Bouncer( String imageFileName, int x, int y, int dx, int dy )`

Constructs a new Bouncer with its upper-left corner at position (x, y), having velocity of (dx, dy) per move, and reading its image from the given file name.

`public int getX( )`

Returns this Bouncer's x coordinate.

`public int getY( )`

Returns this Bouncer's y coordinate.

`public int getWidth( )`

Returns this Bouncer's width in pixels.

`public int getHeight( )`

Returns this Bouncer's height in pixels.

`public int getDX( )`

Returns this Bouncer's velocity in the x direction; that is, how many x pixels this Bouncer object will move each time its move method is called.

`public int getDY( )`

Returns this Bouncer's velocity in the y direction; that is, how many y pixels this Bouncer object will move each time its move method is called.

```
public void setDX( int x )
```
Changes this `Bouncer`'s velocity in the x direction; that is, how many x pixels this `Bouncer` object will move each time its `move` method is called.

```
public void setDY( int y )
```
Changes this `Bouncer`'s velocity in the y direction; that is, how many y pixels this `Bouncer` object will move each time its `move` method is called.

```
public String getImageFileName( )
```
Returns the `String` representation of the file name of the image to draw for this `Bouncer`.

```
public void setWidth( int n )
```
Sets this `Bouncer`'s width in pixels to be the given amount.

```
public void setHeight( int n )
```
Sets this `Bouncer`'s height in pixels to be the given amount.

```
public void move( )
```
Adjusts this `Bouncer`'s position by adding its velocity in the x and y directions to its position.

Example: A Bouncer with position (x = 10, y = 10) and velocity of (dx = 5, dy = -2), should have position (x = 15, y = 8) after a call to `move`.

```
public String toString( )
```
Returns a `String` representation of this `Bouncer` object.

The format of this `String` should be a display of the `Bouncer`'s position in parentheses.

Example: A Bouncer object at position x = 50 and y = 22 should return (50, 22) from a call to its `toString` method.

```
public void bounce( Bouncer other, int direction )
```
Notifies this `Bouncer` that it has collided with another object that is in the given direction relative to it. The direction variable must be one of the following integer constants, which must be defined by you in your `Bouncer` class: NORTH, SOUTH, EAST, or WEST.

class BouncerSet

```
public BouncerSet( )
```
Constructs a new empty `BouncerSet`.

```
public void add( Bouncer b )
```
Adds the given `Bouncer` object to this `BouncerSet`, if it was not already present. If the given `Bouncer` is already in this `BouncerSet`, this method does nothing. (No duplicates!)

```
public Iterator getIterator( )
```
Returns an `Iterator` to sequentially access the contents of this `BouncerSet`. This is needed for the graphical interface to draw all of your bouncing objects. *Note:* If you use an `ArrayList` to store the set of `Bouncer` objects, you can simply return an `Iterator` with the `ArrayList` iterator method.

class **BowlingBallBouncer**

`public void bounce( Bouncer other, int direction )`

BowlingBallBouncer is only affected by collisions with the end walls of the screen or other bowling balls. When a bowling ball collides with something else, its velocity is unchanged. When a bowling ball does collide with a wall or with another bowling ball, its behavior is identical to the tennis ball; it rebounds in the appropriate opposite direction (see below).

Examples: If a bowling ball with velocity (dx = 12, dy = -4) bounces off of the wall to the NORTH, its velocity will become (dx = 12, dy = 4).

If a bowling ball with velocity (dx = 1, dy = -4) bounces off of a football that hits it from the EAST, the bowling ball's velocity remains (dx = 1, dy = -4).

class **FootballBouncer**

`public void bounce( Bouncer other, int direction )`

FootballBouncer bounces back in a somewhat random direction.

When a football bounces, the affected directional axis is pointed in the opposite direction and is given a random magnitude between 1 and 10. The other axis is given a random value between -10 and 10. The phrase "affected axis" means the axis where the collision occurred. On a collision from the EAST or WEST, this is the x axis. For a collision from the NORTH or SOUTH, this is the y axis.

Example: If a football with velocity (dx = 6, dy = -3) hits a wall to the EAST, its new velocity could randomly become (dx = -4, dy = -5)

or any pair of values such that -10 <= dx <= -1 and -10 <= dy <= 10.

The football's new velocity could *not* become (dx = 2, dy = -5) because the sign of x would be unchanged (it was positive before the bounce; it must be negative after).

class **TennisBallBouncer**

`public void bounce( Bouncer other, int direction )`

TennisBallBouncer bounces back in a mirror-image style, changing direction but not speed.

If the tennis ball bounces off of something to the EAST or WEST, it reverses its horizontal direction. If it bounces off of something to the NORTH or SOUTH, it reverses its horizontal direction.

Example: If a tennis ball with velocity (dx = 12, dy = -4) bounces off of something to the NORTH, its velocity becomes (dx = 12, dy = 4).

class **YoYoBouncer**

`public void bounce( Bouncer other, int direction )`

YoYoBouncer bounces back in the exact opposite direction, returning back where it came from.

The idea behind the yo-yo is that it starts from some initial position and travels at its initial velocity until it hits a wall or another bouncer object. When it hits something, it reverses direction and returns to its starting position. On any bounce, both its x and y velocities are reversed in direction and unchanged in magnitude.

Example: A yo-yo with initial position of (x = 10, y = 20) and initial velocity of (dx = 5, dy = -1) will move until it collides with something, at which point its velocity will become (dx = -5, dy = 1). When the yo-yo arrives back at its initial position of (x = 10, y = 20), it will bounce back and resume its initial velocity of (dx = 5, dy = -1).

```
public int getStartingX( )
```

Returns the starting x coordinate of this yo-yo, from when it was originally constructed.

```
public int getStartingY( )
```

Returns the starting y coordinate of this yo-yo, from when it was originally constructed.

Some hints:

- This project has several files that you will need to complete. They are located on the diskette in the folder named Ch10. This folder includes the .gif files needed to get the same picture as above (except for the .gif file you need to add for your own bouncer). Just pass the correct file name to the Bouncer constructor. For example, bowlingball.gif is the name of the file with a picture of a bowling ball. BowlingBallBouncer uses this file name as the first argument.

  ```
  BouncerSet bouncers = new BouncerSet( );
  bouncers.add( new BowlingBallBouncer( "bowlingball.gif", 40, 20, 5, 0 ) );
  ```

- Start out by writing "skeleton" versions of all the classes you must implement. Make the methods do anything; make them return 0 or null if necessary. Get the program to compile in this empty state and then incrementally write the classes.

- Do not try to read all of the graphical interface code and understand it! It is complex and beyond the level you should be at right now. The graphical code does call the methods of the code you will write, so it will not compile until you have provided your classes to it.

- Classes that are not going to be instantiated (no objects of the class will be created) should be declared abstract. Methods that you wish to declare in a superclass and implement in its subclasses should also be abstract.

Answers to Self-Check Questions

10-1 A Check-Out Algorithm (your answer may be different):
```
ID = user's ID
currentBorrower = theBorrowList.getBorrowerWith( ID )

callNumber = the call number of the Lendable to borrow
currentLendable = theLendableList( callNumber )

if( currentBorrower.canBorrow( currentLendable ) )
{
    currentLendable.checkSelfOut( currentBorrower )
    borrower.addLendable( currentLendable )
}
else
    tell user he or she cannot borrower
```

10-2 A Check-In Algorithm (your answer may be different):
```
ID = user's ID
currentBorrower = theBorrowList.getBorrowerWith( ID )

callNumber = the call number from the return item
currentLendable = theLendableList( callNumber )
double lateFees = currentLendable.getLateFees( )
if( lateFees > 0.00 )
    Try to get late fees from the borrower and credit borrower if possible
currentLendable.checkSelfIn( )
borrower.removeLendable(currentLendable)
```

10-3 `CheckingAccount`

10-4 `CheckingAccount`

10-5 `getLoanAmount` in `checkingWithLoan`

10-6 `credit, debit, getBalance,` and so on

10-7 `loanAmount`

10-8 `CheckingAccount`

10-9 `Object`

10-10 `one`
```
two/one
one
```

10-11 `aaa`
```
bbb
---
ccc
aaa
ddd
---
eee
```

10-12 `bbb`

   `---`

   `ddd`

   `---`

   `bbb`

10-13 a and b

10-14 -a Compiletime error

   -b OK

   -c Runtime error (a class cast exception)

   -d OK

   -e Compiletime error

10-15 -a Runtime error (a class cast exception)

   -b `ddd`

   -c `two/one`

   -d Compiletime error

Chapter 11
More Arrays

Summing Up

An earlier chapter introduced arrays for storing collections of primitive types and objects. You are now familiar with classes that have array instance variables.

Coming Up

This chapter begins by showing two algorithms used with arrays: selection sort and binary search. It also discusses Java arrays with two subscripts for managing data logically stored in a table-like format (in rows and columns). This structure proves useful for storing and managing data in many applications, such as electronic spreadsheets, games, topographical maps, and student record books. After studying this chapter, you will be able to

- understand how binary search finds elements more quickly than sequential search
- arrange array elements into ascending or descending order (sort them)
- implement and call `static` methods
- sort and search any array of `obj Comparables`
- declare arrays with two and three subscripts
- process data stored in rows and columns
- process two-dimensional array data row by row and column by column
- initialize two-dimensional arrays with file input
- use two-dimensional arrays as instance variables

Exercises and programming projects reinforce one- and two-dimensional array processing.

11.1   Binary Search

The **binary search** algorithm accomplishes the same function as sequential search
(see Chapter 8, "Arrays"). The binary search presented in this section finds things
more quickly. One of the preconditions is that the collection must be sorted (a
sorting algorithm is shown later).

The binary search algorithm works like this. If the array is sorted, half of the
elements can be eliminated from the search each time a comparison is made. This
is summarized in the following algorithm:

Algorithm: **Binary search, used with sorted arrays**

while the element is not found and it still may be in the array
{
    if the element in the middle of the array is the element being searched for
      store the reference and terminate the loop
   else
      eliminate the correct half of the array from further search
}

Each time the search element is not the element in the middle, the search can
be narrowed. If the search item is less than the middle element, you search only
the half that precedes the middle element. If the item being sought is greater than
the middle element, you search only the elements that are greater. The binary
search effectively eliminates half of the array elements from the search. By contrast, the sequential search only eliminates one element from the search field with
each comparison. Assuming that an array of strings is sorted in alphabetic order,
sequentially searching for `"Ableson"` does not take long. `"Ableson"` is likely to be
located near the front of the array elements. However, sequentially searching for
`"Zevon"` takes much more time, especially if the array is very big (with millions of
elements). The sequential search algorithm must first compare all of the names
beginning with A through Y before arriving at any names beginning with Z. Binary
search gets to `"Zevon"` much more quickly. When an array is very large, binary
search is much faster than sequential search.

The binary search algorithm has the following preconditions:

1. The array must be sorted (in ascending order, for now).
2. The indexes that reference the first and last elements must represent the
    entire range of meaningful elements.

The index of the element in the middle is computed as the average of the first and
last indexes. These three indexes—named `first`, `mid`, and `last`—are shown
below the array to be searched.

```
// This array is initialized so the element at index 0 is less than
// all of the others and the largest index stores a reference
// to the element that is larger than all of the other elements.

int n = 7;
String[] name = new String[n];
name[0] = "ABE";
name[1] = "CLAY";
name[2] = "KIM";
name[3] = "LAU";
name[4] = "LISA";
name[5] = "PELE";
name[6] = "ROY";

// Binary search needs several assignments to get things going
int first = 0;
int last = n - 1;
int mid = ( first + last ) / 2;
String searchString = "LISA";

// -1 will mean that the element has not yet been found
int indexInArray = -1;
```

Here is a more refined algorithm that will search as long as there are more elements to look at and the element has not yet been found.

Algorithm: **Binary search (more refined)**

while indexInArray is -1 and there are more array elements to look through
{
   if searchString is equal to name[mid] then
      let indexInArray = mid // *This indicates the array element equaled searchString*
   else if searchString alphabetically precedes name[mid]
      eliminate mid . . . last elements from the search
   else
      eliminate first . . . mid elements from the search
   mid = (first + last) / 2; // *Compute a new mid for next loop iteration (if there is one)*
}
// *At this point, indexInArray is either -1, indicating that searchString was not found,*
// *or in the range of 0 through n - 1, indicating that searchString was found.*

As the search begins, one of three things can happen (the code is searching for a String that equals searchString):

1. The element in the middle of the array equals searchString. The search is complete. Store mid into indexInArray to indicate where the String was found.

2. searchString is less than (alphabetically precedes) the middle element. The second half of the array can be eliminated from the search (last = mid - 1).

3. searchString is greater than the middle element. The first half of the array can be eliminated from the search field (first = mid + 1).

In the following code, if the String being searched for is not found, indexInArray remains -1. As soon as an array element is found to equal searchString, the loop terminates. The second part of the loop test stops the loop when there are no more elements to look at, when first becomes greater then last, or when the entire array has been examined.

```
// Binary search if searchString
// is not found and there are more elements to compare.
while( indexInArray == -1 && ( first <= last ) )
{
  // Check the three possibilities
  if( searchString.equals( name[mid] ) )
    indexInArray = mid; // 1. searchString is found
  else if( searchString.compareTo( name[mid] ) < 0 )
    last = mid - 1;      // 2. searchString may be in first half
  else
    first= mid + 1;      // 3. searchString may be in second half

  // Compute a new mid
  mid = ( first + last ) / 2;
} // End while

// indexInArray now either is -1 to indicate the String is not in
// the array or is the index of the first equal string.
```

At the beginning of the first loop iteration, the variables first, mid, and last are set as shown below. Notice that the array is in ascending order (binary search won't work otherwise).

Data before Comparing searchString ("LISA") to name[mid] ("LAU")

name[0]	"ABE"	⇐ first == 0
name[1]	"CLAY"	
name[2]	"KIM"	
name[3]	"LAU"	⇐ mid == 3
name[4]	"LISA"	
name[5]	"PELE"	
name[6]	"ROY"	⇐ last == 6

After comparing searchString to name[mid], first is increased from 0 to mid + 1, or 4; last remains 6; and a new mid is computed as (4 + 6) / 2 = 5.

name[0]	"ABE"		Because "LISA" is greater than name[mid],
name[1]	"CLAY"		the objects name[0] through name[3] no longer
name[2]	"KIM"		need to be searched through and can be eliminated from
name[3]	"LAU"		subsequent searches. That leaves only three possibilities.
name[4]	"LISA"	⟸	first == **4**
name[5]	"PELE"	⟸	mid == **5**
name[6]	"ROY"	⟸	last == 6

With mid == 5, "LISA".compareTo("PELE") < 0 is true. So last is decreased (5 - 1 = 4), first remains 4, and a new mid is computed as mid = (4 + 4) / 2 = 4.

name[0]	"ABE"	
name[1]	"CLAY"	
name[2]	"KIM"	
name[3]	"LAU"	
name[4]	"LISA"	⟸ mid == 4 ⟸ first == 4 ⟸ last == 4
name[5]	"PELE"	
name[6]	"ROY"	Because "LISA" is less than name[mid], eliminate name[6].

Now name[mid] does equal searchString ("LISA".equals("LISA")), so indexInArray = mid. The loop terminates because indexInArray is no longer -1. The following code after the loop and the output confirm that "LISA" was found in the array.

```
if( indexInArray == -1 )
  System.out.println( searchString + " not found" );
else
  System.out.println( searchString + " found at index " + indexInArray );
```

Output

```
LISA found at index 4
```

Terminating When searchName Is Not Found

Now consider the possibility that the data being searched for is not in the array—if searchString is "DEVON", for example.

```
// Get the index of DEVON if found in the array
String searchName = "DEVON";
```

This time the values of first, mid, and last progress as follows:

	first	mid	last	Comment
#1	0	3	6	Compare "DEVON" to "LAU"
#2	0	1	2	Compare "DEVON" to "CLAY"
#3	2	2	2	Compare "DEVON" to "ABE"
#4	2	**-1**	1	first <= last is false—the loop terminates

When the searchString ("DEVON") is not in the array, last becomes less than first (first > last). The two indexes have crossed each other. Here is another trace of binary search when the searched for element is not in the array.

		#1	#2	#3	#4
name[0]	"ABE"	⇐ first	⇐ first		
name[1]	"CLAY"		⇐ mid		**last**
name[2]	"KIM"		⇐ last	⇐ first, mid, last	**first**
name[3]	"LAU"	⇐ mid			
name[4]	"LISA"				
name[5]	"PELE"				
name[6]	"ROY"	⇐ last			

After searchString ("DEVON") was compared to name[2] ("KIM"), no further comparisons were necessary. Since DEVON is less than KIM, last becomes mid - 1, or 1. The new mid is computed, but it is never used as an index. This time, the second part of the loop test terminates the loop (2 <= 1 is false).

```
while( indexInArray == -1 && ( first <= last ) )
```

Since first is no longer less than or equal to last, searchString cannot be in the array. The indexInArray remains -1 to indicate that the element was not found.

Comparing Running Times

The binary search algorithm can be more efficient than the sequential search algorithm. Whereas sequential search only eliminates one element from the search per comparison, binary search eliminates half of the elements for each comparison. For example, when the number of elements (n) == 1,024, a binary search eliminates 512 elements from further search in the first comparison, 256 during the second comparison, then 128, 64, 32, 16, 4, 2, and 1.

When n is small, binary search is not much faster than sequential search. However, when n gets large, the difference in the time required to search for something can make the difference between selling the software and having it flop. Consider how many comparisons are necessary when n grows by powers of two. Each doubling of n would require potentially twice as many loop iterations for sequential search. However, the same doubling of n would require potentially only one more comparison for binary search.

The Maximum Number of Comparisons during Two Different Search Algorithms

Power of 2	n	Sequential Search	Binary Search
2^2	4	4	2
2^4	16	16	4
2^8	256	256	8
2^{12}	4,096	4,096	12
2^{24}	16,777,216	16,777,216	24

As n gets very large, sequential search has to do a lot more work. The numbers above represent the maximum number of iterations to find an element or to realize it is not there. The difference between 24 comparisons and almost 17 million comparisons is quite dramatic even on a fast computer.

In general, as the number of elements to search (n) doubles, binary search requires only one iteration to eliminate half of the elements from the search. The growth of this function is said to be logarithmic. The following graph illustrates the difference between linear search and binary search as the size of the array grows.

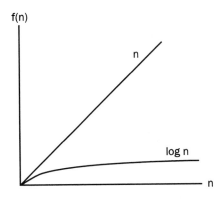

Self-Check

11-1 Give at least one precondition for a successful binary search.

11-2 What is the maximum number of comparisons (approximately) performed on a list of 1,024 elements during a binary search? (*Hint:* After one comparison, only 512 array elements need be searched; after two searches, only 256 elements need be searched, and so on.)

11-3 During a binary search, what condition signals that the search element does not exist in an array?

11-4 What changes would be made to the binary search when the elements are sorted in descending order?

11.2   One Sorting Algorithm

The elements of a collection are often arranged into either ascending or descending order through a process known as **sorting**. To sort an array, the elements must be compared. For int and double, < or > suffices. For String, Integer, and BankAccount objects, the compareTo method is used.

There are many sorting algorithms. Even though others are more efficient (run faster), the relatively simple selection sort is presented here. The goal here is to arrange an array of integers into ascending order, the natural ordering of integers.

Object Name	Unsorted Array	Sorted Array
data[0]	76.0	62.0
data[1]	91.0	76.0
data[2]	100.0	89.0
data[3]	62.0	91.0
data[4]	89.0	100.0

With the **selection sort** algorithm, the largest integer must end up in data[n - 1] (where n is the number of meaningful array elements). The smallest number should end up in data[0]. In general, an array x of size n is sorted in ascending order if $x[j] \le x[j + 1]$ for j = 0 to n - 2.

The selection sort begins by locating the smallest element in the array by searching from the first element (data[0]) through the last (data[4]). The smallest element, data[3] in this array, is then swapped with the top element, data[0]. Once this is done, the array is sorted at least through the first element.

Placing the Smallest Value in the "Top" Position (index 0)

top == 0	Before	After	Sorted
data[0]	*76.0*	*62.0*	⇐
data[1]	91.0	91.0	
data[2]	100.0	100.0	
data[3]	*62.0*	*76.0*	
data[4]	89.0	89.0	

The task of finding the smallest element is accomplished by examining all array elements and keeping track of the index with the smallest integer. After this, the smallest array element is swapped with data[0]. Here is an algorithm that accomplishes these two tasks:

Algorithm: **Finding the smallest in the array and switching it with the topmost element**

(a) top = 0
// *At first, assume that the first element is the smallest*
(b) indexOfSmallest = top

// Check the rest of the array (data[top + 1] through data[n - 1])
(c) for index ranging from top + 1 through n - 1
      (c1) if data[index] < data[indexOfSmallest]
              indexOfSmallest = index
// Place the smallest element into the first position and place the first array
// element into the location where the smallest array element was located.
(d) swap data[indexOfSmallest] with data[top]

The following algorithm walkthrough shows how the array is sorted through the first element. The smallest integer in the array will be stored at the "top" of the array—data[0]. Notice that indexOfSmallest changes only when an array element is found to be less than the one stored in data[indexOfSmallest]. This happens the first and third times step c1 executes.

Step	top	indexOf Smallest	index	[0]	[1]	[2]	[3]	[4]	my_size
?	?	?	?	76.0	91.0	100.0	62.0	89.0	5
(a)	0	"	"	"	"	"	"	"	"
(b)	"	0	"	"	"	"	"	"	"
(c)	"	"	1	"	"	"	"	"	"
(c1)	"	1	"	"	"	"	"	"	"
(c)	"	"	2	"	"	"	"	"	"
(c1)	"	"	"	"	"	"	"	"	"
(c)	"	"	3	"	"	"	"	"	"
(c1)	"	2	"	"	"	"	"	"	"
(c)	"	"	4	"	"	"	"	"	"
(c1)	"	"	"	"	"	"	"	"	"
(c)	"	"	5	"	"	"	"	"	"
(d)	"	"	"	62.0	"	"	76.0	"	"

This algorithm walkthrough shows indexOfSmallest changing twice to represent the index of the smallest integer in the array. After traversing the entire array, the smallest element is swapped with the top array element. Specifically, the preceding algorithm swaps the values of the first and fourth array elements, so 62.0 is stored in data[0] and 76.0 is stored in data[3]. The array is now sorted through the first element!

The same algorithm can be used to place the second smallest element into data[1]. The second traversal must begin at the new "top" of the array—index 1 rather than 0. This is accomplished by incrementing top from 0 to 1. Now a second traversal of the array begins at the second element rather than the first. The smallest element in the unsorted portion of the array is swapped with the second element. A second traversal of the array ensures that the first two elements

are in order. In this example array, data[3] is swapped with data[1] and the array
is sorted through the first two elements.

top == 1	Before	After	Sorted
data[0]	62.0	62.0	⇐
data[1]	*91.0*	*76.0*	⇐
data[2]	100.0	100.0	
data[3]	*76.0*	*91.0*	
data[4]	89.0	89.0	

This process repeats a total of n - 1 times.

top == 2	Before	After	Sorted
data[0]	62.0	62.0	⇐
data[1]	76.0	76.0	⇐
data[2]	*100.0*	*89.0*	⇐
data[3]	91.0	91.0	
data[4]	*89.0*	*100.0*	

And an element may even be swapped with itself.

top == 3	Before	After	Sorted
data[0]	62.0	62.0	⇐
data[1]	76.0	76.0	⇐
data[2]	89.0	89.0	⇐
data[3]	*91.0*	*91.0*	⇐
data[4]	100.0	100.0	

When top goes to data[4], the outer loop stops. The last element need not be
compared to anything. It is unnecessary to find the smallest element in an array of
size 1. This element in data[n - 1] must be the largest (or equal to the largest),
since all of the elements preceding the last element are already sorted in ascending order.

top == 3 and 4	Before	After	Sorted
data[0]	62.0	62.0	⇐
data[1]	76.0	76.0	⇐
data[2]	89.0	89.0	⇐
data[3]	91.0	91.0	⇐
data[4]	100.0	100.0	⇐

Therefore, the outer loop changes the index top from 0 through n - 2. The loop to
find the smallest index in a portion of the array is nested inside a loop that
changes top from 0 through n - 2 inclusive.

Algorithm: **Selection Sort**

for top ranging from 0 through n - 2
{
   indexOfSmallest = top
   for index ranging from top + 1 through n - 1
   {
      if data[indexOfSmallest] < data[index] then
        indexOfSmallest = index
   }
   swap data[indexOfSmallest] with data[top]
}

Here is the Java code that uses selection sort to sort the array of numbers shown. The array is printed before and after the numbers are sorted into ascending order.

```java
double[] data = { 76.0, 91.0, 100.0, 62.0, 89.0 };
int n = data.length;

System.out.print( "Before sorting: " );
for( int j = 0; j < data.length; j++ )
  System.out.print( data[j] + " " );
System.out.println(  );

int indexOfSmallest = 0;

for( int top = 0; top < n - 1; top++ )
{
  // First assume that the smallest is
  // the first element in the subarray
  indexOfSmallest = top;

  // Then compare all of the other elements, looking for the smallest
  for( int index = top + 1; index < data.length; index++ )
  { // Compare elements in the subarray
    if( data[index] < data[indexOfSmallest] )
      indexOfSmallest = index;
  }

  // Then make sure the smallest from data[top] through data.size
  // is in data[top]. This message swaps two array elements.
  double temp = data[top]; // Hold on to this value temporarily
  data[top] = data[indexOfSmallest];
  data[indexOfSmallest] = temp;
}

System.out.print( " After sorting: " );
for ( int j = 0; j < data.length; j++ )
  System.out.print( data[j] + " " );
System.out.println(  );
```

Output

```
Before sorting: 76.0 91.0 100.0 62.0 89.0
 After sorting: 62.0 76.0 89.0 91.0 100.0
```

Sorting an array usually involves elements that are more complex. The sorting code is most often located in a method. This more typical context for sorting will be presented later.

This selection sort code arranged the array into ascending numeric order. Most sort routines arrange the elements from smallest to largest. However, with just a few simple changes, any primitive type of data (such as `int`, `char`, and `double`) may be arranged into descending order using the `>` operator.

```
if( data[index] < data[indexOfSmallest] )
   indexOfSmallest = index;
```

becomes

```
if( data[index] > data[indexOfLargest] )
   indexOfLargest = index;
```

Only primitive types can be sorted with the relational operators `<` and `>`. Arrays of other objects, `String` and `BankAccount` for example, have a `compareTo` method to check the relationship of one object to another.

Only a few Java classes define a `compareTo` method. However, programmers can add a `compareTo` method to any class. Then a collection of those classes of objects can be sorted (just have the class `implement Comparable` and define what `compareTo` means). To make any Java object sortable, have the class implement the `Comparable` interface. This guarantees that the object understands `compareTo` messages. Then you could write the comparison this way for any type of objects to sort in their natural ordering:

```
if( data[index].compareTo( data[indexOfSmallest] ) < 0 )
```

Self-Check

11-5   Alphabetizing an array of strings requires a sort in which order, ascending or descending?

11-6   If the smallest element in an array already exists as `first`, what happens when the swap function is called for the first time (when top = 0)?

11-7   Write code that searches for and stores the largest element of array x into `largest`. Assume that all elements from `x[0]` through `x[n - 1]` have been given meaningful values.

11.3   static Methods

Sorting and searching routines can sort arrays of different types (as long as all of
the array elements are the same type). This section presents a class to mimic Java's
sort and binarySearch methods from the Arrays class. Both of these methods
are static. A **static method** is called with a class name before the dot instead of
an object name. No object is required.

The static sort method arranges an array of Strings into their natural ordering as defined by the compareTo method of the String class. This sort method
from the Arrays class is similar to the sort method of the Collections class
except an array is being sorted here, not an ArrayList.

```java
// Sort an array with the static sort method of the Arrays class.
// All elements must implement Comparable and be of the same type.
import java.util.Arrays;

public class SortAnyArray
{
  public static void main( String[] args )
  {
    String[] array = { "Ric", "Travis", "Teena", "Sean", "Leo" };
    int n = array.length;

    // Sort the elements from indexes 0 through n - 1
    Arrays.sort( array, 0, n );  // Call a static method

    for( int j = 0; j < n; j++ )
      System.out.println( array[j].toString( ) );
  }
}
```

Output

```
Leo
Ric
Sean
Teena
Travis
```

Java's Collections and Arrays classes both have a binarySearch method that
returns the integer index of where an item was found. If the item is not found,
binarySearch returns a negative integer.

```java
System.out.println( "Teena index: " +
                    Arrays.binarySearch( array, "Teena" ) );
System.out.println( "NoThE index: " +
                    Arrays.binarySearch( array, "NoThE" ) );
```

Output

```
Teena index: 3
NoThE index: -2
```

You have already seen static methods in Java with classes such as `Math`, `Double`, `Integer`, and `JOptionPane`. Static methods differ from most others in that they are invoked by specifying the class name, followed by a dot, followed by the method name and the arguments. Java declares these types of methods with the keyword `static`. Here are a few of Java's `static` method headings from five different classes.

Method Headings from the `Math` Class

```
public static double sin( double a )
// Returns the trigonometric sine of an angle.

public static double sqrt( double a )
// Returns the square root of a double value.

public static double rint( double a )
// Returns the closest integer to the argument. If two integers are
// equidistant, such as when a == 2.5, the result is the integer
// value that is even.
```

Method Headings from the `Double` Class

```
public static double parseDouble( String s )
// Returns a double that represents the numeric value represented
// by the String.
```

Method Headings from the `Integer` Class

```
public static double parseInteger( String s )
// Returns an int that represents the integer value represented by
// the String.
```

Method Headings from the `JOptionPane` Class

```
public static void showMessageDialog( Component parentComponent,
                                       Object message )
// Brings up a confirmation modal dialog box.
```

Method Headings from the `Character` Class

```
public static boolean isDigit( char ch )
// Determines if ch is a digit, such as '2'.

public static boolean isLetter( char ch )
// Determines if the specified character is a letter, such as 'a'.

public static boolean isLetterOrDigit( char ch )
// Determines if the specified character is a letter or a digit.

public static char toUpperCase( char ch )
// Returns the uppercase equivalent of the char argument.
```

Here are calls to some of these `static` methods.

```
System.out.println( "    2? " + Math.rint( 1.5 ) );
System.out.println( "    2? " + Math.rint( 2.5 ) );
System.out.println( " 4.56? " + Double.parseDouble( "4.56" ) );
```

```
System.out.println( "   789? " + Integer.parseInt( "789" ) );
System.out.println( "false? " + Character.isDigit( 'A' ) );
System.out.println( " true? " + Character.isDigit( '3' ) );
System.out.println( "    M? " + Character.toUpperCase( 'm' ) );
```

Output

```
   2? 2.0
   2? 2.0
4.56? 4.56
 789? 789
false? false
 true? true
   M? M
```

Now we'll consider a class with static methods for sorting and searching any array of elements that implements Comparable.

Sorting, Printing, and Searching Arrays with Static Methods

The following main method calls several static methods while providing a more typical example of maintaining a collection. This collection needs to be searched in order to modify specific objects referenced from the array. To use the more efficient binary search, the array must first be sorted.

Once the array is sorted with the static sort method, the static binarySearch method returns the index of the found item (or –1 if it is not found). These sort and binarySearch methods are contained in a separate class. This class has a static method named printArray to display the array elements before the sort, after the sort, and again after two objects are modified.

```java
// Use two methods from the MySorterSearcher class that could
// be used to sort and search any array of objects that have
// the Comparable interface--a compareTo method.
public class TestMySorterSearcher
{
  // Print any array of objects (arrays of primitives not allowed).
  // This method is called three times from the main method below.
  public static void printArray( Object[] array, int n )
  {
    for( int j = 0; j < n; j++ )
      System.out.println( array[j].toString( ) );
  }

  // Make up a small collection, sort it, and modify two
  // object found by the binarySearch method.
  public static void main( String[] args )
  {
    BankAccount[] tinyBank = new BankAccount[10];
    // Initialize the array of references to BankAccount objects
    tinyBank[0] = new BankAccount( "Shauna",  0.0 );
    tinyBank[1] = new BankAccount( "Luis", 111.111 );
```

```
      tinyBank[2] = new BankAccount( "Ursula", 222.22 );
      tinyBank[3] = new BankAccount( "Rob", 333.33 );
      tinyBank[4] = new BankAccount( "Ansel", 444.44 );
      int n = 5;

      System.out.println( "Before sorting: " );
      TestMySorterSearcher.printArray( tinyBank, n );

      MySorterSearcher.sort( tinyBank, n );

      System.out.println( "\nAfter sorting: " );
      printArray( tinyBank, n );

      // Modify two accounts

      // Create an account that will "equal" the
      // one we seek--balance doesn't count
      BankAccount searchAccount = new BankAccount( "Ursula", -9 );

      // Search for an account that has an ID of "Ursula"
      int index = MySorterSearcher.binarySearch( tinyBank,
                                           searchAccount, n );
      if( index > 0 )
      { // Change the object referenced in the collection
        BankAccount ref = (BankAccount)tinyBank[index];
        ref.deposit( 99999.99 );
      }

      // Search for an account that has an ID of "Rob"
      searchAccount = new BankAccount( "Rob", -9 );
      index = MySorterSearcher.binarySearch( tinyBank, searchAccount, n );
      if( index > 0 )
      { // Change the object referenced by the array
        BankAccount ref = (BankAccount)tinyBank[index];
        ref.deposit( 5555.55 );
      }

      // Show the changes were made to the
      // objects referenced by the collection
      System.out.println( "\n After depositing to two accounts: " );
      printArray( tinyBank, n );
  }

}
```

Output

```
Before sorting:
Shauna $0.00
Luis $111.11
Ursula $222.22
Rob $333.33
Ansel $444.44
```

```
After sorting:
Ansel $444.44
Luis $111.11
Rob $333.33
Shauna $0.00
Ursula $222.22

After depositing to two accounts:
Ansel $444.44
Luis $111.11
Rob $5,888.88
Shauna $0.00
Ursula $100,222.21
```

The output shows that after sorting, the object referenced by tinyBank[0] has an ID ("Ansel") that is less than the others. This is because the compareTo method of BankAccount compares IDs only. Once sorted, binarySearch finds the index of the array element that references the BankAccount object being sought.

The object referenced by searchAccount is a "fake" account. It is constructed to allow the array to be searched when only the ID is available.[1] This allows you to write code that asks for the ID and is able to find the correct account (if there is one with that ID) even if you don't know the balance (in fact you may search for an account just to find a customer's balance).

The main method above retrieved references to two different BankAccounts with the binary Search method and made hefty deposits for Rob and Ursula. This showed up in the output when the third call to printArray was made.

Static Sort and Search Methods for Arrays of Comparables

A collection of elements cannot be sorted unless there is some way to compare two objects and determine if one is less than the other. Also, binarySearch does not work unless you can compare two elements to see which object is "less than" the other. To ensure that all objects of a class can be compared, Java offers the Comparable interface. Any class that implements Comparable can have its objects compared for "less than." This influences the design of the methods. In particular, the parameters for both sort and binarySearch are arrays of Comparable. This allows many types of arrays to be sorted and searched. The type of elements referenced by the array must be a class that implements Comparable.

Another feature of this class is that the complexity of selection sort is split up into three methods, which happen to be static. Now the sort routine swaps the smallest element with array[top] for top ranging from 0 through n - 1. Another

---

1. Java has collection classes (HashMap, for example) that require programmers to add a key in addition to the object. This key is all that would be needed to retrieve a reference to the object later.

method named `swapSmallestToTop` finds the smallest element and then asks a
third method named `swap` to do the exchange.

```
// This class has two methods for sorting and binary searching an
// array of objects that can be stored in Comparable type references
public class MySorterSearcher
{
  // Arrange array elements in the natural ordering defined by the
  // compareTo method. The array must have the same type at every
  // index. And the type of class must implement Comparable.
  public static void sort( Comparable[] array, int n )
  {
    for( int top = 0; top < n - 1; top++ )
      swapSmallestToTop( array, top, n );
  }

  // A private helper that avoids nested for loops
  private static void swapSmallestToTop( Comparable[] array,
                                         int top,
                                         int n )
  {
    // First assume the smallest is the first element in the subarray
    int indexOfSmallest = top;

    // Then compare all other elements looking for the largest
    for( int index = top + 1; index < n; index++ )
    { // Compare elements in the subarray
      if( array[index].compareTo( array[indexOfSmallest] ) < 0 )
        indexOfSmallest = index;
    }

    // Then make sure the largest from data[top] through data.size
    // is in data[top]. This message swaps two array elements.
    swap( array, top, indexOfSmallest );
  }

  // Swap two array elements. This code could have gone into
  // the sort method, but that method is now pretty long and complex.
  // A helper method is added.
  private static void swap( Comparable[] array,
                            int top,
                            int indexOfSmallest )
  {
    Comparable temp = array[top]; // Hold on to this value temporarily
    array[top] = array[indexOfSmallest];
    array[indexOfSmallest] = temp;
  }


  // Search for an element that "equals" searchElements,
  // using the rules established by the compareTo method
  // of the class. If searchElement is found in array,
  // the index is returned. Otherwise, this method returns
  // -1 to indicate that searchElement was not found.
```

```
   public static int binarySearch( Comparable[] array,
                                    Comparable elementToFind,
                                    int n )
{
   int indexInArray = -1;
   int first = 0;
   int last = n - 1;
   int mid = ( first + last ) / 2;

   while( indexInArray == -1 && ( first <= last ) )
   {
     // Check the three possibilities
     if( elementToFind.compareTo( array[mid] ) == 0 )
       indexInArray = mid;
     else if( elementToFind.compareTo( array[mid] ) < 0 )
       last = mid - 1;
     else
       first= mid + 1;

     // Compute a new mid just in case
     mid = ( first + last ) / 2;
   } // End while

   return indexInArray;
  }
}
```

Self-Check

11-8 Write the output of the following code:

```
public class TestMySorterSearcher2
{
   // Print any array of objects (arrays of primitives
   // not allowed). This method is called three
   // times from the main method below.
   public static void printArray( Object[] array, int n )
   {
     for( int j = 0; j < n; j++ )
       System.out.println( array[j].toString( ) );
   }

   // Make up a small collection, sort it, and modify two
   // objects found by the binarySearch method.
   public static void main( String[] args )
   {
     String name[] = { "Chris", "Jig", "Andy", "Zach",
                       "Mary Lou" };
     int n = name.length;

     MySorterSearcher.sort( name, n );
     printArray( name, name.length );
```

```
        System.out.println( "---Search---" );
        int index = MySorterSearcher.binarySearch( name,
                                              "Mary Lou", n );
        System.out.println( name[index].toUpperCase( ) );
    }
}
```

11.4   Two-Dimensional Arrays

Consider this table of data that represents a score sheet of six quizzes for 11 students.

Figure 11.1: **Quiz data**

This data will be used in several examples of two-dimensional array processing.

```
     Quiz #0        1        2        3        4        5
  0    67.8     56.4     88.4     79.1     90.0     66.0
  1    76.4     81.1     72.2     76.0     85.6     85.0
  2    87.8     76.4     88.7     83.0     76.3     87.0
  3    86.4     54.0     40.0      3.0      2.0      1.0
  4    72.8     89.0     55.0     62.0     68.0     77.7
  5    94.4     63.0     92.9     45.0     75.6     99.5
  6    85.8     95.0     88.1    100.0     60.0     85.8
  7    76.4     84.4    100.0     94.3     75.6     74.0
  8    57.9     49.5     58.8     67.4     80.0     56.0
  9    86.1     76.0     72.0     88.1     55.6     71.3
 10    87.2     95.5     98.1     97.0     98.0     99.0
```

This data could be processed in a variety of ways:

- Use one column to determine one quiz average.
- Use one row to determine the quiz average for one particular student.
- Use the entire table to determine the overall average.

Declaring Two-Dimensional Arrays

Data that conveniently presents itself in tabular format can be represented using an array with two subscripts, henceforth called a **two-dimensional array**. Two-dimensional arrays are constructed as follows:

General Form 11.1: **A two-dimensional array declaration**

typeOrClass **[ ] [ ]** *identifier* **=** **new** *typeOrClass* **[** *rows* **] [** *columns* **] ;**

- *typeOrClass* must be one of the primitive types or the name of any Java class
- *identifier* is the name of the two-dimensional array
- *rows* specifies the total number of rows
- *columns* specifies the total number of columns

Examples of Two-Dimensional Array Declarations

```
double[][] matrix = new double[4][8];

String[][] name = new String[5][10];

// Construct with int constants or expressions
int rows = 10;
int columns = 20;
GridIntersection[][] gridMap = new GridIntersection[rows][columns]
```

These declarations allocate memory to store 32 floating-point numbers, 50 strings, and 200 GridIntersection objects, respectively.

Referencing Individual Items with Two Subscripts

A reference to an individual element of a two-dimensional array requires two subscripts. By convention, programmers use the first subscript for the rows. The second subscript represents the columns. Each subscript must be bracketed individually.

General Form 11.2: **Accessing individual two-dimensional array elements**

two-dimensional-array-name[*rows*] [*columns*]

- *rows* is an integer value in the range of 0 through the number of rows - 1
- *columns* is an integer value in the range of 0 through the number of columns - 1

Examples of Subscripting Two-Dimensional Array Elements

```
String[][] name = new String[5][10];
name[0][0] = "Upper Left";
name[4][9] = "Lower Right";
System.out.println( "At row 0, column 0: " + name[0][0] );
System.out.println( "At row 4, column 9: " + name[4][9] );
System.out.println( name[0][0].toUpperCase( ) + "  " +
                    name[4][9].toUpperCase( ) );
```

Output

```
At row 0, column 0: Upper Left
At row 4, column 9: Lower Right
UPPER LEFT  LOWER RIGHT
```

Nested Looping with Two-Dimensional Arrays

Nested looping is commonly used to process the data of two-dimensional arrays. This initialization allocates enough memory to store 40 floating-point numbers—a two-dimensional array with five rows and eight columns. Java sets all values to 0.0.

```
final int ROWS = 5;
final int COLUMNS = 8;
double[][] table = new double[ROWS][COLUMNS];   // 40 elements set to 0.0
```

These nested `for` loops initialize all 40 elements to -1.0. (Java had already initialized all elements to 0.0 when they were constructed with `new`.)

```
// Initialize all elements to -1.0
for( int row = 0; row < ROWS; row++ )
{
   for( int col = 0; col < COLUMNS; col++ )
   {
      table[row][col] = -1.0;
   }
}
```

After some assignments, the following code uses nested loops to display each row on its own separate line:

```
table[1][1] = 1.1;
table[2][2] = 2.22;
table[3][3] = 33.3333;
table[4][4] = 444.444444;
table[4][5] = 4.5;
table[4][6] = 4.6;
table[4][7] = 4.7;
table[0][7] = -7;
table[1][7] = 171.7;

DecimalFormat doubleFormat = new DecimalFormat( "0.00" );

for( int row = 0; row < ROWS; row++ )
{ // Display one row
   for( int col = 0; col < COLUMNS; col++ )
   {
      // Numbers are seven columns wide with two decimal places always
      String numberAsString = doubleFormat.format( table[row][col] );

      // padWithBlanks prepends a string so it has a length of at least 7
      // See page 569 to see this method added to a class.
      System.out.print( padWithBlanks( numberAsString, 7 ) );
   }
   System.out.println( );
}
```

Output (decimal places align because all are padded strings with two decimals)

```
 -1.00   -1.00   -1.00   -1.00   -1.00   -1.00   -1.00   -7.00
 -1.00    1.10   -1.00   -1.00   -1.00   -1.00   -1.00  171.70
 -1.00   -1.00    2.22   -1.00   -1.00   -1.00   -1.00   -1.00
 -1.00   -1.00   -1.00   33.33   -1.00   -1.00   -1.00   -1.00
 -1.00   -1.00   -1.00   -1.00  444.44    4.50    4.60    4.70
```

Self-Check

Use this construction to answer the following questions:

```
int[][] a = new int[3][4];
```

11-9   Does Java check the range of the subscripts when referencing the elements of a?

11-10 How many ints are properly stored by a?

11-11 What is the row (first) subscript range for a?

11-12 What is the column (second) subscript range for a?

11-13 Write code to initialize all of the elements of a to 999.

11-14 Write code to display all of the rows of a on separate lines, with eight spaces for each element. Assume that the method padWithBlanks from QuizData is available.

11-15 Declare a two-dimensional array named sales such that 120 floating-point numbers are stored in 10 rows.

11-16 Declare a two-dimensional array named sales2 such that 120 floating-point numbers are stored in 10 columns.

11-17 Construct a DecimalFormat object that when used with the following code will generate output like that shown below:

```
int[][] intTable = { { 1, 22, 333, 4444 },
                     { 55555, 666666, 7777777, 88888888 } };

int nRows = intTable.length;
int nCols = intTable[0].length;  // Number of columns in
                                 // the first row

// Need the DecimalFormat object constructed here

for( int row = 0; row < nRows; row++ )
{
  for( int col = 0; col < nCols; col++ )
  { // The first argument is an integer concatenated to an
    // empty String
    System.out.print( numberFormatter.format(
                      intTable[row][col] ) + " " );
  }
  System.out.println( );
}
```

Output

```
**1.0 **22.0 **333.0 **4,444.0
**55,555.0 **666,666.0 **7,777,777.0 **88,888,888.0
```

Row and Column Processing

A two-dimensional array manages tabular data that is typically processed by row, by column, or in totality. These forms of processing are examined in an example class that manages a grade book. The data consists of six quizzes for each of the 11 students. The 66 quizzes shown in Figure 11.1 are used throughout this section to demonstrate several forms of processing data stored in two-dimensional arrays.

The quiz average for each student is computed by processing a 2-D array one row at a time—using **row-by-row processing**. The average, highest, and lowest score of each quiz is found by processing the data one column at a time—using **column-by-column processing**. The overall quiz average is computed only after referencing all meaningful elements. However, before any processing occurs, the two-dimensional array must be declared and given a defined state. These forms of array processing are represented in the context of a class. Here is an outline of the instance variables for a `QuizData` class and the headings of the method that will be described:

```java
public class QuizData
{
    // Instance variables
    private double[][] quiz;
    private int numberOfStudents;
    private int numberOfQuizzes;
    private int columnWidth;
    private DecimalFormat doubleFormat;

    // Constructor
    public QuizData( String fileName )   {...}

    // A helper method to initialize the array with file input
    private void initArray( String fileName )   {...}

    // Return data formatted as a String
    public String toString( )   {...}

    // Display a row-by-row report
    public String studentStatistics( )   {...}

    // Display a column-by-column report
    public String quizStatistics( )   {...}

    // Returns the overall quiz average
    public double quizAverage( )   {...}

    // A helper method for formatting numbers
    private String padWithBlanks( String numAsString, int width )   {...}
```

The constructor sets up a few small formatting details and then uses a private helper method named `initArray` to completely initialize the two-dimensional array.

```
public QuizData( String fileName )
{
  // First set up formatting conventions for output
  columnWidth = 8;
  doubleFormat = new DecimalFormat( "0.0" );

  // Then initialize this object's quiz data with file input
  initArray( fileName );
}
```

Initializing Two-Dimensional Arrays with File Input

In programs that require little data, interactive input suffices. However, initialization of arrays quite often involves large amounts of data. The input would have to be typed in from the keyboard many times during implementation and testing. That much interactive input would prove to be tedious and error-prone. It is best to read the data from an external file instead.

The first line in `quiz.dat` specifies the number of rows and columns of the input file. Each remaining line represents the quiz scores of one student.

```
11  6
  67.8    56.4    88.4    79.1    90.0    66.0
  76.4    81.1    72.2    76.0    85.6    85.0
  87.8    76.4    88.7    83.0    76.3    87.0
  86.4    54.0    40.0     3.0     2.0     1.0
  72.8    89.0    55.0    62.0    68.0    77.7
  94.4    63.0    92.9    45.0    75.6    99.5
  85.8    95.0    88.1   100.0    60.0    85.8
  76.4    84.4   100.0    94.3    75.6    74.0
  57.9    49.5    58.8    67.4    80.0    56.0
  86.1    76.0    72.0    88.1    55.6    71.3
  87.2    95.5    98.1    97.0    98.0    99.0
```

The author-supplied `TextReader` object referenced by `inFile` will be associated with this external file in the constructor, and the number of rows and columns will be read from the first line in the file (11 and 6) with this statement:

```
TextReader inFile = new TextReader( fileName );
numberOfStudents = inFile.readInt( );
numberOfQuizzes = inFile.readInt( );
```

Because these private data members are known throughout the `QuizData` class, the two-dimensional array named `quiz` can, from this point forward, communicate its subscript ranges for both rows and columns at any time and in any method. The next step is to allocate memory for the two-dimensional array:

```
quiz = new double[numberOfStudents][numberOfQuizzes];
```

Now with a two-dimensional array precisely large enough to store 11 (numberOfStudents) rows of data with six (numberOfQuizzes) quiz scores in each row, the two-dimensional array gets initialized with the file data using nested for loops. These steps are encapsulated in the private helper method named initArray.

```
// Read the size of the 2-D array and the array data from a file
private void initArray( String fileName )
{
  TextReader inFile = new TextReader( fileName );

  // Get the dimensions of the array from the input file
  numberOfStudents = inFile.readInt( );
  numberOfQuizzes = inFile.readInt( );

  // Allocate memory for the two-dimensional array
  quiz = new double[numberOfStudents][numberOfQuizzes];

  // Initialize a numberOfStudents-by-numberOfQuizzes array
  for( int row = 0; row < numberOfStudents; row++ )
  {
    for( int col = 0; col < numberOfQuizzes; col++ )
    {
      quiz[row][col] = inFile.readDouble( );
    }
  }
}
```

As with one-dimensional arrays, immediately displaying all of the initialized elements of a two-dimensional array can help prevent errors. This input data can be seen with the help of nested loops in QuizData's toString method. The String is meant to show what the data looks like in the input file.

```
public String toString( )
{
  String result = "    Quiz #0";

  for( int j = 1; j < numberOfQuizzes; j++ )
    result += padWithBlanks( ""+j, columnWidth );
  result += "\n";

  for( int row = 0; row < numberOfStudents; row++ )
  {
    result += padWithBlanks( "" + row, 3 );
    for( int col = 0; col < numberOfQuizzes; col++ )
    {
      result += padWithBlanks( doubleFormat.format( quiz[row][col] ),
                               columnWidth );
    }
    result += "\n";
```

```
  }
  return result;
}

// A private helper to align decimal places by
// prepending " " until numAsString.length() == width.
private String padWithBlanks( String numAsString, int width )
{
  int blanksToPad = width - numAsString.length( );

  // If numAsString.length( ) >= width, prepend nothing
  for( int j = 1; j <= blanksToPad; j++ )
    numAsString = " " + numAsString;

  return numAsString;
}
```

The following program constructs a QuizData object and displays the data
stored in the input file named quiz.dat.

```
public class TestQuizData
{
  public static void main( String[] args )
  {
    QuizData cmpSc = new QuizData( "quiz.dat" );

    System.out.println( cmpSc.toString( ) );
  }
}
```

Output

Quiz #0	1	2	3	4	5
0 67.8	56.4	88.4	79.1	90.0	66.0
1 76.4	81.1	72.2	76.0	85.6	85.0
2 87.8	76.4	88.7	83.0	76.3	87.0
3 86.4	54.0	40.0	3.0	2.0	1.0
4 72.8	89.0	55.0	62.0	68.0	77.7
5 94.4	63.0	92.9	45.0	75.6	99.5
6 85.8	95.0	88.1	100.0	60.0	85.8
7 76.4	84.4	100.0	94.3	75.6	74.0
8 57.9	49.5	58.8	67.4	80.0	56.0
9 86.1	76.0	72.0	88.1	55.6	71.3
10 87.2	95.5	98.1	97.0	98.0	99.0

This two-dimensional array is now correctly initialized and stores 66 quiz scores.
Each row represents the record of one student. Each column represents the record
of one quiz.

When working with two-dimensional arrays, take a little extra time to output all
of the elements and the number of assigned elements. Do this immediately after
the code that initializes the objects. Do not continue until you are satisfied that the
two-dimensional array has been properly initialized. Otherwise, a lot of debugging

effort could be wasted on the wrong portion of a program. It may appear that there is a bug later on in the program when, in fact, the array was never initialized correctly to begin with.

Student Statistics (Row-by-Row Processing)

The average for one student is found by adding all of the elements of one row and dividing by 6 (the number of quizzes taken by each student). Dropping the lowest quiz score provides an interesting twist. To drop the lowest, find the column with the lowest score and subtract it from the total of all six quizzes. Then divide by numberOfQuizzes - 1 instead of numberOfQuizzes. Since the data for each student are stored in one row of the two-dimensional array, they are processed in a row-by-row manner.

Row-by-row processing is characterized by nested loops, where the row subscript changes in the outer loop and the column subscript changes more quickly in an inner loop. The column subscript changes more quickly than the row subscript. One complete row of data is processed before proceeding to the next row. The following code shows row-by-row processing.

```java
// Return a report of student averages
public String studentStatistics( )
{
  // Precondition: numberOfQuizzes > 1
  // This is an example of row-by-row processing
  System.out.println( );
  String result = "Student     Average\n";
  result +=       "=======     =======\n";

  double sum, lowest, average;

  for( int row = 0; row < numberOfStudents; row++ )   // Outer loop
  {
    // Assume the first quiz is the lowest
    lowest = quiz[row][0];
    // Assign sum the value of the first quiz
    sum = lowest;
    // Process the remaining quizzes (start with the second quiz
    // in the row)

    for( int col = 1; col < numberOfQuizzes; col++ )   // Inner loop
    {
      sum = sum + quiz[row][col];
      if( quiz[row][col] < lowest )
        lowest = quiz[row][col];
    } // End the inner loop
    // Drop the lowest quiz
    sum = sum - lowest;
```

```
      // Average is based on dropping lowest, so divide by one less
      average = sum / ( numberOfQuizzes - 1 );
      result += padWithBlanks( ""+row, columnWidth - 1 );
      result += padWithBlanks( doubleFormat.format( average ),
                               columnWidth );
      result += "\n";
   } // End the outer loop

   return result;
}
```

This method reports on the quiz averages for each student.

```
System.out.println( cmpSc.studentStatistics( ) );
```

Output

```
Student     Average
=======     =======
      0     78.3
      1     80.8
      2     84.6
      3     37.1
      4     73.9
      5     85.1
      6     90.9
      7     86.1
      8     64.0
      9     78.7
     10     97.5
```

Quiz Average (Column-by-Column Processing)

Column-by-column processing occurs when the data of a two-dimensional array are processed such that all the rows of one column are examined before proceeding to the next column. The row subscript changes faster than the column subscript. Since each quiz is represented as one column, processing the data column by column generates quiz statistics such as the lowest, highest, and average scores for each quiz.

Output

```
Quiz    High    Low Average
====    =====   ===== =======
   0    94.4    57.9    79.9
   1    95.5    49.5    74.6
   2   100.0    40.0    77.7
   3   100.0     3.0    72.3
   4    98.0     2.0    69.7
   5    99.5     1.0    72.9
```

The implementation of quizStatistics is left as a programming project.

Overall Quiz Average (Processing All Elements)

Finding the overall average without dropping any quiz scores is a simple matter of summing every single element in the two-dimensional array and dividing by the total number of quizzes. The following message shows the output that follows:

```
DecimalFormat averageFormat = new DecimalFormat( "0.00" );
System.out.println( "Average of all quizzes (no quizzes dropped) = "
                  + averageFormat.format( cmpSc.quizAverage( ) ) );
```

Output

```
Average of all quizzes (no quizzes dropped) = 74.51
```

Most students should appreciate the fact that they appear to have done better than the class average. This is because the report by student dropped the lowest quiz score, but the overall average included the lowest quiz score. The implementation of `QuizData.quizAverage` is left as a programming project.

Self-Check

11-18 In row-by-row processing, which subscript increments more slowly, row or column?

11-19 In column-by-column processing, which subscript increments more slowly, row or column?

11-20 Write code that declares a `TextReader` object using a file named `t.dat`. Use the data in the file to initialize a two-dimensional array of integers named `t`. Assume that the file has the number of rows and columns written as the first two pieces of data (as was shown earlier in the file `quiz.dat`).

11-21 Write code that determines the sum of all of the elements in `t`.

11-22 Write code that displays the largest element in each row of `t`.

11.5   Arrays with More than Two Subscripts

One- and two-dimensional arrays occur more frequently than do arrays with more than two subscripts. However, arrays with three and even more subscripts are sometimes useful. Three-dimensional arrays are possible because Java does not limit the number of subscripts. For example, the declaration

```
double[][][] q = new double[3][11][6];
```

could represent the quiz grades for three courses, since 198 (3 x 11 x 6) grades can be stored under the same name (q). This three-dimensional array:

q[1][9][3]

is a reference to quiz index 3 of student index 9 in course index 1.

In the following program, an array with three subscripts is initialized (with meaningless data). The first subscript—representing a course—changes the slowest. So the array object q is initialized and then displayed in a course-by-course manner.

```java
// Declare, initialize, and display a 3-D array
public class Show3DArray
{
  public static void main( String[] args )
  {
    int courses = 3;
    int students = 11;
    int quizzes = 6;
    int[][][] q = new int[courses][students][quizzes];

    for( int c = 0; c < courses; c++ )
    {
      for( int row = 0; row < students; row++ )
      {
        for( int col = 0; col < quizzes; col++ )
        { // Give each quiz a value using a meaningless formula
          q[c][row][col] = ( col + 1 ) * ( row + 2 ) + c + 25;
        }
      }
    }

    // Display
    for( int c = 0; c < courses; c++ )
    {
      System.out.println( );
      System.out.println( "Course #" + c );
      for( int row = 0; row < students; row++ )
      {
        for( int col = 0; col < quizzes; col++ )
        {
          System.out.print( "   " + q[c][row][col] );
        }
        System.out.println( );
      }
    }
  }
}
```

Output

```
Course #0
    27    33    41    49    57    65
    28    34    43    52    61    70
    29    35    45    55    65    75
    30    36    47    58    69    80
    31    37    49    61    73    85
    32    39    46    53    60    67
    33    41    49    57    65    73
    34    43    52    61    70    79
    35    45    55    65    75    85
    36    47    58    69    80    91
    37    49    61    73    85    97

Course #1
    28    34    42    50    58    66
    29    35    44    53    62    71
    30    36    46    56    66    76
    31    37    48    59    70    81
    32    38    50    62    74    86
    33    40    47    54    61    68
    34    42    50    58    66    74
    35    44    53    62    71    80
    36    46    56    66    76    86
    37    48    59    70    81    92
    38    50    62    74    86    98

Course #2
    29    35    43    51    59    67
    30    36    45    54    63    72
    31    37    47    57    67    77
    32    38    49    60    71    82
    33    39    51    63    75    87
    34    41    48    55    62    69
    35    43    51    59    67    75
    36    45    54    63    72    81
    37    47    57    67    77    87
    38    49    60    71    82    93
    39    51    63    75    87    99
```

The table below provides another view of this 3-D array. The first subscript is the same for each course. For example, every quiz for course #0 has 0 as the first subscript. The second and third subscripts represent the student (row) and quiz (column), respectively.

An Array with Three Subscripts

```
Course #     +-----------------------------------------------------------------+
2--------->  | q[2,0,0] | q[2,0,1] | q[2,0,2] | q[2,0,3] | q[2,0,4] | q[2,0,5] |
             +----------+----------+----------+----------+----------+----------|
             | q[2,1,0] | q[2,1,1] | q[2,1,2] | q[2,1,3] | q[2,1,4] | q[2,1,5] |
         +-----------------------------------------------------------------+---|
1----->  | q[1,0,0] | q[1,0,1] | q[1,0,2] | q[1,0,3] | q[1,0,4] | q[1,0,5] |5] |
         +----------+----------+----------+----------+----------+----------|---|
         | q[1,1,0] | q[1,1,1] | q[1,1,2] | q[1,1,3] | q[1,1,4] | q[1,1,5] |5] |
     +-----------------------------------------------------------------+---|---|
0->  | q[0,0,0] | q[0,0,1] | q[0,0,2] | q[0,0,3] | q[0,0,4] | q[0,0,5] |5] |5] |
     +----------+----------+----------+----------+----------+----------|---|---|
     | q[0,1,0] | q[0,1,1] | q[0,1,2] | q[0,1,3] | q[0,1,4] | q[0,1,5] |5] |5] |
     +----------+----------+----------+----------+----------+----------|---|---|
     | q[0,2,0] | q[0,2,1] | q[0,2,2] | q[0,2,3] | q[0,2,4] | q[0,2,5] |5] |5] |
     +----------+----------+----------+----------+----------+----------|---|---|
     | q[0,3,0] | q[0,3,1] | q[0,3,2] | q[0,3,3] | q[0,3,4] | q[0,3,5] |5] |5] |
     +----------+----------+----------+----------+----------+----------|---|---|
     | q[0,4,0] | q[0,4,1] | q[0,4,2] | q[0,4,3] | q[0,4,4] | q[0,4,5] |5] |5] |
     +----------+----------+----------+----------+----------+----------|---|---|
     | q[0,5,0] | q[0,5,1] | q[0,5,2] | q[0,5,3] | q[0,5,4] | q[0,5,5] |5] |5] |
     +----------+----------+----------+----------+----------+----------|---|---|
     | q[0,6,0] | q[0,6,1] | q[0,6,2] | q[0,6,3] | q[0,6,4] | q[0,6,5] |5] |5] |
     +----------+----------+----------+----------+----------+----------|---|---+
     | q[0,7,0] | q[0,7,1] | q[0,7,2] | q[0,7,3] | q[0,7,4] | q[0,7,5] |5] |
     +----------+----------+----------+----------+----------+----------|---|
     | q[0,8,0] | q[0,8,1] | q[0,8,2] | q[0,8,3] | q[0,8,4] | q[0,8,5] |5] |
     +----------+----------+----------+----------+----------+----------|---+
     | q[0,9,0] | q[0,9,1] | q[0,9,2] | q[0,9,3] | q[0,9,4] | q[0,9,5] |
     +----------+----------+----------+----------+----------+----------|
     | q[0,10,0]| q[0,10,1]| q[0,10,2]| q[0,10,3]| q[0,10,4]| q[0,10,5]|
     +-----------------------------------------------------------------+
```

Self-Check

Use this declaration to answer the questions that follow:

```
int x[3][4][5];
```

11-23 How many elements are properly stored by x?

11-24 Which of the following references to x can be properly used as the variable to the left of an assignment operator? Write "Valid" for each reference that can be properly used or "Invalid" and the reason why the reference is invalid.

- **-a** x[0][0][0]
- **-b** x[1][1][1]
- **-c** x[3][4][5]
- **-d** x[0, 0, 0]
- **-e** x[2][3]
- **-f** x[1]

Chapter Summary

- Binary search usually finds an array element much more quickly than sequential search. However, the array must first be sorted.
- Selection sort uses nested loops to rearrange integers in ascending order. The selection sort algorithm is used to sort arrays of `Comparables` into their natural ordering, as defined by the `compareTo` method.
- Some of the new ideas presented with data stored in a two-dimensional array format include:
    - A two-dimensional array manages data that is logically organized in a tabular format—that is, in rows and columns.
    - The first subscript of a two-dimensional array specifies the row of data in a table; the second represents the column.
    - The elements stored in a two-dimensional array can be processed row by row, column by column, or by rows and columns.
    - `for` loops are commonly used to process arrays. In the case of a two-dimensional array being processed row by row, the outer loop usually increments the row index and the inner loop usually increments the column index.
- Java arrays can have many dimensions. One-dimensional arrays are the most common, but occasionally it becomes convenient to store data in a two-dimensional array and perhaps even a three-dimensional array.

Key Terms

binary search   selection sort   static method
column-by-column processing   sorting   two-dimensional array
row-by-row processing

Exercises

The answers to exercises marked with ☼ are available in Appendix C.

☼   1. Write the output generated by the following program.

```
public class StringArray
{
  public static void main( String[] args )
  {
    String[] str = new String[10];

    int n = 5;
    str[0] = "Aimee";
    str[1] = "Bob";
```

```
        str[2] = "Lauren";
        str[3] = "Alex";
        str[4] = "Morgan";

        for( int top = 0; top < n - 1; top++ )
        {
          int subscript = top;
          for( int j = top + 1; j <= n - 1; j++ )
          {
            if( str[j].compareTo( str[subscript] ) < 0 )
              subscript = j;
          }
          String temp = str[subscript];
          str[subscript] = str[top];
          str[top] = temp;
        }

        for( int j = 0; j <= n - 1; j++ )
        {
          System.out.println( str[j] );
        }
      }
  }
```

2. Write the output of this program that uses the `DebuggingBinarySearcher` class. The output statements are in boldface.

```
public class DebuggingBinarySearcher
{
  // Store a collection of BankAccounts
  private BankAccount[] my_data;
  private int my_size;

  public DebuggingBinarySearcher( )
  { // Construct an empty collection
    my_data = new BankAccount[1000];
    my_size = 0;
  }

  public void add( BankAccount newAcct )
  { // Add a bankAccount to this collection
    my_data[my_size] = newAcct;
    my_size++;
  }

  public BankAccount referenceTo( String searchID )
  { // Return a reference to the BankAccount
    // that has the ID searchID. If not found
    // return null. PLEASE NOTE THE DEBUGGING OUTPUT.
    BankAccount result = null;
    int first = 0;
    int last = my_size - 1;
```

```
System.out.println( "First Mid Last" );
// Perform a binary search

while( result == null && ( first <= last ) )
{
  // If n == 7, mid = ( 0 + 6 ) / 2 = 3
  int mid = ( first + last ) / 2;
  System.out.println( first + "        " + mid + "      " + last );

  // Check the three possibilities
  if( searchID.compareTo( my_data[mid].getID( ) ) == 0 )
    result = my_data[mid];
  else if( searchID.compareTo( my_data[mid].getID( ) ) < 0 )
    last = mid - 1;
  else
    first= mid + 1;
} // End while

return result;
}

public static void main( String[] args )
{
  DebuggingBinarySearcher list = new DebuggingBinarySearcher( );
  list.add( new BankAccount( "ABE" , 0.00 ) );
  list.add( new BankAccount( "CLAY", 1.00 ) );
  list.add( new BankAccount( "KIM" , 2.00 ) );
  list.add( new BankAccount( "LAU" , 3.00 ) );
  list.add( new BankAccount( "LISA", 4.00 ) );
  list.add( new BankAccount( "PELE", 5.00 ) );
  list.add( new BankAccount( "ROY" , 6.00 ) );

  // Get a reference to LISA or null if
  // searchName is not in the array
  String searchID = "LISA";
  BankAccount reference = list.referenceTo( searchID );

  // Display the results
  if( reference != null )
    System.out.println( reference.getID( )
                        + " has a balance of "
                        + reference.getBalance( ) );
  else
    System.out.println( searchID + " not found" );
}
}
```

3. Write the output generated by the preceding program when searchID is initialized with each of the following string constants:

a. searchID = "ROY";

b. searchID = "CLAY";

c. searchID = "LAURIE";

d. searchID = "KIM";

e. searchID = "PELE";

f. searchID = "ABE";

4. List at least one condition that must be true before a successful binary search can be implemented.

5. Using a binary search, what is the maximum number of comparisons (approximately) that will be performed on a list of 256 sorted elements? (*Hint:* After one comparison, only 128 array elements need be searched; after two comparisons, only 64 elements need be searched; and so on.)

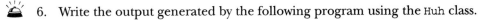 6. Write the output generated by the following program using the Huh class.

```java
public class Huh
{
  public static void main( String[] args )
  {
    Huh h = new Huh( 4, 4 );
    h.show( );
  }

  private int lastRow;
  private int lastCol;
  private int[][] m;

  public Huh( int initLastRow, int initLastColumn )
  {
    lastRow = initLastRow;
    lastCol = initLastColumn;
    // The array of arrays must be initialized in the constructor
    m = new int [lastRow][lastCol];
    for( int row = 0; row < lastRow; row++ )
    {
      for( int col = 0; col < lastCol; col++ )
      {
        m[row][col] = ( row + 1 ) + ( col + 1 );
      }
    }
  }

  private String padWithBlanks( String numAsString, int width )
  {
    int blanksToPad = width - numAsString.length( );
    for( int j = 1; j <= blanksToPad; j++ )
      numAsString = " " + numAsString;
    return numAsString;
  }

  public void show( )
  {
    for( int row = 0; row < lastRow; row++ )
    {
```

```
            for( int col = 0; col < lastCol; col++ )
              System.out.print( padWithBlanks( "" + m[row][col], 5 ) );

            System.out.println( );
          }
        }
      }
```

7. Add a method to Huh that is named incrementBy and that adds the value of the parameter named increment to every element in the two-dimensional array. The message h.incrementBy(5) must add 5 to every element in the array.

8. Add a method to Huh that is named rowSum and that returns the sum of all the elements in a given row. A valid call to rowSum is shown in this output statement:

```
int sumOfRow2 = h.rowSum( 2 );
```

9. Declare a two-dimensional array with three rows and four columns of floating-point numbers.

10. Write the Java code to accomplish the following tasks:
    a. Declare a two-dimensional array named aTable that stores 10 rows and 14 columns of floating-point numbers.
    b. Set every element in aTable to -1.0.
    c. Write a for loop that sets all of the elements in the fourth row (index 3) to 9.9.

11. Show the output from the following program:

```
public class TableOfInts
{
  public static void main( String[] args )
  {
    TableOfInts aTable;
    System.out.println( "a." );
    aTable= new TableOfInts( 2, 3 );
    System.out.println( aTable );

    System.out.println( "b." );
    aTable= new TableOfInts( 3, 2 );
    System.out.println( aTable );

    System.out.println( "c." );
    aTable= new TableOfInts( 3, 2 );
    System.out.println( aTable );

    System.out.println( "d." );
    aTable= new TableOfInts( 4, 4 );
    System.out.println( aTable );
```

```
      System.out.println( "e." );
      aTable= new TableOfInts( 1, 1 );
      System.out.println( aTable );
  }

  private int[][] my_data;
  private int my_lastRow;
  private int my_lastCol;

  public TableOfInts( int maxRow, int maxCol )
  {
    my_lastRow = maxRow;
    my_lastCol = maxCol;
    my_data = new int[my_lastRow][my_lastCol];
    // Initialize the two-dimensional array elements
    for( int row = 0; row < my_lastRow; row++ )
    {
      for( int col = 0; col < my_lastCol; col++ )
        my_data[row][col] = row * col;
    }
  }

  private String padWithBlanks( String numAsString, int width )
  {
    int blanksToPad = width - numAsString.length( );
    for( int j = 1; j <= blanksToPad; j++ )
      numAsString = " " + numAsString;
    return numAsString;
  }

  public String toString( )
  { // Display the table elements
    String result = "";
    for( int row = 0; row < my_lastRow; row++ )
    {
      for( int col = 0; col < my_lastCol; col++ )
        result += padWithBlanks( "" + my_data[row][col], 5 );
      result += "\n";
    }
    return result;
  }
}
```

12. Using this two-dimensional array named t:

```
int nRows = 12;
int nCols = 15;
int[][] t = new int[nRows][nCols];
// Assume that all 12*15 elements of t are initialized
```

and assuming that all of the elements of t have been properly initialized, write code that displays the range of elements (highest - lowest) for each row on its own separate line.

Programming Tips

1. **There are many searching algorithms besides sequential and binary search.**
   These two searching algorithms are only two of many known searching algorithms. However, for small amounts of data, sequential search works very nicely. For larger amounts of data stored in sorted arrays, binary search works very nicely. There are many other ways to store very large amounts of data that can be searched rapidly, such as hash tables and binary search trees.

2. **There are many sorting algorithms besides selection sort.**
   Selection sort is only one of many known sorting algorithms. There are several others that have approximately the same runtime efficiencies. There are some that are much better.

3. **When initializing an array, display the values before continuing.**
   As soon as you believe that you have initialized an array, print the elements back to the screen before continuing to use it. This allows you to visualize the contents of the array and to verify that the array has been initialized correctly. A lot of debugging effort could potentially be wasted on the wrong portion of a program. It may appear that there is a bug later on in the program, when, in fact, the array had never been correctly initialized to begin with.

4. **When you have nested loops, try splitting the inner loop into its own method.**
   When processing 2-D arrays, it is usually preferable to use nested `for` loops to do the bulk of the processing. However, if you have nested loops doing almost anything else, it may make things clearer to place the inner loop into a separate method that is called from the outer loop. The `static sort` method in `MySorterSearcher` did just that.

5. **Many of the programming tips for arrays with one dimension can be applied to two- and three-dimensional arrays:**
   a. Subscripts must be integers.
   b. The range of subscripts is 0 to capacity - 1 (initialized size - 1).
   c. Subscript range-checking is always in force.

Programming Projects

11A `QuizData.quizAverage`

Write a method that returns the overall quiz average. Do not drop any quiz scores. This message must show the output that follows (the answer is rounded to the nearest hundredth):

```
DecimalFormat averageFormat = new DecimalFormat( "0.00" );

System.out.println( "Average of all quizzes (no quizzes dropped) = "
                    + cmpSc.quizAverage( ) );
```

Output

```
Average of all quizzes (no quizzes dropped) = 74.51
```

11B `QuizData.quizStatistics`

Implement and test `QuizData.quizStatistics`. This method must generate a report for each of the quizzes. For each quiz, show the highest and lowest quiz scores followed by the average. Do not drop the lowest quiz from the average. The method must generate output exactly like this:

Output

Quiz	High	Low	Average
====	=====	=====	=======
0	90.0	56.4	74.6
1	85.6	72.2	79.4
2	88.7	76.3	83.2
3	86.4	0.0	30.1
4	89.0	55.0	70.8
5	99.5	45.0	78.4

11C Initializing a Two-Dimensional Array with File Input

Write a program (the `main` method only) that reads data from an external file to initialize a two-dimensional array. The first line of the file contains the number of rows and columns for the table data that follows.

```
2  3
 -7.5     8.1    12.3
 22.19   16.7    -9.99
```

This file stores data to represent an array that is two rows by three columns and where 12.3 is the third element in row 1. Your program should be able to store two-dimensional arrays of any size. The elements may be `int`s or `double`s. The output should show the elements of the two-dimensional array. Using the file shown above, your output should look exactly like this (but your code should work on arrays of different sizes):

```
Initialized Table
    -7.50     8.10    12.30
    22.19    16.70    -9.99
```

11D Adding Matrices

The sum of two matrices a and b stored into the two-dimensional array c is defined
as follows:

c[j][k] = a[j][k] + b[j][k] for j ranging from 0 to m-1 and k ranging from 0 to n-1

Write a program (the main method only) that initializes two two-dimensional
arrays, named a and b, using data stored in a file. Since a and b must have the
same number of rows and columns, the first line of the input file will be used to
specify the number of rows followed by the number of columns. First create the
following input file:

```
3 4
1    2    3    4
5    6    7    8
9   10   11   12

-1    2    0    0
 3    0   -1    3
 3    2    1    0
```

Store the sum of the two matrices into a two-dimensional array named c. Display all
three two-dimensional arrays. Your output should look exactly like this:

```
two-dimensional array a:
   1    2    3    4
   5    6    7    8
   9   10   11   12

two-dimensional array b:
  -1    2    0    0
   3    0   -1    3
   3    2    1    0

two-dimensional array c: (a + b)
   0    4    3    4
   8    6    6   11
  12   12   12   12
```

11E A Statistics Report

Write a complete class that initializes a two-dimensional array through file input.
The row and column sizes are written as the first two integers in the file. The
output should include the entire two-dimensional array, with the highest and
lowest number in each row displayed to the right of each row. A sample input file is
shown with the output that should be generated. First create the following input
file:

```
3 5
11  53   6   -1   5
21  34   6   12   0
31  91   3  -12  55
```

Then complete a method that generates this output, appearing as close to the
following as possible (assuming that you use the previous input file):

```
      Col# 1    2    3    4    5    Hi    Lo
Row#      ----------------------    --    --
      1|   11   53   6   -1   5     53    -1
      2|   21   34   6   12   0     34     0
      3|   31   91   3  -12  55     91   -12
```

11F   Odd-Sized Magic Squares

A magic square is an n-by-n array where the integers 1 to n^2 appear exactly once
and the sum of the integers in every row, column, and on both diagonals is the
same. For example, the following is a 7-by-7 magic square. Notice that each row,
column, and both diagonals total 175 (in general, the sum is $n * (n^2 + 1) / 2$):

```
30   39   48    1   10   19   28

38   47    7    9   18   27   29

46    6    8   17   26   35   37

 5   14   16   25   34   36   45

13   15   24   33   42   44    4

21   23   32   41   43    3   12

22   31   40   49    2   11   20
```

Implement `MagicSquare` with a constructor and a `display` method. With the
algorithm given below, the argument must be odd. Throw an
`IllegalArgumentException` if the size is an even integer, less than 3, or greater
than 19.

```java
public class MagicSquare
{
  public static final int MAX_SIZE = 19;
  // ...

  public MagicSquare( int initSize )
  {
    if( initSize > MAX_SIZE || initSize < 3 || ( initSize % 2 == 0 ) )
      throw new IllegalArgumentException( "initSize = "+ initSize );
    // ...
```

The following code should generate output like that shown above:

```
MagicSquare magic = new MagicSquare( 7 );
magic.display( );
```

Also test other magic square sizes:

```
MagicSquare magic3 = new MagicSquare( 3 );
magic3.display( );

MagicSquare magic5 = new MagicSquare( 5 );
magic5.display( );
```

You should be able to construct an n-by-n magic square for any size from 3 through 15. When j is 1, place the value of j in the middle of the first row. Then, for a counter value ranging from 1 to n^2, move up one row and to the right by one column and store the counter value unless one of the following events occurs (*Note:* There are other algorithms for handling even numbers):

1. When the next row (j) becomes 0, make the next row equal to n - 1.
2. When the next column (j) becomes n, make the next column equal to 0.
3. If a position is already filled or the upper-right corner element has just obtained a value, place the next value (j) in the position that is one row below the position where the last counter value had been placed.

11G Verifying Magic Square

After implementing the `MagicSquare` class above, add a method that shows the sums of all the rows, columns, and both diagonals to ensure that each sum is the same. When n == 7, the output generated by the `MagicSquare` test method should look like this:

```
Sum of row 0 = 175
Sum of row 1 = 175
Sum of row 2 = 175
Sum of row 3 = 175
Sum of row 4 = 175
Sum of row 5 = 175
Sum of row 6 = 175

Sum of col 0 = 175
Sum of col 1 = 175
Sum of col 2 = 175
Sum of col 3 = 175
Sum of col 4 = 175
Sum of col 5 = 175
Sum of col 6 = 175

Sum of diagonal from (0, 0) to (6, 6) = 175

Sum of diagonal from (0, 6) to (6, 0) = 175
```

11H John Conway's Game of Life

The "Game of Life" was invented by John H. Conway to simulate the birth and death of cells in a society. The following rules govern the birth and/or death of these cells between two consecutive time periods. At time T:

1. A cell is born if there was none at time T - 1 and exactly three of its neighbors were alive.
2. An existing cell remains alive if at time T - 1 there were either two or three neighbors.
3. A cell dies from isolation if at time T - 1 there were fewer than two neighbors.
4. A cell dies from overcrowding if at time T - 1 there were more than three neighbors.

A neighborhood consists of the eight elements around any element:

```
O  O  O
O     O
O  O  O
```

The following patterns would occur for times ranging from 1 to 5, if the first society was that shown for T = 1. O represents a live cell; a blank indicates that no cell exists at the particular location in the society.

```
T=0     T=1     T=2     T=3     T=4
O O     O O
OOO     O O     O O      O                // Society dies off at T=4
         O       O       O
```

Other societies stabilize like this:

```
T=0     T=1     T=2     T=3     T=4
         O               O
OOO      O      OOO      O      OOO        // This pattern repeats
         O               O
```

Implement a class named GameOfLife that works with the following driver:

```java
public static void main( String[] args )
{
  GameOfLife society = new GameOfLife( "society1.dat" );
  while( society.hasMore( ) )
  {
    society.display( );
    society.update( );
  }
}
```

Suggestions

- Use two two-dimensional arrays to represent two consecutive societies. Use one to store the current society and the other to store the next society.
- Allow users to view a society for as long as they wish (ask them if they want another iteration).
- The input should consist of an initial society contained in an external file with no more than 72 columns and 22 lines (rows), where a live cell is represented by 'O'.
- Use an input file to more easily initialize your beginning society. Reading blanks from input streams can be a bit tricky, so this file uses periods (.) to represent empty cells and Os to represent live cells. Here is one possible file.

```
18 52
....................................................
....................................................
....................................................
....................................................
....................................................
....................................................
.............................................O......
......O.O.........O...........O........OO...........
......OOO........O.....OOO.....OOO.......OOO.........
.................O.............O........OO..........
..............................................O.....
....................................................
....................................................
....................................................
....................................................
....................................................
....................................................
....................................................
```

- Consider allowing the outer rows and columns to be used as a border where no cell may be placed. The rules no longer apply once the border is in a neighborhood. When this occurs, display a meaningful message and terminate the program with `System.exit( 0 );`. Or just imagine that you can no longer get any life or death from the outer edge.
- Implement the `GameOfLife` constructor first, the `display` method second, and the `update` method to do nothing.
- Complete the `hasMore` method. Your program should display the same society until the user desires to quit. The society will not change.
- Once you get the bugs out of a nonchanging society, concentrate on the `update` method. This will likely be the most difficult to implement.

Answers to Self-Check Questions

11-1   The array is sorted.

11-2   1,024; 512; 256; 128; 64; 32; 16; 8; 4; 2; 1 == 11

11-3   When `first` becomes greater than `last`.

11-4   Change the comparison from less than to greater than.
```
if( searchString.compareTo( str[mid] ) > 0 )
   last = mid - 1;
else
   first= mid + 1;   // ...
```

11-5   Ascending

11-6   The first element is swapped with itself.

11-7   ```
int largest = x[0];
for(int j = 0; j < n; j++)
if(x[j] > largest)
   largest = x[j];
```

11-8   ```
Andy
Chris
Jig
Mary Lou
Zach
---Search---
MARY LOU
```

11-9   Yes, as do all Java arrays.

11-10 12

11-11 0 through 2

11-12 0 through 3

11-13 ```
for(int row = 0; row <3; row++)
{
   for(int col = 0; col < 4; col++)
     a[row][col] = 999;
}
```

11-14  ```
for( row = 0; row < 3; row++ )
{
   for( col = 0; col < 4; col++ )
      System.out.print( padWithBlanks( ""+b[row][col], 8 ) );
   System.out.println( );
}
```

11-15 `double[][] sales = new double[10][12];`

11-16 `double[][] sales = new double[12][10];`

11-17 ```
DecimalFormat numberFormatter
      = new DecimalFormat("**###,###,##0.0");
```

11-18  row

11-19  column
```

```
11-20 TextReader in = new TextReader( "t.dat" );
      int nRows = in.readInt( );
      int nCols = in.readInt( );
      int[][] t = new int[nRows][nCols];
      for( int r = 0; r < nRows; r++ )
      {
        for( int c = 0; c < nCols; c++ )
          t[r][c] = in.readInt( );
      }
11-21 int sum = 0;
      for( int r = 0; r < nRows; r++ )
      {
        for( int c = 0; c < nCols; c++ )
          sum += t[r][c];
        System.out.println( "Sum = " + sum );
      }
11-22 for( int r = 0; r < nRows; r++ )
      {
        int largest = t[r][0];
        for( int c = 1; c < nCols; c++ )
        {
          if( t[r][c] > largest )
            largest = t[r][c];
        }
        System.out.println( "Largest in row " + r + " = " + largest );
      }


      int x[3][4][5];
11-23 60
```

11-24 -a Valid   -d Invalid, need [] for each subscript.
      -b Valid   -e Invalid, missing one subscript.
      -c Invalid, each subscript is too high. -f Invalid, missing two subscripts.

Chapter 12
Simple Recursion

Summing Up

Chapters 1 through 8 presented challenging concepts for a one semester introductory course on object-oriented programming in Java at the university level. Chapter 9 introduced exception handling and enough of Java's I/O streams to have persistent objects. Chapter 10 introduced an informal object-oriented software methodology where a small inheritance hierarchy was designed and built. Finally, Chapter 11 showed a couple of 1-D array algorithms, 2-D arrays, and static methods.

Coming Up

This chapter introduces simple recursive methods—methods that invoke another instance of the same method. This brief introduction hints at problems that cannot be easily solved without recursion. After studying this chapter you will be able to

- compare iterative and recursive solutions to the same problem
- identify the recursive case and the base case of recursive algorithms and methods
- implement simple recursive methods
- solve a problem where the recursive solution is better than the iterative solution

Exercises and programming projects help understand recursion.

12.1   Recursion

One day, an instructor was having difficulties with a classroom's multimedia equipment. The bell rang, and still there was no way to project the lecture notes for the day. To keep her students occupied while waiting for the AV folks, she asked one of her favorite students, Kelly, to take attendance. Since the topic of the day was recursion, the instructor proposed a recursive solution. Instead of counting each student in the class, Kelly could count the number of students in her row and remember that count. The instructor asked Kelly to ask another student in the row behind her to do the same thing—count the number of students in your row, remember the count, and ask the same question of the next row.

By the time the question reached the last row of seats in the room, there was one person in each row who knew the number of students in that particular row. Andy, who had just counted eight students in the last row, asked his instructor what to do since there were no more rows of seats behind him. The teacher responded that all he had to do was return the number of students in his row to the person who asked him the question moments ago. So Andy gave his answer of eight to the person in the row in front of him.

The student in the second to last row added the number of people in her row (12) to the number of students in the row behind her, which Andy had just told her (8). She returned the sum of 20 to the person in the third row from the back of the room.

At that point the AV folks arrived and discovered a bent pin in a video jack. As they were fixing this, the students continued to return the number of students in their row plus the number of students behind them until Kelly was informed that there were 50 students in all the rows behind her. At that point, the lecture notes, titled "Recursion," were visible on the screen. Kelly told her teacher that there were 50 plus the 12 students in her first row for a total of 62 students present.

The teacher adapted her lecture. She began by writing the algorithm for the head count problem. Every row got this same algorithm.

if you have rows behind you
    return the number of students in your row plus the number behind you
otherwise
    return the number of students in your row

Andy asked why Kelly couldn't have just counted the students one by one. The teacher responded, "That would be an iterative solution. You just solved a problem using a recursive solution. This is precisely how I intend to introduce recursion to you, by comparing recursive solutions to problems that could also be solved with iteration. I will suggest to you that some problems are better handled by a recursive solution."

Here is another example of a recursive solution to a problem that has moments when nothing more needs to be done—this is the **base case**—and moments when the same thing needs to be done again while bringing the problem closer to a base case. **Recursion** involves partitioning problems into simpler subproblems. Recursion requires that each subproblem be identical in structure to the original problem. Imagine the teacher needed to call all of her students to cancel a class. She could call all 62 students using this iterative solution:

for all students in the class
    call a student and give that student the cancellation message

Another solution would be for the class to develop a phone tree in advance. A phone tree works like this: The instructor calls two students and gives them a class cancellation message. These two students do the same thing—call two more students and give them the cancellation message. In this manner, each phone call simplifies the original problem until the base case occurs. The base case occurs when there are no more students to call.

The base case in the head count problem occurred at the last row. The last row had part of an answer. There were no more calls to make to the rows behind. In the case of the phone tree, the base case occurs many times—whenever there is no one else to call. The recursive phone tree solution can be illustrated as follows, where each o represents a phone call that has been made.

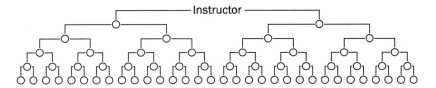

This recursive-like solution is more elegant than its iterative solution for two reasons:

1. the instructor needs to make only two phone calls instead of 62 and
2. the entire class is notified in a much shorter time.

Each phone call results in a problem that is closer to the final solution. There are fewer and fewer phone calls to be made. Eventually, an occurrence of the base case is obtained when a student does not have to call anyone else.

Here are two characteristics of recursive algorithms that can be applied to these noncomputer examples.

1. It must be possible to partition the problem into subproblems that have the same structure as the original problem.
2. A base case must eventually be reached so no more recursive calls are made.

What should students do when they receive a phone call? Either they will do what their caller did or, in the case of the final 32 people, they will do nothing at all. This means that each time a phone call is made, the solution to the subproblem is either another similar occurrence of the original solution or nothing more to do.

The recursive phone tree solution has subproblems with the same exact structure as the original problem. Only the data (the phone numbers) are different. Each time a student is called, he or she could use the following algorithm to help solve the problem:

if I need to make two phone calls
  simplify the problem by making two phone calls
otherwise
  do nothing

Before looking at some recursive Java methods, consider a few more examples of recursive solutions and definitions. Recursive definitions define something by using that something as part of the definition.

Recursion Example 1

Look up a word in a dictionary:

  find the word in the dictionary
  if there is a word in the definition that you do not understand
    look up that word in the dictionary

  Example: Look up the term **object**

  look up **object**, which is defined as "an instance of a **class**."

  What is a class? *Look up* **class** to find "a collection of **method**s and data."

  What is a method? *Look up* **method** to find "a **method heading** followed by a collection of programming statements."

  What is a method heading? *Look up* **method heading** to find "the name of a method, its **return type**, followed by a **parameter list** in parentheses."

  What is a parameter list? *Look up* **parameter list** to find "a **list** of **parameters**." *Look up* **list**, *look up* **parameters**, and *look up* **return type**, and you finally get a definition of all of the terms using the same method you used to *look up* the original term. And then, when all new terms are defined, you have a definition for **object**.

Recursion Example 2

A definition of a *waiting line*:

> empty
> or has someone at the front of the waiting line followed by a *waiting line*

Recursion Example 3

An arithmetic expression is defined as one of these:

> a numeric constant such as 123 or –0.001
> or a numeric variable that stores a numeric constant
> or an *arithmetic expression* enclosed in parentheses
> or an *arithmetic expression* followed by a binary operator (+, -, /, %, or *) followed by an *arithmetic expression*

Characteristics of Recursion

A **recursive definition** is a definition that includes a simpler version of itself. One example of a recursive definition is given next: the power method that raises an integer (x) to an integer power (n).

$$x^n \begin{cases} 1 \text{ if } n = 0 \\ x * x^{n-1} \text{ if } x \geq 1 \end{cases}$$

This definition is recursive because x^{n-1} is part of the definition itself. For example,

$$4^3 = 4 \times 4^{(n-1)} = 4 \times 4^{(3-1)} = 4 \times 4^2$$

What is 4^2? Using the recursive definition above, 4^2 is defined as:

$$4^2 = 4 \times 4^{(n-1)} = 4 \times 4^{(2-1)} = 4 \times 4^1$$

and 4^1 is defined as

$$4^1 = 4 \times 4^{(n-1)} = 4 \times 4^{(1-1)} = 4 \times 4^0$$

and 4^0 is a base case defined as

$$4^0 = 1$$

The recursive definition of 4^3 includes three recursive definitions. The base case is n == 0:

$$x^n = 1 \text{ if } n = 0$$

To get the actual value of 4^3, work backward and let 1 replace 4^0, 4 * 1 replace 4^1, 4 * 4^1 replace 4^2, and 4 * 4^2 replace 4^3. Therefore, 4^3 is defined as 64.

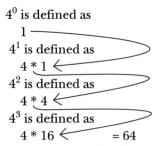

4^0 is defined as
   1
4^1 is defined as
   4 * 1
4^2 is defined as
   4 * 4
4^3 is defined as
   4 * 16   = 64

To be recursive, an algorithm or method requires at least one recursive case and at least one base case. The recursive algorithm for power illustrates the characteristics of a recursive solution to a problem.

1. The problem can be decomposed into a simpler version of itself in order to bring the problem closer to a base case.
2. There is at least one base case that does not make a recursive call.
3. The partial solutions are managed in such a way that all occurrences of the recursive and base cases can communicate their partial solutions to the proper locations (values are returned).

Comparing Iterative and Recursive Solutions

For many problems involving repetition, a recursive solution exists. For example, an iterative solution is shown below along with a recursive solution in the PowFunctions class, with the methods powLoop and powRecurse, respectively.

```
// A class with two methods

public class PowFunctions
{
  public static int powLoop( int base, int power )
  { // Precondition: base and power are positive && base != 0
    int result;
    if( power == 0 )
      result = 1;
    else
    {
      result = base;
      for( int j = 2; j <= power; j++ )
        result = result * base;
    }
    return result;
  }

  public static int powRecurse( int base, int power )
  {
    // Precondition: base and power are positive && base != 0
    if( power == 0 )
```

```
      return 1;
   else               // Make this recursive call \\
      return base * powRecurse( base, power - 1 );
}

public static void main( String[] args )
{
   System.out.println( "powLoop( base, power )" );
   System.out.println( "4^0 is " + powLoop( 4, 0 ) );
   System.out.println( "4^1 is " + powLoop( 4, 1 ) );
   System.out.println( "4^2 is " + powLoop( 4, 2 ) );
   System.out.println( "4^4 is " + powLoop( 4, 4 ) );

   System.out.println( "\npowRecurse( base, power )" );
   System.out.println( "4^0 is " + powRecurse( 4, 0 ) );
   System.out.println( "4^1 is " + powRecurse( 4, 1 ) );
   System.out.println( "4^2 is " + powRecurse( 4, 2 ) );
   System.out.println( "4^4 is " + powRecurse( 4, 4 ) );
   }
}
```

Output

```
powLoop( base, power )
4^0 is 1
4^1 is 4
4^2 is 16
4^4 is 256

powRecurse( base, power )
4^0 is 1
4^1 is 4
4^2 is 16
4^4 is 256
```

In powRecurse, if n is 0—the base case—the method call evaluates to 1. When n > 0—the **recursive case**—the method is invoked again with the argument reduced in value by one. For example, powRecurse(4, 1) calls powRecurse(4, 1 - 1), which immediately returns 1. For another example, the original call powRecurse(2, 4) calls powRecurse(2, 3), which then calls powRecurse(2, 2), which then calls powRecurse(2, 1), which then calls powRecurse(2, 0), which returns 1. Then 2 * powRecurse(2, 0) evaluates to 2 * 1 or 2, so 2 * powRecurse(2, 1) evaluates to 4, so 2 * powRecurse(2, 2) evaluates to 8, so 2 * powRecurse(2, 3) evaluates to 16, so 2 * powRecurse(2, 4) evaluates to 32.

Tracing Recursive Calls

Tracing recursive methods requires diligence, but it can help you understand what is going on. Consider tracing a call to the recursive power method to get 2^4.

```
System.out.println( "2^4 is " + powRecurse( 2, 4 ) );
```

Output

```
2^4 is 16
```

After the initial call powRecurse(2, 4), powRecurse calls another instance of itself until the base case of power == 0 is reached. The following picture illustrates a method that calls instances of the same method. The arrows that go up indicate this. When an instance of the method can return something, it returns that value to the method that called it. The arrows that go down with the return values written to the right indicate this.

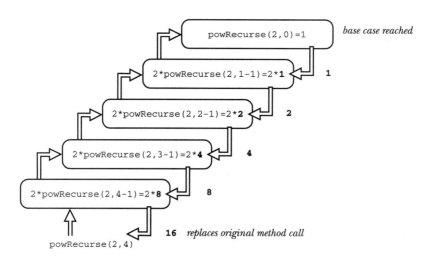

The final value of 16 is returned to the main method, where the arguments of 2 and 4 were passed to the first instance of powRecurse.

Self-Check

12-1 What is the value of PowerFunctions.powRecurse(3, 0)?

12-2 What is the value of PowerFunctions.powRecurse(3, 1)?

12-3 Fill in the blanks with a trace of the call
PowerFunctions.powRecurse(3, 4).

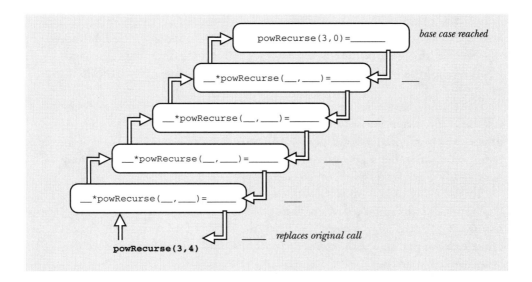

12.2 How Recursion Works

How does a method that calls itself so many times know when to quit calling itself? And how does a program know where to continue when a method has finished? Consider the analogy of a pile of boxes that can be stacked one on top of another (without ever falling down). Each box contains certain vital information that allows a method to execute correctly. At the beginning of a program, there are no boxes on the stack. When a method is called, the vital information needed by that method is stored into a box. This box is then placed onto the stack of boxes.

Next, the computer begins to execute the statements in the method. As the method executes its statements, the information is available from the box on top of the stack. For example, if a change is made to a local variable or the value of a parameter is needed, that information can be found in the box.

When a method has finished executing its own statements, the return point must be available in order to continue from the point of the method call. A return point is the place the program returns to when a method has finished executing. More specifically, the return point is the address of the next machine instruction to be executed.

So where is the value of the return point stored? It is in the box on top of the stack. It was stored there along with the other vital information when the method was originally called.

A recursive method is handled in the same manner. When a method calls itself, the vital information is stored into a new box. This box is placed on top of the stack of boxes. The only thing that may appear to be different is that the return point happens to be in another instance of the same method that has just been called. The computer then begins executing the statements of the method associated with the vital information in the top box. Every instance of the method is associated with a box on the stack. The stack of boxes "remembers" the vital information for all methods that have been called but have not yet finished executing.

When one instance of a method is finished, the top box is removed from the stack and the program continues from the correct return point. The vital information for the current method is now in the box at the top of the stack. This allows a method to remember its own set of vital information even though there may have been many other boxes piled on top of it.

This stacking of boxes provides a useful tool for tracing recursive methods. Let's illustrate this stack of boxes analogy with a simple recursive method that displays the integers 1 through n, where n is a parameter. The recursive method forward contains a comment to show the return point stored into the box before the recursive call is made.

```java
public class ShowDirection
{
  public static void forward( int n )
  {
    if( n > 1 )
      forward( n - 1 );
    // RP# FORWARD
    System.out.println( n );
  }

  public static void main( String[] args )
  {
    int number = 3;
    forward( number );
    // RP# MAIN
    System.out.println( "back in main" );
  }
}
```

Before the program begins executing, there are no boxes. When main is called, the main method's information is placed on top of the stack of boxes. When main completes later, the program will be done. This main method is represented by this box.

```
Program done
number = 3
```

When forward is invoked from main, the return point, RP# MAIN, and the value of n (3) are stored into a new box and placed on top. The stack of boxes is now represented as two boxes, where the top box contains the return point (RP# MAIN) and the value of the single parameter n.

```
RP# MAIN
  n   3
Program done
number = 3
```

Since n > 1 is true, the recursive call is made that causes the return point and the value of n to be stored into another new box on the top. During the second call to forward, the recursive call within the if statement executes once again, causing the stack to look like this:

```
RP#  FORWARD
  n   2
RP#  MAIN
  n   3
Program done
number = 3
```

During the third call to forward, the recursive call within the if statement executes once again, causing the stack to look like this:

```
RP#  FORWARD
  n   1
RP#  FORWARD
  n   2
RP#  MAIN
  n   3
Program done
number = 3
```

The code in forward begins to execute again, but now the recursive call within the if statement is skipped because n > 1 is false. The last statement in the third instance of forward is executed: System.out.println(n);. Even though there are three different values of n, the method knows which one to print. It prints its own value of n (in the box on the top). Therefore, the integer 1 is displayed and the third execution of forward is completed.

Once the program is about to continue from the return point stored in the box on the top of the stack, that top box can be removed. Now the stack contains only three boxes, and the program continues executing from RP# FORWARD in the previous instance of forward.

| RP# FORWARD |
| n   2 |
| RP# MAIN |
| n   3 |
| Program done |
| number = 3 |

RP# FORWARD is located at the end of the if statement. So the next statement executed is the first statement after RP# FORWARD: the println in the previous instance. This causes the value of n to be printed. Since the value of this variable was stored in the box at the top, the system knows that n has the value of 2. The output is 2.

Now that the second instance of forward has finished executing, the program returns to RP# FORWARD in the first instance of forward. The stack of boxes now looks like this:

| RP# MAIN |
| n   3 |
| Program done |
| number = 3 |

The value of n (3) is then output and control returns to main at RP# MAIN. The println message in main executes. Here is the complete output from the program above.

Output

```
1
2
3
back in main
```

The stack of boxes analogy is similar to the stack used by computer systems to control the execution of methods. The difference is that the computer uses memory to store the vital information. Each time a method is called, more memory is used up because each method must have its own set of vital information stored (values of parameters, local variables, and the return point). The space reserved for this stack has a limit. If an attempt is made to store another set of vital information when there is no more memory, an OutOfMemoryException occurs.

Here is another view that traces this recursive forward method. It goes left to right.

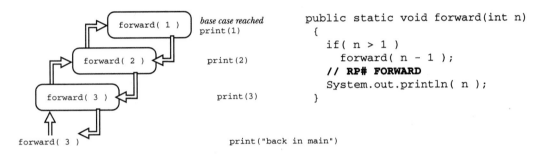

The main method calls forward, which calls forward, which calls forward until the base case is reached. The integer 1 is printed, and the most recently stacked box is removed from the top. Control returns to RP# FORWARD in the new top box where 2 is printed. Control then returns to the original call to forward where 3 is printed. Then control returns to main, "back in main" is printed, and the program is done. Here is another way to look at it.

```
forward( 1 )      base case reached    public static void forward(int n)
                  print(1)             {
                                         if( n > 1 )
forward( 2 )      print(2)                 forward( n - 1 );
                                         // RP# FORWARD
forward( 3 )      print(3)               System.out.println( n );
                                       }

forward( 3 )      print("back in main")
```

Self-Check

12-4 Write the output from calling direction(10).

```
public static void direction( int n )
{
  if( n >= 2 )
  {
    System.out.print( n + " | " );
    direction( n - 2 );
  }
}
```

12-5 Write the output from calling forwardAgain(10).

```
public static void forwardAgain( int n )
{
  if( n >= 2 )
  {
    forwardAgain( n - 2 );
    System.out.print( n + " | " );
  }
}
```

> **12-6** Write a method named `backward` that takes two `int` parameters named `high` and `low` and recursively displays the integers from `high` down to `low`. Use recursion. Do not use a loop.

Defining the Base and Recursive Cases

Being able to determine the base case and the recursive case is a requirement of recursive programming. In `forward`, the base case occurred when n == 1. When this base case was reached, n was printed; no recursive call was made. Even if nothing happens when the base case is reached, it is critical that a base case is available. Without an appropriate base case, a method may call itself endlessly.

Returning to the first recursive definition, which defined the method of raising an integer to an integer power (x^n), the base case occurred when n == 0. At this point, x^0 was defined as 1. The recursive case occurred whenever n > 0. At that point, x^n was defined as $x * x^{(n-1)}$. Whereas `forward` had a do-nothing base case, `powRecurse` had a base case of returning 1 back to the method that called `powRecurse( 0 )`.

Recursive Methods

Consider another method, `mystery`, that contains two parameters (`mystery` serves no useful purpose other than illustrating a recursive method). The recursive definition of mystery is

$$\text{mystery}(j, k) \begin{cases} 1 \text{ if } j <= k \\ j + k + \text{mystery}(j - 1, k + 2) \text{ if } j > k \end{cases}$$

From this definition the recursive and base cases can be easily determined:

Base Case
```
if( j <= k )
   mystery = 1;
```

Recursive Case
```
if( j > k )
   mystery = j + k + mystery( j - 1, k + 2 );
```

When the base case is encountered, `mystery` simply returns 1. Otherwise, the method is called recursively with the first argument decreased by one and the second argument increased by two. Note that the return point after the recursive method call is in an expression. Only after `mystery( j - 1, k + 2 )` is evaluated can the entire expression be evaluated and then returned.

```java
public class Mystery
{
  public static int mystery( int j, int k )
  {
    if( j <= k )
      return 1;
    else
      return j + k + /* RP# MYST */ mystery( j - 1, k + 2 );
  }

  public static void main( String[] args )
  {
    System.out.println( "mystery(2, 4) = " + mystery( 2, 4 ) );   // 1
    System.out.println( "mystery(4, 2) = " + mystery( 4, 2 ) );   // 7
    System.out.println( "mystery(9, 0) = " + mystery( 9, 0 ) );   // 31
  }
}
```

Output

```
mystery(2, 4) = 1
mystery(4, 2) = 7
mystery(9, 0) = 31
```

The first call to mystery finds the base case immediately and returns 1. The second call returns the sum of its arguments plus mystery(3, 5) or $4 + 2 + 1$. Let's trace the third call of mystery(9, 0), which finds the recursive case three times before reaching the base case.

Tracing mystery(9, 0)

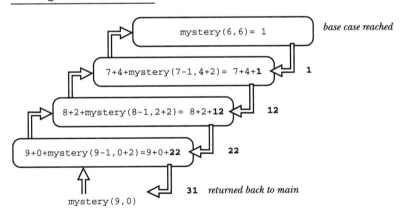

The base case has mystery return 1. Then the previous expression can be returned as $7 + 4 + 1$, the value of mystery(7, 4). We can move backwards until the first call to Mystery can return $9 + 0 + 22$ as 31. Here is another trace using the stack of boxes analogy to show how the stack grows and shrinks. When each call to mystery finishes, the expression within the previous method call can finally be evaluated (return values are shown in boldface).

Another Way to Trace the Recursive Method Mystery.mystery(int n)

```
                                    RP# MYST   1
                                    j == 6     base case
                                    k == 6

                         RP# MYST  RP# MYST  RP# MYST   j+k+mystery(6,6)
              Start      j == 7    j == 7    j == 7     7+4+  1  = 12
              Point      k == 4    k == 4    k == 4

                |    RP# MYST  RP# MYST  RP# MYST  RP# MYST  RP# MYST   j+k+mystery(7,4)
                |    j == 8    j == 8    j == 8    j == 8    j == 8     8+2+ 12  = 22
                V    k == 2    k == 2    k == 2    k == 2    k == 2

 RP# MAIN  RP# MAIN  RP# MAIN  RP# MAIN  RP# MAIN  RP# MAIN  RP# MAIN   j+k+mystery(8,2)
 j == 9    j == 9    j == 9    j == 9    j == 9    j == 9    j == 9     9+0+  22  = 31
 k == 0    k == 0    k == 0    k == 0    k == 0    k == 0    k == 0
```

A Factorial Method Using Iteration

Consider the factorial method (designated by !, an exclamation mark). n! has the following nonrecursive definition:

Iterative Definition for factorial

$$n! \begin{cases} 1 \text{ if } n = 0 \text{ or } n = 1 \\ n * (n-1) * (n-2) * (n-3) * K * 3 * 2 * 1 \text{ if } n > 1 \end{cases}$$

Examples:

0! = 1

1! = 1

5! = 5 * 4 * 3 * 2 * 1 = 120

The following factorial method is written to return n! iteratively. It is assumed that the only values for n are fairly small. (13! would be too large to be represented even as an int.) The factorial method is undefined for n < 0.

```
public class FactorialLoop
{
  public static int factorial( int n )
  { // Precondition: n >= 0 and n is not too large (n < 13)
    int result = 1;
    for( int j = 2; j <= n; j++ )
    {
      result = result * j;
    }
    return result;
  }
```

```
public static void main( String[] args )
{
  System.out.println( factorial( 0 ) );   // 1
  System.out.println( factorial( 1 ) );   // 1
  System.out.println( factorial( 2 ) );   // 2
  System.out.println( factorial( 3 ) );   // 6
  System.out.println( factorial( 4 ) );   // 24
  System.out.println( factorial( 12 ) );   // 479001600
}
}
```

The `factorial` method also has a recursive definition.

$$n! \begin{cases} 1 \text{ if } n = 0 \\ n * (n - 1)! \text{ if } n \geq 1 \end{cases}$$

This definition of the `factorial` method uses the method itself as part of the definition when n > 0. Here are some examples:

```
0! = 1
5! = 5*(5-1)! = 120
```

Now 5! can be calculated by repeatedly bringing the solution one step closer to the base case (n == 0):

```
5! = 5*(4)! = 5*4*(3)! = 5*4*3*(2)! = 5*4*3*2*(1)! = 5*4*3*2*1*(0)!
```

At this time 0! is assigned the value of 1 and we can start moving backwards by replacing previous calls with the partial solutions.

```
           0!            1!          2!         3!      4!     5!
           |             |           |          |       |      |
5*4*3*2*1*1  = 5*4*3*2*1 = 5*4*3*2 =  5*4*6 = 5*24 = 120
```

When `main` calls `factorial( 12 )`, the first occurrence of `factorial` sees n == 12. The method will call itself 12 more times for n = 11, 10, 9, . . ., 0, where each recursive call uses the argument n - 1. The base case is finally reached when the method is called with n == 0 and 1 is assigned to the method.

```
public class FactorialRecursively
{
  public static int factorial( int n )
  { // Pre: n >= 0 and n is not too large
    if( n == 0 ) // Base case
      return 1;
    else
      return n * /* RP# FACT */ factorial( n - 1 );   // Recursive case
  }

  public static void main( String[] args )
  {
    System.out.println( /* RP# MAIN */ factorial( 3 ) );   // 6
  }
}
```

Tracing `factorial(3)`

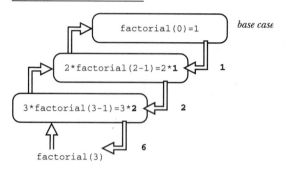

	RP# FACT n == 0	1 *base case*					
	RP# FACT n == 1	RP# FACT n == 1	RP# FACT n == 1	n*factorial(0) 1* 1			
	RP# FACT n == 2	RP# FACT n == 2	RP# FACT n == 2	RP# FACT n == 2	RP# FACT n == 2	n*factorial(1) 2* 1	
RP# MAIN n == 3	RP# MAIN n == 3	RP# MAIN n == 3	RP# MAIN n == 3	RP# MAIN n == 3	RP# MAIN n == 3	RP# MAIN n == 3	n*factorial(2) 3* 2 == 6

Infinite Recursion

As shown in Chapter 7, "Repetition," care must be taken to avoid infinite loops. Care must also be taken to avoid infinite recursion. **Infinite recursion** occurs when a method keeps calling other instances of the same method without making progress towards a base case. For example, the following slight change of – to + in the `factorial` method just shown will result in the method going away from rather than reaching the base case (unless it is called with n <= 0). The arguments to `factorial` get larger, not smaller.

```
public static int factorial( int n )
{ // Pre: n >= 0 and n is not too large
  if( n == 0 ) // Base case
    return 1;
  else
    return n * factorial( n + 1 );    // Change - to +
}
```

Instead of getting the correct answers, the program terminates with an exception. Eventually, there is no computer memory left to store any more instances of the method.

Self-Check

12-7 What value is returned from f(-3)?

```java
public static int f( int n )
{
  if( n < 0 )
    return n;
  else
    return n + f( n - 2 );
}
```

12-8 What value is returned from f(1)?

12-9 What value is returned from f(3)?

12-10 What value is returned from f(7)?

12-11 What could happen if the recursive call f(n - 2) is changed to f(n + 2)?

12.3 Converting Decimal Numbers to Other Bases

This section presents a recursive solution to the problem of converting a decimal number to different number bases. Although you are already familiar with the base 10 (decimal) number system that uses the digits from 0 to 9, other number systems can be better understood by reviewing base 10 numbers. A decimal number such as 9507 can also be written in an expanded form in this way:

$$9507 = 9 \times 10^3 + 5 \times 10^2 + 0 \times 10^1 + 7 \times 10^0$$
$$9000 + 500 + 0 + 7$$

Each digit in the decimal number system represents a coefficient of a power of 10. The rightmost coefficient is multiplied by 10^0, the second rightmost coefficient is multiplied by 10^1, and so on.

The base 8 (octal) number system contains the eight digits in the range of 0 to 7. Each digit is a coefficient of a power of the base, which in this case is 8. Therefore, the octal number 1567 can be written in this expanded form:

$$1567_8 = 1 \times 8^3 + 5 \times 8^2 + 6 \times 8^1 + 7 \times 8^0$$

or in decimal notation as

$$512 + 320 + 48 + 7 \qquad (887_{10} = 1567_8)$$

So 1567 octal is equivalent to 887 base 10. The problem now is to write a recursive method that converts a decimal number to other number systems with bases in the range of 2 through 9. The method must be tested with calls like this:

Method Call	Output
`printInDifferentBase( 99, 2 )`	`1100011`
`printInDifferentBase( 99, 3 )`	`10200`
`printInDifferentBase( 99, 4 )`	`1203`
`printInDifferentBase( 99, 5 )`	`344`
`printInDifferentBase( 99, 6 )`	`243`
`printInDifferentBase( 99, 7 )`	`201`
`printInDifferentBase( 99, 8 )`	`143`
`printInDifferentBase( 99, 9 )`	`120`

A decimal number can be converted to another number system by dividing the decimal number by the new base and writing the remainders in a right-to-left order. Each time the decimal number is divided, the quotient becomes the next dividend. This process continues as long as the decimal number is greater than 0. The divisor is always the base of the number to be converted. For example, converting 5_{10} to its binary equivalent (base 2) goes like this:

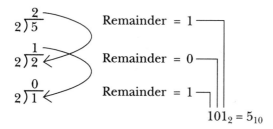

$$101_2 = 5_{10}$$

Another Example: **Converting 99_{10} to its base 8 (octal) equivalent**

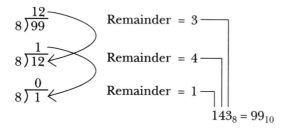

$$143_8 = 99_{10}$$

An iterative algorithm is given where `decimalNumber` is the number to be converted and `newBase` is the base of the new number (2 or 8, perhaps):

```
while decimalNumber > 0
{
    decimalNumber = decimalNumber / newBase
    write the remainder decimalNumber % newBase
}
```

One of the problems with this algorithm is that Java does not include a method for printing digits in a right-to-left order. This problem can be overcome with a recursive solution. In either an iterative or a recursive solution, a method that converts a decimal number to a specified base requires two arguments:

1. decimalNumber: the decimal number to be converted
2. base: the base of the number system that the decimal number is to be converted to

Recall that the division of decimalNumber by base should occur until the quotient is 0. This leads to the base case.

Base Case

if decimalNumber <= 0
    Stop-do nothing

Therefore, the recursive call should be invoked whenever this is true.

Recursive Case

if decimalNumber > 0

Recursion is being used here to postpone the printing of the remainder until the base case is reached. Therefore, the first thing to do is to convert the quotient, decimalNumber / base, using the same base. By stacking the value of each quotient, each remainder can then be displayed in a reverse order. This leads to the recursive case.

Recursive Case

if decimalNumber > 0
{
    printInDifferentBase(decimalNumber / base, base)
    display decimalNumber % base   // Postponed until decimalNumber is 0
}

All of the remainders will be stored until the quotient becomes 0. As the methods finish, the remainder, decimalNumber % base, is output followed by the second to last, and so on. The statement System.out.println(decimalNumber % base); does not execute until the quotient of decimalNumber / base becomes zero.

The following program tests the input described earlier in this demonstration. The decimal number 99 is converted to base 2 through the base 10 number system.

```java
public class NumberConverter
{
  public static void printInDifferentBase( int decimalNumber, int base )
  {
    if( decimalNumber > 0 )
    {
```

```
        printInDifferentBase( decimalNumber / base, base );
        System.out.print( decimalNumber % base );
    }
  }

  public static void main( String[] args )
  {
    for( int base = 2; base <= 10; base++ )
    {
      System.out.print( "99 base " + base + " = " );
      printInDifferentBase( 99, base );
      System.out.println( );
    }
  }
}
```

Output

```
99 base 2  = 1100011
99 base 3  = 10200
99 base 4  = 1203
99 base 5  = 344
99 base 6  = 243
99 base 7  = 201
99 base 8  = 143
99 base 9  = 120
99 base 10 = 99
```

Self-Check

12-12 True or False: The decimal number 5 is represented by 101 in the binary number system.

12-13 True or False: The decimal number 10 is represented as 25 in the base 8 number system.

12-14 What is 8 in binary (base 2)?

12-15 What is 15 in binary (base 2)?

12-16 Write the output of the following program:

```
public class NumberConverter
{
  public static String numberAsString( int decimalNumber,
                                        int base )
  {
    if( decimalNumber == 0 )
      return "0";
    else  // + concatenates here, it does not add
      return numberAsString( decimalNumber / base, base ) +
                            ( decimalNumber % base );
  }
```

```
   public static void main( String[] args )
   {
      System.out.println( numberAsString(  0,  2 ) );
      System.out.println( numberAsString( 99, 10 ) );
      System.out.println( numberAsString( 99,  8 ) );
   }
}
```

12.4   Palindrome

Suppose that you had a word and you wanted the computer to check whether or not it was a palindrome. A palindrome is a word that is the same whether read forward or backward; radar, madam, and racecar, for example. To determine if a word is a palindrome, you could put one finger under the first letter, and one finger under the last letter. If those letters matched, move your fingers one letter closer to each other, and check those letters. Repeat this until two letters don't match or your fingers touch because there are no more letters to consider.

The recursive solution is similar to this. To solve the problem using a simpler version of the problem, you can check the two letters on the end. If they match, ask whether the String with the end letters removed is a palindrome.

The base case occurs when the method finds a String of length two with the same two letters. A simpler case would be a String with only one letter, or a String with no letters. Checking for a String with 0 or 1 letters is easier than comparing the ends of a String with the same two letters. When thinking about a base case, ask yourself, "Is this the simplest case? Or can I get anything simpler?" Two base cases (the number of characters is 0 or 1) can be handled like this (assume str is the String object being checked).

```
if( str.length( ) <= 1 )
   return true;
```

Another base case is the discovery that the two end letters are different when str has two or more letters.

```
else if( str.charAt( 0 ) != str.charAt( str.length( ) - 1 ) )
   return false; // The end characters do not match
```

So now the method can handle the base cases with Strings such as "", "A", and "no". The first two are palindromes; "no" is not.

If a String is two or more characters in length and the end characters match, no decision can be made other than to keep trying. The same method can now be asked to solve a simpler version of the problem. Take off the end characters and check to see if the smaller string is a palindrome. String's substring method will take the substring of a String like "abba" to get "bb".

```
// This is a substring of the original string
// with both end characters removed.
return isPalindrome( str.substring( 1, str.length( ) - 1 ) );
```

This message will not resolve on the next call. When `str` is `"bb"`, the next call is
`isPalindrome( "" )`, which returns `true`. It has reached a base case—length is 0.
Here is a recursive palindrome method inside a class with its own test driver. The
expected result is shown after =?.

```java
public class PalindromeChecker
{
  // Return true if str is a palindrome or false if it is not
  public static boolean isPalindrome( String str )
  {
    if( str.length( ) <= 1 )
      // Base case when this method knows to return true
      return true;
    else if( str.charAt( 0 ) != str.charAt( str.length( ) - 1 ) )
      // Base case when this method knows to return
      // false because the end characters do not match
      return false;
    else
      // The first and last characters are equal so ask
      // isPalindrome if the shorter string (a simpler
      // version of this problem) is a palindrome.
      return isPalindrome( str.substring( 1, str.length( ) - 1 ) );
  }

  public static void main( String[] args )
  {
    System.out.println( isPalindrome( "" )       + " =? true"  );
    System.out.println( isPalindrome( "A" )      + " =? true"  );
    System.out.println( isPalindrome( "no" )     + " =? false" );
    System.out.println( isPalindrome( "abba" )   + " =? true"  );
    System.out.println( isPalindrome( "racecar" ) + " =? true"  );
    System.out.println( isPalindrome( "oh-no" )  + " =? false" );
  }
}
```

Output

```
true =? true
true =? true
false =? false
true =? true
true =? true
false =? false
```

If the length of the `String` is greater than 1 and the end characters match,
`isPalindrome` calls another instance of `isPalindrome` with smaller and smaller

String arguments until one of the base cases is reached. Either a String is found that has a length less than or equal to 1, or the characters on the ends are not the same. The following trace of isPalindrome("racecar") visualizes the calls that are made in this way.

isPalindrome Recursive Calls (true result)

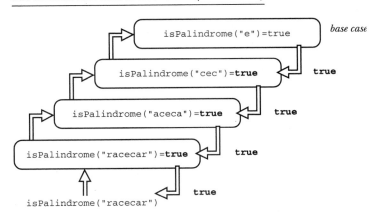

Since the fourth (topmost) call to isPalindrome is called with the String "e", a base case is found—a String with length 1. This true value gets returned to its caller (argument was "e"), which in turn returns true back to its caller (the argument was "cec"), until true gets passed back to the first caller of isPalindrome, the method call with the original argument of "racecar", which returns the value true. Now consider tracing the recursive calls for the String "pooltop".

isPalindrome Recursive Calls (false result)

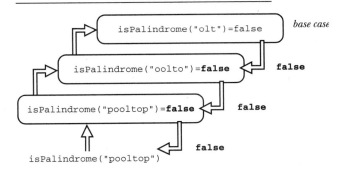

The base case is reached when the method compares the letters at the ends—"o" and "t" do not match. That particular method call returns false back to its caller (whose argument was "oolto"), which returns false to its caller. The original call to isPalindrome("pooltop") is replaced with false to the method that asked if "pooltop" was a palindrome.

Self-Check

12-17 What value is returned from PalindromeChecker.isPalindrome("yoy")?

12-18 What value is returned from PalindromeChecker.isPalindrome("yoyo")?

12-19 Write the output generated by printing the return results from the method huh.

```
System.out.println( huh( "+abc+" ) );
System.out.println( huh( "-abc-" ) );
System.out.println( huh( "-a-b-c-" ) );
System.out.println( huh( "------abc-----" ) );

public static String huh( String str )
{
  if( str.charAt( 0 ) == '-' )
    return huh( str.substring( 1, str.length( ) ) );
  else if( str.charAt( str.length( ) - 1 ) == '-' )
    return huh( str.substring( 0, str.length( ) - 1 ) );
  else
    return str;
}
```

12.5   Recursion with Arrays

The sequential search algorithm uses an integer subscript that increases if an element is not found and the index is still in the range (meaning that there are more elements to compare). The same algorithm can be implemented in a recursive fashion. The two base cases are

1. if the element is found, return true
2. if the index is out of range, terminate the search by returning false

The recursive case is to look in the subportion of the array that has not been searched. With sequential search, it does not matter if the array is searched from the smallest index to the largest or the largest index to the smallest. So the first call to the exists method below compares the search element with the largest valid array index. If that is not it, the next call narrows the search field from the back. This happens when the recursive call simplifies the problem by decreasing the index. If the element does not exist in the array, eventually the index goes to -1 and false is returned to the preceding call, which returns false to the preceding call, until the original method call to exists returns false to main.

```
public class ShowRecursiveSequentialSearch
{
  // Preconditions: The objects in the array are the same
  // type and they override equals
  public static boolean exists( Object[] array, int lastIndex,
                                Object searchElement )
  {
    if( lastIndex < 0 )
      return false;      // Base case 1: Nothing left to search
    else if ( array[lastIndex].equals( searchElement ) )
      return true;       // Base case 2: Found it
    else
      // Recursive case
      return exists( array, lastIndex - 1, searchElement );
  }

  public static void main( String[] args )
  {
    String[] array = { "Kelly", "Mike", "Jen",
                       "Marty", "Stuart", "Grant" };
    int lastIndex = array.length - 1;

    System.out.println( exists( array, lastIndex, "Kelly" ) +
                        " =? true" );
    System.out.println( exists( array, lastIndex, "Jen" ) +
                        " =? true" );
    System.out.println( exists( array, lastIndex, "Not" ) +
                        " =? false" );
  }
}
```

Output

```
true =? true
true =? true
false =? false
```

Recursive Binary Search

Assuming an array is sorted, the binary search algorithm can eliminate half of the array from the search rather than just one element, as was done in the sequential search above. The same binary search algorithm can be implemented in a recursive fashion. The two base cases are

1. If there is nothing left to compare, terminate the search by returning false
2. If the element is found, return true

With binary search, there are two recursive cases:

1. If the element is less than the middle element, search through the lower indexes of the array

2. If the element is greater than the middle element, search through the higher indexes of the array

Each call needs the array being searched, the object being searched for, and two indexes to mark the subarray that needs to be searched. In the beginning, `first` is 0 and `last` should be `array.length - 1`.

```java
public class ShowRecursiveBinarySearch
{
   public static boolean exists( Object[] array, int first, int last,
                                 Object searchElement )
   {
     if ( first > last )
       return false;         // Base case 1: Nothing left to search
     else
     {
       // There is at least one more element to compare
       int mid = ( first + last ) / 2;

       if( searchElement.equals( array[mid] ) )
         return true;        // Base case 2: Found it
       else if( ( (Comparable)searchElement ).compareTo( array[mid] ) < 0 )
         // Recursive case 1
         return exists( array, first, mid - 1, searchElement );
       else
         // Recursive case 2
         return exists( array, mid + 1, last, searchElement );
     }
   }

   public static void main( String[] args )
   {
     String[] array = { "Kelly", "Mike", "Jen", "Marty", "Stuart",
                        "Grant" };
     int lastIndex = array.length - 1;
     // Make sure the array is sorted
     java.util.Arrays.sort( array );

     System.out.println( exists( array, 0, lastIndex, "Mike" ) +
                         " =? true" );
     System.out.println( exists( array, 0, lastIndex, "Grant" ) +
                         " =? true" );
     System.out.println( exists( array, 0, lastIndex, "Not" ) +
                         " =? false" );
   }
}
```

Output

```
true =? true
true =? true
false =? false
```

12.6 Backtracking to Escape an Obstacle Course

All of the problems presented so far have iterative solutions that do not need recursion. This section presents a problem that has an elegant recursive solution that would be rather difficult to do with iteration.

One common use of recursion is finding all of the ways of doing something. Recursion is often used in game-playing strategies to try all of the possibilities in searching for the best move. In order to try all of the possibilities, you must have some form of backtracking available to you. **Backtracking** is the process of taking steps towards the final solution while recording the details. The details could be recorded as an instance of a method. If the desired solution has not been reached, some steps may have to be retraced. This trial-and-error process often requires trying a very large number of possible solutions.

Imagine that you are in a maze, and you want to find the exit. Most people would try a path and follow it until they run into a dead end or get out of the maze. If you reach a dead end, you will want to back up to the most recent place where you had a choice, mark the path you were just on as not good, and try another direction. You could continue to do this until you either tried all of the paths or got out of the maze. Another way to do this is to keep walking while your left hand touches the wall to your left. If the maze is a proper maze, you will get out even if you have to try all paths.

Now consider a problem that demonstrates backtracking that is related to the maze. Instead of escaping from a maze, this problem finds the path out of an obstacle course. An obstacle course may have multiple paths and exits. Keeping a wall to the left will not work when the starting position has no nearby wall. The path has a starting point marked as s and shows a path to any one of the exits. It does not need to be the shortest path. Here is one picture of an obstacle course that shows the before and after state of the course. Notice that the shortest path is not found. There is a tendency in this solution to search down first and then to the right.

Initial Obstacle Course	A Path Out (not always the shortest)
++++++	++++++
+S + +	+SOO+ +
+ +	+.+OOO
+ + + +	+.+.+O+
+++++ +	++++O+

The symbols are defined as follows:

'S'   The starting point where the mover finds itself.

'+'   A place where the mover cannot go.

' '   A place the mover can still try.

'.'   A place the mover has tried and may later become part of the path to the exit.

'O'   Part of the path for a successful escape.

It is also possible that there is no path out. Here is an example that shows that all possibilities have been tried. At this point, one of the base cases has been reached. There are no more paths to attempt.

Initial Obstacle Course	Trying All Possible Paths
++++++	++++++
+S + +	+S..+.+
+ + +	+.+...+
+ + + +	+.+.+.+
++++++	++++++

An earlier programming project asked to have the Grid mover get out of the single exit (see Programming Project 7K, "Finding a Grid's Exit"). The suggested algorithm was to find a wall and keep it to your side. However, the idea of holding a wall to one side won't always work. Consider this obstacle course that would have the mover go around in circles forever when keeping its left hand on the wall in the middle. All four exits would be missed.

```
++++ +++
+       +
+       +
   ++
+   S   +
+       +
+++ ++++
```

An iterative solution would be difficult. Consider a recursive solution that tries all possibilities.

The heart of the solution will be a method named tryThisWay. Assume that there is a two-dimensional array of characters where every element has been initialized to one of the char values '+', ' ', or 'S'. When another method asks the obstacle course to mark the path to the exit, this escape method will be called, with the initial row and column as the row and column where the 'S' was found in the input file. For each position, the return result escaped will be set to false initially. It is likely that the current position (row and column) has been blocked as '+' or previously tried. If it is found that the current location is a possible part of the solution, it will be set as TRIED with the symbol '.'. Then a check will be made to see if the current location may actually represent an exit—the current row or the current column is on one of the four borders. If the current location is not on a border, the algorithm will try other possibilities.

In the algorithm below, the first try is to go south. In anticipation of tracing this algorithm, the success of finding an exit by going to the row below is marked with a down arrow ↓. Because the algorithm uses four different return points, they are marked as directional arrows ↓, →, ↑, and ← to indicate the direction the algorithm is trying.

Algorithm: Escaping from the starting point to the first found exit

boolean tryThisWay(int row, int column)
{
  boolean escaped = false;

  if current row and column is a possibility (not blocked and not tried)
  {
    set current location to TRIED;

    if current location is on the border, the mover is out so
      set escaped = true
    else
    {
      let escaped = ↓ success of escaping using the row below

      if still not escaped
        let escaped = → success of escaping using the column to the right

      if still not escaped
        let escaped = ↑ success of escaping using the row above

      if still not escaped
        let escaped = ← success of escaping using the column to the left
    }

    if the mover was known to escape (escaped is true) during this current method
      let current location = PART_OF_PATH;
  }

  return escaped back to the caller, which is usually this very same method

} // end tryThisWay

If the exit is immediately found below (south), no further recursive calls are made. If it is possible, the algorithm will keep trying to the south until one of the base cases occurs:

1. An exit is found.
2. The location is not a possible way out (it may be blocked or already tried).

If the try to the south fails to find an exit, `false` is assigned to the `boolean` variable `escaped` marked with ↓. The algorithm backtracks to an attempt to try to the right (east). So if the mover has not escaped to the south, an attempt is made to try to the right (east). If the east direction reaches a dead end, `false` is assigned to the `boolean` variable `escaped` marked with →. The algorithm backtracks to try to the north. If an exit is found, `true` is assigned to the `boolean` variable `escaped` marked with ↑. At this point, `escaped` is `true`, so there is no attempt to the left. Then the most recent intersection (the exit) is assigned the symbol for PART_OF_PATH, which is `'O'`.

> // *This would be skipped*
> if still not escaped
>   let escaped = ← success of escaping using the column to the left
}

Whenever `escaped` is `true`, the current location is changed to `'O'`.

if the mover was known to escape (`escaped` is `true`) during this current method
  let current location = PART_OF_PATH;

Then the successful value of `escaped` is returned back to the caller; that row and column intersection is assigned the PART_OF_PATH symbol `'O'`. This continues back to the original location. As was suggested earlier, tracing recursive methods requires diligence. Let's take a look at a more concrete example.

The arrows were added to the algorithm above in order to help trace this very complex recursive algorithm. Consider the following detailed trace to escape from this obstacle course starting at the second row in the second column. Since this can be represented by a 2-D array, consider this data to be stored in this array:

```
char[][] course = new char[4][5];
```

The array data will be initialized from a text input file.

The Initialized 2-D Array of `char` Values Used in the Trace That Follows

```
        01234 columns
rows 0  +++++
     1  +S  +
     2  + + +
     3  +++ +
```

Here is a trace of the escape attempt from this small obstacle course. The algorithm begins with `tryThisWay( 1, 1 )`. This makes a recursive call to try to the south as it calls `tryThisWay( row + 1, column )`. Another recursive call occurs to try to the south. It calls `tryThisWay( row + 1, column )` again, only to discover that there is a block at `course[3][1]`. That instance of the method (`row == 3`, `column == 1`) is not a possibility. One base case has been reached, and the value of `escaped` (`false`) is returned to ↓. The trace could look like this, where the values in gray with double strikethroughs, such as ~~false~~, have been assigned values during the method call (the top call is removed as it returns `false` back so it can be assigned to `escaped` near ↓).

	return	course[row][col]		row	col	escaped?
	↓	'+'		3	1	false
	↓		'.'	2	1	~~false~~ false
tryThisWay's caller			'.'	1	1	false
return point		*course[row][col]*		*row*	*col*	*escaped?*

The algorithm now backtracks to try to the east (col+1) from `course[2][1]`. Since this path is blocked, it returns `false`. The method calls show the attempt to go east and its return value.

		course[row][col]		row	col	escaped?
	→	'+'		2	2	false
	↓		'.'	2	1	~~false~~ false
tryThisWay's caller			'.'	1	1	false
return point		*course[row][col]*		*row*	*col*	*escaped?*

The north has already been tried, so going up (row-1) returns `false`.

		course[row][col]		row	col	escaped?
	↑	'.'		1	1	false
	↓		'.'	2	1	~~false~~ false
tryThisWay's caller			'.'	1	1	false
return point		*course[row][col]*		*row*	*col*	*escaped?*

Finally, the fourth possible move from `course[2][1]`, to the west (col-1) is blocked; so going west returns `false`.

		course[row][col]		row	col	escaped?
	←	'+'		2	0	false
	↓		'.'	2	1	~~false~~ false
tryThisWay's caller			'.'	1	1	false
return point		*course[row][col]*		*row*	*col*	*escaped?*

At this point, all recursive calls have been tried. At the end of the method, guarded action prevents the current location from becoming PART_OF_PATH. The algorithm then returns `false` and backtracks to the original call so the east path from `course[1][1]` can be tried. At this point the method calls look like this.

tryThisWay's caller	'.'	1	1	~~false~~	false
return point	*course[row][col]*	*row*	*col*	*escaped?*	

The 2-D array named `course` now looks like this.

```
        01234 columns
rows 0  +++++
     1  +.   +
     2  +.+  +
     3  +++  +
```

After backtracking to ↓, the direction at `course[1][1]`, the algorithm checks the column to the right with `tryThisWay( row, col + 1 )`.

if still not escaped
    let escaped = → success of escaping using the column to the right

An attempt is made to go east. Then since `course[1][2]` is free, it is marked as tried.

```
        01234 columns
rows 0  +++++
     1  +..  +
     2  +.+  +
     3  +++  +
```

Then an attempt is made to go south from `course[1][2]`, where the return point is the down arrow, ↓. However, this is found to not be a possibility (it is blocked) and `false` is returned. The method calls look like this with the top "box" about to be removed.

↓	'+'	2	2	false	
←	'.'	1	2	~~false~~	false
tryThisWay's caller	'.'	1	1	false	
return point	*course[row][col]*	*row*	*col*	*escaped?*	

At this point an attempt is made to go east from `course[1][2]`. The new top has column == 3 and the space ' ' is changed to the tried character '.'. Then the attempt is made to go south, which is possible. At this point the trace of method calls looks like this:

			course[row][col]	row	col	escaped?
↓	□	'.'		2	3	false
↓	□	'.'		1	3	false
←	□	'.'		1	2	false
tryThisWay's caller		'.'		1	1	false
return point		*course[row][col]*		*row*	*col*	*escaped?*

And the 2-D array course looks like this:

```
      01234 columns
rows 0 +++++
     1 +...+
     2 +.+.+
     3 +++ +
```

From `course[2][3]`, an attempt is made to go south again. Since this soon-to-be-discovered exit has not been tried, it is marked as tried before checking for an exit. At the beginning of this call to `tryThisWay`, escaped is set to `false` initially. But then since the current location is on a border, escaped is set to `true`, a base case. The recursive calls in the big `else` part are skipped. The following guarded action allows the algorithm to change the current symbol of `course[2][3]` to `'O'` (PART_OF_PATH):

if the mover was known to escape (escaped is `true`) during this current method
    let current location = PART_OF_PATH;

Then `true` is returned back to the caller with this action that always returns `true` or `false`:

  return escaped back to the caller, which is usually this very same method
} // End tryThisWay

The current method calls now have only those that are part of the path to the first found exit.

				course[row][col]	row	col	escaped?
↓	□	□	'O'		3	3	~~false~~ true
↓	□	'.'			2	3	true
↓	□	'.'			1	3	false
←	□	'.'			1	2	false
tryThisWay's caller		'.'			1	1	false
return point		*course[row][col]*			*row*	*col*	*escaped?*

The 2-D array named course now looks like this.

```
        01234 columns
rows 0  +++++
     1  +...+
     2  +.+.+
     3  +++O+
```

Once an exit has been found, there is no need to try other paths. That is why the same exit at course[3][3] would be found even if there had been an exit at course[2][4]. Instead, the method returns true to assign the direction to escaped marked with ↓. Then the remaining recursive calls—to the east, the north, and the west—are skipped, since they are all guarded actions. The value of true was returned and assigned to the caller's local escaped variable, causing the other recursive calls to be skipped. At the end of this method, PART_OF_PATH is stored into course[2][3] and true is returned to its caller. The method calls look like this:

return point	course[row][col]	row	col	escaped?
↓	___ '.'	1	3	~~false~~ true
←	___ '.'	1	2	false
tryThisWay's caller	'.'	1	1	false

And the 2-D array named course looks like this:

```
        01234 columns
rows 0  +++++
     1  +...+
     2  +.+O+
     3  +++O+
```

The process continues to return true so the caller can store the success of escaping, skip the other paths, assign PART_OF_PATH into course[row][col], and return true to its caller. This continues until the original call to tryThisWay returns true to the original caller to indicate the success of the escape attempt. At the end, the 2-D array named course looks like this.

```
        01234 columns
rows 0  +++++
     1  +OOO+
     2  +.+O+
     3  +++O+
```

Implementing the Escape Obstacle Course Algorithm

The Java solution to this problem is left as a programming project. The file named ObstacleCourse.java is provided to initialize the 2-D array named course by reading from a disk file and to allow the course to be printed as follows:

```
+++++
+SOO+
+  +O+
+++O+
```

The code to do this is the toString method that prints the tried values as spaces again. Also, another method makes the recursive call to tryThisWay and remembers to replace the initial starting position with 'S'.

Chapter Summary

- A recursive definition has some part that includes a simpler definition of itself. Some examples are the power and factorial methods.
- For many problems, both recursive and iterative solutions exist.
- The base case of a recursive algorithm refers to the time when a recursive call is not needed.
- The recursive case is when a method invokes another instance of the same method. The recursive method call should make progress toward a base case to avoid infinite recursion.
- The characteristics of recursion are
    1. The problem can be made into a simpler version of itself in order to bring the problem closer to a base case.
    2. There are one or more base cases.
- Infinite recursion occurs when a method makes recursive calls that do not make progress towards a base case. Eventually the program terminates, as it has no memory left to store any more instances of the method.
- One common use of recursion is that of finding all the ways of doing something.
- Backtracking is a process of taking steps towards the final solution while recording the details so some steps can be retraced. This trial-and-error process often requires trying a very large number of possible solutions.

Key Terms

backtracking	infinite recursion	recursive case
base case	recursion	recursive definition

Exercises

 1. Write the output generated when this class runs.

```java
public class One
{
  public static int mysteryOne( int n )
  {
    if( n <= 2 )
      return 0;
    else if( n == 5 )
      return 1;
    else
      return n + mysteryOne( n - 1 );
  }

  public static void main( String[] args )
  {
    System.out.println( mysteryOne( 2 ) );
    System.out.println( mysteryOne( 5 ) );
    System.out.println( mysteryOne( 7 ) );
  }
}
```

 2. Write the output generated when this class runs.

```java
public class Two
{
  public static void mysteryTwo( int n )
  {
    if( n >= 1 )
    {
      System.out.print( "<" );
      mysteryTwo( n - 3 );
      System.out.print( n );
      System.out.print( ">" );
    }
  }

  public static void main( String[] args )
  {
    mysteryTwo( 2 );
    System.out.println( );
    mysteryTwo( 5 );
    System.out.println( );
    mysteryTwo( 7 );
    System.out.println( );
  }
}
```

3. Write the output generated when this class runs.

```java
public class Three
{
  public static boolean mysteryThree( int a, int b )
  {
    if( a >= 10 || b <= 3 )
      return false;
    if( a == b )
      return true;
    else
      return mysteryThree( a + 2, b - 2 ) || mysteryThree( a + 3,
                          b - 4 );
  }

  public static void main( String[] args )
  {
    System.out.println( mysteryThree( 14, 7 ) );
    System.out.println( mysteryThree( 3, 6 ) );
    System.out.println( mysteryThree( 4, 8 ) );
  }
}
```

4. Write the output generated when this class runs.

```java
public class Four
{
  public static int MysteryFour( int n )
  {
    if( n < 1 )
      return 0;
    else if( n == 1 )
      return 1;
    else
      return 2 * MysteryFour( n - 1 );
  }

  public static void main( String[] args )
  {
    System.out.println( MysteryFour( -5 ) );
    System.out.println( MysteryFour(  1 ) );
    System.out.println( MysteryFour(  2 ) );
    System.out.println( MysteryFour(  3 ) );
    System.out.println( MysteryFour(  4 ) );
  }
}
```

 5. Write the output generated by the following code.

```java
public class Five
{
  public static void MysteryFive( int[] x, int first, int last )
  {
```

```
        if( first < last )
        {
          int temp = x[first];
          x[first] = x[last];
          x[last] = temp;
          MysteryFive( x, first + 1, last - 1 );
        }
      }

      public static void main( String[] args )
      {
        int x[] = { 1, 2, 3, 4, 5, 6, 7, 8 };
        for( int j = 0; j < x.length; j++ )
          System.out.print( x[j] + " " );

        MysteryFive( x, 0, x.length - 1 );

        System.out.println( );
        for( int j = 0; j < x.length; j++ )
          System.out.print( x[j] + " " );
      }
    }
```

 6. Write a method backward that displays the integers 10, 9, 8, . . ., 1 on separate lines with the method call backward(10). Use recursion to implement the iteration.

7. Write a recursive method for the strange numbers, which are defined as

$$\text{strange}(n) \begin{cases} 5 \text{ if } n = 0 \\ 3 \text{ if } n = 1 \\ 2 * \text{strange}(n\text{-}2) \text{ if } n > 1 \end{cases}$$

The following code should generate the output shown:

```
System.out.println( strange( 0 ) );   // 5
System.out.println( strange( 1 ) );   // 3
System.out.println( strange( 2 ) );   // 10
System.out.println( strange( 3 ) );   // 6
System.out.println( strange( 4 ) );   // 20
System.out.println( strange( 5 ) );   // 12
```

8. What is the value of strange(4)?

9. List one argument to strange that would cause infinite recursion.

10. List the base and recursive cases for the following definition. For each case, list the action taken.

$$\text{binomial}(n, k) \begin{cases} 1 \text{ if } k = 0 \\ 1 \text{ if } n = k \\ \text{binomial}(n\text{-}1, k\text{-}1) + \text{binomial}(n\text{-}1, k) \text{ if } 0 < k < n \end{cases}$$

11. Write a recursive method `binomial` in Java that implements the recursive definition above.

 12. Evaluate `binomial( n, k )` for the following values of n and k or write "Undefined" if `binomial` is not assigned a value:

n	k	binomial(n, k)
1	0	
0	1	
8	8	
2	1	

13. The Fibonacci sequence begins as

1 1 2 3 5 8 13 21 34

where each Fibonacci number is the sum of the preceding two except for the first two. Write a recursive definition for the Fibonacci function.

14. Write the output generated by the following program:

```java
public class TestWeird
{
  public static int anotherMystery( int x, int y )
  { // Pre: both arguments are >= 1
    if( y == 1 )
      return x;
    else
      return x * anotherMystery( x, y - 1 );
  }

  public static void main( String[] args )
  {
    System.out.println( anotherMystery( 4, 1 ) );
    System.out.println( anotherMystery( 4, 2 ) );
    System.out.println( anotherMystery( 4, 3 ) );
  }
}
```

15. Using recursion, complete the method `goingUp` so it displays all the numbers from the first argument to the last in ascending order (separated by a space). You cannot use a loop. Consider the base case. Consider what the recursive case is and if the arguments increase, decrease, or stay the same.

```java
public class TestGoingUp
{

  // Write the method goingUp

  public static void main( String[] args )
  {
    goingUp( 1, 5 );
    System.out.println( );
```

```
        goingUp( 2, 7 );
        System.out.println( );
        goingUp( 3, 3 );
        System.out.println( );
    }
}
```

Output

```
1 2 3 4 5
2 3 4 5 6 7
3
```

Programming Tips

1. **Before developing a recursive algorithm, identify the base and recursive cases.**
   There may be one or more recursive and base cases. Once these are identified, the algorithm is more easily developed. Don't forget that when a base case is encountered, it is possible that nothing occurs; in other words, no recursive call is made.

2. **Make sure each recursive call brings you closer to the base case.**
   When you write recursive methods, you must have a step that brings the problem closer to the base case. This could involve incrementing or decrementing a parameter for the argument to the next call or making a string smaller.

   ```
   // Increment an index or decrement an index
   reverse( array, first + 1, last - 1 );

   // Make the String referenced by str smaller
   showSmaller( str.substring( 0, str.length( ) - 1 ) );
   ```

3. **Recursion can be elegant, but it can also be costly.**
   In future studies you will find very nice recursive solutions to difficult problems. Examples you would see in a subsequent course might include the recursive quick sort algorithm and the binary tree traversal. While such elegant uses of recursion provide runtime efficiency, some recursive methods are tremendously slow. An iterative solution can be much better. You can verify this by completing the programming problem with the Fibonacci numbers and counting how many seconds it takes to compute `fibonacci( 40 )` recursively.

Programming Projects

12A Fibonacci

The Fibonacci sequence begins as

```
1   1   2   3   5   8   13   21   34
```

where each Fibonacci number is the sum of the preceding two except for the first two. Write a recursive method named `fibonacci` that returns the correct Fibonacci number. For example, `fibonacci( 1 )` should return 1, `fibonacci( 2 )` should return 1, `fibonacci( 3 )` should return 2, and `fibonacci( 8 )` should return 21.

12B Number Conversions

Modify the `printInDifferentBase` method shown earlier in the chapter so it converts decimal numbers up to base 16 (hexadecimal). Use the following conversion table to allow single digit symbols (letters A through F) that represent the decimal numbers 10 through 15:

Decimal Value	Symbol to Display
10	A
11	B
12	C
13	D
14	E
15	F

A method call that would convert 142 base 10 to its base-16 equivalent should be `convert( 142, 16 )`. Test your program by converting the decimal numbers 1 through 15 to their hexadecimal equivalents (1, 2, 3, 4, 5, 6, 7, 8, 9, A, B, C, D, E, F) and some others such as these:

```
printInDifferentBase( 62, 16 );     //   3E
System.out.println( );
printInDifferentBase( 63, 16 );     //   3F
System.out.println( );
printInDifferentBase( 64, 16 );     //   40
System.out.println( );
```

12C Adding Reciprocals

Write a method `addReciprocals` that takes an integer as a parameter and returns the sum of the first n reciprocals. `addReciprocals( n )` returns $(1.0 + 1.0/2.0 + 1.0/3.0 + 1.0/4.0 + ... + 1.0/n)$.

12D SumRecursively

Write a method sumRecursively that uses recursion to return the sum of the integers in the array of integers passed as an argument. You cannot use a loop as your answer. You must use recursion. Add another method named show to display the array elements as shown in the output below.

```
public static void main( String[] args )
{
  int[] x = { 1, 2, 3, 4, 5, 6 };
  // Display the array
  show( x, x.length );

  // Note: The second argument to sum is the LARGEST legal index in
  // the array. This makes it easier for you to get sumArray correct.
  int sum = sumArray( x, x.length - 1 );

  System.out.println( "Sum = " + sum );
}
```

Output

```
[1 2 3 4 5 6]
Sum = 21
```

12E reversePrintString

Write a recursive method reversePrintString that prints out the characters of a string in reverse order. Do not use a loop. The method call reversePrintString("abcdef") should generate the output fedcba.

12F Decimal Values of Other Bases

Write a method stringToDecimalNumber that takes a String argument and the base of the valid number represented by the String to get the integer value. The following test driver code should have the method return the value after =? in each case.

```
// The second argument is the base of the number as a string
System.out.println( stringToDecimalNumber( "0", 2 ) + " =? 0" );
System.out.println( stringToDecimalNumber( "1", 2 ) + " =? 1" );
System.out.println( stringToDecimalNumber( "10", 2 ) + " =? 2" );
System.out.println( stringToDecimalNumber( "11", 2 ) + " =? 3" );
System.out.println( stringToDecimalNumber( "100", 2 ) + " =? 4" );
System.out.println( stringToDecimalNumber( "1111", 2 ) + " =? 15" );

// Convert some octal numbers
System.out.println( stringToDecimalNumber( "1", 8 ) + " =? 1" );
System.out.println( stringToDecimalNumber( "11", 8 ) + " =? 9" );
```

```
System.out.println( stringToDecimalNumber( "111", 8 ) + " =? " +
                    (64+8+1) );
System.out.println( stringToDecimalNumber( "1111", 8 ) + " =? " +
                    (512+64+8+1) );
System.out.println( stringToDecimalNumber( "27", 8 ) + " =? 23" );

// Convert a decimal number (should be the same)
System.out.println( stringToDecimalNumber( "56789", 10 ) +
                    " =? 56789" );
```

Suggestions: Include the recursive `pow` method that takes two `int` arguments and returns an `int`. For example, `Math.pow( 8, 3 )` should return 512. Also, you will need to grab the end character in a `String` and convert it to an integer. The trick is to subtract the `char` `'0'` to get the integer value of the rightmost digit. Here is the code to do that.

```
// Get rightmost digit
char rightChar = numberAsString.charAt( numberAsString.length( ) - 1 );
// Convert the char into the correct integer from 0 to 9 ('5'-'0' is 5)
int coefficient = rightChar - '0';
```

12G Implementing the Escape Obstacle Course Algorithm

Complete the `ObstacleCourse` class so it finds a path to an exit. The exit need not be the closest. You are given everything but the recursive method `tryThisWay`. You will probably find it useful to add a few private helper methods for the complex `tryThisWay` method. You will need the files `ObstacleCourse.java`, `TextReader.java`, and `obstacleCourse.data` to complete this project.

```
import java.io.*;

// This file is on the accompanying disk
public class ObstacleCourse
{
  private static char TRIED = '.';
  private static char PART_OF_PATH = 'O';

  private char[][] course;
  private int startRow;
  private int startColumn;

  public ObstacleCourse( String fileName )
  {
    TextReader obstacleCourseFile = new TextReader( fileName );

    int rows = obstacleCourseFile.readInt( );
    int columns = obstacleCourseFile.readInt( );

    // Cursor must be beyond the end of the first line
    // (TextReader does that)
```

```
      course = new char[rows][columns];
      for( int r = 0; r < rows; r++ )
      {
        for( int c = 0; c < columns; c++ )
        {
          course[r][c] = obstacleCourseFile.readChar( );
          if( course[r][c] == 'S' )
          {
            startRow = r;
            startColumn = c;
            // Need to make this space available as part of a path.
            // The toString method will substitute the S back in.
            course[r][c] = ' ';
          }
        }
        obstacleCourseFile.readLine( );
      }
    }

    public String toString( )
    {
      String result = "";
      for( int r = 0; r < course.length; r++ )
      {
        for( int c = 0; c < course[0].length; c++ )
        {
          if( course[r][c] == TRIED )
            result += ' ';
          else
            result += course[r][c];
        }
        result += "\n";
      }
      return result;
    }

    public boolean markPathToExit( )
    {
      // Call the recursive method to find a path to an exit
      // (it may return false)
      boolean result = tryThisWay( startRow, startColumn );
      course[startRow][startColumn] = 'S';
      return result;
    }


    // Write boolean tryThisWay and any private helper methods
    // inside this class


    public static void main( String[] args )
    {
      ObstacleCourse aCourse = new ObstacleCourse( " obstacleCourse.data" );

      System.out.println( aCourse.toString( ) );
```

```
      // Call the method that calls your private method tryThisWay
      boolean foundExit = aCourse.markPathToExit( );

      if( ! foundExit )
        System.out.println( "Could not solve" );

      System.out.println( aCourse.toString( ) );
    }
}
```

Output (this is not the shortest path)

```
++  +++  +++++++++++++++
+     +     ++ ++
       +          +++++ ++
+ +      ++   ++++ + + ++
+ +    + + ++      +++   +
            ++   ++   + +
+++++ + +         ++   + +
+++++ +++   + +   ++     +
+           + +     + +
+++++ +   + + +       + +
+++++++++  +++++++++++++


++  +++  +++++++++++++++
+     +     ++ ++000000000
       +      OOOO+++++ ++
+ +      ++OO++++ + + ++
+ +    + +O++ OO +++   +
           O ++OO++   + +
+++++ + +OOOOOO++   + +
+++++ +++OO+ +OO++     +
+         OO+ + OS +   +
+++++ +   + + + OO   + +
+++++++++  +++++++++++++
```

12H Ways to Climb a Ladder

Given a ladder with n rungs that can be climbed in steps of one rung or two rungs, determine how many ways are there to climb a ladder given the number of rungs. A person can climb either one or two rungs at a time. When rungs == 5, there are eight ways to climb the ladder:

```
1 1 1 1 1
1 1 1 2
1 1 2 1
1 2 1 1
2 1 1 1
1 2 2
2 1 2
2 2 1
```

Other examples include

> 1 rung   1
> 2 rungs   1 1 or 2
> 3 rungs   1 1 1 or 1 2 or 2 1
> 4 rungs   1 1 1 1 or 1 1 2 or 1 2 1 or 2 1 1 or 2 2

Your output should only show the number of ways to climb the ladder, not the actual ways (which is a much more difficult problem). Your output should look just like the output below. Look for the pattern; it's like the Fibonacci sequence described in Programming Project 12A except the second number is 2, not 1).

```
Rungs    WaysToClimb
  1          1
  2          2
  3          3
  4          5
  5          8
  6          13
```

12I   Showing the Different Ways to Climb a Ladder (Difficult)

For a real challenge, show the different ways to climb a ladder with n rungs. Each step can be to climb one rung or two rungs. For example, the function call showMeTheWays(5) should generate these eight lines of output (but not necessarily in this order). *Warning:* This is a difficult problem and may take many hours with no correct result.

```
1 1 1 1 1
1 1 1 2
1 1 2 1
1 2 1 1
2 1 1 1
1 2 2
2 1 2
2 2 1
```

Answers to Self-Check Questions

12-1   1
12-2   3

12-3

```
powRecurse(3,0)=1              base case reached

  3*powRecurse(3,1-1)=3*1        1

  3*powRecurse(3,2-1)=3*3        3

  3*powRecurse(3,3-1)=3*9        9

3*powRecurse(3,4-1)=3*27        27

                          81    returned back to main

powRecurse(3,4)
```

12-4 10 | 8 | 6 | 4 | 2 |

12-5 2 | 4 | 6 | 8 | 10 |

12-6
```java
public static void backward( int high, int low)
{
   if( high >= low )
   {
      System.out.print( high + " " );
      backward( high - 1, low );
   }
}
```

12-7 -3

12-8 1 + f(-1) = 1 + -1 = 0

12-9 3 + f(1) = 3 + 1 + f(-1) = 3 + 1 + -1 = 3

12-10 7 + f(5) = 7 + f(5) = 7 + 8 = 15

12-11 For all values >= 0, you would get infinite recursion.

12-12 True. 5_{10} == 101_2

12-13 False. The decimal number 10_{10} is represented as 12_8 ($1*8^1 + 2*8^0$).

12-14 100

12-15 1111

12-16 0
   099
   0143

12-17 true

12-18 false

12-19 +abc+
   abc
   a-b-c
   abc

```
12-20 public static void printReverse( Object[] array, int last )
      {
        if( last >= 0 )
        {
          System.out.print( array[last] + " " );
          printReverse( array, last - 1 );
        }
      }
12-21 public static void printForward( Object[] array, int last )
      {
        if( last >= 0 )
        {
          printForward( array, last - 1 );
          System.out.print( array[last] + " " );
        }
      }
```

Appendix A

A Little Javadoc

Java has three types of comments to help explain the purpose of code, methods, and classes:

- The one-line comment that begins with // and ends with a new line.
- The multi-line comments that begin with /* and end with */.
- The javadoc style of comments, which begin with /** and end with */.

The first two styles of comments are written among the source code for purposes such as explaining the purpose of a class, explaining what a method does, clarifying a complicated piece of code, and providing documentation, such as the programmer's name and the revision date. Comments provide internal documentation of the source code for programmers who are working on the code. Javadoc comments can provide the same internal documentation. When used with the associated program named javadoc, they also provide external documentation for programmers trying to understand the purpose of existing classes, to understand what the methods do, and to write valid messages. The external documentation takes the form of hyperlinked HTML pages.

Consider a simple example class that has three javadoc comments enclosed in /** and */. The first provides an overview of the class. The second describes the constructor, and the third describes the debit method. There are two javadoc tags: 1) @param to describe what the parameters are for and 2) @return to describe what non-void methods return.

```
/**
    This simple class is used only to illustrate the javadoc program.
*/
public class Account
{
  private String my_ID;
  private double my_balance;

/** Construct one Account object and return a reference to it.
  * @param initID A String meant to uniquely identify this Account.
  * @param initBalance This BankAccount's starting balance.
  */
  public Account( String initID, double initBalance )
  {
    my_ID = initID;
    my_balance = initBalance;
  }

/** Reduce this Account's balance by debitAmount if argument is positive.
  * @param debitAmount The amount of money to debit this Account.
  * @return true if successful or false when debitAmount is not positive.
  */
  public boolean debit( double debitAmount )
  {
    boolean result = true;
    if( debitAmount <= 0.0 )
      result = false;
    else
      my_balance = my_balance - debitAmount;
    return result;
  }
}
```

The Web page documentation shown below is generated by the javadoc program. The input is a file containing the Java class (Account.java). The output is several HTML documents (only Account.html is shown). All of this happens with the following operating system command:

```
javadoc Account.java
```

Figure A.1: **The first part of the HTML documentation**

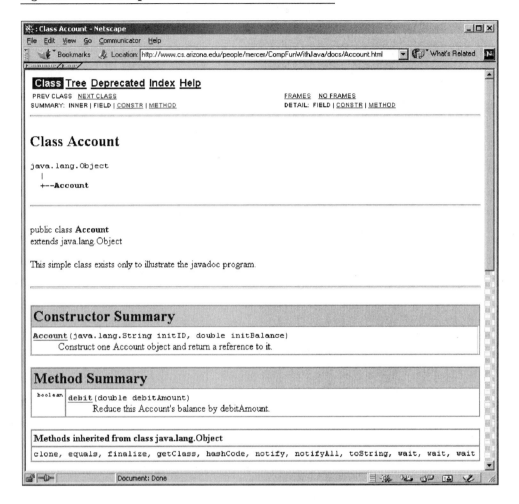

The javadoc program parses the class heading, the method headings, and the javadoc comments to generate hyperlinked HTML pages. Assuming that it compiles, each class begins as shown above, with links to Class, Tree, Deprecated, Index, and Help. The inheritance relationship is shown, followed by an overview of the class that was written as a javadoc comment before the class heading. The constructor and method summaries and a listing of the method names this class has inherited follow. Since this class extends only the Object class, the 11 methods are all that this Account class inherits.

The parameters described after the @param tag in the javadoc comments show up in the constructor and method details. The next screen shot shows the result of describing what a method returns after the @return tag. Notice that only the first sentence in the javadoc comments shows up in the summary section (shown in the screen shot above). All javadoc comments and all of the descriptions following the tags show up in the details section (shown in this second screen shot of the HTML documentation):

Figure A.2: **The second part of the HTML documentation**

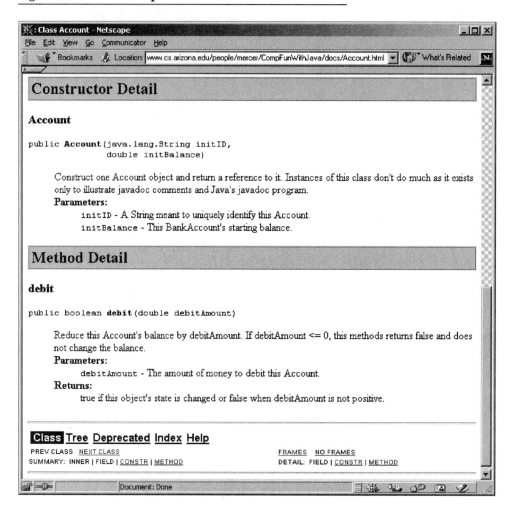

Javadoc comments may also use HTML to format the documentation. The next example shows how to format text as code (bracketed by <code> and </code>), to underline text (bracketed by <u> and </u>), and to format text as bold (bracketed by <b> and </b>). The HTML code <br> causes a line break in a document loaded into a Web browser. Without <br>, the lines would extend to the right. A new line in the source code does not equate to a new line in the Web page.

```
/**
The <code>JukeboxAccount</code> class is part of the jukebox system
specified in Chapter 4 of <u>Computing Fundamentals with Java</u>,
Rick Mercer, Franklin, Beedle and Associates. Programmers can do the
following:
<br>1. Ask for the account ID.
<br>2. Ask a <code>JukeboxAccount</code> if it can play a specific
track.
<br>3. Update time remaining and songs played with
<code>debitOneSong</code>.
<br>
<br>Here is some sample code that shows a <code>JukeboxAccount</code>
is responsible for deciding if it can or cannot play a particular
song. Actual output is shown immediately to the right of the
<code>println</code> messages as comments. All messages of this class
are shown in boldface.
<br><pre>
// Start this account with only 15 minutes of time remaining
JukeboxAccount anAccount = new <b>JukeboxAccount("Olson",15*60,0);</b>
System.out.println( "ID: " + anAccount.<b>getID( )</b> ); //ID: Olson
System.out.println( anAccount.<b>toString( )</b> ); //Olson has 10 minutes
CdTrack selection = new CdTrack( "A 5 minute song", 5 * 60, 0 );
System.out.println( anAccount.<b>canSelect( selection )</b> ); //true
anAccount.<b>debitOneSong</b>( selection );
System.out.println( anAccount.toString( ) ); //Olson has 5 minutes
</pre>
*/
public class JukeboxAccount
{
/** The default play time given to a new JukeboxAccount object.
  */
  public static int INITIAL_SECONDS_OF_PLAYTIME = 1500;

/** The number of songs one JukeboxAccount can play on a given date.
  */
  public static int MAXIMUM_PLAYS_PER_DAY = 2;

// Instance variables
  private String my_ID;
  private int my_secondsRemaining;
  private int my_songsPlayedToday;

/** The time remaining and plays per day are set to the default values
  * INITIAL_SECONDS_OF_PLAYTIME and MAXIMUM_PLAYS_PER_DAY, respectively.
  * @param ID Every one of these objects must have a valid ID.
  */
  public JukeboxAccount( String ID )
  {
    my_ID = ID;
    my_secondsRemaining = INITIAL_SECONDS_OF_PLAYTIME;
    my_songsPlayedToday = MAXIMUM_PLAYS_PER_DAY;
  }
        // Code deleted to save space
```

The following screen shot shows that the HTML tags cause formatting such as bold text, underlined text, and code in a fixed-pitch font. Notice that since the class constants were declared public, they both show up in a section titled "Field Summary."

Figure A.3: **The third part of the HTML documentation**

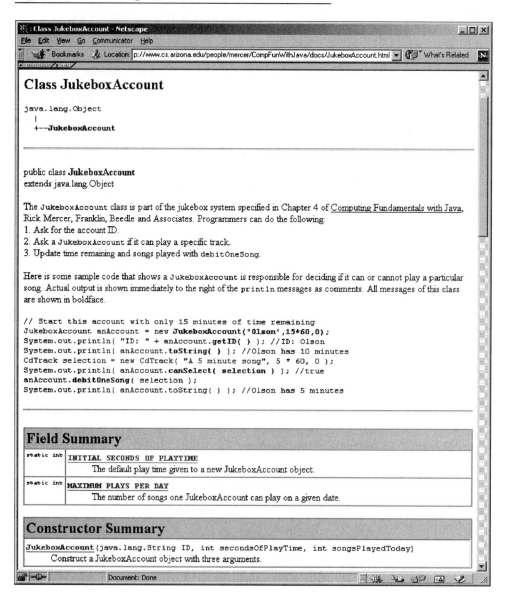

Appendix B

HTML Documentation of Author-Supplied Classes

This appendix provides some HTML documentation of the classes that are not part of the Java library, but are used on numerous occasions in this book. This external documentation is meant to provide a quick reference when you are completing programming projects that need any of the required author-supplied classes TextReader, BankAccount, or Grid. Each screen shot shows only the constructor and method summaries.

Figure B.1: **A summary of constructors and methods for the `TextReader` class**

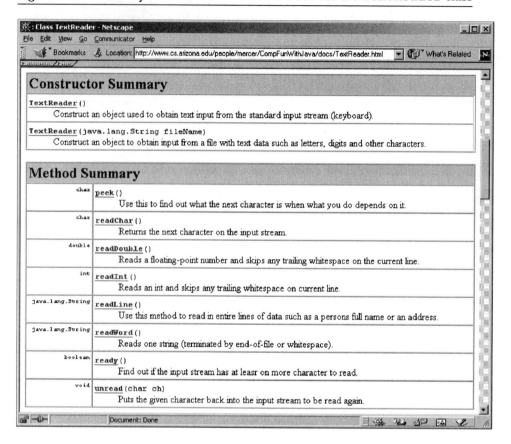

Figure B.2: **A summary of constructors and methods for the BankAccount class**

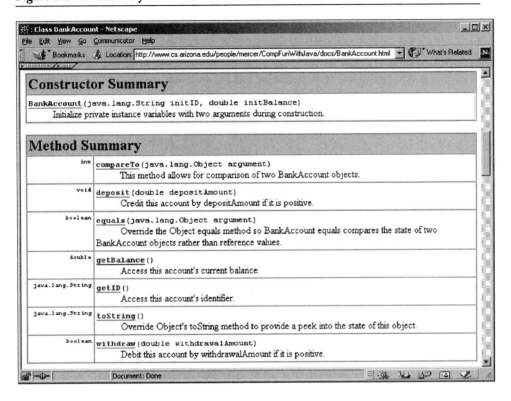

Figure B.3: **A summary of constructors and methods for the `Grid` class**

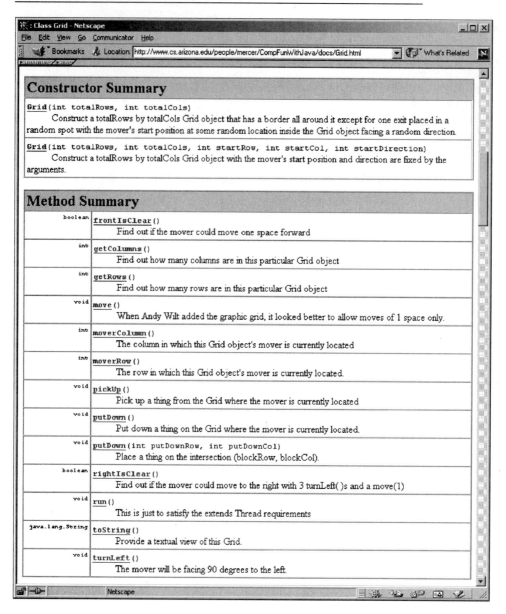

Appendix C
Answers to Selected Exercises

Chapter 1 — Program Development

1. There are many similarities, but data that stores input requires the programmer to write code that will ask (prompt) the user for input.

3. Develop an algorithm that describes the proper steps in the proper order that will solve the problem.

5. It does what it is supposed to do.
   It is detailed enough to indicate an understanding of the problem.
   Someone could simulate a computer-based solution by reading it.

7. The user is getting something that doesn't work. The consequences could be quite dramatic, from minor inconvenience to death. It is easier and less costly to make sure the software works.

8. Search for a phone book listing:
   Start at the first listing and call it the current listing
   repeat the following process
       if the current listing is what you are looking for, stop
       otherwise look at the next listing
   Always successful? No, the listing may not be published (an unlisted number), there may not be such a person, or that person may not have a phone.

10. *Note:* The problem did not say if they are to be sorted by artist, title, category of music, or year released. So you should ask the author, "How do you want them sorted?" The author says, "By artist."

Algorithm 1

- Place all records on the floor near an empty record rack that can hold more records than you have.
- Go through all records and find the record with an artist name that precedes all others alphabetically.
- Place that record as the leftmost record in the record rack (or the top tray of a CD holder).
- Repeat steps 2 and 3 until there are no more records to arrange.

Algorithm 2 (this should eventually work; however, it could take many years)

- Place all records in the rack randomly.
- Check to see if they are in order.
- If they are not in order, take them all out, spread them around, and repeat the previous two steps.

1A   Simple Arithmetic

1. Complete an analysis deliverable for the Simple Arithmetic problem.

Problem	Variable Name	Input/Output	Sample Problems	
Compute a sum and	a	Input	3	5
a product and the	b	Input	7	20
difference between	sum	Output	10	25
the two	product	Output	21	100
	difference	Output	11 (or -11)	75

2. Complete a design deliverable (algorithm) for the Simple Arithmetic problem.
    1. Input two numbers named numberOne and numberTwo.
    2. Compute sum as numberOne + numberTwo .
    3. Compute product as numberOne * numberTwo.
    4. Compute difference as product - sum.
    5. Display sum, product, and difference.

1E   Grade Point Average

1. Complete an analysis deliverable for the GPA problem.

Problem	Variable Name	Input/Output	Sample Problem
Compute a student's	credits1, grade1	Input	4.0, 2.67
GPA for three courses	credits2, grade2	Input	3.0, 3.67
	credits3, grade3	Input	1.5, 4.0
	GPA	Output	**3.26**

2. Complete a design deliverable (algorithm) for the GPA problem.
    1. Input credits1 and grade1.
    2. Input credits2 and grade2.
    3. Input credits3 and grade3.

4. Compute totalCredits = credits1 + credits2 + credits3.
5. Compute totalQualityPoints =
$$(credits1*grade1) + (credits1*grade1)+ (credits1*grade1)$$
6. Compute GPA = totalQualityPoints / totalCredits.
7. Display GPA.

Chapter 2 — A Little Java

2. `* + -  also  / %`

3. To explain what the program does.

    -or-

    Provide internal documentation so other programmers can more easily understand what sections of the program are doing.

6. | **Valid** | **Invalid** |
    |---|---|
    | b, c, d, f, h, l | a. Cannot have - |
    | | e. Does not start with a letter or _ |
    | | g. Cannot begin with a digit |
    | | i. Cannot have a space |
    | | j. This is a string literal |
    | | k. Cannot have { or } |

9.  ```
    Enter a number: 5.2
    Enter another number: 6.3
    Answer: 37.96
    ```

11. a. 4   c. 8.0
    b. ERROR   d. 8.9
    c. ERROR   e. ERROR

12. ```java
    public class RelativeError
    {
       public static void int main( String[] args )
       {
          double relativeError;
          TextReader keyboard = new TestReader( );

          System.out.println( "Enter relativeError [0.0 through 1.0]: " );
          relativeError = keyboard.readDouble( );
          System.out.println( "You entered: " + relativeError );
       }
    }
    ```

13. a. `+--++--++--+`

    b. ```
        +--+
        +--+
        +--+
        ```
        ```

    c. 123

    d. 1
       2
       3

16. `1.65`
    `0.1515`
    `0.2174    // You might get this number as 0.2173913043478261`

19. There is an attempt to assign a floating-point value (`keyboard.readDouble`) to an integer variable `anInt`.

21. No. This expression is actually (x + y) + (z / 3.0), which will not evaluate to the average of x, y, and, z.

23. **slope**

    `1.0`

    `-1.0`

    Division by zero—Java evaluates this to `NaN` (*Not a Number*).

Chapter 3 — Using Objects

2. ```
First and last name (on one line): Your Name
initial balance: 111.11
deposit? 22.00
withdraw? 44.00
Ending balance for Your Name is 89.11
```

4. `"def"`

6. ```
GregorianCalendar today = new GregorianCalendar( );
int year = today.get( today.YEAR );
int month= today.get( today.MONTH );
int day  = today.get( today.DATE );
String dayAsString = "" + day + "/" + ( month + 1 ) + "/" + year;
```

8. a. `int`

   b. `double`

   c. `String`

   d. `int`

   e. `BankAccount`

   f. `TextReader`

   g. `System`

   h. `GregorianCalendar`

   i. `ArrayList`

10. No.

14.
```
String firstName = name.substring( name.indexOf( ", " ) + 2,
                         name.length( ) );
```

16.
```
import javax.swing.*; // Gain access to all Swing components
import java.awt.*;    // Container, BorderLayout
public class SomeComponents
{
  public static void main( String[] args )
  {
    JFrame aWindow = new JFrame( "Five components" );
    aWindow.setSize( 300, 120 );
    aWindow.setLocation( 100, 200 );
    aWindow.setDefaultCloseOperation( JFrame.EXIT_ON_CLOSE );
    // Construct and add five components
    JButton eastButton = new JButton( "One" );
    JButton southButton = new JButton( "Two" );
    JButton westButton = new JButton( "Three" );
    JTextField textF = new JTextField("You can change this text");
    JLabel label = new JLabel( "Center of JFrame" );
    Container contentPane = aWindow.getContentPane( );
    contentPane.add( textF, BorderLayout.NORTH );
    contentPane.add( eastButton, BorderLayout.EAST );
    contentPane.add( westButton, BorderLayout.WEST );
    contentPane.add( southButton, BorderLayout.SOUTH );
    contentPane.add( label, BorderLayout.CENTER );
    aWindow.show( );
  }
}
```

Chapter 4 — Classes and Interfaces

7.
Valid	Invalid
a, e, f	b. No method name
	c. ; after parameters
	d. Need a type or class name before it

8.
```
0
1
2
3
0
1
```

9.
```
// Sets this clickCounter's count back to 0
public void reset( )
{
  my_count = 0;
}
```

10. `aCounter.reset( );    // This clickCounter`

12. a) `20.0`
    b) `24.0`
    c) `22.0`
    d) `23.0`
    e) `26.0`

Chapter 5 — Events, Listeners, and a Little Polymorphism

1.
```
Container contentPane = this.getContentPane( );
contentPane.setLayout( new GridLayout( 2, 3, 8, 4 ) );

// Let the human bank teller enter new account IDs
contentPane.add( new JLabel( "One" ) );
contentPane.add( clearButton );
contentPane.add( new JLabel( "Three" ) );

contentPane.add( leftField );
contentPane.add( new JTextField( "Centered" ) );
contentPane.add( new JTextField( "Right" ) );
```

2.
```
private class ButtonListener implements ActionListener
{
   public void actionPerformed( ActionEvent e )
   {
      theTextField.setText( "Always" );
   }
}
```

3.
```
ButtonListener leftFieldListener = new ButtonListener( );
clearButton.addActionListener( leftFieldListener );
```
-or-
```
clearButton.addActionListener( new ButtonListener( ) );
```

7. `toString` and `equals` (also `getClass`)

8. a, b, and f

Chapter 6 — Selection

3. a. `not 10`   c. `abc`
                        `ghi`
   b. `not`   d. `less not eq.`

5. a. `50`   c. `THREE`
   b. `ONE`   d. `FIVE`

6.  ```
    if( anInt > 0 )
       System.out.println( "YES" );
    if( anInt < 0 )
       System.out.println( "NO" );
    if( anInt == 0 )
      System.out.println( "NEUTRAL" );
    ```

8.  ```
    if( hours < 8 )
       System.out.println( "Hello" );
    else
       System.out.println( "Goodbye" );
    ```

11. ```
    public class LittleStatistician
    {
       private double n1;
       private double n2;
       private double n3;

       public LittleStatistician( double a, double b, double c )
       {
         n1 = a;
         n2 = b;
         n3 = c;
       }

       public double largest( )
       {
         double result = n1;

         if( n2 > result )
           result = n2;
         if( n3 > result )
           result = n3;

         return result;
       }
    }
    ```

13. a. 2   d. Seven
    b. ccc   e. Eight
    c. 25 Three   f. Ten Eleven Hmmmm

16. ```
    public class LittleCalendar
    {
       private int my_day;

       public LittleCalendar( int dayOfWeek )
       {
         my_day = dayOfWeek;
       }

       public String stringDay( )
       {
         String result = "?";
    ```

```
      if( my_day == 0 )
        result = "Monday";
      else if( my_day == 1 )
        result = "Tuesday";
      else if( my_day == 2 )
        result = "Wednesday";
      else if( my_day == 3 )
        result = "Thursday";
      else if( my_day == 4 )
        result = "Friday";
      else if( my_day == 5 )
        result = "Saturday";
      else
        result = "Sunday";

      return result;
  }
}


// Here is a test driver and the output
public class TestLittleCalendar
{
  public static void main( String[] args )
  {
    LittleCalendar a = new LittleCalendar( 0 );
    System.out.println( a.stringDay( ) );
    a = new LittleCalendar( 1 );
    System.out.println( a.stringDay( ) );
    a = new LittleCalendar( 2 );
    System.out.println( a.stringDay( ) );
    a = new LittleCalendar( 3 );
    System.out.println( a.stringDay( ) );
    a = new LittleCalendar( 4 );
    System.out.println( a.stringDay( ) );
    a = new LittleCalendar( 5 );
    System.out.println( a.stringDay( ) );
    a = new LittleCalendar( 6 );
    System.out.println( a.stringDay( ) );
  }
}
```

> **Output**
> Monday
> Tuesday
> Wednesday
> Thursday
> Friday
> Saturday
> Sunday

Chapter 7 — Repetition

1. a. 5
   b. 6
   c. Infinite. The loop subtracts 1 from j each time it adds 1. j remains the same.
   d. Zero

2. 1 2 3 4 5 Loop One
    10 9 8 7 6 5 4 3 2 1 Blast Off

3. a. `for( int j = 10; j >= 0; j-- )`
    `    System.out.print( j + " " );`
    b. `for( int k = 0; k <= 50; k = k + 5 )`
    `    System.out.print( k + " " );`
    c. `for( int counter = -1000; counter <= 0; counter += 100 )`
    `    System.out.print( counter + " " );`

6. a. Unknown. j is undefined. It could be either 0 or infinite.
    b. 7
    c. Zero
    d. Infinite. The statement j++ is not inside the loop.

7.
```
int counter = -4;
while( counter <= 6 )
{
  System.out.print( counter + " " );
  counter++;
}
```

9.
```
TextReader keyboard = new TextReader( );

int perfects = 0;
System.out.println( "Enter test or -1 to quit: " );
while( true )
{
  int test = keyboard.readInt( );
  if( test == -1 )
    break;
  if( test == 100 )
    perfects = perfects + 1;
}
System.out.println( "Number of 100s: " + perfects );
```

13. Opt: B
    Opt: D
    Opt: W
    Opt: B

15.
```
int counter = 10;
do {
    System.out.print( counter + " " );
    counter --;
} while( counter  >= 0 );
```

18.  ```
     // Note: This only reports one error even though
     // you might think that input of -3 would report two errors.

     public int evenNumber( int min, int max )
     {
       // Return an int in the range of min through max inclusive
       int result = 0;
       do
       {
         System.out.print( "Enter an even integer in the range of "
                             + min + " through " + max + ": " );
         result = keyboard.readInt( );

         if( result % 2 != 0 )
           System.out.println( "**Error: Integer was not even" );

         if( result < min || result > max )
           System.out.println( "**Error: Integer was not in range" );

          // Keep going if either error occurred
       } while( ( result % 2 != 0 ) || ( result < min || result > max ) );

       return result;
     }
     ```

Chapter 8 — Arrays

1.  ```
    0. 0
    1. 2
    2. 4
    3. 6
    4. 10
    5. 16
    6. 26
    7. 42
    8. 68
    9. 110
    ```

5.  ```
    double[] z = new double[100];
    // Assume z[0] through z[42] are meaningful
    int n = 43;

    double sum = 0.0;
    for( int j = 0; j < n; j++ )
    {
      sum += z[j];
    }
    double average = sum / n;
    ```
    ```

6.
```
TextReader keyboard = new TextReader( );
System.out.print( "How many lines? " );
int n = keyboard.readInt( );
String[] s = new String[n];

for ( int j = 0; j < n; j++ )
{
  s[j] = keyboard.readLine( );
}

System.out.println( "Lines reversed: " );
for( int j = n - 1; j >= 0; j-- )
{
   System.out.println( s[j] );
}
```

11.
```
c b e d a
a d e b c
```

16.
```
Aimee
Alex
Bob
Lauren
Morgan
```

17.
```
2 16
4 14
6 12
8 10
```

Chapter 9 — A Few Exceptions, a Little Input/Output, and Some Persistent Objects

2. All Exception classes that extend RunTimeException are unchecked. Your code may, but is not required, to place the code in a try/catch.

3.
```
else
{ // Get index in range to find the
  // value of the element in the list
 int index;
 do
 {
    System.out.print( "Enter an index from 0.."
                   + ( list.size( ) - 1 ) + ": " );
    index = keyboard.readInt( );

    try
    {
      System.out.println( "The String at " + index + ": "
                    + list.get( index ) );
    }
```

```
   catch ( IndexOutOfBoundsException iobe )
   {
     System.out.println( "Index out of range, try again" );
   }

   } while ( index < 0 || index >= list.size( )  );
}
```

4.  ```java
    // Create the input stream
    InputStreamReader standardInput =
                            new InputStreamReader( System.in );
    BufferedReader keyboard =
                            new BufferedReader( standardInput );

    // Create output file
    System.out.print( "\nSave input into which file? " );
    String outputFileName = keyboard.readLine( );
    PrintWriter diskFile =
                    new PrintWriter( new FileWriter( outputFileName ) );

    // Read until SENTINEL is on a line with no other characters
    System.out.println( "Enter lines or 'SENTINEL' as the last line:" );
    String line = keyboard.readLine( );

    // Write each line of the input from the user to a disk file
    while( line.compareTo( "SENTINEL" ) != 0 )
    {
      diskFile.println( line );
      line = keyboard.readLine( );
    }
    // Store SENTINEL as the last line--avoid an empty line at end
    diskFile.print( line );

    // Make sure the buffered output actually gets written to the file
    diskFile.close( );
    ```

Chapter 10 — Designing an Inheritance Hierarchy

3.  ```java
    public abstract class USEmployee
    {
      private String my_name;
      private double my_hoursWorked;
      private double my_hourlyRate;

      public USEmployee( String name, double hourlyRate )
      {
        my_name = name;
        my_hoursWorked = 0.0;
        my_hourlyRate = hourlyRate;
      }
    ```

```java
        public void setHours( double hoursWorked )
        {
          my_hoursWorked = hoursWorked;
        }

        // All subclasses will get this one
        public double getGrossPay( )
        {
          double result = my_hoursWorked * my_hourlyRate;
          if( my_hoursWorked > 40.0 )
            result = result +
                       1.5 * my_hourlyRate * (my_hoursWorked - 40.0);
          return result;
        }

        // All subclasses must implement this
        public abstract double getIncomeTax( );
      }
```

4.
```java
   class WeeklyEmployee extends USEmployee
   {
     public static final double TAX_RATE = 0.15;

     public WeeklyEmployee( String name, double hourlyRate )
     {
       super( name, hourlyRate );
     }

     public double getIncomeTax( )
     {
       return TAX_RATE * getGrossPay( );
     }
   }
```

5. a. I am an animal.
   b. I am a Calico and I am an animal.
   c. I am an animal.
   d. Compiletime error
   e. MEOW SCRATCH
   f. RUFF BITE
   g. Prrr I am an animal.
   h. Prrr I am a Calico and I am an animal.
   i. Compiletime error
   j. I am an animal.
   k. Compiletime error
   l. Compiletime error
   m. Compiletime error (attempt to instantiate an abstract class)
   n. Compiletime error (attempt to assign down the hierarchy)

Chapter 11 — More Arrays

1. Aimee
   Alex
   Bob
   Lauren
   Morgan

2. First Mid Last
   0   3   6
   4   5   6
   4   4   4
   LISA has a balance of 4.0

6. 2   3   4   5
   3   4   5   6
   4   5   6   7
   5   6   7   8

7. ```
   public void incrementBy( int increment )
   {
      for( int row = 0; row < lastRow; row++ )
      {
         for( int col = 0; col < lastCol; col++ )
         { // Give each item a meaningless value
            m[row][col] += increment;
         }
      }
   }
   ```

8. ```
   public int rowSum( int currentRow )
   {
      int result = 0;
      for( int col = 0; col < lastCol; col++ )
      {
         result += m[currentRow][col];
      }
      return result;
   }
   ```

11. a.
    0   0   0
    0   1   2

    b.
    0   0
    0   1
    0   2

c.
```
    0   0
    0   1
    0   2
```

d.
```
    0   0   0   0
    0   1   2   3
    0   2   4   6
    0   3   6   9
```

e.
```
    0
```

Chapter 12 — Simple Recursion

1. 0
    1
    14

2.  ```
    <2>
    <<2>5>
    <<<1>4>7>
    ```

3. false
    false
    true

5. 1 2 3 4 5 6 7 8
    8 7 6 5 4 3 2 1

6.  ```
    public static void backward( int n )
    {
       System.out.println( n );
       if( n > 1 )
         backward( n - 1 );
    }
    ```

12. **binomial(n, k)**

    1

    Undefined

    1

    2

14. 4
    16
    64

15.
```java
    public static void goingUp( int numberToPrint, int stop )
    {
      if( numberToPrint == stop )
        System.out.print( numberToPrint + " " );
      else
      {
        System.out.print( numberToPrint + " " );
        goingUp( numberToPrint + 1, stop );
      }
    }
```

Glossary

abstract class A class that captures the common responsibilities of a set of objects. An abstract class cannot be instantiated. An abstract class often implements the methods that are common to all objects while specifying the methods that subclasses must implement. See *subclass* and *superclass*.

abstract method A method heading with no implementation (; instead of a block). Abstract methods are added to abstract classes to require that all subclasses implement the methods in a manner appropriate to the subclass. Abstract methods represent the differences of the objects instantiated from a class hierarchy.

abstraction The ability to understand something without the details. In programming, abstraction refers to using and understanding a class or a method without knowledge of the implementation.

accessing method A method in a class with the main purpose of returning information to the sender of the message. For example, sending a `size` message to an `ArrayList` object and sending a `getBalance` message to a `BankAccount` object return information about the state of those objects. See *modifying method*.

algorithm A step-by-step procedure for solving a problem or accomplishing some task, especially by a computer. A good algorithm must list the activities that need to be carried out and list those activities in the proper order. Algorithms are often written in pseudocode and programming language statements.

algorithm walkthrough A simulation of what a computer would do moving through the steps of an algorithm by hand. Programmers can simulate a soon-to-be-implemented electronic version of an algorithm by following the steps of the algorithm and manually performing the activities; such as storing, retrieving, and processing data; using pencil and paper.

667

algorithmic pattern A guide to help develop programs. It represents a common type of action that occurs over and over again in programs. Some algorithmic patterns have a general solution that a programmer must make up, such as Input/ Process/Output. Others occur so frequently that programming languages implement them with statements such as `if`, `for`, and `while`.

alias Another name that can be used to send messages to an object referenced by another reference variable. A parameter is often an alias to an object referenced by the associated argument. An alias is "another name for" the same object in memory. See *parameter.*

Alternative Action pattern The pattern of choosing between one set of statements and another. This pattern arises so often that Java provides the `if...else` statement to implement it.

analysis The effort spent to understand a problem specification. Analysis activities include reading the problem specification, determining the input and output, solving a few sample problems, and asking the intended users of the program what they need. Analysis is about understanding. See *design.*

application programming interface (API) Documentation of the set of classes, interfaces, exceptions, and methods that provide a wide variety of help to programmers. It is also known as a "library" when considered with implementations that you can use.

argument An expression between parentheses in a message that is needed by the method to fulfill its responsibility. An argument may be a literal, a primitive type variable, a reference type variable, or a more complex expression.

array An object that allows programs to store a collection of object references or primitives under one name. Individual elements in an array are referenced with integer subscripts. Arrays must be initialized with an initial capacity that is often larger than necessary. See *index.*

array processing The algorithms and/or code associated with arrays, such as printing all meaningful values, finding the largest element, finding a specific element, sorting the elements, and so on.

assignment An operation that gives primitive values to primitive type variables and references values to class type variables.

assignment compatibility The notion that only certain expressions can be assigned to certain variables. For example, the value of an integer expression cannot be stored into a variable declared to reference a `String` object.

assignment operator   One of several operators for assigning the value of an expression to a variable. The most common is =, which copies the value of the expression to the right into the variable to the left. That value may be a reference to an object or a primitive value such as 1. Other assignment operators include += and -=.

bag   A collection of values that need not be unique. It is also known as "multi-set."

base case   In a recursive definition or recursive method, the definition or code that does not refer to itself or call itself, respectively.

binary search   A searching algorithm that assumes an array is sorted so the element can be found quickly. For each unsuccessful comparison, the algorithm can eliminate half of the elements from the search. If an array had 1,024 elements, a binary search would need to loop through only 10 times. If the array size were to double, only one additional comparison would be necessary. See *array*, *sequential search*, and *sorting*.

boolean expression   An expression that evaluates to either true or false. Boolean expressions often include relational operators such as < and != and/or the boolean operators !, &&, and ||. Boolean expressions are used as part of if, for, do, and while statements.

boolean type   A primitive data type with the values true and false.

branch   One path through code with multiple selections.

branch coverage testing   The effort to run a program many times in order to ensure that all branches through multiple selection behave correctly.

break   A Java reserved identifier to exit a loop or a switch statement.

bug   A logic error in a program that runs but doesn't do what is supposed to do. See *intent error*.

case   A reserved identifier that identifies the path through a switch statement. See *switch statement*.

cast   An operation for converting certain primitive types to other primitive types, for example int anInt = (int)aDouble;. The same casting syntax is also used to promise the compiler that a reference to a superclass will be storing a reference to one of its subclasses, as in BankAccount anAccount = (BankAccount)Object;. If this promise isn't kept, the program will throw an exception at runtime. You can cast down the inheritance hierarchy but not up. See *one-way assignment*.

catch A reserved identifier in Java that begins a block of code that will execute if the code in the associated `try` block throws an exception. See *exception*.

char A primitive data type that stores single characters such as "A" and "z."

checked exception An exception that must be handled. Any code that may throw a checked exception must be placed inside a `try` block and followed by a `catch` block. Examples of unchecked exceptions include `IOException` and `FileNotFoundException`. See *exception* and *unchecked exception*.

class A mechanism that provides a template for defining the methods and data of many objects. Each object (instance of a class) can have its own state—the set of values for that instance. The Java class acts as a blueprint for the construction of from 1 to many objects.

class constant An identifier in a Java class declared with the reserved identifier `final` and given a value that cannot be changed while the program is running. There is only one of these for all objects of a class. See *final* and *static*.

class diagram A picture of a class that shows the instance variables and methods of a class and the relationship between classes. See *class*.

class hierarchy See *inheritance hierarchy*.

class variable An identifier in a Java class declared as `static`. There is only one of these for all objects of a class, so a change to a class variable during a message to one object changes that value for all objects. See *instance variable*.

cohesion How well the methods and instance variables of a class are related to one another. High cohesion is a sign of good design. Low cohesion is a sign of bad design.

collaborator In responsibility design, an object is a collaborator if it helps another object fulfill its responsibility. There is a two-way trust between these objects that work together.

collection An accumulation of objects that have some reason to be treated as one unit.

collection class A class with the main purpose of storing a collection of elements with operations that allow programmers to easily add, find, and remove elements (`ArrayList`, for example).

column-by-column processing The processing of all the data in one column of a two-dimensional array before going on to process the next column.

command line argument The value that is entered after a program name from an operating system's command line. The input value can be referenced from the main method as the array of String objects that main declares as its single parameter.

comment Internal and external documentation for programs and APIs. There are single-line comments after //, multiple-line documents after /* and before */, and javadoc comments after /* and before */. See *javadoc.*

compiler A program that translates the high-level programming language source code (such as Java) into lower-level code. In the case of Java, the compiler generates *byte code.* This byte code can then be sent to any computer with a Java virtual machine (JVM) installed as a program.

compiletime error An error detected by the compiler while it is attempting to translate source code into a lower–level code. Compiletime errors must be corrected to get a program to run.

computer A programmable electronic device that can store, retrieve, and process data.

computer program A sequence of activities executed by a computer.

constructor A special method in a class that allocates memory for objects and initializes instance variables. A constructor returns a reference to an object so the object can be found later.

coupling How strongly objects are dependent on one another. Low coupling is good design.

CRC cards Index cards or pieces of paper that record a Candidate object name (a class that may be needed later), Responsibilities, and the Collaborators the candidate object would need to help fulfill its responsibilities. CRC cards are usually developed when programmers are trying to understand and design a system.

debugging output statement A print or println statement with the sole purpose of informing the programmer about what is going on while a program is executing. These statements should be commented out or removed once the code has been debugged and the testing is completed.

declaration A statement that brings a name into a program.

decrement Subtract from a numeric type variable. See *numeric type.*

default constructor   A constructor that has no parameters. If you do not include a constructor for a class, Java provides you with a default constructor. If you provide a constructor with one or more parameters, Java does not provide the default constructor.

deliverable   A tangible result. In software development, a deliverable could take the form of an algorithm, a class, a class diagram of an inheritance hierarchy, a CRC card, or doodles on a napkin.

design   The set of activities for defining the components of a system, specifying the algorithms for those components, and assigning responsibilities to objects. Design also includes choosing appropriate patterns; naming things; setting styles, such as indentation; deciding the access level of methods and instance variables (public or private); and doing anything else that helps make a system easier to understand, build, and maintain, while providing value to those who use the system. Design is about making decisions. See *analysis*.

design guideline   A principle intended to help produce quality object-oriented software; a rule of thumb to guide design decisions. It is also known as an object-oriented design heuristic.

Determinate Loop pattern   The pattern of a set of statements that execute a specific number of times; the number of times can be determined before the loop begins to execute. Java provides the for loop to capture this pattern. See *for statement*.

do statement   A Java statement that ensures that the body of a loop executes at least once by placing a loop test at the end. See *while statement* and *for statement*.

double type   A primitive type that stores floating-point numbers within a limited range.

element   An item stored in a list. Specifically in Java, an item referenced from within an array or ArrayList object.

event-driven programming   A style of programming that assumes a loop is continuously running to allow the program to respond to any number of events. It is typically associated with a graphical user interface.

exception   An error that occurs when a program encounters an awkward situation while it is running. For example, an exception would occur if a user entered a string of characters that did not represent a number, 1oo for 100. Another example is if a file name supplied as an argument to the FileReader constructor did not exist. See *checked exception* and *unchecked exception*.

expression A sequence of operators and operands that evaluate to some value. For example, `Math.sqrt( 4.0 )` evaluates to `2.0` and `5 > 2` evaluates to `true`.

extends A Java reserved word to specify that a subclass inherits the methods of a superclass. For example, `public class MyFrame extends JFrame` means that `MyFrame` obtains instance variables and methods from the `JFrame` class. More instance variables and methods may be added and methods can be overridden. See *inheritance* and *override.*

final A Java reserved word that turns a variable into a constant. A `final` variable must be initialized immediately. You can also declare a method as `final` to prevent any subclass from overriding it. See *abstract method* and *class constant.*

for statement A statement to implement the Determinate Loop pattern. It is a construct for executing a set of statements a predetermined number of times.

general form A language for describing the syntax necessary to write valid source code for a particular programming language. In this textbook, text in **boldface courier** must be written as is. The programmer must supply the text written in *italic,* which is defined elsewhere.

graphical component An object with a graphical appearance, such as `JButton` and `JTextField`. Many graphical components construct event objects and send messages to registered listeners when users interact with them.

graphical user interface (GUI) A graphical presentation to the user of a computer program that has buttons, text fields, menu bars, and other graphical components that the user can communicate with.

Guarded Action pattern The pattern of choosing whether or not to execute a set of statements based on the state of the program. This pattern arises so often in software development that Java provides the `if` statement.

helper method A method designed to help another method accomplish its task. Helper methods are useful when two or more methods of a class need the same task accomplished or when one method is getting too long or too complex to be easily understood.

identifier A name that represents a variable's value, object reference, method, class name, or any other programming element. Java provides many identifiers, such as `main`, `sqrt`, `print`, `readInt`, and `String`. Programmers make up their own identifiers.

if statement A statement that provides the ability to either execute a set of statements or skip over them, depending on the value of its boolean expression.

if...else statement   A statement that provides the ability to determine which set of statements to execute. It is used to select from two or more sets of statements.

implementation   The activities required to complete a program so someone else can use it on a computer. Activities performed during implementation include writing code in a programming language, compiling, testing, verifying that the program does what it should, and documenting the system.

implements   A Java reserved identifier that signifies to the compiler that a class will include the methods specified in the interface.

import   A Java reserved word that makes one or more identifiers available to a program without having to be qualified each time. For example, with `import javax.swing.*;` the name `JFrame` can be used to mean the `java.swing.JFrame` class.

increment   Add to a numeric type variable. See *numeric type*.

Indeterminate Loop pattern   The pattern of a set of statements that execute an unknown number of times; the number of repetitions cannot be determined before the loop begins to execute. The loop needs some way to figure out when to stop. The `while` statement is provided to handle these situations. See *Determinate Loop pattern*.

index   An integer used to reference a specific array or `ArrayList` element. The first element has index 0.

infinite loop   A loop that executes virtually non-stop. This is not usually desirable. Adding a debugging print statement inside a loop can help you discover why the loop may be running longer than it should.

inheritance   One class extends another to get (inherit) the instance variables and methods of the other class. For example, `public class MyFrame extends JFrame` means that `MyFrame` has all of the public methods of `JFrame`. You can still add more instance variables and methods to `MyFrame`. See *subclass, superclass, extends,* and *override*.

inheritance hierarchy   A set of classes with the common responsibilities captured in abstract classes, and the different behaviors captured in subclasses. It is used to implement a system that recognizes a set of two or more classes that have commonalities and one or more differences. Subclasses inherit methods and instance variables from superclasses. See *inheritance*.

initialization   A variable declaration that gives a specific value to a variable.

inner class   A class written inside of another class. A common use of inner classes is to implement a listener interface, because the `actionPerformed` method often needs access to the graphical components of the enclosing class. An inner class can reference the private instance variables of the enclosing class.

input   Information or actions that a program can react to. It could be a `String` entered at the keyboard or a button clicked with the mouse.

Input/Process/Output pattern   In a text-based or GUI event-driven environment, the pattern of a program gathering input data somehow, using that input to determine what to do, and then displaying the results or changing the state of some object (if appropriate).

instance   One occurrence of a class. It is a synonym for *object.*

instance variable   A variable inside a class that can be referenced from all methods of the class. Instance variables are initialized when the object is constructed, either through the default value or inside the constructor itself.

int type   A primitive type that stores integer values in the range from -2,147,483,648 to 2,147,483,647.

integer arithmetic   An informal term that serves as a reminder that 5 / 2 is 2, not 2.5, and that the % operator returns the integer remainder.

integral type   Any of Java's primitive types that represent whole values. The integral types in Java are `byte`, `short`, `int`, `long`, and `char`. Expressions of these types can be used with a `switch` statement.

intent error   An error that occurs when a program does what it was programmed to do, not what was intended.

interface   A collection of methods with no instance variables and no method bodies. An interface exists so it can be implemented by any number of classes. This allows programmers to know that an instance of a class is guaranteed to have certain methods. An interface allows different classes of objects to be treated the same.

iteration   One pass through a loop.

iterator   A method that allows a programmer to traverse all of the elements in a collection without knowing how they are stored. In Java, this is done with a separate `Iterator` or `ListIterator` object.

Java virtual machine (JVM)   A program that translates byte code into instructions for the specific type of machine that a Java program is running on.

javadoc A program that uses Java source code as input to generate hyperlinked HTML files that document the classes in a system. If special tags are used (@param and @return), the documentation of your classes can be made to look just like that of the classes that come with Java. See Appendix A, "A Little Javadoc."

keyword An identifier that is reserved by a programming language to mean a specific thing. You cannot use keywords for anything else. Examples are `int`, `double`, and `new`.

layout manager An object that collaborates with a `JFrame` to arrange its graphical components. By default, a `JFrame` uses an instance of `BorderLayout`, but this can be changed to an instance of `GridLayout`.

library The collection of classes and interfaces that comes as part of Java that is included to help programmers more easily implement their applications.

list A collection of indexed elements that can be iterated over. A list is either empty or has a first element, a last element, and a distinct predecessor (except for the first element) and successor (except for last element).

listener An object that implements a specific interface (usually ending with `Listener`).

literal A source code symbol for a value, such as `123`, `4.56`, `true`, `null`, `'h'`, and `"string"`.

local variable A variable declared inside a method that can be referenced only within that method. All parameters are local to the method in which they are declared.

logic error See *intent error.*

main method The first method executed when a class is run (if present). Each class may have its own `main` method even if it is never executed. The method heading must be written like this:

```
public static void main( String[] args )
```

message A way for a program to get something done by an object or to obtain information about an object's state. A message has an object (`System.out`, for example), followed by a dot (`.`), followed by the method name, followed by a set of parentheses. You may have to supply arguments between the required parentheses.

method An operation that performs a well-defined responsibility while hiding details (code written by other programmers). For example, `println` sends the value of the argument to the place where you want it to go with one relatively simple message.

method call (invocation) The invocation of a `static` method using the class name and a dot before the method name. When an object reference is used before the dot instead of a class name, the operation is usually referred to as a message. See *message* and *static method*.

modal dialog box A window for presenting messages and requests for information that maintains focus to prevent users from accessing other windows while it is showing.

modifying method A method in a class whose main purpose it is to modify the state of an object.

multiple constructors More than one constructer. Since all constructors have the same name as the class and no return type, there must be a unique parameter list for each constructor. See *default constructor*.

Multiple Selection pattern A pattern of choosing among three or more alternatives based on the state of the program. This can be implemented by nesting `if...else` statements. The false part of one `if...else` statement can be another `if...else` statement.

nested `if...else` An `if...else` statement that is within another `if...else` statement. It is often used as the false part of an `if...else` statement.

nested loop A loop within another loop. It is often used as a statement to repeat.

new A Java operator for constructing an instance of a class.

null A literal value used to indicate that a reference variable does not currently reference an object.

numeric type Any of Java's integral types—`byte`, `short`, `int`, and `long`—or floating-point types, `float` and `double`.

object An instance of a class that stores its own values. It is an entity in computer memory that has a name, a collection of messages it understands (the methods), and from 1 to many values (the state of the object).

object-oriented design (OOD) The activities involved in partitioning a system into objects, assigning responsibilities to those objects, and striving to build a system that is easy to understand, enhance, and maintain. OOD includes defining the relationships of objects, such as passing one object to another as an argument; retrieving objects as return values; and storing references to objects as instance variables. OOD also includes relationships between classes through inheritance and interfaces.

one-way assignment The ability to assign a reference up the inheritance hierarchy but not down. A `String` reference can be assigned to an `Object` reference variable, but not the other way around, for example.

operator precedence The order in which Java executes operations. Method calls and the dot operator are evaluated first. Assignments operations are performed last—they have the lowest precedence.

output Information supplied by a program to communicate information. Output may go to the computer screen, a file, or another computer on the Web.

override Change the meaning of a method in a superclass to fit the purpose of the subclass. The `toString` method of the `Object` class is often overridden by subclasses, for example.

package A collection of related classes and interfaces. For example, `import java.io.*;` makes available to the program all classes and interfaces stored in the `java.io` package.

parameter A variable declaration in a method heading that is used to get the values of the arguments in a function call or message. A reference type parameter is an alias for the object referenced by the argument. See *argument* and *alias*.

parameter list Zero or more parameters in a method heading that specify the number and type of arguments that must be used in a message so the method can do what it is supposed to do. See *argument* and *parameter*.

pass by value The process of copying the value of an argument to a parameter during a message or method call. It is a way to provide input to a method. All arguments in Java are passed to their associated parameters by value. It is not uncommon that the values passed to a method are references to objects. This means that the parameter is an alias for the argument. See *alias, argument,* and *parameter*.

pattern Anything designed to serve as a guide in making something else. A pattern is a general solution to a problem that can be reused in many different contexts in many different ways. See *algorithmic pattern*.

persistence The ability of an object to stay in existence after a program terminates. Chapter 9 describes how to write any object to a disk so it is saved to be read back into a program at some later point in time.

pixel The smallest recognizable area on the computer screen. A window is made up of many thousands of pixels, each with its own color.

polymorphic message A message that may result in two or more different methods being invoked. Either there must be an inheritance hierarchy with at least two classes implementing the same method or there must be two or more classes that implement the same interface. See *inheritance hierarchy* and *interface*

polymorphism The ability to have the same message sent to different types of objects, resulting in different behaviors.

precondition Something that must be true before a method is called so the method can correctly do what it promises to do. Preconditions may simply be written as comments for a method. Or a method could include code to ensure the preconditions are met.

primitive type One of Java's eight predefined types for storing primitive values. The primitive types are `double`, `int`, `float`, `boolean`, `long`, `short`, `byte`, and `char`.

private An access mode that states that a method or instance variable is known only inside the class where it is declared. Instance variables are declared to be private. See *public*.

problem specification The written description of a desired program or system. See *system* and *computer program*.

program See *computer program*.

Prompt and Input pattern A pattern of asking users for information and then obtaining the information. One way to implement this pattern is with a `print` message followed by a `read` message for text-based input. Or a `JLabel` could be used for the prompt and a `JTextField` for the input.

pseudocode A natural language version of an algorithm. Pseudocode is not compiled, so you can express the solution in your own way (and it can look like a programming language at times). See *algorithm*.

public An access mode that allows an identifier to be known outside of the class. Many methods are declared to be public.

readChar, readDouble, readInt, readLine, readWord, and ready Methods of the author-supplied `TextReader` class for reading text input from the keyboard or a file. For further information, see the javadoc documentation for the `TextReader` class in Appendix B.

recursion A computer programming technique involving the use of a method that calls itself until a base case is reached.

reference   A value stored in a class variable used to locate an object in memory. Java distinguishes primitive variables from reference variables.

referential attribute   A instance variable of a class that refers to an object constructed elsewhere. One object may have several references to it.

repetition control   The notion that a set of statements will execute from zero to many times. See *Determinate Loop pattern* and *Indeterminate Loop pattern*.

responsibility   A task that an object promises to do.

return   A statement used in a method to give the value of a message back to the caller that requested that value.

row-by-row processing   The processing of all the data in one row of a two-dimensional array before going on to the next row.

searching   The act of looking through a collection to get a reference to a specific object or to realize that the object is not in the collection. See *binary search* and *sequential search*.

selection   The ability to choose which sets of statements execute depending on program state.

selection sort   An algorithm that arranges an indexed collection of elements— array and ArrayList, for example—into their natural ordering or their reverse natural ordering. Each value is placed into its final position after it is found to be smaller (or larger) than the remaining elements that need to be sorted. See *sorting*.

sentinel   A specific value that is valid input, but not a valid value that allows users to terminate the loop with one additional input. The loop terminates when this value is found in the input. For example, -1 would be a good sentinel value for reading integer test scores that are in the range of 0 through 100.

sequential search   A searching algorithm that examines all array elements beginning with the first element (index 0). An array index variable gets incremented by 1 until the element is found or there are no more elements to consider.

short circuit boolean evaluation   The requirement that Java compilers generate code that will not evaluate unnecessary boolean expressions. This saves execution time and can allow you to write simpler code. With the expression r1 && r2, r2 is not evaluated when r1 is false because the only possible choice is that the entire expression is false. With the expression r1 || r2, r2 is not evaluated when r1 is true because the only possible choice is that the entire expression is true.

sorting   Arranging a list of elements into ascending or descending order.

special symbol Punctuation with a special meaning in a programming language. In Java, special symbols can be one or two characters, such as (and ==.

state The values stored by an object.

statement A sequence of tokens that comprise some activity such as a message or an assignment.

static A Java reserved word to modify an identifier such as a variable or method. A static variable is also known as a class variable since it is shared by all instances of the class. When a static variable is declared with final, the value cannot be changed and is referred to as a class constant.

static method A method declared with the reserved word static so no instance needs to be constructed to invoke the method. To call a static method, you use the class name and a dot rather than an object name and a dot.

String A Java class that stores a collection of from zero to many characters.

string A sequence of characters. A string can be stored as a Java String object that has the characters between " and ". An empty string is "".

subclass A class that is derived from an existing class through inheritance. A subclass inherits the instance variables and methods of its superclass. A subclass can override methods of its superclass. A subclass can add its own instance variables and methods that the superclass is unaware of. See *extends, inheritance,* and *superclass.*

superclass A class that provides common instances variables and methods (data and behavior) for subclasses through inheritance. Typically a superclass captures the common data and behavior for two or more subclasses. See *extends, inheritance,* and *subclass.*

switch statement An implementation of the Multiple Selection pattern for determining the statements to execute based on the value of an integral expression. See *case* and *break.*

syntax The rules of a language. A compiler expects certain things in certain places. For example, if a { is expected and an identifier is found instead, the compiler will report that as a syntax error at compiletime.

syntax error An error in source code due to a sequence of tokens that does not follow the rules of the language. Among other things, a compiler is designed to detect and report syntax errors.

system An interacting set of objects forming a unified whole.

test driver   Code that exercises the methods of a class to see if they do what they are supposed to do. A test driver could be one `main` method in a class. At a minimum, a test driver should construct several instances of a class and send all possible messages.

testing   Verifying that a program is correctly doing what it is supposed to be doing. Testing occurs at any phase of program development. During analysis, establish sample problems to confirm your understanding of the problem. During design, walk through the algorithm to ensure that it has the proper steps in the proper order. During final testing, run the program (or method) several times with different sets of input data. Confirm that the results are correct. Review the problem specification and make sure the running program does what was requested.

TextReader   An author-supplied class that has several methods for reading numbers and strings from the keyboard: `readInt` and `readDouble`. To use it, copy `TextReader.java` into your working folder. See *readChar, readDouble, readInt, readLine, readWord, and ready.*

this   A Java reserved word that allows an object to refer to itself from inside one of its own methods. `this` comes in handy to pass a reference from itself as an argument in a message (when `equals` calls `compareTo`, for example). `this` refers to the object that sends a message (the instance of a class before the dot). `this` is an alias for the receiver of the message. See *alias.*

throw   A Java reserved word that is used to begin exception handling. For example, `throw new IllegalArgumentException( );` results in output describing what exception was thrown and where it was thrown (the file name with the line number) before the program is terminated.

throws   A Java reserved word indicating that a method may throw an exception.

token   The smallest recognizable piece of source code. See *special symbol, identifier,* and *literal.*

two-dimensional array   An array with two subscripts, used to store data that is considered to be in the format of a table. The first subscript refers to a row. The second subscript refers to a column.

unchecked exception   An exception that does not need to be handled. Any code that may throw an unchecked exception does not need be placed in a `try` block. This includes all classes that extend the `RuntimeException` class, such as `IndexOutOfBoundsException`, `IllegalArgumentException`, and `ArithmeticException`.

variable A named piece of computer memory that stores a primitive or reference value. The value may be changed through assignment while the program is running.

virtual machine An abstraction that represents a view of a computer. Most people view the computer at the highest level of virtual machine—the application software. Programmers view the computer at the level of a programming language. Hardware designers view the computer at the level of digital logic. See *Java virtual machine*.

void A Java reserved word to indicate that a method returns nothing. A void method cannot have a return statement in it.

while statement A statement that allows a set of statements to execute from zero to many times.

white space Any characters that separate input values, including blank spaces, tabs, and new lines.

word A string with no blank spaces. See *string*.

Index